ENCYCLOPEDIA OF INDIAN PHILOSOPHIES

ENCYCLOPEDIA OF INDIAN PHILOSOPHIES

Advaita Vedānta up to Śaṃkara and His Pupils

EDITED BY

KARL H. POTTER

PRINCETON UNIVERSITY PRESS
Princeton, New Jersey

Published by Princeton University Press, Princeton, New Jersey
In the United Kingdom: Princeton University Press, Guildford, Surrey

Library of Congress Cataloging in Publication Data will
be found on the last printed page of this book

This book was composed in India by Shantilal Jain
at Shri Jainendra Press, New Delhi

Clothbound editions of Princeton University Press books are
printed on acid-free paper, and binding materials are
chosen for strength and durability

Printed in the United States of America
by Princeton University Press, Princeton, New Jersey

Contributors:

Edeltraud Harzer, University of Washington
S. Subrahmanya Sastri, Varanasi
Allen W. Thrasher, University of Washington

CONTENTS

PREFACE ix

PART ONE :

INTRODUCTION TO THE PHILOSOPHY OF ADVAITA VEDĀNTA (*Karl H. Potter*)

1. Historical Résumé 3
2. Theory of Value 22
3. Philosophy of Language 46
4. Identity and Difference : The Theory of Relations 62
5. Advaita Metaphysics 74
6. Advaita Epistemology 92

PART TWO :

SUMMARIES OF WORKS

1. Gauḍapāda 103
   Gauḍapādakārikās, or Āgamaśāstra (*Karl H. Potter*) 105
2. Śaṃkara 115
   Brahmasūtrabhāṣya (*Karl H. Potter*) 119
   Bṛhadāraṇyakopaniṣadbhāṣya (*Karl H. Potter*) 180
   Taittirīyopaniṣadbhāṣya (*Karl H. Potter*) 204
   Upadeśasāhasrī (*Karl H. Potter*) 217
   Chāndogyopaniṣadbhāṣya (*Karl H. Potter*) 254
   Aitareyopaniṣadbhāṣya (*Karl H. Potter*) 270
   Īśopaniṣadbhāṣya (*Karl H. Potter*) 278
   Kaṭhopaniṣadbhāṣya (*Karl H. Potter*) 280
   Kenopaniṣatpadabhāṣya (*Karl H. Potter*) 281
   Muṇḍakopaniṣadbhāṣya (*Karl H. Potter*) 284
   Praśnopaniṣadbhāṣya (*Karl H. Potter*) 289
   Bhagavadgītābhāṣya (*Karl H. Potter*) 294
   Māṇḍūkyopaniṣadbhāṣya with Gauḍapādakārikābhāṣya (*Karl H. Potter*) 308
   Dakṣiṇāmūrtistotra (*Karl H. Potter*) 317
   Pañcīkaraṇa (*Karl H. Potter*) 318
   Aparokṣānubhūti (*Karl H. Potter*) 320

Ātmabodha (*Karl H. Potter*) 323
Śataślokī (*Karl H. Potter*) 324
Bālabodhinī, or Ātmajñānopadeśavidhi (*Karl H. Potter*) 326
Ātmanātmaviveka (*Karl H. Potter*) 328
Tattvabodha (*Karl H. Potter*) 331
Daśaślokī (*Karl H. Potter*) 333
Vākyavṛtti (*Karl H. Potter*) 334
Vivekacūḍāmaṇi (*Karl H. Potter*) 335
Sarvavedāntasiddhāntasārasaṃgraha (*Karl H. Potter*) 339
Advaitapañcaratna, or Ātmapañcaka (*K. Raghavan Pillai*) 343
Vākyasudhā, or Dṛgdṛśyaviveka 344
Upadeśapañcaka 344
Māyāpañcaka 344
Laghuvākyavṛtti 345
Commentaries on other Upaniṣads 345
3. Maṇḍana Miśra 346
Brahmasiddhi (*Allen W. Thrasher*) 347
4. Sureśvara 420
Bṛhadāraṇyakopaniṣadbhāṣyavārttika (*S. Subrahmanya Sastri*) 420
Taittirīyopaniṣadbhāṣyavārttika (*Karl H. Potter*) 521
Naiṣkarmyasiddhi (*Karl H. Potter*) 530
Dakṣiṇāmūrtivārttika, or Mānasollāsa (*Karl H. Potter*) 550
Pañcīkaraṇavārttika, or Praṇavavārttika (*Karl H. Potter*) 560
5. Padmapāda 563
Pañcapādikā (*Karl H. Potter*) 564
6. Toṭaka, or Troṭaka, 598
Śrutisārasamuddhāraṇa (*Karl H. Potter*) 598
7. Hastāmalaka 601
Hastāmalakaślokāḥ (*Edeltraud Harzer*) 601

NOTES 603

INDEX 613

PREFACE

This volume, the third in the *Encyclopedia of Indian Philosophies*, is the first of those devoted to the philosophy of Advaita Vedānta. It covers the writings of Gauḍapāda, Śaṃkarācārya, Maṇḍana Miśra and Śaṃkara's pupils : Sureśvara, Padmapāda, Toṭaka, and Hastāmalaka (the last according to traditional authorities only)..

The remarks offered in the preface to volume two in this series relating to the general intent of the *Encyclopedia* apply to this volume and others to follow. To review briefly: this volume is intended, not as a definitive study of the works summarized, but as an invitation to further philosophical attention to them. The plan has been to make available the substance of the thought contained in these works, so that philosophers unable to read the original Sanskrit and who find difficulty in understanding and finding their way about in the translations (where such exist) can get an idea of the positions taken and arguments offered. The summaries, then, are intended primarily for philosophers and only secondarily for Indologists, and certain sections of the works have been omitted or treated sketchily because they are repetitious or deemed less interesting for philosophers, though they may be of great interest to Sanskritists. I might also add that the summaries are not likely to make interesting consecutive reading; they are provided in the spirit of a reference work. It is hoped, on the other hand, that the editor's Introduction will provide a readable account of some of the pertinent features of Advaita Vedānta for those hitherto unacquainted with that system of thought.

Preparation of this volume has been assisted materially by the gracious assistance provided by several agencies and individuals. The Bureau of Educational and Cultural Affairs of the U.S. Department of State, represented by Ms. Evelyn Barnes, kindly provided the project a generous grant in PL-480 rupees to cover preparation of this and other volumes. This grant made possible contacts with Indian colleagues and provided honoraria for a number of the summaries here included. The grant has been administered through the American Institute of Indian Studies, which has provided generous assistance in easing administrative details connected with the gathering of summaries, in arranging editorial travel and consultation, and in providing secretarial assistance and supplies. I wish especially to thank Pradip R. Mehendiratta and Edward C. Dimock for their good offices. In 1975 I received a fellowship from the American Council of Learned Societies through the Joint Committee on South Asia of the American Council of Learned Societies and Social Science Research Council that enabled me to make use of the unparalleled collections at the India Office Library and British Museum in London, without which opportunity a number of the summaries could not have been completed and much scholarly information could not have been conveyed or alluded to through references. I wish to thank James Settle of the American Council of Learned Societies as well as the authorities and staff members at the libraries mentioned. Finally, there are several individual scholars who are probably not aware of the extent of their contribution to this volume through their helpful and provocative conversation with me over the years in connection with Advaita. I wish especially to record my appreciation and debt to Anthony J. Alston, Daniel H. H. Ingalls, T. R. V. Murti, and Allen W. Thrasher for sharing their scholarship and thought with me. I am, needless to say, responsible for all misinterpretations of the materials that have crept into what follows.

1980 KARL H. POTTER

PART ONE

INTRODUCTION TO THE PHILOSOPHY OF ADVAITA VEDĀNTA

1

HISTORICAL RÉSUMÉ

1. What is Vedānta?

The Vedic literature represents the thought of the Aryans, Indo-European-speaking folk who perhaps entered India in the middle of the second millennium B.C. Consisting of a wide variety of materials, notably hymns and directions as to the proper performance of ritual, this literature also contains the beginnings of the philosophical and theological speculations that flowered eventually in classical Hinduism. Many of these speculations, usually reported in the form of discussions between teachers, pupils, and interlocutors, sometimes encased in mythological or didactic stories, are to be found in those portions of the Vedic corpus which reflect the later stages of philosophical development. These sections are termed 'Upaniṣads' (a term of doubtful etymology). The distinction between Upaniṣads and other parts of the Veda such as Āraṇyakas and Brāhmaṇas likewise seems to follow no established rules; presumably it is a matter of tradition. One must always remember that the Vedic 'literature' represents what primarily was, and is even today, an oral tradition.[1] Brahmin families pass from father to son that portion of the Veda which has been entrusted to them to preserve since ancient times.

The Upaniṣads are literally "the final sections of the Veda," which is what the term 'Vedānta' also means. Thus Vedānta philosophy, properly speaking, is that philosophy which takes its lead from the Upaniṣads. However, since the meanings of Upaniṣadic utterances are ambiguous, there came to be several Vedānta philosophies, corresponding to differing interpretations of the essential genius of the texts that inspired them. Despite an evident similarity in terminology, which is derived from their common allegiance to the same basic literature, these Vedānta philosophical systems vary substantially among themselves, and there is a polite but perfectly clear rivalry among them as to which system 'really' represents the teaching of the Upaniṣads. It is an issue that, in the nature of the case, may well be insoluble.

Vedānta philosophers are a particular section of those who specialize in *mīmāṃsā*, or exegetics of the Vedic scriptures. Mīmāṃsā is sometimes divided into Pūrvamīmāṃsā, the school of exegetics that interprets the 'older' scriptural hymns, and Uttaramīmāṃsā, which interprets the 'later,' Upaniṣadic materials. The two exegetical systems differ in the emphasis they place on the injunctive and ritual aspects of the Vedas as opposed to those passages that apparently convey information, especially information about things beyond immediate sensory awareness. The style of the oldest Vedantic philosophical works is overwhelmingly influenced by the exegetical tradition. Great portions of these works are concerned with the niceties of language, and it is mainly in later times that philosophers make bold to compose independent treatises (*prakaraṇa*) in which the elements of Vedānta philosophy are set forth according to the logic of the views themselves, rather than in an order determined by that of scriptural authority.

Much of the Vedānta literature is composed following the tradition of *sūtra* and commentary that reflects the oral tradition in which it was born. *Sūtras* are aphoristic phrases designed to remind their memorizer of the elements of the literature so summarized. Both Pūrva and Uttaramīmāṃsā have their *sūtras*, one set for each being known to us now, though others may have existed at an earlier time. The *(Pūrva)mīmāṃsāsūtras* of Jaimini form the basis of the older variety of Vedic exegesis, as well as provide a taking-off point for commentators such as Śabara, Kumārila, and Prabhākara, who pioneered systematic Mīmāṃsā philosophical systems through their commentaries. It is difficult to date the *Mīmāṃsāsūtras*—the tradition they represent must go back at least to the time of the writing of the Upaniṣads themselves, that is, to before 600 B.C., but the *sūtras* as we now have them need not be credited with such antiquity: it seems unlikely that they are earlier than 200 B.C. The set of *sūtras* ascribed to Bādarāyaṇa, variously called *Vedāntasūtras*, *Brahmasūtras*, or *Śārirakamīmāṃsāsūtras*, provides the corresponding vehicle for the 'later' (Uttara) exegetical tradition. Since the two sets of *sūtras* refer to each others' authors one might suspect they are of roughly the same age, although one cannot rule out the very real possibility of multiple authorship.

Various sorts of commentaries are composed on *sūtras*, and then subcommentaries and further commentaries on those. Traditionally, a *bhāṣya* is an extensive explanation of the meaning of the *sūtras*, a *vṛtti* is a briefer explanation, a *vārttika* a critical treatment of a *bhāṣya*, and so on. Frequently a writer will compose verses of his own for ease of memorization on the part of his reader or pupil, then provide his own commentary on those stanzas.

In addition to the Vedic scriptures, notably the Upaniṣads, and the *sūtras* that are intended to capture the essence of scripture, Vedānta philosophers will on occasion cite as authoritative, and occasionally even write separate commentaries on literary monuments that are not commonly accounted as part of Vedic scripture. Sometimes this tendency represents particular sectarian religious movements, as in later times led members of the Viśiṣṭādvaita Vedānta system to comment on old Tamil works of Pañcarātra persuasion. Far and away the most important instance of this phenomenon concerns the famous *Mahābhārata* poem, the *Bhagavadgītā*. Although the epics (the *Mahābhārata* and *Rāmāyaṇa*) are not accounted as *śruti*, that is to say, as works having unquestioned scriptural authority, they are pre-eminent among those works generally regarded as *smṛti*, 'tradition.' To both older and later Mīmāṃsakas *śruti*, connoting that which is 'heard,' is either authorless or of divine authorship; not being a human production, it cannot be mistaken, though we may be mistaken about what it means—thus the necessity of exegetics. By contrast *smṛti*, what is 'remembered,' comprises works of admitted human authorship, and thus there is the possibility of human error contaminating what they say, although this possibility is rendered academic by the venerability and sagacity of those who composed them. Vyāsa, the alleged author of the *Mahābhārata*, is one of the hoariest of sages, and the didactic portions of that epic, among which the *Bhagavadgītā* stands foremost, have an authority for all practical purposes equivalent to the scriptures themselves. Thus it is that many Vedantic philosophers have written commentaries on the *Bhagavadgītā*, finding in Kṛṣṇa's teachings an appropriate foil for expressing their particular slant.

The Upaniṣads—at least the oldest of them—the *Gītā*, and the *Brahmasūtras*, then, comprise what is considered to be the triple basis (*prasthānatrayī*) for Vedantic philosophy.

II. What is Advaita Vedānta?

So far we have been discussing the general background that all Vedānta philosophy shares. However, the present volume deals with only one Vedānta system, and indeed with only the earliest part of its literature. This system is properly known as Advaita Vedānta, though so important has it become in the eyes not only of scholars but also of those who have been influential in molding the attitudes of enlightened Hindus toward India's past, that one will frequently find the term 'Vedānta' used to indicate *only* Advaita Vedānta. This tendency is a confusion to the uninitiated as well as a constant source of irritation to those who are affiliated with one of the other Vedānta systems. Still, it serves to emphasize the importance that is now attributed to Advaita among the Vedāntas, and especially that attributed to its most famous figure, Śaṃkarācārya, a thinker with whom we shall be dealing at length in this volume.

Just as it is a mistake, though a common one, to identify all Vedānta with Advaita, so it is also a mistake, and a common one, to identify all Advaita with Śaṃkarācārya's philosophy. Through the efforts of a number of diligent scholars, we can now safely say that Śaṃkara did not found Advaita Vedānta and that there are points of interpretation on which others—also properly called Advaitins—differ from Śaṃkara. These points of distinction will become clear as we proceed. First, however, it will be well if we attempt to state as clearly as possible what is shared by and constitutive of the Advaita Vedānta philosophical position. I shall do this in rather summary form here; a fuller explanation is in the sequel.

We may divide the Advaita philosophy, rather arbitrarily for the moment, into a theoretical and a practical basis. Some propositions that characterize the theoretical basis are :

1. The purpose of philosophy is to point the way to liberation (*mokṣa*) from the bondage of rebirth (*saṃsāra*).

2. Bondage is a product of our ignorance (*avidyā*); the true Self (*ātman*) is not bound, does not transmigrate, is eternally liberated.

3. Bondage is beginningless and operates with regularity as long as ignorance is not removed.

4. Since bondage depends on ignorance, liberation is manifested upon the removal of ignorance by acquiring its opposite, namely, knowledge (*vidyā*).

5. The operation of ignorance consists in its creating apparent distinctions (*bheda*) where none actually exist.

6. Therefore, knowledge involves the awareness that all distinctions are false, especially the distinction between the knower and the known.

7. This awareness, which constitutes liberating knowledge, which is free from subject-object distinctions, is pure, immediate consciousness (*cit, anubhava*).

8. The true Self is itself just that pure consciousness, without which nothing can be known in any way.

9. And that same true Self, pure consciousness, is not different from the ultimate world Principle, Brahman, because if Brahman were conceived as the object of Self-awareness it would involve subject-object distinction and, as said above, this is a product of ignorance.

10. The real is that which is not set aside as false, not sublated (*bādha*), in contrast to products of ignorance, which are eventually sublated.

11. Assuming the above criterion of reality, it follows that Brahman (=the true Self, pure consciousness) is the only Reality (*sat*), since It is untinged by difference, the mark of ignorance, and since It is the one thing that is not sublatable, for sublation itself depends on there being consciousness.

12. Pure consciousness is experienced during deep sleep; since we awake refreshed, it is inferred that pure consciousness (reality, Brahman, the true Self) is also the ultimate bliss.

This is by no means an exhaustive list of Advaita tenets, but it will serve for the moment to indicate the tenor of the theory. Now for some 'practical' propositions.

13. Since all distinctions are the product of ignorance, any positive account of a path to liberation, involving distinctions, must be ultimately false.

14. However, some false views are less misleading than others. By criticizing worse views one arrives by stages at better ones.

15. For example, the view that effects are different from their causes (*asatkāryavāda*) is worse than the view that the effect is essentially identical with its cause (*satkāryavāda*); within the latter, the view that the cause transforms itself into its effect (*pariṇāmavāda*) is worse than the view that it manifests its appearance as effect without itself changing in so doing (*vivartavāda*); still, all views that take causation seriously are inferior to nonorigination (*ajātivāda*), since causal relations, as any relations, involve differences and are thus tinged with ignorance.

16. Or, for example, the view that one needs a distinct judgment to verify or justify true knowledge (*parataḥprāmāṇyavāda*) is worse than the view that true knowledge justifies itself (*svataḥprāmāṇya*); however, both these views are ultimately inferior to the view that truth is not to be found in judgments, that therefore one cannot attain ultimate understanding or truth through the *pramāṇas* or 'instruments of knowledge.'

17. Or, again, atheism and agnosticism are worse views than theism; within theism, again, monotheism is preferable to polytheism; but ultimately preferable to all theisms is monism.

18. Or, again, the skeptical or materialist view (Cārvāka or Lokāyata) is inferior to those views which accept the authority of scripture; among the latter, those views (Buddhism, Jainism, etc.) which accept as authority scriptures other than the Vedas are inferior to those views which accept the Vedas as authoritative; among the latter, the view that holds that only the injunctive sections (*karmakāṇḍa*) of scripture are authoritative (or that scripture is exhausted in injunctions) is inferior to that which holds that both the injunctive and declarative (*jñānakāṇḍa*) sections are authoritative; within this last, those who think that both sections speak of liberation—that both actions enjoined and knowledge conveyed in scripture are directly relevant to gaining liberation—hold an inferior view compared to those who believe that the two sections speak to different ends—injunctions leading one to heaven, declarations to liberation, Ultimately, however, scripture can provide no positive key to liberation, because the key lies in removing ignorance, a negative step; so the highest view of all is that of *apavāda*, that reality is "not this, not this" (*neti neti*).

The 'dialectical' aspects of these last four examples of stages along the way toward understanding explain why so many apparent contradictions—paradoxes, if you will—are apparently condoned and indeed frequently celebrated in Advaita. No contradictions are ultimately acceptable to Advaita, to be sure, because contradictions are clearly in the scope of ignorance, if only because they involve language and so distinctions. But it doesn't follow that any contradiction is as good as any other: some are instructive paradoxes, puzzles, which inspire questions from pupils that sympathetic *gurus* can turn to advantage in bringing their pupils to a higher stage of understanding. Frequently Advaita texts read as *verbatim* reports of teacher-pupil interviews.

The feature illustrated in the last four examples likewise suggests the kind of richness that makes Advaita so impressive when contrasted with philosophies such as Nyāya-Vaiśeṣika, which believe that the ultimate truth can and should be literally expressed in language. It must also produce feelings of irritation among nonbelieving Advaita scholars, for apophasis coupled with dialectic renders it difficult at all times to know with what degree of seriousness one should construe what is being said at any moment.

Of particular relevance for our present purposes, the 'dialectical' features of Advaita also make it especially difficult to distinguish an Advaita Vedantin from other Vedantins, especially in cases where we only have fragmentary passages or references to go on in determining his views. A good deal of scholarship—to be reviewed below and in the historical introductions to the philosophers whose views are summarized in the body of this volume—has been expended in attempts to establish how Advaita developed prior to the time of Śaṃkara. But which were the Advaitins? Who are the philosophers that this volume should treat?

III. Who Were These Philosophers?

As we have seen, Vedānta in general can be safely stated to have arisen in the Upaniṣads. It was later epitomized in the *Vedānta-sūtras.* Commentators on these writings interpreted them in different ways and with different emphases: one finds old commentators referred to frequently in Śaṃkara, Rāmānuja, and the other great Vedantins, as well as in their commentators in turn. Unfortunately, the dictates of style and manner entailed that these references do not necessarily identify by name the old teacher-commentator whose opinion is being quoted or reported; frequently it was left to a much later writer, removed from the time of the old commentator by more than a millennium in many instances, to tell us that Śaṃkara meant so-and-so by "they say" in a given passage. As a result, one views these identifications with a mixture of gratitude and skepticism.

Our business is with Advaita Vedantins, however. Did an Advaita tradition exist in the first half of the first millennium A.D.? Śaṃkara certainly thinks so: he refers to his 'tradition' (*sampradāya*) and quotes certain old writers with the reverence appropriate to the elders of a tradition one accepts. He even goes so far as to say that even a man wise in all the sciences is still like a fool if he has no tradition.[8] Despite this, scholars of pre-Śaṃkara Vedānta have had little success in identifying beyond question more than one or two names of writers who may have been associated with an Advaita tradition.

One could, of course, argue that the great teachers whose instruction is reported in the Upaniṣads, men such as Yājñavalkya and Uddālaka Aruṇi, were Advaita Vedantins, since they propounded views and arguments that are interpreted by Advaita as expressing the philosophy outlined above. This would be tendentious in the extreme, however, since important representatives of other Vedānta systems—notably Viśiṣṭādvaitins and Dvaitins—also claim the authority of those very same teachers. Thus the truth of such a claim seems to rest on the acceptance of the truth of Advaita in contrast to other Vedāntas, not on historical arguments of a nondoctrinal sort.

The same consideration weighs against *our* uncritically counting

Bādarāyaṇa, the author of the *Brahmasūtras*, as an Advaitin, although it doesn't stop Advaitins from doing so. In any case, we know nothing of Bādarāyaṇa, not even his date or place of origin, and a summary of his Advaita leanings, if they existed, will arise naturally from the commentaries of his Advaita interpreters, which *are* summarized below.

Bādarāyaṇa mentions on occasion views of others by name. In one passage[3] he contrasts the views of three old teachers—Āśmarathya, Auḍulomi, and Kāśakṛtsna, in that order—on the question of the relation between the individual self and the true Self. Śaṃkara interprets Kāśakṛtsna's position indicated in the *sūtra* in question as representing the monistic Advaita position, and one might therefore wish to count Kāśakṛtsna—whoever he may have been—as an old Advaitin. Unfortunately, once again other Vedantins claim him too: Rāmānuja does so by interpreting the *sūtra* in a way consistent with Viśiṣṭādvaita. Since the *sūtra* in question consists of precisely one word[4] it is not hard to construct divergent readings.

The date of the *Brahmasūtras* is not closely identified—the best scholarly guesses put it a century or two before or after Christ.[5] It seems safe to say, for reasons of the sort mentioned, that we have no firm evidence at this time of an Advaita tradition prior to the time of the *Brahmasūtras*, though there were doubtless Vedantins of some sort, and the *sūtras* do on occasion suggest that older teachers had offered differing interpretations of the Upaniṣads, quite possibly in the form of systematic treatises. Once past the time of the *sūtras*, however, we hear of a few names that may perhaps be linked with Advaita.

The dislike Indians had for identifying people by name is a constant headache in this connection. Instead of naming previous commentators, or even their traditional affiliations, it is characteristic of Indian philosophers to introduce an opponent's view by a laconic "some say." Indeed, we are lucky to get even that; the bane of the efforts of the translator of Sanskrit philosophical texts is making sure when one is dealing with an opponent's view, since so frequently no signal whatsoever is given. Slightly better chances for identification are afforded in passages where an author is making passing reference to someone's position. Unfortunately, even here the given name is either not known or not deemed sufficiently respectful; the person in question may well be identified by the work he wrote. Even this wouldn't be so problematic if we had the *whole* name, but as the work is likely to be a commentary and the author is addressing a knowledgeable audience, the identification may well be only to the *type* of commentary the person is reputed to have written. For example,

Śaṃkara is frequently referred to by his disciples as the *Bhāṣyakāra*, since he wrote a *Brahmasūtrabhāṣya.*

The relevance of all this to our present context is that, in many Vedānta works by Śaṃkara and his pupils, in those of some Mīmāṃsakas, of Rāmānuja and his followers, and of Bhāskara and others, there are constant references to one or more persons called 'Vṛttikāra.' A Vṛttikāra is someone who wrote a brief commentary (*vṛtti*), but the simple allusion to that fact fails to distinguish those who commented thus on one work from those who commented thus on another. Presumably there were *vṛttis* on many of the Upaniṣads, on the *Bhagavadgītā*, and on the *Brahmasūtras*, all of which are now lost; there were also *vṛttis* on other works—for example, on the *Mīmāṃsāsūtras*—which in a given context may be the work alluded to.

Śaṃkara speaks frequently of Vṛttikāras. He speaks, more specifically, of a *Śārīrakamīmāṃsāvṛtti*, that is, a commentary on the *Brahmasūtras*, whose author he names as Upavarṣa.[6] His reference there implies that Upavarṣa also wrote a commentary on the *Mīmāṃsāsūtras*, and this is confirmed by Śabara, author of the major existent commentary on the *Mīmāṃsāsūtras*, who summarizes some of Upavarṣa's views.[7] It is also indirectly confirmed by the fact that Bhāskara also quotes Upavarṣa in the same connection as does Śaṃkara, although under different *sūtras*.[8] Later commentators such as Padmapāda, Govindānanda, Ānandagiri, and even the Naiyāyika Jayanta Bhaṭṭa, have also cited certain views they attribute to Upavarṣa.[9] It seems from all this that there must have been an Upavarṣa who wrote commentaries on the *Mīmāṃsā* and *Brahmasūtras* (or perhaps, some scholars[10] have suggested, a single commentary on both), and furthermore that Śaṃkara, who refers to Upavarṣa as 'Bhagavān,' counted Upavarṣa as a member of the tradition he follows.

Upavarṣa's date has been hazarded as between 100 B.C. and A.D. 200, since Śabara's date is around A.D. 200.[11] Viśiṣṭādvaita writers, notably Rāmānuja himself, speak of a Vṛttikāra named Bodhāyana,[12] and Vedānta Deśika, the great Viśiṣṭādvaita scholiast, identifies Bodhāyana with Upavarṣa.[13] For various reasons that identification seems suspect, and it is more likely that Bodhāyana wrote a different *vṛtti*, and quite possible that Śaṃkara is criticizing that in places.[14] Padmapāda, for instance, speaks of 'another *vṛtti*' (*vṛttyantara*) with which Advaita differs.[15] There is no reason to identify either Upavarṣa or Bodhāyana with the Vṛttikāra who is cited in Śaṃkara's commentary on the *Bhagavadgītā*, although Ānandagiri, many centuries later, seems assured that not only are the *vṛttis* on

Brahmasūtras and *Bhagavadgītā* by the same hand, but that the same author also wrote *vṛttis* on several Upaniṣads.[16]

Śaṃkara, in commenting on some of the oldest Upaniṣads, makes three references to old teachers who apparently addressed themselves to the interpretation of the *Chāndogya Upaniṣad.* Ānandagiri identifies these as referring to Draviḍācārya, who, according to Sarvajñātman (a pupil of Sureśvara's), wrote a *bhāṣya* on some *Chāndogya* "sentences" (*vākya*) ascribed by him to Brahmanandin.[17] On these rather flimsy bases one may take Brahmanandin and Draviḍācārya as two more early Advaitins, since Śaṃkara once again seems highly respectful toward the author of the views he makes reference to. Not all modern scholars have been willing to accept these two as Advaitins. There are authorities and arguments, though by no means conclusive ones, for identifying Brahmanandin with Ṭaṅka, an old teacher mentioned by Yāmunācārya as an opponent but by Rāmānuja as a forerunner in his own tradition.[18] Again, the dates of these two commentators on the *Chāndogya* are almost entirely uncertain.

A final name to be mentioned here is that of Sundara Pāṇḍya, who seems to have written a *vārttika* on Upavarṣa's *vṛtti*.[19] Scholars have identified some passages in Advaita and Mīmāṃsā works that are identified by later Advaitins as referring to Sundara Pāṇḍya,[20] but little or nothing is known of his identity or date.

Other old Vedantins, such as Bhartṛprapañca, Brahmadatta, and Bhartṛmitra, appear not to have been Advaitins, although Brahmadatta may have had strong leanings in that direction despite his espousing theses at odds with those we listed above.[21]

So far we have been dealing with figures who, except for Bādarāyaṇa, wrote works now apparently lost. The first complete Advaita philosophical work is all, or at least a large part, of some stanzas (*kārikās*) that Advaita tradition construes as constituting a kind of commentary on the *Māṇḍūkya Upaniṣad.* The same tradition identifies the author of these stanzas as Gauḍapāda. Śaṃkara speaks of Gauḍapāda as his *paramaguru* and teacher's teacher.[22] The stanzas are called by several names : *Māṇḍūkyakārikās, Gauḍapādiyakārikās,* or *Āgamaśāstra.*

Modern scholarship has blossomed forth in vast controversy over a variety of matters relating to Gauḍapāda. The details must be gathered from the literature itself;[23] here we merely mention the problem areas as they affect our general understanding of Advaita development.

First, there is the question of the date of the *Māṇḍūkyakārikās.* If Śaṃkara's identification is to be accepted one would naturally place the *Kārikās* no more than fifty to one hundred years prior to Śaṃkara's date, which many scholars feel should be fixed at A.D. 788-820. On this understanding the *Kārikās* can date from no earlier than the end of the seventh century. On the other hand, a Buddhist philosopher, Bhāvaviveka, appears to allude to several of the *Kārikās* and quotes one verbatim, and Bhāvaviveka's date is clearly fixed as prior to 630, since one of his works was translated into Chinese around that year. Thus the *Kārikās* must date not later than the early seventh century. But if we place the *Kārikās* in the sixth-seventh century we must either reinterpret Śaṃkara's remark about his teacher's teacher, or else recompute Śaṃkara's date.

Second, there is the name 'Gauḍapāda.' 'Gauḍa' is an old term referring to the northeast portion of the subcontinent, roughly North Bengal. It has been suggested that the *Kārikās* really constitute more than one work, but that the collection came to be known as *Gauḍapādiyakārikās* because the several authors came from that region, or perhaps because the tradition they pioneered flourished in that region. Predictably, this view has not found favor among proponents of the Advaita tradition, who believe the entire set of stanzas constitutes a single Advaita treatise. Nevertheless, given the pronouncedly Buddhistic flavor of the fourth book of stanzas, which contrasts in terminology with the rest, the possibility that we are dealing with more than one work and/or author cannot be ruled out.

Third, there is the matter of the alleged Buddhistic leanings of the *Kārikās*. Even the most ardent Advaitin can hardly deny that the terminology used, especially in the last book, is redolent of Buddhism. That fact alone does not bother those who are willing to admit Advaita's affinities with certain Buddhist systems (Vijñānavāda, Mādhyamika) and who thus have no objection to allowing a general 'influence' on Advaita by Buddhism. Not all Advaitins are so tolerant, however, especially when their opponents have raised what Advaitins consider to be the malicious charge that Śaṃkara was a 'crypto-Buddhist,' citing Gauḍapāda as evidence. There is little reason to doubt that Śaṃkara viewed Buddhism as one of the worst of heresies and criticized it as roundly as any opposing philosophy of which he was aware. This issue, more than any of the others discussed in the scholarly literature, has raised as much heat as light.

Fourth, there is the very interesting question of the relation between the stanzas and the *Māṇḍūkya Upaniṣad* itself. The accepted Advaita tradition is that the *Māṇḍūkya Upaniṣad* consists of a dozen sentences explaining the syllable *aum/om* as having four parts (waking, dream, deep sleep and the 'fourth') and as being symbolically identical with Brahman, the Self. The first twenty-nine *kārikās*, constituting the first book of Gauḍapāda's treatise, provide explicit commentary on these twelve sentences: the relationship between sentences and stanzas is indicated in the commentary attributed to Śaṃkara. The remainder of the *Kārikās*—the last three books—are not specifically comments on the Upaniṣad, although it is contended that they are relevant to its subject matter in a general way. This is not the only relationship that has been suggested, however. The great Dvaita Vedantin Madhva and his followers consider the twenty-nine *kārikās* of the first book, though not the remaining *kārikās*, to be scripture (*śruti*), although they think the Upaniṣad and the stanzas were separate treatises. Rāmānuja also thought those *kārikās* were scripture. It has even been suggested by one modern scholar that the first book of *kārikās* antedated the Upaniṣad itself, so that the Upaniṣad was based on the stanzas rather than the reverse.

There are other issues surrounding Gauḍapāda and the *Kārikās*. However, no one really doubts that there are one or more works preserved in what we call the *Gauḍapādīyakārikās* and that at least one of these works (say, the second and third books) teach Advaita Vedānta in clearcut terms. And since Śaṃkara and Maṇḍana Miśra both know these stanzas they must have been written prior to the time of those philosophers. Thus, despite the many interesting questions raised by scholarship it still seems safe to say that the *kārikās* of at least the second and third books constitute the earliest extended Advaita treatise that has been preserved for us.

Gauḍapāda is according to tradition supposed to have taught Govindabhagavatpāda, Śaṃkara's teacher. Tradition also makes Govinda a Kashmiri who, while traveling south toward Cidambaram happened on Gauḍapāda on the banks of the Narmadā River and became his pupil. It was also on the Narmadā that Śaṃkara subsequently studied with Govinda. These traditions are embellished with interesting stories but can in no way be authenticated at this time. We know nothing at all about Govinda except that he was Śaṃkara's teacher. He apparently wrote little or nothing.

This brings us, then, to the time of Śaṃkarācārya. As mentioned above, many scholars tend to believe that he flourished around the end of the eighth and beginning of the ninth century, but this date is not conclusive, and we favor placing him a century earlier. It is extremely difficult to differentiate traditional stories from fact in his case—no other Indian philosopher has been celebrated in so many legends, and these are reported as unquestionable by his followers. He is reputed to have lived a very short life of only thirty-two years, yet if in that time he was indeed responsible for the vast quantity of literature that is attributed to him, he must have been composing every hour of the day !

The basic problem however, not only for arriving at Śaṃkara's date but also for arriving at reasoned conclusions about much else about him and his philosophy, concerns the authenticity of the works attributed to him. If we could be certain which works are by Śaṃkara we could then draw up a list of references found in those works, and provided we could identify their sources or the authors they presuppose, we would then be able to provide at least an upper limit for his date.

It is difficult if not impossible to be sure which works Śaṃkara wrote. We may start by assuming that he wrote the *Brahmasūtra-bhāṣya*—the Śaṃkara we are interested in is, by definition, the one who wrote this work. No one seems anxious to question the same person's authorship of the *Bhāṣyas* on the *Bṛhadāraṇyaka* and *Chāndogya Upaniṣads*. Beyond these, the questions begin. We shall not try to deal with these questions at this juncture—the issues will be summarized later when the data and arguments are reviewed.

Even in the three works mentioned, there are enough references to give us some purchase on Śaṃkara's date. The author of these works clearly knows Kumārila and Prabhākara, the two philosophical Mīmāṃsakas. They are usually held to have flourished in the seventh century. Advaita traditional accounts of Śaṃkara's life relate a meeting between Śaṃkara and Kumārila. It seems likely that Śaṃkara also knew Dharmakīrti's work. These facts are enough to insure that Śaṃkara did not flourish before the seventh century but do not determine whether he lived in the seventh, eighth, or even the ninth century.

The situation is further complicated by uncertainty about the identity of Maṇḍana Miśra, whose *Brahmasiddhi* constitutes an extremely important source of Advaita. Maṇḍana wrote several Bhāṭṭa Mīmāṃsā works and is reputed to have studied with Kumārila. Tales are told about Śaṃkara's meeting with Maṇḍana and his wife, and their eventual conversion. According to the Advaita tradition, Maṇḍana then changed his name to Sureśvara and became a pupil of Śaṃkara. Some scholars have thought it evident that both Advaitins were aware of each other's works, which confirms their contemporaneity.

The reader will find a review of the arguments concerning Śaṃkara's date in the body of this volume at the outset of the section assigned to that writer. For reasons given there I incline to believe that he flourished at the beginning of the eighth century.

Śaṃkara is said by some of his biographers to have been born in

Kalāḍi, a small town in the Malabar region now included in the state of Kerala. His father died when Śaṃkara was very young, and he developed as a child prodigy, very learned and very religious. At an early age he left home, studied with Govinda, and eventually, arrived at Banaras where he attracted some followers, notably Padmapāda, Hastāmalaka, and Toṭaka. On a journey to Allahabad, he is supposed to have met Kumārila, then very old, who sent his pupil Maṇḍana to debate with Śaṃkara. Maṇḍana brought his wife along, and after Śaṃkara had defeated Maṇḍana (so goes the story) the wife took up the cause. During the course of their further discussion, the wife, Bhāratī by name, pointed out that Śaṃkara was not fully experienced in worldly ways, not having mastered *kāmaśāstra* or the science of passion. Śaṃkara then asked for a month's delay in the proceedings, occupied the body of an amorous king and quickly mastered *kāmaśāstra*. After the month was over, he returned to the debate, defeating Bhāratī, who along with her husband became Śaṃkara's devoted disciple. Maṇḍana, according to tradition, was renamed Sureśvara and proceeded to compose several important Advaita treatises.

The entourage then returned to Kerala by way of Śṛṅgeri, where a *maṭha* was founded. When Śaṃkara's mother died, he fulfilled his childhood promise by performing the last rites despite the fact that he was an avowed *saṃnyāsin*, that is, he had renounced all religious ritual acts.

Śaṃkara then began extensive journeying that took him throughout India. At Dwarka in the west he founded another *maṭha*; he founded a third *maṭha* at Badrinath in the Himalayas and a fourth at Puri in the east. He founded the sect of the Daśanāmis, the "ten-named ones," and installed his most important followers as the heads of the four *maṭhas*. Some stories have it that he met the famous Kashmir Śaiva savant Abhinavagupta, who cursed him with an ulcerous disease of which he eventually died, but not before Padmapāda had transferred it back to its donor, who also died of it. At the age of thirty-two then, having lived a remarkably full life in such a few years, Śaṃkara passed away.

The above account draws a few stories and traditions from the indefinite number found in the many traditional biographies. It is hardly possible to discriminate fact from fiction among these at this late date. Their number attests the particular reverence felt for Śaṃkarācārya by Advaitins in particular, but also to a remarkably great degree by Indians of all walks of life, whether or not their philosophical and/or religious persuasions agree with his.

Overshadowed as an object of traditional reverence, Maṇḍana Miśra must not be underrated as a philosopher. His alleged identity with Sureśvara has been severely questioned by scholars.[24] As mentioned, tradition makes him a pupil of Kumārila and an elder contemporary of Śaṃkara's. His single Advaita work, the *Brahmasiddhi*, is an independent treatise developing the major tenets of Advaita. The sources of the thought expressed in this work have been the subject of speculation. Yet it seems to have been quite original. There is some reason to think that for several centuries following Śaṃkara's and Maṇḍana's lifetimes it was Maṇḍana who was viewed by other schools as the major figure in Advaita.[25] Vācaspati Miśra is said to have continued Maṇḍana's brand of Advaita in a commentary, now lost, on the *Brahmasiddhi* and in his *Bhāmatī* on Śaṃkara's *Brahmasūtrabhāṣya*.

Śaṃkara had many pupils, but only four of them are remembered by name. Padmapāda, a native of Cidambaram (?), is supposed to have been one of his first followers. Padmapāda's *Pañcapādikā* is a commentary on Śaṃkara's commentary on the first four *Brahmasūtras*; it is not clear whether Padmapāda's work carried beyond that point—in any case it is all we have. Although there are one or two other works attributed to Padmapāda, his authorship of them is doubtful.

Sureśvara is now associated especially with the history of the Kāmakoṭi Pīṭha at Conjeeveram (old Kāñchi), which may or may not have been one of the original *maṭhas* established by Śaṃkara but which has become since then one of the great centers of Advaita activity. Tradition, as we have seen, makes him Maṇḍana before conversion; we have no hard evidence about any other facts pertaining to his life. Śaṃkara is said to have assigned to him the writing of subcommentaries (*vārttikas*) on two of his own Upaniṣadbhāṣyas, those on the *Bṛhadāraṇyaka* and the *Taittirīya*. The former is a truly vast work—Mahadevan says it is about half the length of the *Rāmāyaṇa* ! Sureśvara also wrote an independent treatise of great beauty and skill, the *Naiṣkarmyasiddhi*. Other works attributed to him are probably spurious.

A third disciple of Śaṃkara's was, according to tradition, originally named Giri but was given the name of Toṭaka when he joined Śaṃkara's group. He is supposed to have been very devoted but was apparently not a quick learner until one day after Śaṃkara, to the irritation of the other pupils, had delayed lessons so that Toṭaka might attend. He eventually arrived and amazed all by producing first a poem of eight verses, *Toṭakāṣṭaka*, and then a longer work, entitled

Śrutisārasamuddhāraṇa, which is supposed to have been spontaneously composed in the presence of his teacher and fellow pupils.

A final name of interest is that of Hastāmalaka, whom tradition identifies as a son of Prabhākara (not necessarily the famous Mīmāṃsaka), and of whom his father had despaired, for he had been cataleptic from birth. When addressed by Śaṃkara, however, asking "Who art thou?" the boy blossomed forth with a fourteen-verse poem on the Self, now called *Hastāmalakastotra*.

When Śaṃkara established the four *pīṭhas* at Śṛṅgeri, Dwarka, Badrinath, and Puri, he is supposed to have put one of his pupils in charge of each. However, the traditional lists of the different temples disagree on the details of who was installed where, and in addition the Kāmakoṭi temple at Conjeeveram has since become extremely important as a center of Advaita sectarianism. So we cannot say with certainty at this point which pupils are to be associated with which temples.

The following list names the authors treated in this volume, those works which are accepted by practically all scholars as authentically theirs, and also the most important of the spurious works. An approximation, based on evidence to be summarized below, is given of the dates we are at present inclined to assign to these writers.

A CHECK LIST OF AUTHORS AND WORKS

Abbreviations : d. date; p. place; w. work(s); T, edited and translated; E, published but not translated; M, manuscript(s) available but not published; *, probably spurious

Upavarṣa; d. before A.D. 200 (?); p. ?; w. *Brahmasūtravṛtti*

Brahmanandin; d. ?; p. ?; w. *Chāndogyopaniṣadvākya*

Draviḍācārya; d. ?; p. "the South"; w. *Chāndogyopaniṣadvākyabhāṣya*

Sundara Pāṇḍya; d. ?; p. ?; w. *Brahmasūtravṛttivārttika*

Gauḍapādācārya; d. A.D. 600 (?); p. North Bengal; w. *Māṇḍūkyopaniṣadkārikās* (also called *Gauḍapādakārikās* or *Āgamaśāstra*), (T)

Śaṃkarācārya; d. A.D. 725 (?); p. Kerala; w. *Brahmasūtrabhāṣya* (T), *Bṛhadāraṇyakopaniṣadbhāṣya* (T), *Taittirīyopaniṣadbhāṣya* (T), *Upadeśasāhasrī* (T), *Chāndogyopaniṣadbhāṣya* (T), *Aitareyopaniṣadbhāṣya* (T), *Īśopaniṣadbhāṣya* (T), *Kaṭhopaniṣadbhāṣya* (T), *Kenopaniṣad (pada)bhāṣya* (T), *Kenopaniṣad (vākya)bhāṣya* (E), *Muṇḍakopaniṣadbhāṣya* (T), *Praśnopaniṣadbhāṣya* (T), *Bhagavadgītābhāṣya* (T), *Māṇḍūkyopaniṣadbhāṣya* with *Gauḍapādīyakārikābhāṣya* (T), **Dakṣiṇāmūrtistotra* (T), **Pañcīkaraṇa* (T), **Aparokṣānubhūti* (T), **Ātmabodha* (T), **Śataślokī* (T), **Ātmajñānopadeśa* (T), **Ātmānātmaviveka* (T), **Tattvabodha* (T), **Daśaślokī* (T), **Vākyavṛtti* (T),

*Vivekacūḍāmaṇi (T), *Sarvavedāntasiddhāntasaṃgraha (T), *Advaitapañcaratna or Ātmapañcaka (T), *Vākyasudhā or Dṛgdṛśyaviveka (T), *Upadeśapañcaka (T), *Māyāpañcaka (T), *Laghuvākyavṛtti (T), *Śvetāśvataropaniṣadbhāṣya (E), *Nṛsiṃhottaratāpanīyopaniṣadbhāṣya (E), *Kauśitakyupaniṣadbhāṣya (E)

Maṇḍana Miśra; d. A.D. 680-750 (?); p. Mithila (?); w. *Brahmasiddhi* (T [French])

Padmapāda; d. A.D. 750-(?); p. Cidambaram (?); w. *Pañcapādikā* (T)

Sureśvara; d. A.D. 750 (?); p. ?; w. *Bṛhadāraṇyakopaniṣadbhāṣyavārttika* (E; partly T), *Taittirīyopaniṣadbhāṣyavārttika* (T), *Naiṣkarmyasiddhi* (T), **Dakṣiṇāmūrtimānasollāsa* (T), **Pañcikaraṇavārttika* (E), **Kāśimokṣavicāra* (E), **Svārājyasiddhi* (E)

Toṭaka; d. A.D. 750 (?); p. ?; w. *Toṭakāṣṭaka* (E), *Śrutisārasamuddhāraṇa* (E)

Hastāmalaka; d. A.D. 750 (?); p. ?; w. **Hastāmalakaślokāḥ* (T [German])

IV. Relation to Other Systems

Śaṃkara is very much aware of the variety of philosophical views current in his time as well as those relevant to his purpose and which flourished at earlier periods. It would be instructive to measure the amount of time he gives specific systems. Impressionistically, in default of such a measure, we can say that the early Advaitins devote the greatest amount of time to dealing with the views of Mīmāṃsakas and other types of Vedānta. But in the *Brahmasūtrabhāṣya* Śaṃkara considers at length Sāṃkhya. In that work also, there are extended criticisms of Nyāya, Vaiśeṣika, Yoga, Buddhist, Jain, and Cārvāka theories. By consulting the index to this volume the reader can quickly trace the most important passage in which each school is criticized.

One may also raise the question of the influence of the various systems on the development of Advaita. Defenders of the tradition point out that their philosophical stance goes back a long way—in their eyes, it was developed by the sages of whom we hear in the Upaniṣads and by their predecessors. On the other hand, as was implied in the foregoing, there seems to be a remarkably small number of identifiable Advaitins prior to Śaṃkara, and one not disposed to accept tradition uncritically may well speculate that the Advaita interpretation of the Upaniṣads, although no doubt receiving a good many cues from the scriptures themselves, also owes something to other influences, blossoming forth for the first time especially in the works of Śaṃkara and Maṇḍana. Once the question of influence is opened up in this way there does indeed seem to be some reason to suspect certain factors that conditioned the Advaita interpretation.

Some of the influences are relatively uncontroversial. It is clear enough, for example, that Maṇḍana Miśra's brand of Advaita incorporates the doctrine of *sphoṭa*, a grammatical theory held by Bhartṛhari the grammarian, whereas, Śaṃkara and his followers reject the *sphoṭa* theory. Again, Maṇḍana's explanation of false judgments tries to assimilate the Advaita view to that of the Bhāṭṭa Mīmāṃsaka, whereas Śaṃkara is ambivalent and Sureśvara definitely critical of the Bhāṭṭa view on error. Maṇḍana also appears to owe something to Mīmāṃsā in his attitude toward the place of meditation in achieving release, and in his tendency to accommodate to some extent a "combined-path" view (*jñānakarmasamuccayavāda*).[26] These tendencies are not surprising : Maṇḍana was indeed a major figure in the history of both Grammarian philosophy—as the author of the *Sphoṭasiddhi*, a masterful exposition of the theory—and of Bhāṭṭa Mīmāṃsā—as the author of several works about the system and (possibly) as a student of Kumārila himself.

It is also evident that either Advaita takes over some of the Sāṃkhya psychology or that the two systems have a common source. Advaita and Sāṃkhya both develop their account of the world through a model of reflection, according to which the pure consciousness of Self (one Self in Advaita, many in Sāṃkhya) is reflected by the *buddhi*, in various forms, including egoity (*ahaṃkāra*), internal organ (*manas*), and eventually the physical bodies and qualities of the empirical world. The parallels between the two theories on such issues clearly make it important in Śaṃkara's eyes that he carefully distinguishes the peculiar Advaita version, involving *avidyā* as a positive force though nevertheless ultimately unreal, from the Sāṃkhya account featuring a *prakṛti* that undergoes real transformations and in which *avidyā* is only a negative fact, the failure to discriminate.

The greatest notoriety has surrounded alleged Buddhist influence on Śaṃkara's Advaita. On the face of it the charge is absurd. Śaṃkara not only shows no self-conscious leanings toward Buddhism he saves some of his choicest disrespectful language for the Buddhists.[27] Nevertheless, the issue has attracted considerable scholarly discussion. As we have already seen, Gauḍapāda uses Buddhist terminology to draw Advaita conclusions. Furthermore, there are important parallels—up to a point—particularly with Vijñānavāda. Majumdar argues that Gauḍapāda got his philosophy straight out of the *Laṅkāvatārasūtra*.[28] The handling of *avidyā/māyā* in Vijñanavāda resembles

Advaita's in certain respects. Comparisons with Mādhyamika are also possible : both Mādhyamika and Advaita profess the doctrine of nonorigination (*ajātivāda*) and both Advaita and Buddhism appeal to dreams as illustrations taken to show the unreality of the world. Other points of comparison can also be found.[29]

Loyal Advaitins have almost universally rejected the suggestion of any influence, and many of them will argue that the parallels just noted are accidental or the result of misunderstandings or foreshortened views. For example, K. A. K. Aiyar[30] points out five aspects in which Advaita and Buddhism are entirely distinct, and most of them relate to the alleged parallels. (1) Both schools say that the world is "unreal", but whereas the Buddhists mean that it is only a conceptual construct (*vikalpa*), Śaṃkara does not think the world is merely a concept. (2) Momentariness is a cardinal principle of Buddhism—consciousness is fundamentally momentary for them. But in Advaita consciousness is pure, without beginning or end, thoroughly continuous; the momentariness of empirical states of consciousness overlies this underlying continuity. (3) In Buddhism the "self" is the ego, a conceptual construction and quite unreal; in Advaita the Self is the only really Real, the substratum of all conceptions. (4) In Buddhism *avidyā* causes us to construct continuants, such as the self; in Advaita it causes us instead to take what is unreal to be real and vice versa. (5) Removal of *avidyā* leads to a "blowing out" (*nirvāṇa*) for Buddhists, but for Śaṃkara it leads to perfect knowledge (*vidyā*).[31]

2

THEORY OF VALUE

I. Bondage : Life, Death, and Rebirth

As do all Indian philosophical systems (except for the Cārvākas), Advaita orients its entire approach around the quest for liberation (*mokṣa*), the release from bondage (*saṃsāra*). Although there are various levels on which this quest can be understood or interpreted, it seems quite evident that the Advaita philosophers studied here construed bondage quite literally as a more or less mechanical process (though under divine control) describable in very specific detail. In order fully to understand the Advaita theory about liberation it is necessary first to comprehend what constitutes bondage, that is, to review the cycle of life, death, and rebirth as it is conceived in Advaita. For reasons that will become clear, it seems best to begin this account at the time of a man's death and to trace his continuation around to the time of his subsequent death in his next life.

A. *Death.* Death may be due either to "natural causes," construed here as one's having lived through his allotted years as determined by his past karma, or to violence, which interrupts the natural working out of karma. In either case, however, a man comes to the point of death endowed with several relevant bits of equipment. These include his gross body, made up of material substances such as earth, water, etc.; his sense organs and "action" organs (organs of speech, locomotion, grasping, sex, and excretion); his intellectual organ (*manas*); his sense of ego (*ahaṃkāra*); and his internal organ (*buddhi* or *antaḥkaraṇa*), which is the basis of his ability to engage in intentional awareness and consequent activity.

In addition, he has stored up in the form of traces (*saṃskāra*), or tendencies, the residues (*anuśaya*) of acts he has performed in the life just ending, as well as the residues of acts performed in previous lives, which have not as yet come to "fruition" or "maturation" (*vipāka*), that is, which have not as yet produced their results. Karmic residues are of three kinds. (1) There are those residues that were determined at birth to work themselves out during the present life (the one just ending)—these residues are called *prārabdhakarman.* (2) There are those residues that were produced by acts performed either in this life or in a previous one, but which remain latent during this present life—called *sañcitakarman.*[1] (3) Then there are the results of acts performed during this very lifetime, which will mature in some subsequent lifetime in the normal course of events. This kind of karma is called *sañciyamāna* or *āgamin karman.*

As karmic residues mature they are influenced by what are called "impressions" (*vāsanās*) to determine the way in which the karmic potentials will in fact be worked out, the kind of experience (*bhoga*) that will accrue to the agent in consequence, and the future karmic residues that will be laid down by the act(s) so determined. These *vāsanās* appear to be decisions arrived at by the internal organ to seek certain kinds of outcomes. For instance, K. S. Iyer[2] divides *vāsanās* into impure and pure types and subdivides the impure into those, for example, that relate to worldly pride, those that relate to over-intellectualizing (addiction to study, ritualism), and those that relate to one's body (taking the body to be one's true Self, use of cosmetics to beautify or medicines to remove blemishes from one's body). At any moment in one's conscious lifetime one is guided in acting by such *vāsanās*, which develop into desires (*kāma*).[3]

The Upaniṣads themselves suggest several accounts of what happens to these various things at the time of death. It is not altogether easy to rationalize all these into a single consistent account, although presumably that is what a commentator such as Śaṃkara will attempt to do. What we provide next follows Śaṃkara (*Brahmasūtrabhāṣya* IV.2.1-21) where there are disagreements.

The process goes as follows :

1. The speech function becomes absorbed into the intellectual organ or power of thought (*manas*).

2. It is followed by the functions of all the other organs. Śaṃkara emphasizes that it is only the functions that merge, not the organs themselves. (One must keep in mind that a sense organ, for example, is not to be confused with the physical locus—the visual organ is different from the eyeball).

3. Then the *manas*, having absorbed these various functions, has its own functions absorbed into breath (*prāṇa*). That this is so is evidenced by the fact that a dying person—and for that matter one

asleep and not dreaming—is seen to breathe though his senses and his mind is not functioning.

4. Next, breath so endowed merges with the individual self (*jīva*), that is, with the internal organ as limited by the awarenesses, karmic residues, and *vāsanā*s present at this moment. The man stops breathing.

5. Now the *jīva*, thus encumbered, joins the subtle elements (*tanmātras*). These are five in number, corresponding to the five gross elements—air, fire, earth, water, and *ākāśa*. The "subtle" elements apparently are conceived of as minute particles that form the seeds from which grow their gross counterparts. The cluster of the five subtle elements provides a (material) "subtle body" (*sūkṣma-śarīra*) that now encloses the *jīva* along with its appurtenances, just as the gross body did during life.

6. All these factors collect in the heart.[4] The *jīva* arrives replete with awarenesses (both true and false), karmic residues, *vāsanās*, desires, and internal organ and so is perfectly capable of consciousness. However, since the external organs have stopped functioning, its consciousness at this point, like consciousness in dreams, is completely controlled by past karma. Thus at the "moment of death," the *jīva* is caused by its karma to develop a *vāsanā* that determines the direction the subtle body will go as it leaves the heart—by which veins and point of exit, by what path, and to what kind of birth.

7. Thus decided, the *jīva*-controlled subtle body leaves the heart by one or another of the many veins and arteries and eventually gains egress from the dead gross body by one or another opening.

B. *The Progress of the Subtle Body.* To this point, the Upaniṣadic sources appear relatively consistent in their implications. When they turn to the account of what happens immediately after death the versions diverge slightly.

Basically, the texts distinguish two paths for the subtle bodies to follow. One of these is referred to as the "northern path," the "way of the gods" (*devayāna*), which lies through fire or light and leads to the sun. The other is the "southern path", the "way of the fathers" (*pitṛyāna*), which leads through smoke to the moon. Śaṃkara tells us that it is those who observe ritual obligations but do not have knowledge of God (i.e., Brahman with qualities, *saguṇa* Brahman) who follow the southern path; those who know God follow the northern path.

What happens to those who do not fulfill their ritual obligations and do not have knowledge? They follow a third path, which leads to Yama's world or city— called *saṃyamanam* here and also in Manu, the Epic, and elsewhere—or else they are immediately reborn as small animals, insects, perhaps plants, etc.[5]

How does the passage along these paths proceed? In the *Bṛhadāraṇyaka Upaniṣad*, we are told that the self proceeds from this body to the next like a leech or caterpillar. Śaṃkara comments that the idea is that the self creates a link from the old body to the new one by means of its *vāsanās*.[6] This serves to remind us that as the self encased in its subtle body moves along its path it is not unconscious—it is having experiences, determined by its karmic residues as in a dream, and is forming plans and following them out as it goes along. It is thus exhausting some of its stored-up karmic residues as it proceeds and continues doing so in the place (sun, moon, or *saṃyamanam*, as the case may be) at which it in due course arrives.

Some details of the stages along the northern path are discussed in the third section, fourth chapter of the *Brahmasūtras*. For one thing, Śaṃkara argues that though by having meditated on certain symbols one person may experience things appropriate to those symbols and another may experience other things appropriate to other symbols, still there is only one northern path. The *Chāndogya Upaniṣad* tells us that these transmigrating selves go to light, day, the waxing half of the moon, the six months when the sun is going north, the year, Āditya, the moon, lightning.[7] What sort of travel is this? Śaṃkara explains that these are references to divinities that conduct the self along the path, since in its state it is not capable of finding its own way.

The *Chāndogya* also gives us an account of the details of the southern path. It leads from smoke through night, the dark fortnight, the months when the sun is moving south, to the realm of the fathers, thence to *ākāśa* and thus to the moon. Again, these are identified by Śaṃkara as deities who act as guides for the transmigrating self.

C. *Heaven and Hell.* The selves of those who follow the third path—to Yama's world, perhaps—are "reborn" almost immediately in bits of grain and other such things. They retain consciousness all the while, and the "hellish" experiences they earn—ascribed sometimes to instruments of torture controlled by Yama—are more plausibly construed as the natural concomitants of existing in such a state, considering the violent changes wrought on them as they are prepared for use in meals to be consumed by animals and human beings. These embodiments—plants, grains, etc.—being determined by the karmic residues of the selves that inhabit them, are rather quickly lived through, and the subtle-body-enclosed self may move on quickly from one "body" to various others, all the while experiencing appropriate pains "as in a dream." When they are deserving, they in due course find their way into the food of humans and so get into the blood and semen and eventually gain a new human birth.

As for those who arrive at the moon, the Upaniṣads tell us that they become the "food of the gods," which Śaṃkara explains does not mean that they are actually eaten by the gods, but that they serve the gods. Actually, the sojourn in the moon is a period during which the meritorious residues are exhausted, and it is thus basically a happy interim. Those who have arrived there have come to experience their just rewards in heaven for ritual observances practiced in the preceding worldly life. They do so until a small amount of karmic residue remains. There is an extended discussion in the *Brahmasūtrabhāṣya* defending this interpretation. They are also said to take on a watery "body" that supports the organs and allows them to generate pleasant experiences.

Those traveling the northern path, or "way of the gods," proceed, as we have seen, through the sun (Āditya) to lightning. From there they are conducted to the realm of that which they have worshiped and upon which they meditate. If that thing is God, (*saguṇa*) Brahman, they will be led to the Brahmaloka. If they meditated on God under some symbolic manifestation, however, they will arrive at an appropriately different kind of heavenly place.[8]

It seems likely that Bādarāyaṇa thought that the Brahmaloka amounted to the state of liberation. Śaṃkara, though, cannot allow that one can literally "arrive at" the higher (*nirguṇa*) Brahman, since he claims that Brahman is quite unrelated to any second thing, and so he is forced here to interpret the Brahmaloka as a highest heaven, not liberation. That raises the question whether the selves who go there return to be reborn or not. The text, of course, asserts that they do not return—presumably once again speaking of liberation—and Śaṃkara is caught in a dilemma.[9] Either he must reject Bādarāyaṇa's and the Upaniṣads' teaching on the point, or else he must accept the Brahmaloka as liberation and so capitulate to the view that one can obtain liberation without knowing the nature of the highest Brahman. The solution that Śaṃkara finds is rather complex. On the one hand, he argues that the texts saying that the selves do not return from Brahmaloka mean they do not return to rebirth in this world; they do, however, return to other forms of existence, presumably on a divine plane. On the other hand, he is willing to admit that those attaining the Brahmaloka, provided they have in the meantime attained knowledge of the highest Brahman, will be liberated at the time of reabsorption (*pralaya*). *Brahmasūtrabhāṣya* IV.3.10

tells us that such selves proceed, along with the god (Hiraṇyagarbha) who rules the Brahmaloka, to "the pure highest place of Viṣṇu," and that this is what is meant by "progressive liberation "(*krama-mukti*), since the highest Brahman cannot be (literally) "reached."

Maṇḍana Miśra[10] suggests still another way of resolving the dilemma. The nonreturning may be only relative : it may mean that those who go to the Brahmaloka remain there until the next reabsorption, but that after that they return to bondage in the next cyclical universe.

D. *Descent from Heaven to Earth.* For those in the moon the time eventually comes when they have exhausted their good karmic residues. At this point the watery body, which had supported the organs, etc., through their stay on the moon dissolves, and the subtle body with its remainder of bad karma begins to fall back toward the earth. It is said to descend inversely through the stages by which it ascended—through *ākāśa* to air, to smoke, into mist and cloud, and then to the earth's surface in the rain. This process does not take long, and the self loses consciousness during this period, just as one loses consciousness when falling from a tree (according to one account) or because the karmic residues that remain do not become operative again until they determine the next birth.

Having arrived in the rain, the subtle body finds its way into plants. It is not reborn in the plants, that is, it does not experience the pains of plant existence, as do those who follow the third path and who may indeed be reborn as plants and suffer the torments involved. Instead, the subtle body eventually attaches itself to a plant—as a grain of rice, say—which is ground up, cooked, eaten, and digested by an animal. Throughout all this the attached subtle bodies remain unconscious (fortunately for them). It is pointed out in the *Chāndogyopaniṣadbhāṣya*[11] that this part of the cycle is subject to multifarious accidents; a subtle body might spend a long time stuck in some inaccessible place where the rain water had carried it and then evaporated, or it may be carried along in the ecological cycle for a long time, passing through various bodies, occasionally into the ocean, back up into clouds, down again in rain, and so on.

E. *Birth.* Eventually, as was said, the subtle body finds its way into an animal's vital juices—blood, semen—and, depending on the kind of animal it is, becomes involved in the reproductive process. In the case of many animals, including humans, this means that it enters the womb in semen. The *Aitareyopaniṣadbhāṣya*[12] notes that the *jīva* is in a sense born twice—the first time in the semen when it enters the womb, the second time when it leaves the mother's body. In each case there is influence of the parent on the new gross body, through the food eaten by the parent, which interacts with the elements in the subtle body; this is why the child when born resembles his parents, both in the fact that it is a human child that is born (and not some other species of animal) as well as in its facial and other features.

What is not well explained in this account is : what is responsible for a *jīva* destined for highborn caste status, say, getting into the bodily fluids of the right kind of parents, rather than suffering a lower birth among humans, or even among other animals ? It is perhaps not altogether speculative to suggest that this may have a good deal to do with the importance Indians place on the food they eat. The purer *jīvas* find their way into purer foodstuffs (although exactly why still constitutes a mystery, it seems); then since the higher castes eat the purer foods, and so on down the natural order, it will ordinarily work out that the right *jīvas* will turn up with the right parents.

In any case, the food eaten by the mother during gestation becomes transformed into the various physical and mental substances that make up the new body, as determined by the relevant aspects of the subtle body. *Taittirīyopaniṣadbhāṣyavārttika* II.181-186 spells out the details of this process, and Śaṃkara refers to it in more general terms in various places. Sureśvara also dwells, as do other authors, on the misery of the *jīva* as it lies in the womb;[13] here once again it has regained consciousness, apparently, and it develops its organs as the gross portions of its body corresponding to them grow. Although we are not explicitly told so, it would appear that this development takes place as determined by karmic residues through the mechanism of *vāsanās*. If so, it would seem that the process of maturation of a *jīva*'s karma begins again at least at the time it enters the womb, if not before. Although our texts are vague as to details, it is apparent that the Hindu's understanding of these matters must have had tremendous influence on his eating, sexual, and other habits.

An interesting story, corroborating some of the speculations indulged in above, is provided in the *Aitareya Upaniṣad* and its *Bhāṣya* by Śaṃkara and concerns Vāmadeva, who was liberated while in his mother's womb.[14] Vāmadeva is said to have realized the identity of his self with the Highest Self while in the womb, and he immediately obtained release there. The idea is that Vāmadeva was so pure and so close to enlightenment in his previous life that his liberation was accomplished before his next birth. But this suggests several things. First, something happened in the womb to Vāmadeva that led to his liberation; since this could hardly have been a hearing of the scripture or the words of a teacher, we must suppose that his purity resulted in removal of ignorance without special occasion. Second, since Vāmadeva is said to have subsequently been born and lived through a life determined by his *prārabdhakarman*, we must assume that the determination of his length of life and his experiences, as well as of his type of birth, were in fact fixed prior to his liberation in the womb. This means, I infer, that what the *Aitareya Upaniṣad* called the "first birth," in which the subtle body enters the womb in the semen, is that point at which the operation of karmic residues through *vāsanās* is resumed, along with the *jiva*'s consciousness. Third, it suggests that the distinction between Vāmadeva's *prārabdhakarman* and his other karmic residues was already fixed prior to this "first birth", since presumably at the point of liberation all the other residues became inoperative.

F. *Life*. All of this brings us to what we ordinarily call the birth of the child, the "second birth" of the *Aitareya*. It would seem from the foregoing that, viewed in karmic perspective, this is a relatively unimportant event, though for obvious reasons it is a critical occasion viewed from the perspective of human society. All the karmic processes are already under way, and have been for about nine months in the case of a normal child.

This child is, then, endowed with the three kinds of karmic residues noted earlier, that is, *prārabdha*, *sañcita*, and *āgamin*. The *Bhagavadgitābhāṣya*[15] likens *prārabdhakarman* to an arrow already in flight—it will continue until its energy is exhausted, unless something obstructs it. Likewise, the child as he lives through the present life will experience the ripening of the residues of his *prārabdhakarman* unless something obstructs it, such as premature death due to violence or other unnatural causes. So it is the same balance of *prārabdhakarman* that determines the length of his normal life and the type of experiences he will have during that lifetime.

The method by which karmic residues determine experience needs to be discussed, for it lies at the center of the supposed problems about the fatalistic, or at least deterministic, implications of the "law of karma." It seems to me that there is little cause for such problems in the Advaita context. The key to the puzzle, if any, lies in distinguishing karma from *vāsanā*. A *vāsanā*, as we have seen, is explained as a man's determination to aim for certain objectives of a general sort. Now these determinations are the effects of one's karmic residues—one's *vāsanās* will be purer the purer one's karma. Further, pursuing a purer determination will get one, on balance, happier experiences, whereas pursuing impure determination will get one, on balance, less happy or indeed painful experiences. It is in this sense that past actions determine future experiences. However, this is a very loose relation. It is not, for instance, the case that a certain act *x* in a past life specifically determines a certain type of experience *y* in this life. At best, *x* generates a determination on the agent's part to pursue a life plan or style, or a specific element in one, that will lead him to do something, if nothing interferes, productive of *y*. Much may interfere. One aware of the dangers of following his instincts may perform yoga, etc., to counteract the influence of his *vāsanās*. Furthermore, the agent, aware of the relation between his life plans and his type of experience, may decide to take a certain attitude to his life as a whole. This is not an alternative life plan, but a way of looking at life plans. Thus the karmic residues must keep working themselves out—that is, a man must live some life and follow some style or plan, experiencing the appropriate results—but he may remain, as it were, aloof from involvement in the process. In this second-order attitude toward bondage lies the key to liberation.

In living one's life plan or style, however, one necessarily performs actions. The primary meaning of the word "karma" is action. There are a number of relevant kinds of actions. For example, one may divide actions into bodily (*kāyika*), vocal (*vācika*), and mental (*mānasa*) acts. Then again, one can divide actions into those which are ritual acts and those which are not. The former group can be subdivided into those which are positively enjoined (*vidhi*) and those which are proscribed (*niṣedha*). Of the positively enjoined acts there may be said to be four kinds—(1) the regular daily rites (*nityakarman*), such as the baths prescribed for a Brahmin each day; (2) the occasional rites (*naimittikakarman*), ritual observances for particular occasions, for example, those performed at a certain point in the life cycle, such as investiture, succoring the ancestors, and so forth; (3) desired acts (*kāmyakarman*), that is, those acts prescribed for one who wishes to obtain a certain result, say, increase in wealth, or heaven; (4) expiatory actions (*prāyaścitta*), acts performed to purify oneself because one has failed to do certain prescribed acts either in this life or in past lives.[16]

On Śaṃkara's view all these kinds of acts are equally capable of producing karmic residues, which in turn will condition the type of birth, length of life, and kind of experience the *jīva* will inherit in the next life. For that matter, some of a man's acts may produce residues that have their results in the same life. As we shall see, however, there is a condition the presence of which is necessary for residues to be produced by any action, and that is attachment, explained by Śaṃkara as deriving from lack of Self-knowledge.

Which karmic residues work themselves out sooner, which ones constitute the *prārabdhakarman* for a given lifetime, and which are *sañcita*, stored up for later fruition ? Śaṃkara seems to think that in general the more intense and proximate residues, whether sinful or meritorious, tend to mature first, but that this general rule is subject to many exceptions because there are incompatibilities between several residues that have equal claim but only one of which can mature at a given time.

How does maturation actually come about ? One performs an act in lifetime A at time *t*, and this act is supposed to have something to do with the experience the same agent has in lifetime B at time $t+n$. In *Brahmasūtrabhāṣya* III.2.38-41 Śaṃkara explains the difference between the views of Jaimini and Bādarāyaṇa on this score. The Mīmāṃsā view of Jaimini is that the act produces at time *t* something called an *apūrva*, which somehow reflects the act and presages the eventual outcome; this *apūrva* constitutes in a literal manner the karmic residue and works itself out automatically in lifetime B, having been passed along with the other elements of the subtle body. Bādarāyaṇa's view, as Śaṃkara interprets it, is that (1) it is clear that the act itself cannot produce the experience in lifetime B, because an act is a short-lived event; (2) whether or not there is something like an *apūrva*, it cannot by itself produce the experience that constitutes its maturation, because it is an unintelligent thing like a piece of wood and cannot pick out the appropriate time and place for the pleasure and/or pain that constitute the experience produced. As a result, (3) the correct view must be that God arranges things so that the resulting experiences match the merit or demerit characterizing the agent's past acts. It will, I trust, be appreciated that this in no way conditions what was said above about determinism and free will. It is logically possible that A should do *x* in lifetime A, that the karmic residue should breed a *vāsanā* in lifetime B that leads him to do a *y* that is productive of great sin but immediately accompanied by pleasant experiences. Indeed, not only is it logically possible but it seems to happen all the time : why else would people do such things ! God does not ordinarily match experience to simultaneous act on the ground of the merit-value of that act but rather on the ground of the merit-value of one or more past acts.

The child grows into a young, a middle-aged, and an old person. He is constantly forming plans under the influence of those actions from his past and present lives, carrying them out through present actions that are accompanied by types of experience—a mixture of pleasure and pain—arising from situations arranged by God but appropriately reflecting the valence of the past actions. As long as a person lacks Self-knowledge, the acts he performs will themselves breed future lives and experiences. So he arrives in due course at the end of this life, carrying with him the residues of acts in this life and previous ones, and he dies once more, eventually to be reborn again in one of the fashions we have described.

II. Liberation in Advaita

Practically all Indian philosophical systems view liberation as the highest aim of mankind, and Advaita is no exception. In terms of the account of bondage just recounted one might say that liberation consists of release from the process of birth, life, death, and transmigration. This way of viewing liberation characterizes what all systems would agree to be the final desired result of their efforts, but it does not define the specific Advaita doctrine of liberation.

The Advaita view is simple to state and devastating in its implications. Liberation is nothing more nor less than being, knowing, and experiencing one's true Self. In this disarming statement we can find the key to many of the Advaita teachings.

As the Advaitin sees it, the process of rebirth described in the preceding section is the product of our ignorance (*avidyā*). We cannot help being, knowing, and experiencing our Self; thus we are always liberated. It follows, first, that liberation does not require a positive change in us. We do not have to become something, or someone, else. Liberation is not a product; it has no beginning or end; it has no degrees. Liberation is not some other place, like heaven, that one seeks to travel to.

Other systems, viewing bondage as entirely a matter of the individual's somehow falling from grace through performing evil actions, seek to attain liberation by purifying their actions. But the mechanics of bondage will operate for them as much as for those whose actions are bad; pure acts bind as much as impure ones, the *Bhagavadgītā* reminds us.[17] One has to escape the realm of actions altogether. One may contemplate desisting from performing any actions whatever, but the *Gītā* also warns us away from that : no ordinary person can avoid acting even for a moment; refusing to act is itself a kind of action.[18]

One must, therefore, identify a necessary condition for the workings of the mechanism of bondage, something removable and in whose absence the mechanism will cease to function. That condition, says the Advaitin, is *avidyā*. It is only as long as *avidyā* operates that desires for things and ends are formed in us. Without desires the *vāsanās*, or tendencies, will not be carried through into action, and without functioning *vāsanās* the karmic residues cannot determine birth, length of life, and experiences.

However, if *avidyā* were something—like Sāṃkhya's *prakṛti*—that itself functioned through action, that is, if it were an independent and real something, different from oneself, under another's control or out of control entirely, it would not be removable by me, and release, if it occurred at all, would be accidental or at the whim of someone else. Furthermore, under those circumstances, to remove it or destroy it would require another action, which in its turn would breed residues, *vāsanās*, and desires, and the round would go on as before.

But *avidyā*, fortunately, is not something that requires action to destroy it. It is destroyed by its natural opposite, perfect knowledge (*vidyā*). Knowing is not an act and so does not breed further karmic residues. And perfect knowledge is something not under someone else's control or under no control—it is something we already have, and we will immediately recognize ourselves as having it if we only have it called to our attention under appropriate circumstances.

How it is to be called to our attention is a question leading to the main doctrines of Advaita metaphysics and epistemology. Here we are merely considering some implications of what liberation is and is not. We can now see what it is not : it is not the result of an action; it is not like arriving at a place (e.g., heaven) one has not already reached; and it is not dying or just losing consciousness (one is reborn or wakes up eventually).

Still, one may well say, "I am now bound and I want to be free, so liberation must at least be a state I'm not now in. Granted getting into that state is not like going from here to another place; yet, what *is* it like ?" Śaṃkara tells us in one place that it is like what happens to the space inside a pot when the pot breaks, that is, nothing.[19] As Gauḍapāda says, there is no liberation really.[20] Or, using another common Advaita analogy, it is like what happens to the light reflected in a dirty mirror when the mirror is cleaned.

Yet these are only analogies. What, specifically, happens to a man when he becomes liberated ? As we have seen, bondage arises because actions automatically—or with God's help—produce karmic residues, which in turn produce *vāsanās* and experiences. The condition under which this happens is *avidyā*. When *avidyā* is removed, two of the three kinds of action (karma) are rendered inoperative. The residues that have been stored up but are not stated to reach fruition in this life lose their potency; they are "burned," suggests the etymology of the common verb used here, and like burned seed they no longer have the power to produce sprouts. As for the actions still to be performed in this life, they will no longer bind. Behavior after liberation is not action at all, since for a bit of behavior to be an action it must be done with desire for something distinguished as different from oneself, a something that one desires to obtain or avoid; when one realizes through the perfect knowledge that constitutes liberation that there are no other things, the necessary condition for action is annulled, and so no future actions can take place.

That leaves the question of the karmic residues that determine the birth, length of life, and experiences of this very lifetime during which liberation is achieved. The Advaita doctrine here is that this *prārabdhakarman* has to work itself out—it cannot be destroyed by Self-knowledge as the other two kinds of karma can; it cannot be "burned" for it has already begun to bear fruit. Thus the liberated person normally continues in bodily existence, working out his *prārabdhakarman*, and this state is known as "liberation while living," *jīvanmukti*.

The *jīvanmukti* state seems paradoxical. The liberated self has achieved Self-knowledge and thus no longer recognizes any distinctions; yet he moves among us, performs the necessary activities of eating, drinking, etc., that suffice to keep him alive through his allotted years. Having no desires he does not act, but he nevertheless does act insofar as he is impelled by the *vāsanā*s produced by those karmic residues that are still working themselves out. Not recognizing anything as a possible object to be experienced, and not recognizing any organs through which he might experience anything, it follows that he has no experiences; yet because of the operation of *prārabdhakarman* and the *vāsanā*s he is visited with objects experienced through the organs of sense.

Indeed, the *jīvanmukta* or liberated person can be viewed from two perspectives : from the "higher standpoint" (*pāramārthika*) he is liberated and thus incapable of ordinary knowledge, action, and experiences, but from the "lower standpoint" (*vyāvahārika*) he is a *saṃnyāsin* or renunciate, capable of all such things. The Advaitin tends to switch back and forth between the two standpoints in describing one and the same individual.

Saṃnyāsa is generally held by Hindus to be the last of the four ideal "stages of life" (*āśrama*) and is preceded by studentship (*brahmacarya*), householdership (*gārhasthya*), and forest-dwelling (*vānaprasthya*). Whereas most Hindus view *saṃnyāsa* as an advanced spiritual state it is a peculiarity of Śaṃkara's thought that he construes this stage as identical with liberation while living, that is, with *jīvanmukti*. This is because of his relatively uncompromising insistence on the necessity of Self-knowledge for release, coupled with his thesis that Self-knowledge necessarily renders action of any kind impossible. It is for this reason that Śaṃkara, when speaking of *saṃnyāsa*, frequently describes it in terms that seem appropriate only to the liberated person. For example, whereas other philosophers think that one may obtain liberation from any of the four "stages of life," which is sometimes cited as a sign of their tolerant moral attitude, Śaṃkara insists that one can only "become liberated" from the fourth stage. This is taken by some as a sign of relative intransigence in social morality. However, because *saṃnyāsa is* liberation—so that it is tautologous to say one must pass through it to be liberated—and because Śaṃkara insists also that one can reach *saṃnyāsa* directly from any of the other three stages, the alleged intransigence turns out to be a verbal phantasm.

For the same reasons the apparent problem about the possibility of backsliding from *saṃnyāsa* comes to nought. Having received liberation through Self-knowledge and thus passing into a state (like Yoga's *nirvikalpakasamādhi*, perhaps) in which no distinctions are recognized, one subsequently seems to come out of this state to live a life in which knowledge and actions presupposing the recognition of distinctions recommence; thus the charge of backsliding. But again the problem is semantic only. From liberation there is no backsliding : once one has realized that everything is identical with Brahman, there is no possibility of losing that realization. But the stage one reaches, that is, *saṃnyāsa*, is not a kind of *samādhi* at all, since *prārabdhakarman* is still operating. The *saṃnyāsin* does not stop behaving and experiencing, for karmic forces are still at work on him; thus *qua* behaver and experiencer he does not reach a state from which he might backslide; yet he is at the same time identical with the liberated man.

This paradoxical double-level view of the liberated man has not always been well understood by writers on Advaita.[21] A number of Western authors, as well as a few Indians, have found fault with the moral implications of Śaṃkara's position, charging it with being austerely intellectual, antinomian, and failing to reflect adequately the social virtues of love and service to mankind.

It is evident that Śaṃkara does not teach withdrawal from the world at any point along the path of spiritual progress, even at the *saṃnyāsa* or *jīvanmukta* stage. The *saṃnyāsin* is working out his karma, and although from the higher standpoint he is not "acting," this makes no difference at all from the lower standpoint, which is the only standpoint from which questions about social mores matter. As far as the rest of us are concerned, the *saṃnyāsin is* acting—he eats, sleeps, and moves around—and, furthermore, he is doing so motivated by *vāsanās* determined by his karmic residues. What kind of *vāsanās* these are must, then, depend on what kind of residues he has stored up, which in turn must depend on the kind of acts he has performed in previous lives, or earlier in this one.

Now in order to be a true *saṃnyāsin* our individual must have Self-knowledge. But Śaṃkara is quite specific about what kind of a life one must lead before *avidyā* is removed and Self-knowledge results. He specifies four requirements for the "adept" (*adhikārin*) : (1) that he be able to tell what is eternal from what is not; (2) that he be nonattached to present and future experiences; (3) that he have acquired moral virtues such as tranquillity (*śama*), restraint (*dama*), etc., and (4) that he desire liberation. When we learn that the remaining moral virtues include faith (*śraddhā*), concentration (*samādhāna*), and forbearance (*titikṣā*) it becomes very apparent that a person must be imbued with strong positive moral inclinations when he enters the *saṃnyāsa* stage. Because he is no longer desirous of objects after entering that stage([2] above) and is no longer ignorant of what is good for him (following [1] and [4] above), it follows that there is nothing to obstruct his moral *vāsanās* from working themselves out in the natural course for optimally beneficial results. He has no evil karmic residues to spawn opposing *vāsanās*.

These remarks may help explain why the Advaitin does not admit the charges of austere intellectualism or of lack of social virtues in the *saṃnyāsin*. There is another aspect to the criticism, however, that requires further explanation. The charge is that the *saṃnyāsin* is antinomian, that is, that he is outside the obligations of social morality and thus likely to do anything at all, in particular, some harmful or antisocial thing.

Now it is, to be sure, Śaṃkara's position that householders, students, and forest-dwellers are obligated to perform moral actions, whereas *saṃnyāsins* are not. But this does not mean that *saṃnyāsins* are permitted to perform immoral actions. The point is, rather, that *saṃnyāsins* cannot perform actions at all, and therefore questions of both obligation and permission are irrelevant to his status. Although Śaṃkara counts the *saṃnyāsin* the liberated man, outside the scope of *dharma*, the rest of the theory makes it impossible for him to act immorally.

It is sometimes also charged that the Advaita system fails to recognize such virtues as love of fellow man and service to mankind. It is evident that these charges are likely to come from the point of view of Christianity or sympathizers with it, for it is in the Christian religion that these particular virtues are especially celebrated.[22] Advaita apologists have not been slow to respond.[23]

Some answers they give are not to be found in the texts we are considering. For example, to the charge that Advaita fails to give a proper place to love for one's fellow man, modern apologists sometimes answer that, because Advaita teaches that there is only one Self, and because everyone loves his own self, which is identical with the one Self, it follows that everyone loves everyone else's self.[24] That this argument is not found in early Advaita is, I believe, entirely to its credit, for the argument is quite fallacious. Just as one may believe that, say, the Evening Star rises in the evening and that the Morning Star does not rise in the evening, even though the Evening Star is identical with the Morning Star, because one does not believe they are identical, so one may love one self (one's own) and not another, even though the two are identical, because one does not identify them. Still, it may be retorted, at least the Self-knower must love his fellow man, since what he knows is precisely that his is the one Self. But that doesn't follow either. To love one's fellow man one must presumably recognize him as one's fellow, but that means to distinguish him from oneself, and for the liberated man there are no distinctions.

In fact, Śaṃkara's theory makes it impossible to raise the question of the liberated man's love for his fellow man, unless one fiddles with the senses of the words in that phrase. But it by no means follows that his is a selfish philosophy. For Advaita, and Hinduism in general, clearly endorses the view that men are expected, to the extent of their several abilities, to serve mankind with a willing nature. The kinds of acts enjoined on those in the first three "stages of life" are calculated to support the social, moral, and spiritual order, to uphold *lokasaṃgraha*, that is, the "hanging together of the world." We have seen that on Śaṃkara's theory no acts are enjoined on the *saṃnyāsin*, but by virtue of his preparatory training (the four requirements, or *adhikāras*, mentioned earlier) he will in fact behave in ways that will contribute to the same end. In his case, indeed, since he is pure and has no selfish ends of his own to pursue, one can to one's advantage consult him for advice and guidance in one's own quest, and (provided he really *is* a liberated man and not a sham *saṃnyāsin*) the theory guarantees an honest response and a helpful one to the limit of the teacher's ability to understand and sympathize with one's questions and progress. This is the Advaita justification for the Hindu theory of the guru or spiritual adviser; the ideal guru is the liberated man. But he is not obligated to teach, for behavior on his part indicating that he expects to reap personal advantage from his teaching is evidence that he is at best not liberated and at worst a sham.

III. The Role of Action in Becoming Liberated.

Liberation, then, is not something new that one acquires; it is nothing but the very nature of one's true Self. What we call "becoming liberated" is the removal of ignorance, of *avidyā*, which hides our nature from us. The question therefore arises : what is it that constitutes the immediate cause of the removal of *avidyā*?

On this point the Advaitin, being a kind of Mīmāṃsaka, faces the defenders of Vedic orthodoxy as well as all the other Vedantins who interpret the Upaniṣads differently than he does. It is with arguments of this kind that Śaṃkara spends most of his time. And it is over this issue as well that what is perhaps the most serious breach between Maṇḍana's and Śaṃkara's Advaita is opened.

Broadly speaking, we may distinguish three kinds of position against which Śaṃkara argues.

A. *Against Pūrvamīmāṃsā.* First, there is the position of orthodox Pūrvamīmāṃsā. The Mīmāṃsaka tends to view liberation as a kind of heavenly state that one reaches by performance of pure actions. This view is evidently compatible with viewing the liberated state as a different state from one's Self-nature. It also contrasts with Advaita's view in that liberation does not feature the perfect knowledge that is an antidote to *avidyā*. The orthodox Mīmāṃsaka is thus calling by the name "liberation" something other than what Śaṃkara has in mind. Liberation of the sort Śaṃkara has in mind involves, as we have seen, the cessation of karmic results of actions through removal of the ignorance that prevents us from having knowledge of our true Self.

But the Mīmāṃsā view may be recast in a form that accepts Śaṃkara's sense of "liberation" while apparently preserving characteristic Mīmāṃsā tenets. The relevant tenets include these : (1) that the Vedas enjoin everything of human value, including liberation; (2) that it is only actions leading to future results that can be enjoined; (3) that knowing is an act; (4) that false knowing—ignorance or *avidyā*—is a result of faults (*doṣa*) in the knower or in his organs; (5) that these faults arise from moral impurity; (6) that the scriptural injunctions enjoin actions upon us that will purify present faults and preclude future ones; (7) therefore, that by performing actions as enjoined in scripture, we may remove ignorance and achieve the

Self-knowledge upon which we are enjoined to meditate, which high meditative state constitutes liberation.

There are several philosophical theses implicit in the above against which the Advaitin argues on fundamental metaphysical and epistemological grounds. Indeed, a major aspect of Advaita philosophy may be understood as providing a philosophical position supporting the rejection of most of the seven propositions just listed. Let us begin to work up to that position by considering Śaṃkara's immediate arguments against this Mīmāṃsā way of looking at liberation and the means thereto.

The Mīmāṃsā view holds that liberation is a result of actions. Śaṃkara has several general arguments against that thesis.

First, if liberation is identical with the true nature of one's Self, then it has no beginning, because the Self has no beginning. But the result of an action is something that has a beginning; it comes into existence when the act has been performed. Therefore, being without a beginning, liberation cannot be the result of an action.

Second, liberation requires the removal of *avidyā*. Therefore, the action(s) whose result constitutes liberation must be such as to remove *avidyā*. But no *action* can remove *avidyā*; the only thing that can remove *avidyā* is knowledge, and knowing is not an act.

This argument clearly needs to be bolstered by arguments showing that knowing is not an act, and that actions cannot remove ignorance. Śaṃkara argues to the first point over and over again. He contrasts acting with knowing in that the result of an action depends on the will of the agent, whereas knowledge does not. For example, to milk a cow someone must collect appropriate implements and make an effort; to know a cow (i.e., to be aware of it) no effort is required; all that is needed is the presence of the cow and appropriate organs of cognition. Furthermore, if one has false knowledge, that is, mistakes a rope for a snake, what corrects that error is the subsequent awareness that the thing is a rope; no amount of activity will correct the error unless it also produces the corrective or sublating awareness.

With regard to the second point, that actions cannot remove ignorance, Śaṃkara in more than one place points out that results of actions are of only four kinds. The result of an action may be (1) the origination (*utpatti*) of a thing, as when the potter creates a pot, or (2) the attainment (*āpti*) of a state, as when one arrives at the village, or (3) the purification (*saṃskāra*) of a thing through addition to it of meritorious features or the subtraction from it of polluting features, as in certain ritual activities, or (4) the modification (*vikāra*) of a thing involving a change in its features, for example, when one melts ice by heating it. Now liberation, the removal of ignorance, can be none of these four things, for reasons spelled out in infinite ways within Advaita. The basic reason may be said to be that all of these four things involve differentiation between a prior causal state and a subsequent effect state and on the Advaita view liberation must be free of differentiation, being identical with the true Self, which is without beginning or end and without change of any sort.

Note also that knowing is incapable, even according to common sense, of producing an effect of any of the above four kinds. Thus knowing is not an act, since it is incapable of having results of the type actions have. Whereas acts have results, knowing has only content, or subject matter. Either that content exists or it does not. If it does exist, it did not become existent through any activity of the cognition of which it is the content. And if it does not exist (a possibility Advaita ultimately rejects, as we shall see), cognition cannot bring it into existence. Liberation is analogous to the actual entity that is the content of a cognition; indeed, it is ultimately the Advaita position that liberation is the *only* actual entity there is, namely, Brahman, that entity being in truth the real content of all awareness. These lines of development lead directly into the heart of Advaita epistemology and philosophy of language.

These, then, are the major reasons Śaṃkara adduces against identifying liberation as the result of an act. That does not silence all opponents, however, for there are other ways of thinking of the relations among knowing, acting, and liberation.

B. *Against Bhedābhedavāda.* According to a second account, achieving liberation involves both action and knowledge, a combined path of the two (*jñānakarmasamuccaya*). Versions of the combined-path view were held, scholars believe, by certain pre-Śaṃkara Vedāntins such as Bhartṛprapañca, whose works are now for the most part lost, by the writer whom Śaṃkara identifies as the "Vṛttikāra" in his *Bhagavadgītābhāṣya*, by Bhāskara, a near-contemporary of Śaṃkara's and by others who espoused some version of Bhedābhedavāda.

According to the combined-path thesis the way to liberation involves the achievement of Self-knowledge followed by the practice of nonattached action. The virtue of the theory, it would seem, is that it promises to account properly for the central place of Self-knowledge in gaining liberation while maintaining throughout the authority of scriptural passages enjoining observance of prescribed acts and avoidance of proscribed ones. That is, on the combined-path view it is not necessary to make the Self-knower out to be beyond the scope of morality altogether. The antinomian aspects of the doctrine that liberation is gained solely by knowledge are one extreme to be avoided, and equally to be avoided is the other extreme, that, as the Mīmāṃsaka holds, liberation is the result of action. Although agreeing that knowing is not an act, the combined-path theorist maintains that the liberation-seeker must meditate on the passages in scripture identifying the self with Brahman and that such meditation properly performed, though not an action, will remove the conditions of bondage. However, the conditions of proper meditation involve faithful observance of religious ritual; the seeker must continue to perform prescribed actions while he is securing his understanding of the Self, and specifically, even after he has achieved the understanding of his self-identity with Brahman he must continue to observe the scriptural prescriptions as he works off the remaining karma accreted from previous actions.

As we have seen, Śaṃkara agrees that prior to the achievement of Self-knowledge the seeker must satisfy high moral requirements, so that observance of scriptural injunctions is insisted on up to this point by both parties. Śaṃkara parts company with the combined-path view over the latter's insistence on observance of scriptural injunctions *after* liberation—on Śaṃkara's interpretation, when one has arrived at the stage of the *saṃnyāsin*.

Śaṃkara's reasoning is clear and simple, given his presuppositions. The knowledge that occasions liberation—that is, that removes *avidyā*—is the realization that all distinctions are unreal, nonexistent from the highest standpoint. But any action can only proceed on the basis of the assumption of a difference between agent and action, action and result. Precisely because the liberated self is one who no longer recognizes any such distinctions, it follows that one who knows his Self cannot perform any action at all, whether enjoined by scripture or otherwise. By the same token, as Śaṃkara sees it, the notion that scripture enjoins actions upon the Self-knower must necessarily be mistaken. It is only the unenlightened who are subject to obligations to perform actions; it is a type of category-mistake to suppose that a liberated man—a *saṃnyāsin*—is obliged to do anything, for that would be to suppose that the liberated man is aware of differences between himself and other things.

In short, it is Śaṃkara's view that Self-knowledge and action are entirely incompatible—the conditions for the presence of one constitute the conditions for the absence of the other. Of course, prior to gaining Self-knowledge, the seeker practises action combined with meditation; but, once true knowledge is gained, no further action is possible.

C. *Against Maṇḍana Miśra's Type of Advaita.* There is a third position to consider, arising within the Advaita system itself. Maṇḍana Miśra does not accept the thesis of the incompatibility between Self-knowledge and action. Maṇḍana's position seems to be as follows. Knowledge in general requires a distinction between a knower, an instrument of knowledge (*pramāṇa*), and a content or object known. If Śaṃkara persists in his view the result will be that Self-knowledge is not knowledge, since the required distinction is precluded by hypothesis. Further, consider an empirical case of achieving valid knowledge when previously there had been error. For example, consider the well-known example of seeing two moons because of double vision. When one comes to know, through a trustworthy authority, that there are not two moons, but only one, the illusion of two moons does not automatically cease. Thus, a false appearance continues to exist even after valid knowledge has been achieved. Likewise, in the case of Self-knowledge, the false appearance of diversity continues to exist even after one has learned that there is only the one Self. To rid oneself of the false appearance of diversity which remains even after realization of the truth, meditation of a certain kind is required and indeed enjoined by scripture, a meditation that inculcates the vision of unity over and over until the traces of past karma either mature and wither away or else are somehow rendered inoperative. Now to be sure it is the meditations that accomplish the exhausting or anesthetizing of *prārabdhakarman*, but the meditation should also be accompanied by ritual action (*nityakarman*), as we are told by the Vedas. Through a combination of meditation and action, then, traces of two kinds are dealt with—mental traces that would otherwise produce error, and moral traces that would otherwise lead a person into further sins. Just as one who has been confused by his double vision and been told truly that there is only one moon may nevertheless slip back into his confusedly seeing two moons because his affliction leads him to forget the truth, so the Self-knower may backslide into bondage because the operation of the traces of past acts leads him to forget what he has learned.

In this way, although liberation is not an effect of action or of knowledge (since true knowledge does not have its content, reality, as its effect), still the eradication of the karmic traces remaining after realization is an effect and requires causal conditions. These conditions, according to Maṇḍana, include as a major factor meditation, and as accessory factors ritual acts of prescribed sorts.

Thus Maṇḍana provides a third position contrasting with Śaṃkara's, a more subtle challenge perhaps, but still diverging plainly from Śaṃkara's teachings. Both Śaṃkara's pupils Sureśvara and Padmapāda appear to be aware of Maṇḍana's views and rush to their teacher's defense.

Sureśvara points out that if the cessation of bondage depends on causal factors like meditation and action, it cannot be deemed necessarily everlasting once attained, for whatever is subject to dependence on causal conditions is noneternal. Even the authority of the Vedas is not sufficient to assure the eternality of liberation thus conceived.

Padmapāda's treatment of Maṇḍana is quite extensive.[25] In addition to Sureśvara's objection, Padmapāda raises some difficult questions for Maṇḍana with regard to how meditation accompanied by action can produce the direct realization of reality (Brahman) that constitutes the final state of liberation.

Although neither Sureśvara nor Padmapāda specifically allude to it, Maṇḍana at one point challenges himself to explain how any set of causal conditions can remove *avidyā* completely without leaving anything else foreign to the Self in its place. After all, the challenge goes, causes are always found to have effects that are something different from those causes and that in turn are potential factors in other causal nexuses; thus meditation cum actions can never completely expunge from reality (the Self) all foreign conditions, and liberation will never be achieved. Maṇḍana answers himself by citing the analogy of the *kaṭaka*-nut, or soap-nut, which was understood to have the remarkable ability, when thrown into dirty water, of clearing away all the dirt in the water and itself as well. This appears to be an attempt at answering the major thrust of the kind of criticism aimed at Maṇḍana by Sureśvara and Padmapāda.

It will be evident that three positions, the Mīmāṃsaka, the Bhedābhedavādin, and that of Maṇḍana, all of which try to find a place for action in the path to liberation, are largely motivated by sentiments of Brahmanical orthodoxy. All three views have at least this in common : they assume that the Vedic passages that apparently enjoin continued performance of ritual actions (the *nityakarmans*) are to be respected and applied in all stages of life, specifically including the stage of *saṃnyāsa*. Now that stage is interpre ed by Śaṃkara as being identical with the stage of Self-realization, that is of liberation, or *jīvanmukti*, an identification that proponents of the three other positions may not accept. "Even supposing the *saṃnyāsin* is a liberated person," we may imagine the three opponents saying, "still the Vedas clearly enjoin actions upon him."

We have seen Śaṃkara's response to this : because the Self-knower does not recognize any distinctions he is not subject to any injunctions, and so, whatever the appearances, those Vedic injunctions cannot be addressed to him. Śaṃkara nevertheless appreciates the pious motivations of the other positions. From their point of view he is advising them that at a certain stage in life one can stop performing religious rites. All their religious training runs counter to the implications of that, for orthodoxy counsels them that only by regular performance of prescribed acts and avoidance of prohibited ones can a person maintain whatever merit he may have earned; without such ritual action he will surely quickly gather demerit and subside once again into the lower sections of the great chain of Being.

To allay these moral and religious scruples Śaṃkara offers some words of counsel and comfort. The orthodox believer accepts the Mīmāṃsā distinction between *nitya-*, *naimittika-* and *kāmyakarmans*[26] and takes it very seriously. His notion is that, although the last two kinds of acts are undertaken for specific purposes, so that they involve attachment and so may plausibly be supposed to be improper for a *saṃnyāsin* to perform, still the regular (*nitya*) rites—the *agnihotra*, or daily fire-sacrifice, and the like—are to be performed as a matter of duty and not in order to achieve any specific results. Thus these particular regular acts can incur no sinfu' results : nd involve no attachment, and the orthodox Hindu assumes they should continue to be performed as long as life persists. Śaṃkara points out in response that, first, a certain type of act, for example, the *agnihotra*, is not *nitya* or *kāmya* by nature. Rather, a particular ritual act is *kāmya* if it is performed in order to gain a particular result, whereas it is *nitya* if it is performed out of a natural desire to avoid evil. So it is not that the Vedas enjoin on everyone the performance of a specific set of actions.

Second, the desire to avoid evil, however natural, is a desire; thus in an ultimate sense *nitya* and *kāmya* acts are essentially on the same footing, and there is no consistent way of maintaining that performance of one is essential for the *saṃnyāsin* whereas performance of the other is not.

As a result, there is no specific act omission of which by the Self-knower will incur sin, and the Vedas when properly understood do not imply anything to the contrary. Scripture does not enjoin any ritual action on the *saṃnyāsin*. But that raises the general question : how *does* a *saṃnyāsin* behave ?

IV. Stages of Life, and the Role of Yoga.

We have been discussing the place of ritual action in the achievement of liberation. Nonattached action is one of a number of kinds of discipline, or yoga, spoken of regularly in Indian thought, and one may at this point raise the question whether any of these kinds of discipline other than the gaining of Self-knowledge (*jñānayoga*) has a place in the proper path.

The arguments Śaṃkara adduces against a combined-path view apply equally against the supposition that any kind of activity whatsoever is possible in the state of *saṃnyāsa*, since the *saṃnyāsin* has realized the nondifference of everything else from his Self. The fact remains, of course, that many of the texts on which Śaṃkara chooses to comment speak in ways that *prima facie* run against his view.

In his comments on the *Bhagavadgītā* and the *Brahmasūtras*, for example, as well as on several Upaniṣadic passages, Śaṃkara carefully distinguishes alternative assumptions from his own.

Whenever he can Śaṃkara interprets references to "yoga" as referring to *jñānayoga*. He has no special problem, for instance, interpreting Gauḍapāda's *asparśayoga* as the discipline of Self-knowledge. Other passages cause more trouble. For example, in the opening stanza of Book Five of the *Bhagavadgītā* Arjuna asks which is better, *saṃnyāsa* or *yoga*? Clearly here the terms cannot be synonymous. Śaṃkara explains that Arjuna is of course not aware that *saṃnyāsa* is identical with Self-knowledge. Indeed, Lord Kṛṣṇa here recommends yoga over *saṃnyāsa*, which seems to contradict Śaṃkara's doctrine. In this context, however, *saṃnyāsa* means (according to Śaṃkara) Patañjali's kind of yoga, that is, renunciation without Self-knowledge, so Śaṃkara's doctrine is unaffected. Patañjali's yoga, involving action, cannot be practised by Śaṃkara's *saṃnyāsin*; Kṛṣṇa's teaching is meant for householders such as Arjuna.

Although standard Indian tradition speaks of four stages of life—studentship, householdership, forest-dwelling, and renunciation—Śaṃkara, without rejecting this classification, provides at one point[27] what he would take to be a more accurate division between (1) householders who respect scriptural injunctions, (2) ascetics who have renounced the world but do not have Self-knowledge, (3) "lifelong students," who study, teach, and practise penance throughout their lives without raising a family, and (4) the true *saṃnyāsin*, the one who "rests in Brahman," that is, the Self-knower. The point of this passage is to indicate why *saṃnyāsa* is the only stage of life from which one can gain liberation; it is so, we can see, because Śaṃkara has defined it so that it is identical with liberation.

3

PHILOSOPHY OF LANGUAGE

I. Exegetics

In the previous chapter we saw that there are three main alternative views about the role of action in gaining liberation and that Śaṃkara distinguishes his own position from all of them. The argumentation over these points consumes a large proportion of classical Advaita literature, and it may not be altogether evident to the casual reader why this is so. One must remember that Vedānta is first and foremost a kind of Mīmāṃsā or exegesis, and thus it functions, in the classical way of looking at these things, primarily to interpret the true meaning of the Vedic scriptures. It follows that the fundamental application of Advaita comes in connection with an assessment of the role scripture plays in achieving liberation.

The three alternative positions receive extended discussion as possible lines of scriptural interpretation. And it is the implications of some of the arguments developed in defending Śaṃkara's practically motivated exegetical views that lead him to characteristic theses in epistemology, philosophy of language, metaphysics, and philosophy of religion. Most English-language expositions of Advaita, having a Western audience in mind, reverse this order and make the Advaita theory appear more abstract and impractical than it was intended to be. In this introductory essay I am trying to develop Advaita theory in a fashion more nearly reflecting the order of the Advaitin's practical concerns.

The Vedic corpus, including ritual formulae (*saṃhitā*), directions for sacrifice (*brāhmaṇa*), and *upaniṣads*, may be viewed as having two distinguishable sections, one dealing with actions (*karmakāṇḍa*), the other with knowledge (*jñānakāṇḍa*). Broadly speaking, this distinction separates those passages in scripture that are related to ritual actions, as in sacrifice, from other passages that state the nature of Brahman, the Self. These sections do not necessarily occur in separate places in the scripture : although the Upaniṣads feature passages of the second kind, the other parts of the Vedas feature passages of the first kind. A basic question of scriptural exegesis is : what is the relation between these two sections?

There are, logically speaking, three possible relationships : (1) the *karmakāṇḍa* is primary, the *jñānakāṇḍa* subsidiary; (2) the two sections have equal weight; (3) the *jñānakāṇḍa* is primary, the *karmakāṇḍa* subsidiary. The three alternative views considered in the previous chapter concerning the role of action in liberation in fact correspond closely to the above-listed three positions on the present question. It is Pūrvamīmāṃsā that takes position (1), Bhedābhedavāda that takes position (2), and meditation-theory of Maṇḍana's sort that takes position (3).

A. *Critique of Niyogavāda.* The exegetical tradition of Pūrvamīmāṃsā, which is of hoary antiquity, promulgates the view that the primary purpose of scripture is to provide advice to men as to how to achieve the ultimate human purpose (*puruṣārtha*). It does this by issuing injunctions as to how a man should act. By performing *nityakarmans* and avoiding *kāmya*- and *niṣiddhakarmans*[1] a man can purify himself and become eligible to attain prosperity of various sorts culminating in heavenly bliss. Originally, it seems apparent, heaven was the highest human goal recognized in this tradition; liberation as a further goal came to prominence after the basic traditional stance had been established. Later Mīmāṃsakas tailored the tradition to suit the new development by taking the view that liberation constitutes a further goal to be obtained by action, if only the action of meditation. Thus the view came to be that scripture's primary function is to ordain actions, including meditation, leading to the highest human goals. As a result, the orthodox Mīmāṃsā view claims that *all* of scripture is governed by an overriding injunctive mood—whatever is said in scripture must be tied to the context of some injunction to act. If such a method of understanding scripture is not practiced, the Mīmāṃsā argues, the anomaly will follow that at least some of scripture will not be valid since it will not lead us to the highest human end. Scripture's validity depends on its relevance to matters lying beyond the sphere of ordinary experience; the other means of knowledge cannot operate successfully there, and if scripture's function were confined to this world it would have no specific role to perform and thus would not be valid. Its proper role, then, concerns future lives and goals.

This argument from scripture's role as a *pramāṇa* is only one line of argumentation put forth by the Mīmāṃsaka. Another important line is grammatical. Some sentences in the Vedas are grammatically injunctive : their verbs appear in the optative mood (*liṅ*, in technical Indian grammatical terminology). Other sentences do not have verbs in the optative mood, but the Mīmāṃsā proposes to construe such sentences as ancillary to injunctions, as what are technically called *arthavāda*. *Arthavāda* sentences do, indeed, provide information rather than enjoin, but they are nevertheless subsidiary to injunctions, since the information they provide relates in every case to future events and things that are to be produced or achieved by actions of the sort enjoined in the injunctions. This might not seem to us the most evident way of analyzing the meaning of declarative sentences, but the Mīmāṃsaka has additional arguments with which he bolsters his position. Prominent among these is an argument stemming from a theory about the acquisition of language. Children learn the meanings of words from their roles in injunctions, so it is argued. A child hears his grandfather order his father, "Bring the cow !" and sees his father leading the cow in. Later, he hears his grandfather order his father, "Bring the horse !" and, observing his father bringing a different animal in, draws the correct conclusion that "cow" means the first and "horse" the second kind of animal. Generalizing, and treating declarative sentences as a special kind of word or phrase, the Mīmāṃsaka concludes that understanding of information-disseminating segments of language presupposes a context of injunctions.

The refutation of these views is carried on at some length by Śaṃkara, notably in the commentary on the *Bṛhadāraṇyaka Upaniṣad*. It is, however, Sureśvara who provides the most generous treatment. The discussion is elaborate and is carried on through technical terminology that is not easy for an outsider to understand. Among these technical terms, we may note one of the most important.

There are various terms for injunctions,[2] but Sureśvara frequently uses the term *niyoga* to connote the notion of injunctive force. Thus a *niyogavādin* is someone who believes that enjoining is the primary function of scriptural sentences. *Niyoga* can also be used to designate, by extension, the optative mood, or *liṅ*—since it is the regular sign of *niyoga*—as well as the expected result (*kārya*) of the action enjoined, the thing-to-be-done—since an expected result is a regular concomitant and unique sign of injunctive force.[3]

The reader is directed to the summaries for a review of the many arguments developed by Śaṃkara and Sureśvara against the *niyogavādin*.[4] Here we shall be content to note a few aspects of these arguments that influence other developments in Śaṃkara's system.

As we have seen, one of Śaṃkara's major arguments against this sort of theory stems from the thesis that liberation, unlike heaven, is not a thing to be achieved. Thus it cannot properly be enjoined as something *to be* achieved. The *niyogavādin* may seek to turn this point to his advantage : scripture does not enjoin us to become liberated, but it does enjoin us to do things that will put us in a position from which we can become liberated. Śaṃkara's argument, however, is deeper than that : the point is, for him, that liberation is not in any way a future state or goal; rather, it is something that exists in the present, always has existed, and always will exist. The Mīmāṃsaka seeks to make the declarative statements in the *jñānakāṇḍa* subsidiary to the injunctive ones on the ground that scripture can only speak of entities to be known in the future. Śaṃkara insists that the main entity of which the *jñānakāṇḍa* speaks, that is, Brahman, is now existent and so cannot in any way be made out to be subsidiary to action.

The Mīmāṃsaka feels that this undercuts scriptural claim to authority, for to be a *pramāṇa* scripture must make known something that other *pramāṇas* cannot, and the only such things the Mīmāṃsaka envisages are events and things in future time. Śaṃkara's answer to this is that the Self is not made known by the other *pramāṇas* and that the sentences in the *jñānakāṇḍa* have a function in preparing the way for Self-knowledge. Thus the *karmakāṇḍa* does, as the Mīmāṃsaka suggests, make known future states that result from action, and the *jñānakāṇḍa* helps make known the Self : in both cases scripture's content is previously unknown and thus scriptural passages of both sorts are authoritative.

B. *The Combined-path View.* Other Vedānta philosophers agree that both the *karmakāṇḍa* and the *jñānakāṇḍa* are authoritative; in their view both kinds of passage in combination conduce to liberation. Sureśvara at one point implicitly classifies all such combined-path views into three varieties, according to whether such a view makes actions superior to knowledge or knowledge superior to action or whether it accords them equal status.

A view that might fall into the first class is that known as *kāmavilayavāda*,[5] which postulates that the primary path to liberation involves destruction of desires. The means to this is through fulfilling all one's desires, after which one gains a divine state from which liberation will follow automatically, for all that obstructs Self-knowledge is one's desires. Thus knowledge and action are both required, but action is primary. Sureśvara's response to this is to point out that no one can ever succeed in fulfilling all his desires; the so-called "law of karma" guarantees that every activity that fulfils one's desire will breed more desires. Only by abandoning actions can one hope to destroy the influence of desires.

A combined-path view that makes knowledge superior to action is known as *prapañcavilayavāda*.[6] On this view the *karmakāṇḍa* injunctions are subsidiary to superior injunctions found in the *jñānakāṇḍa*. These latter injunctions—to know the Self, etc.—are superior to the *karmakāṇḍa* injunctions addressed to those who desire heaven—that they should sacrifice, etc.—for what these *karmakāṇḍa* injunctions do is tell us how to destroy worldly actions. Such destruction of all worldly activity requires the eventual removal of difference; indeed, the various *karmakāṇḍa* injunctions—*nitya*, *kāmya*, etc.—are intended to remove some part of the notion of difference whose ultimate and complete removal is enjoined in the *jñānakāṇḍa*. Sureśvara's answer here is to point out that the *karmakāṇḍa* enjoins action, not dissolution of action, on us in order that we may gain heaven, a different state from liberation, so that the attempted compromise is inconsistent with the texts. Furthermore, he adds, the world involving its myriad distinctions cannot be destroyed by actions, which merely breed more distinctions; only by destroying the cause of such notions of difference can the world be destroyed, and the cause is *avidyā*. Activity cannot destroy *avidyā*; only knowledge can.

The third possibility, which is the one most commonly associated with the term "combined-path view" (*jñānakarmasamuccayavāda*), is that the *karmakāṇḍa* and *jñānakāṇḍa* have equal roles in constituting the path to liberation. This is the view that was apparently propounded by Bhartṛprapañca, and Śaṃkara invokes considerable argumentation in dealing with it. This view, like the previous one, finds both the *karmakāṇḍa* and the *jñānakāṇḍa* to be comprised of injunctions, injunctions in the former to act and in the latter to meditate. As Hiriyanna[7] understands Bhartṛprapañca, the view distinguishes two stages on the path, corresponding to heaven and liberation respectively. The path to the first stage lies in the performance of the *nityakarman*s as enjoined in the *karmakāṇḍa* while meditating on God in the form of Sūtra or Hiraṇyagarbha, which Bhartṛprapañca views as a lower form of Brahman. By this combination of methods, one will then achieve *apavarga* or escape from *saṃsāra*, which is a necessary stage on the way to, but not identical with, liberation. The self that has gained this stage is not yet liberated precisely because *avidyā* has not yet been eliminated. To eliminate *avidyā*, another combination of action and knowledge is required—the "knowledge" this time involving meditation upon the higher Brahman itself, with which one in due course achieves identity, this identity constituting liberation.

Śaṃkara is unhappy with this account for several reasons. First, the notion that Brahman has a lower nature suggests that Brahman is not completely free from difference; Bhartṛprapañca's view is termed *bhedābhedavāda*, "identity-in-difference-ism" for this reason. Śaṃkara thinks the notion of Brahman both containing difference and being free from it is a fudge—plainly inconsistent. Second, he professes not to understand the second part of Bhartṛprapañca's story. Either the self who has gained *apavarga* is ready to hear the great sentences such as "that art thou" and be immediately liberated as a result, which would imply that he has given up all notions of difference, or he is not ready because he still recognizes distinctions among things. If the former, since he recognizes no distinctions he cannot act and need not meditate; liberation will arise from hearing the scriptural sentences alone. If the latter, if he is not ready, he can act and he can try to meditate as much as he pleases, but he will never be liberated as long as ignorance—his recognition of difference—continues. Thus Śaṃkara's conclusion is that Bhartṛprapañca's solution makes the worst of the various other solutions.

C. *Meditation Theory* (*Prasaṃkhyānavāda*). A final way of reconciling the two parts of scripture will be to make the *jñānakāṇḍa* superior to the *karmakāṇḍa*. This is in fact the view that Advaita takes. However, there is more than one way of interpreting that common Advaita doctrine, and it is over the interpretation of this point that Maṇḍana Miśra and Śaṃkara seem most notably to part company. The view that Maṇḍana espouses was in all likelihood not original with him, however, for Śaṃkara considers it in the *Brahmasūtrabhāṣya* in a manner that suggests he is not merely setting aside the vagaries of a contemporary upstart.

The attitude of meditation theory toward our present problem is that the *karmakāṇḍa* passages are indeed subsidiary to the *jñānakāṇḍa* ones, but that both sections are partly injunctive in function, the Upaniṣadic passages enjoining meditation and informing us what we should meditate on, the *karmakāṇḍa* passages enjoining actions and informing us of their results. However, the emphasis is different in the two sections : in the *karmakāṇḍa* the emphasis is on injunctions, and the informative material is subsidiary as explanatory (*arthavāda*), whereas in the *jñānakāṇḍa* the statements about Brahman and the Self are primary and do not depend on injunctions for their sense, although there is implied an injunction on us to meditate on the things these statements make known to us. Thus the Vedas as a whole enjoin us to do two things—to perform prescribed acts and to meditate on Brahman—and they give us the information necessary for us to successfully follow these commands; it remains true, though, that the supreme message of the Vedas is found in the Upaniṣadic passages that tell us of the identity of the Self with Brahman.

This interpretation avoids many of the most glaring deficiencies of the Mīmāṃsā and Bhedābheda theories. Notably, it is apparently consistent with Advaita's penchant for monism; Maṇḍana is an even more damaging critic of difference than Śaṃkara. Yet Maṇḍana's view is not acceptable to Śaṃkara and his school. The major difficulty with it is that the meditation that is made out to be the practical point of the *jñānakāṇḍa* has no possible function. The argument here is much the same as the one just mentioned as used against Bhartṛprapañca : if the aspiring self is eligible to hear the great sentences; ignorance will be removed immediately thereby; if he isn't ready, meditation won't help. Meditation, if enjoinable, is an action, and actions both presuppose and foster differences. Śaṃkara charges that the meditation theorist misconstrues the famous passage in scripture that advises us to "hear, think, and reflect" (*śravaṇa, manana, nididhyāsana*); thinking and reflecting are not acts, and thus this passage cannot properly be construed as an injunction, at least in the same sense as passages advising sacrifice are. Another way of making this point is by reminding us that liberation is not a result and so cannot be "reached" by any activity, even meditation. Of course, this is not to say that meditation doesn't play a role in Śaṃkara's philosophy, only that it plays the same subordinate role that actions in general do.

D. *Śaṃkara's Positive Account.* These, then, are the rival views on the subject and Śaṃkara's reasons for rejecting them. How then does Śaṃkara think the two sections are related ? Śaṃkara's basic point is that the two sections are addressed to two entirely distinct classes of people. The *karmakāṇḍa* consists of injunctions to act; it presupposes in those it enjoins a recognition of themselves as agents wielding ritual and other objects in a variety of ways in order to achieve various sorts of results. Since liberation is not a result to be achieved, since the true Self is not an agent, there is no way in which these injunctions can be construed as relating to liberation, except in the indirect way of specifying how one should purify himself in order to become eligible for Self-knowledge. On the other hand, the *jñānakāṇḍa* consists, not of injunctions, but of declarations of fact, statements whose subject matter exists already, that is, Brahman, or the Self. These statements are addressed to a person who has become eligible to hear them by virtue of his moral purity, intelligence, and spiritual motivations. Since the statements' whole point is to imply that there are no differences in reality, they can only be comprehended by one who is just on the verge of appreciating the truth that Brahman, the true Self, is without distinctions.

As a result, the two sections of the Vedas really have no logical relation to each other, which is to say that there is no possibility of applying some common exegetical method to them collectively. In particular, one cannot apply Mīmāṃsaka methods of exegesis to the *jñānakāṇḍa*. Yet that does not in any way impugn the Mīmāṃsā method as applied to the *karmakāṇḍa*, provided no implications are drawn that affect the *jñānakāṇḍa*. Insofar as meditation theory tries to do this it too is defective.

Scripture is authoritative throughout, but again its authority has to be understood with respect to distinct subject matters for the two sections. What the *karmakāṇḍa* enjoins about actions is valid; what the *jñānakāṇḍa* states about Brahman is likewise valid. Both kinds of passages tell us something we did not know before and could not know otherwise, the injunctions telling us what actions to perform for what future results, the statements telling us truths about a reality that is not available to the other *pramāṇas*. The function of both kinds of passages is to make something known (*jñāpaka*), not to produce activity (*kāraka*). If hearing any passage, injunctive or declarative, prompts one to act in some way it must be because one desires something, so that it is the desire that does the prompting. But, though both kinds of passages make something known, the things they make known are entirely different.

Yet there *is* a sense in which the *jñānakāṇḍa* is primary and the *karmakāṇḍa* subsidiary, and that is evident from the above. Assuming that the common purpose of scripture is to tell us how to achieve the ultimate human purpose or goal, and assuming that it is agreed that that ultimate purpose is liberation, which Śaṃkara equates with true knowledge of the Self, then it is clear that the *jñānakāṇḍa*'s subject matter pertains to that ultimate purpose in a way that the *karmakāṇḍa* does not. By hearing "that art thou" and other passages from the *jñānakāṇḍa*, one, if properly prepared, rediscovers his true Self, thus gaining liberating Self-knowledge; this result is not possible from hearing passages from the *karmakāṇḍa*. This is not to say, of course, that passages of either kind cannot be misused or misconstrued; the point is that the *karmakāṇḍa*, whether properly or improperly construed, cannot make the Self known, whereas the *jñānakāṇḍa*, when properly construed by an eligible person, can.

II. Theory of Meaning.

All of this brings us to consider how the sentences of the *jñānakāṇḍa* are to be construed. False views of the nature of language and meaning obscure an adept's ability to understand the real meaning of sentences that could make the Self known to him; part of becoming "eligible" for Self-knowledge involves adopting a correct view about language.

Śaṃkara's overall view of language is ambivalent. He is, on the one hand, suspicious of language—it is the instrument of ignorance, breeding mental constructions that distort reality by hiding our true Self from us and distracting us to consider other things.[8] But on the other hand, he finds the mechanism of liberation ultimately in an act that requires speech. Although even the great sentences of the Upaniṣads (*mahāvākyas*) are ultimately false, says Śaṃkara, because they are language and so the products of ignorance, still one can be liberated by hearing a falsehood, just as one can be killed by being frightened by an illusory snake.

Maṇḍana appears to have resolved this ambivalence by endorsing Bhartṛhari's thesis that Brahman is language (*śabdādvaita*). His thesis appears to be that Brahman is consciousness, that consciousness is the power of speech, and so the conclusion follows that Brahman is of the nature of speech; the whole universe is a manifestation (*vivarta*) of speech. It is through words that we are able to discriminate and identify the contents of our ideas, which is to say the objects of our world. Maṇḍana adduces a striking series of arguments for this conclusion.

With such a basis for a positive attitude toward language it is perhaps not surprising that Maṇḍana develops the view we sketched earlier, on which it is possible to approach Brahman positively through meditation. By contrast, Śaṃkara and Sureśvara emphasize the impossibility of using language directly to designate reality. Although hearing a *mahāvākya* is the occasion for the liberating knowledge, that knowledge is a direct intuition (*anubhava*) free from the taint of words or any of the other means of ordinary knowing; what one learns is no positive description of reality. No reflective consideration is possible after Self-knowledge, for there is no discriminate content to reflect upon. The last word on this, from the viewpoint of Śaṃkara's school, is that Brahman is "not this, not this" (*neti neti*).

Nevertheless, Śaṃkara's position is that one cannot be liberated merely by hearing a "great sentence" without understanding what the sentence means. One may wrongly think that the words that make up a sentence such as "that art thou" directly denote Brahman, or that they can do so indirectly or figuratively, but the hearer must not understand them this way if liberation is to result. Furthermore, wrong views about syntax can also obstruct understanding : if the hearer does not realize that the "art" in "that art thou" is the "is" of identity and not the "is" of predication (as Western philosophers might put it) he will not appreciate the significance of the sentence and will remain in ignorance.

Indian theories of meaning concentrate on a number of problems familiar to Western theorists. Enormous subtleties abound in Indian treatments of these issues. Some of these subtleties are hinted at in the summaries offered in this volume. Here in the Introduction I attempt only to place the Advaita views among those with which they compete.

Indian grammatical tradition identifies at least three meaningful segments of language. A morpheme or syllable (*varṇa*) is the smallest meaningful segment. *Varṇas* combine to form words (*pada*), and words compose sentences (*vākya*). Let us ignore questions about the meaning of *varṇas* and limit ourselves to the last two segments. The theory of meaning concentrates on questions such as (1) what are the meanings of words, and of sentences ? (2) how are meanings established ? (3) how are meanings learned or made known ? and (4) how does all this apply to the proper interpretation of the *mahāvākyas* ?

A. *Word-meaning*. The characteristic view of the Nyāya-Vaiśeṣika is that the primary meaning (*abhidhā*, *śakti*) of a word is a particular (*vyakti*) characterized by a universal (*jāti*) and a "form" (*ākṛti*). The Mīmāṃsaka, by contrast, finds that the universal alone is the primary meaning; the particulars characterized by that universal are indicated by the word but only through secondary meaning (*lakṣaṇā*). Some theorists take the particular alone to be the primary meaning;[9] others take the "form" to be that meaning. In addition, there are, at least two more complex views to consider. The Buddhists, disbelieving in universals and facing tensions arising from their theory of momentariness of particulars, developed a unique account according to which the function of a word is to exclude everything to which the word does not apply. This view, known as *apohavāda*, is difficult to state in a way that does not invite its rebuttal, but in the process of teasing out its implications Dignāga's school of Buddhist logic seems to have developed an intriguing and subtle view that one hardly knows whether to classify as nominalism or conceptualism.

All the views catalogued so far identify the meaning of a word with something nonlinguistic —a universal or a particular, even a function of excluding. The other complex view is that of the grammarians, who take a different tack by hypostatizing *meaning* as what is called a *sphoṭa*, literally something that "bursts forth" when revealed by speech. Kunjunni Raja refers to it as "the partless, integral linguistic symbol".[10]

Maṇḍana Miśra defends the *sphoṭa* theory in his *Sphoṭasiddhi*, and one infers that the author of the *Brahmasiddhi* defends it also, although it is not specifically invoked there. Properly, discussion of that theory belongs below, as an answer to the question of the way meanings are made known. Śaṃkara, on the other hand, specifically rejects the *sphoṭa* theory and identifies the meaning of a word as the *ākṛti*, by which, however, he apparently means the universal property—that which is more normally termed the *jāti*. This is the view of most Advaitins after Śaṃkara.

B. *How are Meanings Established?* Here the issue concerns the role of convention in the establishment of relation between a particular word and its object. Classically, the Naiyāyikas and Vaiśeṣikas hold that meaning-relations are established by God's will, whereas the Mīmāṃsakas argue that meanings are inherent in the very nature of words. Advaita Vedāntins agree with the Mīmāṃsakas here.

An allied question relates to the manner of word-meaning connection. Maṇḍana considers as an objector he who believes that the connection requires mediation through ideas—that it is because the word evokes an idea that in turn is connected to the object. Maṇḍana rejects such a theory for a number of reasons and concludes that words are connected naturally to their objects.

C. *How are Meanings Made Known?* This is by far the richest of our first three questions and involves numerous subtleties. One of the most interesting of these, anticipating contemporary issues in philosophy of language, is the question whether the meaning of a collection of meaningful items is made known by those items, or whether the collection has a holistic meaning of its own, logically antecedent to those of its parts. In the form most pertinent to Advaita concerns, this issue comes up in connection with sentences.

First we may divide relevant theorists into two camps, those who take sentence meaning as a complex of word meanings, and those who do not. The main proponents of the latter view are the believers in *sphoṭa* and those who follow in their wake, including, as we have seen, Maṇḍana Miśra. For Bhartṛhari there is a "sentence-*sphoṭa*" (*vākyasphoṭa*), which is expressed or manifested by the words making up the sentence, just as the word-*sphoṭa* is expressed or manifested by the syllables making it up. Maṇḍana explores several ramifications of this position, notably its application to language learning. To see fully his position, though, we need to introduce the members of the other camp, those who think sentence meanings are complexes of word meanings. In Sanskrit parlance, the first camp's view is known as the "partlessness" thesis (*akhaṇḍārtha*), whereas the second camp's view is known as the thesis in which meaning is derived from the parts (*khaṇḍārtha*).

The latter group is in turn divided into two major sections. The Bhāṭṭa Mīmāṃsakas and Nyāya-Vaiśeṣikas hold that not only is the meaning of a sentence composed of the meanings of the words in it, but also that one understands the meaning of the sentence by first understanding the meanings of the words. This view is known as *abhihitānvayavāda*. The contrasting (*anvitābhidhānavāda*) view, held by the Prābhākara Mīmāṃsakas, although agreeing that sentence meaning is composed of word meanings, nevertheless believes that one understands the meanings of the sentence directly from hearing the words : one doesn't have to have understanding of the word meanings first. One may, on this view, subsequently come to understand the meanings of the words, but sentence meaning is made known by hearing the words alone, not by synthesizing their meanings.

One might infer from the above account that the Prābhākara position is a clever compromise between *sphoṭavāda* and the *abhihitānvayavāda*, and so indeed it may be considered. But Maṇḍana, at any rate, finds it objectionable. One may conjecture that Maṇḍana, as a former pupil or follower of Kumārila as well as a proponent of *sphoṭavāda*, deems it his mission to be particularly polemical against Kumārila's rival. On the other hand, it may rather be that Prabhākara's position only accidentally has the feature that might qualify it as a halfway house, since the basic inspiration for the theory stems from an even more fundamentalist version of Mīmāṃsā than that of Kumārila.

Maṇḍana brings in Prabhākara as one who insists that a sentence is meaningless without a verb and that the function of the verb is to signify an action to be done. Without such an action providing the overriding context, Prabhākara argues, the words are not properly connected and no sentence meaning results. This is, of course, part of the Mīmāṃsaka attack on the Vedāntin's assertion that the *jñānakāṇḍa* provides a source of knowledge independent of the injunctive context provided in the *karmakāṇḍa*. Maṇḍana points out that Prabhākara is able to say that sentence meaning arises directly from hearing words, without needing other *pramāṇas* to provide the meanings of those words, precisely because Prabhākara assumes that there is a primary injunction that gives the context for their meaning. Or, turning the same point around, Prabhākara is saying that on the *anvitābhidhāna* theory no understanding of a sentence can occur without something providing the connection among the words, and in the case of scripture (since *ex hypothesi* scripture has no author) it must be the injunctive character of the words that provides the connection. It is this assumption that Maṇḍana is concerned with refuting in the *Brahmasiddhi*.

The refutation leads Maṇḍana to make some interesting points about language learning. Prabhākara's thesis can apparently be bolstered by considering a plausible reconstruction of how a child learns the meanings of words. He hears grandfather tell father "bring the cow," sees father bringing the cow, then hears "bring the horse," sees a horse brought, and infers what "cow" and "horse" must mean. Note that he is assumed to understand the meanings of the two sentences first : this is the nub of the *anvitābhidhānavāda* theory. Now, how does he come to understand the meanings of those injunctions ? Prabhākara insists the understanding comes from language itself (*śabdapramāṇa*), arguing that one understands the injunctive force from the intention of the speaker. Maṇḍana's reply is that we understand meanings from their capacity—that is, from the fact that they mean something—and not from the intention of the speaker; if it were otherwise, a speaker could mean anything by his words just by intending it! This discussion has a very modern ring to it, lying at the heart of issues between some of the speech-act theorists and other, more traditional linguists.

Maṇḍana offers to account otherwise for the connection among the words in a sentence, the connection that Prabhākara finds necessary in order that sentence meaning be grasped. All that is required, Maṇḍana points out, is that we have some way of eventually coming to know of the connection; the requirement is that there is connection, and if the connection is there the condition Prabhākara insists on is satisfied whether or not we are aware that it is at that stime. Later on, Maṇḍana declares, we can become aware of the connection by the instrument of knowledge called *arthāpatti*. The argument continues at length, with Prabhākara's position being developed in mentalistic directions (the word is connected to an idea, not to an object). This position is also subject to criticism by Maṇḍana.

In the end, although Maṇḍana is not very explicit about it, one presumes that he follows Bhartṛhari and *śabdādvaita*. In the remarkable, rather self-enclosed section in the *Brahmasiddhi* where he explains that view, he makes it clear that, because difference is ultimately unreal and modifications ultimately nothing but what they are modifications of, it follows that, whereas speech (*vāk*, *śabda*) is real, collections of words, meanings, and so forth are not ultimately real but are instead reflections or manifestations (*vivarta*) of speech. Whereas one may conjecture that Maṇḍana prefers *abhihitānvayavāda* to *anvitābhidhānavāda*, given the arguments reviewed above plus the evidence of the masterful *Sphoṭasiddhi*, still it would seem that even Kumārila's theory proves acceptable only up to a point for Maṇḍana.

Śaṃkara, on the other hand, clearly rejects *sphoṭavāda*. Sureśvara finds nothing in his master's remarks to mitigate against a rather clearcut espousal of the *abhihitānvayavāda* view, and he makes a spirited defense of that view himself in more than one place. It is interesting to notice, also, that Sureśvara makes generous use of Maṇḍana's arguments, choosing language so close to Maṇḍana's as to make one sure that he knew the *Brahmasiddhi*. Indeed, these passages provide some of the most powerful evidence for the traditional identification of the two. However, Sureśvara's treatment lacks the characteristic *śabdādvaita* aspects.

D. *Interpretation of the Mahāvākyas*. For Advaita, the success of any theory of meaning arises from its relative success in explaining, consonantly with Advaita teachings, the meaning of the great sentences of the Upaniṣads. Sometimes there are said to be four of these great sentences, one from each Veda : "Brahman is wisdom" (*prajñānaṃ brahma* [*Aitareya Upaniṣad* III.5.3]); "I am Brahman" (*ahaṃ brahmāsmi* [*Bṛhadāraṇyaka Upaniṣad* I.4.10]); "That art thou" (*tat tvam asi* [*Chāndogya Upaniṣad* VI.8.7]); and "this Self is Brahman" (*ayam ātmā brahma* [*Māṇḍūkya Upaniṣad* IV.2]).[11]

Let us consider "that art thou." Uttered by Uddālaka Āruṇi to his son Śvetaketu, the context suggests that by "that" the sentence refers to Brahman, by "thou" it refers to Śvetaketu's self, and by "art" it is indicated that these two referents are identical. However, this straightforward explanation presents several problems for the Advaitin. For one thing, Śaṃkara explains in several places that Brahman is ineffable in the sense that words (even "Brahman") cannot denote It directly. It would seem to follow that if "that" means Brahman it must mean it indirectly, consistently with Śaṃkara's thesis.

Is "that art thou" metaphorical, then, a figurative identification—one's self is like Brahman, or Brahman is like one's true Self? No,

Śaṃkara replies : figurative language presupposes the speaker's knowledge that the things identified are really different, whereas "that art thou," insofar as it provides Self-knowledge, presupposes that the speaker knows that the things are really identical. If one says "Devadatta is a lion" figuratively, he knows Devadatta is not a lion.

It is not Śaṃkara's contention that Brahman cannot be indicated by words—what he is saying is that Brahman cannot be directly designated by any word. However, It can be indirectly designated for example, by the word "I." The word "I" directly denotes my ego (*ahaṃkāra*), but since the ego is a reflection of the true Self, as the mirror image is a reflection of the fact reflected in it, one can use the word "I" nonmetaphorically to indicate the Self. But all such usage presupposes, as has been said, the operation of ignorance, a failure on our part to discriminate the true Self from the *jiva* , ego, or whatever. Now if one truly appreciates the difference between self and Self and understands the nature of the Self, one will also appreciate why no word can directly designate It. All words indicate particulars by means of alluding to them through the universals that characterize them. But no universals characterize the true Self—It is "not this, not this". So if one says "that art thou," knowing the truth about the Self, it follows that he is not using the words "that" and "thou" to directly denote Brahman.

Which leaves us still seeking understanding of what "that art thou" means. Sureśvara is perhaps the most helpful writer on this point. He asks us to consider a sentence like "the space in the pot is the space in the sky". Read literally, this sentence is false—the space in the pot is there where the pot sits, the space in the sky somewhere else and unconfined, and so on. Yet the sentence indicates something beyond the direct meaning of its terms, namely, that both the pot space and the sky space are aspects of space *simpliciter*. Thus the sentence points beyond its literal meaning, and Sureśvara emphasizes that it does so immediately—that one does not have to reflect on it to appreciate this meaning it has provided; one already knows the difference between space *simpliciter* and confined parts of spaces. The analogy with "that art thou" is evident.

Notice that this refutes certain interpretations of "that art thou" that might seem tempting or obvious. Of these the most common is to suppose that "that art thou" means that Śvetaketu's self (*jīva*) is identical with his true Self or Brahman. The sentence does not mean that. Indeed, on Advaita tenets, the *jiva* is a product of ignorance or *māyā*, whereas the true Self or Brahman is not, so they are quite distinct, and it would be as false to identify them as it would be to identify the space in the pot with that outside the pot.

Nor does "that art thou" assert that one Reality goes under two names, for examples, "Self" and "Brahman." For one thing, the sentence is not about names. And "that" and "thou" do not name the one Reality directly.

Sureśvara explains the function of "that art thou" as a negative one. That the sentence cannot be interpreted literally should be evident when one reflects that the designation of "that" excludes thou and the designation of "thou" excludes that and yet they are identified in the sentence. So we are immediately led to forget the literal meaning as well as the figurative ones inasmuch as this is an identity statement, and given proper preparation we should immediately grasp the sense of the statement even though no literal "translation" is possible. This grasping will necessarily be accompanied by a realization that no words, which is to say no properties, properly apply to that which is conveyed through the sentence.

4

IDENTITY AND DIFFERENCE : THE THEORY OF RELATIONS

It has become clear in the preceding chapters that the major thrust of Advaita, as its title implies, is that even though practical affairs of men require a belief in the difference among things, that belief is false, and, indeed, eradication of it constitutes a critical part of achieving release. The liberating knowledge is awareness of nondifference, of nonduality.

But, one may well object, not every awareness constitutes knowledge. For an awareness to be an instance of knowledge it must be true—and why in the world should we suppose the awareness of nondifference to be true ? The way we discover truth is through using our eyes and other senses, as well as by using our reason. But the clear testimony of our senses as well as of reason is that there are distinctions among things. For instance, it is surely evident that at p_1 and t_1 certain things are the case, whereas at some other p and some later t they are different. Change does occur. Again, as another example, consider the relation between the subject of awareness and its object : some such relations support the predication of "truth" for the resulting judgment, whereas others do not support such a predication; therefore, at the least it must follow that judgments of the one kind are distinct from judgments of the other kind and that there is something about the one kind that makes them true that is lacking in the others.

The Advaitin's answer to this objection has already been indicated. One has to recognize a difference in levels of understanding, between reality and appearance. On the highest level, on which awareness of reality (or perhaps better, the reality that *is* awareness) occurs, there is no possibility of difference. From the lower level, the level of appearance, myriad distinctions are of course apparent, but this is entirely the work of *avidyā* or "ignorance."

The objector will hardly be satisfied, of course. He will reiterate his challenge : "I have asked for proof," he will say, "and the Advaitin has given me a pronouncement that merely avoids the challenge. Where is his *proof* that there are in reality no distinctions ?"

A great deal of the literature summarized later in this volume suggests answers to this challenge. But we can perhaps capture one major point of the discussion by focusing on those aspects of difference that the objector himself cited—the experience of change, or a thing arising when it was not there before, and the experience that one's own judgments differ from each other in significant respects. There are also some general arguments, chiefly pioneered by Maṇḍana Miśra, which we need to consider.

A. *Change and Causality*—1. *Gauḍapāda's Ajātivāda.* Gauḍapāda combines the denial of causal change with a general metaphysical principle to arrive at an unconditional monism. The principle is that any (putative) object that is nonexistent at the beginning, that is, that originates, and that is nonexistent at the end, that is, is destroyed, is also nonexistent in the middle, that is, is completely nonexistent. The argument for this principle stems from dreams. Everyone accepts that dream objects are unreal—why ? Because, though they appear to originate, exist for a time, and then go out of existence, it is clear on waking that none of these appearances are veridical : as we say, "it was all a dream." Accepting the unreality of dreams, we can then formulate the following inference : waking objects are unreal, because they originate, like dream objects. And Gauḍapāda assumes that this inference is unobjectionable.

Assuming that the inference is unobjectionable, all that needs to be done is to show that no waking objects actually originate. The view that no objects are ever born, that nothing originates, is known in Sanskrit as *ajātivāda* and is especially associated with Gauḍapāda. He presents several arguments for the thesis.

The major argument is predicated on a familiar assumption in Indian thought, that a thing's nature cannot change. We have seen, on the basis of the preceding argumentation, that if there were a real object it could not have origination as its nature, for that which has origination as its nature is unreal, as the objects of dreams are unreal. Therefore, if there are any real objects they cannot have origination as their nature. But if so, they cannot originate, for a thing cannot lose its nature.

One might respond here that Gauḍapāda has taken us in by verba manipulation. He has commandeered the word "real" for himself, meaning by it that which does not originate and has proved that real objects (in that sense) do not originate, which is hardly news. But the question, after all, was : does anything at all originate? And the argument doesn't prove anything about that.

Gauḍapāda handles this objection by dividing all things into two varieties, real (*sat*) and unreal (*asat*). A real object is taken to be nonoriginating on the basis of the argument already provided. But what the objection indicates is the possibility that unreal objects are really born, that is, become real, or that some other causal relations hold between the real and unreal as, respectively, cause and effect. To deal with this, Gauḍapāda considers what he takes to be an exhaustive list of possibilities.

First, both the effect and the cause cannot be real. If the effect is different from the cause, then it cannot be real, since that which originates does not exist (yet). And, if the effect is the same as (has the same nature as) the real cause, it cannot originate, since that nature involves nonorigination. So if there are causal relations either the cause, or the effect, or both must be unreal.

Second, suppose that the cause is unreal but becomes real as effect. But that is absurd—an unreal object such as a son of a barren woman cannot come to exist.

Third, if the cause is real and the effect not, and if the cause and effect are the same object, either that object exists (is real) or it does not (is not). If it (already) exists it cannot originate as effect, and if it doesn't exist (already) it cannot also exist as cause. On the other hand, if the cause and effect are different objects, the one real, the other unreal, and yet the effect originates from this cause, this will force us to suppose, says Gauḍapāda, "that what is born has already been born."

Or else we are led to the fourth alternative, that both cause and effect are unreal, in which case nothing ever comes to exist or goes out of existence, which is Gauḍapāda's conclusion.

Gauḍapāda buttresses this line of argument with some others. One interesting point he mentions is that if causality is accepted, then, since whatever originates must have an end, either *saṃsāra* has a beginning or else liberation must have an end. Neither result is acceptable.

Gauḍapāda's arguments are reminiscent of Buddhism. Conio[1] and Vidhusekhara Bhattacharya[2] trace the Buddhist originals of some of the arguments. Not every scholar accepts the implications of that parallel, however. Anantakrishna Sastri[3] feels that the Buddhist *ajātivāda* is different from that of Gauḍapāda. Gauḍapāda's view, he says, "does not mean natural non-origin but non-origin of the effected universe in the form of its cause (*sadbhāvena*). The effect, when viewed from the standpoint of its cause, will be found to have no origin; while viewed in its own form as mere effect it certainly possesses some kind of origin (i.e., *vivarta* or illusory appearance)."[4] That is to say, Gauḍapāda is not denying the obvious fact that causal relations characterize the world of appearances. That world appears, just as dreams appear, but the appearance is the result of "construction" (*vikalpa*), of ignorance, or *māyā*. This is evidently his view; whether the Buddhist view is any different we shall not try to judge here. Even if it is different, it is not clear that Anantakrishna Sastri is right in assimilating Gauḍapāda's view to Śaṃkara's; this may be an overreaction to the charge of Advaita parallelism with Buddhism.

A. *Change and Causality—2. Śaṃkara's Theory.* Śaṃkara provides numerous arguments relating to causality. Perhaps the richest resource is in *Brahmasūtrabhāṣya* II.1.15-20, where Deussen[5] counts some eight different arguments, not all of which will be summarized in this volume.

Some of Śaṃkara's arguments resemble standard reasons provided, for example, in the *Sāṃkhyakārikās*, for the theory of *satkāryavāda*, the theory that the effect preexists in its cause. For example, such an argument is that the effect must exist there already, for otherwise anything might arise anywhere. Another argument suggests that when scripture says that "in the beginning the universe was nonexistent (*asat*)" it means that the effect, before it arises, is the causal stuff but not yet developed in name-and-form.

In a somewhat more original vein, Śaṃkara points out that it is common experience that when the perceptibility of something, call it x, depends on the persistence of another thing y we assume x and y to be identical in nature, whereas conversely, when $x \neq y$, the perceptibility of x does not depend on the persistence of y, for example, a horse can be perceived without a cow being present.

Still another argument, which is both complex and difficult for a Western scientific mind to sympathize with, is predicated on the thesis that every causal process must have an "agent" (*kartṛ*). The assumption seems to be developed on the basis of one kind of Sanskrit grammatical theory. The verb from which the basic causal terms come (*kāraṇa*, "cause"; *kārya*, "effect"; *karman*, "causal object or action," etc.) literally means "to make" or "to produce" something. As with Aristotle, the paradigm in this kind of grammatical theory seems to be the production of formed stuff out of unformed stuff. In such a context, say in producing a pot from a lump of clay, the stuff clay is the cause, the pot the effect. But in addition we may want to identify whatever it is that is responsible for the form—here the shape—that the stuff takes in its effect state. That determining force is termed the "agent" or *kartṛ*. Characteristically, an agent brings about the effect by producing an action (*karman*) that gives the stuff the effect's nature. Thus it is the agent that is responsible for the nature of the effect.

The argument of which I speak begins in such a context. It is noted that without an agent an effect will be without a nature. But furthermore, Śaṃkara argues, the only thing that can properly function as agent is the effect itself. It must, therefore, preexist its own manifestation, for nothing else can serve as agent. The agent is that which gives the form to the effect, and only if it already has that form can it perform its function.

A major objection to this reasoning arises from the suggestion that the effect gets its form upon its manifestation through some kind of relation with the agent. Śaṃkara's response is evident : if the effect doesn't already have a nature it cannot come into a relation with anything, so on this view too one will have to admit the preexistence of the effect before its manifestation.

But suppose, someone suggests, the "agent" is simply the prior nonexistence of the effect; then the effect is the "counterpositive"[6] of that absence, and a relation between an absence and its counterpositive is perfectly appropriate. Śaṃkara disagrees : absences or nonexistents cannot be causal agents; a son of a barren woman cannot produce anything.

Causality must involve a relation between an agent with a nature and an effect with a nature, as Śaṃkara sees it. The function of the agent is to act so as to bring the effect to manifest itself in our experience. This effect, say the pot, is made of the substance that prior to production was known as the lump of clay; the effect is thus identical in substance with its cause, preexisting in it in potency. This is the view known throughout Indian thought as *satkāryavāda*, the view that the effect exists in its cause.

However, Śaṃkara, like Gauḍapāda, does not admit that the effect really exists at all. In commenting on a famous passage in the *Chāndogya Upaniṣad* he makes it quite clear that in the production of, say, a pot from some clay it is the clay that is real; the pot is "based merely on speech" (*vācālambanamātra*). For this reason most Advaita scholars prefer to term Śaṃkara's view *satkāraṇavāda*, or the view that the cause is existent, especially since other systems, notably Sāṃkhya, accept *satkāryavāda* in a fashion objectionable to Śaṃkara.

The point is perhaps more clearly made by considering the distinction between two models of causation called in Sanskrit *pariṇāmavāda* and *vivartavāda*. The Sāṃkhya provides an example of a system that adopts the *pariṇāma* model. On its view the pot is a transformation of the clay that constitutes it, both cause and effect existing at their appropriate times, neither being in any relevant way "unreal." By contrast, the *vivarta* model views the effect, the pot, as not an actual object but an appearance or construction due to our imagination conditioned by ignorance (*avidyā*). It should be evident that the *vivarta* model fits Gauḍapāda's theory; the *pariṇāma* model does not.

However, one can also look at the issue from a different angle. The reality of the cause, it may be pointed out, is a reality only relative to the effect. By contrast with the pot the clay is real; but on Śaṃkara's account the clay is not ultimately itself real. This allows for different ways of handling causal relations in the world. Consider : one might say that *all* causality, whether the relation between the ultimate cause (Brahman) and all appearance or the relation between a particular lump of clay and the pot it becomes—all such relations must be thought of according to the *vivarta* model, so that everything except Brahman is an appearance, a construction from *avidyā* relative to something else, its cause. But one doesn't have to say that. One might say instead that everything is a construction of *avidyā* when compared with Brahman, the only real existent, but that within the realm of phenomenal experience the relation between cause and effect corresponds to the *pariṇāma* model, so that cause and effect, though both ultimately unreal from the "highest standpoint" (*pāramārthika*), are equally real from the empirical standpoint (*vyāvahārika*). Or one might complicate things still further and hold that, though ultimately all is unreal by contrast with Brahman, within the world of appearances some causal relations are *pariṇāma*, some *vivarta*.

Which of these stories Śaṃkara tells is a matter of dispute among scholars. When we discuss the workings of *avidyā* below, we shall reconsider that point. Here I shall merely note, by way of transition, that the use of the *vivarta* model at whatever level puts the question of relations, including the causal relation, in a new and different light. *Vivarta* causality is an apparent relation between an effect that is (at least comparatively) unreal and a cause that is (at least comparatively) real, between a thought construction and that on which such a construction is grounded. Attention therefore shifts to the epistemic or awareness relationship, and away from scientific accounts of the relations of objects occupying a common, "external," and real world.

B. *The Awareness Relation*. We are led, then, to look more closely at knowing or awareness, in particular at what constitutes a "construction" and at error in general,

Returning to Gauḍapāda, we need a closer look at his use of the notion of construction (*vikalpa*). The term *vikalpa* is one of the most difficult Indian philosophical terms to interpret : the precise sense of some of its meanings is not always clear, and a great deal is made to hang on those senses. My best guess as to what Gauḍapāda means by it is "wrong interpretation." His own example of a *vikalpa* is the taking of a rope in the dusk to be a snake, a wrong interpretation of what is presented to the senses. This example is offered as an analogy to the relation between the Self (*ātman*) and its "states" (*bhāva*) such as living, etc. Again, the person who is aware of difference (*bheda*) is termed a *vikalpaka*, one who wrongly interprets.

Whether Gauḍapāda takes wrong interpretation as merely a negative state, a failure on our part, or whether he views it more positively as an activity, "constructing," is less clear. My own view is that he distinguishes between *kalpanā* and *vikalpanā*, the former bearing the sense of apparently producing something, the latter merely connoting our failure to properly understand something.[7] If that is right, the fact that I wrongly interpret something, say, the rope as snake, does not necessarily imply that I apparently produce the snake. There seems some reason to think that in fact Gauḍapāda supposes that the mechanism of apparent production ultimately stems from God and works through the *vāsanās*, the karmic traces. If this account is correct, Gauḍapāda's view would correspond to some degree with the view of the Yogācārin Vasubandhu, who distinguishes imaginary (*parikalpita*) from dependent (*paratantra*) natures of things, both of those distinguished from their absolute (*pariniṣpanna*) nature, a correspondence that may or may not be construed as lending credence to the association of Gauḍapāda with Buddhism.

Gauḍapāda is also fond of the term *māyā*, which figures elsewhere in Advaita. For the most part, it seems to me, Gauḍapāda uses *māyā* synonymously with *vikalpa*. If so, Gauḍapāda seems to be saying that we regularly wrongly interpret and so find differences where none exist, this occurring in both the dreaming and waking states. But these wrong interpretations are not forged out of whole cloth, so to speak; they are, rather, misinterpretations of something apparently produced by God through traces (in waking) or by us through traces (in dream).

The apparent-production aspect carries the idea of *ajātivāda*, reviewed above; thus even that diversity which we wrongly interpret as different sorts of states is unreal. Our wrong interpretations are doubly unreal. This idea recurs in Śaṃkara and later Advaitins, who sometimes use "wrong interpretation" to help us understand apparent production and thus, by contrast, the ultimate ground of both, the nondual Brahman.

It is remarkable that in the entire *Brahmasūtrabhāṣya* Śaṃkara nowhere uses the term *vikalpa* in Gauḍapāda's sense.[8] But Śaṃkara develops a related theory, with his own terminology for expressing it.

The fundamental text on this, a passage more studied and memorized by students of Indian philosophy than probably any other passage in the entire literature, is the famous introduction to the *Brahmasūtrabhāṣya*. Here, Śaṃkara develops the idea of "superimposition" (*adhyāsa*), which he defines as "the appearance, in the form of a memory, of something previously experienced in some other place." This would seem to be an analysis of the mechanism by which "wrong interpretation" takes place. Śaṃkara himself claims that his definition captures the common core of everyone's theory of error, that whatever differences in detail there may be, all the other systems agree that, in erroneous cognition the properties belonging to one thing appear to us as belonging to another.

In particular, says Śaṃkara, we are prone to superimpose the properties of the object of awareness on its subject, and vice versa. That is, we identify ourself *qua* seat of consciousness with ourself *qua* body, mind, memory, etc., all of which are objects, not subjects, and so have at least one property that the self *qua* subject cannot have. It is this primary superimposition that constitutes ignorance (*avidyā*), and it is this confusion in particular that needs to be eradicated through knowledge (*vidyā*).

Śaṃkara's account implies the important consideration that superimposition is not the free exercise of the imagination. It is the attribution of something experienced previously to something experienced now. Questions naturally arise : where did these things come from, and are they distinct from each other? If they are not distinct, how can they be superimposed, and if they are distinct, what happens to nondualism? It is questions such as these that later Advaitins spend much time answering, attempting to square their accounts with Śaṃkara's to the best of their ability.

Śaṃkara's own answers to these questions are not entirely free from ambiguity. Broadly, they are as follows. Ultimately, that on which everything is superimposed is pure consciousness, otherwise known as Brahman. So when one mistakes a rope for a snake, at the empirical level the snaky properties are attributed to a rope (of course not recognized as such at the time), but more fundamental is the basic superimposition involving attributing external-world attributes to pure consciousness (of course not recognized as such at the time). In this sense, Śaṃkara says, all practical affairs are dependent on *avidyā*, on superimposition.

At the heart of our confusion is the notion, due to *avidyā*, that my consciousness is different from yours or from anything else at all. This, then, suggests the answer to one of the questions posed above : all difference is unreal, and so the ground of superimposition is ultimately one, nondual, undifferentiated; distinct grounds are not required to have superimposition, although ordinary perceptual errors like the rope-snake happen to be built on more fundamental errors and so appear to involve one thing superimposed on another.

This line of explanation, however, inevitably leads us to inquire how the first superimposition could take place, which provided the distinctions that subsequently provide the grounds for the "ordinary perceptual errors." Sometimes Śaṃkara's answer to this is to disallow the question : *avidyā* is beginningless, and there was no first superimposition. Sometimes he confesses inability to explain the mysterious ways of *avidyā*.

Neither reply seems to do justice to a concern that motivates the question asked. If superimposition, *avidyā*, is the lack of awareness (*ajñāna*) that I, a knowing subject, am responsible for, then it would seem that if the grounds for every error are themselves the result of superimpositions, which in turn are things I am responsible for, I am caught up in a narcissistic game with myself. One can imagine a critic going on from this though to conclude that : either I didn't need to begin this game and thus ought to be able to end it at will, or else if not I am mysteriously subject to it in a way that awareness of it will not end, so that I am unable to escape at all. Śaṃkara seems to be exploring this worry in the *Upadeśasāhasrī*, and his answer appears to go something like this. In a sense you are caught up in a game with yourself, but you fail to appreciate the different levels of "yourself." The grounds for superimposing something on something else in this life include sense presentations in this life and the results of traces produced by yourself in previous lives. In turn, these are manipulated by a higher yourself, God. What is provided by that higher self is not fully in control of the lower self : thus the feeling that one is subjected to conditions for experience not created by oneself.

If these speculations are generally accurate it would seem that Śaṃkara follows a line much the same as Gauḍapāda, the "three-tiered" account mentioned previously as resembling the Yogācāra view, but with an important emphasis. Though the ordinary level of experience constitutes a double error—the misinterpretation superimposed on grounds that are themselves unreal because only apparently produced—it seems that for Śaṃkara it is the Self that is responsible for the apparent production, and that the mechanism by which apparent production occurs is a "higher-level" wrong interpretation. That is, *avidyā* is not only a failure to comprehend, a wrong interpretation, it is also the power of projecting as objects of awareness things that, ultimately unreal, themselves, are then misinterpreted once more as practical life continues. We shall return to consider this "positive" aspect of *avidyā* below.

C. *Maṇḍana's Critique of Difference.* It is Maṇḍana Miśra who develops the most devastating arguments against the reality of difference. These arguments are based on the logical incoherence of difference in general and are not tied to the particular cases of causation or awareness.

The Buddhists base their whole philosophy on distinctions. For them, difference is the very nature (*svabhāva*, *svarūpa*) of every thing, as is clearly indicated in their theory of meaning as *apoha*, the theory that a word can only designate its object by excluding everything else, since the object has no character of its own other than this difference. Maṇḍana argues that this is logically untenable. Difference is a relation between at least two things that are different from each other. If difference is the essence of these things they will both be identical with it, and then by the principle that if two things are identical with the same thing they are identical, these two different things will be identical, which is absurd.

If difference is real and not intrinsic to things, it must be a relation among things. Maṇḍana moves on to consider relations in general, arguing *their* unreality. Relations cannot be the natures of things, for this would result in mutual dependence, which precludes the thing ever coming to be. Therefore, it must be concluded that all relations are dependent on human purposes (*pauruṣeyāpekṣa*) and not intrinsic to things at all.

Various responses, stemming not only from Buddhism, but also from Kumārila, Nyāya-Vaiśeṣika, Jainas, and other Vedāntins will be considered at length, and I shall not attempt to summarize them here, except to point out that Maṇḍana's knowledge of the systems he treats is very acute : he picks out critical aspects of his opponents' theories. For example, in treating Kumārila and Nyāya he concentrates on the substance-attribute distinction, which is surely central to those ontologies, and on the use by Kumārila and Nyāya of negation, by using which they hope to avoid the force of the arguments we have cited.

Maṇḍana's approach contrasts with Śaṃkara's perhaps because Maṇḍana is writing an independent treatise, whereas, Śaṃkara is commenting. It contrasts with Gauḍapāda's approach, perhaps because Maṇḍana writes in prose and Gauḍapāda composed stanzas. Some scholars profess to find more significant contrasts among these writers than merely those brought about by stylistic necessities, however. There certainly do seem to be differences between Maṇḍana and Śaṃkara on other matters, notably, the issues over the path to liberation, but on the criticism of difference it is not clear that any substantial disagreement exists among the three. They each have their predilections—Gauḍapāda for the dream analogy, Śaṃkara for exegetics, Maṇḍana for philosophical argument. Still one finds considerable treatment of all three topics in the works of each writer. And the message is consistent : difference is unreal.

D. *Sureśvara's Synthesis.* Sureśvara develops all the themes and arguments reviewed in this chapter so far. He is very clearly aware of both Śaṃkara and Maṇḍana (and doubtless Gauḍapāda as well) and follows them both closely, indeed, so closely that some scholars have suggested that if the two are different writers Sureśvara must "plagiarize" Maṇḍana.[9] Presumably the same charge might be made that Sureśvara plagiarizes Śaṃkara, too, but since Sureśvara spends much of his time commenting explicitly on Śaṃkara rather than on Maṇḍana it seems inappropriate to tax him on that score !

Thus, Sureśvara develops Gauḍapāda's *ajātivāda,* Śaṃkara's superimposition, and Maṇḍana's arguments versus difference in various parts of his vast *Bṛhadāraṇyakavārttika.* He does not seem to develop any new ideas of his own on the epistemological points involved. If he has a distinct thesis to argue on difference, it will become relevant when we discuss the "positive" side of ignorance.

E. *Padmapāda's Contribution.* By comparison with Sureśvara, Padmapāda is temperamentally much more akin to Maṇḍana—interested in the logical and epistemological arguments for their own sake. Even though his ideas are developed in the apparent context of a commentary on Śaṃkara's opening sections of the *Brahmasūtrabhāṣya,* it is evident almost immediately that Padmapāda takes Śaṃkara as an occasion for developing his ideas rather than as a context limiting the relevance of his remarks. What Padmapāda does is to take Śaṃkara's idea of superimposition and erect a whole theory of knowledge on it. Whereas Śaṃkara and Sureśvara, and even to a large extent Maṇḍana, bring in epistemology only to the extent necessary to make certain points pertaining to "the path" and its teaching, minimizing the difficulty of the notions so developed,

Padmapāda spares his reader nothing. His method is startlingly "modern" : by far the largest portion of his work is a painstaking expansion of Śaṃkara's definition of superimposition, each word and nuance explained, analyzed, justified, and expanded by relating it to the richness of systematic criticism and response from the standpoint of other epistemological theories.

It is Padmapāda who pioneers the epistemology we most likely associate with Advaita. He provides the bridge between Śaṃkara and later Advaita, which is as obsessed with epistemology as Śaṃkara was with the contrast between knowledge and action.

With respect to the specific topic under discussion—the critique of difference—Padmapāda embarks on a new road, one that some find an extremely dangerous one. In all the other Advaitins we have so far studied, difference and relations have been argued to be unreal using completely negative arguments. Indeed, the very knowledge that liberates is held to be incapable of formulation in positive terms—in the final analysis the only formulation that is safe is "not this, not this." Even "that art thou" has to be unpacked in negative fashion : each term, according to Śaṃkara and Sureśvara, removes a source of ignorance and it is only the ignorant who will construe it as a positive assertion having a subject-predicate form.

Padmapāda's approach is to emphasize the positive identity between *jīva* and the *ātman*. To illustrate the relation between them he appeals at length to the analogy of the relation between one's face and its reflection in a mirror. Thus the function of "that art thou" for Padmapāda is not merely to remove error or ignorance, as it seems to have been for Śaṃkara and Sureśvara, but it actually propounds a declaration of identity between a reflection and its prototype. That, says Padmapāda, is why it is a positive rather than a negative judgment. Later developments in Advaita, to be dealt with in a subsequent volume in this series, feature extensive development of this line of thought among the writers belonging to the so-called "Vivaraṇa school," who take their point of departure from Padmapāda.

5

ADVAITA METAPHYSICS

We turn now to a positive account of the "categories" of Advaita philosophy. As we have seen, there is only one real thing according to this school, and it is alternatively called "Brahman" or "Ātman." We begin by inquiring more closely into the nature of this Real and follow this by exploring the workings of *avidyā* and *māyā*, by recourse to which the appearance of diversity is explained. In this way we shall be led on to consider how apparent creation takes place, and thence to consider the phenomenal world and the empirical selves we take to inhabit it.

I. Brahman

We have seen, in passages such as "not this, not this," that no positive language is adequate to describe Brahman. This does not prevent our authors from saying a good deal about Brahman. If pressed, they will of course admit that the predicates are applied only from the empirical standpoint conditioned by ignorance. Still, the choice of such predicates seems to matter enough to warrant some extended discussion.

Śaṃkara clearly distinguishes a higher from a lower Brahman in the *Brahmasūtrabhāṣya* and elsewhere. The higher Brahman, Brahman viewed from the aspect of knowledge (*vidyā*), is free from all adjuncts, all name and form. It is *nirguṇa* Brahman, and it is knowledge of this Brahman that constitutes liberation according to Śaṃkara. *Saguṇa* Brahman, or God, is the lower Brahman; it is Brahman viewed from the aspect of ignorance (*avidyā*).

It is, of course, the higher Brahman about which one cannot properly speak positively. Many of the adjectives used in our texts are negative : Brahman is without qualifiers (*nirviśeṣa*), without form (*arūpa*), without change, without parts, without end (*advitiya* or *advaita*). These perhaps require no further comment here.

Three positive properties are commonly invoked in alluding to Brahman. These are truth (*sat* or *satya*), consciousness (*cit* or *caitanya*), and bliss (*ānanda*). (In later Advaita these are combined into a stock triad—*saccidānanda*—but this combination is not found in Śaṃkara's works.[1] The closest passage is the *satyaṃ jñānam anantam brahma* of *Taittirīya Upaniṣad* II.1.) These three properties, or each of them singly, are said by Padmapāda to constitute the essential definition (*svarūpalakṣaṇa*) of Brahman, in contrast to the accidental definition (*taṭasthalakṣaṇa*) that according to Padmapāda is provided in the second *Brahmasūtra*. The discussion of each of the three properties is instructive.

The term *sat*, being, occurs in the earliest Vedic texts. A theme there is whether the universe sprang from *sat* or *asat*, being or non-being, and texts are found that argue for each side of the issue. Advaitins, who naturally view *sat* as the origin, explain away texts appearing to favor the converse view as saying something else.[2] The explanations are rather forced.

What is it to have or be *sat*? Later Advaitins search explicitly for a properly formulated criterion of reality. In the texts here covered the nature of reality has to be inferred from contrast with what it is not, and we have seen that it is not composite, not subject to origination and destruction, not subject to relations or change, etc. The *Bṛhadāraṇyaka Upaniṣad* declares that the secret name (*upaniṣad*) of the Self is *satyasya satya*, "truth of truth," and Śaṃkara and Sureśvara in commenting on this and similar passages treat this as a pronouncement more or less parallel to "not this, not this."

In Vaiśeṣika *sattā* is understood as a very comprehensive universal property (*sāmānya*). Maṇḍana Miśra, in the course of his extended attack on difference, describes Brahman as a universal in which all different individuals are absorbed, and in commenting on this verse he explicitly identifies Brahman as *sattā*. He appears to retract this later in the same passage, dismissing the identification as metaphorical, but apparently Sureśvara is not willing to leave it at that, for he pointedly refers to Maṇḍana's view (though without identifying the author) and rejects it on the grounds that it allows for complexity and so internal differentiation within Brahman.

Far more informative is the second property in the triad. The Highest Brahman is pure consciousness (*cit*) or awareness (*jñāna*), the Witness (*sākṣin*), which is not Itself an object of thought. Brahman is self-luminous; indeed It is the sole source of consciousness. By Its light everything else shines, that is, is known to awareness. In Itself It has no specific form; whatever appears to It as cognized is not intrinsic to It. Thus the consciousness that is Brahman is not a relational consciousness between knower and known. The closest approximation in our experience to pure consciousness occurs in deep sleep, which according to Advaita is a state of consciousness without any objects. When objects appear to this witnessing consciousness they are the work of *avidyā*; they are superimposed on pure consciousness, which remains unaffected by that relationship.

Although Brahman is self-luminous it should not be inferred that It is the object of Its awareness. Brahman can never be the object of knowledge, properly speaking. By the same token Brahman cannot be literally identified as the knower, the subject that knows objects. Both knower and known are products of *avidyā* and not ultimately real; likewise the relation between them is unreal. This we have seen above, and we shall return below to distinguish pure consciousness from empirical awareness.

The third member of the triad is bliss. Although the Upaniṣads frequently comment on this aspect of Brahman, Śaṃkara is peculiarly hesitant to attribute this property to It. Śaṃkara's reasons can be easily guessed. Bliss is pleasure, and pleasure is a temporary state, the experiencing of which requires a body, organs, etc. So if Brahman is bliss it must be so in some sense that cannot be translated into empirical analogues. In *Bṛhadāraṇyakopaniṣadbhāṣya* III.9.28.7, for example, Śaṃkara remarks that though no doubt Brahman is bliss, nevertheless that bliss is not cognized as an object by us. Our happiness has nothing to do with Brahman's bliss, he implies; the case is unlike that of consciousness, since we do experience pure consciousness (Brahman) in deep sleep, etc., whereas Śaṃkara seems to suggest that even the liberated Self does not cognize or experience Brahman's bliss.

Doubts about Brahman's having a blissful nature are addressed at length by Maṇḍana, and his spirited defense provides no room for the kinds of misgivings that Śaṃkara's approach invites. Pleasure is not just the absence of pain, argues Maṇḍana, nor does our attraction toward Brahman's bliss constitute any kind of passion.

Sureśvara emphasizes a point made by both Śaṃkara and Maṇḍana, that bliss is not a content of consciousness, something we think of and have experience of in an empirical way. The Upaniṣads suggest that the basis of the bliss of Brahman lies in Its being "full" (*pūrṇa*), not lacking anything. We share this bliss to the extent that we are or become self-complete; our pleasures are fleeting expressions of the joy that is our very nature.

II. God

The Higher Brahman, then, is unrelated to anything else, without internal differentiation, a very abstract though perhaps not austere reality. It is the one without a second. But then whence all this world of distinctions? What does it have to do with Brahman, after all? The answer is that the lower Brahman, God (*īśvara*), is the cause of all the diversity.

This basic point is set forth in the second *Brahmasūtra*. Brahman is that from which the origination, maintenance, and destruction of the world proceeds, and of course the Brahman that is meant is *saguṇa* Brahman. Advaitins are very concerned, in interpreting this *sūtra*, to insist that God is both the efficient and the material cause of the world. He is both immanent and transcendent, to use theological language; though different from His effects—being omnipotent and omniscient where those effects are not—He is yet within the world as inner controller (*antaryāmin*). It is His light, that is, His consciousness, that is reflected in *avidyā* as individual selves and the objects they cognize.

What is difficult to comprehend from the standpoint of ordinary theism is that the Advaitin can say all this about God and yet view Him as conditioned by ignorance. Brahman is the Supreme, the texts say, and yet in the same breath they affirm that He is not only not the Highest, His properties are unreal, false attributions of our ignorant superimpositions.

These properties, as we have seen, include omnipotence and omniscience. These notions are given Advaitic twists, however. God's omnipotence, for example, does not mean that He is responsible for the evil and imperfection in the world. God is subject to the karmic potentialities of individual selves in creating. He provides the opportunities for the *jīvas* to experience and thus work off their karmic residues. Again, His omniscience is hardly a matter of knowing everything in the discursive way we think we know some things. His omniscience is a feature deriving from the mere fact that He *is* consciousness; it is His awareness—Him—on which we superimpose the contents we believe ourselves to be experiencing as we go through the world.

Other problems about His creative ability are easily dismissed by Śaṃkara. Why should God create? He has no unsatisfied desires, no selfish interests providing Him with motivations to act. The answer is that God creates out of "play" (*līlā*). The meaning is that God responds in an appropriate manner to the karmic potencies without any personal interest of His own in the outcome; He "cannot help expressing Himself in creative activity."[3] This is an important reason why Brahman's fullness is emphasized.

Whatever the uninitiated may make of this apparently ambivalent attitude to the deity, it is undeniable that some, including Śaṃkara, are able to work up a fervent devotional attitude toward God despite His involvement with ignorance. A source for this side of Śaṃkara is found in the commentary on the *Bhagavadgītā*. He is also believed (but probably wrongly) to have composed devotional poetry.

III. Avidyā and Māyā

We saw the subjective side of *avidyā* as superimposition in an earlier section, but that suggests only a small part of this critical concept in Advaita. It is *avidyā* or *māyā* that provides the adjuncts (*upādhi*) that, by conditioning Brahman, produce the occasion for the apparent creation of the world. Clearly we have to do here with more than a merely negative notion.

Scholars have carried on lengthy investigations of the origins of these notions. R. B. Joshi suggests that at least four theories about the origins of the theory have been propounded, each by influential scholars.[4] The word *māyā* occurs as early as the *Ṛg Veda* (X. 54, 2), and it is used there and in a few Upaniṣads to mean a "mysterious power."[5] Deussen and others think, therefore, that Advaita's interpretation is firmly based in early Hindu tradition. A thorough study of references to *māyā* in the traditional literature exclusive of Buddhism and Jainism can be found in P. D. Devanandan's *The Concept of Maya*.[6] It appears that, although the term *avidyā* appears frequently in the older Upaniṣads, the word *māyā* does so only once—in the *Praśna Upaniṣad.* Furthermore, study of the occurrences of *avidyā* shows it to be used in the Upaniṣads as a negative notion—the opposite of *vidyā*, equivalent to *ajñāna*, nonknowledge. In the *Bhagavadgītā* also, one finds *māyā* used to speak of God's power, but it is in no way related to *avidyā*.

R. D. Ranade, however, argues that, although the Advaita notion of the equivalence of *māyā* to *avidyā* is not explicitly stated in the Upaniṣads, it is nevertheless implicit there.[7] As was noted, however, the term *māyā* occurs only in the *Praśna* among the older Upaniṣads, along with the *Maitrī* and *Śvetāśvatara Upaniṣads* among the later but still not "modern" ones. Joshi pertinently asks why, if the *Śvetāśvatara* (for example) sets forth *māyā* in Śaṃkara's sense, Śaṃkara didn't even comment on that Upaniṣad, much less quote it extensively.[8]

By contrast with these infrequent instances of *māyā* in Hindu scriptures, Gauḍapāda uses it in sixteen places. Furthermore, Joshi argues, Gauḍapāda uses it not only to mean the power of apparently creating things but also to speak of the things so created.[9] This latter usage is found in Buddhism and represents one of the numerous aspects of Gauḍapāda's work that point toward Buddhist influence. Still, Gauḍapāda does not identify *māyā* with *avidyā* as Śaṃkara appears to do.

Joshi concludes that Śaṃkara gets the notion of *māyā* from Buddhism through Gauḍapāda but that he develops it in his own special way.[10] Specifically, where Gauḍapāda did not equate *avidyā* and *māyā*, Śaṃkara does. A second contrast is that in the main Śaṃkara uses the term *avidyā* to speak only of that which produces the world of *māyā* or name-and-form but does not refer to the world itself as *avidyā* (though Joshi admits that Śaṃkara is not always consistent on this score). Still another contrast is that, whereas Gauḍapāda seems to speak only of real and unreal, Śaṃkara's explication indicates a three-level view with the empirical world occupying a position midway between Brahman and pure nonexistence.

Maṇḍana Miśra divides *avidyā* into two sorts, covering (*ācchādika*) and projective (*vikṣepika*), and explains that the former is nonapprehension (*agrahaṇa*, *ajñāna*) whereas the latter equals false apprehension (*viparyayagrahaṇa*). The covering *avidyā* is the cause, projective *avidyā* the effect. This is the basis for a notorious distinction, introduced by Vācaspati Miśra following Maṇḍana, between a root ignorance (*mūlāvidyā*) and a secondary ignorance (*tulāvidyā*). Although Śaṃkara does not use this terminology, he may have made such a distinction in some places between a causal ignorance and an effect ignorance, perhaps sometimes calling the former *māyā*.

Modern scholars have argued vociferously and at length about this distinction. Sacchidanandendra Sarasvati, perhaps the most vehement critic of the distinction of two *avidyās*, feels that it was Padmapāda who was responsible for the introduction of the distinction into Śaṃkara's school of Advaita.[11] On Sarasvati's view *avidyā* in Śaṃkara is superimposition, whereas *māyā* is equivalent to *prakṛti* or *nāmarūpa*. It is a confused notion to suppose that God has a power called *māyā*. *Nāmarūpa* is not a power; rather, it is what illusorily appears when occasioned by (not caused by) superimposition. Superimposition doesn't need a cause, since as Śaṃkara says it is beginningless. And Śaṃkara does not mean by *avidyā* to designate the empirical objects in the world but rather to speak of our false awareness of those objects. On Sarasvati's showing Śaṃkara is a realist,

True knowledge does not remove the objects of the world but rather removes our false awareness of them.

The two-*avidyās* problem also bears on another much discussed issue, the question of the locus of ignorance. The issue is supposed to arise as follows : on the one hand ignorance is something we *jīvas* experience, so presumably it belongs to us. On the other hand, if *avidyā* equals *māyā* and *māyā* is God's power to produce the world illusion, presumably *avidyā* belongs to God. Furthermore, there really are no individual selves or *jīvas*, so for that reason also the locus of ignorance has to be Brahman—presumably *nirguṇa* Brahman, although this seems to present a logical inconsistency.

When Śaṃkara raises the question "whose is *avidyā* ?" he conspicuously avoids the above issues by simply denying that *avidyā* belongs to anything. It is never really connected to either the *jīva* or to Brahman or God. And he drops the matter there. Later Advaitins propose to force the issue further by developing the idea that ignorance is *anirvacanīya*, "not describable (as either real or unreal)," but Śaṃkara does not use the term that way. Maṇḍana seems to.[12]

Maṇḍana, in fact, finds that *avidyā* must belong to the *jīva*. Otherwise, he argues, Brahman would be subject to *saṃsāra*, and when It obtains release everyone will be released at once. Furthermore, since Brahman is perfect knowledge (*vidyā*) by nature It cannot be visited with error.

Sureśvara's position on this issue is still different. He has no use for the distinction between *mūla* and *tula*, but he has an answer to the question "whose is *avidyā* ?"—it is Brahman's. Does this mean that Brahman is ignorant ? No, says Sureśvara, because *avidyā* is unreal and thus does not affect Brahman. However, since the *jīva* mistakes this *avidyā* for something real, it is he who is termed "ignorant."

Ingalls points out that in the passages where Śaṃkara raises the question of the status of *avidyā* he never speaks of *avidyā* as unreal, though he suggests that its relation to other things is unreal.[13] We may also note that, although Śaṃkara does not have standard terminology to regularly reflect the distinction, he does seem to speak of *avidyā* or *māyā* as *causing* us to experience (superimpose) things the way we do, which is to give it a positive function beyond that of merely veiling or covering Brahman. This might seem to imply that *avidyā* is not the same as superimposition after all, but one must recall that Advaita's view of causality makes the effect identical with its cause.

IV. Creation

It is God, then, who creates the world-appearance, according to our authors, and not the individual selves. If the world is an illusion, at least it is not completely fabricated by us. We do, to be sure, ordinarily misconstrue the world God apparently creates, taking it to be a real creation. But Śaṃkara's Advaita is not idealism in the usually accepted epistemological sense of the word : there is a world, not projected by our thought, that is independent of our thinking and will not go away just by our thinking it away. The world is "false," not in the sense of being a figment of our imagination, but in the sense that it is not real—the only real ultimately being *nirguṇa* Brahman.

In explaining creation Advaita combines psychology, epistemology, and metaphysics in a fashion bewildering to the untrained student. The nature of the Advaitin's problem is evident : he has to explain how diversity can even apparently arise from undifferentiated unity. But the complexity arises because there are several distinct kinds of diversity to account for. First, one must explain how undifferentiated, *nirguṇa* Brahman can develop into God, *saguṇa* Brahman. Second, one must try to explain how the one Self, the *paramātman*, can appear as many individual selves or *jīvas*. Third, one must show by what process a world-appearance is apparently created and how that world is related to God on the one hand and to the *jīvas* on the other, not to speak of accounting for the attributes of the world as we find them in our experience. In discussing all this, we will try to be careful to speak only of what *our* authors suggest on the topic : later Advaita is largely occupied with working out these details, but that story will be taken up in another volume of this series.

In explaining these various relationships Śaṃkara and his fellows have recourse to a number of analogies or models. (Some of them play a major part in post-Śaṃkara developments.) These are all invoked to make plausible the generation of multiplicity from unity, or, alternatively, to illuminate the phenomenon of superimposition and erroneous awareness, for it is by such awareness that the multifariousness of our perceptual contents is grasped. We shall briefly review the most important of these models, starting with those found appealed to in Gauḍapāda's *Kārikās*.

A. *Rope-snake.* Perhaps the best-known example utilized by Advaita is that of the perception of a snake at dusk, when what is there is actually a rope. Gauḍapāda uses this analogy to explain how the self or *jīva* constructs various things from itself through its own *māyā*. The mechanism is through memory, and the notion clearly fits Śaṃkara's account of superimposition. Gauḍapāda appears to think not only that the analogy helps explain the way we *jīvas* construct our experiences from our own past memory traces, but also that it helps explain how the higher Self—perhaps God ?—constructs the individual *jīvas*. It also helps to illustrate the process called "sublation" (*bādha*), by which error and ultimately ignorance is removed. The commentator on Gauḍapāda's *kārikās* (perhaps Śaṃkara ?) has an objector complain that, because the rope is, on Advaita tenets, as unreal as the snake, it cannot serve to explain apparent creation of the world from positive reality : the objector points out that it is just as likely that such creation is from nonexistence, or the void. The commentator's answer is that, when the snake is detected as being illusory, the rope remains as a positive substratum on which the illusion was based; likewise, he implies, there must be a positive Reality, Brahman or the Self, on which all error projected out of ignorance is based.

The author of the *Gauḍapādakārikābhāṣya* also invokes the rope-snake analogy in another place to explain how the Self (here, *puruṣa*) can produce individual streams of consciousness (*citta*) through the life breath (*prāṇa*). This use of the rope-snake analogy is more sophisticated, as it explicitly recognizes that the snake *is* in a sense the rope, or an appearance thereof : likewise, this author argues, all beings are in breath before they are apparently created or manifested. The idea here seems to be that creation occurs through a series of manifestations (*vivarta* rather than *pariṇāma*) in each of which something contains within itself effects that flow forth into a manifest state.

Śaṃkara, in the *Upadeśasāhasrī*, appeals to the rope-snake analogy to answer an objector who questions what it is that transmigrates. The puzzle is that the Highest Self cannot transmigrate, since it is changeless, but the individual self cannot do so either, since it is not real. The answer is that transmigration itself is not real; it is just like the snake that though unreal, exists, wriggles, and hisses through the rope's existence until sublation takes place.

A final instance of the rope-snake example may be noted in Padmapāda's *Pañcapādikā*. An objector complains that, where the problem is to explain the appearance of an individual self, neither the reflectionist analogy nor that of the red crystal (both will be discussed below) can apply, since there is no real substratum to act as adjunct (*upādhi*) in generating the *jīva* appearance. This is a grave difficulty, since in order for there to be appearances there need to be *jīvas* for things to appear to, and the objector's point is that the models regularly appealed to in Advaita, though they may help us understand error once we have *jīva*s as percipients, cannot help us understand the appearance of *jīva*s themselves. Padmapāda's reply is to point to other models—the rope-snake, for one, and even better the pot-space model (see below). In both cases memory traces produce the appearances of things (a snake, the space in a pot) though nothing like those things is nearby to be reflected through any medium. This implies, then, that the rope-snake and pot-space models may be better able to help us understand the production of *jīva*s, whereas the reflectionist and red-crystal analogies may be preferable when the problem is to account for the world appearance.

B. *Pot-space.* Gauḍapāda invokes the pot-space metaphor to explain how nonduality can apparently produce duality without being affected. Just as space (*ākāśa*), which is single and continuous, may be apparently enclosed within a pot without harming the unity and continuity of space in general, just so, says Gauḍapāda, the Self is manifested as many individual *jīva*s without being affected thereby. Furthermore, when the pot is destroyed the space it enclosed is "merged into space" without anything changing really; likewise, when a *jīva* is liberated, it is "merged into Brahman" without any real change taking place.

Śaṃkara has in mind the same points when he utilizes the analogy. God is like *ākāśa* in that He is limited by bodies, sense organs, etc. thus apparently creating portions of space. But such differentiation is merely a result of our failure to discriminate the Self from its adjuncts such as body, senses, etc.

Sureśvara puts it a different way. It is the pot that originates, remains, and is eventually destroyed, not the space it contains—that is always there, unchanged by the change in its surroundings.

C. *Wheel of fire* (*ālātacakra*). This notoriously Buddhistic figure is appealed to by Gauḍapāda in the fourth book of the *Kārikās*. In illustrating how one and the same thing, a burning firebrand, when waved about can appear as a series—say, as a flaming circle—Gauḍapāda hopes to shed light on how consciousness (*vijñāna*), though itself not discrete, when it "flickers" may appear as a series of perceivings and perceptions, but when it does not "flicker" does not appear as anything and is thus "unborn." Furthermore, he argues that just as the appearances of the flickering stick are not produced from anything different from the stick nor do they become real external, or for that matter internal, properties, likewise, consciousness alone produces the apparent objects we experience, but those objects cannot be said to exist either outside or inside consciousness. This is an interesting use of the wheel-of-fire example in that it was used by Buddhists to make the reverse point, that a series of momentary flashes of light can generate the illusion of constancy. One is constrained to note : that Gauḍapāda's use of it does not work very well it is left unexplained who or what is analogous to the one who waves the stick. It is also not clear whether Gauḍapāda invokes the analogy to help explain the generation of selves or empirical objects from God, or of empirical objects by individual selves. His comments seem to suggest the latter, but this appears to conflict with more realistic passages elsewhere in the work.

D. *Water and foam.* An ancient analogy likens the world's relation with its creator to the relation between foam and the water from which it bubbles. The point clearly is to emphasize the identity between cause and effect, water and foam, as well as to illustrate how, even in the empirical world, production sometimes does not require any distinction between a creator and the materials from which he creates. The contention of Śaṃkara that God is both the efficient and the material cause of the world is well illustrated in this analogy. Its defect is that it is as amenable to being construed in terms of *pariṇāma* causality as of *vivarta* causality.

In the *Upadeśasāhasrī* the model is complicated so that it is *dirty* foam arising from clear water, but the point is not developed.

E. *Sun's rays, spider's web, sparks from a fire.* These and other like illustrations are appealed to by Śaṃkara in various of his works, notably in the commentary on Gauḍapāda's *Kārikās*, where they are all offered along with the rope-snake to help explain how the Self can produce individual awareness through *prāṇa*.

F. *Reflection analogies.* These are probably the most complex and sophisticated of the models offered by Śaṃkara and his contemporaries. They are invoked by Śaṃkara to explain the relation between God and the *jīvas*. Śaṃkara says that the *jīvas* are mere "appearances" or "reflections" (*ābhāsa*) of the Highest Self, as when the sun is reflected in rippling water. The analogy is used to rebut an argument by an opponent who wonders why, if there is only one Self operating the various bodies, the actions of the various bodies do not get mixed up. Śaṃkara's answer is that when the sun is reflected in several *ābhāsa*s the trembling of one such reflection does not require that the next one also tremble; no more so in the case of one individual self's actions—they need not affect the next self.

Śaṃkara also invokes the reflection analogy to explain how qualityless Brahman, consciousness only, can appear as many objects in our experience. In *Brahmasūtrabhāṣya* III.2.11 21 an objector points out that in the case of the sun there is something different from the sun, namely, rippling water, for the sun to be reflected in, whereas there is nothing different from Brahman. Śaṃkara admits that this is a dissimilarity—no analogy is perfect—but argues that there are a number of points of similarity nevertheless. For example, Brahman, like the sun, appears to be affected when the nature of the reflecting medium changes—when, for example, it becomes dirty and the light becomes pallid—but neither Brahman nor the sun are really affected.

Again, Śaṃkara uses reflection to explain the Upaniṣadic passage that says that the Self enters into the universe.[14] Of course the Self, being nondifferent from the universe, cannot literally enter it, but it enters it just as the sun "enters" the water by being perceived there in its reflection, though of course it doesn't literally enter the water. This use of the analogy implies that the undifferentiated universe, like Sāṃkhya's *avyakta prakṛti*, is the medium that reflects pure consciousness, Brahman, with the *jīvas* perceiving the Self and themselves in that medium in varied ways.

In the commentary on the *Chāndogya Upaniṣad* the analogy is developed further. Here the reflection is of a man, or of the sun, in a mirror : the man reflected is not affected by being reflected, and no more is God affected by the multiplicity of *ābhāsa*s that result from His apparent connection with *buddhi*, etc. The defects of the resulting appearances are the result of imperfections in the reflecting medium, not in the thing reflected.

Just what does constitute the reflecting medium is not clearly answerable on the basis of Śaṃkara's writings. We have seen so far that undifferentiated *prakṛti* or the internal organ (*buddhi*) can be cast in the role. In other places other items are so cast—*prajñā*, *prāṇa*, and *citta* among them. But of course , it is Śaṃkara's view that ultimately there is no medium distinct from Brahman Itself. This would seem to suggest that the first projection cannot be understood on the reflection model, though later ones can, and Śaṃkara's discussion in one or two places seems to endorse that idea. The original projection is more like dreaming, or a magic show.

Another kind of reflection analogy is exemplified in the red crystal. A piece of rock crystal sitting on the shelf may appear to be red in color because there is a red flower behind it undiscriminated by the observer. Although Śaṃkara appeals occasionally to this analogy, Maṇḍana Miśra explains it most completely. The advantage of this model is that it sheds light on the necessity of removing the medium so that the prototype—the crystal, or Brahman—may be directly seen, even though the form of the crystal was not entirely obliterated by the flower it reflected.

Padmapāda develops the reflection analogy at some length. He utilizes both the red-crystal and the face-in-the-mirror examples to suggest a contrast. Padmapāda is the first of our authors to work out in detail a "map" of the process of creation. In a remarkable passage he presents it quite explicitly for us.[15] *Avidyā* (the list of synonyms is informative) veils the natural awareness of Brahman, and the result is a transformation (*pariṇāma*) of that *avidyā* which has God as its locus and which is termed *ahaṃkāra*, the sense of ego, of awareness, agency, and enjoyership. This *ahaṃkāra* is not, however, an evolute of *prakṛti* or *avidyā*, since this would make it completely different from the Self; rather, it is falsely attributed to the Self as a crystal is falsely held to possess red color because it is near the flower. The analogue of the flower., according to Padmapāda, is the internal organ (*antaḥkaraṇa*), that is, the *buddhi*.

Padmapāda proceeds to contrast the analogy of the red crystal with that part of the process which is like reflection in a mirror. The difference is that in the case of the red crystal the crystal's nature (its color) is different from that of the flower, so that our error comes in identifying them, but in the case of the face in the mirror the prototype is identical with its reflection, the reflected face is not different from the face. And the mirror reflection model is ultimately the right one, Padmapāda concludes. The ego is identical with Brahman, not just similar to It. There is a lengthy dialogue to prove this important point of identity, to show that the *jīva* has the same nature as Brahman, even though, like the face and its reflection, they appear in different places.

An implication of Padmapāda's analysis is that when one appreciates the identity of *jīva* and Brahman it does not follow that the medium —the internal organ—is destroyed, any more than it is the case that when one realizes that one's face is identical with its reflection in the mirror the mirror is thereby destroyed. This is handy, for it explains why upon liberation the *jīva* does not immediately disappear. When pressed about this with the objection that his model requires a distinct, separate medium, Padmapāda immediately has recourse to the rope-snake analogy, or, alternatively, the pot-space analogy. In both the latter cases, the prototype (analogous to Brahman) is not related to the rest of the items in the model (analogous to the adjuncts, including the medium).

Padmapāda, however, is constrained to confess that after all none of the models is quite sufficient to completely explain the mystery of creation. Later Advaitins continue to explore these models with the hope that they can ultimately be shown to resolve the mystery.

By comparison with his predecessors, however, Padmapāda's description is lucid. One must engage in substantial reconstructive analysis to manufacture an account from Śaṃkara's writings, voluminous though they are. Śaṃkara does appeal to the *ahaṃkāra* as the specific adjunct involved in the manifestation of the *jīva*.[16] Elsewhere, he seems willing to settle for saying that the *jīva* is a "part" of God, provided that isn't taken seriously but interpreted according to the reflectionist model. But most of Śaṃkara's thoughts on the topic of the relation between Self and self seem to come in criticizing other people's views. In a well-known passage in the *Brahmasūtras* Bādarāyaṇa refers to three old sages, Āśmarathya, Auḍulomi, and Kāśakṛtsna, who differed over the question of the relation between self and Self. Śaṃkara understands Kāśakṛtsna's view to be that they are nondifferent and argues that this is the correct view, in contrast to that of the other two, who admit at least some degree of difference. In other places,[17] he is largely concerned with controverting the views of his archrivals, the Bhedābhedavādins such as Bhartṛprapañca. We learn how not to interpret the relation in question but are left singularly uninformed as to how Śaṃkara wishes us to interpret it.

It is the apparent production of individual selves that most requires explanation, for the materials with which to develop the explanation are sparse. Once we assume that somehow attributeless Brahman has been veiled (by itself? by *avidyā*, anyhow) and become apparently diversified into many *jīva*s, along with an omniscient, omnipotent God, the rest of the story becomes much easier to tell. With internal organs to function as reflecting media, projection of a variety of objects for the *jīva*s to cognize is understandable along lines sketched above. Gauḍapāda lists a large catalogue of kinds of things that people become aware of, erroneously supposing them to be real and different from the Self.

In Śaṃkara and Sureśvara creation is only discussed when the textual occasion demands it. Usually in such passages the Upaniṣads are repeating various creation myths that are found throughout scripture. These myths feature Vedic deities such as Prajāpati, Hiraṇyagarbha, Sūtrātman, Brahmā, and Virāj as well as things such as the "breaths" (*prāṇa*). Such a myth is found in the first chapter of the *Bṛhadāraṇyaka Upaniṣad*. Sureśvara explains the order of creation based on this myth as follows. In the absence of Brahman-awareness things are created through *māyā*. From Viṣṇu—God supreme—comes Sūtrātman or Hiraṇyagarbha—knower and agent—and from him comes Virāj, which is apparently equivalent to

Sāṃkhya's unmanifest *prakṛti*. Creation takes place cyclically in Hinduism, as is well known; Sureśvara explains that after each intermediate cycle ends a new one is initiated by Virāj through the creation of gods such as Indra, Agni, and so forth, whereas after a major *pralaya* or end of a cycle the new creation is initiated by Brahmā. The myth is developed so as to involve the gods of creation in the very same kinds of fear and ignorance that humans are subject to, so that the world is the trials and tribulations of our experience projected onto a divine level. At this level Prajāpati, God as seeker after liberation, does appear to be thought of as projecting his own world-illusion; Vedānta is idealistic on this symbolic level at any rate, God subjecting Himself to ignorance. And this Upaniṣad applies its idealism to humans also in some places, although Advaitins like Śaṃkara tend to interpret such references as meaning that the individual self creates the stuff of its experiences from the traces of its past works with the assistance of God.

In the *Chāndogya Upaniṣad*, creation is explained as occurring through the process of triplication, according to which the differentiation of things proceeds according to the involvement of three "divinities" corresponding to the three elements fire, water, and food (or earth). Śaṃkara's comment indicates that he is not very particular about this and that the alternative account in terms of quintuplication is equally or more appropriate in explaining certain things. Indeed, in his *Upadeśasāhasrī* he provides a quintuplication explanation.

Sureśvara develops other themes found in the *Bṛhadāraṇyaka Upaniṣad*, such as the role of the breaths and of *vāsanās*. But generally the treatment by our authors of standard topics in metaphysics or science is unsatisfactory or nonexistent. One is reduced to speculations about what our authors might have said about the origins or analysis of certain interesting kinds of entities. For example, time and space are said by Śaṃkara to be the effects of *avidyā*, but scripture also alleges that Brahman "precedes the world." U. C. Bhattacharjee concludes that "Vedānta . . . does not give a quite satisfactory . . . account of Time,"[18] but one might better have said that it, or at least its earliest advocates, give no account at all.

V. States and Sheaths of the Self

We have seen that our authors use many analogies to try to indicate how the one Self becomes many, and that none of them is quite without difficulty. All the analogies so far discussed—reflection, pot-space, rope-snake, etc.—are defective on at least one count :

they require that there already be at least two things, namely, a percipient and an obstruction or adjunct. That is, all these analogies are taken from the kinds of experiences we have of what is commonsensically taken as an external world, and since the theory dismisses the adjuncts as ultimately unreal the theory goes outside of the analogy, which is therefore inadequate for the job.

There is another type of analogy, however, that might succeed where the previous ones failed, because it does not require the prior existence of something distinct from the percipient. The most obvious example is dreaming. Whatever one's ultimate explanation of dreams is, common sense suggests that the objects seen in dreams are not produced, even by reflection, from anything external to the mind of the dreamer. The thought suggests itself—a thought not unique to India—that perhaps the objects seen in the waking state are internal to that state just as those seen in dream are internal to the dream state, and that, just as we wake up from a dream and the dream objects are no more, so we can "wake up" from what we call waking experience and the ordinary objects of the empirical world will be no more. This is the thought that dominates Gauḍapāda's *Kārikās*, and which he relates there to the categories of the *Māṇḍūkya Upaniṣad*.

The idea is that there are four states of the Self to be distinguished. The waking state, called *Viśva* in the Upaniṣad, is mentioned first and identified with the syllable "*a*" in *aum* the sacred symbol of Brahman. Second is the dream state, called *taijasa*, equivalent to *u*. Third is the state of deep sleep called *prajña*, which is associated with *m* and in which no objects are confronted. Finally there is the fourth state, *turīya*, the state of liberation, which is associated with the silence following the utterance of the sacred syllable. Gauḍapāda indicates that the objects of waking, like dream objects, arise from erroneous awareness coupled with nonawareness of the truth about things, which is that nothing exists out there. Although there are no objects presented in deep sleep, all sleep is accompanied by traces, seeds of future experiences; thus one cannot be liberated directly from deep sleep or unconsciousness.

Śaṃkara (in *Brahmasūtrabhāṣya* III.2.1-6) points out that despite the analogies between waking and dream there are still important differences. We *jivas* construct our dream objects, but God creates the objects of waking. He also distinguishes unconsciousness as in a faint from deep sleep, though his grounds are not quite clear. Most important, in *Brahmasūtrabhāṣya* II.2.29, he rejects the dream analogy by pointing out that only some waking objects are sublated, whereas all dream objects are. He seems to think that in deep sleep Brahman is experienced, perhaps not so in a faint. Elsewhere he explains in some detail the mechanism of dreaming, which represents the results of past karma and anticipations of future results.[19] To manage this the *jīva*, while asleep, has to create for itself a dream body made out of *vāsanās*, since experience shows that no awareness of objects is possible without a body. Nevertheless, in dreams, unlike in waking, no contact through sense organs with any objects external to that body occurs.

As for deep sleep, Śaṃkara's explanation is that this occurs when from tiredness the organs, including the internal organ, are temporarily absorbed into breath, so that no objects are presented. Presumably the difference between deep and dreaming sleep is that in the latter the self has created a dream body to serve as "subject" of awareness of the dream objects.

Elsewhere Śaṃkara equates deep sleep with ignorance (*ajñāna*) and with *māyā*;[20] it is this ignorance, that evolves into the three states over and over, and the process is likened to a magic show, with the Self the magician and the magically created apparition.

Sureśvara provides a graphic account of what happens in sleep,[21] as well as of the process of waking. Another analogy is offered to show how the Self can create without any independent stuff from which to create : the example is that of a spider who spins the thread out of himself. Sureśvara also makes the important point that in dream it is not that the Self creates dream objects from the *vāsanās*, but rather that the *vāsanās* are themselves the objects experienced.

It is a popular notion in India that one should not wake up a person who is in deep sleep. Sureśvara explains why : each of the states involves the *jīva*'s residing temporarily in an appropriate set of "nerves" (*nāḍī*), one set for waking, another for sleeping, and while the *jīva* resides in the sleep set the sense organs do not operate. If one deeply asleep were woken up suddenly the *jīva* might be unable to find its way back to the waking nerves and so the person might be struck deaf, dumb, or blind for life.

Maṇḍana's example of the clearing nut (*kaṭaka*) is used by Sureśvara in explaining how the Self can be devoid of all *vāsanās* in deep sleep. Also, one in deep sleep is not attached to the objects of his dreaming, since he frequently does not remember them after he wakes up.

Sureśvara, furthermore, presents a fresh theory of his own (apparently) when he specifies that *each* of the three stages—waking, dream, deep sleep—must be divided into three states along the same lines.

The waking state of the waking stage is true knowledge; the dream state of waking is erroneous awareness (e.g., sensory awareness), and the deep sleep state of waking occurs when one is so carried away by passion or desire that one "loses one's senses," that is, one's discrimination altogether. As for the dream stage, its waking state occurs when one dreams he is behaving as he would while awake, its dream state occurs when one dreams he is dreaming, and the deep sleep state involves inability to recall dream objects. As for deep sleep itself, its waking state form is sattvic, its dream state is rajasic, and its deep-sleep state is tamasic.

Another ancient theory, related to the four stages theory just reviewed, is that of the five "sheaths" (*kośa*). Its major textual locus is in the *Taittirīya Upaniṣad.* There the Self is described as having five forms, frequently symbolized as five concentric circles, each subsequent one within its predecessor. The outermost sheath is the *annamayakośa*, the sheath made of food; this represents the gross embodiment of the *jīva.* Within this lies the *prāṇamayakośa*, the sheath made of breath, signifying the vital element in living things. Within this lies the *manomayakośa*, the sheath made of the internal organ or "mind" this is construed as indicating the form of the self in its function as perceiving and conceiving. The fourth sheath, still more subtle, is the *vijñānamayakośa*, the sheath of consciousness, which illuminates the internal organ. Finally, the fifth sheath is *ānandamayakośa*, the sheath made of bliss.

The Upaniṣad describes each of these sheaths in turn as "different from" the previous one and yet the same as it. Furthermore, it does not explicitly identify the fifth sheath with the supreme Brahman, although in a later passage it does say that the liberated man reaches the *ānandamayakośa*. Gauḍapāda nevertheless endorses the identification. Śaṃkara and Sureśvara refuse to identify the fifth sheath with Brahman, perhaps another instance of Śaṃkara's reticence on the point about the bliss of Brahman.

6

ADVAITA EPISTEMOLOGY

The most distinctive notion in Advaita is probably that of pure, undifferentiated or objectless consciousness. To be sure, a distinction between two kinds of awareness—*nirvikalpaka* or construction-free and *savikalpaka* or construction-filled—is a common one in Indian philosophy by Śaṃkara's time, especially as found in the Yoga systems of Buddhism and Hinduism. But Advaita elevates the distinction to new heights by identifying construction-free awareness with reality, Brahman.

Much of what needs to be said about the Advaita view of knowledge or awareness (*jñāna*) has been anticipated in the preceding discussion. It may be helpful to bring it together now. The basic contrast is between pure consciousness—called variously by names such as *anubhava*, "Witnessing" (*sākṣijñāna*), the Self, Brahman, etc.—and ordinary awareness involving the functioning (*vṛtti*) of the internal organ.

First, pure consciousness is not an act of any sort. Śaṃkara traces the mistaken views of numbers of his opponents to the fallacious assumption that knowing is an act; as we saw, much of his polemic against Mīmāṃsā stems from this point. In acting, an agent uses some instrument(s) to bring about a change in some object(s). Acting requires differentiation, and pure consciousness is precisely that which is undifferentiated. There are no instruments or objects to contrast with the Self as knower. That whole model for understanding awareness has to be abandoned. Even to talk of the Self as Witness is ultimately incorrect, because it suggests the improper model once again. Indeed, *any* way of speaking, if taken seriously, will be misleading in this way. This difficulty is an accurate measure of how difficult it is to eradicate *avidyā*.

Even ordinary knowing isn't an act, for that matter, or at any rate it differs from standard doings, as we have seen, in that one does something to get something else, whereas knowing is not necessarily a means to something else. However, it resembles acting in that it involves something coming into a relation with something different from itself, though once again the important distinction to note is that, whereas in acting something changes in the object as a result, in knowing nothing happens to the object.

Second, consciousness proper is not adventitious; it does not come and go but persists eternally. On this point Advaita agrees with Sāṃkhya and disagrees with Buddhism and with Nyāya and Mīmāṃsā. Ordinary awareness is dependent on the apparent presence of instruments (e.g., sense organs) and objects, and being so dependent it can exist only as long as those organs and objects are there. Pure consciousness on the other hand, not being dependent on anything, continues to shine regardless of what it may be taken to be shining upon, or even (as in dreamless sleep) if it appears to be shining on nothing at all.

One of the most acute discussions of the logic of this and of the preceding contrast occurs in the second chapter of the prose section of the *Upadeśasāhasrī*. After reviewing the reasons for Advaita's view on the nonact and the persisting nature of consciousness, an important objection is raised by the pupil in the dialogue. In deep sleep consciousness ceases; we say, "I knew nothing." And thus consciousness is adventitious after all. The teacher replies that the pupil's analysis of deep sleep is incorrect. How could we know enough to report that we knew nothing in deep sleep unless we were conscious during that period ? It is that consciousness, which is never lost, that is constitutive of the true Self about which the pupil asks.

A corollary of this second point about consciousness is that, whereas ordinary awareness not only has an object but also requires it as the occasion for that specific piece of awareness or judgment, pure consciousness has no more relation to its objects than does the sun that shines on everything without being in the least affected by or dependent on things. This important contrast provides the basis for Śaṃkara's answer to a very important objection to his theory of superimposition.

The objection is this : superimposition is explained as general error analogous to the rope-snake, red crystal, and so on, the analogy being that in all cases we are misled by a similarity between what is presented to us and something we remember from previous experience, and thus misled we erroneously project something false onto the presented item and consequently minisnterpret it. The Advaitin wishes to take this model of empirical error and expand it to explain cosmic creation; the projective *avidyā* leads us to misinterpret the presented objects of the world along lines dictated by our *vāsanā*s, our memories of past experiences. But the expansion carries with it an awkward implication : there must be something really presented that the projective *avidyā* leads us to misinterpret, and the only real thing is consciousness itself. Now consciousness is characterized in scripture as that which is never an object—Brahman is that by which all else is known but which is itself not known. The objector points to the inconsistency : if Brahman is not known It cannot be the object that is misinterpreted through the cosmic *avidyā*.

This objection is the very first that Śaṃkara raises against superimposition in the introduction to the *Brahmasūtrabhāṣya*, so one infers he feels it to be important. The bright pupil of the *Upadeśasāhasrī* I.1.2 also raises it. Śaṃkara's answer has several parts. First, though the Self is not an object of pure consciousness, it does not follow that it can't be the apparent object of empirical or ignorant awareness. Indeed, whenever we speak of ourselves in the first person as knower we are (though we do not know it) aware of the Self. Thus it is in a sense an object, although not of pure consciousness. Second, inasmuch as a person has ordinary awareness, which as we now know Advaita construes as a reflection of the "light" of the pure Self, of pure consciousness, he is constantly aware of that "light," aware of pure consciousness, or Brahman, just as one who mistakes a rope for a snake is aware of the rope in a sense even though he calls it a snake. And third, there are types of error that do not seem to require that something be presented as an object on which to superimpose; consider our supposing that the sky is a blue-colored dome, whereas in reality there is only space (*ākāśa*). For Śaṃkara, apparently, *ākāśa* is not a presented object. This last response is not, I think, to be taken altogether seriously, inasmuch as Śaṃkara insists in other places that every awareness must have an *ālambana* or supporting object; since our blue-domed-sky awareness is an awareness it must have a supporting object, namely *ākāśa*. Śaṃkara uses this realism to rebut the Vijñānavāda Buddhist in several places. The resolution of this apparent inconsistency on Śaṃkara's part can be found, I suspect, by reminding ourselves that though in one sense the object misinterpreted in superimposition must be really there to be misinterpreted, it doesn't follow that it must be "real" in the Advaitin's rather technical sense. Thus though in the cosmic projection there must be an analogous something for the world-illusion to be projected on, this something need not be pure consciousness or

Brahman and indeed cannot be insofar as we are speaking of and conceptualizing it. Granted we cannot explain that about which we cannot speak; the account seems to hang together with respect to that about which we can speak.

This point, however, continually recurs as a theme in Advaita, the theme of the self-luminosity of the Self. In a remarkable passage in the *Bṛhadāraṇyakopaniṣadbhāṣya* Śaṃkara is found defending realism against a Buddhist who uses the self-luminous character of consciousness as a reason for concluding that there is nothing other than consciousness. The Buddhist likens consciousness to a lamp, which lights itself at the same time it lights up the objects around it. Śaṃkara counters by pointing out that there is an important difference between light and consciousness: the lamp requires consciousness to reveal it, since for something to be "revealed" it must be possible for it to be present or absent to the revealer, and since the lamp cannot be absent from itself it cannot be its own revealer.

The lesson Śaṃkara draws from this is a remarkable one for a monist : consciousness must be distinct from its object, and so there must be external objects distinct from the awareness that knows them, contrary to the Vijñānavādin's tenets. The apparent dualistic implication of this does not trouble Śaṃkara at all, it would seem, because, though awareness requires external objects, consciousness does not, for one can have objectless consciousness as in deep sleep. Further, the objects need not be real, and consciousness has no actual relation to any objects they are the result of superimposition. It is in this very odd sense that Śaṃkara believes in the self-luminous character of consciousness.

What is *not* accepted, on Śaṃkara's view of self-luminosity, is that consciousness knows itself. Consciousness is pure subject, never object; it never has anything to do with objects. Thus Brahman, the Self, is not an object of pure consciousness; whatever Brahman we think we know must have an element of *avidyā* involved in it. This is the key to Śaṃkara's answer to another conundrum posed early in the *Brahmasūtrabhāṣya.* "Is Brahman known or not ?" asks someone; "if It is known we need not inquire further, and if it isn't known, given Advaita assumptions, It can never be known and once again inquiry is pointless." This dilemma, perhaps reminding us of one in Plato's dialogues, is shrugged off by Śaṃkara without much fuss. We know of Brahman's existence, he notes, on the grounds of tradition and experience, but the Brahman we know of is one on which there are various erroneous opinions. To remove these false notions is the point of Advaita teaching. As we now know, Śaṃkara interprets these teachings ultimately in a negative fashion, so that in fact we never do know Brahman in a positive way; when all characterizations have been rejected, pure consciousness will remain unqualified by adjuncts, and that state of understanding will constitute liberation.

This clever solution allows Śaṃkara to argue both sides of the issue when it is appropriate for him to do so. Thus in the *Bhagavadgītābhāṣya* and elsewhere he can affirm the possibility of Self-knowledge in the sense that it will be known when awareness of objects ceases, whereas at other places he denies that the Self can be known, following the Upaniṣadic dictum that "you cannot see the seer of seeing," etc.

We are left, nevertheless, with questions about the justification of the Advaitin's method of proceeding. Does he play the philosophical game by any of the same rules as anyone else ? What are those rules ? What philosophy is regularly supposed to aim for is truth, that is, true awareness. What the Advaitin recommends would seem to be a kind of consciousness that it would be presumptuous to call true, though equally presumptuous to classify as false—it seems to be beyond that dichotomy. Śaṃkara endorses that thought completely : if "truth" means what is provided by the instruments of valid knowing (*pramāṇa*), Self-knowledge is not ultimately true or false—it just *is*.

In a memorable passage in the *Brahmasūtrabhāṣya* (II.1.14), Śaṃkara faces the methodological issue squarely. An objector complains that on Advaita tenets the *pramāṇas* must be invalid, since they give us knowledge — allegedly "true knowledge" — about objects and Advaita says those objects are unreal. Thus in crediting our perceptions of pots and tables we are superimposing on something the impressions produced by our *vāsanās*, and this is precisely what error consists in. That's right, says Śaṃkara, all the *pramāṇas* can only operate as long as *avidyā* holds sway, as long as differences are recognized and accepted as such. Thus the *pramāṇas* fail to tell us about reality and so are "false"—at any rate, not "true."

The admission cuts deep, however. The objector points out that, if the *pramāṇas* do not tell us the truth, the point of instruction is lost; the teacher is unable to give veridical proofs to convince the pupil what to do or believe in order to gain liberation. And since instruction is required in order to realize one's Self the impossibility of receiving that instruction would seem to preclude the possibility of liberation, and Advaita is reduced to a kind of skepticism or worse.

Śaṃkara's response is astonishing when first heard, although it is not new with him : Nāgārjuna the Buddhist had offered it centuries earlier. It is that even though the *pramāṇas* are unreal they may nevertheless assist in "producing" liberation that is real, just as one may die from a fancied snakebite The objector retaliates that the analogy won't do : the effect—dying—is just as unreal as its cause, the snakebite, whereas the supposed analogue is between an unreal cause and a real effect. But we know by now that Śaṃkara's response will be to deny that liberation is an effect at all—as effect, it is unreal. The point, however, is that one may be jogged to an improved awareness by something in the realm from which he is escaping, as something violent happening in one's dream may cause one to awaken. There is no rule that requires that all the causal conditions producing a result be as real as that result.[1] The teacher's business, then, is to gauge the level of his pupil's confusion and to use the pupil's mistaken categories to jog him to higher and higher levels of understanding, a process that is admirably illustrated in the prose passages of Śaṃkara's *Upadeśasāhasrī*.

Although ultimately, therefore, none of the *pramāṇas* are veridical in quite the sense one might have expected, it doesn't follow at all that the Advaitin has no interest in the subject of truth in that commonly accepted sense. The teacher must use arguments and other procedures in accordance with the *pramāṇas* to convince his pupil, at least to convince a pupil with intellectual training and inquisitiveness. Thus Advaitins spend a good deal of time discussing the number and nature of the *pramāṇas*, in particular the number and nature of those they feel are especially critical in bringing the adept to the brink of Self-knowledge.

Discussions of that sort are not found among our authors, however, although references to numerous *pramāṇas* can be found. Traditionally, the *pramāṇas* accepted by Advaitins are held to be six : perception (*pratyakṣa*), inference (*anumāna*), comparison (*upamāna*), verbal testimony (*śabda* or *āgama*), presumption (*arthāpatti*), and negation (*abhāva*).[2] Among these, the priority in terms of importance is clearly with verbal testimony, which, for an Advaitin, mainly means scripture (*śruti*). Yet Śaṃkara emphasizes that even scripture is ultimately "false," presupposing the workings of *avidyā* as do the other *pramāṇas*

All of this may appear somewhat surprising. Advaita places a lot of emphasis on direct realization, on the immediacy of Self-knowledge. Perception, among the *pramāṇas*, is regularly identified as providing direct knowledge, and one might suppose that it would ultimately be perception that delivers the immediate awareness that constitutes liberation. Furthermore, if one is put in the position of defending the possibility of Self-knowledge, surely verification through direct experience constitutes the most fundamental proof. Yet Śaṃkara and his fellows look to scripture, to language, as the critical means of proof.

A Śaṃkara views Self-knowledge it is not given by any *pramāṇa* at all. It is true that Self-knowledge is immediate intuition (*anubhava*), but that is quite different from perception. The difference is the one, noted earlier, between those two kinds of awareness; perception involves instruments and objects and distinctions, whereas Self-knowledge does not. And in some Pickwickian sense *anubhava* may constitute a "proof," but it is not a proof that will ever be used. When one has Self-knowledge one no longer has doubts or needs proof, and when one needs proof one is not in a position to have Self-knowledge, since one is under the sway of ignorance.

It also follows that opponents cannot use perceptual evidence to disprove Advaita theory. Śaṃkara points out[3] that perception of difference does not disprove unity; just as *ākāśa* is one though sounds perceived in it are many, and a universal property is single though its particular instances are many, so Brahman may be one though its manifestations are many. Differences are due to adjuncts and do not affect the Real. And if perception is unable to disprove Advaita for that reason, the other *pramāṇas* are equally without force against it.

The importance of scripture becomes evident under the circumstances. A critic of Advaita, unable to use the usual kinds of reasons to oppose the system, can only turn and ask why he should pay any attention to, much less believe, a system that has no rational basis. To this the Advaita answer is that the basis, rational or not, is provided by scripture, which all reasonable parties accept as the *pramāṇa* that tells us about transempirical facts. We have seen how the Advaitin defends the veridicality of scripture (Chapter Three). Exegetical methods, including the use of inference and other *pramāṇas*, provide the rational basis for Advaita in an important sense, then, but it is scripture itself that, on the Advaitin's own view, bears the weight.

But this appears to provide the critic with the opening he was looking for after all. Maṇḍana elaborates a series of objections based on the proposition that perception is a more trustworthy *pramāṇa* than verbal testimony and so should be preferred where the two conflict. And clearly they do conflict, says the opponent, for perception shows us a multitude of different things, whereas according to Advaita scripture denies all difference.

The opponent argues that perception should be preferred to verbal testimony because verbal testimony depends on perception, because scripture is inconsistent, because perception precedes testimony in life, because one must first perceive a word before one can understand its meaning, and because one can explain away language but not the evidence of the senses. Maṇḍana answers that neither *pramāṇa* depends on the other, that they don't conflict, because perception affirms whereas scripture negates, that is, removes or sublates error. The notion that temporal precedence among *pramāṇas* implies greater trustworthiness is simply mistaken; the *pramāṇa* that comes later, undermining the results of the earlier use of another *pramāṇa*, is the one that carries the day. Scripture is not inconsistent; it does not teach duality; rather, assumes it in order to later remove it.

Later in the *Brahmasiddhi* Maṇḍana returns to the question of scripture's authority as a *pramāṇa*. This time an objector argues that since another *pramāṇa* such as perception can contradict scripture it follows that verbal testimony depends on perception and the other *pramāṇas*. Maṇḍana rejects this argument easily : perception may be contradicted by inference, but it doesn't follow that it depends on inference; no more does perception depend on verbal testimony. The *pramāṇas* are independent of one another. The discussion leads on to consideration of the characteristic Mīmāṃsā view of the injunctive force of scripture mingled with further points about the authority of verbal testimony. Maṇḍana insists that scripture is the only *pramāṇa* for knowing Brahman. But, he adds, even if one were to admit that Brahman can be known by another *pramāṇa* it wouldn't follow that scripture was not authoritative because dependent. When one tells us about something he has seen, our belief about the object is dependent on his perception, but our belief that he has seen the object is not. In any case, Maṇḍana concludes, the proof of Reality is not to be found in our knowing it by a *pramāṇa* : rather, a *pramāṇa*—scripture—leads us to direct knowledge of the Real, a direct knowledge that is in fact the Real itself and therefore not an instrument in knowing It.

Another objection is raised somewhat later still, one that the reader may well have anticipated. If our understanding of scripture depends on inference and other *pramāṇas*, those must be the ultimate source of Self-knowledge, for it is they that enable us to make sense of language. Maṇḍana lists a series of rebuttals to this argument, of which the first is sufficient. It is that the hearer of a sentence conveying information, about a speaker's perception, for example, does not himself use perception to grasp that information; *his* knowledge depends on testimony alone. Sentences can be understood whether true or false; since a false sentence cannot very well be known by any *pramāṇa* this is also sufficient to meet the argument.

As one works his way through these arguments one begins to realize that these points have been made or implied before. Advaita is a difficult philosophy to summarize, in contrast to, for example, Nyāya-Vaiśeṣika (see the previous volume in this series), for its points are much more thoroughly intertwined and much less dependent on precise empirical detail for their appreciation. Listening to an Advaitin is deliciously, or irritatingly, repetitive, depending on one's receptivity to the message. As we terminate this essay at this point in what may seem an abrupt fashion, the explanation stands : Advaitins can weave these points and patterns in endlessly varied ways —the summaries below and others to follow in later volumes bear witness to this—but the major lines of the argument, as announced early in the essay, are simple enough. An introduction must remain just that. For further insights, whether scholarly or spiritual, we need to consult the literature itself.

PART TWO

SUMMARIES OF WORKS

GAUḌAPĀDA

The first extant piece of literature that can be safely classified as exclusively Advaitic is attributed in Advaita tradition to an author referred to as Gauḍapādācārya. Almost everything about this identification has been questioned; the literature on Gauḍapāda is vast and complicated. Some doubt there was any one author responsible for the four books that now comprise the *Gauḍapāda-kārikās*. Assuming there was at least and (for argument's sake) at most one author, when did he live?

The major piece of relevant hard data is that the Buddhist philosopher Bhāvaviveka, while quoting a number of Vedāntic passages including some Upaniṣadic texts, offers one stanza that is identical with the fifth stanza of Book Three of the *Kārikās*. Now Bhāvaviveka is known to have been a junior contemporary of Dharmapāla, who is reported by Chinese travelers in India to have been flourishing in the fifth century A.D. One of Bhāvaviveka's works was translated into Chinese in A.D. 630, which also confirms this evidence.[1]

The major difficulty with this date stems from the fact that Śaṃkara refers to Gauḍapāda as his "highest teacher," *paramaguru* (*Gauḍapādakārikābhāṣya* (IV.100) or "teacher's teacher," *guror garīyase* (*Upadeśasāhasrī* II.18.2), and Śaṃkara's date is most frequently estimated at A.D. 788-820. If two centuries elapsed between Gauḍapāda and Śaṃkara this relationship cannot be taken literally. Thus either the ascription must be explained away, or else either Gauḍapāda's or Śaṃkara's dates must be revised. Surprisingly, it proves easier to revise Śaṃkara's date than to seriously question the evidence cited above relating to Gauḍapāda's.

Max Walleser has suggested that the word "Gauḍapāda" is not the name of one person but a more general reference to the lines (*pāda*) stemming from Bengal (*gauḍa*).[2] This suggestion has been rejected by all scholars who have concerned themselves with Gauḍapāda. S. L. Pandey summarizes the responses and adds an important piece of evidence, that is, that Śaṃkara (in the *Chāndogyopaniṣadbhāṣya*) clearly thought that the four books of the *Kārikās* were written by one person.[3]

Vidhusekhara Bhattacharya points out that the term "Gauḍa" need not refer to a resident of Bengal, though it suggests some association with that area through family background. Indeed, a late Advaitin, Bālakṛṣṇānanda Sarasvatī, takes the view that Gauḍapāda was a member of a sect of Gauḍas who lived in the "Kurukshetra country."[4] Another late author, Nārāyaṇa the *ṭikākāra* on the *Māṇḍūkya Upaniṣad*, places Gauḍapāda as writing his work in the Himalayas at Badarikasrama.[5] These opinions are not worth much, to be sure, but they do suggest we need not take the term "Gauḍa", overly seriously, for learned pandits do not.

A number of works are ascribed in manuscripts to Gauḍapāda, including an *Uttaragītābhāṣya*, a commentary on the *Nṛsiṃhatāpanīya Upaniṣad*, a *Durgāsaptaśati*, a *Śrī Vidyāratna Sūtra*, and a *Subhāgodaya* on Śrī Vidyā. None of these identifications can be authenticated. It is also possible that the same author who wrote these *Kārikās* also wrote the commentary on the *Sāṃkhyakārikās* attributed to Gauḍapāda. But the somewhat naive character of the Sāṃkhya commentary seems so alien to the depths of reflection suggested in the Advaita stanzas that the identity seems unlikely.

As noted in the introductory essay, scholarly excitement has been raised on several scores concerning Gauḍapāda's text. Fundamental to these discussions is the authenticity of the commentary on the *Kārikās* that is attributed to Śaṃkara. Since authoritative Advaita scholarship now favors the ascription of this work to Śaṃkara we shall assume, in this discussion, that the work is authentic.[6]

An important textual question concerns the status of the *Māṇḍūkya Upaniṣad* and the first twenty-nine *Kārikās* of Gauḍapāda's text. The *Māṇḍūkya Upaniṣad* is composed of prose passages, or *mantras*, concerning the mystic syllable *om* that relate each letter of the syllable to one of the four states—waking, dream, deep sleep, and the fourth, or liberation—referred to here by technical terms of Upaniṣadic ontology—*viśva*, *taijasa*, *prajña*, and *turīya*. The first twenty-nine *kārikās*, constituting Book One of the *Gauḍapādakārikās*, are usually thought to be a commentary on the prose passages. But a tradition reported in some of the other Vedāntic schools takes the *Kārikās* as well as the prose passages as scripture (*śruti*), and some scholars have argued that Śaṃkara implies that he too takes that view. Vidhusekhara Bhattacharya has advanced even more startling hypothesis that the prose passages of the Upaniṣad were composed subsequently to the *Kārikās* and were based upon *them.*[7] He suggests that the entire *Māṇḍūkya Upaniṣad* may have been composed after Śaṃkara's time. B. N. Krishnamurti Sarma, basing his views on the tradition that the first twenty-nine *Kārikās* are scripture, argues that both Rāmānuja and Madhva held that view and that Madhva, furthermore, did not think that the *Kārikās* were part of the Upaniṣad—indeed, he thought the authors were different from each other.[8] Sarma agrees with Bhattacharya that the *Kārikās* are older than the prose passages.

These suggestions have invited a torrent of criticism. One of the implications of Bhattacharya's and Sarma's hypotheses is that "Gauḍapāda's *Kārikās*" is not one work but several. This is spelled out by Bhattacharya, who suggests that we do not have all of the *Kārikās*, that they have been rearranged, and that there are four or more independent treatises involved[9]. The commentator Śaṃkara says he is commenting on four *prakaraṇas*, which is ambiguous and has been cited in argument by both sides of the discussion, for a *prakaraṇa* may be a chapter in a book or a separate treatise altogether. Various scholars have found fault with the arguments of Bhattacharya and Sarma on grounds of using unauthentic works as evidence, of misinterpreting passages, of ignoring relevant evidence (especially from the subcommentary of Ānandagiri, a much later Advaitin, who views the *Kārikās* as commenting on the prose passages).[10] Others have apparently been persuaded, at least partly. One could hardly say at this point that any consensus has emerged.[11]

Another vexed question concerns Buddhist authorship or influence. Vidhusekhara Bhattacharya has stressed the Buddhist terminology used in Books Two to Four especially in the last book. He thinks that two *Kārikās* in Book Four, actually refer to the Buddha under that name, and he argues that *asparśayoga* is Buddhistic in origin.[12] Again devout Advaitins have inveighed against this thesis. However, most recent writers seem willing to admit Buddhist influence to the extent implied by the use of Buddhist terminology but do not interpret such use as showing that Gauḍapāda is any less a Vedantin.[13]

GAUḌAPĀDAKĀRIKĀS on the *MĀṆḌŪKYA UPANIṢAD* also called *ĀGAMAŚĀSTRA*

(Summary references "ET"refer to the edition and translation by Vidhusekhara Bhattacharya University of Calcutta, 1943).

BOOK ONE : TRADITIONAL DOCTRINE (ĀGAMA)

1. *Kārikās* 1—5 (ET 1-2). The one (Self) resides in three forms in the body, it is in the waking state, the dream state, and the state of deep sleep. In the first state the Self is called *viśva,* in the second *taijasa,* and in the third *prajña. Viśva* is visible to us, conscious of external objects, and its activities and enjoyments pertain to the sphere of the gross (*sthūla*). *Taijasa* is conscious of internal objects (that is, dream presentations); it dwells in the mind (*manas*) and has to do with what is fine (*pravivikta*). *Prajña's* consciousness is not polarized (*ghana*—without distinctions); it resides in the heart, and its fruits and enjoyments consist of bliss (*ānanda*). The person who understands these three forms of the Self and their respective enjoyments is not affected through enjoying.

2. *Kārikās* 6-9 (ET 2-4). The person (*puruṣa*) produces through the vital breath (*prāṇa*) all the different rays of thought (*citta*). Some say that creation occurs through the expansion of the self; some say it is like a dream or a magic show. Others hold that it is God's desire; still others hold that beings are created from (or by) time (*kāla*). Some say God enjoys the results; others say it is for the sake of His play (*krīḍā*), but that it must be natural to Him, for how can one who has accomplished everything have any desires ?

3. *Kārikā* 10 (ET 4). There is a fourth state of the self, called *turīya* (here, *turya*). This form of the self is without duality (*advaita*), is the remover of all frustrations (*duḥkha*), is shining, without change, and all-pervading.

4. *Kārikās* 11-18 (ET 5-8). *Viśva* and *taijasa* can be both cause and effect, *prajña* can be cause only, and *turīya* is neither cause nor effect. *Prajña* knows nothing, whereas *turīya* is always seeing, is omniscient (*sarvadṛk*). Both *prajña* and *turīya* are not cognizant of duality, but *prajña*, unlike *turīya*, is accompanied by sleep that operates as a seed (*bīja*). *Viśva* and *taijasa* are said to be accompanied by "sleep" and "dream"; these are then explained respectively as any erroneous awareness and as nonawareness of the nature of things (*tattva*). "Sleep" visits the *jīva* because of beginningless *māyā*; when the *jīva* "awakens" (*prabudhyate*) it experiences *turīya,* which is not produced and is without duality, "sleep," or "dream." (When this happens) if the world (*prapañca*) were existent it would have to cease to exist. But this duality (of the world) is merely *māyā*; really there is only nonduality. If conceptual constructions (*vikalpa*) were constructed by someone they would cease. But this way of putting it is for didactic purposes only; when (the truth) is known there is no duality.

5. *Kārikās* 19-29 (ET 9-14). The four states are identified with the three letters comprising the sacred syllable *aum* / *oṃ* plus the undifferentiated ground of them—the *turīya*. Reasons are found for identifying *viśva* with *a*, *taijasa* with *u* and *prajña* with *m*. By meditating on each letter, one reaches the corresponding state; meditating on the *turīya* gets one nowhere, for *turīya* has no measure. The results accruing from meditation on *Om* are extolled. *Om* (or *praṇava*) is Brahman—both the higher (*para*) and lower (*apara*)—as well as God (*iśvara*) residing in the hearts of everyone; it is both without measure and of unlimited measure; the cessation of duality, it is bliss.

BOOK TWO UNREALITY (VAITATHYA)

6. *Kārikās* 1-3 (ET 15-17). Dream objects are unreal, since they are inside (*antaḥsthāna*) insofar as they are covered up (*saṃvṛta*). The dreamer does not go to the (actual) place about which he dreams —there isn't enough time—and when he wakes up he isn't in the same place he dreamed of. This reasoning is consonant with scripture (cf. *Bṛhadāraṇyaka Upaniṣad* IV.3.10).

7. *Kārikā* 4 (ET 17-18). The same argument shows objects of the waking state to be unreal. They are inside insofar as they are covered up.

8. *Kārikās* 5-10 (ET 18-21). The states of waking and dream are in fact identical, since their objects are alike unreal. Any object that is nonexistent at the beginning and at the end is also nonexistent in the middle. Dream objects can serve a purpose as easily as can waking ones. (*Kārikā* 8 is obscure). Furthermore, when dreaming, the dreamer believes those objects he dreams of as external to be real, whereas those he dreams of as internal he takes to be unreal; in fact we know them both to be unreal. Likewise, in the waking state, though we take what we apprehend as external to be real and what we apprehend as internal to be unreal, both kinds of objects are unreal.

9. *Kārikās* 11-15 (ET 22-26). *Objection* : If both internal and external things do not exist, who is it that apprehends them?

Answer : The Self (*ātman*) apparently creates (*kalpayati*) the self by the self through its own *māyā* and cognizes various things. This is the view of the Vedānta (i.e., the Upaniṣads). Some of the things are constructed in internal thought as fleeting (*avyavasthita*), others are constructed in external thought as fixed (*niyata*) through time; both are alike unreal, however. The difference between the internal and external constructions pertains to the kinds of organs used to grasp them, not to the respective reality or unreality of their objects.

10. *Kārikās* 16-30 (ET 26-37). First the *jīva* is constructed and from it the various things, which in turn condition subsequent memories. Just as a rope in the dusk is imagined to be various things—a snake, a line of water—so the *jīvātman* is imagined to be various things; and just as when we know the rope to be what it is the imagining of its being other things disappears, so it is with the self.

Stanzas 19-38 describe some of the kinds of things different people construct. Various fundamental categories of things are mentioned—some know the Self as breath (*prāṇa*), elements (*bhūta*), *guṇas*, *tattvas*, *padas*, *viṣayas*, worlds (*loka*), gods (*deva*), sacrifices (*yajña*), enjoyers (*bhoktṛ*) and enjoyables (*bhojya*), subtle (*sūkṣma*), gross (*sthūla*), material (*mūrta*), nonmaterial (*amūrta*), time (*kāla*), space (*dik*), discussion or views (*vāda*), worlds (*bhuvana*), mind (*manas*), *buddhi*, *citta*, *dharma* and *adharma*. Different numbers of categories are distinguished by different systems. When one thinks of the Self as created, it appears so; and so it is when one thinks of It as destroyed, or as ongoing. All these things are not different from It (the Self) but are imagined to be so.

11. *Kārikās* 31-38 (ET 38-47). All these things that people construct on the basis of the *jīva* appear as the objects of dream and illusion do. Nothing originates or disappears; no one is in bondage, no one seeks anything, liberation or anything else; there are no liberated ones—this is the highest truth (*paramārthatā*). All such things are really nonexistent, imagined through the nondual Self—thus nonduality is bliss. Wise men know that there is no manifoldness or separateness, or for that matter nonseparateness; they see what is nonconstructed, the quiescence of the world (*prapañcopaśama*). Having understood this, they should fix their memories on nonduality, and having thus realized nonduality they should move in the world as if inert (*jaḍa*). Such wise persons should be without praise or salutation, beyond participation in ritual, homeless wanderers, acting only as the occasion demands. Thus having realized the truth both inwardly and outwardly, they remain steadfastly true to nature (*tattva*).

BOOK THREE : NONDUALITY

12. *Kārikās* 1-10 (ET 48-54). Duties of worship arise only for those who think something is born and who are thus miserable. The author speaks, rather, of the nonmiserable state in which there is no birth and which is the same throughout to show how that nonduality can give rise to apparent duality and yet remain unaffected. An apt analogy is the way in which space (*ākāśa*), which is without

duality, nevertheless is manifested as portions of space, for example, as that part of space enclosed in a pot (*ghaṭākāśa*); just so, the Self is manifested as *jīvas*. Likewise, just as when the pots are destroyed the space they enclosed becomes merged into space *simpliciter*, so likewise are the *jīvas* merged into the Self.

13. *Kārikās* 11-16 (ET 54-58). What is *jīva*? In the *Upaniṣads* it is indicated that, among the five sheaths (*kośa*) of food, breath, mind, understanding, and bliss, the bliss sheath is the Highest Self and is also the *jīva*. The same thing is taught in the *madhukāṇḍa* of the *Bṛhadāraṇyaka Upaniṣad*, namely, that the self within the body and the self of things outside the body are identical with the Self or Brahman. Although some Upaniṣadic texts imply a difference between *jīva* and *ātman*, they are speaking of the apparent distinction that arises after an apparent creation. In reality nothing is born; there is no creation. References to it and its consequent distinctions are made only, out of kindness, for the purpose of spiritual instruction (*upāya*).

14. *Kārikās* 17-18 (ET 59-60). Although dualists may think they disagree with us, there is no real conflict; we both admit duality, but we, unlike them, hold that duality is confined to the realm of appearances and is not found in reality.

15. *Kārikās* 19-32 (ET 60-67). Duality is not found in reality, for what is real is naturally immortal and thus cannot become mortal, any more than what is naturally mortal can become immortal. In scriptures we find it said in some places that creation arises from what exists or "is real" (*sat*), in other places, that it arises from what is nonexistent or "is unreal" (*asat*). But neither position is reasonable ultimately; the only reasonable position is that no creation takes place at all. This is the proper interpretation of texts such as "not this, not this" (*neti neti*). It is unreasonable to think that what exists is really born, since to think that one has to think that what is born has already been born (which is absurd). On the other hand, it is unreasonable to think that anything is created from what is *asat*, either in reality or through *māyā*. For a son of a barren woman is not born either in reality or through *māyā*. This leaves the possibility only that what is "born" is born through *māyā* from reality (*sat*). Just as the mind (*manas*) flickering (*spandate*) in dreams has the appearance of a duality, even though in reality there is only one *manas*, not several, so it is in the waking state also. When the mind becomes nonmind no duality is experienced. And the mind "becomes nonmind" when it does not construct images (*na saṃkalpayate*); then, there being nothing to be grasped (*grāhya*), there is no grasping.

16. *Kārikās* 33-36 (ET 68-70). The *jñāna*, or awareness, that is without conceptual construction and is unborn is declared to be non-different from the object of that awareness, which is Brahman. Thus the unborn Brahman becomes manifest through the unborn (awareness). The awareness in question is not like that in deep sleep; in deep sleep the mind becomes oblivious, whereas in the awareness of the suppressed mind (about which we are speaking) the light of awareness shines forth free from fear, on all sides as Brahman. This kind of awareness is unborn, without sleep or dream, without name and form, all-knowing once and for all; it is not merely an approximation metaphor (*upacāra*).

17. *Kārikās* 37-48 (ET 72-82). Rather the awareness (of the nonmind) is *samādhi* (concentration), which is beyond language and thought, very calm and unwavering, full of light and without fear. Since there are no thoughts about objects, the awareness rests in itself and attains equanimity. It is contactless concentration (*asparśayoga*), difficult even for yogis, who shrink from it, seeing fear in what is without fear. But it can and must be attained through control of the mind (*manaso nigrahaḥ*). The means for this is constant remembrance that all is *duḥkha*; even when one is distracted by desires and pleasant experiences, even when one is at ease in *laya* (sleep? or at least mentally inactive), remembering that all is frustration (*duḥkha*) one turns away from desires and enjoyments. If awareness slackens (in *laya*) one should awaken it; if it becomes distracted, one should pacify it; if it becomes stiffened (*sakāṣāya*), one should understand it; when it reaches equanimity one should see that it stays there. The adept should not allow himself to experience pleasure (*sukha*) leading to attachment to his skill; he must be free from attachment through his understanding (*prajñā*). He should make his awareness fixed in itself. Such awareness, when it is not again distracted or affected by *laya* and when it has no movement and projects no images, is Brahman. It is then independent, calm, quiescent (*sanirvāṇa*), beyond language, blissful, unborn, all-knowing, and identical with its unborn "object" (viz., Brahman). Thus no *jīva* is born in reality.

BOOK FOUR : THE PEACE OF THE FIREBRAND (ĀLĀTAŚĀNTI)

18. *Kārikās* 1-2 (ET 83-94). The book begins with an invocation to "the greatest of men," to him who has understood the *dharmas*, which are like the sky, through an awareness that is nondifferent from its object, and to him who has taught the contactless

concentration that is free from self-contradiction and confutation by other systems.

19. *Kārikās* 3-5 (ET 101-107). Some argue that birth is from something already existing, whereas others argue that it is from something as yet nonexistent. Neither is possible.

20. *Kārikās* 6-10 (ET 108-112). Argument of Book Three, *kārikās* 20-22, repeated in the same language, except that there the discussion is about *bhāvas* and here it is about *dharmas*.

21. *Kārikās* 11-13 (ET 112-114), (The Sāṃkhya says that) the cause itself is what is born as its effect. How can they consistently maintain that that very thing which is born and is different be nevertheless unborn and eternal? If they insist that the effect is unborn, being nondifferent from the cause, then they cannot explain how the cause can be eternal when the effect (which is also the cause) is produced. Further, a person who thinks things are produced from something already existing cannot give an example if the view is that the cause is eternal; if his view is that the cause is some already existing but noneternal thing he lands in infinite regress.

22. *Kārikās* 14-20 (ET 115-125). This last contention is examined and defended, and it is claimed that the thesis of nonorigination (*ajātivāda*) has been explained by *buddhas*. If one replies "it is like the seed and the sprout—there is a beginningless series of causes and effects, but that's how it is," Gauḍapāda answers that the reply commits fallacies, specifically that of offering as example what has yet to be proved (*sādhyasama*).

23. *Kārikās* 21-23 (ET 126-129). *Objection* : If we do not know the point of origin or the end of a thing we admit that attests to its nonorigination; but as to something that is produced we *do* know its point of origin, so the *ajātivādin* conclusion doesn't follow.

Answer : Since nothing (really) originates we do *not* know the point of origination of any effect. And so the conclusion does follow after all.

24. *Kārikās* 24-28 (ET 131-138) *Objection* : Since we have ways (through language and thought) of identifying things (*prajñapti*), there must be an occasion (*nimitta*) for the identification, and so the identification must be dependent (*paratantra*) on something else, that is, an (external) object. Furthermore, since we experience impurities (*saṃkleśa*) there must be (objects that are the) causes of those experiences.

Answer : What the opponent takes as an occasion is not real. Our awareness (*citta*) does not touch any object or an appearance of an object, because objects are unreal and appearances of objects are no different. Neither awareness nor its objects are originated; those who see origins are like those who see marks made in the sky by birds flying there.

25. *Kārikās* 29-41 (ET 140-147). One who believes in the reality of origination cannot maintain consistently that *saṃsāra* is beginningless but has an end or that liberation has a beginning but no end. For if something has as its nature to be unborn it cannot be born, and if its nature is that it has been born it must have an end. Neither *saṃsāra* nor liberation has a beginning or end.

The argument of Book Two concerning the unreality of dream objects and the implications for the unreality of objects of waking states is repeated.

26. *Kārikās* 42-44 (ET 149-153). The *buddhas* sometimes speak of birth in order to help those who fear the doctrine of nonorigination. And the evil that might accrue for one who trusts such teaching is slight. In any case, the mere fact that someone speaks in practical terms of, say, an elephant cannot prove that elephants are real; we say that something exists whenever there is some practical reason for dealing with it.

27. *Kārikās* 45-52 (ET 153-157). Only consciousness (*vijñāna*) is real, though it appears in various guises as objects with beginnings and ends, movements, etc. It is analogous to a burning stick that, when swung about, appears as a continuant (say, a fiery hoop); in the same way, awareness when it flickers appears as perceiver and perceived. But when the burning stick does not flicker it fails to appear at all and is thus "unborn"; so it is with awareness. The appearances of the flickering burning stick are not produced from anything other than the stick; they do not go out to become real qualities of anything external. When the stick is at rest those fiery appearances don't reside somewhere else, nor do they reside in the stick. All this is analogous to awareness : the objects of our consciousness are not produced from anything other than our consciousness; they do not go out to form real external objects, and when our mind is calmed those objects don't reside somewhere else, nor do they reside in our mind.

28. *Kārikās* 53-56 (ET 158-160). There is no causation, for it is an accepted rule that substances may cause other substances to arise and that one thing causes a different thing to arise. But there are no substances, and there is only one real thing—consciousness—so it follows that there is no causation and in particular, that consciousness does not cause its objects to arise or vice-versa. In fact our attachment to the world and its objects depends on our adherence to a

belief in causal relations; when we lose that belief we will lose the attachment and thus there will be no causes, no effects.

29. *Kārikās* 57-60 (ET 161-165). On the level of ordinary affairs (*saṃvṛti*) everything is coming into and going out of existence all the time; thus nothing is eternal. On the other hand everything is by nature without origination, and thus without destruction either, so eternal. But we do not hold either of these views, for the things apprehended on the level of ordinary affairs are only *māyā*. Thus, for example, the illusory sprout that arises from an illusory seed is neither eternal nor is it subject to origination and destruction. In such a case the words "eternal" and "noneternal" don't demarcate anything from anything else and so are useless.

30. *Kārikās* 61-72 (ET 165-172). These stanzas repeat points already made about dream objects, etc.

31. *Kārikās* 73-81 (ET 174-188). Things that exist in the *saṃvṛti*, or practical level, do not exist from the highest (*paramārtha*) standpoint because they are dependent. So we cannot even assert that they are from the highest standpoint "unborn," since from that standpoint they do not exist at all. It is rather our attachment to unreality that is responsible for our viewing things under the subject-object modality; when this manner of viewing ceases there is nothing to classify as unborn. When this happens one reaches a state free from sorrow, desire, and fear (i.e., the state of *samādhi* mentioned before, here once again described in the same terms).

32. *Kārikās* 82-86 (ET 190-195). Through adhering to notions about things (such as : it is, is not, both is and is not, or neither is nor is not) happiness is obscured and frustration becomes manifest. One who realizes that the Lord (*bhagavān*) is not touched by these four alternatives (*koṭi*) is all-seeing (*sarvadṛk*) and desires nothing more.

33. *Kārikās* 87-89 (ET 196-198). Three stages in understanding are distinguished : ordinary (*laukika*), in which both objects and a subject are cognized as real; purified ordinary (*śuddha laukika*), in which perceiving, but not the objects, is cognized as real; and supramundane (*lokottara*), in which neither objects nor perceiving is cognized.

34. *Kārikās* 90-100 (ET 199-217). The *agrayāna* explains what is to be avoided, what is to be known, what is to be attained, and what is to be developed (made more mature). Of these four, what is to be known is not perceived, whereas the other three are. All *dharmas* are without beginning and without variety; they are by nature consciousness only, quiescent from the beginning by nature; they are all

the same, not different. The unwise follow difference and are pitiable; the wise are certain about the unborn, undifferentiated Reality, but the people do not grasp it. This knowledge of the wise is free from attachment (*asaṅga*) because it does not relate to the *dharmas*. If any difference among *dharmas* is cognized that cognition is not nonattached, and removal of the covering is *a fortiori* impossible. Not that the *dharmas* are really covered—they are primary awareness (?) (*ādibuddha*) and likewise liberated (*mukta*). This the *buddhas* understand. The Buddha instructs us that consciousness does not reach the *dharmas*—yet the Buddha said nothing about either consciousness or *dharmas* !

ŚAṂKARA (ŚAṂKARĀCĀRYA, ŚAṂKARABHAGAVATPĀDA)

As noted in the introductory essay, the date of Śaṃkara is not agreed on by scholars. A great deal of traditional lore has been built up around Śaṃkara's name; some of it may well be accurate, but much of it surely is not. To be able to defend a hypothesis on Śaṃkara's date, one must have weightier evidence than mere tradition. Without any inscriptional evidence to rely on, internal evidence deriving from references in Śaṃkara's writings is critical in arriving at his *terminus a quo*. But which are Śaṃkara's writings?

Tradition is at work here also. Śaṃkara is credited with a great many works, most of which are highly unlikely to be by him. The most careful work on the criteria for deciding which works are Śaṃkara's has been done by Paul Hacker, with applications by Sengaku Mayeda.[1] In the following discussion we follow these authors wherever possible.

Hacker and Mayeda propose the following tests, all of which are satisfied by the *Brahmasūtrabhāṣya* (by common consent the work of the Śaṃkara we are interested in): (1) Use of the term *avidyā* to mean superimposition (*adhyāsa*), and not as synonymous with such terms as *jaḍa*, *bhāvarūpa*, *āvaraṇa-* or *vikṣepa-śakti*, or *anirvacanīya*, which identifications Hacker and Mayeda find non-Śaṃkaran; (2) use of the term *nāmarūpa* to mean the original world stuff, like Sāṃkhya's *prakṛti*; (3) relatively infrequent use of the term *māyā* in comparison with *avidyā*; (4) frequent occurrence of the term *īśvara* (it is found less frequently in later Advaitins, including Śaṃkara's pupils); (5) reluctance or refusal to accept *ānanda* as a positive property of Brahman; and (6) nonoccurrence of the term *vivarta* in its "illusionistic" sense as the relation between a cause and its only apparent, unreal effect. These are among the main tests; various others are also proposed. Using these tests Mayeda has argued for Śamkara's authorship of the *Bhagavadgītābhāṣya*, *Upadeśasāhasrī*, *Gauḍapādakārikābhāṣya*, and *Kenopaniṣadbhāṣya* (as well as the *Brahmasūtrabhāṣya*, of course). The method is highly scientific and does not give completely unambiguous results; in particular, the *Gītābhāṣya* and *Gauḍapādakārikābhāṣya*, whose authenticity has been questioned by some scholars, show both similarities and differences with the *Brahmasūtrabhāṣya.*

Different but rather clearer evidence is available for those *Upaniṣadbhāṣyas* on which Sureśvara comments, that is, the *Bṛhadāraṇyaka-* and *Taittirīyopaniṣadbhāṣyas.* Unless we find the ascription of the subcommentaries to Sureśvara spurious—and no one has—we have no reason to refuse to ascribe these commentaries to Śaṃkara.

The same tests are appealed to by Hacker and Mayeda to support the rejection of other *prakaraṇa* works frequently ascribed to Śaṃkara, notably the *Vivekacūḍāmaṇi* and *Ātmabodha,* both very popular in Advaita circles. Ingalls has also contributed additional reasons to reject the *Vivekacūḍāmaṇi.*[2] Fuller evidence on the various ascriptions is reviewed in the material provided below.

The upshot of the most careful scholarship to date on the works of Śaṃkara, therefore, is that the following may without question be accepted as the work of the author of the *Brahmasūtrabhāṣya* : the *Bṛhadāraṇyakopaniṣadbhāṣya,*[3] the *Taittirīyopaniṣadbhāṣya,* and the *Upadeśasāhasrī.*[4] There seems no real reason to question the inclusion of the *Aitareyopaniṣadbhāṣya,* the *Chāndogyopaniṣadbhāṣya,* the *Muṇḍakopaniṣadbhāṣya* and the *Praśnopaniṣadbhāṣya* on this list. Beyond this point, however, is only speculation. Therefore, we shall limit ourselves to these works in arriving at an estimate of Śaṃkara's date.

Authors whom Śaṃkara, the author of the above works, presupposes include Kumārila, Bhartṛhari and Dharmakīrti,[5] and, of course, Gauḍapāda, to whom Śaṃkara refers deferentially.[6] Now Bhartṛhari lived in the middle of the fifth century, Gauḍapāda (as we saw), in the sixth century, and Kumārila and Dharmakīrti, most likely in the seventh century. As a result Śaṃkara cannot precede the middle of the seventh century. No firm evidence forces us to date Śaṃkara any later than mid-seventh century, however. The arguments of Belvalkar[7] and, more recently, Kunjunni Raja[8] are not conclusive for a later date. Finally, very recent work by Allen Thrasher based on a study of Maṇḍana Miśra confirms the dating of Śaṃkara in the late seventh and early eighth centuries rather than the frequently cited 788–820 date of Dasgupta and others.[9]

So far we have confined ourselves to scholarly data of a relatively firm sort. There is a vast traditional literature on Śaṃkara's life and times that any Śaṃkara scholar must be aware of, whatever he may decide to do with it. Thrasher, for instance, argues that much of what we know on scientific grounds agrees nicely with the traditions. Given what we know, it is possible that Śaṃkara was the pupil of Gauḍapāda's pupil, met Kumārila, and debated with Maṇḍana Miśra. Other traditional theses, for example, that Maṇḍana was defeated and became Sureśvara, are less clear from the evidence and in all likelihood are not true, although the particular thesis of the Maṇḍana-Sureśvara identity is still being argued in the journals.[10]

Of the traditional accounts of Śaṃkara's life—*Śaṃkaravijayas* by Ānandagiri, Mādhava, Cidvilāsa, and Sadānanda[11]—all except Ānandagiri agree that Śaṃkara was born in Kaladi, a small village in modern Kerala. Ānandagiri insists that the birthplace was Cidambaram in Tamil Nadu. There are various stories, clearly apocryphal, about the circumstances surrounding Śaṃkara's birth. His father is identified as Śivaguru, son of Vidyādhirāja, and is said to have died shortly after the child Śaṃkara was born. A famous story concerns the taking of vows of *saṃnyāsa* by the child who, then eight years or so old, assured his despairing mother that he would return to give her the last rites even though this is not required—and possibly not even allowed—for a *saṃnyāsin.* There is also a story, regarded by some as infamous, that Śaṃkara tricked his mother into consenting to his taking the vows by pretending a crocodile was about to swallow him in a river and would not release him except to a religious life.[12]

After leaving home the young Śaṃkara is said to have met his guru Govinda on the banks of the Narmadā river, but he soon continued to travel and began his teaching in Banaras. There he attracted disciples, initially Padmapāda, and with Padmapāda he went on pilgrimage to Badrinath, the headwaters of the Ganges. He remained there for four years and, according to one account, though not yet sixteen he wrote his major works. He then returned to Banaras for more teaching and converting. After several more years he was off to Prayāga (Allahabad), where he met the elderly Kumārila, who sent him on to Maṇḍana. A popular story ensues: debating with Maṇḍana with the understanding that the loser would become the winner's pupil, he defeated that Mīmāṃsaka, but Maṇḍana's wife Bhāratī challenged him to further debate and temporarily embarrassed Śaṃkara by pointing out to him that he was woefully inexperienced in worldly ways, specifically in first-hand knowledge of sex. Śaṃkara is supposed to have asked for a temporary leave of absence from the debate to gain the necessary experience, which he did by entering the body of a powerful king for a few months.

Returning, he defeated Bhāratī, and both she and her husband are supposed to have become his disciples, Maṇḍana taking the name of Sureśvara.

After returning to his birthplace to attend to his mother's funeral Śaṃkara set out on a far-flung tour during which he established the four great monasteries of Advaita in the four corners of India—at Śṛṅgeri in the south, Dwarkā in the west, Badrināth in the north, and Puri in the east. (A powerful tradition claims a fifth *pīṭha* at Kāñci, that is, Conjeeveram.[13]) At each of these *āśramas* he appointed one of his favorite disciples as pontiff.

Another story tells of his meeting with the Śaiva philosopher Abhinavagupta, who cursed Śaṃkara with a nasty disease,[14] but Padmapāda caused the curse to rebound to Abhinavagupta himself, who died of it.

Those who take the vows of Śaṃkarācārya's order of the Daśanāmīs, or "ten-names," receive one of ten names—Giri, Puri, Bhāratī, Sarasvatī, Tīrtha, Āśrama, Vana, Āraṇya, Pārvata, Sāgara. The order also designates four grades of realization—*brahmacārin, daṇḍin, parivrājaka,* and *paramahaṃsa.*

Śaṃkara's life is agreed by all to have been a very short one in years, though remarkable in productivity. He died at the age of thirty-two in the Himalayas according to most sources, although Ānandagiri again disagrees, locating his place of death at Kāñci.

The foregoing has been based, as has been said, on traditional accounts. At least two Western scholars of modern times have offered suggestions toward reconstructing some features of the development of Śaṃkara's thought. Daniel Ingalls, studying the relations between Śaṃkara and Bhāskara, a rival Bhedābhedavādin commentator on the *Brahmasūtras* and *Bhagavadgītā,* suggests that Śaṃkara began his career as a Bhedābhedavādin, then was influenced by Gauḍapāda's thought, taking certain elements of Buddhism through Gauḍapāda (the "two truths"), others from Bhartṛhari (*vivarta*), and still others from Sāṃkhya (superimposition).[15] On Ingalls' interpretation, Śaṃkara's philosophical polemics are mainly directed toward Pūrvamīmāṃsā. Paul Hacker proposes an even more startling intellectual biography for Śaṃkara.[16] Basing himself on the ascription to Śaṃkara of a commentary on Vyāsa's *Yogabhāṣya,* which Hacker finds reason to accept, he suggests that Śaṃkara started as a follower of Pātañjala Yoga, was brought by an Advaita master to study Gauḍapāda's "new doctrine of Oṃ and new Yoga," and was moved to prepare a commentary on the *Māṇḍūkyakārikās*—the *Gauḍapādakārikābhāṣya*—from which he moved through composition of the

Taittirīyabhāṣya and part of the *Upadeśasāhasrī* (section II.19 at least) into his mature works such as the *Brahmasūtrabhāṣya.*

Hacker has also studied Śaṃkara's probable religious affiliation, which he finds to have been Vaiṣṇava,[17] despite the widespread adoption by Śaivites of Advaita philosophy.

The works summarized below are not ordered by any attempt at reconstructing the order in which they were written. Rather, they are arranged in two groups : first, the works argued above as likely to be authentic; then, and more briefly, summaries of a number of works that are probably not the work of the author of the *Brahmasūtrabhāṣya,* but that are important in Advaita literature because they have some intrinsic interest or are widely commented on by later Advaitins and are regularly ascribed by tradition to Śaṃkara. We have not tried to summarize all such works, whose number runs into the hundreds.

BRAHMASŪTRABHĀṢYA

This is Śaṃkara's major and most authoritative work. It is safe to say that it is the single most influential philosophical text in India today, a status it has enjoyed for at least a century, possibly much longer. Countless Indian adepts commit portions of this text to heart, especially the introduction to and commentary on the first four *sūtras,* known as the *Catuḥsūtrī,* in which Śaṃkara sets forth some of his most characteristic and striking views and arguments.

Influential as it is, neither Indian nor Western scholars agree on the accuracy of Śaṃkara's interpretation of Bādarāyaṇa's *Sūtras.* The *Sūtras,* as one of the fundamental works of all Vedānta systems, is interpreted in appropriately disparate ways by each of those systems. Several works in English indicate the disparity among the interpretations of a single *sūtra* by the various Vedānta authors.[18] Among "impartial" scholars, mostly Westerners without suspected doctrinal affiliation, there has been continued debate over whether (in particular) Rāmānuja or Śaṃkara is the more faithful interpreter of Bādarāyaṇa's thought, debate stemming at least in part from Thibaut's remarks in the introduction to his standard translation of the *Brahmasūtrabhāṣya,* in which he expresses the opinion that Śaṃkara's philosophy is closer to that of the Upaniṣads than Bādarāyaṇa's own, but that Rāmānuja's reading of Bādarāyaṇa is more accurate than Śaṃkara's.[19] Numerous writers have expressed reservations about Śaṃkara as commentator, some finding him careless, confused, or even downright dishonest.[20] However that may be, there can be little question that the work stands at the pinnacle of Indian philosophical compositions.

In the following summary, "E" refers to the edition by Narayana Ram Acarya, (Bombay : Nirnayasagara Press, 1948). "T" refers to George Thibaut's translation in the Sacred Books of the East (republished, New York : Dover Press, 1962).

FIRST CHAPTER (ADHYĀYA), FIRST SECTION (PĀDA)

Introduction (E1-4; T3-9). It is evident that "I" and "That" are different, as are their properties. So it is erroneous (*mithyā*) to superimpose (*adhyāsa*) upon the subject (*viṣayin*), whose nature is awareness (*cit*) and whose sphere is the notion of "I," the object (*viṣaya*), whose sphere is "That"; it is also an error to superimpose the subject on the object; furthermore, superimposition of the properties of each on the other is also erroneous. Nevertheless it is a natural propensity of men to do just that, superimposing the nature and attributes of each upon the other when they say, for example, "I am that" or "that is mine."

Now what is superimposition ? It is the appearance (*ābhāsa*), in the form of a memory, of something previously experienced in some other place. Other philosophers define superimposition in slightly different ways. Some say it involves the nongrasping of the distinction of two things leading to one being superimposed on the other. Others say it is the attribution to a thing of properties contrary to those belonging to that thing. In any case all agree that it involves the appearance of the properties of one thing in another. And this agrees with ordinary experience as reflected in the reports of illusions such as "the shell appears as silver" or "the single moon appears double."

Objection : How can one superimpose an object on the interior Self (*pratyagātman*), which is not an object ? One can superimpose an object only on another object that is before him, and you have just told us that the Self is entirely different from "That."

Answer : The Self isn't nonobject in an absolute sense, for It is the object of our notion of "I" and is directly known to everyone. Furthermore, your alleged rule that one can superimpose an object only on another object that is before him has exceptions: we superimpose blue color on *ākāśa* (the sky), which is not an object of perception. So our position is not inconsistent.

Superimposition is *avidyā*; understanding the true nature of reality by discrimination is *vidyā*. Since it is so, faults present in an *x* that is superimposed on a *y* are not transferred to *y*. Superimposition, that is, *avidyā*, provides the necessary condition on which all distinctions of practical speaking (*vyavahāra*) are based, whether such speaking is ordinary or scriptural. Such distinctions involve means of knowledge (*pramāṇa*), their objects (*prameya*), injunctions and prohibitions, and even liberation (*mokṣa*).

How is it that means of knowledge, that is, perception, inference, etc., operate only in dependence on *avidyā*? It is because they can operate only if there is a knower (*pramātṛ*), and the existence of a knower depends on notions of "I" and "mine" with respect to the body, sense organs, and such, which notions in turn depend on the operation of the senses, the body, and the superimposition of the Self on that body, so that without all this the Self cannot become a knower. Men become attracted or repelled by sense objects just as animals do in depending on their senses; since it is evident to everyone that animals do not discriminate their Self from what is not their Self, it follows that the same applies to men. In the same way, though a man who sacrifices following scriptural injunctions realizes that the Self has a relation to other worlds, still his activity does not depend on his understanding the difference between his Self and what that Self is not; indeed, once he understands that difference he realizes the uselessness of such actions. Thus even the Vedic texts have as their purport that which is dependent on *avidyā*. Texts enjoining sacrifices presuppose that on the Self is superimposed caste status, stage of life, age, etc. Attributes reflecting notions about a man's relations with others, with his body, his senses, or with his internal organ, are superimposed on the Self, which is in actuality the witness (*sākṣin*) of all, and that witnessing Self is in turn superimposed on the internal organ, sense, and so on. This natural, beginningless, and endless superimposition, taking the form of erroneous notions, is why everyone supposes himself to be agent and enjoyer.

It is in order to get rid of these false notions and to acquire understanding (*vidyā*) of the unity of the Self that the study of the Vedānta (texts) should be taken up.

I.1.1 (E4-6; T9-15). The *sūtra* reads : "Then, therefore, the desire to know." "Then" in the *sūtra* does not mean that something new is being started, nor is it merely an invocation (*maṅgaia*). Rather it means that this teaching is intended to follow immediately upon acquaintance with the Vedas, although it is not necessary that a man has inquired into *dharma* in order to undertake the inquiry about Brahman. "Then" does not mean "following performance of (certain kinds of) acts," since the inquiry into *dharma* and that into

Brahman differ not only in themselves but also in their results. Understanding of *dharma* results in prosperity that is dependent on acts; understanding of Brahman results in liberation or perfection (*niḥśreyasa*) that depends on no actions. *Dharma* is something to be accomplished in the future by action; Brahman is already existent, since eternal, and so not dependent on human activity. Dharmic injunctions instruct man in order to make him act in certain ways to achieve results; scriptural texts relating to Brahman merely instruct man without enjoining him, the results following directly upon understanding the texts.

Then what is it that constitutes the unique antecedents of the inquiry into Brahman? It is discrimination of what is really eternal from what is not; nonattachment to enjoyments of objects both now and hereafter; acquisition of tranquillity, restraint, and other instruments; and the desire for liberation. When these conditions exist a man may successfully inquire about Brahman, whether or not he has already inquired about *dharma*.

The word "therefore" in the *sūtra* indicates that one should inquire into Brahman for the reason that the Veda indicates that the results of that inquiry constitute the highest aim of man.

The meaning of the word "Brahman" will be explained in the next *sūtra*.

Objection : Is Brahman generally known to us or not? If It is known we need not inquire about It; but if It is not, we cannot inquire about It.

Answer : Brahman is known to us, because once we understand that the word "Brahman" connotes something that is "great" (an understanding we derive from etymology) and realize that Brahman is therefore omniscient, omnipotent, eternally pure, intelligent, and free, we know Brahman exists; and because Brahman is known to each person as his Self : no one ever says (or thinks) "I do not exist," but if the Self's existence were not generally known we would think and speak that way.

Objector : Then, since Brahman is already known, we need not inquire about It.

Answer : No, since there are mistaken opinions about Brahman. Ordinary people and Lokāyatas believe the body qualified by awareness is the Self; others, that It is the organs plus awareness; others that the internal organ is the Self; others again, that the Self is momentary cognitions; and still others, that It is the void (*śūnya*). Some say there is an agent and enjoyer different from the body and that it transmigrates; some say that that being is enjoyer only, not agent;

others think that in addition there is a God; and still others think that God is the Self of the enjoyer. So there are all these conflicting opinions, based on both reasoning (*yukti*) and authority but which are only apparently authoritative. That is why one should proceed to study Brahman, that is, the Vedānta texts, using the help of arguments (*tarka*) and aiming for perfection.

I.1.2 (E7-9; T15-19). The *sūtra* says "[Brahman is that] from which birth, etc. (proceed)." "Et cetera" in the *sūtra* includes maintenance and destruction. The sense is that Brahman is the omniscient, omnipotent cause from which proceed the beginning, maintenance, and destruction of the world of name-and-form, of agents and enjoyers, of fruits of actions that are determined spatially, temporally, and causally, of a world that is not thinkable through the internal organ. Only from such a God as has just been described can the birth, etc., of the world arise; it cannot arise from an unconscious *prakṛti*, or from atoms, or from a transmigrating being. And it cannot arise, etc., from the world's own nature, because natural causation needs special spatial and temporal occasions.

This last argument is by itself not sufficient to prove the existence of God, however. Though inference, as well as sense perception, can help in providing understanding of Brahman insofar as it does not contradict scripture, still it is the proper understanding of the Vedānta texts (that is, the Upaniṣads) that alone produces that understanding. Not that this excludes arguments (*tarka*), for scripture itself tells us that, for example, the Self is to be considered (*mantavya*) as well as heard (*śrotavya*).

Scripture (*śruti*) as well as immediate awareness (*anubhava*), etc., are both to be used in appropriate ways in the inquiry into Brahman, unlike the inquiry into *dharma* in which only scripture is pertinent. The reason is that Brahman, unlike *dharma*, already exists. Again, the arising of *dharma* depends on man's efforts and so involves injunctions, prohibitions, rules, exceptions, etc., but the existence of something that already exists is not dependent on man's efforts. The truth of a judgment concerning a matter of fact depends on the world, unlike the truth of a judgment concerning what is to be done.

Objection : Since Brahman exists already other *pramāṇas* can provide knowledge of it as well as scripture; so we need not study the Vedānta texts after all.

Answer : No, since Brahman is not an object of the senses. We might know that Brahman is the cause of the world by perception or inference if we could see both Brahman and the world with our sense organs, but we only grasp the world that way and not Brahman.

The *sūtra* does not provide an inference to show Brahman's causality, but rather reflects scriptural passages (found at *Taittirīya Upaniṣad* III.1 and 6). As for the omniscience of Brahman, it follows :

I.1.3 (E9-10; T19-20). "From (1) (Brahman's) being the source of scripture (or, as an alternative reading) from (2) scripture's being the source (of knowledge of Brahman)."

On interpretation (1), we must take it that scripture itself is omniscient, and so how much more so its author, Brahman. On interpretation (2), the passage is to be understood as showing that *sūtra* 2 does not present an inference to God's existence independent of scripture.

(E10-12; T20-23) *Objection* : Scripture is not the means of knowing Brahman, for, according to *Mīmāṃsāsūtra* I.2.1, all scriptural passages have actions as their purport. Either scriptural texts enjoin actions or else they provide supplementary information to someone intending to perform actions. Scripture is not needed to give information about existing things, since perception, etc., can do that; in any case, even if it could give information, the information would *ex hypothesi* be irrelevant to action and so of no use to us. All scriptural passages are directly or indirectly injunctive, and one cannot enjoin the existence or nature of an already existing thing. Thus if the texts you have in mind do not themselves enjoin they must either supply ancillary information in aid of such injunctions or, if you insist that their subject matter is different, they must concern meditation (*upāsana*) and other actions mentioned in those particular texts.

I.1.4. *Answer* : "But that (is so, that is, Brahman is known from scripture), because (the passages in question) are connected (to Brahman) through (their) meaning." These texts cannot merely provide ancillary information, since many of them clearly preclude any reference to action (e.g., *Bṛhadāraṇyaka Upaniṣad* II.4.13 : "Then by what should he see whom ?"). Again, scripture is needed to give information about some already existing things, for example, the information that the Self is Brahman ("that art thou"). And some information is relevant even though it does not speak of what is to be gained or avoided : the Self, Brahman, which is not something to be gained or avoided, is such that understanding of It produces an end to all frustration. And though some texts do concern meditation those concerning Brahman cannot, since once knowledge of Brahman occurs there is no longer anything to be gained or avoided, all conceptions of difference are destroyed.

(E12-14 ; T23-29) *Objection*: Just as the Vedas give information about the implements of the sacrifice, information not known in common parlance, to those who are enjoined to perform sacrifices if they desire to get to heaven, so information about Brahman, not known in common life, is imparted by the Vedas to those who are enjoined to learn to understand Brahman if they wish to attain immortality, that is, liberation. But information irrelevant to any action, merely stating facts about what already exists without any reference to any possible action, is senseless and cannot occur in scripture.

Answer : If someone says "this is a rope, not a snake" intending to remove the fear of another person who has mistaken the one for the other, it is not senseless; likewise it is not senseless for the Vedānta passages to make statements about the Self intending to remove the error of one who thinks that It transmigrates.

Objector : The analogy fails, because though fear of snake is dispelled by hearing that it is a rope, merely hearing that the Self doesn't transmigrate doesn't stop men from undergoing transmigration. And in fact it is for this very reason that the scriptures enjoin us to consider and meditate on the Self in addition to hearing of It.

Śaṃkara : The objector's whole line of argument fails because it depends on the fallacious assumption that liberation, like *dharma*, is something not yet existent that is to be obtained. But in truth liberation is eternal and disembodied (*aśarīra*). It is eternal, not in the sense (*pariṇāminitya*) that a continuant undergoing change may be said to be, but in the sense (*kūṭasthanitya*) that it doesn't undergo any changes at all, that it is omnipresent, partless, absolutely self-sufficient, self-luminous. Since liberation is eternal in that sense, as well as not involving any body, it cannot be an effect of actions enjoined in scripture. In fact, liberation follows immediately upon knowledge of Brahman, and thus that knowledge cannot be viewed as a means conducive to some action designed to gain liberation.

(E14-16; T29-31) Śaṃkara now shows by citing appropriate passages that the identity of Self with Brahman cannot be dismissed as a mere figure of speech or as a kind of imaginative association constituting an element in meditation. Knowledge of Brahman is, like knowledge of an object by perception, dependent on its object, not on human activity. Brahman has no connection whatsoever with actions.

(E16-18; T31-34) Brahman is not even the object of an "act" of knowing or other activity of mind or speech.

Objector : If so, scripture cannot tell us about Brahman.

Answer : True, scripture does not speak of Brahman as an object but rather turns aside all distinctions produced by *avidyā*. Scripture in fact tells us that Brahman is always subject, never object. Realizing this one realizes as well that liberation is not transitory but is rather the very nature of the eternally liberated Self. Those who believe that liberation is a result of actions of mind, speech, or body, or who think it to be a modification (of something), properly conclude that liberation is noneternal, for in experience we find that modifications such as curds, as well as effects such as jars, are noneternal. Liberation is not something to be obtained, since it constitutes (a person's) Self and is all-pervading, thus ever present to everyone, like *ākāśa*. Nor is it a thing to be acted toward by ritual activities of purification (*saṃskāra*), for purification involves either the adding of some quality or the removal of some fault, but neither is relevant in the case of liberation, for liberation is just Brahman, to which no quality can be added and which is without fault.

Objection : Liberation may be a quality of the Self that needs purifying action to manifest it, just as a dusty mirror needs the action of rubbing to clear it.

Answer : No, the Self is not the locus of any action, since an action must modify its locus; if actions could modify the Self It would be noneternal, and this contradicts scripture. And it cannot be purified by actions relating to something else, since the Self does not bear any relation to anything else.

Objector : Surely the embodied Self is purified by ritual actions such as bathing.

Answer : No, for what is purified there is not the Self but a self joined to the body through *avidyā*, that is, the ego principle (*ahaṃkāra*). Common sense will tell you that when we say, having recovered from a disease, "I am well," we are speaking of the ego and not the Self. And since there are no other ways in which liberation could be connected with action than those mentioned here, it follows that liberation stands in no relation to action.

(E18-19; T34-36) *Objection* : But knowledge (which you claim produces liberation) is itself a mental act.

Answer: No indeed. An action is something not dependent on what now exists but on human intelligence, whereas knowledge is (just the reverse) dependent on what exists and not dependent on human intelligence. Thus even though some actions such as meditation, as well as knowledge, are, if you like, "mental," they are entirely unlike each other. Therefore one's meditative object is something that depends on human action and so can be enjoined, but Brahman is not dependent on human action and so cannot be enjoined, since it cannot be gained or avoided.

Objection : Then what about the Upaniṣadic passage that enjoins us that the Self should be seen and heard ?

Answer : The purpose of this injunction is to divert men's thoughts from the objects of ordinary activities and toward the Self. Many passages (which are quoted) tell us that Brahman is not an object to be sought or avoided.

(E19-21 ; T36-40) *Objection* : There is nothing in the Vedic scriptures that speaks only to describe existing things; all scriptural texts are either injunctions, prohibitions, or supplements to those two.

Answer : No, because the Upaniṣads are surely about the Self, and the Self cannot be an aspect (*śeṣa*) of something else. If someone should claim that the Self, since it is made known by other means (that is, perception, inference), is only incidentally referred to by scripture, we reply that the Self is again being confused with the object of self-consciousness; the Self with which we are here concerned cannot be the object of self-consciousness but is rather the witness of all that. It is inconsistent to deny that Self, for it is that very Self that would do the denying ! So those (*Mīmāṃsā*) authorities who first made the claim that all scriptures consist of injunctions must have been speaking about that portion dealing with injunctions. And when they aver that whatever Vedic passages that do not refer to actions are without purpose, it would mean, if strictly construed, that all information (given there) is without purpose (which is absurd); if it is not taken strictly but is relaxed to allow that information may be conveyed about things that are related to possible actions, then why shouldn't it give information about the Self, since to do so wouldn't require objects, for example, the Self, to be acts.

Furthermore, some Vedic passages (for example, "don't kill Brahmins") enjoin avoidance of certain kinds of acts. Avoidance of action is neither action nor instrumental to action, so it would follow from your (Mīmāṃsā) principle that those Vedic passages are without purpose, which is absurd. And you can't assume that the "not" (in "do not kill Brahmins") itself denotes some other (opposed) action, for that's not the way the word "not" is used in contexts such as this: what "not" means is passivity—inaction, except in special cases, such as vows.

(E21-24; T40-45) As for the objection (at E12-14 above) that although a man who is told that something is not a snake but a rope no longer is under an illusion, when he is told that his Self is Brahman, he still remains in *saṃsāra* : we hold that the latter man is not in *saṃsāra* in the same way as before. He is no longer subject to frustration and fear. It is like a person who is proud of his earrings while he has them; after he loses them he may lose his pride and his pleasure in his ownership; when a person loses his body he loses his concern for pleasure or pain.

Objector : Only a dead person loses his body.

Answer : No, because the cause of embodiment is false awareness. The Self is eternally disembodied; thus when wrong knowledge is corrected by the understanding of the Self, he "loses his body" and is no longer in *saṃsāra* in the same way.

Objector : Embodiedness is caused by merit (*dharma*) and demerit (*adharma*).

Answer : But merit and demerit are caused by embodiment, so there will be the fallacy of mutual dependence (*itaretarāśraya*) as well as of a beginningless chain of blind leading blind. Anyway since the Self cannot be an agent this view is invalid.

Objection : The Self is "agent" in the same sense that a king is, by (producing action by) Its mere presence.

Answer : No, because kings get action by offering wages, whereas the Self can do nothing analogous. It is false awareness alone that can explain the notion of the Self as agent.

Objection : The notion in question is not false but is, rather, figurative (*gauṇa*).

Answer : A figurative use of a word that primarily means *x* to apply to *y* can only be appealed to if *x* and *y* are known to be different. If they are not known to be different we assume instead that there is an illusion present. For example, a man who, seeing something in the dusk, calls it a "post" when it is in fact a man, does not use figurative language, but, rather, usesl anguage expressive of his error.

Finally, with respect to the argument (at E12-14 above) that merely hearing "the Self is Brahman" doesn't stop men from transmigrating, since the scriptures enjoin us to consider and meditate on the Self in addition to hearing It, Śaṃkara claims that the meditation and the consideration are parts of the process by which Brahman comes to be known; they are not additional acts.

(E24-25; T45-47) The Sāṃkhya philosophers use inference to prove that there is a material cause of the world called *pradhāna* (or *prakṛti*) and interpret scripture as referring to that. They say that the cause of the creation of the world is the contact between selves (*puruṣa*) and the material cause (*pradhāna*). *Pradhāna* is, according to them, a nonconscious (*acetana*) composite of the three *guṇas*. They contend that the Upaniṣadic passages that the Advaitin interprets as referring to Brahman can be interpreted consistently as applying to *pradhāna*. It is omnipotent, since all objects arise as modifications of it. Although nonconscious it can be said in a figurative sense to be omniscient; since what you think of as "knowledge" is really a property of the *guṇa sattva* and since it is only the *pradhāna* (and not *puruṣa*) that can be held to know something or everything, *pradhāna* is said in scripture to be "omniscient" as a way of praising its supreme sattvic nature. Omniscience can only mean the potentiality (*śakti*) for knowing everything: if Brahman were to know everything always he would depend on the act of knowing, but if Brahman's knowledge is not permanent (and knowledge is the essence of Brahman) then when knowledge ceases Brahman would also cease. Again, Brahman prior to the creation of the world is without instruments of action, and knowledge cannot occur without the presence of the appropriate instruments of the act of knowing, that is, the body, senses, etc. Finally, *pradhāna*, being composite, can become modified and thus be a material cause, whereas Brahman, being noncomposite, cannot be so.

In answer, the *Sūtra* (I.1.5) says : Since (the cause of the world is said in the Upaniṣads) to "see" (*īkṣati*), (the *pradhāna*) is not (that cause, because) it is not based on scriptural authority.

(E25-28; T47-52) The Upaniṣads attribute consciousness to the cause of the world. The Sāṃkhya argument that the *pradhāna* is omniscient because knowledge is a property of *sattva* won't do because *pradhāna* is a state, not of pure *sāttva*, but of balance among all three *guṇas*. So we would have to call it "little-knowing" (because of the other *guṇas*) as well as "all-knowing" ! As for the argument about Brahman's depending on his knowledge unless he is only *capable* of omniscience, there is no difficulty in Brahman's knowledge being essential to Him, any more than the fact that the sun gives off light by nature makes the sun depend on its light. As for what Brahman knows prior to creation, He knows name-and-form, and He needs no body, senses, etc., to know, any more than the sun needs anything else in order to shine. On the other hand the transmigrating self requires a body before knowledge can arise, since it is governed by *avidyā*.

Objection : Scripture says there is no transmigrating self other than God. How then can you say that the one requires a body for knowledge but not the other ?

Answer : True, they are not different in reality. But just as *ākāśa* is limited by adjuncts (*upādhi*) such as jars, caves, etc., but the resulting spaces are not different from *ākāśa*, so the Lord is limited by the body, senses and so on, but the result (the transmigrating self) is not different from the Lord. The ideas that there are separate spaces or separate Selves respectively are just false ideas, born of our failure to discriminate the Self from its adjuncts.

To return for a moment to the last of the Sāṃkhya's original objections, to the effect that only a composite like *pradhāna* can be material cause, we reply that *pradhāna* is not endorsed by scripture; our positive arguments for Brahman's being the material cause will come later (in Book Two).

(E28-29; T52-54) *Sāṃkhya* : Nonconscious things are sometimes figuratively spoken of as conscious ("the riverbank is inclined to fall"); in the same manner *pradhāna* is spoken of figuratively as conscious since it performs actions, just as in scripture fire and water are figuratively spoken of as (if) conscious ("the fire thought; the water thought).

Answer (I.1.6) : If (the consciousness of the world-cause is) said to be figurative, no, because of the use of the word "Self" (in scripture to apply to the world-cause).

Scripture, for example, *Chāndogya Upaniṣad* VI.8.7 and elsewhere ("that art thou, Śvetaketu"), identifies the world-cause as the Self and affirms the identity of that Self with Śvetaketu, who is certainly conscious. As for the attribution of consciousness to fire and water, that certainly is figurative, since there is no independent reason—as there is in the case in question—for retaining the literal sense, and good reason, from common sense, to adopt a figurative one.

(E30-31; T54-57) *Sāṃkhya* : The fact that the word "Self" is used to denominate the world-cause is not sufficient for your purpose, since that word itself is frequently used figuratively, as when a king says of his servant "that man is my (other) 'Self' "; since *pradhāna* is the servant of the *puruṣa* it may be termed "Self" in that sense.

Answer (I.1.7) : (*Pradhāna* is not the Self) because it is taught that there is release for one who takes his stand on That (that is, Brahman or Being.)

If the *pradhāna* were truly the Self, then scripture, when it teaches Śvetaketu "that art thou," would be telling him that he is nonconscious, and he would conclude that liberation is not possible for him. We should not suppose that scripture would provide such a misleading teaching. Furthermore, we should not assume figurative meaning unless there is a clear-cut and well-recognized distinction between the primary object and its analogue.

I.1.8 (E31-32; T57-58). And (the *pradhāna* cannot be the Self) because it is not referred to (in scripture) as something to be avoided.

If *pradhāna* is Being (Brahman) but not the Self, and if "that art thou" refers to the *pradhāna*, the teacher (speaking through scripture) would eventually say that one should distinguish the two; but in fact he says the opposite.

I.1.9 (E32-33; T59-60). Further, (the Self is not the *pradhāna*) because it is said to "go to" (the Self in sleep).

Chāndogya Upaniṣad VI.8.1 tells us that in sleep a man's self (*jīva*) becomes united with Brahman. (There is an etymological explanation involved.) But the conscious Self cannot become united with the unconscious *pradhāna*.

I.1.10-11 (E33-34; T60-61). Further, because (the Vedānta texts) agree (that the world-cause is conscious Brahman, that cause cannot be *pradhāna*), and (sūtra 11) because scripture (states it, that is, that Brahman is the cause of the world).

Compare *Śvetāśvatara Upaniṣad* VI.9.

(E34-43; T61-77. This section is known as the *Ānandamayī* section.),

Question : Since the main thesis of Vedānta is now established why does the work go on further ?

Answer : Brahman is understood in two ways : as qualified by adjuncts—different kinds of name-and-form; and as the opposite of that, that is, free from all adjuncts. Many passages show this. The first is Brahman viewed from the perspective of *avidyā*; the second is Brahman viewed from the perspective of *vidyā*. We are taught that in worshiping the first we get different results according to the mode of worship determined by the adjuncts distinguishing the Lord. Now when we turn to the question of liberation, the question arises which form of Brahman must be known to gain liberation, and whether it is devotion or knowledge that leads us to release, and how that can be. Further refutation of opposing views will also be set forth.

I.1.12 (E36-37; T64-66). (The Self) consisting of bliss (is the Highest Self) because of the repetition (of the word "bliss").

In *Taittirīya Upaniṣad* II.1.5 scripture says that the Self consisting of knowledge (*vijñāna*) is different from the Self consisting of bliss (*ānanda*). This Self of bliss is said to experience joy and be embodied, so it may be thought that it must be merely the transmigrating self and not the Highest Self. But, because scripture repeatedly uses the word "bliss" to describe the Highest Self, we must assume that in this passage too the Highest Self is being mentioned, and we shall have to explain the references to experiencing and to embodiment as applying to the self of knowledge, etc., or as being a secondary usage.

Objection : A self "consisting of" bliss cannot be the Highest Self since it is composite.

I.1.13-19 (E37-43; T66-77). *Answer* : The objection does not stand, since the word "consisting of" (*maya*) need not involve composition but instead may suggest "being full of (bliss)." Scripture says Brahman is the cause of bliss, and the context of the passage leaves no doubt which Brahman is meant, namely, the supreme Self and not the other (individual self [*jīva*]). That the reference is not to the *jīva* is shown by the explicit declaration of scripture. Incidentally, the attribution of consciousness, indeed of desire, in the passage in question (from the *Taittirīya Upaniṣad*) shows that we surely cannot be talking about *pradhāna*. Finally, since scripture teaches that the *jīva* gains union with That, that is, the Self of bliss, that Self cannot be either *jīva* or *pradhāna*.

Śaṃkara's exposition of these *sūtras* initially clarifies the meaning reflected in the exposition given above, but in his comments following *sūtra* 19 he provides a different interpretation and debates the first one at some length. According to this alternative interpretation *sūtras* 12 through 19 are addressed to *Taittirīya Upaniṣad* II.5.1, which mentions Brahman as the "tail" and "support" of the Self of bliss. The problem is : how can Brahman be a mere member of the Self—isn't it the principal, not the appendage ? The *sūtras* answer yes, because scripture says so. The suffix-"*maya*" is analyzed as involving *prācurya*, which the previous interpretation took as meaning "being full of" but on this second interpretation is a technical term meaning a stylistic device. The point of the *sūtra* in which it is mentioned is to explain why II.5.1 speaks of Brahman as "tail" : the answer is that it's merely a manner of speaking, a device, and not to be taken seriously. Since Brahman is spoken of as the cause (the *sūtras* go on) it cannot be a mere appendage. And so forth.

I.1.20 (E43-46; T77-81). (What is spoken of in *Chāndogya Upaniṣad* I.6.6ff. as) the one within (the sun and the eye is the Highest Lord), because (His) properties are taught (in that passage).

Opponent : That Upaniṣad is speaking of some transmigrating self, since it attributes hair, fingernails, and eyes to this person, since he is spoken of as spatially located, and since his power appears to be limited.

Answer : No, it refers to the Highest Lord. "Freedom from all sin (*pāpma*)" can only be attributed to God, as well as being the cause of all. As for the attribution of bodily qualities, a location and limited powers, these are appropriate descriptions of that same God when He presents Himself as an object of devotion and meditation with a body formed out of *māyā*.

I.1.21 (E46; T81). And (God is) other (than an individual transmigrating self whose body is the sun), because the difference is taught (in scripture).

The scripture in question is *Bṛhadāraṇyaka Upaniṣad* III.7.9.

I.1.22 (E46-48; T81-84). *Ākāśa* (is Brahman) since its marks (are mentioned in *Chāndogya Upaniṣad* I.9).

Opponent : In this passage the word "*ākāśa*" means a particular elemental substance, since that is what the word commonly means and since the properties attributed to it in the passage fit the properties ascribed to that elemental substance.

Answer : No, because the passage doesn't say that *ākāśa* is the cause of only some things but of *all* things, and only Brahman can be so described, certainly not that elemental substance.

I.1.23 (E48-50; T84-87). For the same reason the life breath (*prāṇa*) (in *Chāndogya Upaniṣad* I.10-11) (is Brahman).

The passage in question once again speaks of characteristic marks of Brahman qualifying what is referred to by another word here "*prāṇa*."

I.1.24-27 (E50-56; T87-97). (In *Chāndogya Upaniṣad* III.13.7, the word) "light" (indicates Brahman) because of the mention of feet. If it be objected that (Brahman is) not (the subject of this passage) because the meter (*chanda*) is named, no !—because by that (naming) consciousness is directed (toward Brahman); it is so also elsewhere. So Brahman is the subject, since Brahman is the only thing that can have beings, etc., as its feet. There is no reason to suppose that both passages (*Chāndogya Upaniṣad* III.12.6 and III.13.7) do not refer to Brahman.

I.1.28-31 (E56-62; T97-106). The life breath is Brahman, because that is what is indicated (in *Kauṣitakī Upaniṣad* III.1 and) in many different passages. Just because Indra says that he is breath doesn't disprove this : just like Vāmadeva, he must have gained insight through scripture.

FIRST CHAPTER, SECOND SECTION

I.2.1-8 (E62-69; T107-116). (The one who consists of mind, spoken of in *Chāndogya Upaniṣad* III.14, is Brahman) because what (that passage teaches) is well known everywhere; because the passage attributes qualities appropriate to Brahman though not to the *jīva*; because agent and act are separated; because the words used for each are different; and because of *smṛti*.

Objection : The passage talks about a self "in the heart"—that must be the *jīva*, not Brahman.

Answer : No, because Brahman "in the heart" is a form in which we are to meditate upon Brahman, and because it is like the case of *ākāśa*.

Objector : But *jīva* and Brahman are said to be identical.

Answer : No, they are different. Although Brahman and *jīva* are in a certain sense identical, it does not follow that Brahman enjoys anything. In respect to the possibility of enjoyership they are opposite.

I.2.9-10 (E69-70; T116-118). The eater (in *Kaṭha Upaniṣad* I.2.25) (is Brahman), because he is said to "eat" what is both movable and immovable, and because of the context.

I.2.11-12 (E70-74; T118-123). The two in the cave (in *Kaṭha Upaniṣad* I.3.1) are the *jīva* and the Highest Self, because it is seen and because of the qualities (mentioned in the passage).

Objector : In the passage the two in the cave are said to drink the results of their actions, and this makes it impossible to suppose the passage refers to either the *buddhi*, which is nonconscious, or to the Highest Self, which cannot drink anything.

Answer : One can explain this by appeal to figurative usage.

Objector : The two are the *buddhi* and the *jīva*, because "the cave" must be the body or the heart, and both *buddhi* and *jīva* can appropriately be said to enter there, but not Brahman.

Answer : As is seen (in ordinary life), we sometimes speak this way, for example, we say "the men with the umbrella are walking" but don't mean they all have an umbrella. Anyway, many passages speak of the Highest Self as in the cave.

I.2.13-17 (E74-79; T123-130). The person within the eye (in *Chāndogya Upaniṣad* IV.15.1) is Brahman, because the properties attributed are appropriate, because locations are attributed to Him (in scripture), because of the context, and because of inferences from other scriptural passages. That person cannot be some other self, because of impermanency and impossibility, that is, this person in the eye cannot be someone reflected in the eyeball or the *jīva*, or some deity, since they are impermanent, and because the qualities imputed in the passage are not compatible with those other selves.

I.2.18-20 (E79-81; T130-135). The inner ruler (in *Bṛhadāraṇyaka Upaniṣad* III.7.1) is Brahman, for His properties are mentioned; it is not *pradhāna*, nor is it the *jīva*.

It cannot be *pradhāna* since *pradhāna* is, according to Sāṃkhya, nonconscious, but the Upaniṣad (at III.7.23) says this inner ruler sees. Why can't it be the *jīva* then? Because the Upaniṣad explicitly distinguishes the inner ruler from the individual self.

I.2.21-23 (E82-86; T135-142). "That which is not seen" (in *Muṇḍaka Upaniṣad* I.1.5-6) is Brahman, not the *jīva* or *pradhāna*, because of the properties and form attributed to him (in the passage).

Sāṃkhya : The passage refers to *pradhāna*, because the subject is said to be the source of all beings (*bhūtayoni*) ; *pradhāna* spins out creation like a spider. Further, the qualities mentioned here are compatible with a nonintelligent creatrix; attributes such as knowledge and perception are attributed to something higher (*akṣara*).

Śaṃkara : No, because later in the same Upaniṣad that same all-knowing Being is said to be the material cause as well. As for "*akṣara*," this term refers to Brahman. We have no great objection to using the term "*pradhāna*" to refer to that which is the potentiality of names and forms, abides in God, forms His limiting adjunct, etc., provided it not be supposed that it is an independent thing.

I.2.24-32 (E86-93; T143-153). Vaiśvānara (in *Chāndogya Upaniṣad* V.11.18) is Brahman, because the two terms are such as to indicate that, and because of an inference from *smṛti*.

Objection : No. "Vaiśvānara" means something different, something that dwells within, that is, the digestive mechanism (a kind of "fire").

Answer : No. The Highest Lord (Brahman) is taught as present in the digestive mechanism, and also other things are said of Vaiśvānara that can't be said of digestion. For the same reason Vaiśvānara is not the fire-god or the fiery element. Jaimini doesn't think the term "Vaiśvānara" need have anything to do with fire, even as a limiting condition.

Objection : The Upaniṣad says that this "Vaiśvānara" has spatial size; how can it refer to Brahman?

Different answers are ascribed to Āśmarathya ("because the size is a feature of the Lord's manifestation"), Bādarī ("because the Lord is to be meditated upon in a form with size"), and to Jaimini ("because He is to be identified imaginatively with spatially located parts for the purposes of meditation"). Anyway, the Jābālas (i.e., the *Jābāla Upaniṣad*) say that the Lord is in the space between the forehead and the chin.

FIRST CHAPTER, THIRD SECTION

I.3.1-7 (E93-98; T154-162). (In *Muṇḍaka Upaniṣad* II.2.5) the "support of heaven, earth, etc." is Brahman, because of the use of the word "own" (self), and because it is specified as what is to be gained by the liberated. The phrase cannot refer to *pradhāna* or *prāṇa* because they are declared to be different and because the whole context indicates the proper interpretation; besides, the passage (in the *Muṇḍaka*) about (the two birds) one of whom stands and one of whom eats leaves no doubt as to the meaning.

Opponent : The passage cannot refer to Brahman, since it speaks of the "support of heaven, earth, etc." as "the bridge of the immortals," and Brahman cannot be a bridge, since there is nothing beyond for it to be a span toward.

Answer : It's a bridge in the sense that it binds, not in complete analogy to a bridge over a stream.

The two birds must be the Lord (which stands) and the individual self (which eats).

Objector : But then the *jīva* is different from the Self, despite your denials.

Answer : It is not the purpose of the Upaniṣad to teach the highest truth about the individual self here; rather it concerns the nature of Brahman. The individual self is erroneously distinguished from Brahman, just as limited parts of space are erroneously distinguished from all-pervading space.

I.3.8-9 (E98-102; T162-169). *Objector* : In *Chāndogya Upaniṣad* VII.23-24 we are told that the "Bhūman" ("earth") is that where one sees nothing else, hears and understands nothing else. The reference here must be to *prāṇa*, since the passage concludes a series of questions about what is greater than the preceding item, but when we get up to *prāṇa* no such question is asked; instead we are told that one who views *prāṇa* as greater speaks most wisely, and, further, that *prāṇa* is the greatest because it is what remains awake during deep sleep. It is also described as "bliss," "immortality."

Answer : The "Bhūman" is Brahman (not *prāṇa*) since it is something superior to deep sleep and the bliss of deep sleep belongs to *prāṇa*, and because of the characteristics attributed. The one who speaks most wisely is one who speaks truly, not one who speaks about *prāṇa*; in the passage, Nārada asks for truth and Sanatkumāra leads him up to the knowledge of *Bhūman*, that is, Brahman, which must therefore be the truth. Further, that which one sees and hears, understanding nothing else, surely must be Brahman, not *prāṇa*; compare other Upaniṣadic statements for confirmation. Likewise the other attributes—bliss, immortality—belong to Brahman, not to *prāṇa*.

I.3.10-12 (E102-104; T169-171). *Objector* : In *Bṛhadāraṇyaka Upaniṣad* III.8.7-8, the word "*akṣara*" indicates that the syllable ("*om*") is the Self of all, following Pāṇini.

Answer : No. The *akṣara* is Brahman (not the syllable), since it supports all things up to the sky (or space) and does so on command of the *akṣara*, that is, the Lord. Further, *akṣara* is described by unambiguous attributes.

I.3.13 (E104-105; T171-174). *Objector* : In *Praśna Upaniṣad* V.2, it is the lower Brahman that is being discussed, for the rewards offered to one who knows Him are confined to a certain world, which would be inappropriate if we were speaking of the omnipresent Highest Lord.

Answer : No. (The reference is to the Highest Self,) since He is referred to as the object of sight. Seeing is different from meditating: a something that is the object of sight must be real, whereas in meditation one can imagine things in various forms. Here, however, the object that is to be meditated upon (the Self) is identified as the object of sight as well and so must be the really Real, the Highest Brahman.

I.3.14-18 (E106-111; T174-182). *Objection*: In *Chāndogya Upaniṣad* VIII.1.1 we hear of a "small space" (*dahara*) in a lotus in a palace in the city of Brahman. The reference here must be to the element *ākāśa*, that is, space or "ether," given what is said about its size and position.

Answer : The *dahara* is Brahman, because of what the passage goes on to say, that is, that the individual selves go into the world of Brahman — this going being an inferential mark that *dahara* refers to this Brahman world. Further, this small space is said to support the worlds. Again, in other passages words suggesting "space" are used to designate Brahman.

Objector : Then, since in VIII.3.4 the *dahara* is spoken of as having risen from his earthly body, it must be the individual self, not Brahman.

I.3.18. The individual self is not meant, because that is impossible. Attributes like freedom from evil cannot be attributed to the *jīva*.

Objector : Surely they can, as witness Prajāpati's teachings in *Chāndogya Upaniṣad* VIII.7-11, where the individual self is taught as being free from evil.

I.3.19 (E111-115; T183-191). (In *Chāndogya Upaniṣad* VIII.7-11) the reference is to the *jīva* insofar as its true nature has become manifest (as Brahman). That is, Prajāpati is speaking of the realized self, which has discovered itself to be the Highest Self, which is to say that he is speaking of Brahman, not the lower self.

Objection : How can we speak of the "true nature" of Brahman, which is alleged to be unchanging and eternal; how can It have any other form than Its own true one?

Answer : True, Brahman cannot lack Its true nature. But just as a pure crystal, without lacking its true nature, is seen as red by an observer who fails to see the distinction between it and the color of some limiting adjunct (e.g., a red flower), likewise Brahman's true nature is "discovered" by an observer—the individual self—who learns to discriminate that nature from its adjuncts. Prajāpati's instruction has to be understood in this way. The whole process by which the individual self discovers its true nature as the Highest Lord is analogous to that by which an imagined snake becomes a rope as soon as the observer has discovered its true nature.

Some of us (?) believe the individual self to be real. The whole purpose of these *sūtras* is to disprove this view by citing scripture and reinforcing those citations with arguments.

I.3.20-21 (E116-118; T191-195). The reference (of *dahara*) is not (to space or the *jīva* but to Brahman). We have already explained that the Lord may be termed "small" (in I.2.7 above).

Opponent : In *Muṇḍaka Upaniṣad* II.2.10 and *Kaṭha Upaniṣad* V.15 the shining one mentioned must be some luminous substance and not Brahman. The passage speaks of something which, though luminous, causes other luminous bodies not to shine. For example, the moon and stars do not shine when the sun is shining, so that which causes the sun not to shine must likewise be another luminous body.

I.3.22-23 (E116-118; T192-195). *Answer* : No. Because it is said "After Him, when he shines, everything shines" (it must be the Highest Self and not a luminous body referred to), and because of the words "of Him" (in the passage "by the light of Him all this is lighted"); moreover, *smṛti* (*Bhagavadgītā* XV.6-12) speaks of the Highest Self as universal light.

The sentence "after Him, when he shines, everything shines" can only make sense if the reference is to the Highest Self. For it is not evident that any other luminous body makes the sun not to shine. But what is evident is that nothing can be known to shine except through the functioning of the light of knowledge itself, which lights up all.

I.3.24-25 (E118-120; T195-198). The person the size of a thumb (in *Kaṭha Upaniṣad* II.1.12-13) is not the "self of knowledge" (*vijñānātman*) but is the *puruṣa*, the Highest Self. It is appropriate to speak of the Self as having a size appropriate to dwelling in the human heart, since after all only humans are entitled to study the Vedas.

I.3.26-33 (E120-135; T198-223). Not that the gods cannot seek release and practice meditation, etc., leading to it, for they have bodies and we hear in the Upaniṣads of a god like Indra living as a disciple with another god (Prajāpati), etc. Granted, they cannot sacrifice to gods, because they are gods! They can, however, be present at sacrifices made to them, since they are capable of assuming various forms at once.

An objector finds an inconsistency between holding that the gods have bodies and the proof of the Vedas' authoritativeness, in *Mīmāṃsā-sūtra* I.1.5, on the basis of the eternal connections between words and their meanings. The answer is offered that gods, men, and the world originate from *śabda*, word (specifically, the Vedas). But, says the objector, I thought you said (in *sūtra* I.1.2 above) that the world originates from Brahman! And anyway, he continues, it is evident that words are given to things only after the things have come into being—so the notion of eternal connections between words and meanings is in any case false.

In answer Śaṃkara develops his theory of the meaning of words. First, words are connected, not with individual things, but with their kinds or species (*ākṛti*); since the gods also fall into species, they constitute no difficulty. Second, the sense in which the world arises from *śabda* does not entail that *śabda* is the world's material cause; that cause is Brahman, as affirmed in I.1.2. We know by perception and inference—that is, from *śruti* and *smṛti*—that words precede things; it is so affirmed over and over again in the Upaniṣads and elsewhere.

Specifically, however, what is the nature of a word that it can "precede" and so "create" the world? Two hypotheses are reviewed and rejected. The first is that of the *sphoṭavādin*, who presents arguments to show that the letters it contains cannot comprise a word if that word is to be endowed with the required powers. Knowledge of the letters comes serially, and the earlier parts of the sequence are lost before the later ones arise. Therefore the *word* must be a unitary meaning, which we grasp in one mental act after having heard the several sounds. The second is the view of the Mīmāṃsaka (Upavarṣa), that the letters are after all the word, since letters are not transitory individuals but permanent properties whose presence can be recognized in a single act that requires no additional *sphoṭa* to be postulated.

Objection: After each *kalpa* a *pralaya* or dissolution ensues, after which an entirely new production takes place; how then can the connection between word and thing be eternal, even on your view?

Answer: It is like going to sleep; when we wake up there is a new creation, but in the same forms and with the same names as before.

Objector: But *mahāpralaya*—complete dissolution of the entire world—isn't like merely going to sleep; we can't merely take up in the next *kalpa* where we left off before.

Answer : For the gods it is just like the temporary cessation in sleep. Furthermore, the karma of beings in the world prior to *pralaya* cause the creation of a world after *pralaya* in which that karma can be worked off.

The last three *sūtras* return to the question of the capacity of the gods to have personalities and know Brahman.

I.3.34-38 (E135-139; T223-229). *Śūdras*, however, are not entitled to Brahman-knowledge, since they do not study the Vedas, do not receive the *upanayana*, etc. Nevertheless, some *śūdras* do acquire such knowledge by other means than Vedic study, admits Śaṃkara.

I.3.39-43 (E139-144; T229-236). A few more passages are studied and interpreted as referring to Brahman.

FIRST CHAPTER, FOURTH SECTION

I.4.1-7 (E144-155; T237-252). In this section Śaṃkara returns to deal with the Sāṃkhya system. There are texts, says the Sāṃkhya, that suggest that *pradhāna* is after all the material cause of the world—for example, in the *Kaṭha Upaniṣad* I.3.11 we seem to be told that "beyond the *buddhi* is *prakṛti* and beyond that is *puruṣa*." Thus our Sāṃkhya view is based on Vedic authority. Śaṃkara labors to show that the passage need not be interpreted that way, since the term used is not "*prakṛti*" (or "*pradhāna*") but rather "*avyakta*." Śaṃkara suggests that "*avyakta*" here refers to the body that is being compared to a chariot in which rides the Self. Not the gross body, of course, but the subtle body is intended, and it is called "*avyakta*" because it is the potential state of what will become actualized in the gross state.

Objector : Then you admit our contention, for that is precisely what we mean by "*pradhāna*," that is, a potential form of the world.

Answer : Not precisely, for you think that the potential form is independently capable of producing the world, whereas our view is that its capacity is dependent on God (*parameśvara*). Of course we admit, as you do, that some form of the world exists prior to its gross manifestation. But in my (Śaṃkara's) view this "potential form" or subtle body is in fact *avidyā*, made of *māyā*, having God as its abode, a great sleep (*mahāsupti*) in which the transmigrating selves (*jīva*) wait free of their particular characters. It is also sometimes called "*ākāśa*" or "*akṣara*". Another difference between my view of the *avyakta* and yours is that, where you suppose the *pradhāna* needs to be distinguished from and by the *puruṣa* to achieve liberation, nothing in the text (the *Kaṭha*) suggests this; rather, the Upaniṣad goes on to advise one to perceive what is without qualities and thus one will be "freed from the jaws of death"—but Sāṃkhya does not suppose that by merely perceiving *pradhāna* one will be liberated, so the passage is after all not referring to *pradhāna* but rather to the Highest Self, meditation upon which will result in liberation—which is just my view and not yours.

I.4.8-14 (E155-161; T252-263). *Śvetāśvatara Upaniṣad* IV.5 is not a reference to *pradhāna*. Furthermore, in *Bṛhadāraṇyaka Upaniṣad* IV.4.17 the "five groups of five" does not refer to the twenty-five Sāṃkhya categories, for those categories cannot be subdivided into pentads.

I.4.14-15 (E161-165; T263-268). *Objection* : It is impossible to prove that the Upaniṣadic texts refer to Brahman as the origin, etc. of the world, because these texts contradict each other.

Answer : The texts are entirely consistent in their description of the ultimate cause of the world, although they do differ in their accounts of the specific order in which creation comes about. But this inconsistency is of no importance, since the ways of the world are not what scripture teaches, and man's welfare doesn't depend on their so teaching.

Certain texts (for example, *Taittirīya Upaniṣad* II.1; *Chāndogya Upaniṣad* III.19.1; *Bṛhadāraṇyaka Upaniṣad* I.4.7,) seem to say that the world was created from nonbeing (*asat*), but in order to fit the contexts we must assume that the reference is to *nirguṇa* Brahman, which precedes *saguṇa* Brahman.

I.4.16-18 (E165-168; T268-274). *Kauśītakī Upaniṣad* IV.19 is interpreted. It does not refer to *prāṇa*, and according to Śaṃkara the *sūtras* also refute the notion that it refers to the individual self. The reference is rather to Brahman.

I.4.19-22 (E168-174; T274-283). The discussion here is about the well-known text in which Yājñavalkya counsels his wife Maitreyī in *Bṛhadāraṇyaka Upaniṣad* IV.5.6 to know *ātman*. The objector thinks the reference is to *jīvātman* since it is that self that can be "dear" to us in the way a husband, etc., can be; further, the passage concludes "how should one know the knower?" and the individual self is the knower.

Answer : The context requires that the reference be construed as applying to the Highest Self, not the *jīva*. It is only knowledge of the Highest Self that provides immortality, and it is only by knowledge of the Highest Self that everything becomes known.

Sūtras 20-22 refer to the views of three ancient sages, Āśmarathya, Auḍulomī, and Kāśakṛtsna, concerning the relation between the individual self and the Highest Self. Śaṃkara takes it that Āśmarathya's view is that the individual self should be viewed as nondifferent from the Highest Self whereas Auḍulomī's is that the individual self, initially different from the Highest Self, becomes identical with it at the time of liberation. Kāśakṛtsna, however, holds the correct view, which is that the two selves are absolutely nondifferent. It is correct because it is the only view of the three on which liberation results from Self-knowledge alone.

I.4.23-27 (E174-178; T283-289). *Opponent* : Brahman is only the efficient (*nimitta*) cause of the world, and not the material cause (*prakṛti*), because, one, efficient causes, but not material causes, are capable of consciousness, two, we refer to efficient causes, but not material ones, as "Lords" and, three, the material cause should resemble its effects in nature, so that the world—having parts, nonsentient and impure—should have as material cause something with parts, nonsentient and impure, and Brahman is the opposite of that.

Answer : Scriptural passages clearly indicate that Brahman is the material cause as well as the efficient cause; if it were not so we could not know everything by knowing Brahman; the Self could not reflect "Let me be many"; the Self could not transform (*pariṇāma*) itself into its own self. As for objection one, it is an argument depending on inference, which in turn depends on ordinary experience; but we are speaking of matters beyond ordinary experience, so that scripture here holds sway, and it tells us that the cause of the world is conscious.

Special and prior attention has been given to Sāṃkhya theories, because Sāṃkhya, like Advaita, holds the theory that the effect pre-exists in the cause (*satkāryavāda*). Theories that assume the opposite need also to be considered, however.

SECOND CHAPTER, FIRST SECTION

II.1.1-2 (E179-182; T290-296). The purpose of this chapter is to refute objections to our doctrine that are founded on nonauthoritative texts (*smṛti*) or on reasoning.

Objection : Certain traditional texts, called *smṛti*, would have no purpose unless we assume they are intended to tell us that *pradhāna* is the cause of the world; for example, the *Kapilasmṛti* (i.e., the *Sāṃkhya śāstra*). We need such texts to help us understand the Vedānta texts, and because such *smṛtis* were composed by sage-like authorities we must believe what they say. If your view, that Brahman is the material cause of the world, were true, these *smṛtis* would have no point; so your view must be false.

Answer : But there are other *smṛtis* that teach our doctrine, and your thesis would leave no purpose for them ! So that argument only produces a standoff, and then we have to choose, and naturally we must choose that thesis which is favored by scripture, as is enjoined by the *Mīmāṃsāsūtras*. And we have shown that scripture favors our doctrine.

Objection : Kapila and other sages have perfect knowledge and must therefore be considered authoritative.

Answer : No. Any perfect knowledge, they have, depends on performance of *dharma* in conformity to Vedic injunctions; thus scripture, the Vedas, precedes those sages, and its meaning cannot be called into question by them. Furthermore, since the various alleged sages contradict each other, one can only decide by appeal to scripture. And anyway, there were various "Kapilas"—which one does the *Śvetāśvatara Upaniṣad* refer to ? It might not be the Sāṃkhyin—there are lots of others.

There is also a limit to the scope of the appeal to *smṛti*, that is, it must speak of things that are known to either common sense experience or are spoken of in the Vedas. Now Kapila's *smṛti* speaks of things like *mahat*, which are found in neither place; therefore it is untrustworthy and we need not trust it when it speaks of *pradhāna* either. We have seen how those passages in the Vedas that appear to speak of such things are to be interpreted: they do not speak of Sāṃkhya things but rather of Vedānta topics.

II.1.3 (E182-184; T296-299). *Objection* : In the Upaniṣads we find references to yoga practices, so the *smṛti* that expounds them (the *Yogasūtras*) should be accepted as authoritative.

Answer : No, although that part of them which speaks in accordance with scripture can be accepted, it cannot be accepted as a whole for the reasons given in the previous section.

Question : Why do you limit this claim to the Sāṃkhya and Yoga *smṛtis*; do not the arguments apply to all systems not based on scripture?

Answer : There is special room for confusion with respect to Sāṃkhya and Yoga, since some of their tenets are identical with ours and since there is a Vedic passage (*Śvetāśvatara Upaniṣad* VI.3) that might appear to corroborate the claims of those systems to authority.

II.1.4-11 (E184-198; T299-317). So much for objections to our view based on *smṛti*. We now turn to those objections based on reasoning (*tarka*).

Question : How can reasoning even be relevant here ? The tenet in question is the Vedāntin's thesis that Brahman is both the efficient and material cause of the world, and with respect to Brahman as with respect to *dharma*, there is no other authority save scripture.

Opponent answers : No, because Brahman, unlike *dharma*, is an existing thing (not one to be accomplished), and so other *pramāṇas* besides scripture are relevant to it. In such a case, where there is doubt as to the interpretation of scripture, one should choose that interpretation which best accords with the other *pramāṇas*. After all, you hold that Brahman is finally realized through direct experience; reasoning, which provides knowledge of unseen objects on analogy with seen ones, is nearer to experience than scripture, which is entirely dependent on tradition. Too, scripture itself tells us that Brahman is to be reflected upon as well as heard (*Bṛhadāraṇyaka Upaniṣad* II.4.5). So, since reasoning is clearly relevant in this instance, we proceed now to deny your Advaita thesis on the basis of arguments.

Brahman cannot be the material cause of the world, because the effect (the world) is entirely different from the cause (Brahman). The world is nonconscious (*acetana*) and impure (*aśuddha*) and thus the opposite in character to Brahman. But in the world effects always resemble in character their material causes. That the world is impure and nonconscious is clear : it consists of pleasure, frustration, and delusion, marks of impurity, and as bodies and organs it subserves the intentions of conscious beings, such subservience being a mark of nonconsciousness.

Another objector (objecting to the first one) : Right you are; the effect must resemble its cause; and since Brahman, a conscious being, is its cause, the world too must be conscious. The reason why we do not perceive the consciousness in a lump of clay or a log is that they are asleep or in a faint—for when humans are in those states we don't perceive their being conscious either.

First objector answers : Well, but you haven't explained the other disparity, concerning impurity. And anyway, you've asserted that the whole world is conscious on the basis solely of scripture, but scripture doesn't bear you out; it says that the world is partly conscious, partly not. Even though scripture frequently seems to attribute consciousness to material elements like fire and water, this is a misinterpretation; that to which consciousness is attributed in such passages is the presiding deity, not the material itself. So my objection to the Advaita tenet stands.

Answer (beginning with II.1.6.) : In the world we do find that nonconscious effects arise from conscious causes, for example, from conscious humans, nonconscious hairs, etc., arise, and for that matter the reverse is true too : scorpions come from cowdung. An effect must have some disparate characteristics from its cause, otherwise it would be indistinguishable from it and be not an effect at all. So the general premise of your argument, that effects cannot differ from their causes, cannot be maintained.

Earlier you argued that Brahman, unlike *dharma*, can be known by other *pramāṇas*. But that is mistaken, since Brahman has no perceptible, and thus no inferential, marks by which it could be perceived or inferred. When the *Bṛhadāraṇyaka Upaniṣad* exhorts reasoning as well as hearing it does not mean that Brahman can be grasped by reasoning alone, but that one should use one's head in understanding the implications of scriptural pronouncements.

Finally, *tu quoque* ! If difference in properties makes it impossible for a conscious being, Brahman, to have nonconscious effects, then in the same way a nonconscious being, *pradhāna*, cannot have conscious effects—*mahat*, etc.

Objection (II.1.7): If Brahman is the cause of the impure world, and It is pure, that world cannot exist in It. But your view on causation is that the effect pre-exists in the cause, so you are caught in an inconsistency.

Answer : No. Our view is that the effect only has its being in and through its cause, Brahman, and not otherwise. Therefore your talk of an effect "not existing before its origination" is empty talk about nothing. Or if it is about something, something that exists prior to its coming into being, then you cannot very well say that it doesn't exist !

Objection (II.1.8) : (1) At the end of a cycle, at the time of dissolution of the world (*pralaya*, or here, *āpīti*), the impure world will be absorbed into Brahman and pollute it. (2) Furthermore, if the world loses its distinctions in Brahman at *pralaya*, the specific occasions for subsequent differentiations in the next cycle will be lost. And finally (3) we would have the untoward consequence that the *muktas*—the liberated selves—would be reborn again into the world. And you cannot maintain that the world remains distinct from Brahman at *pralaya*, since then there will be no *pralaya* and anyway it will violate your rule that an effect cannot exist apart from its cause.

Answer (II.1.9) : Not so. (1) We find examples in experience of things that return to their original state without being visited by the qualities of their effects ; for example, clay that has been made into a pot and then returns to a state of mere clay does not have the qualities of the pot. If any such thing were found, indeed, there would be no possibility of *pralaya*. Furthermore, why do you confine your argument to *pralaya*? The effect *would* pollute its cause all the time, were it not that, on our view, it is a mere superimposition of *avidyā*, just as the illusion produced by a magician, or a dream, the fantasies of which do not affect the magician or the dreamer. Likewise, the fantasies that appear in the waking, dreaming, and deep-sleep states do not touch the Highest Self, any more than the snake affects the rope for which it is mistaken.

(2) Again, in deep sleep all distinctions are dissolved into the Self, but because of ignorance the old distinctions reappear as soon as one awakes. And that also explains why (3) the freed selves will not be reborn, since they have no ignorance that will determine future births.

Anyway, the arguments the Sāṃkhya urges against the Vedāntins afflict his own system as much as theirs. If the world cannot arise from Brahman because it has different qualities, the same is true of *pradhāna*, which lacks sounds, etc., and so cannot produce a world that has them. *Pralaya* presents parallel difficulties for Sāṃkhya and Vedānta.

Reasoning is an unstable foundation as a basis for understanding things that should be realized from scripture; for it is notorious how arguments may be found to contradict any thesis, and the most profound logical philosophers have contradicted one another.

Objection: That cannot stand as a valid refutation of the utility of reasoning, for it is itself an instance of reasoning. Again if all reasoning were unstable practical affairs would be impossible, for we depend on predictions based on observed similarities to get through life. Again, reasoning is required in even understanding the scripture. Finally, the fact that past logicians have contradicted each other is no reason why in future they should.

Answer (II.1.11): No, for then there will be no liberation. No doubt reasoning works well for some things, but liberation is not a matter of perception and therefore cannot be reached by inference; scripture is the only means by which we can arrive at any knowledge of it. After all, everyone who argues about the nature of liberation agrees that it results from true knowledge, and true knowledge must be absolute, not changing all the time. You cannot say that the Sāṃkhya view is accepted by everyone as truth, for many reject it. Nor can you collect all the logicians—past, present, and future—and achieve a consensus! The Vedas, however, being eternal, are not subject to this difficulty and can provide the perfectly true knowledge required.

II.1.12 (E194-195; T317-318). In the same manner views based on reasoning, but with even less authority than the Sāṃkhya (as, for example, the Vaiśeṣika view), are refuted.

II.1.13 (E195-196; T318-320). *Objection* : When scripture is contradicted by another *pramāṇa* it indicates that its authority is being extended beyond its proper province, and it must give way to the other *pramāṇa*, just as you Advaitins argue that reasoning should give way to scripture when it is incompetent to grasp things beyond *its* proper province. Very well : everyone knows the distinction between persons who enjoy things, for example, by eating them, and the things enjoyed by, for example, being eaten. Your view would rub out this distinction by making enjoyers and their objects identical. Therefore you should give up the view of Brahman being the material cause of the world.

Answer : Your argument is based on the notion that nondifference entails the absence of distinctions. But it is not so in ordinary experience—for example, foam, waves, and bubbles are distinct from each other although they are all nondifferent from the ocean. Likewise, enjoyers and their objects are distinct from each other although they are nondifferent from Brahman.

II.1.14-20 (E196-208; T320-343). To pursue the same point further, scripture indicates clearly that the distinctions among effects are merely words, the result of speech, whereas the truth is that these effects are really nondifferent from the cause. Thus in *Chāndogya Upaniṣad* VI.1.4 we are told that just as a lump of clay, a single cause, gives rise to multiple effects by virtue of being called "pot," etc., so it is with Brahman and its effects, the world. The effects are unreal; only the cause is real, and the effects are only real insofar as they are modifications of that cause. Otherwise we couldn't understand the teaching that by knowledge of the one cause all the effects become known. So, just as the parts of space limited in jars, etc., are not different from space itself, or just as the mirage is not different from the surface of the desert, so the world is not different from Brahman; in each case the effects have no existence except in dependence on the cause.

Objection : It is more plausible to explain the situation as involving identity-in-difference. Just as the ocean is one *qua* ocean but many *qua* waves, foam, and bubbles, or just as the clay is one *qua* clay but many *qua* pots, etc., so Brahman is one *qua* Brahman but many *qua* the manifold world. Then knowledge of the unity of Brahman leads to liberation, whereas knowledge of the manifoldness of the world leads to both the ordinary and Vedic doctrines about action.

Answer : No, for then both kinds of knowledge would be equally true, since both unity and multiplicity are equally true, and there would be no reason why knowledge of the former should lead uniquely to liberation. Scripture indicates the unreality of the effects as well as their nondifference from Brahman.

Objection : If what you say is true, then the *pramāṇas* such as perception, inference, etc., become invalid, since there are in reality no objects for them to grasp. Furthermore, scriptural injunctions will lose their force, since they require the existence of objects that on your view are nonexistent. Finally, the entire science of liberation (*mokṣaśāstra*) is undermined if the distinction between pupil and teacher is unreal; and if liberation is not real, what good is your doctrine ?

Answer : As long as we are not liberated all these distinctions are accepted as real and the *pramāṇas* , injunctions, and distinctions referred to can operate in precisely the way we ordinarily suppose. When we become liberated it is as if we awake from a dream—all the dream distinctions are set aside as unreal at that point, whereas a moment before, in the dream, they were accepted without question.

Objection: But then how can the Vedānta texts, if untrue, tell us the truth about Brahman ?

Answer : We sometimes find that unreal causes produce real effects, for example, a man bitten by a fancied snake may die, or a person who bathes in a dream may feel cleansed.

Objector : But these results are unreal !

Answer : Yes, but the awareness one has of them is quite real. When one wakes from a dream he says that the things he dreamt of are unreal, but he doesn't deny he dreamt. (This also shows that consciousness, not the body, is our real Self.)

We think Brahman has multiplicity in it by nature because in our worldly state we are visited by desires that call for distinctions between desire, desirer, and things desired; once the unity of Brahman is appreciated, however, no further desires arise and thus the conditions leading to drawing distinctions are removed. Various passages from scripture support this view.

Objection : If Brahman is without modifications then how can that Brahman be described as the Lord, controller of the world, since there is no room for a distinction between controller and controlled ?

Answer : The Lord's qualities, such as omniscience, omnipotence, etc., depend on *avidyā*, the limitations of name-and-form, just as the particular parts of space depend on the limiting adjuncts like pots, etc. But none of these qualities—omniscience, etc.—belongs to Brahman, which is without any adjuncts whatever.

Further (II.1.15), it is only when the cause exists that we perceive the effect, and this relationship shows the nondifference of cause and effect.

Objection : We find things in the world that are distinct, but one depends upon the other—for example, smoke depends on fire.

Answer : No, since we sometimes see smoke even after the fire has gone out ! And in any case our idea is that the dependence in question is more a matter of the awareness of something depending on the awareness of (what is supposed to be) something else—when *that* relationship holds we have nondifference, not otherwise. And that relationship does not hold between smoke and fire. (An alternative explanation of the *sūtra* is also offered.)

Further (II.1.16), if something *x* is different from a *y* that precedes *x*, then *x* cannot arise from *y*—for example, oil does not arise from sand. Thus, since any effect *x* must be nondifferent from its cause *y* prior to its production, it must be inferred that it remains nondifferent after its production.

Objection (II.1.17) : But scripture sometimes describes the effect as nonexistent prior to its production.

Answer : That is not what those texts mean. What is meant is that prior to the effect's production it lacks properties that it takes on at the time of production, not that it doesn't exist at all then.

II.1.18 (Here is an argument for *satkāryavāda*) : If *asatkārya-vāda* were true, since the effect is nonexistent prior to its production what would stop our producing curds from clay or pots from milk ?

Opponent (the *asatkāryavādin*) : Each substance has a certain power (*śakti*) to produce certain kinds of effects and not others.

Śaṃkara : And this "power" to produce a certain kind of effect is precisely the nature of the effect as existent in the cause prior to its production !

Naiyāyika : We hold that cause and effect are different, being related to each other by the relation of inherence (*samavāya*).

Śaṃkara : Then what connects this inherence with its relata ? You must either postulate an infinite series of connections or give up your thesis that inherence is distinct from its relata.

Naiyāyika : Inherence connects itself to its relata without requiring further relations.

Śaṃkara : Then contact (*saṃyoga*) should likewise relate itself to its relata without any further relation. And anyway, since we experience the cause (say, a substance) and the effect (say, its quality) as identical (*tādātmya*), the postulation of inherence is superfluous.

Again, does the whole effect reside by inherence in all its causal parts collectively or only in each part distributively? If the former, we can never see wholes, which contradicts your theory. If the latter, that alleged "whole" cannot be a unity but must be a collection of many parts itself.

Naiyāyika : Wholes, like universal properties, are fully present in each of their instances without losing their unity.

Śaṃkara : No, for although we see potness in each pot, we do not see the whole in each of its parts.

Furthermore, in ordinary language we find ourselves saying "the pot arises"; if the *asatkāryavādin* were right, we should say "the potter arises," since only the potter, and not the pot, would on his view exist to perform any action of arising at the time in question. But we don't say that.

Naiyāyika : What happens is that the effect comes into the inherence relation with its cause.

Śaṃkara : But it doesn't exist yet, and so can't come into any relation! Furthermore, your way of describing your view is incoherent. You say "the effect is nonexistent prior to its production"; if you really mean that the effect doesn't exist, then we can't talk about that nonexistence as "prior to production"—a barren woman's son is not properly described as "nonexistent prior to production"; he is merely nonexistent, period. But effects are not like that; therefore they are not nonexistent.

Objection : If the effect already exists nobody would exert himself to produce it.

Answer : It exists already, but not in the form it is to take as effect, and it is to bring about the cause's assuming the form of the effect that the exertion is directed. And that does not imply difference of effect from cause, for a mere difference in form does not entail difference in essence. Devadatta with legs together is not a different person from Devadatta with legs apart. This refutes the momentariness doctrine of the Buddhists.

II.1.19-20. The nondifference of effect from cause is like the nondifference of a folded piece of cloth from the cloth unfolded. Or it is like the relation between the breath when held and the various breaths that support the motions of a living body—the latter are manifestations of the former but nondifferent from it.

II.1.21-23 (E208-210; T343-346). *Objection* (II.1.21) : If what you say is true, that is, that Brahman and the individual self are nondifferent, then It would not have produced effects such as bondage and suffering, or, if It did, since It would have had the power to liberate Itself from them It would certainly have long since done so. But here is the world, full of bondage and suffering, and therefore what you say must be wrong, and the world was not created by an intelligent agent.

Answer (II.1.22) : Brahman, not the *jīva*, is the creator of the world and is not identical with it. Brahman is not at fault for creating bondage and suffering, since for It, as opposed to the *jīva*, there is nothing to be achieved or avoided.

Objection : But in scriptural statements like "*tat tvam asi* (that art thou)," Brahman and the self are said to be nondifferent. Are you now denying that?

Answer : They are both different and nondifferent, like space and the portion of space enclosed in a jar. Furthermore, as soon as awareness of nondifference arises all distinctions are sublated, including that between Brahman and individual self; the world-illusion vanishes and with it the question of creation of bondage and suffering.

II.1.23. Brahman may have various distinctions in It, including distinctions of value—just as the earth generates stones of different value—but this does not adversely affect its ultimate unity.

II.1.24-25 (E210-211; T346-349). *Objection* : An intelligent cause requires materials and instruments to carry out its intentions—for example, a potter requires clay, a wheel, etc. But Brahman can have no such aids, so how can It create?

Answer : In some cases the material has within it the capacity to cause effects without assistance : for example, milk becomes curds, or water ice, without any help.

Objection : Milk requires heat to become curd.

Answer : No. Heat hastens the process, but it becomes sour eventually. In Brahman's case, since Its powers are perfect, no help of any kind is needed.

Objector (II.1.25) : Well, all right, nonconscious things like milk and water can do that, but our point is that conscious agents require instruments.

Answer : Gods, sages, and others do not require instruments, yet they are conscious. For that matter, the spider spins its own web.

Objection : But all these create from material substances that are distinct from their conscious selves, whereas Brahman is alleged to create from His very consciousness; thus the analogy does not apply.

Answer : It applies, since its point was merely to show that not all cases of creation by an intelligent being were precisely like that of the potter.

II.1.26-29 (E212-215; T349-354). *Objection* : Either Brahman has parts, or else when It creates It transforms Itself wholly into something entirely different. But then Brahman will be destroyed; the texts that tell us to seek to "see" It are without point, there being nothing left to "see" except Its effects, which we see quite readily; and scripture will be violated.

Answer (II.1.27) : Scripture shows both that Brahman is without parts and that It does not transform Itself wholly into something different.

Objector : Even scripture cannot make us agree to something incoherent. Our argument is not met.

Answer : Your dilemma is not a real one. The change in Brahman due to Its creative capacities is not a matter of transforming Itself either in whole or in part, but rather it is a matter of illusory plurality produced from ignorance, as two moons are produced by double vision but the moon is not thereby changed either totally or partly. Or as in the case of a dream, the dreaming person is not totally or even partly changed. And anyway, your argument applies equally against you (Sāṃkhyas), since if *prakṛti* produces it must either change totally or in part, and it has no parts.

Sāṃkhya : Surely it does have parts, namely, the *guṇas*.

Śaṃkara : But the *guṇas* have no parts, though they are responsible for that part of the world that resembles each of them in nature respectively. And if you say that even they have parts, then *prakṛti* cannot be eternal. The same argument applies against atomic theory (e.g., of Vaiśeṣika). Either atoms have parts or they haven't; if they have they aren't atoms, and if they haven't they can't combine.

II.1.30-31 (E215-216; T354-356). Brahman has all the powers required for creation, for scripture tells us so, even though It lacks the kinds of organs that the gods are said to require in order to create.

II.1.32-33 (E216-217; T356-357). *Objection*: An intelligent creator always acts for some purpose, but Brahman has nothing left to achieve, hence no purposes.

Answer : Some acts are the manifestation of mere sport (*līlā*).

Objection : Then His acts are merely senseless.

Answer : No, for scripture tells us He is omniscient.

II.1.34-36 (E217-219; T357-361). *Objection* : God gives different selves differing amounts of happiness and suffering and thus treats men unequally. Furthermore, He is cruel, for He produces pain and destruction (at *pralaya*).

Answer : God is not free in this matter; He is bound to create according to the karmic potentialities of each bound self.

Objection : This might be an excuse as regards creations subsequent to the first one, but since scripture tells us that Being existed prior to all differentiation, God is necessarily responsible for that first creation and thus for the inequality and cruelty alleged.

Answer : No, it is like the seed and the sprout; *saṃsāra* is beginningless. If the world had a beginning it would have arisen without a cause, and then it would follow that the liberated selves would return to *saṃsāra,* that a person would become liable for what another did, and soon, and this is unreasonable. In the same manner, scripture affirms the truth of the beginninglessness of *saṃsāra.*

II.1.37 (E219; T361-362). So the various properties ascribed to Brahman, such as being both material and efficient cause of the world, are thus seen to be appropriate.

SECOND CHAPTER, SECOND SECTION

II.2.1-10 (E220-228; T363-381). In an introductory passage it is explained that in this section other systems, for example, Sāṃkhya, will be dealt with purely in terms of reasoning, without reference to scripture.

Sāṃkhya : Just as pots require clay as their causes, since they are made of clay, so the world, which is made up of pleasure, frustration, and delusion, requires something made up of these qualities as its cause. This something is *pradhāna.* Since it is nonconscious it evolves into varied modifications to effect the purposes of conscious things, namely, *puruṣas.*

Śaṃkara : Since we never see nonconscious things modifying themselves to suit the purposes of conscious beings, but rather we see that transformations of nonconscious things into effects such as pots, etc., always require the activity of a conscious agent, for example, a potter, in shaping the result, this argument of yours fails to prove what you intend it to. On the basis of your own example you should admit that conscious agency plays a part in the production of the world.

Sāṃkhya : We never observe activity on the part of isolated consciousness; activity is always located in a nonconscious substratum—for example, a chariot. Thus it is all right to attribute agency to the nonconscious *pradhāna.*

Śaṃkara : True, activity is always observed in nonconscious beings, but only when a conscious being is also present. Since the presence of consciousness is the peculiar occasion of activity, always there when activity occurs and never there when it is absent, we find it appropriate to denominate it as the agent-cause.

Sāṃkhya : Since pure consciousness cannot move, it cannot induce activity in another.

Śaṃkara : It can do so like a magnet, which though immobile induces motion in others.

Sāṃkhya : Nonconscious things can, after all, move by themselves; for example, milk and water flow naturally without requiring a conscious agent.

Śaṃkara : On our view we can infer a conscious cause for any motion, including those. For example, the milk flows from a cow by virtue of her conscious intention to provide sustenance to her calf. At best these examples beg the question—they stand in need of being proved as much as the major contention (about *pradhāna*).

II.2.4. Again, why does *pradhāna*—which consists of three *guṇas*, you say—sometimes produce one thing, sometimes another, or sometimes not produce at all?

Sāṃkhya : It transforms spontaneously, just as grass spontaneously becomes milk (when eaten by a cow).

Śaṃkara : Hardly, since it doesn't become milk when it is not eaten at all, or is eaten by a bull. And anyway, you hold that transformation is always for the benefit of a conscious being—so how can it be "spontaneous" in the sense you now maintain?

Sāṃkhya : Although activity on the part of nonconscious stuff may occur spontaneously, that is, without any cooperating conscious agent, it must, we agree, occur for the benefit of something conscious.

Śaṃkara : What benefit—pleasure for the self, or its liberation? It can't be pleasure, for on your view the self (*puruṣa*) can't gain or lose pleasure. So it must be liberation. But the *puruṣa* is already liberated before *pradhāna* acts ! So that can't be it. Or is it the satisfaction of the *puruṣa's* longing for liberation? But a *puruṣa* can't long for anything, and the *pradhāna*, being nonconscious, can't either !

Sāṃkhya : It is as if a lame man rode on the back of a blind one : being able to see, he moves the other to act; so it is with *puruṣa* and *prakṛti*.

Śaṃkara : I see; you give up, then, the notion that *pradhāna* can move spontaneously. And how does the *puruṣa* make *pradhāna* act? A lame man may speak to his blind friend, or steer him by touch; nothing like that is possible in the case of *prakṛti* and *puruṣa*. The *puruṣa* cannot be said to induce activity in *prakṛti* merely by its proximity, since then, it being eternally proximate, *prakṛti* would never cease acting and there would be no liberation.

Again, how precisely does *pradhāna* act? The three *guṇas* are in equilibrium initially; what is responsible for disturbing that equilibrium? If *guṇas* are said to be like that, that is, unsteady, the result will be that we will be unable to explain the order in the world, since these *guṇas* are nonconscious. And if consciousness is attributed to *pradhāna,* our position has been accepted—this *pradhāna* is our Brahman.

II.2.10. Again, the Sāṃkhya is inconsistent : Sāṃkhya philosophers give differing accounts of the number of sense organs, the origin of the *tanmātras,* and so forth.

Sāṃkhya : Your view, that Brahman is both the nature of the suffering in the world and the cause of that same suffering, is objectionable on several counts. For one, if these attributes belong to the same Brahman release will be impossible, for the cessation of suffering would involve Brahman's losing an essential property. Furthermore, it is evident to everyone that the cause of suffering and the suffering caused are distinct things, as are the desirer and the thing desired; if the latter two were not distinct we could not ascribe the property of being desirous to the desirer, since he would have nothing lacking in him to desire.

Śaṃkara : Your argument rests on the premise that the two properties—being the nature of suffering and being its cause—must have distinct abodes, but this we deny. Fire, although it has different properties such as giving off heat and giving off light, and although it is capable of change, doesn't burn itself up or light itself up, since it is only one thing, not two; likewise with Brahman. The appearance of suffering and the cause of it reside entirely in the realm of *avidyā* : the body is the sufferer, and the sun (say) the cause of suffering (through sunburn).

Sāṃkhya : But the body is nonconscious; how can it undergo suffering?

Śaṃkara : It only seems to : that is my point. How can consciousness itself undergo suffering? In fact, on your view, what does undergo suffering? Your own metaphysics does not account for it, so you too must accept it as a result of *avidyā.*

Sāṃkhya : No. Suffering must be held to be real, not apparent.

Śaṃkara : Then liberation will be impossible, since its cause (*pradhāna*) is eternal.

II.2.11-17 (E228-238; T381-400). *Vaiśeṣika* : The qualities that inhere in a substance that is a cause produce qualities of the same kind in the effect; for example, white threads produce a white cloth. But the Vedānta view is that conscious Brahman produces nonconscious world, which violates the principle.

Śaṃkara : As a matter of fact that is not even the Vaiśeṣika view. For Vaiśeṣika postulates as the ultimate causes atoms, which have by nature a size called "atomic" (*parimāṇḍalya*); the atoms are held to produce dyads, which in turn produce triads of dyads, and so on. Doubtless it is true that by this theory white atoms produce white dyads; however, from the "atomic size" of the atoms, a like "atomic size" is not produced in the dyads; rather the dyads have a size called "small" (*aṇu*). Again, when two dyads combine to form a quatrad we have a small substance being the cause of a large (*mahat*) one. There is no reason, therefore, why conscious Brahman should not produce the nonconscious world.

Vaiśeṣika : You misunderstand the principle we appeal to. The qualities of the effect must resemble those of the cause except where the effect has by nature qualities contrary to those of the cause. Now largeness is a quality that the quatrad has by nature, so the dyad cannot produce its opposite; but in the case of the world it has no quality contrary to consciousness—"nonconsciousness" is not a positive quality but a mere lack. Thus here the principle should apply, but since Brahman and the world violate it, your Advaita theory should be rejected.

Śaṃkara : No, for your own view requires that the effect and its qualities not exist until after the cause has operated. Indeed, you even hold that the effect must exist for a moment without qualities before they arise in that effect. Thus the effect has no "natural" qualities of the kind you allude to.

Vaiśeṣika : The cause of the size of the dyad is not the sizes of the atoms but rather their multiplicity (*bahutva*), etc.

Śaṃkara : No matter; at the time of origination all the qualities of the cause are related to their abode by the same relation, namely, inherence, so the principle in question is violated. For that matter, it is violated even more evidently on your own view when you allege, for example, that substances are produced by contact, for contact is not even a substance.

II.2.12. Śaṃkara now proceeds to outline the atomic theory of Vaiśeṣika, according to which the bodies that inhabit the world are built up from initial contact among atoms following *pralaya*. Śaṃkara's criticism directs our attention to the first motion, allegedly in the atoms of air, which produce contacts and lead to further contacts, etc. According to the theory this first motion is due to something "unseen" (*adṛṣṭa*). Now no matter what this *adṛṣṭa* may be—an effort on the part of the selves, an original impact, an invisible cause—it cannot operate during *pralaya*, since at that time the internal organs are not in contact with the selves, and the selves are in *pralaya* not conscious and so incapable of causing motion. And nonconscious atoms cannot move except as impelled initially by conscious causes. Where is this *adṛṣṭa* located—in the selves or in the atoms? If in the selves, then it cannot produce motion, not being connected with the atoms. Or if you say that the omnipresent selves, having *adṛṣṭa* as their qualities, are in contact with the atoms, the result will be that the atoms will never stop acting, and there will be no *pralaya* at all.

Further, how can we even make sense of contact between atoms, which have no parts? If they touch at all they must interpenetrate, and thus no increase in size will occur when they combine.

II.2.13. Again, the postulation of inherence as the relation connecting the dyad to its two constituent atoms won't do, since it leads to infinite regress. Inherence is postulated to connect relata that are absolutely different; but as it is absolutely different from its relata, it will require still another inherence to relate itself and one of its relata, and so on *ad infinitum*.

Vaiśeṣika : Inherence is experienced as being present where it does occur, and not as depending on other relations for its presence.

Śaṃkara : But then, contact is also so experienced, but on your theory *it* requires inherence to connect it to its relata!

II.2.14. Again, either the atoms are mobile by nature or are immobile by nature, or both or neither. But none of these is possible. If mobile by nature, no *pralaya* could take place. If immobile by nature, no creation could take place. The third possibility is contradictory. And if they are neither mobile nor immobile by nature their motion depends on something else, like *adṛṣṭa*; but as before, either *adṛṣṭa* is in contact with the atoms, in which case *pralaya* is precluded, or it is not in relation to the atoms, in which case no creation will take place.

II.2.15. Again, since whatever has qualities such as color, etc., is gross and impermanent by comparison with its more subtle cause, and since on the Vaiśeṣika theory atoms are held to have color, it follows that they must have more subtle causes, being themselves gross and impermanent. Kaṇāda argues that atoms are permanent because otherwise we should not have the expression "impermanent" in our language; but this does not prove that atoms are permanent—something else, for example, Brahman, will do as well. Anyway, one cannot prove the existence of something merely from facts about verbal usage.

II.2.16. The substance earth is said in Vaiśeṣika to have four kinds of sense qualities and to be gross; water has three and is more subtle; fire, two and is still more subtle; and air has one quality and is subtlest. What, then, about the atoms of each of these four kinds of substance—do they have differing numbers of qualities or the same? Since substances with more qualities are bigger than those with fewer, if earth atoms have more qualities than air atoms they should be bigger, but this contradicts atomic theory according to which all atoms are without parts and so of the same size. If they all have the same number of qualities, however, then either we won't be able to touch earth or we will find all sense qualities in all four kinds of substance, contrary to actual experience.

II.2.17. Still other objections to Vaiśeṣika. For one, Vaiśeṣika holds that two things can be different and yet related to each other by a relation of dependence called *ayutasiddha.* (Two things are *ayutasiddha* if one cannot exist without the other.) We ask : between two such things what constitutes the inability of one to exist without the other ? Is it that they must occur at the same place, or at the same time, or with the same character ? Not the first, since your view is that the cloth and the threads occupy different places. Not the second, since if so the two horns of a cow will be *ayutasiddha* ! And surely not the third, since if so qualities and substances will be identical in character.

Again, the notion of inherence as the peculiar relation, distinct from contact, which connects effect with cause, is a pointless one. Since the effect does not exist before it is produced (on Vaiśeṣika theory) it cannot be connected to the cause at that time in any fashion. Once it is produced, being a substance in relation to another substance, the cause, the appropriate relation is contact, for that is a proper relation between two substances.

Relations such as inherence and contact do not, in any case, exist separately from their relata. The fact that we have words in our language referring to relations does not prove that they are not in fact words referring to aspects of the relata. Devadatta, though one, is described in many ways according as we have in mind his various activities.

Contact only occurs between entities that have parts, as far as our observation goes; thus it cannot be postulated between atoms, selves, and internal organs.

Finally, the Vaiśeṣika assumes that composition and decomposition take place by, respectively, the combining and separating of their parts, but it need not always be so. For example, some substances—ghee, gold—decompose by melting, a process wherein no parts are separated but rather the substance gradually passes back into an undifferentiated condition. And some substances are produced, not by combining parts, but, for example, as milk produces curds or water ice.

II.2.18-27 (E239-246; T400-418). Turning to the Buddhists, we find three principal viewpoints among them : (1) everything is real (*sarvāstivāda*); (2) only consciousness (*vijñāna*) is real; and (3) everything is void (*śūnyavāda*).

Sarvāstivāda holds that both external and internal entities are real, externals including elements (*bhūta*) and elementaries (*bhautika*), internals including mind (*citta*) and mental associates (*caitta*). The elements are earth, fire, etc.; the elementaries are color, etc., and the sense organs. Internals make up the five *skandhas*. It is by the aggregating of such entities that the external and internal objects and states of experience are produced.

But the Sarvāstivādins cannot explain how this aggregating comes about. For on their own assumptions there is nothing of the appropriate kind that can function to bring about the aggregation. The Buddhists do not admit any God, and their view is that consciousness depends on the prior existence of an aggregate of atoms—so what brings that about ? It can't be the *ālayavijñāna*, for either that is another name for the self (*ātman*), which they deny, or else it is momentary and cannot bring about motion in the atoms.

Sarvāstivādin : The aggregating comes about through operation of the mutual causality (of the twelvefold chain) beginning with *avidyā*, etc.

Answer : Members of this chain can be explained as caused by other members, but our question is about the aggregates that are required in order that *avidyā*, etc., can function at all.

Sarvāstivādin : Yes, they must be assumed, as we say.

Śaṃkara : But our question is : what occasions the aggregating, and this you haven't answered.

Sarvāstivādin : *Saṃsāra* is beginningless; aggregates produce other aggregates, and *avidyās* reside in these aggregates, producing other members of the chain.

Śaṃkara : Do the aggregates produce on principle or not ? If they only produce others of the same kind, a human body could never be reborn in a different form; or, if they operate without principle, anyone might at any instant become something else entirely !

Furthermore, liberation cannot occur or even be desired, since you admit no permanent self to enjoy or desire it.

II.2.20. For that matter, *avidyā* and the rest cannot even function to cause other members of the (twelvefold) chain (of *pratītyasamutpāda*), since they are held to be momentary, for a momentary thing has ceased before it can operate. And further : are the origination and destruction of an entity the very nature of that entity, or another state of it, or something altogether different ? None of these exhaustive alternatives fits the Buddhist position. If a thing is identical with its origination and destruction, we should find ourselves using the words "origination," "destruction", and "pot" interchangeably, and we don't. If these are states of the pot, then the pot exists for at least three moments, contrary to the Buddhist assumption. And if they are altogether different, then the pot must be eternal, since it never comes into any connection with origination and destruction.

II.2.21. And things cannot arise without causes, since you yourself hold that mind and mental associates arise depending on causal factors (*pratyaya*) and since without causes operating anything might originate at any time.

II.2.22-24. *Sarvāstivādin* : We believe in three kinds of absolute cessation (*nirodha*) : a kind that involves will (*pratisaṃkhyā*), a kind that does not involve will (*apratisaṃkhyā*), and mere space (*ākāśa*).

Śaṃkara : None of these kinds of cessation is possible. As to the first two, they would involve either the cessation of the stream (*saṃtāna*) to which they belong, or else the nonorigination of a member of that stream. But the stream cannot stop, since each of its members occasions another. And it is observed that when a thing is "destroyed" it enters into a different state but does not cease altogether in any form whatsoever. Anyway, you believe that such cessations arise either as a result of true knowledge or all by themselves. But if the former, destruction is not natural but occasioned, and if the latter, what is the point of the path (being practiced) ? As for *ākāśa* , it is not a mere absence but a positive entity. It is to be inferred as the substratum of sounds. If it were a mere nothing, there would be no room for more than one bird to fly at once ! Again, your own scriptures indicate that wind is grounded on *ākāśa*. Finally, though you say that *ākāśa*, and for that matter all three *nirodhas*, are nondescribable, yet you aver they are eternal. You can't have it both ways.

II.2.25. Further, all things cannot be momentary, since then we could not account for memory and recognition, which requires that one and the same person sees and later recalls.

Sarvāstivādin : What happens is that two momentary cognitions occur that are closely similar to each other.

Śaṃkara : But to grasp the similarity one cognizing subject is required. Otherwise we should not say "this is similar to that" but merely "look, similarity" ! The conscious subject is never in doubt as to whether it is itself or only similar to itself.

II.2.26-27. The Buddhist holds that entities arise from non-entities, that is, after the destruction of their causes. But if it were so anything could arise from anything, even from hare's horns. If the Buddhist, to meet this, says there are different kinds of nonentity, we merely point out that he has then made his "nonentity" into an entity, since it has a character that determines a certain kind of effect. And furthermore, labor would become exceedingly easy, since everyone has nonentity at his disposal and could produce whatever he needs. And then no one would wish or work for liberation.

II.2.28-32 (E247-252; T418-428). Versus Vijñānavāda. According to Vijñānavāda, means of knowing (*pramāṇa*), objects (*prameya*), and results (*phala*) are all internal to our cognizing, for there are no external objects. External things must be either atoms or aggregates of atoms, but atoms are too small to be represented, and aggregates of atoms are either nondifferent from atoms (after all) or else (if they are different) they cannot be composed of atoms. In the same fashion we can show that there are no external universal properties, etc.

Furthermore (continues the Vijñānavādin) ideas do differ among themselves according as they represent different objects, and this difference is a function of consciousness, so the object form (*viṣayākāra*) is just consciousness and external objects are merely construction (*kalpanā*). After all, we are never conscious of the one without also being conscious of the other, and this shows they are nondifferent. Just like dream objects, objects of waking experience are internal only; there are no external objects.

Question : If there are no external objects what is responsible for the differentiations among our ideas ?

Answer : The variety among the traces (*vāsanā*).

Śaṃkara's reply to all this : Since consciousness is *of* an external object, there must necessarily be such objects. We are not conscious of consciousness but rather of things. If the Buddhist's point is that external objects are impossible and therefore cannot be apprehended, we reply that he has got the case backward—what is possible or impossible is to be justified by appeal to *pramāṇas*, the *pramāṇas* cannot in turn be justified by appealing to preconceived possibilities or impossibilities. Since perception grasps external objects and the other *pramāṇas* confirm that they are indeed external, it is not possible to doubt that there are external objects.

In addition, since the Buddhist adopts his thesis of extreme momentariness, according to which ideas last no more than a moment, the things that he alleges about ideas will not stand examination. We could not know, on the assumption of momentariness, whether two ideas are different from each other, which idea leaves a trace, what is real and what is not, and so on, since all such judgments presuppose a categorical difference between knower and known, which is what is denied by the Vijñānavādin.

Further, an idea cannot illuminate itself, any more than fire can burn itself; to explain consciousness one must posit a knowing Self, which is entirely different from Its ideas. Even the lamp does not become evident to consciousness by itself; it requires a knower for that, like any other object. And whereas an idea cannot illuminate itself, not lasting long enough for that, a permanent cognizing Self can.

II.2.29. As for the analogy drawn between dream objects and those of the waking state, by reference to which the Vijñānavādin argues that both are unreal, Śaṃkara points out that there is a great difference : dream objects are always sublated when we wake up, but only some waking objects—those we denominate as illusory—are sublated; the rest are never negated in any state. Again, there is the further difference that dream objects are the results of memory impressions, whereas perceptions in the waking state are immediately presented without the intermediacy of memory.

II.2.30. Anyway, how can one possibly individuate momentary ideas except in terms of their disparate contents ? But what is responsible for the disparate contents ? You deny that external objects can be and must say that it is due to traces. But traces cannot operate without a substratum in which to reside—and no such substratum is admissible in your system.

Vijñānavādin : We believe in the existence of an *ālayavijñāna*, a "storehouse of traces," which provides the required substratum.

II.2.31. But it cannot, since it is momentary—or else you give up your thesis that everything is momentary.

Thus we have refuted the first two Buddhist viewpoints mentioned above, that is, those of the Sarvāstivādins and Vijñānavādins. As for the third, that of the Śūnyavādins (Mādhyamikas), who maintain that all is void (*śūnya*), it does not merit discussion, for the *pramāṇas* clearly refute the thesis and the Śūnyavādins put forth no fresh positive reason to justify their contention.

II.2.32. Indeed, that the Buddha's words could have spawned three positions so widely different suggests that either intentionally or unintentionally he did not make himself clear, and we can safely dismiss the whole theory.

II.2.33-36 (E252-256; T428-434). Śaṃkara considers Jain philosophy, mentioning the most prominent features of it—its categories of *jīva* and *ajīva* and others and its method of *saptabhaṅgī* or "sevenfold predication," according to which seven different ways of viewing a proposition are distinguished and combined.

II.2.33. Contradictory attributes cannot belong to one thing. The upshot of your sevenfold-predication method is that nothing definite is claimed—your categories are neither categorically affirmed nor denied; everything is indefinite and thus doubtful, and so cannot be made the basis for action with an aim to gain release; no clear advice is forthcoming.

II.2.34. One characteristic Jain thesis concerns the size of the self (*jīva*); it is said to be of the same size as the body it inhabits. Śaṃkara points out that in that case either it is fixed—and would be too big to enter some bodies and too small to fill up others—or else it is flexible, expanding or contracting to suit. But if the latter is the case, it must have parts that it loses or gains to attain the right dimension. In that case the Jains adopt a form of the atomic theory (previously refuted) and must in effect hold that the self is noneternal.

II.2.35. The notion that the self may undergo change of size by adding or dropping particles contradicts another characteristic Jain theory, according to which upon release the self rises to the top of the universe like a pot emerging from the mud, for there is no reason to hold that any particular particles are essential to the self, and in any case it has been shown to be impermanent.

II.2.36. Anyway, upon release the size of the self is presumed to be fixed, so we should properly infer that the size of the self is fixed always, or at least that its initial size and its intervening size must have been permanent as well, which would then entail the same conclusion—that it is fixed in size.

II.2.37-41 (E256-259; T434-439). (*Sūtra* 37) This *sūtra*, which appears to state that theism is inadequate, is interpreted by Śaṃkara as intended to refute the thesis that God is only the efficient, but not the material, cause of the world (otherwise, Śaṃkara contends, this *sūtra* would be inconsistent with, for example, I.4.23-24, and others, where God is affirmed to be the cause in both senses). Thus he takes it to address theistic Sāṃkhya and Yoga as well as Śaivas and Vaiśeṣikas,

On these views, Śaṃkara contends, God is just another self like us, and if in particular He willfully causes evil and ignorance resulting in differential status for animals, men, etc., He is subject to passions and is no better than any other self and doesn't deserve our devotion. To say, as is sometimes said, that He creates in response to and determined by the merit and demerit of the other selves will produce mutual dependence between God and the selves' karma, neither being ultimately responsible; that the series of reciprocal influences is beginningless doesn't help. Again, since agency requires imperfection (according to *Nyāyasūtra* [I.1.18]) God must be imperfect. And if He is a self in the Yoga system's sense like their *puruṣas*, He must be inactive.

II.2.38. Further, it is impossible to conceive how God could be related to the other selves or to *prakṛti* consistently with His agency. What could the relation be? It can't be contact, since all three relata are all-pervasive. It can't be inherence : which is the substratum and which the superstratum ? It can't be any other relation inferred from God's agency, because that is precisely what is in question.

Objection : How does the Advaitin relate God to the world, then ?

Answer : We have no difficulty; for us the relation is one of identity (*tādātmya*). And whereas these theists we are discussing must invoke a relation whose knowledge is possible through empirical means so that they may prove it through inference, we Advaitins, who depend entirely on scripture, do not have to posit a perceptible relation. If the theist retorts that he, too, can appeal to scripture, he will be begging the question in a different manner, for he, unlike ourselves, considers scripture to be a creation of God.

II.2.39. The theist says that God produces changes in *prakṛti* just as a potter produces changes in clay. But this cannot be right; *prakṛti* does not have qualities like color, etc., and is not an object of perception, so cannot be manipulated in the required manner.

II.2.40. *Theist* : We say that the way God rules *prakṛti* is analogous to the way the self rules its sense organs.

Śaṃkara : The analogy is unconvincing : we infer that the self rules its sense organs because it experiences pain and pleasure resulting from them, but God does not experience pleasure and pain resulting from *prakṛti*.

II.2.41. According to the *tārkikas* both God and *prakṛti* are of infinite duration. But if God is omniscient, he must know the extent of *prakṛti* and of the *jīvas*. But then their extent must be finite, since it is a matter of experience that everything whose extent is measurable is of finite duration. Thus God is not omniscient.

II.2.42-45 (E259-261; T439-443). (*Sūtra* 42) Śaṃkara explains that this section deals with the view of the Bhāgavatas. This view is described as follows : God, namely Vāsudeva, is both the material and efficient cause of everything; specifically, He is the cause of the individual selves (*saṃkarṣaṇa*), the internal organ (*pradyumna*), and the ego principle (*aniruddha*). Śaṃkara dissents only from the view that God creates the selves. If that were the case the selves would be impermanent and release would be impossible.

II.2.43. The Bhāgavatas apparently hold that *pradyumna* arises from *saṃkarṣaṇa*, and *aniruddha* from *pradyumna*. But this disagrees with experience : we never observe that an instrument, like an axe, arises from the agent. And there is no scriptural authority for it either.

II.2.44. Bhāgavata : Let us then understand "*saṃkarṣaṇa*" and the other two words as denoting, not the individual self, internal organ, and ego principle, but rather their presiding deities (thus not participating in *prakṛti*).

Śaṃkara : Are these deities equal to the Lord in excellence ? In that case they are unnecessary. Or are they equal to one another in excellence, but less than the Lord ? Then the objection in *sūtra* 42 remains in force, since given two things of equivalent attributes one cannot be the cause of the other. Experience shows that when *x* causes *y*, *x* is superior to *y* in certain respects—for example, the clay that causes a pot is more flexible.

II.2.45. Furthermore, the Bhāgavata theories are internally inconsistent, as well as being inconsistent with the Veda.

SECOND CHAPTER, THIRD SECTION

II.3.1-7 (E262-270; T [volume 2] 3-18.) We have charged other systems with inconsistencies arising from their ways of handling problems about creation. But one may in turn suspect that such inconsistencies infect our own system. This section allays this doubt by studying the purport of Vedānta texts concerning the origination of various elements.

The first element to be discussed is *ākāśa*. The opponent (in *sūtras* 1-6) charges that *ākāśa* does not originate since there is no scriptural passage saying it does. *Chāndogya Upaniṣad* VI.2.3 says that water, fire, and air were produced, but not *ākāśa*.

There are, however, passages that appear to assert the origination of *ākāśa*, for example, *Taittirīya Upaniṣad* II.1. The apparent contradiction by this passage of the previously cited *Chāndogya* passage is explained away. But this passage must be understood in a secondary sense, since well-known theses about origination—for example, the

Vaiśeṣika analysis of causation involving inherence, noninherence, and instrumental causes—show that *ākāśa* cannot be an effect.

II.3.7. *Answer* : *Ākāśa* is an effect. The principle is that whatever is found distinct from other things is an effect. Since *ākāśa* is found distinct from earth, etc., it is an effect. In this way also spatial direction (*dik*), time, internal organs, and atoms are also proved to be effects.

Opponent : Then the Highest Self is an effect, since It is distinct from *ākāśa*, etc.

Answer : We infer that the Self is not distinct from the fact that scripture mentions nothing beyond the Self that It could be an effect of. If there is not an ultimate something that is not an effect we will end up in *śūnyavāda*.

As to the opponent's argument above, that effects require inherence causes, noninherence causes, etc., cited on Vaiśeṣika authority, counter-examples are cited to refute the Vaiśeṣika theory. A rope, for example, may be made of things of different kinds—threads and cow-hair—which shows that the inherence cause of an effect need not be of the same genus as that effect. Again, one atom is the inherence cause of its initial motion.

Again, we argue thus : *Ākāśa* is noneternal because it is the substratum of a noneternal quality (namely, sound), like jars. And the argument cannot be extended to the Self, since we do not admit that the Self is the substratum of noneternal qualities.

II.3.8 (E270; T18-19). Likewise, air is an effect, even though there are apparently inconsistent passages.

II.3.9 (E271; T19-20). *Opponent* : Then Brahman too is an effect !

Answer : What could be Its cause ? It would have to be superior to Brahman in some fashion (as we saw above). Brahman cannot arise from particulars, since we never find generals produced from particulars. It cannot spring from nonbeing (*asat*), as *Chāndogya Upaniṣad* VI.2.2 shows.

II.3.10-13 (E271-274; T20-25). Fire comes from air, water from fire, and earth from water. None of them arises directly from Brahman. But of course Brahman is indirectly the cause of them, as of everything.

II.3.14-15 (E275-276; T25-28). The order in which the elements are reabsorbed into Brahman is precisely the reverse of that in which they came out (even though scripture does not speak precisely to the question), since experience as well as *smṛti* point to this conclusion. Apparently conflicting scriptural passages are explained away.

II.3.16 (E276-277; T403-404). The Self is not born and does not die; expressions that seem to say so refer primarily to the body.

II.3.17 (E277-279; T29-33). The Self is, in fact, eternal. A variety of opposing arguments, mostly already dealt with, are reviewed and rejected.

II.3.18 (E280-281; T33-35). *Opponent* : Consciousness is adventitious to the self, produced by contact between self and internal organ; if the self were essentially conscious there could be no unconsciousness.

Answer : The self is essentially conscious, as scripture proves. "Unconsciousness" is not the absence of consciousness but rather the absence of intended objects (*viṣaya*).

II.3.19-32 (E281-289; T35-49). (*Sūtras* 19-28) *Opponent* : The self is of atomic size, since it goes out and comes into the body, and since scripture alleges it to be infinitesimal.

Question : If the self is atomic, how can one feel a sensation throughout his body ?

Opponent's answer : It can do so, just as sandal-paste, though applied in one place, gives pleasure over the whole body. Further, just as a lamp, occupying one place in a room, illuminates all of it, so the self, though occupying only the heart, disseminates consciousness throughout the body.

Śaṃkara (II.3.29-32): Atomic size belongs properly to the *buddhi*, and is improperly attributed to the Self, which is actually all-pervasive. The answers the opponent gives above to the questions raised won't do. When we step on a thorn we do not experience pain all over the body. And the analogy of the lamp is misplaced : light is a substance that pervades the room, but the quality of an atom cannot spread beyond the space occupied by the atom. The existence of the atomic-sized *buddhi* must be admitted in order to explain why everything is not perceived at once, and also to explain individuation in *saṃsāra*.

II.3.33-42 (E289-297; T49-61). That the self is an agent is proved in various ways, because scripture enjoins actions, attributes motion to the self, has instruments, meditates. It is not just the *buddhi* that does these things. However (*sūtra* 40), the self's agency is adventitious, not natural, to it; it is due to adjuncts. If it were a natural property of the self to be agent, release would not be possible, since activity breeds bondage.

Objection : Release might still be possible, by avoiding the results of activity through avoiding the occasions (*nimitta*) for acting, just as burning is avoided, even though fire has a natural capacity to burn, provided no fuel is present.

Answer : Since in the case of activity the occasions are connected to the self through the capacity (*śakti*) to act, they cannot be altogether avoided.

Objector (II.3.41) : The agency of the self is independent of God, since each self has its own specific problems, motives, passions, etc., as well as its own instruments, etc., to carry out actions and has no need of God for that. Furthermore, if activity depended on God it would follow that God is cruel and unjust because responsible for unequal frustrations for different selves.

Answer : Because scripture teaches that God is a causal agent in all activity we infer that each self's activity is a result, in part, of God's permission, and by the same token we must infer that release is in part a result of God's grace.

II.3.42. As for the objection that God is cruel and unjust, it cannot stand. God allots appropriate results corresponding to the merit or demerit of the selves, merit or demerit that was earned by each self through its previous activities. Just as the rain causes all kinds of seeds, good and bad, to sprout, so God causes all kinds of seeds of action to sprout, whether good or bad.

II.3.43-53 (E297-304; T61-73). *Sūtra* 43 states that the self is a part (of God), which Śaṃkara says cannot be meant literally, since Brahman has no parts. Then why isn't Brahman identical with the self? Because scripture, for example, *Chāndogya Upaniṣad* VIII.7.1, says they are different. Then mustn't we view the self as the servant of its master, God ? No, because other passages declare their identity. Thus the part-whole relation is appropriate (provided it isn't taken seriously !). *Sūtras* 44-45 cite scripture and *smṛti* to support this interpretation.

Objection : If the selves are parts of God then God must suffer as the selves do in *saṃsāra*, and those who realize Brahman must suffer more as a result.

Answer : No, the selves suffer because they, out of ignorance, identify themselves with the body, etc. Their suffering is conditional upon ignorance, whereas God does not suffer, not being ignorant. Analogies are provided : a holy man, not identifying himself as a man with relations, does not suffer from hearing that a relation has died; light is not affected by conditioning adjuncts.

Objection (II.3.47-48) : If there is only one inner Self for all beings how can there be Vedic injunctions and prohibitions ?

Answer : The possibility of such injunctions and prohibitions is contingent upon the Self identifying itself through ignorance with bodies, etc.

Objection : Then Vedic injunctions have no purport for one who knows rightly.

Answer : No, the injunctions are not purportless, they simply don't apply to such a one, since obligations can only arise with respect to things to be acquired or avoided, and for the realized Self there are no such things.

Opponent : These injunctions and prohibitions pertain for anyone who has discriminated the self from the body. Since one who knows rightly has made this discrimination, he is obligated.

Answer : No, obligation is, rather, contingent on the self identifying himself with the body. It doesn't follow that the realized person can act any way he likes, for he does not *act* at all, the very possibility of action depending on self-body identification.

Objection (II.3.49-50) : Since there is only one Self operating the various bodies the results of the actions of the various bodies will be mixed up.

Answer : No, it is the individual *jīvas* that are connected to bodies, so the difficulty does not arise. The *jīvas* are merely reflections (*ābhāsa*) of the Highest Self. Just as, if the sun is reflected in water, the trembling of one reflected image does not mean the next one has to tremble also, so the connections of *jīvas* with the results of actions do not get mixed up.

Actually, it is those (like Sāṃkhya and Vaiśeṣika) who hold that there are a plurality of all-pervading selves who get into this difficulty (of the results of actions getting mixed up), because the connection of action with all selves are contingent upon the same factors.

Sāṃkhya : The differences among the results of the actions of the several embodied selves is due to *prakṛti's* questing for release. If it were not so there would not be any liberation.

Śaṃkara : This merely assumes what you wish to prove but gives no reason for it. If no reason can be offered to differentiate the results of different selves' actions, we should conclude that liberation is not possible.

Vaiśeṣika : In our case the differences among the results of the actions of the various selves is due to their connection with their respective internal organs.

Śaṃkara : But since each self is all-pervading it is in connection with all the internal organs as much as any, and the difficulty is not removed.

Sāṃkhya and Vaiśeṣika : Then the difference is due to *adṛṣṭa*, the karmic potentialities.

Śaṃkara (II.3.51) : But in Sāṃkhya *adṛṣṭa* resides in *prakṛti*, which is common to all embodied selves, and in Vaiśeṣika it is created by the contact of internal organ and self, which contact as we have just seen is equally present for each internal organ and every self. So the difficulty is still not removed.

Vaiśeṣika (II.3.53) : Even though selves are all-pervading, since the contact is between the internal organ and that part of a self enclosed within a body, the difficulty does not arise for us.

Śaṃkara : No, since all selves are equally within each body. And various absurdities arise if the critical connection is made to depend on presence in a certain place—suppose one body moves out of that place and another into it, then the two internal organs occupy the same place, and confusion of results again occurs.

Anyway, there cannot be more than one all-pervading self, since we never experience many things occupying the same place.

Vaiśeṣika : Yes we do; various qualities reside in one locus at the same time.

Śaṃkara : But they have different characteristics, whereas your all-pervading selves are all precisely alike ! We never see anything like that.

SECOND CHAPTER, FOURTH SECTION

II.4.1-4 (E304-308; T74-79). Despite some passages (e.g., *Śatapatha Brāhmaṇa* VI.1.1) that say that the vital breaths (*prāṇa*) existed before the beginning (of the worlds), they actually arise from Brahman (like everything else), as many scriptural passages in fact assert.

II.4.5-7 (E308-312; T79-84). There are not merely seven "breaths," but eleven, all told : five sense organs, five action organs, and the internal organ. They are held to be "small" (*aṇu*) in size, though not atomic, for they could not then produce effects throughout the body.

II.4.8-13 (E312-317; T84-91). The chief breath is produced from Brahman, is different from wind and from the functioning of the organs, has the other breaths as its functions, and is limited in size and is subtle like the sense organs.

II.4.14-16 (E317-319; T91-93). The "breaths"—that is, the organs—are dependent on, and supervised by, their respective deities but produce experiences in the embodied self, not in those deities.

II.4.17-19 (E319-321; T93-96). The chief breath is distinct from the sense organs (called "breaths" also here), because (among other things) when the sense organs are "asleep" the chief breath remains active.

II.4.20-22 · (E321-323; T96-100). *Chāndogya Upaniṣad* VI.3.2 says "That divinity thought 'let me enter the three divinities (associated with the three elements) with this *jīvātman* and let me then develop name-and-form.' " Does this mean that the *jīva* created the specific characteristics of things? No, it is God who did that, as other passages in the Upaniṣads clearly indicate. All gross things are constructed from the three subtle elements—earth, water, fire.

THIRD CHAPTER, FIRST SECTION

III.1.1-7 (E324-330; T101-112). This section deals with the mechanics of *saṃsāra*. These *sūtras* consider whether the subtle transmigrating body includes, in addition to sense organs, *manas*, karma, etc., also the subtle elements that will constitute the seeds of the next body. Śaṃkara understands the answer to be yes and that in fact elements of earth and fire, as well as water, help make up the transmigrating body.

III.1.8-11 (E330-335; T112-121). Śaṃkara here explains how it is that the transmigrating body goes to other worlds, experiences there the results of previous actions, and then is reborn into this world in a body determined by karma. The problem is that if all the fruits of karma are experienced before rebirth, what is left to determine the new body? The opponent argues that the texts tell us that the *adṛṣṭa* (karma) earned in this life has results that are to be entirely experienced in heaven—the fruits of sacrifice, etc.—and that therefore nothing is left over to determine rebirth into this world. Śaṃkara's view is that some of one's karma produces experiences in heaven (as a god, say) whereas the rest (*anuśaya*) remains and determines the next body here—the good karma produces heavenly experiences, the bad determines the new body.

III.1.12-21 (E335-339; T121-126). Only those who perform sacrifices go to the lunar heaven; the others go to hell, the abode of Yama, or rather to one of the seven hells ruled over by Yama. Those in hell can be reborn into earthly form even without performing the requisite sacrifices occasioning conception, etc., as we find that various sorts of beings come into the world in other fashions than by birth from the womb.

III.1.22-27 (E339-343; T126-132). *Sūtras* 22-23 concern details of the descent of the subtle body from the lunar world to this one—it assumes a subtle form but does not become *ākāśa*, etc., and it stays in that form for a very brief period. When it arrives here (*sūtra* 25) it enters into foodstuffs—plants, etc.—but it does not become embodied in those things, it does not experience states as a result of its presence there; it resides there merely on the way to entering into new animal bodies through digestive processes. There are embodied selves in plants, but they do not get there by descending from the lunar regions. It is not that plants embody sacrificers who have killed animals, etc.—done unholy things—and so have earned this reward; sacrifice of animals is not unholy, for Vedic authority, which is our only guide in these matters, condones it. The last two *sūtras* review the process of conception and birth.

THIRD CHAPTER, SECOND SECTION

III.2.1-6 (E343-348; T133-141). The world of our dreams is not real, it is merely *māyā*, since things happen in dreams that cannot happen in reality (that is, in the waking world). For example, there isn't room for dreamt of chariots in the actual body; the sleeper cannot go to points far away in a single moment; the sleeper's body cannot remain visible to others on a couch while it is far away experiencing things in quite another place; he dreams it is day when it is night, and it can't be both at once. Nevertheless these illusory dreams may be prophetic. The waking world—"real" by comparison with the dream world—is still not absolutely real, as we have seen earlier; the dream world is sublated each morning when we awake, whereas the waking world remains until ultimate realization of Brahman's identity with the Self. As long as the self is blinded by ignorance it cannot produce for its experience anything real, even though it is ultimately nondifferent from God; thus whereas God can create the waking world, which is relatively real, the self bound by ignorance can only produce unreal dream objects, its true powers concealed by ignorance.

III.2.7-9 (E348-353; T141-149). *Question* : Where does the *jiva* reside in deep sleep—in the arteries (*nāḍi*), the heart (*puritat*), or the Highest Self?

Answer : In all of these, but essentially in the latter, that is, Brahman.

Question : How can we be sure that the self that wakes up from deep sleep is the same one that entered that state, any more than we can be sure that the same drop of water is extracted from a lake after it has once been dissolved in that lake?

Answer : There are several reasons : the person waking from deep sleep is seen to complete work left unfinished, he remembers his experiences before,—injunctions would otherwise be meaningless,—and, finally, a person could become liberated merely by falling asleep and scriptural injunctions would be pointless. The drop of water dissolves into the water completely—that is, without adjuncts—but the *jīva* is conditioned by adjuncts even while it is "dissolved" in Brahman in sleep—so the analogy is not apt.

III.2.10 (E353-355; T149-152). What kind of a state is attained when in a faint? None from waking, dream, deep sleep, or death seems appropriate; a person does not see objects as one awake or dreaming, his body behaves differently from one deeply asleep, and he is not dead. Śaṃkara's solution is that in faint we are in a state of half union with the deep sleep state.

III.2.11-21 (E355-363; T152-166). These *sūtras* state the nature of Brahman, experienced in deep sleep. Brahman is without qualities (*nirviśeṣa*), without form (*arūpa*) though capable of assuming form as light can, consciousness-only (*caitanyamātra*) though appearing as objects because reflected like the sun, etc.

Objection : Whereas the sun's light is reflected in an entirely different body, the water, for Brahman there is no comparable reflecting medium; thus the analogy suggested won't work.

Answer : No analogy is perfect. Brahman, like the reflected sun, appears affected when certain adjuncts change, but neither are really affected, and it is in these features that the analogy has point.

The commentary on *sūtra* 21 contains a long section dealing with someone who suggests that the Vedas enjoin us to annihilate the duality of the world-appearance (*dvaitaprapañcavilaya*). Śaṃkara is puzzled how the Vedas can enjoin such a thing. Either it would be like literally enjoining us to destroy all the objects in the world, which is quite beyond our capacities, or it is to enjoin an effort to destroy something that does not exist, in which case the injunction is not necessary—all that is required is knowledge of Brahman. Those Vedic passages that seem to enjoin us to know something are in fact meant merely to call our attention to it. One cannot enjoin knowledge, for truth depends on what is the case and not merely on human actions or wishes.

III.2.22-30 (E363-369; T166-175). *Sūtra* 22 deals with the famous Upaniṣadic "*neti neti*" ("not this, not this"). An opponent proposes to construe this as denying Brahman altogether, and Śaṃkara shows that it denies everything but Brahman. Brahman is known by yogis in meditation.

Objection : If a yogi knows Brahman in meditation that must mean that one self—a lower self—knows another self—a higher one.

Answer : No, there is no such distinction in reality; it only appears so because of the adjuncts limiting the individual self. So, after having set aside ignorance, the self passes into unity with the Highest Self (*prajñenātmanaikatāṃ gacchati*). The relation of the Highest Self to the bound one may be conceived by analogy with the relation between a snake and its coils, or between light and the fire that is its substratum.

III.2.31-37 (E369-373; T175-180). Scripture is interpreted to show that there is nothing other than Brahman.

III.2.38-41 (E373-375; T180-183). God is responsible for the results accruing from human actions, for the actions disappear immediately and cannot effect results at a later time. There is no proof for such a thing as an *apūrva* to do it, and even if there were such a thing it would require a conscious agent to occasion its operation.

THIRD CHAPTER, THIRD SECTION

III.3.1-10 (E375-384; T184-201). Do the different Upaniṣadic texts teach differing ways to know Brahman or only the same ones ? Śaṃkara holds that the texts, despite their differences, teach a common set of meditative cognitions, that the *Taittirīyaka* , *Vājasaneyaka*, *Kauṣītaki* versions of the Vedas all contain the same message. On the other hand, some apparently identical texts (e.g., *Bṛhadāraṇyaka Upaniṣad* I.3.7 and *Chāndogya Upaniṣad* I.2.7) are different in their subject matter, even though they may pass under the same name (here, the Udgīthavidyā).

Opponent (III.3.9) : When (in *Chāndogya Upaniṣad* I.1.1) it is said "Let a man meditate on *om* as the *udgītha*," what is the relation between *om* and *udgītha* ? It could be any one of four : superimposition (*adhyāsa*), sublation (*apavāda*), identity (*ekatva*), or qualification (*viśeṣaṇa*), and since there is no particular reason to prefer any one of these, we cannot decide.

Śaṃkara : It can only be the last relation (of qualification); thus the text in question enjoins us to meditate on that utterance of *om* which is (a part of) the *udgītha*.

Where different texts have the same essential meaning one should combine together the particular specifications that may only occur in one such text but not the others.

III.3.11-25 (E384-399; T201-225). Thus when different texts mention different essential qualities of Brahman we should combine them all in thinking about Brahman. This principle is applied in a number of contexts.

III.3.26-32 (E399-407; T225-238). A number of problems are considered concerning texts that specify the details of the liberated self's "path to the Brahma-world." The liberated self has to completely burn off his karma while embodied; it is only those who know *saguṇa* Brahman who travel the path of the gods—those who know *nirguṇa* Brahman do not travel at all.

III.3.33-39 (E407-413; T238-249). More cases where different texts are to be understood as conveying identical messages.

III.3.40-52 (E414-423; T249-268). Some points about meditation and sacrifices are made here.

III.3.53-54 (E423-425; T268-272). *Lokāyataka* (i.e., *Cārvāka*) : There is no self distinct from the body; it is the body that is conscious, since we observe that consciousness is found only where a body is.

Answer : But bodies are found where consciousness is not; so your view cannot stand. Further, we are conscious of the elements of the body, but if consciousness is a quality of those same elements this will not be possible, no more than it is possible for fire to burn itself.

III.3.55-66 (E425-432; T272-284). More on meditation and sacrifice.

THIRD CHAPTER, FOURTH SECTION

III.4.11-17 (E433-439; T285-295). Knowledge (*vidyā*) alone is the cause of achieving the goals of mankind (*puruṣārtha*).

Objection (by Jaimini) : Knowledge of the Self cannot by itself produce anything; it is supportive of sacrificial action that may have the results wished for. Thus the passages (in scripture) that appear to say that knowledge has fruits must be taken as *arthavāda*, praise of instruments supportive of actions with beneficial results. Several passages are cited in support of Jaimini's interpretation.

Answer (III.4.8 *et passim*) : Since the Upaniṣads teach a Self (=Brahman) different from the embodied self, they cannot be understood as merely *arthavādas*, as they might if the self taught were just the transmigrating self. Furthermore, knowledge of the Highest Self not only does not support action, it undermines it, for when one realizes Brahman the entire world in which action must take place is destroyed. And since it is *saṃnyāsins*, who no longer work, who have the knowledge in question, that knowledge can hardly be subservient to action.

III.4.18-20 (E439-442; T295-303). Jaimini thinks that the passages that appear to enjoin *saṃnyāsa* only mention that state and do not enjoin it. Bādarāyaṇa's view, on the other hand, is that *saṃnyāsa* is a state to be achieved like the other three *āśramas*.

III.4.21-25 (E443-445; T303-306). Certain other texts are interpreted, and in *sūtra* 25 the conclusion is once more drawn that sacrificial acts are not necessary for one who seeks liberation, since knowledge is what brings that about.

III.4.26-27 (E445-446; T306-309). But action is useful in helping produce knowledge, for one who seeks knowledge must be calm, disciplined, etc., and sacrificial action is propaedeutic to these states. Nevertheless, Śaṃkara insists, it is knowledge alone that brings about the desired result.

III.4.28-31 (E446-448; T309-312). *Chāndogya Upaniṣad* VI.1.2, which might be thought to relax prohibitions on certain kinds of food for the Brahman-knower, is rather an *arthavāda* glorifying the food of the "breaths." The only exception to the laws about which food to take arises when one's life is in danger.

III.4.32-35 (E448-450; T312-315). *Objection* : Since you tell us that actions are for the purpose of gaining knowledge leading to achievement of man's end (that is, liberation) it presumably follows that someone who does not desire liberation need not perform the duties of his *āśrama* ! Or if they are nevertheless duties, they cannot (as you allege) produce knowledge, because then there will be the contradiction that such an instrument is both permanently and impermanently connected with its result.

Answer : The Vedas enjoin ritual action on all *āśramins* regardless of their desire or lack of desire for release. There are two sorts of texts : one kind enjoins actions as "permanent" (*nitya*) duties of members of a certain class of persons; the other kind advises action as a means to knowledge for those who seek release—and the two kinds of texts relate to one and the same action, but that involves no contradiction.

III.4.36-39 (E450-451; T315-317). Can those who do not belong to any one of the *āśramas* still gain the releasing knowledge ? Yes, says Śaṃkara, since scripture speaks of such cases and *smṛti* does too; for example, a widower, though not belonging to an *āśrama*, can through praying, fasting, etc., gain knowledge conducive to liberation.

III.4.40-43 (E451-453; T317-320). These passages concern backsliders. In the first place, no one backslides from *saṃnyāsa*; the texts do not recognize any such thing. If one who has taken the vow of chastity carelessly breaks it he does not lose his class but, rather, must perform expiatory sacrificial acts befitting the situation. In any case these apparent backsliders should not be associated with.

III.4.44-46 (E453-454; T320-321). Concerns a question about who is to perform the subordinate meditations involved in sacrifices. The priest is, not the sacrificer.

III.4.47-49 (E454-456; T322-325). Does *Bṛhadāraṇyaka Upaniṣad* III.5 enjoin the state of being a *muni* (silent meditator) or not? "Yes," says Śaṃkara; it also enjoins achieving the other *āśramas* as well.

III.4.5 (E456-457; T325-327). The same passage (*Bṛhadāraṇyaka Upaniṣad* III.5) enjoins "being a child."

Opponent : Yes, what is enjoined is a state in which one can do whatever one likes without incurring sin, just as a *saṃnyāsin* can !

Śaṃkara : No, what is enjoined is innocence, absence of sensuality, etc.

III.4.51 (E457-458; T327-329). Do the means—meditation, sacrifice, etc.—leading to knowledge of Brahman always do so in this life, or may they have this result in a subsequent life? Śaṃkara says that unless there is some kind of obstruction the knowledge will arise in this life, but when an obstruction exists the result will arise in a subsequent life.

III.4.52 (E458-459; T329-330). Does knowledge always produce liberation as soon and in the same degree?

Śaṃkara : Well, liberation is not a result; it is a permanent state, without degrees; knowledge, also, does not admit of a higher and lower degree, at least the knowledge of *nirguṇa* Brahman, which alone leads to release.

FOURTH CHAPTER, FIRST SECTION

IV.1.1-12 (E459-472; T331-352). How to meditate is here detailed. One should repeatedly meditate on Brahman as constituting the Self.

Objection : Repetition of meditation on, for example, "that art thou" is useless : if one doesn't understand it the first time one isn't going to after countless repetitions.

Answer : But we know from experience that that isn't so; people hear something and don't always understand it the first time but eventually come to do so. Particularly in the case of such a deep truth as is conveyed by "that art thou" one must fully understand the meanings of the constituent words to be able to understand the whole sentence. Or again, the word "self" (*ātman*) has to be understood in some cases as referring both to Brahman and one's own self. When one is advised to meditate on other things (e.g., the *manas*) as Brahman (as in *Chāndogya Upaniṣad* III.18.1) one should not see Brahman in the symbol (e.g., the *manas*), but vice versa, since the purpose is to find the unity (of Brahman) in the diversity of the world Meditation should be carried on seated, not standing up or lying down; Śaṃkara cites scripture and *smṛti* (viz., *Bhagavadgītā* and Yogaśāstra) in favor. One can meditate at any time, at any place, and in any direction; any apparent restrictions on this should be viewed as suggestions and not as rules. Such meditations are to be continued until death or realization.

IV.1.13-19 (E472-478; T353-363). When one attains realization all karma disappears, including both the traces of earlier karma and the future results of one's acts, both good and bad karma. The exception to this is the result of karma that has already begun to operate (*prārabdhakarman*)—such karmic results must work themselves out in a natural manner, and knowledge has no power to affect them. This is attested by observation that the body of the realized person does not disappear immediately.

Objection : The results of permanent actions (*nityakarman*) such as performance of the *agnihotra* sacrifice, since they are different from the result of knowledge, must also disappear, as they are the results of good actions (and thus the only karma left operating after knowledge of Brahman may be bad!)

Answer : No, since these acts contribute to knowledge, as we have seen.

Objection : Then what "good karma" were you talking about before, when you said that both bad and good karma disappear upon knowledge ?

Answer : Acts undertaken to gain some specific good results; these do not contribute toward gaining knowledge of Brahman. These are in general unlike the *nityakarmans*, which as a class contribute in some fashion toward achievement of true knowledge and thus are such that their results continue to death. Now, a knower of Brahman thus has destroyed all karma except the *prārabdha* sort produced by *nityakarmans*—when at death these are exhausted the knower achieves stability in liberation (*sampadyate*).

Objection : Why does he not continue even after that to see multiplicity, just as one who knows there is only one moon may continue to see two of them despite his knowledge ?

Answer : Because there is nothing to produce such a perception—all karma has been exhausted.

Objection : But new actions will produce more karma, etc.

Answer : There will be no more actions; actions presuppose false awareness (*mithyājñāna*), but by this point that has been destroyed by right awareness (*samyagjñāna*).

FOURTH CHAPTER, SECOND SECTION

IV.2.1-21 (E478-489; T364-381). This section describes what happens to the unrealized self at death. Speech (*vāk*) is merged in *manas*; the rest of the organs follow along; the *manas* is then merged in "breath" (*prāṇa*); it is in turn merged in the *jīva*, which then comes to occupy the elements that will make up the next body. The self, whether of a person who knows *saguṇa* Brahman or of one who does not, goes out in the same way, namely, the way just described, except that, whereas the ordinary self is reborn as described above, the knower of *saguṇa* Brahman enters a vein (or artery, *nāḍi*) leading toward a relative immortality. The subtle body endures until liberation and is responsible for the warmth we feel in living bodies, which is absent in dead ones. When death after liberation occurs the subtle body dissolves—it does not depart from the body at all; the various constituents of the subtle body are absorbed into Brahman and are no longer distinct from It in any way. As for the one who knows only *saguṇa* Brahman, the texts tell us his subtle body departs through a certain vein out of the top of the skull and follows the rays of the sun—this is true of those who die at night as well as of those who die in the daytime, and for those who die in the inauspicious half of the year as well as for those who die in the auspicious half.

FOURTH CHAPTER, THIRD SECTION

IV.3.1-16 (E490-503; T382-404). The description of the progress of the knower of *saguṇa* Brahman continues. Despite different accounts in scripture about the path of the gods (*devayāna*) leading to the Brahma-world, they all refer to the same path. The stages along the path, associated with various deities, are detailed; the subtle body is guided along by these divinities, eventually reaching *saguṇa* Brahman (but not *nirguṇa* Brahman), that is, the "Brahma-world" ruled over by Hiraṇyagarbha. Jaimini's view that the Highest Brahman is thus reached is refuted—one cannot literally "go" to *nirguṇa* Brahman.

Here an opponent comes in to suggest that, if one performs no actions other than the permanent (*nitya*) ones and avoids those which are forbidden, then, because the permanent acts are supposed to have their fruition in this life, there will be no cause when one dies for any rebirth and one can thus achieve liberation without Self-knowledge. Śaṃkara refutes this by merely noting that one cannot hope to exhaust all his karma in this lifetime for even if one confines himself to *nityakarmans* the results of former acts will conflict with that of later ones and thus both cannot be worked off simultaneously, with the result that it will take time to work all of them off—meanwhile one is likely to die.

Sūtras 15-16 exclude from the ranks of those who travel the path of the gods to *brahmaloka* those who meditate upon symbols rather than on (*saguṇa*) Brahman; these persons achieve results appropriate to that on which they meditate.

FOURTH CHAPTER, FOURTH SECTION

IV.4.1-22 (E503-513; T405-419). Finally, the nature of liberation is indicated. Liberation is the self's manifesting its own nature; it does not take on any new characteristics but is nondistinct from Brahman. The views about whether the released self is omniscient, omnipotent, and pure, or is merely pure consciousness, or some combination of these, are reconciled by Śaṃkara as speaking to the question from different standpoints. *Sūtras* 8 following, which appear to grant to the released self positive powers, are viewed by Śaṃkara as referring to the knower of *saguṇa* Brahman. The truly "released self," unlike God, has nothing to do with the world of bodies, organs, etc., and so questions about power cannot arise. On the other hand, those who have attained the *brahmaloka* have all lordly powers except that of creation, which is specifically God's business. When it is said they have unlimited powers what is meant is not that they share God's power but rather that they never return into embodiment in this world.

BṚHADĀRAṆYAKOPANIṢADBHĀṢYA

The *Bṛhadāraṇyaka* is the longest and one of the oldest of the Upaniṣads. This Upaniṣad is found in two recensions, the Kāṇva and the Mādhyandina of the *White Yajurveda.*[21] The material is classified with the *Vājasaneyī Saṃhitā* and *Śatapatha Brāhmaṇa.*

There is no reason to doubt Śaṃkara's authorship of this commentary. Sureśvara's vast *Vārttika,* summarized below, develops Śaṃkara's thought as expressed here, following the master closely and shedding occasional light on the references found there. There are scholarly studies proving the authenticity of this work.[22]

Daniel Ingalls has offered some interesting comments on the relationship between this commentary and the *Brahmasūtrabhāṣya.* He writes : "Śaṃkara's *Bṛhadāraṇyakopaniṣad-bhāṣya* is a far more original piece of writing than his *Brahma-sūtra-bhāṣya,*" arguing that in the former work Śaṃkara breaks with tradition frequently, whereas in the *Brahmasūtrabhāṣya* he is "very careful not to depart from tradition."[23]

The "tradition" in question is identified by Ingalls as the work of the "Protocommentator," or Vṛttikāra, and Ingalls suggests that both Śaṃkara and the Bhedābhedavādin Bhāskara followed the Vṛttikāra, even though Bhāskara is quite outspoken in his criticism of Śaṃkara's interpretations of certain features of their common source. By comparing Śaṃkara's theses and arguments developed in the *Bṛhadāraṇyakabhāṣya* with those found in the *Brahmasūtrabhāṣya* —and especially the ones found in Bhāskara's commentary as well— one can distinguish "what is original . . . in Śaṃkara's philosophy" from what goes back to the Vṛttikāra.

The edition followed in the summary below, referred to as "E," is that by H. R. Bhagavat, and is part two of the second volume of *Works of Shankaracharya* (Poona : Ashtekar & Co., 1928). The translation ("T") is by Swami Madhavananda (Almora : Advaita Ashrama, third edition, 1950).

Introduction (E1-3; T1-8). An "*upaniṣad*" means something knowledge of which removes *saṃsāra* together with its cause, which is what this Upaniṣad does. It is large and was taught in the forest, which explains its name (*Bṛhadāraṇyaka*). Now we will explain the connection of this Upaniṣad with the *karmakāṇḍa*—the section of the Vedas concerning action. The Vedas are concerned with providing an understanding of how to obtain what is desired and avoid what is not desired, specifically an understanding of those aspects that are not available to perception or inference, that concern future lives. Thus the first requisite is that one who hears this Upaniṣad must believe that there is a self that persists through future lives; this is taught in various places throughout the Upaniṣads, including this one (at II.1.16-17).

Objection : Knowledge of future embodiments is a matter of perception.

Answer : No, since there are different opinions about it—for example, the materialists and Buddhists deny it—but nobody quarrels about a matter of perception like a pot. And since the self cannot be perceived in its future state, it cannot be known by inference either.

Anyway, if a man believes in future lives he wants to know how to maximize good and minimize bad, and the *karmakāṇḍa* tells him that; it tells him that by two kinds of actions he can improve his lot— by ritual acts he can attain the world of the fathers, and by meditation he can attain the world of the gods. But he naturally wants to remove the ignorance that is responsible for *saṃsāra*—and it is to explain this that this Upaniṣad exists.

Now the horse-sacrifice, which is the first topic here, is the most noble sacrifice of all and leads to identity with Hiraṇyagarbha. Its mention here at the outset shows that all ritual action falls within *saṃsāra*. Not even the *nityakarmans* are without their karmic residue, since scripture speaks of all ritual action collectively, showing that it is produced by desire and produces future births in this world, the world of the fathers or of the gods. Since this is the case, only knowledge of Brahman, not any actions, can gain liberation from *saṃsāra*.

I.2.1 (E6-10; T15-26). The text begins "there was nothing at all here in the beginning. It was covered over by Death . . . ." The second sentence disproves the theory that something can come from nothing—from the void or from prior absence—for then there would have been nothing for Death to cover over. So scripture disproves the *asatkāraṇa* view. Inference also disproves it : seeing that effects only take place when there is a cause, we infer that the cause of the universe too must have existed prior to creation, as in the case of a pot.

Objection : The cause of a pot does not exist prior to its production, for the lump of clay is destroyed as the pot is produced.

Answer : No, the clay (though not the lump) is the cause. The clay persists despite the lump being destroyed, as is evident from perception.

Objection : Nothing persists—we merely notice a similarity between different entities.

Answer : No, for every attribution would become nonsense, including the attribution of "being similar to *x*," if all entities were momentary; or if there were no entities, only momentary ideas based on nothing, then all ideas would be false and nothing could be established at all.

Besides, the effect exists before it is produced, for to be produced means becoming manifested to perception, and we know that a thing becomes manifested to perception which exists unilluminated and then becomes illuminated. A nonexistent jar is not manifested when the sun rises.

Objection : Since according to you the effect pre-exists, if it exists at all it must exist prior to its production, so what is to stop its manifesting itself when the sun comes up ?

Answer : There are two kinds of covering (*āvaraṇa*) : one consists of darkness or something blocking our perception of a jar, the other consists of its parts having some other form, for example, a lump of clay.

Objector : You are equivocating on "covering"; the one kind of covering (darkness, or the wall) does not occupy the same place as the jar, whereas the other kind (the clay) does.

Answer : Not always; water mixed with milk is concealed by the milk, which occupies the same place as the water.

Objector : If you are right one ought to try to make a jar by removing obstructions to it, namely, the clay. But no one makes a jar that way!

Answer : Not necessarily; when one manifests a jar one does it by lighting a lamp. And this is not just to remove darkness; it is to produce the light to illuminate the jar.

Again, the effect must pre-exist because we find people trying to produce an object in the future, and therefore we conclude they must know the object they are trying to produce.

Another argument : God and yogis have infallible knowledge about the future. Now if the future jar did not exist, their perceptions would be false.

However, there is of course a certain sense in which the effect does not exist before its production: it does not exist in its manifested form before production, only in its potential form as, say, a lump of clay. When we say the effect exists before its production we are saying it exists in potential form.

Vaiśeṣika : The prior absence (*prāgabhāva*) of the jar precedes and causes the production of the jar.

Śaṃkara : Then you must be treating prior absence, like the others of your absences, as positive entities—otherwise it could hardly be related to the jar by a causal relation.

Vaiśeṣika : Such a relation is possible with respect to two things that are inseparably related (*ayutasiddha*).

Answer : No, there cannot be inseparability between an existent and a nonexistent thing.

I.3.1 (E16-21; T41-53). Mīmāṃsaka : This section (the Udgītha section) is preface to an injunction to repeat certain *mantras*.

Answer : No, for this Upaniṣad deals with knowledge (*vidyā*). We cannot act correctly without correct knowledge; we cannot meditate properly without having correct knowledge of what we are meditating on.

Objection : No, since the scriptures direct us to look on Brahman, for example, as a name, etc., which is an error (*viparyaya*), like seeing a stump as a man.

Answer : The direction is intended for one who knows the difference between Brahman and Its name—for him there is no error in worshiping Brahman by meditating on Its name, any more than there is in worshiping God by means of images.

Objection : But in fact there is no Brahman, only a name.

Answer : No; because (1) scripture also tells us to look on the Ṛk (hymn) as the earth, and we know there are both a hymn and the earth; (2) a figurative sense presupposes a direct one—so the name "Brahman" presupposes a thing, Brahman; and (3) scripture is authoritative with regard to all supersensuous things, whether they are results of sacrifices or the existence of entities.

Opponent : Scriptural statements are only authoritative as injunctions, and so the only information they give us refers to what has to be done; so declarative statements about the existence of things do not have any authority, or at any rate they have authority only in connection with what has to be done—and Brahman has no connection with purposive action.

Answer : There are texts that make that connection. Anyhow, your rule cannot be correct, since it is the Vedas that tell us what a prohibited act leads to, and a prohibited act is not something that is to be done. One who avoids eating poisoned meat, for example, does so because he comes to know the meat is poisoned; thus, conveying information—through declarative sentences—is the way in which we are able to avoid prohibited acts. Likewise, a man who learns the nature of the Self will come to check his impulses—and it is the Vedas that convey *that* information.

Opponent : Very well, information causes us to avoid prohibited acts; but it is not the case that knowledge of the Self should cause us to stop following Vedic injunctions.

Answer : Why not? They are both alike—both eating poisoned meat and following Vedic injunctions produce results contrary to our purposes (*anartha*), and so both are stopped by the knower of the Self.

Opponent : Perhaps this is so for the (*naimittika* and *kāmya*) acts that you are thinking of, but the *nityakarmans* produce no harmful effects and shouldn't be stopped.

Answer : No, they too are enjoined on persons subject to *avidyā*, passion, and aversion. And anyway, a rite such as the *agnihotra* is not by nature either *kāmya* or *nitya*. It depends on the purpose of the sacrificer—if he wants one kind of outcome—heaven—it is *kāmya*, if he merely acts out of natural desire to do good and avoid evil, it is *nitya*. But the Self-knower is not enjoined to any acts at all, for that requires obliteration of the cause of all acts, namely, awareness of their means. If one thinks he is Brahman—unlimited in space, time, etc.—he cannot act.

Objection : Well, he has to eat !

Answer : Yes, but that is not like a *nityakarman*—eating is not supposed to be compulsory; it is irregular, not enjoined at any particular time.

Objection : Nevertheless scripture does regulate eating.

Answer : It regulates what can be eaten, etc., but these are not injunctions to act or incentives to action, and so they do not impede knowledge.

I.4.7 (E44-55; T111-140). The Upaniṣad is speaking of Virāj or the cosmic Puruṣa and its creation, the universe, and it says at this point "He entered into it," that is, the universe. Śaṃkara says "He" is the Self, who has entered into all bodies "from Hiraṇyagarbha down to a blade of grass."

Objection : If the Self is the universe how can It "enter into" it? Only a finite thing can enter into a space, but an unlimited thing, like *ākāśa*, cannot enter into anything because, being omnipresent, it is already there. And further, if It somehow did so It must be subject to *saṃsāra* and be subject to frustration, etc.

A number of replies to these conundrums are considered and rejected.

With respect to the possibility of the Self's being subject to frustration, Śaṃkara denies it. When the opponent then tries to conclude that if there is only one Self and It is not frustrated there is nothing left to be frustrated and so any knowledge one might get from scripture would be useless, Śaṃkara counters with the tale of the tenth man (keeping track of a group of ten, the leader counts only nine until reminded that *he* is the tenth).

As for the problem about the Self's entering itself, Śaṃkara eventually explains this using the analogy of reflection. Just as the sun "enters into" the water in the sense of being perceived there because of its reflection, so the Self enters into the undifferentiated universe in the sense of being perceived in the differentiated universe by the differentiated *jīvas*.

The Upaniṣad goes on to say "the Self alone is to be meditated upon." Is this an initial injunction (*apūrvavidhi*)? Some say it must be, since the text has in fact just said "He . . . does not know (the Self)," and the next sentence—the one now considered—must therefore enjoin us to meditate for the first time on something hitherto unknown. The case is similar for injunctions to act—illustrations are offered.

Śaṃkara : But there is nothing to be done; therefore it is not an initial injunction. Knowledge of the Self is conveyed in the very sentence under discussion; the sentence is itself the knowledge that is supposed to be enjoined. Now an injunction cannot itself be the very act it enjoins. Therefore this sentence merely removes ignorance about the Self; it does not enjoin any further action such as meditation, for such action is impossible once Self-knowledge is gained.

Objection : The knowledge gained from hearing this passage isn't sufficient to obliterate awareness of everything other than Brahman. A person does not know the Self merely on hearing a statement about its nature; he must be enjoined to do so.

Answer : But he's already gained the knowledge just from hearing it !

Objection : The recollection of Self-knowledge is different from the awareness arising from hearing it stated, and it is this recollection that is enjoined.

Answer : No, for recollection comes automatically. Since Self-knowledge destroys ignorance immediately, memories of the objects known when one was subject to ignorance automatically disappear; all that is left is Self-knowledge.

Objection : Then it is suppression (*nirodha*) that is enjoined, this being different from the knowledge conveyed in the texts. Suppression is prescribed in another system (viz., Yoga).

Answer : But scripture does not indicate that suppression is a means to liberation; it only indicates Self-knowledge is that. Besides, there is no way of suppressing other than Self-knowledge. Then again, once Self-knowledge is gained there is no expectation (*ākāṃkṣā*) about details—what act is required, how to perform it, what to use, etc.—since no further effort is required.

Objection : Being a mere declaration, the sentences (e.g., "that art thou," etc., apparently including the one under discussion) that you hold to vouchsafe knowledge are not authoritative, any more than those ("Fire cried") that merely narrate an event.

Answer : Authority is contingent, not upon the mood of the verb, but on whether or not the passage speaks the truth.

Now, although "the Self alone is to be meditated upon" is not an initial injunction it is nevertheless true that it is a kind of injunction, namely, a restrictive (*niyama*) one, for it does limit the Self-knower to recollection of his knowledge : this is because even after Self-knowledge the residues of *prārabdhakarman* are still operative and so might obscure once again the knowledge gained from hearing a text. So the Self-knower is enjoined to think only on the Self.

I.4.10 (E57-68; T145-172). Two views about who the Brahman is who became all as a result of knowledge (according to this passage): one, it must be the lower Brahman (*brahmāpara*), since effort on its part is indicated and the Highest Brahman is incapable of effort (commentators say this is the Vṛttikāra); two, it must be Brahmins who are referred to, men who attain identity with Brahman (commentators say this is Bhartṛprapañca).

Śaṃkara : Neither of these views is correct, since in each case the identity with all would be noneternal. And since it is eternal, everybody is already identical with all, and the supposition otherwise is due to *avidyā*; therefore it is the Highest Brahman who is spoken of here, who was conditioned by *avidyā* and then uncovered.

Objection : It is improper to suppose that *avidyā* conditions Brahman.

Answer : No, since otherwise it would not be necessary to know Brahman; if there were no superimposition (*adhyāropa*) of *avidyā* on Brahman knowledge of unity would not have been enjoined.

Objector : We mean that Brahman cannot be supposed to be the cause of superimposition, the creator of *avidyā*.

Śaṃkara : That's right. But one should not suppose that therefore something else is the cause of superimposition or the creator of *avidyā*.

Objector : Then scripture will be useless.

Answer : It is, for one who knows the truth.

Objection : But it is also useless to know the truth.

Answer : No, since it removes ignorance.

Objection : But, since Brahman is one, removal of ignorance is impossible.

Śaṃkara : Since it is evident that knowledge of unity does remove ignorance, it cannot very well be impossible !

Objection : It is even impossible that you can say "that is impossible" !

Answer : But you see—I just did !

Objection : From various scriptural texts, from the authority of various systems of philosophy, for example, of Kaṇāda and Gautama, from the fact that everyone speaks of first seeking and then gaining liberation, and because of the difference between action and knowledge being inappropriate for God, the individual self must be different from God. So it is proper to understand the word "Brahman" in this text as denoting someone who aspires to be Brahman.

Answer : Then the transmigrating self is supposed to be liberated by knowing himself, falsely, to be Brahman—and for this scriptural authority is not necessary !

Objector : The identity texts actually counsel a kind of meditation (*sampat*) based on the resemblance (of the individual self) with

Brahman, to be practised by one who knows Brahman fully (and knows It to be different from the transmigrating self).

Śaṃkara : But then why do the scriptures repeatedly assert the identity of the Self with Brahman? If the Self and Brahman are different they cannot be made identical by meditation or by scripture or by anything else. Further, if the knowledge counseled is knowledge of the individual self and not of Brahman, why is it termed "knowledge of Brahman"?

Objector : Suppose we say that "Self" in these passages refers to Brahman and not to the individual self.

Śaṃkara : But the texts explicitly say "I am Brahman," etc. If your assumption were correct they should say "That is Brahman," etc. And a thing can't be both Brahman and not Brahman; to speak in that way merely incurs doubt and does evil thereby.

The text says "It [Brahman] knew only Itself"—that is, Its natural (*svābhāvika*) state. The opponent presses Śaṃkara for a specification of the intrinsic character of this natural Self. Śaṃkara identifies this character as the property of being the seer of sight, the hearer of hearing, etc.

Objector : Surely the seer, whether of sight or of a jar, is the same?

Śaṃkara : No. The seer of sight is identical with sight and is eternal, whereas the seer of the jar is transitory, for jars come and go. There are in fact two kinds of sight (*dṛṣṭi*). One kind is well known to us; it is the transitory kind, as is shown by the fact of blindness in certain people—if the eternal sight were the only kind everyone would have vision. But there is also the eternal fact of consciousness, without which the blind man could not have visions in his dreams, etc. So the text means that Brahman knew only Itself, eternal consciousness, without the transitory, noneternal consciousness superimposed on It.

Objector : But in III.4.2 we are told "One should not try to know the knower of knowledge," so such knowledge as you say Brahman had is self-contradictory.

Śaṃkara : No, since the knowledge of the Self, which Brahman had, does not involve taking the Self as a content (*viṣaya*)—Self-knowledge is just the cessation of *avidyā*, nothing else.

The one who knows Brahman becomes all; even the gods cannot prevail against him—so the text goes on to say. Why should one even suppose the gods had such a power? Because the gods depend on men for ritual support, etc., and fearing that by liberation they would lose that support they may try to hinder liberation.

Objection : If gods can do that, they can also obstruct the good outcome of sacrificing, etc., and then men would become doubtful about the worth of ritual action.

Śaṃkara : No. Everything comes from its appropriate cause; nothing happens from its own nature (*svabhāva*) alone. The good outcome of actions is a result of karma; though gods or God or time or whatever may be auxiliaries in the process, they cannot disturb the karmic mechanism's eventual fruition, although they may temporarily delay it. In the case of Self-knowledge they cannot even do that, since the removal of *avidyā* upon knowledge of the Self is automatic and instantaneous, involving no spatial, temporal, or causal relations with which the gods can tamper.

Objection : Surely it is the stream (*saṃtati*) of consciousness that removes *avidyā*.

Śaṃkara : No, since such a stream can contain thoughts of self-preservation (*jīvana*), etc.

Objector : Well, let's suppose that a stream unmixed with untoward thoughts extending up to death is what liberates.

Śaṃkara : No, for that would make the meaning of the scriptures indefinite, which is not right. We would not be able to tell whether it was the first stream (after the initial moment of Self-knowledge), or the last stream (prior to death) that was the liberating one.

Anyway, the initial Self-knowledge liberates despite the persistence of effects of an opposite nature. What Self-knowledge destroys are the results of past actions that have not yet begun to bear fruit, as well as the potentiality of producing more karmic results in the future. What it does *not* destroy are those results that are responsible for the present body and which have not spent themselves yet, though they have begun to; these (*prārabdha*) results require false notions and faults in order that they be worked off, but only so much as is required will be experienced and no more. Actually, even these false notions are merely memories due to impressions laid down at a time prior to realization; a man of Self-knowledge cannot really entertain false ideas, for there is no content possible for them. A false idea is one of something having a property similar to something else for which it is mistaken, for example, of shell as silver. Just as one who has properly perceived the shell cannot really have false ideas about it, just so one who has realized the Self cannot really have false ideas that something not-Self, for example, the body, is the Self.

II.1.20 (E115-127; T291-318). The Upaniṣadic text says that the secret name (*upaniṣat*) of *ātman*, the self, is "truth of truth."

Question : Is the "self" referred to here the individual transmigrating self, or is it the Supreme Self, Brahman? If these selves are different then the texts that teach their identity are false, and if they are identical there will be no one for the Vedas to instruct, so they will be useless.

One view is this : The self meant cannot be Brahman, for the preceding Upaniṣadic texts in this section have been speaking of the individual self, which wakes, dreams, and sleeps. So the suggestion must be that the individual self is what is under discussion here, a self that creates a world of experience when waking or dreaming and knowledge of which liberates in deep sleep. There is no transcendent Self or Brahman.

A second view is this : The transcendent Supreme Self created the universe, not the transmigrating self, which is different from it. It is by worshiping this transcendent Self that one attains liberation, not by identifying oneself with It.

Śaṃkara : Neither view is correct. The individual self is identical with the transcendent Supreme Self, as the text declares.

Objection : Then either the Vedic teachings become useless or else the transcendent Self loses its transcendence, being infected by the frustrations, etc., of the transmigrating self.

One possible solution to this : The Supreme Self underwent a modification (*vikāra*) before becoming the individual self (*vijñānātman*), so that the individual self is both the same as and different from the Supreme Self. Thus the difficulty cited can be avoided.

Critique of this : There are at least three ways in which the individual self might be a modification of the Supreme Self. One, it may be a modification of a part of Brahman, supposing Brahman has parts, or two, the Supreme Self may retain Its form but a part of It be modified, like hair; or three, the whole Supreme Self may be modified, like milk. On view one, the scripturally affirmed identity between the self and the Self could only be at best figurative, since the Self will be just an aggregate of Its parts. On two, since the whole inheres in its parts anything that affects a part will affect the whole, so that the Supreme Self will become subject to evil. View three is also wrong, being explicitly denied by both scripture and *smṛti*.

Another suggestion : The individual self is a part of the Highest Self as a spark of fire is a part of the fire. Scripture speaks in this way.

Critique of that : Then the Supreme Self must be wounded, which is contrary to scripture. The passages you have in mind, about sparks, are not meant literally but are intended to suggest the unity of the Self. In all the Upaniṣads, unity is first proposed (*pratijñāta*), then by reasons (*hetu*) and examples (*dṛṣṭānta*) the world (*jagat*) is shown to be a part or modification of the Highest Self, and then unity is offered as conclusion (*upasaṃhṛti*). So it is here. The illustration of sparks of fire is sometimes used, as in the story told by earlier proponents of our tradition (*sampradāyavid*; commentators say the reference is to Draviḍācārya) about the fowler's son who, learning that he was actually a prince and realizing his unity with royalty, gave up a fowler's duties and took on royal ways. Likewise, they say, the individual self, separated from the Supreme Self like a spark of fire, takes on worldly attributes, but when it learns of its identity with the Supreme Self it loses those attributes. Here again, the analogy of sparks is meant as illustration of unity.

The Supreme Self is intrinsically invisible, hence without parts; so a part of It cannot become the individual self. And if you say that the individual self is a part because of the imposition of some adjunct or obstruction, as the *ākāśa* enclosed in a jar is a part of the great *ākāśa*, then discriminating people would never think that the self is a part of the Self, since it would appear as something quite distinct. So any such notions about the self's difference from the Self are erroneous (*bhrānta*).

Question : If all Upaniṣads teach only the single Supreme Self, why is there any reference to the individual self at all?

Some say : It is so that the *karmakāṇḍa* or ritual portion of scripture will have purport—if there were no one to sacrifice, etc., that section of scripture would be pointless. Indeed, this is why only the *karmakāṇḍa* portion of the Vedas is authoritative: the Upaniṣads are not authoritative, for in order to make sense of them one must interpret them figuratively.

Answer : We have already answered this. A *pramāṇa* is what leads to valid knowledge; since the Upaniṣads lead to valid knowledge they are authoritative. Furthermore, the Upaniṣads do not contradict themselves, as you imply. Nor are they even ambiguous. First, they do not say that Brahman both is and is not unitary; second, they never contradict the unity of Brahman.

Although you've charged that the Upaniṣads undermine the authority of the *karmakāṇḍa* of the Vedas, it is not so, since they speak of a different thing, namely, the unity of Brahman; they do not negate directions about how to act meant for someone who wants something, etc.; these passages about action are all absolutely correct.

Objection : But if Brahman is the only real thing, the passages about action have nothing to apply to, and so they certainly cannot lead to valid knowledge.

Answer : But it is evident to perception that injunctive passages are about something; since your argument (that their authority is undermined by absence of a real object) stems from inference it must bow to perception. What they are about are things created out of *avidyā*, unreal but the topic of these passages nevertheless.

Objection : But only those who have correct knowledge (*vidyā*) are capable of (successful) action.

Answer : No, quite the contrary; those who have knowledge are incapable of performing actions, as we have shown.

Still other pundits, following their own ways of thinking, argue against us that if Brahman is the only real thing perception is contradicted—since we see different sights, hear many sounds, etc.—and that it also contradicts inference, for example, from the fact of differences in karmic results to a difference in the selves who earned those results—and even that it contradicts scriptural passages that imply that things desired are distinct from those who desire them. To them we reply as follows :

These are the lowest among Brahmins and other castes who, having minds poisoned by bad reasoning, hold views contrary to tradition about the meaning of the Vedas. First, as to perception : does the fact that many sounds are perceived contradict the unity of *ākāśa* ? If not, the fact that many selves are perceived does not contradict the unity of Brahman. Second, as to inference : we ask them, "who are you who do the inferring ?" Suppose they say "we (Naiyāyikas), the experts in logic," and we reply, "but who are you really who call yourselves so ?" Suppose now they say, "evidently we are an aggregation of self, body, organs, and mind." We wish to point out that they have already assumed themselves multiple, that is, they do not know the self they are making inferences about, that "self" they claim is joined with body, mind, and organs. For between one such self and another—on their own view—there is no intrinsic difference, so the differences that they infer exist between the selves are actually accidental differences owing to differences among adjuncts. And indeed no intrinsic differences can be inferred in the Self, for the Self is not a content of inference at all—anything that can be a content of inference is *ipso facto* not the Self—and of course we admit the Self is different from all contents of awareness, all of which is name-and-form. The contention about scripture is answered in the same fashion.

The argument (offered more than once above) that if there is only one Brahman there will be no one to receive the Vedic teachings has no force. If you mean that once Brahman has been realized the Upaniṣads and the rest of scripture will have no use, we agree readily;

on the other hand, if you mean that before realization the scripture has no use, this will contradict the assumption of anyone who believes in the Self at all, including yourselves, since you believe there are selves !

II.3.6 (E134-138; T337-346). This is the famous "not this, not this" (*neti neti*) passage; it begins, according to Śaṃkara, with several characterizations of the subtle body, then contrasts that subtle body with Brahman by indicating that Brahman can only be described negatively, as it were.

Here some other "Upaniṣadists" (commentators say Bhartṛprapañca) argue as follows : the gross and subtle elements are the lowest, the Highest Self is the highest, and in between is a third kind of entity, one that is a combination of the individual self, the agent and experiencer, with its knowledge, actions, and previous awareness. They try to find a middle ground between Sāṃkhya and Vaiśeṣika; although the actions are the cause and the body and organs the effect, these same actions are maintained in that portion of the Highest Self (corresponding to Vaiśeṣika's *ātman*) which becomes conditioned by these actions whose origins are in the elements. This conditioned self is then the agent—experiencer, subject to bondage and liberation, but the actions and ignorance that bind it are adventitious only to that part of the Highest Self, which is not affected by it any more than the earth as a whole is affected by a desert covering part of it.

These philosophers do not see that their theory is contrary to the Upaniṣads as well as to good reasoning, as we have argued previously. The Highest Self cannot have parts; either the individual self is different from or identical with the Highest Self. If it is said to be only figuratively identical, then it can't be held that impressions or ignorance (belonging to the subtle body) somehow qualify that "portion" of the Highest Self. The theory that Brahman has three forms doesn't agree with the text that assigns two forms to It.

How is it that by the expression "not this, not this" the truth of truth is to be described ? Words convey their meanings by relating to adjuncts such as name, form, action, genus, species, quality, etc. Brahman has none of these, so it cannot be described as a cow can be. To be sure, Brahman is sometimes described by expressions such as "knowledge, bliss, Brahman, Ātman", etc., but if we wish to describe its true nature it is impossible. Thus we are reduced to "not this, not this," eliminating all positive characteristics that might be thought to apply to it.

III.2 (E169-170; T429-432). What is this "death" that a liberated man is said (in the text) to be free from? It is the functioning of organs toward their objects, as the Upaniṣad states in those passages (e.g., III.2.2,3,7) that speak of the senses (*graha*)—mind, nose, speech, etc.—and their objects (*atigraha*)—respectively, desires, odors, names, etc. And we have argued previously that what causes bondage cannot be the cause of its cessation.

Some, though, think that everything leads to the cessation of bondage, that we are relatively liberated each time we die, and that everything is therefore a form of death until duality ends, when one really transcends death.

But this is not the view of the *Bṛhadāraṇyaka Upaniṣad*, whose point is that the texts teaching identity provide knowledge that negates all action, not that the injunctions to act are themselves the means of understanding that identity.

Objection : Identity is the purpose of Vedic injunctions, but *saṃsāra* follows automatically from them, just as, when a lamp is lighted to illuminate a certain object everything thereabouts is illuminated also.

Answer : No, for if the Vedic actions have only identity as their purpose there is no evidence to show that bondage follows automatically. Both identity and *saṃsāra* cannot be conveyed by the same sentence; this would be contrary to a proper theory of meaning.

III.2.13 (E174-175; T442-446). Some (commentators say Bhartṛprapañca) say that even when the organs and their objects are destroyed one is not yet liberated—one finds a mediate stage called *apavarga*, after which meditation has to be practiced in order to gain final liberation.

Śaṃkara : But how, on that view, could such a disembodied man, lacking any organs, manage to meditate? It must be, rather, that the man retains his organs and body but turns away from the world to meditate on the Supreme Self. But then he cannot use the same means both to attain an intermediate state of heavenly enjoyment and eventually to gain final release, for one activity cannot produce two opposite results. Finally, if the idea is that after the death of the body he attains the state of heavenly enjoyment and then, with his organs destroyed and being name only, is qualified for attainment of final release (somehow), the result will be that the Vedas cannot teach identity to ordinary folk, because for them it will be meaningless; only those who have reached the intermediate stage will be capable of knowing the identity that gives final release.

III.3 (E175-180; T447-459). The purpose of this section is to show that no matter how excellent action is it cannot lead to liberation.

Some say : Disinterested action combined with *vidyā* can give rise to a different kind of effect (from action), just as poison or curd can (produce effects different from their usual one under certain circumstances).

Answer : No, for liberation has no origin (*anārabhya*); it is not an effect at all; but the destruction of bondage. And we have said that bondage is just *avidyā*, which cannot be destroyed by action, since actions only function with respect to contents that are visible. In other words, actions can produce or obtain or modify or purify something, but they have no other functions.

Opponent : Yes, action by itself is like that, but our point is that combined with *vidyā* it can produce something different.

Śaṃkara : None of the *pramāṇas* give evidence of such an outcome.

Opponent : Well, injunctions to act must be supposed to have an expected outcome (for the action enjoined); in the Viśvajit sacrifice, since no other outcome is mentioned, that outcome should be supposed to be liberation; otherwise no one will act.

Śaṃkara : In the case of the Viśvajit sacrifice the assumption is that heaven is the outcome—and so it should be in general. You can't use an analogy to prove the opposite of what it shows. And you can't very well say that liberation is not a result at all, since that is *our* position.

Opponent : Well, it is like knowledge—although liberation is not produced by knowledge it is said to be so produced. In the same way, our position is that actions "produce" liberation, as it were.

Śaṃkara : No. *Avidyā* is what must be destroyed for liberation to ensue, and only knowledge, not actions, can destroy *avidyā*. A thing destroys what is opposite to it in nature. Now the nature of *avidyā* is nonmanifestation (*anabhivyakti*), so what destroys it is that which has the opposite nature, manifestation, and that is knowledge, not action.

Opponent : Then we shall suppose that action has an unseen (*adṛṣṭa*) power to destroy *avidyā*.

Śaṃkara : It is unreasonable to suppose so when we know something that is seen to destroy *avidyā*.

Opponent : Our position is that the *nityakarmans* must produce liberation, since there is nothing else they can be supposed to produce, it having been specifically excluded that they produce the same kinds of results as the other acts (e.g., heaven, children, etc.).

Śaṃkara : You cannot reason in that fashion, for the kinds of results that might accrue to these acts are infinite, and you have no reason to exclude all of them. The desires and purposes of human beings are indefinite in number. Besides, the results of actions are, as we have said, either the production, attainment, modification, or purification of something, and liberation is none of these. Since it is eternal, it cannot be produced, attained, or modified, and it is surely not something that becomes purified as a sacrificial post might be.

Now we do not deny that, like poison or curds, actions combined with *vidyā* can produce a different effect from actions not so combined, but the results must still be the kinds of things forthcoming from actions, no matter how exalted.

III.4.2 (E184-186; T469-473). The Upaniṣadic passage is the famous one in which Yājñavalkya argues "you cannot see the seer of seeing, you cannot hear the hearer of hearing, etc."

Śaṃkara comments here that there are two kinds of "seeing" (*dṛṣṭi*), an ordinary (*laukika*) and a higher (*pāramārthika*) kind. The ordinary kind involves the internal organ (*antaḥkaraṇa*) combined with the visual organ and is an act, with a beginning and an end. But the higher kind is the very nature of the Witness-Self and has no beginning and no end. Even the distinction of Witness and ordinary vision is a result of adjuncts—ordinary vision is an adjunct. Now ordinary vision displays the colors, etc. of its contents; although it is a reflection of the higher kind that higher kind does not appear as the content of ordinary vision. That is what Yājñavalkya means, that ordinary vision does not display the inner Self, which is the Witness of that ordinary vision.

Others (commentators say Bhartṛprapañca) explain the passage in a different way. They think the expression "seer" means that which sees, the agent of the act of seeing. But that interpretation makes the words "of seeing" redundant, and this makes for a faulty reading. Besides, as we have argued elsewhere the resulting theory is inconsistent with other passages in the text.

III.5.1 (E187-198; T474-491). Yājñavalkya is now dealing with the question of Kahola, who wants a clear account of *ātman*. Some (commentators say Bhartṛprapañca) say that the question concerns the individual self, not the Highest Self, but Śaṃkara rejects this : the answer to this question goes beyond the answer to the previous one in that it makes clear that the Supreme Self is beyond the properties of *saṃsāra* such as hunger, etc.

Question : How can the very same self both have and lack a property like hunger ?

Answer : We have already explained that. It is like a snake, a piece of silver, and the blue color that arise through ignorance in a rope, a shell, and the sky respectively, even though they are contrary in nature to their substrata.

Objection : But the Upaniṣads say that the Highest Self is "one without a second" and "there is no difference in It."

Answer : Those statements are quite true. They stem from the highest standpoint (*paramārthadṛṣṭi*), for then name-and-form (*nāmarūpa*) cease to be separate from their locus, just like the foam on the ocean. But from the standpoint of ordinary vision, since Brahman has not been discriminated from its adjuncts like body and organs—which were produced from (by ?) name-and-form, there is the common experience (*vyavahāra*) of the existence of all sorts of distinct reals (*vastu*). Indeed, this experience, though false, is found alike in those who believe that those things do not exist as different from Brahman and those who do not believe so. But those who believe in the highest truth, though they discuss the question in accordance with scriptural passages concerning it, are confident that Brahman is one alone, without a second, free from all experiencings (*sarvavyavahāraśūnya*).

The remainder of the Upaniṣadic passage dwells on the behavior of the Self-knower, who is said to lead the life of a *bhikṣu*, renouncing all kinds of desires. Śaṃkara takes this to involve giving up the holy thread and quotes various authorities concerning the way of life of the mendicant, defending the literal reading of such passages.

Vidyā and *avidyā* cannot coexist in the same person, being contradictory like light and darkness. Therefore the knower of the Self should not have anything to do with the contents of *avidyā*, namely, actions, their means, and results. Even such objects as the holy thread fall within these "contents." The text means to emphasize that all desires are the same and should be shunned *in toto* by the Self-knower.

III.9.28.7 (E222-224; T563-568). As a kind of postscript to this section Śaṃkara introduces a discussion of the meaning of the word 'bliss" (*ānanda*) as applied to Brahman. "Bliss" is in common parlance a synonym for pleasure or for a kind of pleasure. Now some scriptural texts say that bliss is to be known as Brahman, whereas others imply that no attributes of Brahman can be known.

One disputant argues that Brahman is bliss, but since It is consciousness as well It cognizes Its own bliss, and since liberated selves are essentially Brahman they cognize it too.

Śaṃkara : No, since cognizing something requires a body and organs, which are lacking in liberation, which is (here) final separation of the body (*śarīraviyogo hi mokṣa ātyantikaḥ*). Also if Brahman could cognize Itself It would contradict Brahman's unity. So it is not that Brahman knows Itself as bliss; Brahman *is* bliss, no doubt, but that bliss is not cognized; the happiness of the liberated self is merely a natural manifestation of his state, not a cognition.

IV.3.6 (E235-239; T601-608). The passage says that the Self is the immaterial inner light that helps the body and organs to operate when external sources of light (sun and moon) are inoperative.

Objection (by a materialist): Since we know that the body and senses are helped to act by the light of material bodies like the sun and moon, it is wrong to infer that in their absence there is an immaterial body giving off light, since only things of the same type help each other. The only light that can be inferred, therefore, is that "light" which is the visual organ, which is material. You also argue that that which reveals a thing is different in kind from it, but that inference is faulty, since we see that, for example, the eye reveals the body but is not different from it, both being material. We see that the aggregate of body and senses is quite capable of seeing, etc., so we infer that it is this aggregate that is the self, the agent of the acts of seeing, etc.

Answer : This theory cannot explain the fact that in our dreams we only see things that we have already seen. If the aggregate of body and senses were the seer it could see anything in dream: blind men could see things never known to them when they had eyes, etc. Likewise, in memory we can close our eyes and recall what we have seen previously; what is shut can't be the seer—the seer is that which sees what it saw when the eyes were open. Finally, on your view a dead man should be able to see, since he has body and organs.

Objector : Let us say that the organs alone are the seers, then.

Answer : No, for then one could not know that one is touching the same thing one sees, since the agents of the two sensations would be different.

Objector : Then the seer is the *manas*.

Answer : No, since the *manas* is a content of cognition, like color, etc. and so cannot be the cognizer of contents.

As for your argument that what helps something to act must be of the same type as that something, there is no such regularity—sometimes it is one way, sometimes another. Sometimes men are helped by their own species, sometimes by animals.

IV.3.7 (E239-248; T609-629). The passage begins by asking "which is the self?" and answers that it is the *puruṣa*, made of *vijñāna*, the light within the heart, among the *prāṇas*, that it, being like (*samana*), moves between two worlds, thinking and shaking as it were, and that, being dream (*svapna*) it goes beyond (*atikramati*) this world with its forms of death.

Śaṃkara : "being like . . . . " what? Being like the *buddhi*, which is what is meant by the word "heart." So the *buddhi* is illumined by the self, and we cannot distinguish the two, since light is pure and assumes the image of what it illumines. This is why all beings constantly superimpose the one on the other with constructions (*vikalpa*). So the self, assuming the likeness of the *buddhi*, moves constantly between this world and the next by constant births and deaths, appearing to think and move ("shake"). To show that the self is pure light and that *saṃsāra* does not pertain to it in its natural state the text adds that the self can transcend the waking world in dreams, which shows that it is not dependent on the body and organs, etc.

Objection (by a Buddhist) : There is no self distinct from the *buddhi* and revealing it, for the only evidence we have from perception or inference is of one kind of conscious entity (*dhī*), and nothing attests a second kind. Actually the contents of consciousness just are consciousness, it reveals itself; there is nothing other than consciousness.

Śaṃkara : This is the (Buddhist) view. Some of them hold that consciousness (*vijñāna*) is pure and momentary, untainted by any duality between grasped and grasper (*grāhyagrāhaka*), whereas the Mādhyamikas go even further and hold that both consciousness and external objects are simply void. So some (Buddhists) believe in external objects (*bāhyārtha*) and others do not. To those who do we reply that a pot is not self-luminous—when it is in the dark it does not illumine itself.

Objection : But a lamp does!

Śaṃkara : No, since a lamp, like a jar, requires something else to reveal it even though it, unlike the jar, is luminous.

Objector : The difference is that the jar requires a light to reveal it, whereas a lamp, being self-luminous, does not require another light.

Śaṃkara : No, both are alike revealed by consciousness. For something to be "revealed" (*avabhāsa*) requires that we notice some difference in it in the presence or absence of the revealer; thus what is revealed must be capable of being present or absent to its revealer. But the lamp cannot be absent to itself, so it cannot be its own revealer. Now both the lamp and the jar can be present or absent to their common revealer, consciousness. And this consciousness must, by analogy with other cases, be something distinct from what is revealed. Further, since that consciousness (of lamp or pot) is itself revealed, there must be another consciousness that reveals it, and that consciousness is the Self.

Objector : That will produce an infinite regress.

Śaṃkara : No, the regress would only follow if we adopted as a principle that when A reveals B there must be a different thing C that reveals A. This principle is not generally true, since, for example, the eye, which reveals the lamp that reveals the jar, does not require any other external revealer. Thus since there are counterexamples to the principle we cannot assume it in general, and no regress results.

New objection : There are no external objects like jar or lamp apart from consciousness (*vijñāna*), since we never find them apart from consciousness. In this respect they are like dream objects, which are universally accepted as nothing but consciousness because they are not perceived apart from dream consciousness. Likewise, since the jar, lamp, etc., are not perceived apart from waking consciousness we draw the analogous conclusion. Thus the previous discussion is beside the point.

Śaṃkara : You must admit external objects in some sense, since you suppose that different words like "jar," "lamp," and "consciousness" mean different things. If you didn't suppose there were different things to be meant these words would have to be viewed by you as synonymous, and Buddhist scriptures would have to be condemned as useless—debates would be impossible, etc. Since you admit dream consciousness to be real you must admit that its contents, the things we dream of, are distinct from consciousness, whether you wish to term them "real" or "unreal."

The Buddhist also objects to our view of a permanent Self (=consciousness) because of his doctrine of momentariness. But that doctrine is disproved by the fact that we recognize, for example, a jar to be the same jar as the one seen earlier.

Objector : That recognition is due to similarity (*sādṛśya*), as when we "recognize" hair, fingernails, etc., that have been cut and have grown again.

Śaṃkara : No, your example conflicts with your thesis of momentariness. And anyway, it is an inadequate analogy. When we see hair, nails, etc., that have grown again we do not recognize them as the identical hair, nails, etc.; we only see that these things are the same kind of thing. But in the case of recognizing a jar we see that it is the identical jar. Furthermore, on your doctrine it would not be possible to perceive similarity, since to do that something must persist long enough to perceive two things at different times and to see that they are similar.

Objector : We hold that a single chain-like perception (*eka . . . śṛṅkhalavatpratyaya*) includes both the preceding and the later perceptions.

Śaṃkara : This is inconsistent with the doctrine of momentariness. Further, on your view consciousness is self-conscious (*svasaṃvedya*) only, unwitnessed by anything else; this being the case it cannot be viewed as having parts, being transitory, frustrating, void, etc., unless it is that way in its pure state, in which case liberation will be impossible, purification of consciousness being out of the question. You may say that impurity enters consciousness when the grasper-grasped distinction qualifies it—but, if consciousness is the only thing there is, nothing occasions the grasper-grasped distinction and so again either it is natural to consciousness or it cannot arise there consistently with your view. Finally, there being no persisting self you cannot talk of consciousness as the highest end of life, since it is extinguished upon death.

IV.3.9 (E249-251; T631-636). This passage explains the mechanism of dreaming. Dream is said to be the third state, between this world and the next, in which one experiences the results of past karma and glimpses the results of future actions. In dreams the self, tinged by the impressions of his present waking life, "puts the body aside" by making it unconscious through exhausting some of its karma and creates a dream body (*nirmāṇa*) comprised of past impressions (*vāsanā*) as the consequence of past deeds; the impressions are then illuminated as contents (*viṣaya*) by the self's "own light," that is, by consciousness, and so the self becomes as if the subject of those contents as objects, but actually free from contact with elements (*bhūta*) and their accompaniments (*bhautika*), both external and internal.

IV.3.22 (E265-266; T669-672). Some (commentators say Bhartṛprapañca) hold that desires (*kāma*) and impressions (*vāsanā*) tinge the self and the *buddhi* "as the scent of flowers in the oil in which they have been boiled." The arguments of Vaiśeṣikas and other systems are adduced to support this.

Śaṃkara : The arguments of other systems—Vaiśeṣika, etc.—contradict scripture and thus are fallacious. Furthermore, if desires and impressions inhere in the self they cannot be known as its contents, just as the eye cannot see its own qualities.

IV.3.23 (E266-268; T673-676). The question here is : why doesn't the self "see" in the state of deep sleep, if it is naturally conscious ? How can a thing be conscious by nature and not know ? This puzzle is discussed at some length. The solution Śaṃkara gives is that though the self is eternally conscious, in deep sleep there is no content, because in deep sleep the internal organ, senses, etc., are unified with the Highest Self.

IV.3.30 (E269-270; T678-682). Śaṃkara here defends the above interpretation against an alternative one, which has the text saying that the Self is both one and many (commentators say this is Bhartṛprapañca again), so that perception, etc., are different from one another and yet identical with the Self. Śaṃkara's answer is, first, that this is not what it is intended to prove, and, second, that the view is unacceptable. The apparent diversity among perceptions is due to adjuncts, just as a naturally transparent crystal appears to take on different colors due to reflecting things of those colors. Further, substances with no parts cannot have multiple properties; consider *ākāśa,* which is said to have properties like all-pervadingness, etc., whereas in fact it is due to the presence of other things that *ākāśa* appears all-pervasive. Or again, an atom of earth is said to have smell, but actually it *is* smell, and the appearance that it has other qualities is due to its contact with other substances that are in turn naturally watery, etc.

IV.4.2 (E279-281; T703-709). The discussion here concerns the precise mechanism of death and rebirth. First the organs collect in the subtle body and cease functioning; then the subtle body departs from the heart through its upper portion, leaving the body either through the eye, the top of the head, or another part of the body, depending on the kind of karmic store it takes with it. The experiences the karma-conditioned self now undergoes are, as in the case of dreams, dependent on that karma, and it in turn determines the kind of body the self will be reborn into. As for just how it gets to that next body, Śaṃkara's answer is that the *vāsanās* form a stream that stretches from the old body to the new one, and they finally leave the old body when the new one has been made, the analogy given in the next Upaniṣadic passage being that of a leech's motion along a straw.

IV.4.6 (E285-289; T718-727). Now the text considers what happens at death in the case of "one who is without desires," who is said to "merge into Brahman" (*brahmāpyeti*). Śaṃkara interprets this as referring to the final body of the liberated self. His internal organ, etc., does not depart from the body. The passage about "merging with Brahman" is carefully explained to mean the achievement of liberation while still alive, for if liberation were supposed to be a change of state occurring at death the doctrine of the unity of the self would be undermined and liberation would become the result of action, not of knowledge, and would not be eternal.

Liberation is eternal and therefore must be the inherent nature of the self that is liberated. It is like fire, which is naturally hot and light-producing; its heat and light are not literally produced by one who builds a fire, but, rather, the natural properties of the fire become manifested upon the removal of obstructions. But one should not conclude that liberation is the production of absence (*abhāva*) of something, like breaking one's bonds; for there is nothing else but the Self and thus no real bonds to be broken. Liberation is only the cessation of *avidyā*, like the cessation of a snake mistaken for a rope.

Others hold that in liberation a consciousness and bliss are manifested different from the consciousness and pleasures experienced in this life. But they must say what they mean by "manifested." If these properties are the natural, eternally experienced properties of the self then there is no point in saying they are manifested, since they are never not experienced. But if they are only manifested at certain times because of adjuncts obstructing them, they could never be manifested, since there would then have to be something else to bring about their manifestation and in which they reside, and liberation will be no different from bondage. If, however, these properties are said to reside in the self they cannot be experienced, for one does not experience one's own properties.

Objection : Liberation must make some difference, or no one would care about it and scripture would become useless.

Answer : No, for ignorance must be removed, and both effort and scripture are required for that.

Objection : The self that is under the sway of ignorance is surely affected by it, and so there is some difference in that self that differentiates bondage from release.

Answer : No. One reason is that the Self witnesses ignorance. One cannot witness his own natural property, so ignorance must not be a natural property of the Self.

Objector : But surely the Self is subject to error, since one has the feeling "I am confused, I do not know."

Śaṃkara : No, because the confusion and ignorance are clearly recognized to be the *contents* of that feeling, not its subject ! On our view, one who knows that he is confused is not confused.

IV.5.15 (E312-316; T785-796). The scriptural passages relating to *saṃnyāsa* and the other *āśramas* are inconsistent; thus here we shall discuss the real meaning of the scriptures on this point. One view is that the Vedas enjoin ritual actions for everyone except those who are unfit to perform them because of various shortcomings of their bodies, etc.; for such persons exceptions are made, and the life of the recluse (*saṃnyāsa*) is meant for them. Śaṃkara's view, on the other hand, is that *saṃnyāsa* is recommended for those who seek liberation, because in that state one can cultivate the kind of virtues required for

Self-knowledge, that is, meditation, discrimination, nonattachment, control of the senses.

Objection : But the Vedas explicitly say that the injunction to perform the *nityakarmans* is for life.

Answer : Right, it is for life for those unenlightened who are desirous of their fruits. But it does not follow that others must practise rites forever. The injunctions are graded in their applicability depending on the capacity and knowledge of men. It may be that we can say, in general, that castes (*varṇa*) other than Brahmins are so enjoined.

V.I.1 (E318-322; T804-813). Once again an opponent (commentators say Bhartṛprapañca) argues for a different view of Brahman, according to which Brahman is both dual (*dvaita*) and nondual (*advaita*), just as the ocean is real and nondual and the waves are also real but dual. By adopting this interpretation both the *jñānakāṇḍa* and the *karmakāṇḍa* portions of scripture become valid, since they each deal with their respective aspect of Brahman.

Answer : No. A thing cannot be both one and many. And the view contradicts scripture. The illustration of ocean and waves is applicable only in connection with effects that have parts; the Self, Brahman, has no parts and so is not in this way analogous to the ocean. Nor does your view help make sense of the two parts of scripture, since people do not have to be taught duality; they can see it as soon as they are born. Thus it is proper to assume that the *karmakāṇḍa* is addressed to people in their natural state of ignorance and that the *jñānakāṇḍa* is meant for those who become disgusted with that state, so that each of the two has a distinct audience, and there is thus no conflict between the two. Finally, even supposing your account of Brahman were true, how would it help? How can Brahman instruct Itself, even if It be both one and many? If Devadatta is both one and many (having hands, ears, tongue, etc.) it doesn't make sense to suppose that the tongue will instruct the ear while the unitary Devadatta is unaffected, for Devadatta has only one consciousness, just as the ocean has only one water.

TAITTIRĪYOPANIṢADBHĀṢYA

Because Sureśvara comments on this work its ascription to Śaṃkara is rather straightforward. In addition, Van Boetzelaer briefly tries out some of Hacker's criteria, although his concern is merely to point up Sureśvara's emphases.[24]

The *Taittirīya Upaniṣad* forms part of the *Taittirīya Āraṇyaka* of the

(*Black* ?) *Yajurveda*. It has three chapters: Śikṣāvallī, Brahmavallī, and Bhṛguvallī. The first, Śikṣāvallī, is sometimes referred to as the *Saṃhiti Upaniṣad*, and the latter two chapters together are called the *Vāruṇī Upaniṣad*.[25]

Balasubramaniam points out that "this Upaniṣad has become a classic for three of its outstanding teachings: (1) for the definition of Brahman in terms of its essential nature (*svarūpalakṣaṇa*) as real, as knowledge, and infinite (*satyaṃ jñānam anantaṃ brahma*) and also for the definition *per accidens* (*taṭasthalakṣaṇa*) of Brahman as the cause, etc., of the universe; (2) for the method of discrimination between the Self and the not-Self through an inquiry into the fivefold sheath (*kośa-pañcaka-viveka*), and (3) for the calculus of pleasure (*ānandasya mīmāṃsā*), which points to Brahman as bliss *par excellence*."[26]

"E" references in the following summary are to the edition by H. R. Bhagavat in *Works of Shankaracharya* (Poona : Ashtekar & Co., 1928). "T" refers to the translation by Gambhirananda in *Eight Upanishads* (Calcutta : Advaita Ashrama, 1938), volume one.

CHAPTER ONE : ON PRONUNCIATION (*ŚIKṢĀVALLĪ*)

1. Introduction (E335-336; T231-237). After offering the usual salutations, Śaṃkara explains that the *Taittirīya Āraṇyaka* prior to this point has discussed *nityakarmans* and *kāmyakarmans* and now begins to discuss Brahman-knowledge, which is undertaken for the purpose of avoiding the cause of the performance of actions. That cause is desire (*kāma*), for it incites one to act; nobody acts when his desires have been satisfied. Now, if one "desires," that is, is devoted to the True Self his desires will be satisfied, for the Self is Brahman, and it will be said (below) that the knower of Brahman gains the Highest. Thus to be established in one's own Self, when ignorance has ceased, is to attain the Highest.

2. *Objection* : Liberation consists in being established in one's Self without effort, and it arises from the nonarising of any further *kāmya* and *pratiṣiddha* (prohibited) acts, from the cessation of experiencing of those that have begun (to ripen), and from the absence of sin (*pratyavāya*) from performance of the *nityakarmans*. Or else, liberation comes directly from actions alone, since they are the cause of the unsurpassable state called "heaven."

Answer : No, for acts are of many sorts, and so all karma cannot become exhausted in the experiencings of any single life; thus a new body will arise because of the remaining karma.

3. *Objection* : The *nityakarmans* have the purpose of bringing to an end the good and bad fruits of that karma which has not yet begun to ripen.

Answer : No, for it is stated that notdoing (required acts) produces sin. And even if it were admitted that performance of *nitya-karmans* may bring an end to the fruition of karma not yet operative, still it is only the results of impure acts that could be thus destroyed, not those of pure acts. Since actions that have favorable results are naturally pure there is no opposition between them and the *nityakarmans*; only impure acts oppose pure ones.

4. Furthermore, desires, which cause karma, cannot cease (entirely) unless there is knowledge. Desire belongs to those who know only the not-Self and is inappropriate with respect to one's own Self since that (Self) is eternally realized, and one's Self is the Highest Brahman—so it has been said.

5. Anyway, the nonperformance of an act cannot literally produce sin, since a negation cannot produce a positive entity. Nonperformance of the *nityakarmans* thus "produces" sin only in the sense that it points to the fruition of sinful acts done in the past. So neither performance nor nonperformance of *nityakarmans* can destroy all karma.

6. As for your alternative argument (section 2 above) that "liberation comes directly from actions alone since they are the cause of gaining heaven," that is also wrong, for liberation is an eternal thing and so cannot be produced from actions.

7. *Objection* : But actions together with knowledge (*vidyā*) can produce an eternal thing, just as posterior absence (*pradhvaṃsābhāva*) of pot is produced by destroying the pot but is never afterward capable of being destroyed.

Answer : No, for liberation (unlike posterior nonexistence) is a positive thing (*bhāva*). Anyway, posterior absence cannot have a beginning—there is only one absence (*abhāva*) and it only seems to be differentiated by conceptual constructions (*vikalpa*) endowing it with connections with motions, qualities, and the like. Absences cannot really have qualities, etc., as a lotus can; if they could, they would become positive entities, not negative ones.

8. *Objection* : Well, the subject of knowledge and actions (the Self) is eternal, so Its liberation is eternal.

Answer : No, for agency naturally involves frustration. And further, if it were to cease, liberation would also cease. Therefore liberation involves remaining in one's own Self after the cessation of the material causes (*upādānahetu*) (of bondage), namely, ignorance, desires, and actions. Now the cessation of ignorance follows from knowledge that one's very own Self is Brahman, and that is why the Upaniṣad is begun, for the purpose of conveying Brahman-knowledge.

9. That knowledge is actually denoted by the term "*upaniṣad*," either because it ends birth and old age, etc., or because it takes one near Brahman, or because the highest good is nearby in it. And so this book is also called "*upaniṣad*," since it is meant for that purpose.

10. I.11 (E350-358; T283-294). Here begins a discussion as to whether liberation comes from action alone, or from action assisted by knowledge, or from a combination of action and knowledge, or from knowledge assisted by action, or from knowledge alone.

11. *First opponent* : Liberation comes from actions alone, since according to *smṛti* a man who knows the Vedas thoroughly is prepared for (*adhikāra*) action. And some say that the whole of the Vedas have action as their purport, and if liberation cannot be achieved by action the Vedas will be useless.

Answer : No, since liberation is eternal, and every effect of action is well known in the world to be noneternal.

12. *Objection* : When *kāmya-* and *pratiṣiddha-* actions no longer arise, and when the actions already performed are consumed by experiencing (their fruits), then from the eternal performance of the *nityakarmans*, since sin cannot come from them, liberation accrues without dependence on knowledge.

Answer : No; as was explained in the introduction (see section 2 above) the residual karma of past actions may still produce new births, etc. Now, as for the opponent's assertion that a man who knows the Vedas thoroughly is prepared for action, that is wrong, for meditation (*upāsana*) is a different thing from gaining knowledge through hearing (the Vedas). One becomes competent for action merely by hearing the Vedas; meditation on them is not necessary for that. But meditation is enjoined as a different thing from Vedic study, and it is well known that it is different and that it, rather than mere study, results in liberation.

13. *Second opponent* : So liberation must result from action assisted by knowledge. Actions when accompanied by knowledge can produce different results than actions alone, just as poison, curd, etc., which by themselves cause death, discomfort, etc., when mixed with *mantras*, sugar, etc., produce other results.

Answer : No, since anything produced by action is noneternal.

14. *Opponent* : The *Chāndogya Upaniṣad* (VIII.15.1) says that liberation is both eternal and produced.

Answer : Scripture cannot create something that does not exist—even a hundred passages cannot make something that has an origin into something eternal.

15. This reasoning also disproves the third opponent's position—

which says that action and knowledge in combination can produce liberation. Indeed, liberation is not something that can be produced at all, at least in the sense in which someone has to go to a different place or state to get it, because one's very self, always present, is not a different place or state.

16. *Objection* : This contradicts scriptural texts concerning the paths (*gati*) that are followed by those departing the body, as well as the power (*aiśvarya*) they attain, etc.

Answer : No, those texts relate only to Brahman as effect (*kārya-brahman*). Anyway, knowledge and action are contradictory in nature and so cannot be combined. The latter requires distinctions between agent, action, and result, etc.; the latter presupposes their absence ; thus one or the other must be false (*mithyā*). And the scriptures are very clear that it is the one involving differences that is false, not the other.

17. *Objection* : If actions are false then the Vedas surely would not enjoin them ! But in fact the Vedas do enjoin us to act, and since scripture is a valid means of knowledge it must view action as the means to the highest end.

Answer : No. The purpose of scripture is to instruct us concerning human goals (*puruṣārtha*), that is, to convey knowledge that will cause the cessation of ignorance and so lead to liberation.

18. *Objector* : Even so, scripture establishes the existence of agency, etc., and your account contradicts that.

Answer : No. The scripture proceeds hypothetically, by assuming the existence of distinctions between agent, act, and fruit, etc., and enjoining actions for those who wish for liberation, but it does not establish the existence of those distinctions. Rather, the injunctive portions of the scripture are addressed to those who have desires and other hindrances resulting from past actions, and they enjoin *nityakarmans* in order to remove these hindrances so that desirelessness will result, upon which ignorance may be dispatched and liberation achieved. The Vedic texts that enjoin acts are not contradictory to the requirements of (the Upaniṣadic account of) knowledge. They support that account, but just because of that, actions have no place in the achievement of the highest goal.

19. *Objection* : Then there can only be one stage of life, householdership, since actions are enjoined for householders only.

Answer : Certainly not. There are many actions, and lots of them are practiced in other stages of life—for example, celibacy, truthfulness, nonviolence, meditation, etc. Even before becoming a householder one may gain knowledge from actions performed in previous lives, and in that case, since householdership is intended for performance of acts that will provide just that kind of knowledge, entry into it at this point is unnecessary. Again, one who has lost all desire for worldly ends and has nothing to achieve through action will not perform acts even if he accepts (outwardly) the stage of householdership, and will properly be accounted a monk, etc.

20. *Objector* : Since the Vedas enjoin such difficult actions as the *agnihotra* sacrifice, etc., which involve much effort, and since these injunctions apply to the householder, whereas the other kinds of actions you mention can be more easily performed in all the stages, it is not right to say that the householder's duties are on the same footing as those of the other stages.

Answer : No, for even the householder's actions may be easier due to other acts performed in previous lives. As for the fact that the Vedas dwell on the *agnihotra*, etc., the kinds of acts householders perform with effort, that is true but presents no problem for our account: for those who are not attached to the world other stages are appropriate, whereas for those who are attached there is a variety of actions for which such people have desire, and it is natural that the Vedas should spend a lot of time on them, especially since these actions are beneficial in obtaining the knowledge leading to liberation.

21. *Objection* : Well, if that is true—that actions produce the knowledge leading to liberation—then there is no need for any other kind of effort like, for example, studying the Upaniṣads, etc.

Answer : No, for there is no rule that knowledge arises merely from removal of the obstructions to it; it is not precluded that the grace of God, asceticism, or meditation may be required in addition for gaining the knowledge in question. That is why other stages of life are needed, and it also shows that people in any stage of life may be prepared for knowledge, and that it is through knowledge alone that the highest goal is attained.

CHAPTER TWO : THE BLISS OF BRAHMAN (BRAHMAVALLĪ)

1. (E355-362; T298-318). The Upaniṣad states that the one who knows Brahman attains the Highest, that Brahman is truth (*satya*), knowledge (*jñāna*), and unending (*ananta*), that he who knows Brahman as existing in the secret place (*guha*) simultaneously enjoys all desires. It goes on to say that from Brahman, which is the Self, came *ākāśa*, from *ākāśa* came wind, from wind fire, from fire water, from water earth, from earth plants, from plants food, from food man, who is of the essence of food. The self (*ātman*) is the head, the sides, the tail of man.

2. *Objection* : As it will be said that Brahman is the Self of all, and all-pervading, it follows It cannot be attained. Something is only seen to be attained when it is a limited thing and attained by another limited thing, but Brahman is unlimited.

Answer : That is no fault, for the attainment or nonattainment of Brahman depends on Its being seen or not. Just as the tenth man counting the present company counts nine and fails to count himself, so the self, veiled by ignorance, counts himself as the body, etc., and fails to count his real Self; likewise, just as someone may point out to the tenth man that he is the tenth in the company, so scripture may point out to the ignorant self that the omnipresent Brahman is actually his real Self.

3. The statement that Brahman is truth, knowledge, and unending is meant as a definition of Brahman; it indicates differentia of Brahman by marking out this noun "Brahman" from other nouns.

4. *Objection* : Indication of the meaning of a noun by specifying differentiating features is appropriate only when the differentia stand in contrast to other possible qualifications; for example, a lotus may be singled out by the qualification "blue" but only because "blue" contrasts with "red" and other possible qualities that might qualify other nouns of that class. Now there is only one Brahman, and so there are no other nouns of that class from which "Brahman" can be distinguished. So the sentence in question cannot be a definition.

Answer : No, for the adjectives used here have a defining, though not a qualifying, function. A qualifying adjective distinguishes a thing named by a noun from other things of its own class, but a definition demarcates the thing from everything else. Now the defining adjectives here mentioned distinguish Brahman from everything else, all that is unreal, finite, and characterized by the knower-known relationship.

5. *Objection* : Since it is said (e.g., in Chāndogya Upaniṣad VII.24.1) that one does not know anything else (but Brahman) it follows that the Self is knowable.

Answer : No, that sentence too is a definition; it says that Brahman is (by definition) that in which one does not see anything else, that is, It is that in which that kind of action—seeing other things—does not occur at all. And since there are now such differences in one's Self, knowledge (*vijñāna*) is impossible in It. And if the Self were an object of knowledge (*vijñeya*) there would be no knower.

6. *Objection* : The one Self can be both knower and known.

Answer : No, since the Self has no parts it cannot simultaneously be both knower and known. Again, if the Self were cognizable like a pot instruction about It would be pointless. If, like a pot, It were already familiar there would be no point in the Vedas pointing It out. If the Self were a knower (in that sense) It could not be said to be unending or absolute truth; so the expression "Brahman is knowledge" is intended to exclude all activities such as agency, etc., from It, as well as to deny that It is nonconscious like earth, etc.

7. *Objection* : You say that the purpose of this sentence "Brahman is truth, etc." is only to preclude certain characteristics applying. But since Brahman is not well known to us, as, for example, a lotus is, this "definition" may as well apply to nothing at all (*śūnya*), as is the case with the following sentence : "Having bathed in a mirage and put sky-flowers on his head, the son of a barren woman goes armed with a bow made of hare's horn !"

Answer : No, for our sentence is a definition and there is no point to a definition of nonentities. When we say that the adjectives "truth, knowledge, unending" are used to define but not to qualify we do not mean to imply that they do not distinguish the things they are applied to from other things—indeed they do so by denying their opposites (unlike the terms used in your nonsense example). Even the word "Brahman" has its own specific meaning (and so is not like nondenoting expressions such as "hare's horn," etc.).

8. The text goes on to say "from that Brahman that is the Self," thus indicating that Brahman is the cognizer, the agent of cognition.

9. *Objection* : If Brahman is the cognizer, the agent of cognition, then it follows that It is capable of having desires, that It is impermanent, and that It is dependent. Even if you insist that Brahman is consciousness, and so not the cognizer, still It is impermanent and dependent, because the meanings of verb roots (*dhātu*) are dependent on the cases (*kāraka*) of nouns, and "consciousness", that is, "knowledge," has meaning derived from a verb root (and so is dependent on a noun).

10. *Answer* : No, the consciousness that is the very nature of the Self and inseparable from It is referred to here in only a secondary sense (*upacāra*) as an effect. The cognitions that *are* effects are the transformations of the *buddhi*, which take the form of their objects, having passed out through the openings of the visual organ, etc. These transformations are illuminated by consciousness and so resemble It; it is they that are the cognitions and that relate to the verb root "to know," and it is they that are mistakenly supposed to be properties of the Self and subject to change. But the consciousness of Brahman is inseparable from It, just as the sun's light is inseparable from the sun or the heat of the fire from fire. Consciousness is not

dependent on any other cause. Since everything is nondisjoined from Brahman in time or space, and since Brahman is exceedingly subtle, it follows that there is nothing different from It, subtler than It, or in any way remote from Brahman in such a way that it is unknowable in past, present, or future; thus Brahman is omniscient. So Brahman is not the agent of cognition and cannot even be denoted (properly) by the word "knowledge" (*jñāna*), though that word is used to indicate Brahman figuratively, for knowledge resembles pure consciousness. Likewise, Brahman is not denoted by the word "truth" (*satya*), which naturally means external reality but can be secondarily indicated by it. In this way these words "knowledge," "truth," "unending" when juxtaposed in this way and mutually restricting each other, though they neither separately nor together denote Brahman, can nevertheless serve as a definition. Actually, however, Brahman cannot be spoken of (directly) and unlike the blue lotus cannot be taken to be the meaning of any sentence.

11. Śaṃkara now turns to the next part of the textual passage, which states that one who knows Brahman enjoys all desires. The "secret place" referred to is the *buddhi*. The Brahman-knower is here said to enjoy all desires simultaneously—through a single, eternal consciousness—and not progressively as conditioned by merit and demerit, sense organs, etc.

12. The remainder of the text is construed as a kind of gloss on the preceding—and major—portion and is intended to show how Brahman can be understood as truth, knowledge, and unending. There are three kinds of unendingness—spatial, temporal, and with respect to real things. For example, *ākāśa* is unending spatially but not temporally because it is a product. But Brahman is unending both spatially and temporally. Again, with respect to real things—substances—ordinary substantial things, like cows and horses, limit each other in virtue of their classifications; an idea of cowhood is in opposition to that of horsehood, etc. But Brahman is not differentiated in this way, and so has unendingness in the third sense as well. Why? Because Brahman is the cause of everything.

Objection: In this latter respect Brahman is limited by being dependent on Its own effects.

Answer: No, for those "effects" are unreal (*anṛta*). For there are no real effects distinct from their causes.

13. II.5 (E366-368; T332-338). The *ānandamaya* sheath is not Brahman, but a conditioned self, since the Upaniṣad will say (II.8.5) that the *ānandamaya* self is obtained, and only non-Self can be an

effect. Furthermore, the Self cannot obtain Itself, since It is never divorced from It. Again, the kinds of things the Upaniṣad says about the *ānandamaya* self—that it is the "head" (symbolically) of the "body" consisting of the sheaths—are inappropriate as applied to Brahman. Bliss (*ānanda*) is the result (*phala*) of knowledge (*vidyā*) and action (*karman*); knowledge and action are undertaken in order to acquire bliss. Thus it is appropriate that the self of bliss (*ānandamaya*) should be the inmost sheath.

14. II.6 (E368-374; T338-355). Śaṃkara finds three questions asked in this passage : one, does Brahman exist or not? two, does the unenlightened man reach Brahman or doesn't he? and, three, does the enlightened man reach Brahman or doesn't he?

As to one, Brahman exists, since It has been spoken of as "truth" (*satya*).

15. *Objection* : I suspect that Brahman does not exist, for whatever exists is grasped as possessing distinctive properties (*viśeṣa*), like a pot, whereas what does not exist is not perceived, for example, a hare's horn; now Brahman is not perceived, so It does not exist.

Answer : No, for Brahman is the cause of *ākāśa*, etc. In the world we note that the causes of existing things themselves exist, for example, the earth that is the cause of the pot is held to exist. So Brahman, being the cause of *ākāśa*, exists. An existing thing cannot come from a nonentity.

16. *Objector* : If Brahman is a cause like earth It will be nonconscious (*acetana*).

Answer : No, for Brahman is capable of desires.

17. *Opponent* : Then Brahman must have wants, as we do!

Answer : No, for Brahman is independent, that is, Brahman's desires do not impel Him to activity as ours do us. Brahman's desires are truth and knowledge, and they are pure because they are of Brahman's very nature. Although Brahman is not impelled to act by them He is the inciter of them in accordance with the karma of living beings. And so He has no wants.

18. Furthermore, whereas we are dependent on instrumental causes (*nimitta*) such as merit, etc., and require causes and effects over and beyond ourselves in order to realize our desires, Brahman is not dependent on such instrumental causes.

19. *Question* : Then how is Brahman related to such instrumental causes?

Answer : They are nondifferent from It.

20. *Question* : How can something become many except by entering into something else?

Answer : Through manifestation of name-and-form residing in itself. When the name-and-form that exists unmanifested in the Self are manifested, then they become manifested in all the spatial and temporal states that are not different from Brahman, though without abandoning their own natures. Thus Brahman appears as many. But Brahman does not consist of name-and-form. They are said to be of the nature of Brahman because when Brahman is denied they are too. They are the two adjuncts through which Brahman enters as an aspect of empirical dealings involving knower, known, and knowing.

21. The Upaniṣad goes on to speak of creation, saying that Brahman created all this through austerities (*tapas*), and having created it, entered it. The question then arises : did the Creator enter the world in His own form or another form ?

22. *First opponent* : On grounds of the grammar of the text He must have entered it in His own form.

Second opponent : That's not right, for if Brahman is a cause like clay, Its effects are nondifferent from It, and so It cannot enter into Its effects any more than clay can enter into a pot already made.

First opponent : But the clay may enter into a pot made of clay in some other guise, say as dust; likewise Brahman can enter into the world as, say, name-and-form.

Second opponent : No, for Brahman is single, unlike clay; something made up of many parts can enter in "another form," but not as a single entity.

First opponent : Perhaps, then, Brahman enters as the hand enters the mouth.

Second opponent : No, for there's no empty space that is not already Brahman.

First opponent : Then let's just say that one effect of Brahman, the *jīva*, enters into another effect, name-and-form.

Second opponent : No. A pot doesn't enter into another pot. Again, the Vedas carefully distinguished the *jīva* from name-and-form. And finally, if the *jīva* actually enters into the world liberation will be impossible—one doesn't enter into what he tries to get free of.

First opponent : Then the entry may be in the sense of becoming reflected (*pratibimbatva*), as the sun is reflected in water.

Second opponent : No, for Brahman is not limited and has no features. A thing like the sun, which has features and is limited, may be reflected, but the Self cannot be since It has no shape and is all-pervasive, and since there is thus no place outside the Self where the reflecting medium might be located. So there is no way in which

Brahman can enter the world, and we must disregard the text in question.

23. *Śaṃkara* : The passage has a different meaning, one appropriate to the context, which has to do with gaining knowledge of Brahman. The successive effects beginning with *ākāśa* and ending with food have been introduced in order to induce knowledge of Brahman, and the progress goes on through the "selves" made of breath (*prāṇa*), knowledge (*vijñāna*), and bliss (*ānanda*). When the text here speaks of "entering," it has in mind this progression, that is, that the inquisitive self—which is Brahman itself—enters into its own creation to rediscover itself successively. But all of this way of speaking is empirical (*vyāvahārika*), not from the highest standpoint (*pāramārthika*).

24. II.8.5 (E379-382; T370-382). The Upaniṣad here says that this Brahman is both in the person (*puruṣa*) and in the sun. One who knows the self as made of food (*annamaya*), made of breath (*prāṇamaya*), made of *manas* (*manomaya*), made of knowledge (*vijñānamaya*), and made of bliss (*ānandamaya*), he attains the self of each sort progressively.

25. *Śaṃkara*: Who is this "one who knows the self," and how does he attain the self of each sort? Is the attainer different from the Highest Self? If so, scripture will be contradicted; if not, the same self will be said to attain itself, and the Highest Self will be reduced to a transmigrating being or the "highest absence" !

Now the attainer must be the Highest Self, since it is said that it "becomes that," and one cannot become something other than what one is. And that is not unsound, because the idea is that the attainer must remove the things that are not of the nature of the Self but that are produced from ignorance—things such as the "self made of food," etc. For the instruction has to do with knowledge alone, and the result of knowledge is to remove ignorance.

26. *Objection* : Rather, the situation may be like the information offered to someone who is asking his way—one seeks information about the village he wants to get to, but it doesn't follow that he is that village !

Answer : The example is not apt, for the knowledge provided to one asking his way concerns the path that one should follow by walking, not by knowing, whereas in the present case no path other than knowledge itself is alluded to.

27. *Objection* : The path is knowledge of Brahman coupled with performance of previously enjoined actions.

Answer : No, for it has already been shown that liberation is eternal, and the present texts (about the Self entering) agree with that. The enlightened man sees nothing different from his Self, and so nothing exists for him as a separate thing that could cause bondage (here, "fear" [*bhaya*]). Anyway, it is appropriate that knowledge be adduced to destroy duality if duality is a product of ignorance, just as the absence of a real second moon is not grasped by one whose visual organ is diseased (*taimirika*).

28. *Objection* : But we do not thus grasp absence-of-duality-in-general.

Answer : Yes we do, in deep sleep and in *samādhi*.

29. *Objection* : Duality exists, since we perceive it in the waking and dream states.

Answer : No, since those states are the results of ignorance; when ignorance ceases, perception of duality in waking and dream experiences cease.

30. *Objector* : Then the nonperception of duality in deep sleep is also a result of ignorance.

Answer : No, for there it is natural. The nature of a substance (*dravya*) is unchangeable (*avikriya*) because it does not depend on any other thing. Change is not natural, since it is dependent. Now any differentiating characteristic (*viśeṣa*) of an existing thing is dependent on causal factors, so differentiation is change. And perceptions in waking and dream states are differentiations, thus dependent on something else, and so nonperception of things in those states is not natural, but in deep sleep there are no differentiations, so nonperception in that state is natural.

31. For those for whom God is different from the Self, and for those for whom creation is different, there is no cessation of fear, for fear is caused by something being the cause of another, but if that cause exists it cannot be destroyed, and if it doesn't exist it cannot attain itself.

32. *Objection* : Both knowledge and ignorance are properties of the Self.

Answer : No, because they are perceived, like colors, etc., as states of the internal organ (*antaḥkaraṇa*). Color, etc., cannot be properties of the perceiver. Knowledge and ignorance, being perceptible, are name-and-form, not properties of the Self; name-and-form are only imagined or constructed (*kalpita*), like night and day (are imagined) in the sun; really, they do not occur.

UPADEŚASĀHASRĪ

For the most careful scholarship on this work we are indebted to Sengaku Mayeda, who has examined it exhaustively.[27] Since it is a *prakaraṇa* or topical treatise rather than a commentary, and since so many such treatises traditionally ascribed to Śaṃkara are likely to be spurious, the authenticity of this one is especially worthy of close attention. Mayeda has compared the style and content of the *Upadeśasāhasrī* with the *Brahmasūtrabhāṣya*, using Hacker's criteria. He has also examined the fact, indicated long ago by G. A. Jacob,[28] that Sureśvara's *Naiṣkarmyasiddhi* depends on and quotes voluminously from the *Upadeśasāhasrī*, and he has discussed evidence supporting Sureśvara's having ascribed the *Upadeśasāhasrī* to his teacher Śaṃkara. Evidence from the writings of others—Bhāskara, Vidyāraṇya, Sadānanda—is also adduced. The upshot is overwhelmingly in favor of Śaṃkara's authorship.

This work has two parts, one metrical, the other in prose. Only the metrical sections are quoted by the authors Mayeda studies, and one might therefore question whether the prose part has as much claim to authenticity. Mayeda argues that the prose passages as well as the metrical ones show agreement in doctrine and style with Śaṃkara's unquestioned work. He remarks, in addition, "It is not common in India that works in prose except the Śrutis are quoted verbatim."[29]

Mayeda returns to the question of the two parts in another article,[30] in which he develops the arguments summarized above and adds other information. One conclusion of some interest is that the nineteen chapters of the verse section were each composed independently at different times. Another is that the prose section shows a unity of purpose that suggests it is a complete work in itself. Furthermore, the prose section quotes from the fifteenth chapter of the verse section. The order followed in the summary below places the prose section before the verse section, following the practice of all the printed editions, though some manuscripts (Mayeda points out) reverse the order, and commentators on the work differ in their assumptions about the order.

The edition and translation to which "ET" references are made in the summary are to Swami Jagadananda, *Upadeshasāhasri of Sri Sankaracharya* (Mylapore, Madras : Sri Ramakrishna Math, 1949). Numbering of passages follows Jagadananda's work.

PART I (PROSE)

CHAPTER ONE : TREATISE ON INSTRUCTIONS FOR TEACHERS

I.1.1 (ET1). The instruction is to be used to teach those seekers of liberation who desire and have faith in its purport.

I.1.2 (ET2). The means of liberation, namely, knowledge (*jñāna*), needs to be repeatedly explained to a pure Brahmin pupil who is without desire for anything noneternal, who has abandoned desire for sons, wealth, and for this world or the next, who has taken up the life of a wandering monk (*paramahaṃsa parivrājaka*), who has control over his mind and senses, who has qualities such as compassion, etc., as well as being versed in the *śāstras*, and who has come to the teacher in the manner prescribed and been examined about his background.

I.1.3 (ET2-3). Upaniṣads and *Bhagavadgītā* are quoted in support of the previous passage.

I.1.4-5 (ET4). When the teacher finds that the pupil doesn't understand, he must remove the causes of that lack of understanding, those causes being lack of merit, lax conduct, failure to discriminate between things that are eternal and those that are not, playing to the public, pride in caste, etc. These faults can be removed by practising means such as nonanger and observance of the vows of noninjury, etc., as long as the means are not incompatible with knowledge. The teacher should also encourage the development of virtues such as modesty, etc.

I.1.6 (ET5). The teacher is one who knows the arguments for and against, understands and remembers the pupil's questions, has such virtues as tranquillity, self-control, compassion, and a desire to help others, one who knows the *śāstras* and is nonattached to any pleasures or frustrations both present and future, who has renounced actions and their means, who knows Brahman and is fixed in It, who observes the rules of conduct and lacks faults such as pride, deceit, jealousy, etc. His only purpose is to help others attain knowledge of Brahman. He should begin by teaching those scriptural texts dealing with the identity of Self and Brahman.

I.1.7-8 (ET6-7). Next he should teach the defining marks of Brahman as set forth in scripture. Examples are provided.

I.1.9-11 (ET7). Now, if the pupil has grasped those marks and wishes to achieve liberation, the teacher should ask him "Who are you?" If he says, "I am a member of such and such family, have been a student and am now a monk . . . " the teacher should say "How can you hope to cross the ocean of *saṃsāra* when your body will be eaten by birds or will turn into earth?"

I.1.12-13 (ET8-9). If the pupil should then say "But I am not the body; I enter into and leave bodies beginninglessly and so am bound into an endless cycle of births and deaths. I am tired of this circling and have come to you to terminate it," the teacher should say "You are right; so why did you first say you were a member of such and such a family, etc, . . . ?"

I.1.14-17 (ET9-10). "To say what you first said identifies the self with the body, but the two are quite different."

I.1.18 (ET11-12). When the pupil has remembered the definition of the Self that he was taught (I.1.7-8), the teacher should summarize the truth about that Self. It is different from name-and-form, has no body, is not gross or containing demerit, not touched by *saṃsāra*, is of the nature of eternal knowledge, all-pervading, without inside or outside, omnipotent, the Self of all, without desires, omnipresent. By Its unthinkable power It is the support of name-and-form, the seeds of the world, merely by existing in the world in an indescribable (*anirvacanīya*) way.

I.1.19-20 (ET 12-13). The name-and-form first took the name and form of *ākāśa*; this name-and-form rose from the Highest Self like dirtyfoam from clear water. Becoming grosser as evolution progressed the name-and-form took the form of air, then fire, water, and earth. In this order each preceding element entered each succeeding one, and so the five gross elements came into existence. From earth, made up of all five elements, various food-providing plants are produced, and when they are eaten they form sperm and blood in the bodies of men and women. When these are churned forth by sexual passion springing from *avidyā* and are sanctified by *mantras*, they are poured into the womb, and an embryo is developed, which is delivered in the ninth or tenth month.

I.1.21 (ET13-14). The child, when born, is given a name and form and is purified by *mantras* at various ceremonies. When invested it gets the name of student, and when married it gets the name of householder, etc. Thus the body, which is subject to these changes of name-and-form, is different from the Self.

I.1.22 (ET14). The internal organ and the sense organs are also of the nature of name-and-form.

I.1.23-24 (ET14-16). So you see that your Self is quite different from the "you" that has a caste and a family and which undergoes purification at ceremonies, etc.

I.1.25 (ET16-17). If the pupil says "(I see !) That Self and I are entirely different. So I want to worship Him and by doing so escape from *saṃsāra*. But how can I then *be* that Self?"

I.1.26-29 (ET17-19). The teacher should then say "Don't you believe it; it is prohibited to believe that the Self and oneself are different. Why ? Because the scripture indicates that one who believes in the difference of the two will surely get more *saṃsāra*, but it also declares that those who realize the identity of Self and Brahman will achieve final release."

I.1.30-32 (ET19-21). "Now since it is forbidden to believe in difference, once one has realized that one is identical with the Supreme Self the ritual acts such as investiture are also forbidden, since they involve the assumption of difference and are thus inconsistent with the knowledge gained. Thus the injunctions in the Vedas to perform ritual acts are binding only on transmigrating beings, and not on those who have gained the knowledge of their identity with the Supreme Self. Scripture bears out that rites, etc., have nothing to do with the Self, and scripture wouldn't have stated thus if it was not intended that such actions should be given up."

I.1.33 (ET21-22). The pupil may now say "I perceive directly the pain produced by burning or cutting my body and from my hunger, etc. But the Highest Self I know to be free from pain and hunger, etc. So how can I be identical with that Self?"

I.1.34 (ET 22-23). The teacher should say in answer to this: "It isn't right to localize your pain in your Self, for pain is always localized in the place where the injury occurred. We say 'I have a pain in the head, or the chest, or the stomach,' but we don't say 'I have a pain in my Self' !"

I.1.35 (ET23-24). "Furthermore, if pain were in the Self it couldn't be felt at all, just as the eye's own color cannot be perceived by that eye. Since it is an effect, pain must have a locus, just as cooked rice must be cooked in something. Now the trace (*saṃskāra*) set up by pain must have the same locus as the feeling of pain, since one perceives them in memory. Likewise the aversion to pain must be located in the same place."

I.1.36 (ET24-25). "What is the locus of the traces of pain and of colors, desires, aversions, etc. ? It is the *buddhi*, as scripture shows."

I.1.37-38 (ET25-28). "Therefore the traces of color and form etc., have no relation with you, and thus you are nondifferent essentially from the Highest Self. Perception does not controvert this." Scriptural and *smṛti* passages are adduced.

I.1.39 (ET28). The pupil may now say "If this is all so, what is referred to in the scripture and *smṛi* and ordinary talk when the subject is action, agent, and object, about which there is a great deal of controversy ?"

I.1.40 (ET28-29). The teacher should answer : "Everything experienced or spoken of in scripture is made from *avidyā*. Really there is only the one Self, which appears to be many, as the moon appears many to one with an eye disease."

I.1.41 (ET29-30). *Pupil* : "Then why do the scriptures speak of the differences among ends, means, etc., as well as the origination and destruction of things ?"

I.1.42 (ET30-31). *Teacher* : "Scripture gradually teaches an ignorant man to discriminate what will really achieve what is desirable and to avoid what is undesirable, and it is this that is the purpose of scripture; it does not prove differences among ends and means, etc., since it is just these differences that constitute *saṃsāra*. Scripture, therefore, roots out *avidyā* by demonstrating the unity of origination and dissolution, etc."

I.1.43 (ET31). "And when this has occurred one's knowledge becomes established in the one Self in which the least taint of impurity is inconceivable."

I.1.44 (ET31-32). "One who wants to achieve this highest knowledge must abandon the desires for son, wealth, and worlds, which desires arise from the notion that the self belongs to castes, stages of life, etc. Thus all ritual actions must be given up, since they are the result of ignorance."

CHAPTER TWO : ON KNOWLEDGE OF THE CHANGELESS, NONDUAL SELF

I.2.45 (ET33-34). A student aspiring to liberation approached in the proper manner a knower of Brahman and asked : "Sir, how can I be liberated from this *saṃsāra* ? I possess feelings of the body, senses, and their objects in waking and in dream and again after I have slept. Is this (experiencing) natural to me or is it accidental, my true nature being different ? If it is natural to me I can have no hope of liberation, since one cannot change his own nature. But if it be accidental, liberation may be achieved by removing the cause."

I.2.46 (ET34). *The teacher said* : "Listen, my child, it is not natural, and it is accidental."

I.2.47 (ET34). *Pupil* : "Then what is the cause, and what will remove it, and what *is* my own nature ? Once the cause is removed the effect will become absent and I shall return to my own nature, just like a patient who returns to health when the cause of his disease is removed."

I.2.48 (ET34-35). *Teacher* : "The cause is *avidyā*. Knowledge (*vidyā*) removes it. And when ignorance is removed you will be liberated from *saṃsāra* and will never again feel frustration in the waking and dream states."

I.2.49 (ET35). *Pupil* : "What is this *avidyā* and what does it concern? What is the knowledge by which I may find my own nature?"

I.2.50 (ET35). *Teacher* : "You think you transmigrate, but you are really the nontransmigrating Supreme Self. Likewise, although you are really not an agent or experiencer, you suppose yourself to be an agent, an experiencer, a noneternal being."

I.2.51 (ET35-36). *Pupil* : "But I am an agent and an experiencer. This is not due to *avidyā*, because my awareness cannot have the Self for its object. *Avidyā* involves the superimposition of the properties of one thing on another, and both the properties and thing must be known. For example, one superimposes silver on shell, or a man on a post, and vice versa—and we are acquainted with silver, shells, men, and posts. But nothing can be superimposed on something with which we are not acquainted, and since we are not acquainted with the Highest Self there can be no question of superimposition."

I.2.52 (ET36-37). *Teacher* : "No, that is not an invariable rule, since we regularly experience the superimposition of other things on the Self. For example, properties of the body such as color, etc., are superimposed on the Self when we say "I am white" or "I am black."

I.2.53 (ET37). *Pupil* : "Then we are acquainted with the Self as the object of our consciousness of egoity, and since we are also evidently acquainted with the body, superimposition is all right because it does satisfy the rule I mentioned. So why do you say the rule is not invariable?"

I.2.54 (ET38). *Teacher* : "Listen. It is true that we are acquainted with the Self and with the body, but not everyone is aware of them as different from each other. They are regularly known rather as undiscriminated—the Self is regularly identified with the body. This is what I had in mind when I said the rule was not invariable."

I.2.55 (ET38-40). *Pupil* : "When *x* is superimposed on *y* it is (eventually) discovered that *x* did not exist in *y*. For example, the silver did not exist in the shell, the man did not exist in the post, the snake did not exist in the rope, and the blue-dome-form did not exist in the sky. Now if the Self and the non-Self were superimposed on each other neither would exist. But that is not right; it is the position of the nihilists. Now if the body alone is superimposed on the Self (and not vice versa), the body will be nonexistent in the existing Self, and that also is not right, since it is contrary to sense perception, etc. So, the body and the Self are not mutually superimposed upon each other. Instead, they are in a relation of permanent contact, like pillars and bamboos (making a house)."

I.2.56 (ET40), *Teacher* : "No, if it were a relationship of contact the Self would exist for another's sake and would be noneternal. So the Self cannot be in contact with the body; indeed, it is quite different from the body, being eternal, etc."

I.2.57 (ET40-41). *Pupil*: "Then the nihilist position follows."

I.2.58-59 (ET41-42). *Teacher* : "No, because the Self, like *ākāśa*, is by nature not in contact with anything. Even so, just as nothing is in contact with *ākāśa* and yet it is related to everything, so the Self is related to the body even though It is not in contact with it. So the nihilist position does not come into the situation. And, contrary to what you argued, the nonexistence of the body in the existing Self is not contrary to sense perception, because it is not sense perception or any other *pramāṇa* that tells us that the body is present in the Self it is not like our seeing a fruit in a pot, ghee in milk, oil in sesamum, or a picture on a wall."

I.2.60 (ET42). *Pupil* : "Since the Self is not an object of sense perception, how can the body be superimposed on it and vice versa ?"

I.2.61 (ET42-43). *Teacher* : "There is no problem here. We see that the blue-dome-form is superimposed on the sky even though the sky (*ākāśa*) is permanently known. So there cannot be any rule that superimposition can only be on things that are occasionally known.

The Self, like *ākāśa*, is permanently known, and the body is superimposed on it."

I.2.62 (ET43). *Pupil* : "Sir, is the mutual superimposition of body and Self made by the body, etc., or by the Self ?"

I.2.63. (ET43). *Teacher* : "Why does it matter ?"

I.2.64 (ET 43-44). *Pupil* : "If I am merely an aggregate of body, etc., I am then nonconscious and exist for another's sake only and am incapable of making a superimposition. If, however, I am the Self I am quite different from that aggregate, exist for my own sake only am conscious, and am capable of making the superimposition."

I.2.65 (ET44). *Teacher* : "Well, don't make it if it is the root of all trouble !"

I.2.66 (ET44). *Pupil* : "I can't help making it, for I am dependent on something else."

I.2.67 (ET44). *Teacher* : "Then you are nonconscious and exist for the sake of another, and that other is conscious and exists for itself. You are only an aggregate !"

I.2.68 (ET44). *Pupil* : "If I am nonconscious how can I experience pleasure and frustration and what you are saying ?"

I.2.69 (ET45). *Teacher* : "Are you different from, or the same as, the consciousness of pain and frustration and what I am saying ?"

I.2.70 (ET45). *Pupil* : "Yes, I am different from them, since they are objects of my experience, like jars, etc., and if I weren't different from them I couldn't know them. Furthermore if I were the same as those experiences they would exist for themselves, but that is absurd; so they must exist for another, that is, for me who know them."

I.2.71 (ET46). *Teacher* : "Right ! A conscious being does not exist for another's sake, whether that other be conscious or nonconscious. If one conscious being existed for the sake of another conscious being it would be as if a lamp needed another lamp to illuminate it, which is absurd. And a nonconscious being by its very nature exists for the sake of another."

I.2.72 (ET46). *Pupil* : "But a servant and his master serve each other's purposes even though they are both conscious."

I.2.73 (ET46-47). *Teacher*: "No, for consciousness is analogous to light, which is why I used the example of the two lamps. Consciousness is changeless and eternal and illuminates everything presented to your *buddhi*, like the light of a fire. Now then, since that is the case, were you right when you said what you said at the outset (in I.2.45) ? Has your confusion disappeared ?"

I.2.74 (ET47-49). *Pupil* : "Sir, the confusion has disappeared thanks to you. But I still have doubts about my allegedly changeless nature. Sounds, etc., are known when ideas (*pratyaya*) arise having the form of sound, etc. These ideas in turn require a consciousness to entertain them, a knower for whose sake they exist. Now this knower, the Self, must change, since it entertains these various notions of different colors, (sounds), etc. And yet you say the Self is changeless."

I.2.75 (ET49-50). *Teacher* : "No need to doubt. If you were subject to change like the internal organ or the sense organs you would only know a portion of the objects of your knowledge as they do. But because you are completely aware of the contents of your knowledge it follows that your Self is free from change."

I.2.76 (ET50). *Pupil* : " 'Know' is a verb and suggests (activity and) change; yet you say the knower is changeless. How is this ?"

I.2.77 (ET50). *Teacher* : "No, the word 'know' means an activity only in a secondary sense. The activity of the *buddhi*, an idea, comes to be called 'knowledge' because it is a reflection of knowledge (proper), just as the word 'cut' means the separation into two of something in only a secondary sense."

I.2.78 (ET50-51). *Pupil* : "That example won't do. Just as 'cutting' is used figuratively to suggest a change in the object cut, so 'know' figuratively suggests a change in the Self's knowledge, and so the Self is not changeless."

I.2.79 (ET51). *Teacher* : "That would be so if there were a difference between the knower and knowledge. But there isn't, since the knower is just knowledge itself, unlike the situation as understood by the logicians (*tārkika*)."

I.2.80 (ET51). *Pupil* : "Then how can this knowledge (being eternal) result from an action?"

I.2.81 (ET52). *Teacher* : "Listen. I didn't say that the result was knowledge, but rather, it is the *reflection* of knowledge (cf. I.2.77)."

I.2.82-84 (ET52-53). *Pupil* : "Then how am I the changeless knower, completely aware of the contents of my knowledge (cf. I.2.75) ? If I am so, then it is not *my* fault that ideas of sound, etc., occur in my *buddhi* and result in the reflection of knowledge, since *I* am changeless and eternal knowledge !"

I.2.85 (ET53). *Teacher* : "Correct, you are not at fault. The only fault is *avidyā*."

I.2.86 (ET53). *Pupil* : "But sir, if I am changeless like one in deep sleep, how is it that I experience different states of waking and dream ?"

I.2.87 (ET53). *Teacher* : "Do you experience these states all the time ?"

I.2.88 (ET53). *Pupil* : "No, I experience them intermittently."

I.2.89 (ET53-54). *Teacher* : "So they are accidental features only, and not of your own nature. If they were natural to you you would experience them continuously, as you do experience pure consciousness, which *is* your nature. What is a thing's own nature is never found to be lacking in it. Since waking and dream are sometimes lacking in us, that is, when we are in deep sleep, it follows that they are not natural to us."

I.2.90 (ET54-55). *Pupil* : "But then pure consciousness also must be accidental, since it is not known in deep sleep—or else I am not of the nature of pure consciousness."

I.2.91 (ET55-56). *Teacher* : "No, that's not right; think about it : you may speak of an accidental consciousness, but you cannot prove it. On the other hand, that the Self is pure consciousness is impossible to refute."

I.2.92 (ET56). *Pupil* : "But I have pointed out an exception !"

I.2.93 (ET56-57). *Teacher* : "What you say involves a contradiction. You say that in deep sleep you are not conscious when you are. In deep sleep objects of knowledge are absent, but knowledge is not absent. That consciousness which allows you to say 'in deep sleep I was not conscious of anything' is the consciousness that is your Self. It is self-evident and does not require a *pramāṇa* to prove It. It is analogous to the case of iron or water, etc., which depend on the sun or fire to heat them or light them up, whereas the sun or the fire do not in turn need something else to heat or to illuminate them."

I.2.94 (ET57-58). *Pupil* : "It (consciousness) can only be veridical (*pramā*) if it is noneternal, but not if it is eternal."

I.2.95 (ET58). *Teacher* : "No, for in knowledge there cannot even arise the question about its noneternity."

I.2.96 (ET58). *Pupil* : "But there is such a distinction : eternal knowledge is not dependent on a veridical observer (*pramātṛ*), whereas noneternal knowledge does so depend because it involves exertion of effort on the part of an observer."

I.2.97 (ET58). *Teacher* : "So it is clear that the knower, the Self, is self-evident, since it does not require a *pramāṇa*."

I.2.98 (ET59). *Pupil* : "Well, then, even when there is no *pramāṇa* there should be veridical knowledge, since the knower is eternal."

I.2.99 (ET59-61). *Teacher* : "No. If the knower depends on a *pramāṇa* to be known, to whom will the desire to know belong ? If we postulate another knower who desires to know the first knower, we will land in an infinite regress. Anyway, the Self cannot be an object of knowledge, for a thing is considered to be an object of knowledge when it is arrived at by an intervening desire, memory, effort, or *pramāṇa* on the part of a knower who is distinguished from that thing. Now the knower cannot distinguish himself from himself by desire, memory, effort, or *pramāṇa*, for these varieties of awareness take as their object something distinguished from the subject of that awareness, and as before, an infinite regress would arise if we were to deny this."

I.2.100 (ET61). *Pupil* : "If we cannot know the knower it will remain forever unknown to us."

I.2.101 (ET61-62). *Teacher* : "No, I have already given several proofs that the knower cannot be an object of knowledge."

I.2.102 (ET62-63). *Pupil* : "If the knower is not the locus of veridical knowledge, how can it be properly called a 'knower' ?"

I.2.103 (ET63-64). *Teacher* : "Veridical knowledge remains what it is by nature whether or not it is considered as eternal or noneternal. Just as *standing* is what it is whether it be considered as preceded by motion or not so preceded, so that we say both 'people stand' and 'mountains stand,' so it is in the case of knowing."

I.2.104 (ET64). *Pupil* : "The Self, which is eternal knowledge, is changeless, so it cannot act without being connected with the body and senses, just as the carpenter requires tools to ply his trade. But if the Self, being unconnected with the body and the organs, uses them as instruments (this will require a *tertium quid* to connect them, and so) an infinite regress will result. No regress results in the case of the carpenter since he is always connected with his body and senses."

I.2.105 (ET64-66). *Teacher* : "Indeed, agency requires the use of instruments, but the taking up of an instrument is itself an action, so it will require still other instruments, *ad infinitum.* So the Self cannot be an agent at all.

If someone were to propose that the occurrence of an action causes the Self to become an agent, no, since the action requires an agent to perform it in order that it occur at all. Again, if someone suggests that something else makes the Self act, no, for nothing else except the Self can have an independent existence and be a nonobject, etc. Everything else, nonconscious and so not self-established, depends for its manifestation on its becoming the contents of consciousness. Nor can we accept that there is more than one Self, noncomposite, existing for Its own sake and for another's. And it is impossible to suppose that the body and the senses and their objects exist for their own sake, since they depend on consciousness for their manifestation."

I.2.106 (ET66). *Pupil* : "We don't depend on perceptual ideas in knowing our own bodies."

I.2.107 (ET66-67). *Teacher* : "That is true in the waking state but not after death or in deep sleep. The same is true for the sense organs."

I.2.108 (ET67-68). *Pupil* : "You have said that the Self is the same as that knowledge which is the result of *pramāṇas*. But this is a contradiction."

Teacher : "No it isn't. Knowledge is a result; even though changeless and eternal, it is made manifest by perception and the other *pramāṇas*; the result of their operations produce what we call 'knowledge' and also make it appear that knowledge is noneternal."

I.2.109 (ET68-69). *Pupil* : "If that is so, everything other than the Self, pure consciousness, has existence only for Its sake. But since it is only when apprehended as causing pleasure, frustration, or delusion that anything non-Self serves another's purpose, it follows that everything that is not the Self does not really exist at all except *as* the pure Self; they are like the snake in a rope, the water in the mirage, etc. Thus all duality experienced in waking and dream does not exist except as knowledge itself. So there is nothing else except my Self."

I.2.110 (ET70). *Teacher* : "Right ! It is *avidyā* that brings about waking and dream experiences, and it is *vidyā* that destroys *avidyā*. You have attained fearlessness and will no longer feel frustration in dream or waking. You are liberated from the frustrations of *saṃsāra*."

I.2.111 (ET70). *Pupil* : "*Om* !"

CHAPTER THREE : ON PARISAṂKHYĀNA

I.3.112 (ET71). *Parisaṃkhyāna* is (a type of meditation) intended for those desiring liberation through destroying the merit and demerit that has been accumulated while trying to not collect any more. Faults, caused by *avidyā*, produce efforts of body, internal organ, and speech, and it is through these efforts that karma is accumulated which has effects that are desirable, undesirable, and mixed in nature.

I.3.113 (ET71-72). Things are known—sounds, sights, tastes, etc. —that are of a completely different kind from the knower. It is as connected with one another that these known things come to possess properties such as birth, growth, death, contact and separation, cause and effect, and sex, all of which produce pleasure and/or frustrations. The knower is quite different.

I.3.114-115 (ET72-75). So the knower of Brahman will perform the *parisaṃkhyāna* meditation (as follows) : "I am of the nature of consciousness, changeless, endless, fearless, and subtle, not an object; I cannot be made an object and be connected with sound either in general or in its specific forms such as musical notes, praise, abuse, etc. So what can sound do to me ? Pleasant and unpleasant sound can elevate or injure an ignorant man who does not discriminate, but it cannot elevate or harm one who understands." He should then repeat the same pattern of meditation with respect to touch, color (or form : *rūpa*), taste, and smell.

I.3.116 (ET75-77). (Then he should continue :) "Furthermore, these kinds of things (sound, etc.), when assuming states as body, auditory organ, and of the two kinds of internal organs and their objects, are connected and combined in all actions. Since this is so, for me, who understands, there is no enemy, friend, or even neutral other. So, anyone who through false knowledge tries to connect me with pleasure or frustration, which depend on action, strives in vain, for I am not within the reach of pleasure or frustration, as scripture and *smṛti* aver. The reason is that nothing other than the Self exists." So, since duality does not exist, those parts of the Upaniṣads that deal with the unity of the Self should be carefully studied.

PART II (VERSE)

CHAPTER ONE : INTRODUCTION

II.1.1 (ET79). Invocation to Brahman.

II.1.2 (ET79-80). After the Vedas have dealt with all actions enjoined and prohibited following marriage and the sacred fire established then, they go on to describe the knowledge of Brahman.

II.1.3-5 (ET80-81). *Saṃsāra* is described. Since ignorance is its root, knowledge of Brahman, which liberates man from ignorance, is set forth in the Upaniṣads.

II.1.6-7 (ET81). Actions are not incompatible with ignorance and so do not destroy it, but knowledge (*vidyā*) alone does so. As long as ignorance is not destroyed, desires and aversions cannot be avoided, leading to actions.

II. 1.8-11a (ET81-82). *Objection* : The obligatory rites (*nityakarman*) should be practised as long as life lasts, because they cooperate with knowledge in producing liberation, because they are enjoined, and because failure to perform them breeds sin. Now you may say that knowledge produces a sure result (viz., liberation) and so is independent of anything else, but that is wrong; for just as the *agniṣṭoma* rite produces a sure result (viz., heaven) but nevertheless depends on something other than itself (viz., accessories such as speaking certain *mantras*, etc.), so knowledge depends on other things, namely, obligatory rites, in producing a sure result.

II.1.11b-15 (ET82-84). *Answer* : No, for since actions are incompatible with knowledge it cannot depend on them. Actions are (always) accompanied by egoism (*abhimāna*) and so are incompatible with knowledge, for it is obvious that the Upaniṣads teach that (the liberating) knowledge is the awareness that the Self is without change. Now actions, having their origin in the awareness that one is an agent and in the desire to get results, depend on the agent, whereas knowledge only depends on a real thing (*vastu*). True knowledge undermines the idea of agency as (understanding the mirage undermines the idea of) water. So how can a man both accept the truth and still perform actions? So one who desires liberation should give up actions.

II.1.16-21a (ET84-85). As long as the natural conviction that the Self is not different from the body, etc., prevails, the Vedic injunctions remain authoritative. But when one, through understanding the statement "not this...," understands that the Self is without attributes, *avidyā* is caused to cease. After that, *avidyā* cannot arise again, since it is not present either in the Self—which is without attributes—or in the non-Self. So, since actions depend on our idea of agency, and since such an idea cannot arise from *avidyā* once the knowledge "I am Brahman" has arisen, it follows that knowledge is independent of actions (in producing liberation). Scripture supports this.

II.1.21b-24 (ET85-86). As for the objection (in II.1.8-11a) about the analogy with the *agniṣṭoma*, the analogy is faulty, for each ritual act requires several mutually distinct accessories and differs from the next in the quality of the results it secures, whereas knowledge has an opposite nature. Since each action is intended to secure its own specific results the accessories differ in each case and the action depends on them for its success. But what other thing can knowledge depend on? Only if one has the idea that he is an agent, etc., can he incur sin. But a man who has Self-knowledge has neither an idea of ego (i.e., of agency) nor any desire for the results of actions.

II.1.25-26 (ET87). The Upaniṣads, which teach Brahman-knowledge, are called by that name because it suggests something that will certainly slacken the bondage of birth, etc.

CHAPTER TWO : DENIAL (PRATIṢEDHA)

II.2.1-2 (ET88). It is impossible to deny the Self, for It is what is left after everything else is denied in the words "not this, not this." So, reflecting thus, one comes to know the Self clearly. However, the notion of 'I' concerns what arises from words, and since that is denied (by "not this, not this") the notion of 'I' can never again be regarded as well founded.

II.2.3-4 (ET89). A (right) awareness that follows another always sublates its predecessor. Now consciousness itself (*dṛṣir eka svayam*) is not sublated, being proved through the nature of its fruit. By crossing the forest of the body in which dwell the dangers of grief, delusion, etc., one finds his own Self, just as the man of Gandhāra reached his own country by crossing the forest (cf. *Chāndogya Upaniṣad* VI.14).

CHAPTER THREE : THE SELF IS GOD

II.3.1 (ET90). If God (*īśvara*) were non-Self one could not know that "I am that." But if he is rightly aware that the Self is God, this right knowledge produces the cessation of any other.

II.3.2-3 (ET90-91). Why should scripture (i.e., *Bṛhadāraṇyaka Upaniṣad* III.8.8) describe something as "not large," etc., if these qualities belong to something other than the Self—since we are not seeking knowledge about what is other than the Self? Since the Self is so qualified the opposite ideas ("large," etc.) are denied in It. Understand then that these passages are intended to remove false superimposition (of largeness on the Self), since if they were intended to deny them of what is not Self they would describe a void (*śūnyatā*).

CHAPTER FOUR : KNOWLEDGE OF THE NATURE OF THINGS (TATTVAJÑĀNA)

II.4.1 (ET92). How can the karma, whose seed is egoism and which remains (stored up) in the notion of 'I', still produce results after the acts have been burnt in the fire of the idea of nonegoism?

II.4.2 (ET92-93). *Objection* : Such acts produce results just like the ones that are seen.

Answer : No, the seen results are due to another cause.

Objector : But how can there be action when egoism is destroyed?

II.4.3-5 (ET93-94). *Answer* : (Some acts) produce results by overpowering your knowledge of Brahman through their power of giving rise to bodies, etc. When these acts come to an end, however, that knowledge becomes manifest. It is reasonable that knowledge and experience (*bhoga*) are not incompatible, since they are the results of karma that has already begun to work itself out. But other kinds of karma are different. When one's knowledge of one's identity with the Self becomes as firm as the belief of (another) man that he is a human being, that knowledge will liberate him even against his will!

CHAPTER FIVE : ERROR OF THE BUDDHI

II.5.1 (ET95). Just as Udaṅka did not accept the nectar, thinking it was urine, so Self-knowledge is not grasped because of the fear that one's karma will be destroyed.

II.5.2-3 (ET95-96). The Self seems to move and to stop when it is actually the *buddhi* that moves and stops, just as trees seem to move to one who is in a moving ship. Likewise, the Self is mistakenly thought to transmigrate.

II.5.4 (ET96). The appearances of sounds, etc., should be understood as awareness that belongs to the *buddhi* but is pervaded by the reflection (*pratibimba*) of consciousness (*caitanya*). People are confused by this.

CHAPTER SIX : DENIAL OF DIFFERENTIA (VIŚEṢĀPOHA)

II.6.1-2 (ET98). The Self is not in itself qualified by a limb that has been cut off and thrown away, and likewise, It is not qualified by any other things. Therefore all qualifiers are like the limb cut off and thrown away, for they are all non-Self. Thus the Self is free from all qualifiers.

II.6.3-6 (ET98-100). All these are qualifications only because of superimposition due to *avidyā*; they are like ornaments. They all should be known as unreal when the Self is known. Having realized that the Self is not the object of the ego notion, one should accept the Self as the knower free from all qualifiers. The ego too is like the limb cut off and thrown away. In the sentence "I am Brahman" the word "I" denotes pure consciousness, which was previously (thought to be) the object of the ego notion.

CHAPTER SEVEN : PERVASION BY THE BUDDHI

II.7.1-2 (ET101-102). I am the omniscient, omnipresent, Highest Brahman. Everything seen in whatever manner is seen by me as pervaded by the *buddhi*. Just as I am the witness (*sākṣin*) of my *buddhi's* objects, so I am of the objects of others also. It is not possible for me to be accepted or rejected; therefore I am the Highest Brahman.

II.7.3 (ET102). The Self does not change, is not impure or elemental; because It is the witness of all the *buddhis*, It is not of little feeling like the *buddhis*.

II.7.4 (ET102). Just as, when the sun shines, red color is seen in a crystal, so all is seen when illuminated by my "sunlight."

II.7.5 (ET102-103). Things seen may exist in the *buddhi* when the *buddhi* exists, but not when it is inoperative. The knower, however, is always the knower. Therefore, duality does not exist.

II.7.6 (ET103). Before discrimination the *buddhi's* understanding is erroneous. After discrimination there is neither *buddhi* nor anything other than the Highest (Brahman).

CHAPTER EIGHT : DESTRUCTION OF MIND (MATIVILĀPANA)

II.8.1 (ET104). Oh my mind ! Since I am really consciousness by nature, my connection with tastes, etc., is a delusion created by you. But since I am quite without qualifications no fruit comes to me from your efforts.

II.8.2 (ET104-105). Stop seeking effects made of *māyā*; be at peace in Me; I am the Highest Brahman, as if liberated; I am unborn (*ajā*) and one without a second.

II.8.4 (ET105). Being single, nothing different from Me can belong to Me, nor can I belong to anything else. Therefore, I get no benefit from your activities. As you (oh mind !) are not different from Me you can neither exert effort nor gain results.

II.8.5 (ET105). Since people are attached to effects and causes, this dialogue helps to liberate people by leading them to correct thoughts about the nature of the Self.

CHAPTER NINE : SUBTLENESS AND PERVASIVENESS

II.9.1 (ET107). In the series from earth to the innermost Self each succeeding item is found to be subtler and more pervasive.

II.9.2 (ET107-108). Earth, water, etc., are validly (*pramāṇatas*) known to be external, as bodies.

II.9.4 (ET108). All beings from Brahmā to immobile things (*sthāvara*) are My bodies. So from where should faults like lust and anger come into Me ?

II.9.5 (ET108-109). People think that I, the Lord, who resides in everything and am untouched by faults, am tainted, just as a child thinks the sky is blue.

CHAPTER TEN : RIGHT WAY OF SEEING THE NATURE OF CONSCIOUSNESS

II.10.4 (ET112). I have no sight (*darśana*) in deep sleep, waking, or dream. These states are due to confusion (*mohana*), for they have no independent existence nor do they depend on the Self. Therefore I am just the Fourth (*turīya*), the Seer, and without a second.

CHAPTER ELEVEN : WITNESS

II.11.1 (ET116). All things are by nature pure consciousness and only appear different because of *avidyā*. The apparent difference is caused to cease by the teaching "You are existent (*sadasīti*)."

II.11.5 (ET117). Just as dreams appear true as long as one does not wake up, so the identification of oneself with the body, and the validity of perception, etc., continue in the waking state as long as there is no Self-knowledge.

II.11.6 (ET117). I am Brahman, pure consciousness, without qualities, which like space (*vyoma*) remains in all beings. I am the witness, free from all the faults of beings.

II.11.8 (ET118). Those who think that they are Brahman and yet believe themselves to be agents and enjoyers have fallen from both knowledge and action. They are without doubt heterodox (*nāstika*).

II.11.9 (ET118). Just as the unseen (*adṛṣṭa*) results of merit and demerit are accepted on the basis of scripture (*śāstra*), it must be accepted on the same basis that the Self is Brahman and that liberation comes from knowledge.

II.11.10 (ET118-119). Yellow-colored clothes, etc., are the subconscious impressions (*vāsanā*) experienced by dreamers. The unique Seer (*dṛśi*) is different from them.

II.11.11 (ET119). Just as a sword when taken from its sheath is seen as it is, so the Knower, the Self-existent (*svayaṃbhu*) is experienced in sleep in its self-illuminating nature free from cause and effect.

CHAPTER TWELVE : ILLUMINATION

II.12.1 (ET122). Just as a man supposes his body to have light in it when it is exposed to the sun, so he makes the same supposition about the *citta* when it is reflecting pure consciousness.

II.12.3 (ET123). The ignorant man identifies himself with what is seen and does not know the seer, like the tenth man who got identified with the other nine.

II.12.4 (ET123). Say how there can reasonably be the two contrary ideas "do this" and "you are that (Brahman)" with respect to the same person at the same time.

II.12.6 (ET124). Identifying the seer and seen is like identifying one's self with one's face in the mirror.

II.12.8 (ET124). In "that art thou" it is the Knower of knowledge, the Self, that is denoted by the word "thou," and not the other (the *jīva*)—that other sense is due to superimposition.

II.12.10 (ET125). Just as the light of the sun together with (a part of) the body is what the knower knows, so things' natures together with the things in which they reside are what the Knower knows.

II.12.14-15 (ET126). Discrimination is an idea in the *buddhi*, and since it is something seen it is liable to destruction. The Self's consciousness, on the other hand, is never destroyed, not being produced; its producibility is imagined in it by another consciousness that is actually its object and different from it.

II.12.19 (ET127). Just as space (*vyoma*) is within everything, so I am even within space. So I am changeless, immobile, pure, unaging, without a second.

CHAPTER THIRTEEN : EYELESSNESS (ACAKṢUTVA)

II.13.1-8 (ET128-130). I, who am of the nature of pure consciousness only, have no perception or conception, since I have no sense organs or internal organ. Likewise, I do not act because I have no life breath (*prāṇa*). I am rather the witness of the fluctuations (*vṛtti*) of the internal organ produced by the sense organ together with its objects, as well as other fluctuations such as memory, attachment, dreams, etc.

II.13.9-10 (ET130). Because of failure to discriminate between the Self and the fluctuations of the internal organ men continue in *saṃsāra*, misconceiving themselves to be ignorant or pure, etc., as they identify themselves with various fluctuations.

II.13.14-17 (ET131-132). So, I have neither restlessness (*vikṣepa*) nor *samādhi*; both of these belong to the internal organ, which can change. Since the Self is changeless it cannot act either in *samādhi* or out of it.

CHAPTER FOURTEEN : DREAM (SVAPNA) AND MEMORY (SMṚTI)

II.14.1 (ET136). Since jars, etc., seem to appear in dreams and in memory, we may infer that the knower (*dhī*) having those objects as its form was seen before.

II.14.2 (ET136). Just as one is different from the body wandering about in one's dreams, so the Seer, witnessing the body in the waking state, must be different from that body.

II.14.3-6 (ET136-137). The internal organ—pervading colors, etc.—takes on their form, just as copper takes on the form of the mold when poured into it, or just as light assumes the form of the objects it reveals. It was the internal organ (the knower, *dhī*) in its form as the object that was seen before—otherwise how could one remember or dream of the forms of such objects? But the Self witnesses these modifications.

II.14.15 (ET140). For one who knows *prāṇa* everything is *prāṇa* and so there is no day or night for him; how much more then for the knower of nondual Brahman !

II.14.16 (ET140). Since the Self's consciousness never stops It neither remembers nor forgets itself. If the internal organ remembers the Self that is awareness conditioned by *avidyā*.

II.14.27-28 (ET143-144). For the Self-knower even Brahmā and Indra are pitiful objects. Why should he wish to become (like) Brahmā or Indra if all desires that cause frustration have been cut off?

II.14.33 (ET145). The Self, with *prājña* and *prāṇa* as adjuncts, is reflected in the fluctuations as the sun is reflected in water. The Self is pure and liberated naturally.

II.14.40 (ET147). The internal organ is a pilgrimage place (*tīrtha*) where the gods (*deva*), Vedas, and all other purifying agencies are united. Bathing in that place makes one immortal.

II.14.46 (ET148-149). If your view is that the internal organ takes on the forms of jars, etc., through its fluctuations and yet is not illuminated (by the Self), then the faults and impurities in that self could not be avoided.

CHAPTER FIFTEEN : ONE THING IS NOT ANOTHER

II.15.1 (ET151). Since one thing cannot be another, one should not suppose that Brahman is different from oneself, for if one supposes that they are different the one (the self) will surely be destroyed.

II.15.2 (ET151). Things seen appear like a picture painted on a canvas when it is remembered. That by which they are seen is the *jīva* (here, *saṃjñaka*), that in which they are seen, the *buddhi* (here, *sattvakṣetrajña*).

II.15.14 (ET155). In meditation one assumes the form of the object meditated upon, and the object is different from the meditator. No such action is possible on the part of the Self; it is independent of all actions, including meditation.

II.15.21-23 (ET157-158). The *buddhi*, burning with ignorance, desire, and action, like fuel in the fire of the Self, shines forth through the doors that are the senses. The Self's fire experiences objects when the *buddhi*, ignited by oblations, functions among the senses. If one remembers that all perceptions are but oblations offered to the Self's fire one does not become attached.

II.15.24-25 (ET158). The Self is called *taijasa* when witnessing dream objects produced by the impressions of karma arising from *avidyā*. It is called *prājña* when (in deep sleep) it is not aware of either objects or impressions.

II.15.41 (ET162). Awareness (*bodha*) does not require another awareness so that it be known—it is its own nature to illumine, just as it is the sun's nature to light itself.

II.15.42 (ET163). A light does not depend on another to be revealed; one's own nature does not depend on anything else.

II.15.44 (ET163). When something previously nonexistent comes into existence from something else it is called its effect. But light, being the sun's own nature, does not come into existence as the sun's effect.

II.15.45-46 (ET164). Just as the sun reveals jars or a snake coming out of its hole without exerting any agency in that revealing, so Self-awareness, having revealing as its nature, is a knower but not an agent.

II.15.48 (ET165). In similar fashion the Self, though without effort, is called an agent, just as a magnet is so called, though without agency.

CHAPTER SIXTEEN : EARTHY

II.16.1-2 (ET167). The solid matter in the body is earthy, the liquid part watery; its heat, motion, and the space contained in it consist of fire, air, and *ākāśa* respectively. The senses and their objects are also produced from earth, etc., respectively.

II.16.3-4 (ET168). These senses are called organs of the *buddhi*; the speech organ, the hand, etc., are the organs of action; and the *manas*, situated within, has as its purpose the imaginings (or constructions?) (*vikalpa*) through those (organs). The *buddhi* has as its purpose ascertainment of things. The Self is the Knower, always manifesting by its own nature, that is, illumination, everything that is experienced.

II.16.5 (ET168). Just as light, the manifester, takes on the forms of the objects it manifests but is really different from them, so the Self is different from ideas.

II.16.9 (ET169). One becomes frustrated when one believes himself to be frustrated, not merely by seeing frustration. The seer of the frustration in the body does not experience frustration.

II.16.10 (ET170). Cannot the Self be both subject and object, like the eye? No, for the eye consists of parts (so that one part might be subject, another object), but the Self is (only) the seer and does not become object.

II.16.11 (ET170). *Objection*: The Self is a combination of parts, since It consists of qualities such as knowledge, effort, etc.

Answer: No; like light It has only one quality, knowledge.

II.16.19-20 (ET173). Just as the closing and opening of the eye, which are properties of air (*vāyu*) and not of the eye, are mistaken for properties of the visual organ, which actually has the nature of light, and just as motion, not a property of the *manas* or the *buddhi*, is wrongly attributed to them, so the Self is mistaken for an agent because actions occur when the body, the *buddhi*, the *manas*, the eye, light, and objects are connected with It.

II.16.21 (ET173). The property of the *manas* is to imagine (*saṃkalpa*) and that of the *buddhi* is to ascertain (*adhyavasāya*), and not the other way around. Everything is imagined (constructed?) (*kalpita*) in the Self.

II.16.23 (ET174). *Objection*: Knowledge and its objects are momentary, merely *dharmas* (streaming) continuously. Just as a lamp seems to persist because of the similarity (of the *dharmas* of one moment to those of the next), so it is (with knowledge and its objects). The ultimate human purpose is to destroy this notion.

II.16.24 (ET174-175). *Answer*: One version of this theory has it that *rūpa*, etc., are appearances in another form of existent things that have their own form (*svākāra*). Another version is that no external objects exist. We address ourselves here to the first version.

II.16.25-26 (ET175). (On this version) knowledge has the same form as that of some external thing; but since everything is momentary and the *buddhi* (here, *dhī*) thus also momentary and incapable of supporting traces, there will be no memory.

II.16.27 (ET175-176). Again, it would be futile (on this view) to teach the means to attaining an end, since it needs no effort to destroy the notion of persistence; all things being (naturally) momentary the destruction of the persistence doesn't depend on anything else.

II.16.28 (ET176). *Objection* : The effect (the destruction of the notion of persistence) does depend on something though that something is different from its effect.

Answer : Then the effect depends on a series that is completely different (from the one that exhibits similarity). Anyway, on your view of the momentariness of everything, nothing can depend on anything.

II.16.29 (ET176). For *x* to depend on *y* the two must exist at the same time and be connected with each other so that connection with *x* is of benefit to *y*.

II.16.30 (ET177). We hold, in contrast, that there is false superimposition in the Self and the destruction of that in the same Self. On your view, who will attain liberation, since everything is always being destroyed ?

II.16.31 (ET177). One cannot deny the existence of one's Self, since it is the witness of all.

II.16.32 (ET177). If the witness didn't exist no one would be aware of the existence or nonexistence of anything.

II.16.39-41 (ET179). Liberation is artificial and fleeting according to those who view its attainment as the change of state on the part of the self. Again, liberation can't be union with Brahman or separation (from *prakṛti*); both union and separation being noneternal, liberation cannot consist of the individual going to Brahman or of Brahman coming to it. However, the true nature of the Self is never destroyed.

II.16.45 (ET181). Going out of equilibrium on the part of the *guṇas* is an unreasonable notion; since *avidyā* is at that point merged (into *avyaktaprakṛti*) there is no cause for the alleged going out of equilibrium.

II.16.46 (ET181). If the *guṇas* cause their own changes either they will always change or they never will, and there will be no regulation of those changes.

II.16.47 (ET182). If *prakṛti* works for the *puruṣas* there will be no difference between the bound and the liberated. Again, since *puruṣa* has no desires *prakṛti* cannot serve them !

II.16.49 (ET182). And since there can't reasonably be any relation between *prakṛti* and *puruṣa*, and since *prakṛti* is not conscious, *prakṛti* cannot serve the *puruṣa*.

II.16.51 (ET183). The followers of Kaṇāda—the Vaiśeṣikas—hold that pleasure, etc., are objects of knowledge, but they cannot be so, since they are qualities of the Knower and the Knower cannot know its own qualities, just as heat cannot be revealed by light.

II.16.52 (ET183). Further, since pleasure and knowledge are both produced by mind-self contact, they cannot inhere simultaneously in the self; so pleasure cannot be an object of knowledge.

II.16.53-54 (ET184). As for the other qualities, they too cannot occur simultaneously, being different from one another.

Objection : Knowledge of qualities is just their coinherence in the same self.

Answer : No, since pleasure, etc., are qualified by knowledge, and also since one remembers "pleasure was known by me," and the self is without awareness according to you.

II.16.55 (ET184). The self is changeless according to you, so pleasure, etc., cannot be qualities of it. Furthermore, since pleasure, etc., are as different from one self as from any of them—and from the internal organ, for that matter—why shouldn't they be present in those too ?

II.16.56 (ET185). If knowledge be knowable by a second knowledge an infinite regress will result. And if the two knowledges are produced simultaneously from contact between internal organ and self, then you ought to accept (simultaneous production of other qualities that you hold to arise successively).

II.16.57 (ET185). The Self is not bound since It does not change, It is not impure since It is not attached.

II.16.58-59 (ET185). *Objection* : If that is so, since there is no bondage there is no liberation and the scriptures are useless.

Answer : No, bondage is error (*bhrānti*) of the *buddhi*, and its removal is liberation.

CHAPTER SEVENTEEN : RIGHT THINKING (SAṂYAṄMATI)

II.17.1 (ET191). Nothing exists other than the Self.

II.17.10 (ET194). *Objection* : Scripture states that three things exist besides the Self, namely, form (*rūpa*), name (*nāman*), and action (*karman*).

II.17.11-12 (ET194-195). These three are constructed (or imagined, *kalpita*), for they are interdependent; for example, a painting and its description are mutually dependent and so involve imagination. So, just as form is constructed as related to words and *buddhi*, likewise the whole world is constructed (*vikalpita*) from error and *buddhi*.

II.17.13 (ET195). What is existent (*sat*) and mere consciousness (*ciṅmātra*) is not imagined. It is both knower and known. What is other than that is constructed.

II.17.14-15 (ET195). This thing which is existent and pure consciousness is the knower by which everything in dream is known, as well as what is known in dream by *māyā*.

II.17.16 (ET196). Just as a jewel seems to become colored because of its proximity to colored things, so pure consciousness assumes different form because of the superimposition of different adjuncts.

II.17.17 (ET196). Both in dream and in the waking state different forms are constructed. The difference makes manifest states of the *buddhi* as objects, leading to actions arising from desire through error.

II.17.18 (ET196). What is in the waking state is like what is in dream. The ideas of what is internal (in dream) and external (in waking) are mutually dependent, like reading and writing.

II.17.19 (ET197). When the self imagines different things it desires them and so determines to have them, and then arise actions according to those desires and determinations.

II.17.20 (ET197). Even though it is not perceived in deep sleep the whole universe is perceived as a product of *avidyā*; it is quite unreal.

II.17.22 (ET197-198). When the *citta* is pure like a (clean) mirror, knowledge (*vidyā*) is revealed. So, one should take care to purify it by forbearance (*yama*), performance of the regular duties (*nityakarman*), sacrifices, and austerities (*tapas*).

II.17.23 (ET198). One should practice the best austerities regarding the body, etc., in order to purify the internal organ. One should undertake to control the internal organ, etc., and to wither the body away.

II.17.24 (ET198). The best austerity is the one-pointedness of the internal organ and the senses; it is better than all duties.

II.17.26 (ET199). That which is called deep sleep is darkness or ignorance (*ajñāna*), the seed of sleeping and waking awareness. It ought to be completely burnt up by Self-knowledge like a burnt seed that does not mature.

II.17.27 (ET199). That seed, called *māyā*, evolves into the three states that succeed each other over and over. The Self, the locus of *māyā*, though without change and single, appears as many like reflections in the water.

II.17.29 (ET200). Or, like a magician who comes and goes on an elephant (which he has created), so the Self, though without motion, appears to be undergoing conditions of various sorts.

II.17.31 (ET200). But there is no magic for those whose vision is not obscured or for the magician himself.

II.17.33 (ET201). *Objection* : Since the Self is not perceptible to the sense organs being devoid of sensible qualities like sound, etc., and being different from pleasure, etc., how can it be perceived by the *buddhi*?

II.17.34 (ET201). Just as Rāhu, though invisible, is seen as a reflection in the moon, so the Self, though omnipresent, is grasped in the *buddhi*.

II.17.35 (ET202). Just as the reflection and the heat of the sun, perceived in water, do not belong there, so consciousness is experienced in the *buddhi* though it is not a property of the *buddhi*, since its nature is opposed to the *buddhi*.

CHAPTER EIGHTEEN : THAT ART THOU

The interpretation here follows that of A. J. Alston, *That Art Thou* (London, 1967) on various points.

II.18.2 (ET128). The author pays his respects to his teacher's teacher.

II.18.9-18 (ET220-223). *Objection* : Liberation does not arise when one hears "that art thou"; one must practice meditation (*prasaṃkhyāna*) along with reasoning (*yukti*). Since one doesn't perceive the Self directly just from hearing the sentence, there must be an injunction (*niyoga*) (to some sort of action), just as there is in the case of ritual action. And this is not inconsistent (with knowledge) as long as the knowledge remains fitful. Again, if a man could get Self-knowledge by behaving as he pleases, prescriptions would be pointless; so meditation and reasoning are acts that are (prescribed) to be performed until there is Self-knowledge. The tendencies (*saṃskāra*) produced by perception surely sublate the notion "I am the existent," (*sadasmi*) which one derives from hearing the sentence in question. Also, one is attracted by defects (*doṣa*) toward objects. Perception, which gives us particular knowledge of objects, can certainly contradict ideas arising from hearing or from inference, since those give us general knowledge of things. No one becomes free from pain merely from understanding the meaning of a sentence. And even if someone were to become free, it would be inferred that he had meditated on the sentence's meaning in previous lives. Indeed, if people could become free from pain in this way we would have to conclude that there is no basis in scripture for our actions, which is not desirable. Furthermore, in the Vedas a result (*phala*) has been set forth in this sentence, and so there must be a means (*sādhana*) for its attainment. Since this result can only be an entity that already exists, that is, the Self, the only appropriate means must be meditation. Therefore, meditation should be practiced in order to realize the Self by one who is tranquil (*sama*), etc., and who has given up everything that is inconsistent with the means and its goal.

II.18.19 (ET223-224). *Answer* : This is not right. Liberation is not a goal that depends on action for its achieving.

II.18.20-21 (ET224). Rather, in the text "not this, not this," scripture prohibits the practice of superimposition. Just as a father superimposes his son's troubles on himself, so the ego is superimposed onto the Self, and the text in question removes the superimposition, after which no later injunction to act is possible (since action requires superimposition).

II.18.22-23 (ET224-225). Just as ignorant people superimpose impurities onto the sky and are advised to stop doing so, so there can be both superimposition on the Self and prohibitions of it. But if the prohibited superimposition had been real, liberation would be transient, so superimposition must be unreal and its prohibition must be like a rule against constructing an altar (*agnicayana*) in the sky.

II.18.24 (ET225). Words cannot refer to the Self, since they can only refer to objects. Likewise the ego sense cannot reveal the Self.

II.18.28 (ET226). Words can refer to something associated with a universal or a motion, etc., but since the Self is not associated with such things words cannot refer to It.

II.18.29-31 (ET226-227). Words can indirectly (by *lakṣaṇā*) indicate the Witness when they directly name (*abhidhā*) a reflection (*ābhāsa*) of It; but they cannot directly refer to It. It is as when one uses a word indirectly suggesting fire in referring to torches, etc.

II.18.32-33 (ET227-228). The reflection of a face is different from the face since it conforms to the mirror, whereas the face is different from the reflection because it does not conform to the mirror. The reflection of the Self in the ego sense is like that—they are different, but are not distinguished.

II.18.34 (ET228). Some say that the reflection alone, the ego sense, is the transmigrator (*saṃsārin*). They say that a shadow (*chāyā*) is real, since we learn that from *smṛti*, and also because a shadow causes a (real) result such as coolness, etc.

II.18.35 (ET228-229). Others say that the transmigrator is a part or modification of the Knower and is itself the reflection of that (Knower, that is, the Self). Others again say that the transmigrator is the independent ego sense only.

II.18.36 (ET229). The Buddhists say that the transmigrator is the series (*saṃtāna*) consisting of the ego sense, etc., and that there is no positive (permanent) element (*anvayin*) there. We shall consider these various opinions below (II.18.44ff.).

II.18.37 (ET229). Let us now return to the present topic. The reflection of the face in the mirror is a property of neither the face nor the mirror, for if it were a property of either it would persist when they were parted.

II.18.39 (ET230). *Objection* : It is the property of both together).

Answer : No, because it is not always seen even when both are present (but wrongly positioned).

Objection : But, for example, Rāhu, a real thing, is sometimes seen in the sun and the moon (at an eclipse).

II.18.40 (ET230). *Answer* : If Rāhu is taken to be already proved as real, the reflection of the face is not, and the example is irrelevant. But if Rāhu is taken to be a shadow, then it is unreal as we have shown.

II.18.41 (ET231). The *smṛti* text (referred to in II.18.34) prohibits one from stepping over certain persons' shadows, but being a prohibition it cannot establish the reality of anything.

II.18.42 (ET231). The coolness referred to in II.18.34 arises from avoiding hot substances, and when such behavior has a positive cause it is perceptible, for example, water. But a shadow is not perceptible.

II.18.44 (ET231-232). *Objection* : Then who is the transmigrator? Not the Seer (*dṛśi*) for It cannot change, and not the reflection, for it is not real, and not the ego sense, since it is not conscious.

II.18.45 (ET232). *Answer* : Transmigration must therefore be mere *avidyā* arising from nondiscrimination.

II.18.46 (ET232). Just as the rope-snake, though unreal, has existence by virtue of the rope's existence until discrimination occurs, so likewise transmigration has existence by virtue of the changeless Self (until discrimination occurs).

II.18.47 (ET232). *Second objector* of II.18.35: The self, itself the locus of the reflection of the Self through Its own ideas possessing changes, is the transmigrator; eternal, it experiences pleasures and pains.

II.18.48 (ET233). *Answer*: This opinion arises from misinterpretation of the scriptures and from lack of right knowledge of the Self, as a result of which you identify the Self with the ego. Not discriminating them, you will continue to transmigrate. But accepting my view one can explain how the Vedas can refer to the Self (indirectly) by words meaning "knowledge."

II.18.51-52 (ET234). *Objection* : On your analysis, in the sentence "he knows," the agent and the action belong to different loci. But it is evident and well recognized in the world that the act and its agent, denoted respectively by the verb and the pronoun, belong to the same locus, as in "he does" or "he goes." So you should explain why it is different in the case of "he knows."

II.18.53-54 (ET234). *Answer* : Through nondiscrimination the word "knows" is mistakenly predicated of the Self. Since the *buddhi* has no knowledge and the Self has no activity, the expression "he knows" cannot be properly applied to either of them.

II.18.59-60 (ET236). *Objection* : If a word has no primary sense it cannot have a secondary one either. What is the primary sense of "knows" on your view? If words have no meaning, the Vedas will cease to be an authority, and since you don't want that you'd better admit that the sentence "he knows" refers to the act of knowing as it is ordinarily understood to refer.

II.18.61-62 (ET236). *Answer*: If you accept what seems evident to ignorant people you will end up holding the Lokāyata position, which you don't wish to uphold. But if one takes the position of the learned (in grammar) then it will be hard to understand the meaning of the word "knowledge" as it is used in the Vedas to designate the Self. The Vedas must be held authoritative, however, and there is a way out of this.

II.18.63-69 (ET236-238). Ordinary people's usage construes knowing as an act, since they do not distinguish the thing from its reflection and so superimpose agency, which properly belongs to the *buddhi*, onto the Self. Thus we come to speak of the *buddhi* as the knower. But we know from scripture that knowledge is eternal, so that it cannot be produced by the *buddhi* or indeed by anything at all. We come to speak of the *buddhi* and the Self both as the agents of the act of knowing, just as we speak of our selves as our bodies. The Logicians (*tārkikas*) are deluded also in this way and judge that knowledge is produced. But the correct view is that the word "knows," as well as the experiences corresponding to that word and the memories of them, all proceed from failure to distinguish the Self from the *buddhi* and the reflection of the Self in the *buddhi*.

II.18.72-73 (ET239). The Buddhists deny the existence of a knower by holding that (ideas) are self-illuminating and are themselves knowers. This theory will be hard to refute unless one insists that (ideas are nonconscious and) illuminated by something completely different in nature from them.

II.18.74 (ET239-240). But if you say that there is a persistent knower actively cognizing the ideas, that is no better, for such a knowing agent must itself be nonconscious too, and there would be nothing else to know it.

II.18.75 (ET240). *Objection* : The knower and known are entirely different, but knowledge arises merely from the proximity of the knower to the known (and not from reflection or superimposition).

Answer: No, since the knowing witness is proximate to everything and so everything will become conscious.

II.18.76-77 (ET240-241). Furthermore, is the frustrated hearer-seeker the Witness Itself or something else ? You do not accept that the Witness suffers or strives. But you cannot admit either that the sufferer and striver can understand that he is the Witness, since he is an agent. So the scriptural statement "that art thou" will be false, and that is wrong.

II.18.78 (ET241). This statement makes sense if it is made from the standpoint of nondiscrimination, but if the ego has been discriminated from the Witness and then the two are identified that will bring in the faults mentioned.

II.18.79 (ET241). Now if you say that the word "thou" indirectly refers to the Witness, then you will have to show what relation exists between the Witness and the ego that is the direct meaning of "thou."

II.18.80 (ET241-242). *Opponent* : The relation is of the seer to the seen.

Answer : How can the Witness be a seer, since It is without activity ?

II.18.81 (ET242). If the relation between Witness and ego is identity (*tādātmya*), understanding the Witness to be without activity; still unless one can perceive that relation the idea (of the Witness) could not arise.

II.18.82 (ET242). And if you think that the relation in question is found explained in scripture, that cannot be, for the three defects explained earlier will apply, and in any case the relation must be grasped in the form "there is a witness of mine" (and not "I am the Witness").

II.18.83 (ET242). But when the *buddhi*, not conscious, is reflected as if conscious, then its ideas also are reflected as if conscious, as sparks from a red-hot iron appear to be fire.

II.18.84 (ET243). Only if a Witness exists, which is not rejected when these other things are, can it be explained how people may sometimes experience a reflection of consciousness and sometimes not, and how one can hope to know the Witness.

II.18.88 (ET244). Neither scripture nor reasoning support the notion that *citta* is conscious, since then the body, the eye, etc., would be also.

II.18.89 (ET244). *Objection* : So what if they are ?

Answer : Then you fall into the Lokāyata position. Furthermore there could never be the idea "I am the seer" unless consciousness were reflected in the *buddhi* (here, *cetas*).

II.18.90 (ET244). Unless one is already convinced that he is the seer the teaching "thou are that" will be useless. It can only be meaningful to one who knows the difference between the Self and the not-Self.

II.18.91 (ET245). A thing known as "mine" or "this" is without doubt part of the "thou" (i.e., not Self). A thing known as "I" (alone) is part of the "that" (the Self), whereas what is known as "I am this" belongs to both spheres.

II.18.92 (ET245). All these ideas express the Self more or less directly, but the question which of them qualify which must be worked out by reasoning.

II.18.93 (ET245). "Mine" and "this" are qualifiers of the intermediate one (the "I am this" of II.18.91). Just as for a wealthy man the wealth is the qualifier of the whole man including his body, so the body is a qualifier of the pure Self qualified by the ego sense.

II.18.94 (ET245-246). Everything involving the *buddhi*, including the ego sense, is a qualifier of the Witness. And that pure consciousness, touched by nothing, is reflected in everything.

II.18.95 (ET246). From the ordinary point of view all this is just the reverse of what we suppose. For the undiscriminating everything exists, for those who discriminate, nothing exists (except the Self).

II.18.96 (ET246-247). Only reasoning, considering cases of agreement and difference of words and things denoted by them, can determine the meaning of "I" (and not common sense).

II.18.99 (ET247-248). When the meaning of "that art thou" has been understood on the basis of scripture and worldly analogies the scripture again says "that art thou" to (finally) remove the delusion of the hearer.

II.18.100 (ET247-248). It is as when Brahmā told Rāma "Thou art Viṣṇu, not Daśaratha's son" and removed Rāma's delusion. He did not indicate any further effort that Rāma had to make in order to realize his Viṣṇu-nature.

II.18.101 (ET248). In this way (under these circumstances) the word "I" reveals the innermost Self. The sentence "that art thou" provides the same revelation. The result is liberation.

II.18.102 (ET248-249). If right knowledge were not produced directly from hearing the relevant texts, one would have to assume there is some further act that has to be performed. But even before experiencing it (directly through the text's hearing) the existence of one's Self is admitted.

II.18.103 (ET249). Right knowledge of the meaning of "that thou art" arises immediately on hearing it and results in liberation.

II.18.105-106 (ET250). Does "I am Brahman" mean that I am Brahman or something else? If it means that I truly am Brahman, then the Self and Brahman are identical. But if something else is meant the sentence would be false. So, it is only by taking the Self and Brahman as identical that a contradiction with the experience of liberation can be avoided.

II.18.107 (ET250). Ideas and the *buddhi* exist for the sake of the Self, which is reflected in them. Since they are not conscious, it is supposed (*kalpyate*) that the result of the liberating knowledge belongs to pure consciousness.

II.18.108 (ET250-251). Since the causes of the "result" (liberation)—that is, the activity of the *buddhi* and its ideas—are not of the nature of that "result" (being nonconscious), it is proper to attribute it to the unchanging (Self), just as a victory won by his army can be properly attributed to the king.

II.18.109 (ET251). Just as the reflection of one's face in the mirror may be identified with the face, so the reflection in the mirror of ideas is in fact the Self.

II.18.110 (ET251). Only in this way is the sentence "I am the existent (Brahman)" to be understood. Without a (similar) bridge, the teaching "that art thou" would also be useless.

II.18.111 (ET251). Teaching is useful only when addressed to a hearer. If the Witness is not the hearer, who else could it be?

II.18.112 (ET251-252). If you say that the *buddhi* may be the hearer because of its proximity to the Witness, no, because the Witness cannot help the *buddhi* to hear any more than a piece of wood can!

II.18.113 (ET252). And if the Witness did help the *buddhi* it would follow that it acted and changed, and that is undesirable. But if reflection is accepted this problem does not arise.

II.18.115-116 (ET252-253). *Objection* : In order to know that something is a reflection of the Self we must know that the Self exists independently of the reflection. But in order to know that the Self exists independently of the reflection we must know that the thing *is* a reflection of the Self. So your case depends on mutual dependence (*anyonyāśraya*).

II.18.117 (ET253). *Answer* : No, for in dreams the dream notions and the seer are known to be distinct. In that state there are no (external) chariots, etc., so that the Self must directly apprehend the ideas.

II.18.118 (ET253-254). (In the waking state too) an idea pervaded by consciousness takes on objective form. That whose form it is is called the external object.

II.18.119 (ET253-254). This latter (the external object) is the objective (*karman*) because it is desired, and one who desires it is enjoined to action relating to it. In the present case (of knowing), that which is modified into the form of the (external) object (viz., the *buddhi*) is said to be the instrument by which the object is obtained.

II.18.120 (ET254). And that (ego) which is pervaded by a reflection of consciousness is called the "knower." One who distinguishes between these three (object, instrument, and agent of knowing) knows the Self.

II.18.121-122 (ET254-255). Ideas vary, some being true, some false, some doubtful. Consciousness is one in all of them, and the difference stems from the ideas alone, just as a crystal takes on different colors because of the differences in the adjuncts with which it becomes associated.

II.18.123 (ET255). The ideas are manifested, apprehended, and have their existence proved by something else that is immediately known. This inference may take as an illustration the lamp.

II.18.124 (ET255). Can one get another to know the Self through a *pramāṇa*? Or is it to be done rather by negation of everything else other than the Self without a *pramāṇa*?

II.18.125 (ET255-256). *Opponent*: It is done by negating everything else on the authority of scripture alone.

Answer: That will lead to a mere void (*śūnyatā*), as there would be no familiarity (*prasiddhi*) with the Witness.

II.18.126 (ET256). *Opponent*: One reasons "you are conscious; how can you be the body?"

Answer: No, for one is not familiar (with pure consciousness).

The inference would only be valid if one already had proved the Self as pure consciousness.

II.18.127 (ET256). *Opponent* : Pure consciousness is immediately evident, so the Witness (does not need to be proved).

Answer : If that were the case it should also be evident to the Voidist.

II.18.128 (ET256). *Opponent* : We remember that we saw something. This proves that the agent, object, and instrument exist simultaneously for the witnessing Self.

II.18.129 (ET257). *Answer* : Supposing that memory were a valid means of knowing, still the agent, object, and instrument are known successively, and the memory must likewise cognize them successively. The notion of their simultaneity is a false one.

II.18.130 (ET257). Between the ideas "I knew this" and "I knew myself as agent" there is mutual dependence, and where that is the case there cannot be simultaneous awareness.

II.18.131 (ET257). Furthermore, to know each of the three (agent, object, and instrument) all three are required. When the knower is engaged in knowing the agent it is not available to know simultaneously the object and instrument.

II.18.132 (ET258). In any case, an object is what an agent strives to obtain, and so it helps prove an agent and nothing else (not, e.g., a Witness).

II.18.133 (ET258). When someone does not know something a *pramāṇa*—such as verbal testimony or inference—is required.

II.18.134 (ET258). Is the Witness also established by a *pramāṇa*, or not? It is.

II.18.135 (ET258). And this is so whether the one who doesn't yet know is the Witness itself or something else.

II.18.136 (ET259). What does "established" mean (in II.18.134)? Does it mean "made known" or "made to exist" or something else?

II.18.137 (ET259). If it means "made to exist" all efforts are useless, since it is evident that things come to exist from their natural causes.

II.18.138 (ET259). So here "established" means "made known."

II.18.139 (ET259-260). *Opponent* : Being established means being known through a clear distinction between act, agent, etc.

Answer : No, for "clear" and "unclear" only make sense as applied to something other than the Self.

II.18.140 (ET260). The reason why a pot is not "clear" to a blind man is that he is not a seer. For the agent, instrument, and object of Self-knowledge to be "clear" there will have to be a seer beyond all of them to apprehend this.

II.18.141-143 (ET260-261). *Objection* (by a Vijñānavādin): Why do we need to say that experience requires a Witness different from it? On our view experience is the experiencer. Through error, consciousness, which is really undifferentiated, appears to have distinctions of object (*grāhya*), grasper (*grāhaka*), and knowledge (*saṃvitti*). But since consciousness is the only reality, it is both the act and the agent and object as well.

II.18.143-144 (ET261). *Answer*: If consciousness is destroyed every moment it will require an agent to bring it into existence.

Buddhist: Consciousness has no properties.

Śaṃkara: Then you contradict your own thesis that it is momentary.

Buddhist: Such properties are just the absence of their opposites, for example, the absence of nonexistence.

Śaṃkara: Then consciousness is not momentary, for you hold that it is *svalakṣaṇa* (and so of a positive character).

II.18.145-146 (ET261-262). You define cowhood as absence of noncow, but this will not do. No more will it do to define destruction as absence of nondestruction. For you even a moment is only the absence of the nonmomentary.

II.18.147 (ET262). *Buddhist*: Absence has no distinctions in itself; the distinctions are due to names.

Answer: How can plurality be introduced into a unity merely through names?

II.18.148 (ET262-263). If a word signifies the absence of (all) things different how can it uniquely apply to a particular, say, a cow? An absence cannot create distinctions, nor is it itself particular.

II.18.149 (ET263). And since on your view there are no qualifications of knowledge by names, universal properties, etc., likewise there are no qualifications of negation (which may particularize a cow).

II.18.150 (ET263). But for practical purposes we need perception and inference, which require qualifications in their objects distinguishing acts and their factors (viz., object and instrument).

II.18.151 (ET263). So you must admit pot, blue, yellow, etc., as qualifiers of consciousness, as well as a knower by which these are known.

II.18.152 (ET263-264). And as the perceiver is different from the colors and objects he perceives, so the knower of ideas is different from them since he illuminates them like a lamp.

II.18.154-155 (ET264). Is knowing an act? Or does the knower pervade its object? Neither. Assistance (*upakāra*) is given to the ideas by the constant Knower. We have already said that this assistance consists in the reflection of consciousness. Assisted by it the *buddhi* pervades pots, etc., as their illuminator, like light.

II.18.156 (ET264-265). A pot becomes invested with *buddhi* just as it becomes lit up by standing in the light. This investing of the pot with the *buddhi* is the pervading of it by the *buddhi*, and it is a process with stages.

II.18.157 (ET265). First the idea encompasses the pot, and subsequently it becomes assisted by the Self. But the Self does not participate in the process any more than time or space, etc.

II.18.158 (ET265). Only a knower depending on instruments (*karaṇa*) for grasping objects, since it knows only a part of its field, can be an evolver (*pariṇāmin*).

II.18.159 (ET265-266). Only the *buddhi*, and not the Witness, can have the knowledge "I am the Witness," for there is nothing different from the Witness (with which to make the contrast).

II.18.160 (ET266). On the other hand, the ego is not that which experiences liberation, since it cannot be without pain or pleasure.

II.18.161-162 (ET266). Rather, the undiscriminating notion that one is in pain, which arises from identification with the body, etc., is sublated by the discrimination revealing one's identity with the Self, just as the notion that "I am the one with the earrings on" is sublated when one takes them off. If it were the reverse a *pramāṇa* would lead to unreality and would not be a *pramāṇa*.

II.18.170 (ET268). The words "that" and "thou" (in "that art thou"), which refer to one and the same thing, function as the words in "the black horse" do.

II.18.171 (ET269). The word "thou" loses its meaning of the empirical ego subject to frustration by being set in apposition to "that," meaning the pure Witness not subject to frustration. Likewise, the term "that," set in apposition to "thou," which indicates the inner Self, loses its sense of something not immediately known.

II.18.173 (ET269). So the two words, without completely giving up their own proper meanings, together convey a qualified meaning leading to immediate awareness of the inner Self. Any other way of construing the sentence leads to contradiction.

II.18.174-175 (ET270). The tenth man—led astray by the idea of nine—only needs to know himself (no act is needed). Likewise, the one whose *buddhi* has been led astray by desire because his eyes have been bandaged by *avidyā* needs only to know himself as pure consciousness distinct from everything else.

II.18.177-178 (ET270-271). In understanding the meaning of

a sentence one must first determine the relationships among the words by positive and negative concomitance (*anvayavyatireka*), for the meaning of a sentence is a function of our memory of the words that are heard to compose it.

II.18.179 (ET271). In the case of sentences that state eternal truths, once the meanings of the words have been rightly discriminated resulting in an understanding of the meaning of the whole sentence, no further questioning of the meaning is appropriate.

II.18.180-183 (ET271-272). This method of positive and negative concomitance is only needed for the understanding of the word "thou" as the pure Self. Once this discrimination has occurred, the meaning of the sentence becomes as clear as a piece of fruit in one's palm. In this way the meaning of "that art thou" as meaning the pure Self becomes clear from understanding the meanings of the words therein, through the rejection of the false idea of the Self as sufferer (which is inconsistent with the word "that").

II.18.185 (ET273). Perception, etc., can contradict a sentence such as "cook the pieces of gold" (since one can't cook gold). But how can there be contradiction of a sentence (such as "that art thou") by things caused by the organs ?

II.18.186-188 (ET273-274). *Objection* : As long as one perceives that he is frustrated (or "in pain") the belief that he is free from frustration cannot arise merely from hearing the sentence "I am free from frustration" !

Answer : No, for we regularly realize that we are free from suffering—for example, when we wake up from a nightmare.

Objection : The example is irrelevant; we did not hear a sentence in our dream !

Answer: Nevertheless, once the dream is over we believe the suffering not only not to persist but indeed never to have really occurred at all. A persistence (*saṃtāna*) of error or suffering is never found.

II.18.189 (ET274). Once a man knows that his self is the inner Self through sublation of the notion that is suffering, his knowledge is uncontradictable as was that of the one who realized he was the tenth.

II.18.194 (ET275-276). Truth (*pramā*) does not arise from hearing such texts as "cook the gold pieces," since such texts must be interpreted figuratively. But since "that art thou" does not contradict known truths this is not the case for it.

II.18.201 (ET278). *Objection* : One cannot achieve a concrete experience of satisfaction like that which follows eating merely from hearing a sentence. To analyze a sentence hoping to achieve a concrete experience is like trying to make milk pudding from cow dung.

II.18.202 (ET278). *Answer*: All sentences about the not-Self produce abstract knowledge only, but such is not the case with sentences about the inner Self, for there are exceptions, for example, the tenth man.

II.18.203 (ET278). The Self is its own *pramāṇa*; that is, it is self-known.

II.18.207 (ET279-280). Had the texts said "thou will be Brahman" (instead of "thou art Brahman") then one would have to practice actions like hearing, considering, and meditating. But then liberation would be treated as impermanent, which would involve a contradiction. So to read the Vedas as implying that is incorrect.

II.18.208 (ET280). Or again, if the hearer were different from what was to be heard about, the hearing might be viewed as an enjoined act. But the opponent accepts their identity too. So if the text is interpreted following his principles it becomes quite unintelligible.

II.18.209-210 (ET280). If a man once knows he is liberation itself, self-existent and self-evident, then if he should desire to act he is crazy and flouts the scripture. For that which is self-existent and self-evident there is nothing to do, whereas that which has something to do is not self-existent and self-evident.

II.18.211 (ET281). *Objection* : The words "I am liberation, self-evident and self-existent" just state a fact. But why should there be any activity on the part of the hearer to understand them ?

II.18.212-214 (ET281-282). *Answer* : One knows from perception that one is an agent and feels frustrated, and then arise efforts to avoid that state. The scripture, recognizing this state of the hearer, enjoins reasoning, etc., on his part so that he may understand who he is. But once one has understood this, how can he ever thereafter accept any idea contrary to that ?

II.18.215 (ET282). *Objection* : Then why, if I am in fact contrary in nature, should I have the impression that I am a desirer, an agent, and not the self-existent, self-evident One ?

II.18.216 (ET282). *Answer* : It makes sense to ask why one has the impression of being desirer and agent, but it makes no sense to ask why one is liberated. For one only questions what is contrary to *pramāṇas*.

II.18.217 (ET282). Now the experience "I am liberated" accords with a *pramāṇa*, that is, with verbal testimony in the text "that art thou." However, the impression of being frustrated should be questioned, since it arises from a fallacious perception (*pratyakṣā-bhāsa*).

II.18.220 (ET283). Scripture cannot be doubted in what it says about the nature of the Self, for in this sphere it is the authoritative *pramāṇa*.

II.18.221 (ET283-284). No notion of the Self other than that indicated by scripture is authoritative.

CHAPTER NINETEEN : CONVERSATION BETWEEN SELF AND INTERNAL ORGAN (= MIND)

II.19.1 (ET288). If one treats with the medicines of knowledge and nonattachment the sickness of desire, one will be cured.

II.19.2-3 (ET288-289). Oh mind, your ideas of "me" and "mine" are efforts for someone else other than yourself. Since you are not conscious and I don't want anything, being quite content, you should keep quiet; I am thinking of your welfare.

II.19.4 (ET289). Scripture and the other *pramāṇas* tell me that the one that is beyond the six continual waves is the Self of the world and of us. Your efforts are useless therefore.

II.19.5 (ET289-290). The cause of all wrong notions is the perception of difference. So when you are quieted, the idea of difference disappearing, people will not be deluded.

II.19.15 (ET293). If duality, assumed by us to be real so that there can be inquiry, were nonexistent, then inquiry would be impossible and truth would not be known, and that is not desirable.

II.19.16-17 (ET294). *Objection* : What is called "real" is actually unreal, like a horn on a human's head, because it doesn't serve any purpose.

Answer: Serving a purpose is not a proper criterion of reality. And anyway, the Self does serve a purpose, since it is the subject matter of inquiry as well as the source of creation through *māyā*.

CHĀNDOGYOPANIṢADBHĀṢYA

The *Chāndogya Upaniṣad*, the second longest and one of the oldest and most authoritative Upaniṣads, belongs to the *Sāma Veda*. A. Weber long ago argued that the *Chāndogya* antedates at least the sixth book of the *Bṛhadāraṇyaka*, with which Upaniṣad it overlaps at certain points.[31] The *Chāndogya Upaniṣad* belongs to the *Taṇḍin Brāhmaṇa* of the *Sāma Veda*. I am not aware that the question of the authenticity of Śaṃkara's commentary on this Upaniṣad has as yet been explored using modern standards, but no one has questioned the ascription of the work to Śaṃkara.

"E" references are to the edition by H. R. Bhagavat, *Works of Shankaracharya*, volume two, part one (Poona: Ashtekar & Co., 1927), pp. 113-334. "T" refers to the translation by Ganganatha Jha in Poona Oriental Series 78 (Poona: Oriental Book Agency, 1942).

BOOK ONE

Introduction (E113-114; T1-5). One can fulfill the aims of man neither by action alone, which leads to the region of the moon by the southern path, or "path of smoke," nor by action accompanied by knowledge of *prāṇa*, etc., which leads to the region of the sun by the northern path, or "path of fire." Deviating from either of these paths according to one's nature one merely earns further rebirths. It is only knowledge of the nondual Self, without dependence on any action, that causes the cessation of these three "paths," and this is what is explained in the *Chāndogya Upaniṣad.*

Indeed, this kind of knowledge is absolutely inconsistent with action because it undermines all distinctions involving act, instrument, and result and so cannot in turn be undermined by any idea involving such distinctions.

Objector : But there are injunctions to act (which undermine this kind of knowledge); these are enjoined on those who know the Vedas, and thus, among others, on those who know the nondual Self.

Answer : No, since in the absence of awareness of distinction of agent, experiencer, etc., which lie in the ambit of action, no action is possible. It follows that actions are only enjoined on those visited by the fault of *avidyā*, not on the Self-knower.

In this Upaniṣad knowledge of the nondual Self is the main subject matter, along with several kinds of worship (*upāsana*) and meditative means (*sādhana*) to higher ends (*abhyudaya*), which are close to isolation (*kaivalya*) and which relate to the sphere of modified (*vikṛta*) Brahman—these (worship and meditation) help effect the results of action and yet are like knowledge of the nondual Self in that they involve the functioning of the internal organ (*manas*). The difference, however, is that, whereas worship and meditation work by helping to concentrate the internal organ on some supporting object (*ālambana*) and thus assist one in achieving purity of *sattva*, which in turn illuminates the nature of reality (*vastutattvāvabhāsa*), knowledge of the nondual Self undermines all ideas of difference (including that of any supporting object) that are superimposed on the Self, just as knowledge of rope undermines the idea of snake. Because worship and meditation, involving a supporting object, are easier to practice they are expounded first (in this Upaniṣad). Indeed, the very first to be expounded are those practices which relate to the elements (*aṅga*) of (sacrificial) action, since they are more familiar and overhasty abandonment of action will make any meditation or worship very difficult.

I.1.10 (E117-118; T13-15). This section discusses the role of "*om*" in sacrifice and recommends meditation upon it.

Objector : Why meditate upon it? Pronouncing it is efficacious in sacrifice (as long as it is done correctly) whether one understands it or not, just as a person who doesn't understand medicine is cured by a drug just as much as one who understands.

Answer : Knowledge renders acts more effective; a jeweler, because of his knowledge of jewels, does better in business than the amateur, even though both are qualified to barter; likewise, though both those ignorant of "*om*" and those knowledgeable are fit to worship, the latter are more likely to succeed.

II.23.1 (E158-161; T103-115). This Upaniṣadic passage states that three kinds of persons achieve "a meritorious place" (*puṇyaloka*, i.e., heaven), whereas one who stands in Brahman (*brahmasaṃstha*) achieves immortality. The three kinds of heaven-bound persons are (1) householders who perform sacrifices, study the scriptures, and practice charity to mendicants within their means; (2) wandering ascetics who have achieved the fourth *āśrama* (i.e., *saṃnyāsa*) but do not "stand in Brahman"; and (3) the lifelong *brahmacārin*, who dwells with a teacher throughout his life studying and practicing penance. Those who "stand in Brahman" are a fourth kind; they are wandering mendicants who rest firmly in Brahman and achieve final immortality, not just temporary immortality such as gods, etc. have.

Now some (Ānandagiri says the Vṛttikāra) interpret this passage differently. They say that it is intended to show that persons of all four stages of life reach heaven by performing their proper duty (*svadharma*) even without gaining knowledge. Thus *brahmacārins*, householders, and renunciates alike reach heaven by knowledge, restraints (*yama*), and observances (*niyama*), so that the second type of person, (2) above (the "wandering ascetic"), includes both ascetics and renunciates. The rest of the passage asserts that persons in any of these stages of life will attain immortality and will "stand in Brahman" by meditating on "*om*" and that this outcome is not restricted to members of the fourth stage. There is no authority to suppose that liberation is possible only for the wandering mendicant; indeed, the teaching of the Upaniṣads is that liberation comes from knowledge, which may be combined with the duties of any of the stages of life. Therefore the view must be that anyone performing the duty of his stage of life and gaining knowledge attains immortality.

This interpretation is not correct, for there is a contradiction between the ideas that must be accepted in order to perform actions (or duties) and those that lead to knowledge. For action one must distinguish agent, instrument, action, result, etc., notions that are found in everyone and do not arise from scripture; on the other hand, knowledge arises from scripture but is not attainable until distinctions of all kinds are set aside, just as one who has experienced the double-moon illusion will not correct it until the erroneous idea of difference (between the two moons) is removed, even though the night may end. Now the only kind of person for whom distinctions have ceased is the wandering mendicant. Any other person, seeing other persons and things as different from himself and others and therefore thinking in terms of possession and acquisition, cannot be one who "stands in Brahman," for his ideas are clearly wrong, relating to unreal things that are modifications merely arising from speech (*vācārambhanamātravikāra*).

Objector : Then the injunctions of the Veda become untrustworthy (*apramāṇa*).

Answer : No, the injunctions are valid for those who make distinctions, just as dream ideas are valid before waking.

Objector : But because discriminating men will not follow the injunctions their validity will be impugned.

Answer : No, for the fact that discriminating persons do not wish to perform *kāmya* acts (i.e., acts intended to realize rewards such as wealth, children, etc., does not impugn the validity of injunctions to perform them, for only those who desire such rewards perform them. Likewise, with respect to other kinds of acts.

Objection : Since you must admit that the wandering mendicant continues to perform actions such as begging, etc., even after gaining knowledge, you must also allow that householders, etc., should continue to perform acts even after they have gained knowledge.

Answer : No, no more than the fact that someone has killed someone should make a discriminating person want to kill; since he does not recognize anything to be acted upon, the wise man is not urged to perform the *agnihotra* and other such acts (as are enjoined by scripture). As for the mendicant's begging, this is just a response to hunger.

Objector : Yes, and performance of the *agnihotra* is just a response to fear of doing evil.

Answer : No, for one who does not recognize diversity will not be motivated by such a fear, since a man does not fear evil accruing from actions he is not entitled to perform.

Objector : All right then, a man may become a wandering mendicant as soon as he gains the idea of the unity of everything, while remaining in his stage of life—whichever it may be.

Answer : No, since all the other three stages of life require acceptance of the distinction of owner and owned; the fourth stage is just that involving abandonment of that distinction.

Opponent : Since, then, the mendicant has abandoned distinctions he cannot practice observances and restraints, etc.

Answer : No, he may deviate from the idea of unity because of hunger, etc., temporarily. Observances and restraints are for the purpose of cessation from acts, and practising them cannot involve violating prohibitions, since prohibitions apply to men prior to their realization of unity. Because someone falls into a well in the dark does not mean he will do so when it is light.

The wrong interpretation proposed above is correct insofar as it claims that persons of all stages may gain heaven but wrong in saying that the second type of person mentioned in the text includes both ascetics and renunciates. Asceticism also requires acceptance of distinctions and ceases upon realization that differences do not really exist, whereas the passage clearly speaks of a fourth kind of person who "stands in Brahman," etc., and is different from the others. Now this description must apply, not just to anyone who wanders about with a sacrificial thread, a triple stick and a water pot, etc., but rather to one who is rightly called a "*paramahaṃsa*" by virtue of his having abandoned actions altogether through abandoning the distinctions between agent, result, and so forth, which are their prerequisites.

The Sāṃkhya, Buddhist *śūnyavāda*, and other teachings that counsel renunciation of actions are incorrect inasmuch as they are based on continued recognition of difference.

From all this it follows that the real renunciate is one who has abandoned all notions of distinctions and that a householder who has achieved this becomes thereby a "wandering mendicant" in the sense intended by this passage.

Objection : If a householder were to do this he would destroy his sacrificial fire and thus incur sin—this follows from scriptural authority.

Answer : No, he does not destroy his fire; it merely comes to an end. As scripture says, "its fireness disappears" (cf. VI.4 below) when unity is realized.

III.14.1 (E178-179; T151-152). The Upaniṣad says "All this is Brahman" (*sarvaṃ khalvidaṃ brahma*"), etc. By "all this" is meant this world of modifications of name-and-form, the contents of our perceptions, etc. How is this world Brahman? Everything is born from Brahman in succession through fire, food, etc. Likewise, the world at *pralaya* is progressively absorbed into Brahman. Finally the world lives and moves in Brahman. Thus in all the three times it exists undifferentiated from Brahman, for it is never perceived apart from Brahman. See Book Six for an explanation as to how this same Brahman is one and "without a second." Here it is explained how one should meditate on Brahman.

III.19.1 (E188; T172-173). The Upaniṣad says "In the beginning this was indeed nonexistent; it became existent...." What is meant is not that the universe didn't exist at all before some time *t*, but rather that its name-and-form were undifferentiated (*avyākṛta*) before it became differentiated. The term "existent" (*sat*) is found used here in the sense of "differentiated name-and-form."

V.10.2 (E226-228; T249-255). The Upaniṣad here describes the *devayāna* or way of the gods. This path is meant for celibates, householders who know the doctrine of the "five fires" (discussed prior to this point in the Upaniṣad), and it is also called the "northern path," in contrast to the "southern path," the path of smoke, which is the way of those who perform ritual action without understanding the theories underlying them. This northern path is also followed by "forest-dwellers", that is, hermits and ascetics. The "immortality" that this path leads to is not absolute; however, their rebirth will not be in human form. The same path is also followed by lifelong *brahmacārins* and those who meditate upon Hiraṇyagarbha. The path culminates in the heaven called *satyaloka*.

V.10.3-8 (E228-234; T255-272). The southern path, or way of smoke, is followed by householders who perform sacrifices and works of public service and charity. At death they travel to smoke, to the heaven of the fathers, then to *ākāśa*, and then to the moon. After the karma produced by those works is exhausted they return by some similar reverse route to be reborn in a body determined by other acts, quite possibly acts performed in lives other than the just-prior one.

Objection: When a person dies all his karmic residues become operative in determining the next birth.

Answer: No. A man may have been in previous lives a peacock, an ape, and a man; if his rebirth next time round as an ape is determined by the residues arising from his previous apish existence the other traces—laid down when he was peacock and man—are stored up and passed along. This helps explain how the newly born ape knows how to jump from branch to branch and cling to its mother—if all it had to determine it were traces of the human condition this would be inexplicable.

The route by which those following the southern path re-enter the world is by way of rain, which carries them down onto the earth, where they may or may not be eventually eaten or absorbed into plants or animals. Those who eventually find themselves in a human male body may, if it isn't celibate, pass into the womb as seed, and then, influenced by the humanness of the father, the child's body will be born human and determined by the karmic residues of past human and other bodies conveyed to the father in his food.

A third type of person is he who is burdened by sinful karmic residues. These do not follow the path of smoke but go directly into grains and then perhaps in food into man, or if not, they jump from one plant to another—but all the time they remain conscious and thus have hellish experiences.

Objection : Since those who follow the southern path also are propelled by their karma into new bodies just as these last-mentioned sinful types, they should also have hellish experiences—and then people would stop listening to the scriptures, for it would become clear that performance of ritual acts and acts of service, etc., produce greater unhappiness.

Answer : We must distinguish the cases analogously to the difference between climbing a tree and falling down from it. While climbing a tree one is consciously desirous of reaching the top; when falling one becomes unconscious—one's organs become anesthetized. So it is that both the sinful ones who go into grains and the moon-bound ones on the southern path are conscious and desirous of where they are going, whereas the ones coming back to earth from the moon are unconscious or practically so.

Persons whose lives have been predominantly virtuous and who travel by the southern path are reborn in higher-caste bodies—Brahmin, Kṣatriya, or Vaiśya—whereas those whose conduct has been bad are reborn as a dog or pig or outcaste (*caṇḍāla*). The third kind of person, who has not observed ritual or other kinds of proper action, is reborn over and over as small creatures—insects, etc. That is why the heavens are not overpopulated.

Seeing how much misery and trouble is involved in the karmic process one should develop a feeling of disgust toward *saṃsāra* and try to avoid it.

VI.1.4 (E245; T293-294). Śvetaketu is taught by his father that "all things made of clay are known by knowing a lump of clay, for modifications are dependent on names".

Objection : How is it that when the cause, the lump of clay, is known, the effect, which is a different thing, is also known?

Answer: Because the effect is not different from its cause. The apparent differences between effect and cause are due merely to language; that is, (the effect) is only name, just a supporting object of speech (*vācālambhanamātra*), not an actual object (*vastu*) called a modification, since it is the clay alone that is an actual, real (*satya*) object.

VI.2.1 (E246-247; T295-299). The Upaniṣad says that in the beginning there was only Being (*sat*), without duality (*advitiya*), but that some say that in the beginning there was only Nonbeing (*asat*), without duality, and that being was born from that.

Question : If this Being is here now, why is it qualified as being here only "in the beginning"?

Answer : Because, although now this Being is qualified by name-and-form, in the beginning It had no name-and-form. Just as in deep sleep and just upon waking from it one knows only unqualified Being, so before the world arose there was Being alone.

The passage says that Being is "without a second" in order to reject the supposition that in the beginning there were things other than Being that acted as accessory causal factors analogous to the potter, etc., in the case of the production of pots. Thus the present position is to be distinguished from that of the Vaiśeṣika in two regards—one, the effect does not exist prior to its origination, and, two, before its production there must be, according to them, more than one factor, and these factors by their combination will occasion the production of the effect. So it is clear that what the Vaiśeṣikas imagine as "Being" is a different thing from the Being that we call the cause.

On this point some nihilist Buddhists say that in the beginning Being was absent, though they do not assert that this absence of Being is some other entity additional to Being, as the Naiyāyikas are prone to do, since they (the Naiyāyikas) construe positive (*bhāva*) and negative (*abhāva*) things as both actual entities.

Objection : But the Buddhists also hold that prior to its birth the universe was absence of Being, and that this absence was "without duality."

Answer : True, but it is not a correct view if what is meant is that there was only absence of positive things, since one who says this must be denying his own existence.

Objector : The person who says this exists after his birth but not before.

Answer : No, for there is no proof that there was absence of Being prior to origination; so the notion that in the beginning there was Nonbeing is a misconception (*kalpanā*).

Objection : For a word to be meaningful it must pick out the form (*ākṛti*) of a thing, and a sentence made up of meaningless words is itself meaningless. Now the sentence "there was only Nonbeing, one, without duality" is composed of meaningless words, since none of them pick out the form of anything, and so that sentence must be meaningless and hence unauthoritative (*apramāṇa*). (But it occurs in the Vedas !)

Answer : There is no fault here. The word "Being" does pick out the form of Being, and the adjectives are coordinate (*samanādhikaraṇa*) with it. Then the negative particle "non" is introduced, but not to name something else, rather to contrast the meaningful expression "Being" with a possible wrong notion that someone might have. So the sentence in question serves a purpose and is by no means unauthoritative, since it has a function, though the function involved is one that impugns the truth of the wrong opinion quoted in the sentence.

VI.2.2 (E248-249; T299-304). There is no proof that Being arises from Nonbeing. The Buddhist argues that the sprout arises only after the seed is destroyed. Even though that is true, it remains the case that the parts of the seed persist in the sprout. And further, the Buddhist does not even allow that there is such a thing as the seed in distinction from its constituent parts.

Opponent: What is always destroyed on the arising of the sprout is the *shape* of the seed, a form that is admitted by the Buddhist to exist, though only as *saṃvṛti*.

Answer: What is this *saṃvṛti* ? Is it a positive or negative thing ? If it is a negative thing, there is no corroborative instance to show that a positive entity can arise from a negative one. If it is a positive thing, then the sprout does not arise from Nonbeing but rather from something positive.

Opponent : In any case we do not accept that the parts of the seed persist in the sprout—they are destroyed too (at the time of the birth of the sprout).

Answer : Our argument (about *saṃvṛti*) applies equally to the parts —either they are positive or negative, and so forth. And further, if there is an infinite series of parts of parts . . . of seed, there is no way it can be destroyed, and our view prevails.

Objection : There is no proof for your theory either, since there is no instance of a jar being produced from another jar.

Answer : Right—no entity is produced from another entity; rather, production is when one and the same entity takes on a different form. It is the same clay that takes on the forms of jar, lump, etc.

Objection : Your Being is held to be single, indivisible, without parts, inactive, etc. How can it take on various forms ?

Answer : The parts are imagined (*parikalpita*) by our *buddhi*, just as the snake, etc., is imagined in the rope, etc.

VI.2.4 (E250-251; T306-309). This Upaniṣadic passage and the previous one are describing the gradual production of the world by a series of thoughts and actions, first on the part of Being, which intentionally produced fire, then by fire, which intentionally produced water, and then by water, which intentionally produced food.

Objection : Fire, water, etc., are not the kinds of things that can think and act.

Answer : The sense is figurative; it is meant that Being did the thinking and producing.

Objector : Then we can say that with respect to Being too the sense is figurative !

Answer : No, since we only know about Being from verbal (i.e., scriptural) authority.

Objector : But it is possible to know from inference that Being is unconscious, like clay; thus it must be that the origin of the world is from an unconscious *pradhāna* (i.e., *prakṛti*).

Answer : No, since we shall be told soon that this Being is the Self.

Objector : Yes, this too is figurative, just as in the statement "Bhadrasena is my very Self" spoken by someone to whom Bhadrasena is very dear.

Answer: No, for we are taught that liberation comes to one who identifies his Self with Being.

Objector : Even that is figurative and indicates that by identification one gets close to liberation (but not all the way there), just as one may say "I am in the village" meaning he is heading there quickly.

Answer : The whole present treatment is governed by the statement that Being is that by the knowledge of which everything is known, which clearly indicates the nondifference of everything else and Being. Furthermore, scripture does not declare anything other than Being as "to be known," nor can anything else be inferred from scripture, as would be the case if these usages were merely figurative. If it is imagined that the whole discussion is merely figurative the efforts of its author would be futile, for knowledge of the ultimate purpose of mankind could be had from reasoning (*tarka*) alone. Since our assumption is that the Vedas are authoritative we cannot write its meaning off as entirely figurative.

VI.3.2 (E252-253; T311-313). The Upaniṣad says that this deity (*devatā*) conceived a plan to produce modifications of name-and-form by entering into fire, water, and food as "this *jīvātman*." "This deity" means Being, says Śaṃkara, and the reason the text says "this *jīvātman*" is because Being remembers, prior to the beginning of each creative cycle, its own Self, endowed with breath, which had experiences in the previous cycle and resolves to re-enter the world through this living self or *jīvātman*.

Objection : It cannot be correct to say that Being, which is not subject to transmigration, which is omniscient, should, while It is fully in control of Itself (*svatantra*), wish to subject Itself to embodiment and the resulting experiences.

Answer : True, it would not be correct to say that Being does this in Its unmodified form. But the text does not say that—it says that Being enters into embodiment through the *jīvātman*. Now this *jīvātman* is merely a reflection (*ābhāsa*) of the "deity" (i.e., Being) resulting from its connection with *buddhi*, etc., and the various elements (*bhūta*), just as a man or the sun is reflected in a mirror. The "deity" is not affected by the frustrating experiences of the embodiments, any more than the man, sun, etc., are affected by the defects that the images reflected owe to the reflecting medium.

Objection : If *jīvātman* is merely a reflection it must be untruthfully obtained (*mṛṣaiva prāpta*), and so must its peregrinations in this and other worlds.

Answer : There is no fault; it is truthfully experienced insofar as it has the nature of Being. All name-and-forms, all modifications, are true as having the nature of Being, though in themselves they are untrue (*anṛta*), since they are merely dependent on language. The same is the case, then, with *jīvātman*. The logicians cannot find any fault with this, since it can be shown that all doctrines of duality (*dvaitavāda*) involve mutual contradiction and are merely conceptual constructions (*vikalpa*) of the *buddhi* and so not based in actuality.

VI.4.1-4 (E253-255; T315-318). This section explains by illustration the theory of triplication, according to which Being differentiated things by making fire, water, and food triple. For example, of the various colors we see in fire, the white color belongs to untriplicated water, the black to untriplicated food (or earth), and the red to untriplicated fire. So, when you experience triplicated fire and think of the fire as distinct from its three colors, the fire you are thinking of is not a single entity characterized by fireness and does not answer to the term "fire" in the sense you had in mind before you made the discrimination. It is as in the case of one's experiencing a crystal as a ruby when it happens to be placed in front of a red object; the term "ruby" and this thing's rubyness last only as long as we have not distinguished the crystal from the object—as soon as we have, both the name and the idea of ruby (as a kind of thing characterized by rubyness) disappear. So we conclude that there is no such thing as fire; the idea of fire is untrue (*mṛṣā*), all there is really are the three colors. Now, by the same token, since the whole universe has been triplicated, universeness, and so the idea of a universe, will disappear on discrimination, and all that remains will be the three "divinities" fire, water, and food—but since Being made each of these triplicate in the beginning (according to VI.3.4) fireness, waterness, and foodness will likewise disappear along with the respective notions, and all that will be left is Being, everything else being mere modifications of words.

This reasoning can be extended by analogy to include all things not clearly falling under fire, water, or food, as well as to matters involving qualities other than color, where other patterns such as quintuplication (*pañcikaraṇa*) may apply.

VI.8.1 (E260-262; T328-331). The Upaniṣad says that Uddālaka Āruṇi discussed with his son Śvetaketu the final stage of sleep (*svapnānta*) and explained that when a man is said to be sleeping he has become absorbed into Being and has gone to his own (*svamāpita*).

The "final stage of sleep" Śaṃkara construes as deep sleep (*suṣupti*). Now just as when the mirror has been removed the reflection of a man in the mirror "goes into his own", that is, into the man himself, so when the internal organ, etc., have ceased the deity (Being) that entered the internal organ through the *jīvātman* for the purpose of differentiating name-and-form goes to its own Self. In dreaming, the self clearly has not gone into its own Self, so that cannot be the sleep referred to. Now when a man is said to be in deep sleep he has gone to his own, that is, become absorbed into Being.

Question : How is this "going into one's own" known to ordinary men ?

Answer : By inference from the experience of fatigue. After many experiences in the waking state a man's organs become tired and they are temporarily absorbed into *prāṇa*, which alone lies awake and the resulting state of deep sleep is termed "going to one's own."

VI.13 (E270-271; T348-350). The Upaniṣadic text is the one in which Uddālaka has his son dissolve salt in water. The point of the experiment is to show Śvetaketu how it is that Being may be the root-cause or essence of everything and yet that that fact may not be readily recognized by people. For example, they may become absorbed into Being in deep sleep but not recognize that fact, just as the salt may disappear from sight but still remain as testified to by taste.

Then by what means is Being apprehended? asks Śvetaketu.

VI.14 (E271-273; T351-356). The answer is the parable of the man from Gandhara who arrives blindfolded and only finds his way home by having the right direction pointed out by villagers; just so, one lost in *saṃsāra* must have the way pointed out by a teacher and only then is liberated, merged into Being.

Objection : Being merged into Being does not directly follow on liberation, for the remaining karma that has begun to operate must still be burnt off by further actions. But these will in turn breed more karma, which in turn will generate rebirth, and so on, with the result that even one who knows the truth about Being and the Self will not escape *saṃsāra*. On the other hand, if it should be held that true knowledge immediately destroys all karmic residues then the body should immediately die, and not only would there be no time to find a teacher, but liberation would not necessarily follow from knowledge.

Answer : Two kinds of karmic residue must be distinguished. The kind that has already begun to operate, like the motion of an arrow already shot into the air, ceases only when its momentum is spent; this kind of karma produces experiences that must be lived through to exhaust it. But other residues that have not yet become operative, including those earned in the present life whether before or after the attainment of knowledge, are all burned up by true knowledge just as they are also burned up by ritual acts according to the *Bhagavadgītā*, etc.

VI.15.2 (E274; T357-358). The general sense of this section is to argue that both the wise man and the ignorant one, upon death, are merged into Being by following the same path—by a succession of absorptions of internal organ into *prāṇa*, *prāṇa* into fire, and fire into the Highest Deity, though the ignorant one eventually gets reborn, unlike the Self-knower.

An alternative account of the process of absorption is cited, according to which at death the man goes out through the artery in the top of the head and on to the sun and other "doors" before arriving at Being. Śaṃkara points out that this account cannot be right, at least for the wise man, for one who has recognized the truth has no such notions as time, place, causes, etc., and thus cannot progress through times and places as this account would require.

Śvetaketu naturally wants to know why the wise man is not reborn like the ignorant one.

VI.16 (E275-277; T358-365). The Upaniṣad explains that just as truth protects a man from being burnt by the axe in the ancient form of the lie-detection test, so the wise man is protected from rebirth by the true knowledge he has gained.

Question : (Since the Self is supposed to be self-illuminating) what is the result with regard to the Self that this just-completed chapter is supposed to have brought about ?

Answer : Its point was to eliminate the misconceptions that the Self is the agent or enjoyer and to teach that the *jivātman* is the entity that is referred to by the word "thou" in "That thou art, Śvetaketu" (the repeated conclusions of many passages in this chapter), the entity that is supposed to hear and study the truth. Once that truth has been properly appreciated, however, since all difference is rejected there cannot be any supposition that the Self is agent or enjoyer or that It is supposed to hear or study, since the idea of the *jivātman* will then be known to be an untrue modification.

Objection : What "that thou art" means is that the thing denoted by "thou" has Being just as the sun, internal organ, etc., answer to the notion of Brahman and other deities, just as religious representations are referred to as Viṣṇu, etc.

Answer : No, this assertion has a different form. In the passages about the sun, etc., it is expressly said that "the sun is called 'Brahman' " (*ādityo brahmetyādau*)—the term "called" (*iti*) not being present in "*tattvamasi*."

Objection : "That thou art" is figurative just like "you are a lion" said of a hero.

Answer : A figurative expression, being false, cannot be properly said to bring absorption into Being. Nor can this sentence be viewed as a eulogy, for Śvetaketu is not a person to be eulogized, and it is no eulogy of Brahman for It to be called "Śvetaketu" !

VIII. Introduction (E299; T413-414). Even though the preceding two chapters have expounded Brahman as Being, single, without duality, still for many people of dull intellect (*maṃdabuddhi*) it is not possible to think of anything not located in space and time, etc. So this chapter explains Brahman in a way suitable to their gifts, with the hope that it will lead them along the way gradually. It thus describes Brahman as located in a particular place in the body, as having qualities, as requiring celibacy for its realization, as reached upon death by passing out from the top of the head, etc., even though these characterizations are from the higher standpoint impossible since the distinctions involved in them do not exist.

VIII.5.4 (E310-311; T437-440). In the course of preceding sections there has been reference to various things—oceans, trees, cities—and events—meeting one's ancestors, etc.

Question : Are these things, which have been described as arising from one's wishes (*saṃkalpa*), here in the world like ordinary oceans, trees, etc., or are they mental ideas (*mānasapratyaya*) only ? If they are gross there isn't room for them in the body, and anyway the Purāṇas say clearly that things in the *brahmaloka* are purely mental. But if they only exist in the mind this conflicts with other Purāṇic statements to the effect that oceans, etc., go to Brahman in their gross forms.

Answer : Well, they can't very well go in their gross forms, since they're too big for that. So the most reasonable supposition is that they are mental things, like the bodies of the men and women we see in dreams.

Questioner : But those dream objects are unreal, and the Vedas say that "his desires are real."

Śaṃkara : Well, there is a reality in mental ideas; men and women are actually perceived in dreams.

Questioner : The things perceived in dreams are only forms of traces (*vāsanā*) from the waking world.

Śaṃkara : That's only a small part of the truth. The objects perceived in the waking state are also mental ideas only, since they are merely reflections of Being, and it is said in scripture that all regions are rooted in wishes. Therefore there are mutual causal relations between external and mental things. But even though the mental are just external, and the external just mental, they are not unreal with respect to one's own self.

Questioner : But objects perceived in dreams become unreal upon waking.

Śaṃkara : True, but the unreality is relative, in relation to waking, not in dream itself. Likewise, waking objects are unreal in relation to dream experiences. What is unreal in all cases is the specific form, arising as name in dependence on speech and occasioning false awareness; the three colors alone are real—but then even these three colors are unreal in their particular forms, though as pure Being they are real. So prior to knowledge of Being all ideas are true with respect to their own objects, just as dreams are—so there is no inconsistency.

VIII.12.1 (E324-328; T467-477). The Upaniṣad says here that the embodied being is visited by pleasure and pain and cannot be rid of it, but the disembodied Being is not touched by pleasure or pain.

Objection : If pleasure does not touch the pure Self then in deep sleep a person must become annihilated.

Answer : We are talking of the pleasure produced by meritorious acts from past lives—it is this that is absent in deep sleep. The passage does not deny that bliss is present, for bliss is the very nature of things, as the Upaniṣad asserts that abundance, that is, Brahman, is bliss.

Objection : If abundance (=Brahman) and bliss are identical then either bliss is unknowable or else by Its very nature It will be constantly known—and in either case liberation is impossible.

Answer : There is nothing wrong in the thesis that the All-Self (*sarvātman*) is related to all results, just as clay is related to all pots, jugs, etc.

Objector : Then the All-Self must be related to frustrations also !

Answer: Frustrations are contained within the Self, to be sure; they are constructions born of *avidyā* just like the snake in the rope.

The true Self does not transmigrate, for transmigration is superimposed on the Self through *avidyā.*

VIII.12.3 (E329-330; T478-481). In the course of describing how the enlightened Self laughs and plays it is remarked that in this pure state It does not remember Its previous embodiments.

Objection : If so It cannot be omniscient.

Answer : That the Self does not remember Its experiences in the body when affected by *avidyā* does not impugn Its omniscience, any more than failing to remember what one experienced while insane impugns the knowledge a wise man has.

Objection : We were told that abundance (i.e., Brahman, the true Self) does not see another, hear another, etc., but now we are being told that that same Self is described as seeing the things It plays with in the *brahmaloka*, etc. This is an inconsistency.

Answer : As said elsewhere in the Vedas, It both sees and does not see them—since the Self is consciousness, It does not stop being conscious when liberated, so is aware of and sees things. But since desired objects have no existence apart from the Self, It does not "see" them.

AITAREYOPANIṢADBHĀṢYA

The *Aitareya Brāhmaṇa* of the *Ṛg Veda* is one of the oldest of the Brāhmaṇas. To it are added five Āraṇyakas, or "forest-treatises." A portion of the second of these is known as the *Aitareya* or *Bahvṛcā Upaniṣad*, or sometimes as *Ātmaṣaṭka* since it has six sections.

As in the case of the *Chāndogya*, *Īśā*, *Kaṭha*, *Muṇḍaka*, and *Praśna Upaniṣads*, the authenticity of the commentary traditionally ascribed to Śaṃkara has not been tested by modern methods. However, as the *Aitareya* is generally accepted to be one of the oldest Upaniṣads, and no one has questioned Śaṃkara's authorship of the commentary in question, we here accept the work as genuine.

References ("ET") are to the edition and translation by D. Venkatramiah (Bangalore: Bangalore Press, 1934).

INTRODUCTION

1 (ET1-3). Noting that the *Aitareya Upaniṣad* is a portion of the *Aitareya Āraṇyaka* that follows a section dealing with action and devotion to God and that some philosophers think that salvation is gained by following a combined path of knowledge and action (*jñānakarmasamuccaya*), Śaṃkara argues to the contrary that the way of knowledge alone leads to salvation according to the ultimate view espoused in this Upaniṣad. For though in the earlier section gods are mentioned as subjects of meditation, later on in the Upaniṣad they are shown to be subject to *saṃsāra* inasmuch as they are visited with hunger and thirst, etc. On the other hand, the Highest Brahman is declared in (other) scriptural passages to be free from hunger, etc.

2 (ET4-9). *Opponent* : Yes, knowledge of the Self does lead to liberation. But there is no reason to believe that only *saṃnyāsins* can practice the way of knowledge; indeed, the *Aitareya Āraṇyaka* begins by discussing karma and then passes immediately on to discuss knowledge, suggesting that the person who performs prescribed duties is the one fit to follow the path of knowledge. Various scriptural passages favor the view that the way of action can coexist with the way of knowledge.

An objector to the opponent argues that the combined-path interpretation will have the result of making the second part of the *Āraṇyaka* superfluous, for it will then be taken to repeat the message of the earlier section. The opponent has at hand several ways of answering, each of which finds a purpose for the Upaniṣad that is compatible with the combined-path view.

If one objects that passages enjoining *saṃnyāsa* will be contradicted, the opponent answers that these passages are meant either to praise knowledge of the Self or to apply to those who are for some physical reason unable to perform actions.

3 (ET10-14). *Answer* : No, a combined-path is impossible, for once one knows the Self one will recognize there is nothing to be gained from works and thus one will not engage in them.

Objection : One engages in ritual works merely because scriptures enjoin it.

Answer : No, since Self-knowledge involves the conviction that injunctions no longer carry any force. For no one acts without the belief that some benefit will result from his doing so, and this belief is undermined by Self-knowledge.

Objector : Scripture enjoins actions regardless of the fitness, etc., of those on whom it is enjoined.

Answer : Then it would follow that everyone is enjoined to do all actions at once, which is absurd ! And anyway, the one who has attained Self-knowledge is not subject to commands, even Vedic commands, since those injunctions have sprung from himself, and it is a contradiction for someone to be both enjoiner and enjoined with respect to the same injunction. In addition, it would be absurd for the Vedas, which are God's (= the Self's) creation, to instruct their creator—just as absurd as a servant instructing his master.

Objector : The scripture itself enjoins both action and knowledge for the same individual.

Answer : That would mean that the scripture would enjoin inconsistent things, since (as was argued) action presupposes lack of Self-knowledge and Self-knowledge presupposes lack of action.

4 (ET14-16). *Opponent* : The knower of the Self would not by himself desire the results of actions, but scripture generates such desires.

Answer : No. Scripture supplies the means of obtaining ends, desire for which is already present in someone who cannot obtain those ends by other devices. Having supplied the means to Self-knowledge, which is incompatible with action, it would be absurd to suppose it will turn around and generate the opposite desire !

Opponent : Scripture isn't engaged in supplying the means to Self-knowledge.

Answer : Surely it is, according to various scriptural passages themselves (which are cited). And these passages are intelligible, clear, and not contradicted.

5. (ET16-21). *Opponent*: We are advised (by the *Bhagavadgītā*) that for the knower of the Self "no purpose is served by perform-

ing some deed or not performing it" (*Bhagavadgītā* III.18). Thus renunciation (*tyāga*) is no more appropriate for the Self-knower than action is.

Answer : That is not the point. When one has realized the Self the necessary conditions for action—that is, desire arising from ignorance (*avidyā*)—are absent; it is not through any effort on the part of the person that this occurs. It is merely his very nature.

Opponent : Very well ! Since it is a natural thing, it cannot be the subject of scriptural injunctions. And it follows, too, that the Self-knower may as well remain a householder as become a *saṃnyāsin*.

Answer : No. The stage of householder implies the presence of desires, and the absence of desires implies the stage of *saṃnyāsa*. For that matter, even discipleship under a *guru*, meditation, etc., are incompatible with Self-knowledge. Śaṃkara suggests that those who argue as the last opponent has are afraid of the life of a *saṃnyāsin*. But he maintains that as long as one thinks he owns a home, he must have some desire for it. Once the sense of ownership is lost the life of a *saṃnyāsin* will follow on naturally.

6 (ET21-27). *Opponent* : The scriptures enjoin certain ways in which an ascetic should accept food, bathe, etc. Likewise the householder who has attained Self-knowledge and renounced desires should continue to perform the obligatory duties (*nityakarman*).

Answer : Such a person is not subject to the command of the scripture, although persons who are not yet realized are so subject. There is no analogy between the householder and the *saṃnyāsin*—the injunctions to the householder are binding, whereas those (if any) that may be thought to apply to the *saṃnyāsin* are incidental to him, because he does not have any desires to provide a motive for his actions. Nevertheless the *saṃnyāsin* will continue to act in a disciplined way, but only because he has acquired the habit of doing so and has no motive for departing from that habit.

Self-restraint (*śama*), detachment (*dama*), etc., are necessary for gaining Self-knowledge and are not in the end compatible with any life other than that of the *saṃnyāsin*. Although the householder may practice these in some degree, full accomplishment requires withdrawal from the home; otherwise the means will be inadequate for producing the intended result. Further, scripture tells us that the rites enjoined upon householders, for example, meditation on *saguṇa* Brahman, result in the performer's attaining the divine state but within the limits of *saṃsāra*, whereas the knowledge of the Self has no relation to action. If action alone could gain one knowledge of the Self it could not produce a reward within the limits of *saṃsāra*.

Objection : Why cannot attainment of the divine state within *saṃsāra* be a subsidiary result (*aṅgaphala*)?

Answer : Because the two are quite incompatible. Knowledge of the Self involves going beyond language, form, and acts; it relates to an object without attributes. Action must be toward something capable of being the object of an action; *saṃsāra* involves a distinction between action, agent, and fruit.

7 (ET 27-31). Only the unenlightened are under obligation to men, ancestors, and gods; the enlightened ones who seek the world of the Self are under no such obligation.

Objection : Unenlightened persons, since they have not fulfilled their obligations, cannot enter *saṃnyāsa*.

Answer : No. No obligation exists before a person enters the state of householder.

Opponent : Surely obligations exist even prior to becoming a householder.

Answer : No, since obligations would bind persons in all the stages of life, which would be undesirable. *Saṃnyāsa* can be entered into from any stage of life, provided a person becomes enlightened.

8 (ET 31-34). Certain scriptural texts that appear to contradict Śaṃkara's theses are discussed and interpreted in such a way as to accord with the view maintained.

CHAPTER ONE

The Upaniṣad speaks of the fact that first there was only the Self and nothing else. He thought "let me create" and created the worlds; then He created *puruṣa* from the waters, and brooding like a bird over that *puruṣa* hatched out speech, breath, sight, sound, and touch along with the presiding deities governing their respective objects, followed by the other vital parts.

9 (ET 35-46). *Opponent* : Doesn't the wording "at first there was only the Self" suggest that now there are other things besides? And if so, doesn't that contradict Advaita?

Answer : No. It is like saying "before there was only water, now there is also foam"; since foam is nothing but water, it is still correct to say "there is only water"; likewise here.

Opponent : How can an agent create without any materials? A carpenter can't build without wood to work with!

Answer : Again, it is like water and foam. The Self is both the efficient and material cause of His creation, just as is the water of the particular kinds of bubbles of foam. Or better, He is like a magician who without any material projects himself into another (magically created) self.

Śaṃkara likens the *puruṣa* of this passage to a lump of clay that the Self by merely willing it caused to develop, first the several bodily seats of the senses, then the sense organs themselves, and finally the presiding deity of each of the respective kinds of objects—in that order—and including the inner sense (*antaḥkaraṇa*).

CHAPTER TWO

The Upaniṣad continues : The presiding deities thus created fell into the great ocean and, developing hunger and thirst, requested sustenance. He showed them a horse and a cow but they weren't satisfied, but when he showed them a man they were glad, and He ordered each deity to enter into the appropriate part of the man's body. Hunger and thirst were also allotted a place with the deities in the human body.

10 (ET 47-55). The "great ocean" is *saṃsāra*, says Śaṃkara: it is filled with suffering born of ignorance and desire, endlessly surging with desire but still holding on its bosom the ship of wisdom sailing toward liberation. Śaṃkara extracts from this suggestion a proof that the combined path of knowledge and works is not adequate.

The Lord (=the Self) instilled hunger and thirst into the *puruṣa* initially and so the deities suffered these pangs also. When the deities were transferred to the human bodies, hunger and thirst were assigned to those embodied deities as well, which is why food and drink when offered to the gods also satisfy hunger and thirst (of the priests, presumably).

CHAPTER THREE

The Upaniṣad continues: The Lord next created solid matter as food for the hunger of the gods, now embodied in human beings, but they had difficulty finding a way of ingesting this food, until they discovered the downward breath (*apāna*) and sucked in the food through their mouths. This posed a question for the Lord : He had created speech, smell, vision, hearing, touch, mind, and breath to perform the various functions of the body, and what was left for Him ? So he slit open the skulls of the bodies and entered there, and occupied three seats and three dreams. Then He, having been born within the individual body, named everything he could think of, and then, perceiving Brahman (=*puruṣa*) everywhere, cried "I have seen It" (*idam adarśam*), which is why the Lord is called "Indra" (a contraction of "*idaṃdra*"). The gods love secrecy !

11 (ET 56-72). The question that the Lord reflected on is like a king's reflecting concerning a city : "Since this city and its inhabitants

are by nature intended for the benefit of someone other than themselves, namely me, the lord of the city, I must find some way of becoming available to them as enjoyer of the fruits of their (worshipful) deeds; otherwise they will never come to know of my existence or my nature, and their activities will be in vain." The Lord's reflecting thus led him to the notion that if He entered the human body as its seat of consciousness He would play the appropriate role, and so He did so through the skull—an hypothesis born out by our experience that when the top of the head is anointed with oil it produces a blissful sensation.

The "three seats" may be the visual sense, the mind, and the *ākāśa* in the heart, or it may refer to the father's body, the mother's womb, and one's own body. The "three dreams" are the waking, dream, and deep sleep states—they are all "dreams" since they are conditioned by *avidyā*, the individual self not "waking up" from these states even though hammered by suffering.

(ET 72-76) *Objection* : Since the Self is all-pervading it makes no sense to speak of Him entering a body through a split in the skull. So this whole passage is irrational (*anupapanna*).

Answer : No, the passage is meant to explain the nature of the Self; everything else in it is *arthavāda*, not to be taken literally; or better, it is taught by the Lord in order that the nature of the Self can be more easily comprehended.

(ET 76-82) *Objection* : You have spoken of one Self, but there are in fact three: the individual self (*jīva*), the Lord (*īśvara*) and the *puruṣa* of the Upaniṣads; so how can you maintain Advaita (non-dualism)?

Answer : How do you know of the existence of the *jīva*?

Objector : The *jīva* is inferred as the agent of hearing, seeing, thinking, etc., from the fact something must hear, see, think, etc.

Śaṃkara : When hearing something one is only aware of sounds, and so cannot infer something quite different, that is, an agent-self.

Objector : One can be aware, through mental activity going on simultaneously with hearing, that hearing is going on, and that awareness is itself the *hetu* in the inference.

Śaṃkara : No, for one can hear without this awareness occurring.

Objection : But whatever is known is known through the *manas*.

Śaṃkara : But what knows the *manas*? There must be a knower that is not itself known, and that is the Self. And *that* self (the Self) cannot be an object of inference.

(ET 83-97) *Objection* : But scripture says the Self is to be known as both hearer and thinker.

Answer : Sometimes the Self hears, and other times He thinks. There is no contradiction in that.

Vaiśeṣika : Aha ! So consciousness is an adventitious quality of the Self, now present, now absent, as we contend.

Śaṃkara : So you contend, but scripture can't mean that, since it tells us that the Self is neither hearer nor thinker. This text means that the Self is not something that has these traits; rather, Its hearing, etc.—Its consciousness—is eternal.

Objection : Then we should be conscious of everything at once !

Śaṃkara : We must distinguish two kinds of consciousness of which the Self is the ultimate seat. On the one hand, there is the kind of consciousness that involves the internal organ and the sense organs; it is impermanent and requires sense-object contact. On the other, there is the eternal, nonmaterial consciousness that is the Self. It is of this latter that scripture speaks. The existence of this latter kind of consciousness is shown by the fact that though the senses are destroyed internal awareness (e.g. in dreams) continues. Furthermore, the kind of consciousness that requires the sense organs depends on the second sort, the witness-consciousness, since it provides (as it were) the light that illuminates all, whether dream or waking state objects. The Vaiśeṣikas and others who suppose that consciousness is adventitious confuse the first kind of awareness with the second and so miss the second's peculiar characteristics. Failing to see the eternal consciousness that is the Self, they naturally find the world full of distinctions, for example, between the different "selves" of *jiva*, God, and *puruṣa*. But really all such distinctions are the result of superimposition—which is why scripture tells us "He (the Self) is not this, not this".

Objection : If all this is so, then how can the *jiva* know the Self?

Answer : Only by scripture's telling him he is nothing else. If he doesn't understand that, he won't understand the positive statement "You are Brahman." And without understanding his identity with Brahman he will circle endlessly in *saṃsāra*.

CHAPTER FOUR

The Upaniṣad says : (Let the pregnant women withdraw ! We shall now discuss the mechanics of the birth of the *jiva*.) The *jiva* is first implanted into the father's semen as a minute image of himself; it is then implanted into his mate, and becomes an image of her; in due course a son is born. This is why the father cherishes his son, since that son is truly himself; likewise, when the son grows up, he replaces his father in his place in society. The father dies and eventually takes on another body. Thus the *jiva* is born three times in this process: once in his father's seed, a second time when he emerges from the womb, and a third time when he enters the subtle body when leaving the gross body at death. Vāmadeva gained liberation even while yet in the womb. (We have finished. Let the women return!)

12 (ET 98-110). The *jīva,* having peregrinated to the lunar spheres, comes down with the rain and enters into food, and is thus ingested into the father's body and into his semen. The period of conception and gestation is described, as is the care of the child by its parents. The importance of having sons is brought out: it is in order that *saṃsāra* will continue, and this is binding on ordinary folk, though it has no relevance for one seeking liberation. At whatever point a *jīva* realizes the nature of the Self, however, he becomes immediately liberated, even if this occurs while in the womb, as it did to Vāmadeva, who forced his way out of the womb, shed his body, and rose upwards, attaining bliss and immortality.

CHAPTER FIVE

The Upaniṣad says: Which self of the two is the one we adore? That by which one sees, hears, smells, speaks, tastes, which is the heart, the internal organ, which carries on all sorts of mental and volitional activities—that is Brahman, the Lord of all, also called "Prājña." By this Prājña-Self one obtains the supreme bliss of immortality.

13 (ET 111-127). According to Śaṃkara the two selves referred to are one (*prāṇa*, or *hiraṇyagarbha*) that entered the body by the feet, and the other that entered it through a split in the skull. The question posed is: which of these should we meditate on? The one that came by the feet provided the organs by which we grasp things; but the one that came by the head is that by which we are aware of not only the organs but their functions and objects. Those organs, functions, and objects are all names of Prājña, the lower Brahman (*apara brahman*), who, as Hiraṇyagarbha, has entered the internal organ, the reflecting medium, and is reflected therefrom as different images of the sun are reflected in varied waters. The Higher Brahman, when conditioned by *māyā*, is known as Lord (*īśvara*), inner ruler (*antaryāmin*), Hiraṇyagarbha, Virāj, Prajāpati, and so on down the whole gamut of orders of being. It was this understanding that Vāmadeva got and which led him to liberation.

CHAPTER SIX

Concluding invocation.

ĪŚOPANIṢADBHĀṢYA

The *Īśa Upaniṣad* is sometimes called *Saṃhitā Upaniṣad*, presumably since it occurs in the *mantra* or *saṃhitā* portion of the *White Yajurveda*. It is a short Upaniṣad, only eighteen verses long, but probably among the oldest. Others have found a happy attempt at a synthesis in this Upaniṣad between action and knowledge as paths.[32] Śaṃkara, in contrast to that interpretation, finds that portions of the eighteen verses are addressed to different persons—some verses are meant for Self-knowers (*saṃnyāsins*), the rest for those who have not known the Self. Far from a synthesis, Śaṃkara's notion is that the two paths are mutually inconsistent and so cannot be practiced simultaneously. Although both are aids, action is only an "extrinsic aid" (*bahiraṅga*) whereas knowledge is an "intrinsic aid" (*antaraṅga*) to liberation.[33]

Vidyārṇava[34] points out that the Upaniṣad mentions four kinds of wrong views—(1) *upāsanāvādins*, who spend their time in prayer, (2) *mahāyājñas*, who spend their time in good works, (3) those who spend their time studying *mūlaprakṛti*, i.e., Sāṃkhyas, and (4) those who worship created nature (Hiraṇyagarbha) through yoga. Each gets an appropriate result.

"E" references are to the edition by H. R. Bhagavat, *Works of Shankaracharya* (2d edition : Poona: Ashtekar & Co., 1927), volume 2, part 1. "T" refers to the translation by Swami Gambhirananda in *Eight Upanishads* (Calcutta : Advaita Ashrama, 1957), volume 1.

Introduction (E1; T3-4). The verses constituting this Upaniṣad are not used in rituals, for they reveal the true nature of the Self and do not deal with (ritual) action. This is appropriate, for the Self is not an agent nor can it in any way become involved in action, since action requires attributing qualities to the Self that it does not really have. Thus the point of this Upaniṣad is to reveal the true nature of the Self and thus to remove ignorance.

1 (E1-2; T4-6). This verse is addressed to the knower of the Self and says that for such a person liberation will arise from firm devotion to that knowledge together with renunciation of the threefold desire (for sons, wealth, and worlds).

2 (E2-3; T6-8). The second verse, however, is addressed to one who does not know the Self and advises performing ritual actions such as the *agnihotra*. Why the difference between the audiences addressed in the first two verses? Because Self-knowledge and action are mutually incompatible, as was shown in the introduction.

3 (E3; T8-9). Those who "kill the Self" (*ātmahan*) are those

ignorant common folk from whom the Self is concealed by *avidyā*, just as the consciousness of one who is killed is hidden.

4 (E3-4; T9-12). The verse describes the Self in apparently contradictory terms—for example, it says the Self is both "motionless" and yet "faster than the mind." How can this be? The answer is that some adjectives describe the Self in its unconditioned state, others describe It in its conditioned states.

6-7 (E5; T13-14). When one realizes that all this is just the one Self he will be unable to hate others; for it is common experience that one only hates what is seen as different from oneself. Again, sorrow and delusion do not affect one who knows the Self.

8 (E5-7; T15-18). The point of insisting that action and knowledge are incompatible is in part to recommend to the nonknower of the Self both knowledge and works—as we find in *Bṛhadāraṇyaka Upaniṣad* I.5.16, for example, that by *vidyā* one attains the world of the gods, thus this *vidyā*—that is, meditation and worship—has its own result and should be practiced in addition to ritual acts.

9-11 (E7; T18-21). By construing "*avidyā*" in these verses as meaning karma, and "*vidyā*" as meaning meditation, and taking it that each of the two have their distinct outcomes, that is, progression of the subtle body to the world of the fathers (*pitṛloka*) as the outcome of ritual action, progression to the world of the gods (*devaloka*) as the outcome of meditation on and worship of the gods, these three verses become intelligible.

12-14 (E8-9; T21-24). As for worship, it may be either of the unmanifested (*avyākṛtaprakṛti*) or of the manifested (Hiraṇyagarbha)—these again have different results, for worship of the unmanifested *prakṛti* results in absorption into that *prakṛti* (*prakṛtilaya*). That is the highest state attainable through human and divine methods (i.e., by action or worship); beyond all this is the liberation attainable by Self-knowledge.

15-17 (E9-10; T25-28). These verses proceed to illustrate the meditation on the gods through prayer.

18 (E10-11; T28-31). The verse finishes the prayer.

Question: When the texts talk of "crossing over death, attaining immortality through "*vidyā*," etc., why should they not be construed as speaking of liberation rather than (as you have urged) merely the path of the gods or absorption into *prakṛti*?

Answer: As we have said, Self-knowledge and action are opposed in means and end and cannot be combined.

Question: Well, then, why can't we say that action and Self-knowledge arise successively—that is, first we perform ritual acts, then achieve Self-knowledge and go on performing acts ?

Answer : No, since once knowledge arises action ceases altogether.

KAṬHOPANIṢADBHĀṢYA

The *Kaṭha*, one of the best known of the Upaniṣads, is probably among the dozen or so "earliest." It tells the story of Nāciketas' trip to the netherworld and his reception by Yama, who eventually teaches Nāciketas the truth about liberation.

Śaṃkara's commentary is presumably authentic—no one has questioned it—but it is essentially repetitive of his comments on other Upaniṣads; hence the brevity of our summary.

"E" references are to H. R. Bhagavat's edition in *Works of Shankaracharya* (Poona: Ashtekar & Co., 1927), volume two, part one, pp. 36-77. "T" refers to the translation by Swami Gambhirananda in *Eight Upanishads* (Calcutta : Advaita Ashrama, 1957), volume one, pp. 96-228.

Introduction (E36-37; T97-100). The word "*upaniṣad*" is derived from the root *sad* meaning to split up (*viśaraṇa*), go (*gati*) or loosen (*avasādana*) plus prefixes. As a result an Upaniṣad is something that splits up or destroys the *avidyā* that binds us, or something that goes to Brahman.

CHAPTER ONE, SECTION TWO, OR SECOND VALLĪ

1 (E45-46; T128-129). The better (*śreyas*) is glossed as liberation (*niḥśreyasa*) and is said to be different from the more pleasant (*preyas*), since the former has the nature of knowledge (*vidyā*), whereas the latter has the nature of *avidyā*. One cannot follow both paths. The wise man follows the former, the unintelligent one the latter.

8 (E48; T137-139). That the Self cannot be reasoned out (*atarkya* in the Upaniṣadic text) means that it cannot be reasoned out by one's own *buddhi* alone. Why ? Because there is no end to hypotheses one may invent about It—for example, one person may hold It to be very small, another smaller, a third the smallest, etc.—so there is no end to reasoning.

CHAPTER TWO, SECTION THREE, OR SIXTH VALLĪ

1 (E70-71; T207-210). The Upaniṣad speaks of the peepul or fig tree, which has its roots above and its branches below.

Śaṃkara : The tree symbolizes the world; the root is Viṣṇu, that is, Brahman. The world is like a tree because it is cut down. From Brahman, its root, it grows from the seeds of *avidyā*, desire, karma, and the unmanifest into the sprout called Hiraṇyagarbha, the lower Brahman; its trunk is all living things; it grows through being sprinkled with the waters of thirst; its sprouts are the objects of the senses, its leaves the Vedas and *smṛtis*, its flowers are sacrificial acts, and so forth. Like the peepul tree it is continually shaken by the wind of desires and deeds. Its branches—heaven, hell, the beastly and ghostly states—are below its root.

4 (E71; T212). One should try hard for self-realization while alive on this earth, for except for the *brahmaloka* there is no other world where the Self appears as clearly as a face in the mirror—and the *brahmaloka* is difficult to attain.

KENOPANIṢADBHĀṢYA

There are in fact two commentaries on the *Kena Upaniṣad* ascribed to Śaṃkara, one on the words (*pada*), the other on the sentences (*vākya*). Some scholars have doubted the authenticity of the sentences commentary, though none has questioned that the word commentary is Śaṃkara's.[35] A recent study by Mayeda[36] argues that both are authentic and uses more careful methods than others had previously.

The Upaniṣad belongs to the Tālavakāra Brahman of the *Sāma Veda* and is itself in two parts, half verse and half prose. Its name is taken from the first word of the first verse—"*kena*," "by whom?"

PADABHĀṢYA

"E" references are to the edition by H. R. Bhagavat, *Works of Shankaracharya* (Poona: Ashtekar & Co., 1927), volume 2, part 1, pp. 78-112. "T" refers, to the translation by Swami Gambhirananda in *Eight Upanishads* (Calcutta : Advaita Ashrama, 1957), volume one, pp. 35-94.

PART ONE

Introductory Section (E78-79; T35-39). Śaṃkara reviews the distinctions among the northern and southern paths and the type of rebirth (as "small creatures," e.g., insects) that those who do not even adhere to scriptural injunctions will earn. Distinct from all three of these outcomes is that accruing to the renunciate free from desire, who through meditation on the true Self overcomes ignorance and bondage; he alone can achieve Brahman-realization. It is shown again that knowledge cannot be combined with action.

Let us suppose that someone committed to knowing Brahman

approaches a teacher who understands Brahman and that the following discussion ensues.

I.1 (E79-80; T39-42). The Upaniṣad has the pupil ask "by whom (*kena*) are the internal organ, *prāṇa*, speech, and the sense organs ruled in their several activities?"

Śaṃkara : The questioner is actually asking "by whom is the directed (*preṣita*) internal organ willed to go toward its object?" The implication is that the internal organ, etc., are not independently (*svatantra*) capable of activity or cessation of activity with respect to objects; if they were so, they would not commit evils knowing the consequences. Since they do so it is appropriate to ask who or what impels them to do so.

I.2 (E80-82; T42-47). The answer given in the Upaniṣad is that "He is the ear of the ear, the internal organ of the internal organ. . . ."

Question : We expected an answer to the question in the form "*x* rules the internal organ, *prāṇa*, speech, etc.," with a description of *x* so that the pupil can identify him; the answer provided is not appropriate for the question asked.

Śaṃkara : But in this case no description of the required *x* can be given except by reference to the activities of the ears, etc. It is not that *x* has his own activity apart from that of the organs. Nevertheless, because of the rule that aggregates always serve the purposes of something else, we can presume that there is an *x* whose purposes the ears, etc., serve, and that is the *x* the teacher speaks of here.

Objection : "The ear of the ear" makes no sense, as an ear does not need another ear any more than a light needs another light.

Answer : Though the ear has the capacity of revealing its own objects, it only does so when the light of the Self, i.e., consciousness, is present, and it is in virtue of this that the phrase "ear of the ear" is used to designate that Self.

I.3 (E82; T48-49). Brahman cannot be the object of the activity of the sense organs, speech, or the internal organ—so, says the Upaniṣad, there is no way of instructing concerning It. Śaṃkara says that the text means to suggest that it is very difficult to teach about Brahman. That it is not altogether impossible is suggested by the very next stanza, which invokes scripture to teach about Brahman.

I.4 (E82-83; T49-52). The text says that Brahman is different from what is known and above what is not known.

Śaṃkara : Everything that is known is little (*alpa*), mortal (*mṛtyu*), and frustrating by nature, and Brahman is different from that, so the text means that Brahman is not to be avoided. But since Brahman is nothing different from one's Self, Brahman is not something to be obtained, and that is what is meant by saying that Brahman is above what is not known. And since Brahman is thus shown to be something neither to be obtained or avoided, the disciple will have no desire to treat It as an object of knowledge, realizing that It is his very own Self.

PART TWO

II.1 (E85-87; T58-62). The Upaniṣad : *Teacher* : If you think "I know Brahman well" you do not really know Him, and should study (*mīmāṃsya*) more.

Pupil : I think (Brahman) is known.

Śaṃkara : The knower cannot be known by the knower, any more than fire can burn itself—thus anyone who thinks it is easy to know Brahman is mistaken. Rather they probably comprehend only certain aspects of Him.

Objection : Since a thing is known when one comprehends its essential nature, and since the essential nature of Brahman is consciousness, one knows Brahman well when he knows that It is consciousness.

Answer : That is true. But the point here is that even when one thinks he knows this he really only knows consciousness in relation to its states when limited by adjuncts such as the internal organ and the senses, with which consciousness he is likely to identify his self. Even when Brahman is known as conditioned by divine adjuncts It is still known conditionally and not fully understood.

So the pupil sat and meditated on what the teacher had said, and then approached him and said "I think Brahman is known." And the teacher asked : "Why ?." Said the pupil : "Listen !"

II.2 (E87; T62-64). "I do know Brahman, but also I do not know."

Teacher : Isn't that contradictory ?

Pupil : (Possibly; but) anyone who understands this sentence I have just uttered understands Brahman.

II.3 (E87-88; T64-66). That is to say, those who think they know that Brahman is this or that—say, the organs, or the intellect, they do not know.

But is Brahman wholly unknowable ?

II.4 (E88-90; T66-71). Yes, when the Self, Brahman, is known in relation to all ideas in all states of consciousness as the Witness thereof and thus nondifferent from them, then It is known.

Objection : No, the Self is really known when we understand that

It is the agent in the act of knowing, just as one knows the wind when one understands that which moves the branches of a tree.

Answer : Then you would interpret the Self as a substance possessing the power of knowing, not consciousness itself. Thus on your view knowledge comes and goes, modifying the self when present. It follows that the self you are talking of is changeable, composed of parts, noneternal, impure, etc. (And that is not a proper understanding of the Self).

Vaiśeṣika : Consciousness is an adventitious quality arising from contact between the Self and the internal organ, but it does not follow that the Self is changeable, etc., any more than the pot can be said to change when it is painted a different color.

Answer : Then Brahman, the Self, is mere substance without consciousness and this contradicts scripture. Furthermore, since the Self is without parts the internal organ must always (or never !) be in contact with It, which is contrary to the Vaiśeṣika theory. Finally, only things that have properties can be said to "come into contact" with something else, and then only with something else of the same kind—but on the Vaiśeṣika view the Self—without properties, undifferentiated, etc., is supposed to come into contact with something else—the internal organ—which is of a different kind altogether.

MUṆḌAKOPANIṢADBHĀṢYA

Ranade explains "*Muṇḍaka Upaniṣad*" etymologically as "an 'Upanishad addressed to Shavelings.' "[37] Max Müller explains that "*Muṇḍaka,* in its commonest acceptation, is used as a term of reproach for Buddhist mendicants, who are called 'Shavelings,' in opposition to the Brahmins, who dress their hair carefully, and often display by its peculiar arrangement either their family or their rank . . . ."[38]

Ranade calls the *Muṇḍaka* an emotional work in contrast with the *Kaṭha,* with which he thinks it is roughly contemporaneous. It is an Upaniṣad of the *Atharva Veda.* Since it is in verse it is sometimes called *Mantropaniṣad,* as are other verse Upaniṣads such as the *Īśa.*

"E" references are to H. R. Bhagavat's edition in *Works of Shankaracharya* (Poona: Ashtekar & Co., 1927), volume 2, part 1, pp. 498-531. "T" refers to the translation by Swami Gambhirananda in *Eight Upanishads* (Calcutta : Advaita Ashrama; 2d edition, 1966), volume 2, pp. 77-172.

FIRST MUṆḌAKA, PART ONE

Introduction (E498-499; T79-81). This Upaniṣad is a part of

the *Atharva Veda.* Śaṃkara gives a general account of the purpose of the Upaniṣad, which is to make knowledge of Brahman attractive by distinguishing it from lower knowledge, so that people will engage in it; this is initially accomplished by indicating the great teachers who have passed this knowledge down, and subsequently by showing that Brahman-knowledge comes only to those in *saṃnyāsa* and cannot be associated with actions.

3-6 (E500-502; T84-91). The Upaniṣad relates that Śaunaka, a great householder, asked Aṅgiras what it is by which, when it is known, all this becomes known. Aṅgiras answers that there are two kinds of knowledge, a higher and a lower, and of these the lower consists in knowledge of the Vedas, the sciences of pronunciation (*sikṣā*), ritual (*kalpa*), grammar (*vyākaraṇa*), etymology (*nirukta*), prosody (*chanda*), and astrology (*jyotiṣa*), whereas the higher consists in knowledge of the immutable (*akṣara*). It is by the higher knowledge that wise men understand that which is beyond the senses and is eternal, all-pervading, extremely subtle, etc., and which is the source of all.

An objector complains : This "higher knowledge," since it is outside the *Ṛg Veda*, etc.--how can it be "higher" and the means of liberation ? If it is outside the Vedas it is useless, as Manu (XII.9) shows; furthermore the Upaniṣads will be classed as "outside the Vedas"—or if they are inside, then the distinction between "higher" and "lower" is pointless.

Answer: No, the point being made is that knowledge of the immutable is conveyed only by the Upaniṣads and that knowledge is the "higher"—it does not refer to the collection of words that are found in the Upaniṣads. But by the word "Veda" a collection of words is always meant. The idea, then, is that merely by learning the words in the Vedas one does not necessarily get the higher knowledge.

FIRST MUṆḌAKA, SECOND PART

Introduction (E504; T95-96). The lower knowledge has ignorance as its content, and involves *saṃsāra* with its differences between agent, action, actor, etc.; it is without beginning or end, and since it has the nature of frustration it has to be totally destroyed by each embodied being. The higher knowledge on the other hand has liberation as its content—the destruction of that bondage; it is without beginning or end, without age, fear, death; it is supreme bliss and without a second, since it is nothing but being stabilized in one's own Self. So the text first speaks of the lower knowledge, since eradication of it requires first our understanding that it is there.

11 (E508; T106-108). The text speaks of forest-dwellers, and *saṃnyāsins*, as well as learned householders, who become free from passion (*virāja*) and so, leaving the body, proceed along the "path of the sun"—the "northern path"—to the place where the immortal *puruṣa* lives.

Question : Isn't this liberation?

Answer : No; the Upaniṣad will subsequently explain that liberation takes place right here and involves no journeying. Anyway, the context precludes that we can speak of liberation in this case. The "freedom from passion" mentioned here is a dependent variety since it involves duality.

12 (E508-509; T109-111). The text now advises a Brahmin who has examined the worlds, realized that everything here is only karma and so has renounced them, to find a teacher who knows the Vedas and is stabilized in Brahman.

That is, using the *pramāṇas*—perception, inference, comparison, and scripture—to appreciate that the lower knowledge is meant for ignorant persons and has no capacity for releasing us from bondage, which is to say that such a one realizes that all the worlds are dependent and so like *māyā*, water in a mirage, the Gandharva city, dreams, bubbles in water or foam subject to periodic destruction—realizing all this one should turn away from virtue and vice and renounce everything that has to do with karma. The Brahmin is uniquely qualified for Brahman-knowledge after renunciation. So he should become detached and seek out a teacher.

SECOND MUṆḌAKA, FIRST PART

Introduction (E510; T113). This section explains that the immutable is called "Self" (*puruṣa*), and that it is this Self from which *saṃsāra* arises and into which it becomes dissolved. This is what, being known, leads to all else being known, the subject of the higher knowledge of Brahman.

1 (E510; T113-114). Śaṃkara explains that the immutable Self is the originator and destroyer of things in the same sense that, e.g., different parts of space arise when *ākāśa* is limited by pots, etc., and are dissolved back into *ākāśa* when the pots, etc., disappear, and *ākāśa* is held to be the cause in both such eventuations.

2 (E510-511; T115-117). The text speaks of two "high immutables," of which the Self is the higher. Śaṃkara explains that the lower of these two is the unmanifested, or *māyā*, which is the adjunct of Brahman appearing as name-and-form, which is itself higher than the evolved world of modifications.

3 (E511-512; T117-119). This highest immutable permeates the other one, which is also called *ākāśa,* and becomes empirical content.

Question : How can it do that, since it lacks life-breath, etc.

Answer : If like the Self the life-breath, etc., exist in their own form before origination (of the world), then the Self will possess them since they will occur along with It. But they do not exist in their own form prior to origination. Therefore the Self is without life-breath, etc., just as Devadatta is without a son prior to a son's being born.

The textual passage explains that the life-breath, along with the internal organ (*manas*), sense organs, space (*kha*), air, light, water, and earth, are born from the Self. Śaṃkara explains that they are born as content and modification of *avidyā,* exist only in name, and are "unreal" (*anṛta*) (quoting *Chāndogya Upaniṣad* VI.1.4). For just as a man does not possess a son by dreaming of one, so the Self does not possess the life-breath, etc.

SECOND MUṆḌAKA, SECOND PART

Introduction (E515; T128). This section explains how the immutable is to be known despite Its being without form.

THIRD MUṆḌAKA, FIRST PART

Introduction (E521; T143). This section now turns to consider various aids to the yoga of meditation on the immutable Self, which yoga has been shown to be the means to obtain the realization that destroys completely all causes of *saṃsāra.*

1-2 (E521-522; T143-147). The text of the first of the two passages presents the famous simile of the two birds, constant companions and having the same name, which cling to the same tree, but where one eats the fruit the other looks on without eating. Śaṃkara explains that one of these two is the individual self, or "knower of the field" (*kṣetrajña*), and the other is God—both are conditioned by the limiting adjuncts of the subtle body (*liṅga*) that is the locus of the *vāsanās* of *avidyā,* desire and karma. The "tree" is the body, being like the banyan tree (*aśvattha*) with its roots up and its branches down, the root being the unmanifest, which supports all the results of the actions of living things. God, unlike the individual self, remains the eternal Witness.

The simile is continued in the second passage—the individual self, stuck on that tree, worries about his impotence by reflecting on his inability to maintain the occasions of his enjoyments. But when he sees the other (bird), that is, God, and appreciates His glory, then the individual self becomes free of sorrow (*vitaśoka*). Śaṃkara explains that this will happen if through accumulation of good karma he finds a kindly person who teaches him yoga.

4 (E522-523; T148-151). It becomes clear from Śaṃkara's comment on this verse that the God spoken of in this section is the life-breath (*prāṇa*) and that the individual self who sees him attains pleasure (*rati*) from the Self alone, that is, renounces all other sources of enjoyment like wife, sons, etc., and takes to activities that are spiritual. Śaṃkara takes occasion to show that the text does not imply that knowledge of Brahman and action are to be practised together.

6 (E524; T153). The text says that truth (*satya*) alone conquers, not untruth (*anṛta*), and that by truth the way of the gods is maintained indefinitely. It is this path by which those sages, free from desire, proceed to the place where the optimum treasure truly exists.

THIRD MUṆḌAKA, SECOND PART

3 (E527-528; T161-162). The text says that this Self is not gotten through study (*pravacana*) nor by interpreting (*medha*) nor by listening extensively to scripture. Rather it is that upon abandoning everything else this Self shines through by Its own light when prayed for.

4 (E528; T162-163). Śaṃkara interprets this passage as saying that one cannot pray for the Self successfully without being strong and undeluded, and that one must be a *saṃnyāsin* (he interprets "*liṅga*" here to mean *saṃnyāsa*).

5 (E528; T164). What happens when such a one "enters Brahman"? They "enter into everything" in the sense that all limiting adjuncts are given up, so that the analogy is with what happens when *ākāśa* ceases being confined within pots due to the breaking of the pots.

6 (E529; T165-166). Thus it is not that the liberated self has to go anywhere to achieve liberation; Brahman cannot be approached through change of place. Liberation is not a product, but merely removal of *avidyā*.

7 (E529-530; T167-168). The constituents of the body—the senses, etc.—go to their respective deities (e.g., the sun) at the time of liberation. The karma that has not yet begun to operate, along with the self made of consciousness (*vijñānamaya*), all become unified in Brahman when the limiting adjunct is removed.

9 (E530-531; T169-170). *Objection* : Everyone knows that there are many obstacles to achievement of the highest goal. Therefore,

even one who knows Brahman may, after death, be visited by afflictions (*kleśa*) or by one of the gods or something and so may not reach Brahman.

Answer : No, the only obstacle to liberation is *avidyā*; there is no other source of bondage. Thus one who knows Brahman becomes Brahman, and is not born again, attaining immortality.

PRAŚNOPANIṢADBHĀṢYA

Like the *Muṇḍaka* this work belongs to the *Atharva Veda*; indeed, on Śaṃkara's interpretation it is parasitic upon the *Muṇḍaka*. However, it is in prose rather than verse.

Again, no one has either questioned or studied Śaṃkara's authorship of the work.

"E" refers to the edition by H. R. Bhagavat, *Works of Shankaracharya* (Poona: Ashtekar & Co., 1927), volume two, part one, pp. 393-423. "T" refers to the translation by Swami Gambhirananda in *Eight Upanishads* (Calcutta : Advaita Ashrama, 1957), volume two, pp. 407-506.

FIRST QUESTION

Introduction (E393; T407-408). This Brāhmaṇa is an extensive reiteration of the subject of the *mantra*(-portion) (viz., the *Muṇḍaka Upaniṣad*?). It consists of a story in the form of questions and answers, and is intended to explain who can gain knowledge and who can teach it.

I.16 (E398; T424-425). The text says that the pure Brahmaloka is for those who are not crooked, not false, not *māyā*. Śaṃkara explains that the higher way, or northern path, which is pure like the *prāṇa* or sun and not tainted with passion like the heaven of the moon, is followed by those who are without guile, in contrast to householders for whom crookedness is unavoidable because they are involved in many contradictory purposes characterizing worldly dealings (*vyavahāra*). Likewise, it is to be followed by those who are not false, unlike householders who practice untruthfulness when at play. Again, one who follows this path must be free from *māyā*, unlike householders. *Māyā* is false conduct (*mithyācāra*) involving dissimulation, making an external show of something while acting quite differently. In sum, this path is meant for the *brahmacārins*, forest-dwellers, and monks (*bhikṣu*) in whom such faults are absent.

FOURTH QUESTION

IV.5 (E408-410; T456-461). The text indicates that it is the internal organ (*manas*) that in dreams takes on the various forms experienced and so experiences them.

Objection : The internal organ is an instrument (*karaṇa*) of the one who experiences, that is, the self. So how can it be properly held here that the internal organ is an independent knower ? Only the knower of the field (*kṣetrajña*), that is, the self, is independent.

Answer : There is no fault here. The knower of the field that is independent is precisely that which is conditioned by the internal organ, since the Highest Self is not something that either sleeps or wakes.

Objection : If the Self is conditioned by the internal organ during sleep Its self-illuminatingness will be sublated !

Answer : You misunderstand the purport of scripture. Common language reference to everything from self-illumination to liberation itself with respect to the Self has *avidyā* as its content, and so is caused by the conditioning of the internal organ, etc.

Objection : But scripture tells us, for example, "in this (dream) state the Self is self-illuminating" (*Bṛhadāraṇyaka Upaniṣad* IV.3.9), and on your view the statement is meaningless.

Answer : Your idea is that the intent is that in sleep the Self is unconditioned—but of course there It is still associated with the nerves and heart.

Objector : Well then, what does that passage (IV.3.9) mean ?

Another party : The passage is irrelevant since it belongs to another branch of the Vedas.

Objector : No, for the Vedas must surely all point to a common conclusion. And so the self-illuminatingness of the Self must be upheld, since the scripture speaks truly.

Śaṃkara : Then hear the true meaning of the scripture. Just as the self-illuminatingness of the Self is not sublated when sleeping in the heart or nerves, since it has no relation with them, just so in dream, through the internal organ along with *vāsanās* whose activity is occasioned by ignorance, desire, and karma, the Self remains self-illuminating, being dissociated from all causes and effects while yet witnessing their results.

SIXTH QUESTION

VI.2 (E416-418; T482-491). In answer to a question as to where the *puruṣa* exists the answer is given in this text that it is within the body. Here *puruṣa* is also indicated as "that in which the sixteen parts—*prāṇa*, etc arise.

Śaṃkara argues that the idea is that the partless *puruṣa* appears to have parts by superimposition on it of adjuncts. This *puruṣa* is actually consciousness, invariable, pure, and without properties or parts, but people have various misconceptions about it, such as that it arises afresh at each moment, or that when it stops everything is as if void, or that it is a property of the elements (the view of the Lokāyata). But consciousness is in reality nothing but the Self. That it is unchanging follows from the fact that it remains the same while other objects differ in nature from one another, and from the fact that objects depend on consciousness for their existence, just as color depends on the eye for its manifestation. Knowables may not exist when they are known, but knowledge cannot fail to exist when there is an object.

Objection : Consciousness is not felt in deep sleep and so it changes like its objects.

Answer : No, since knowledge illuminates its objects like light, its absence cannot be inferred in sleep any more than one can infer the absence of light from the absence of anything to be lighted up.

Objection : The nihilist holds that there is no knowledge where there is no object.

Answer : Then he should explain how he can know that that knowledge is absent without knowing something!

Objection : Since knowledge is not nonconcomitant (*avyatireka*) with its object, the nonexistence of knowledge follows from the nonexistence of objects.

Answer : No, since nonexistences—that is, absences—are admitted to be knowable objects by the nihilists. Indeed, they hold that an absence is eternal. So if knowledge is not nonconcomitant with its object, an absence, it too must be eternal, and so to talk of its nonexistence is nonsense. But from the highest standpoint knowledge is neither an absence nor is it noneternal.

Objection : The object is different from knowledge, but knowledge is not different from its object.

Answer : You might as well say that *vahni* (fire) is distinct from *agni* (fire) though *agni* is not distinct from *vahni*. This is mere talk.

Objection : Since there is no awareness (*darśana*) when there is no object, knowledge must be absent if there is no object present.

Answer : No, since the nihilists admit the existence of knowledge in deep sleep.

Objector : Yes, but there knowledge is known by itself alone.

Answer : No, since the difference (between knowledge and objects of knowledge) is established.

Objection : Now if knowledge is known by another knowledge, that knowledge must have another knowledge to know it, etc., and this incurs the fault of overextension (*atiprasaṅga*) (i.e., infinite regress).

Answer : No, we don't accept that knowledge knows itself. Only objects are known, and knowledge is that which knows them. Thus objects and knowledge are completely different in nature, and no regress results.

Objector : But if knowledge is not known, omniscience is impossible.

Answer : That affects only the one who makes the wrong assumption. And one who makes that assumption, unlike us, invites an infinite regress, as he has just argued. Our theory does not invite such a difficulty because we hold that consciousness is single.

Objection : The present text says that the *puruṣa* is in the body like a berry in a cup (*kuṃḍabadaravat*).

Answer : No, for the body, constituted by *prāṇa*, etc., said to be the "products" of *puruṣa*, cannot contain its own source in itself like a berry in a cup.

Objection : Well, it is possible for a mango to contain in itself a seed, which produces a mango tree.

Answer : But the seed it contains is not the same seed that produced the tree on which that mango grew. Anyway, although trees and seeds may be related in this way, *puruṣa* cannot be since it is partless. *Puruṣa* cannot be literally contained in the body, since it is the cause of *ākāśa*, which obviously cannot be contained in the body in a literal sense.

VI.3 (E418-421; T491-499). The text says: "He thought: 'At whose departure shall I come to be, and because of whose maintenance shall I be maintained ?'."

Objection : Now the Self is not an agent, but *pradhāna* is, and is therefore properly viewed as the "creator," organizing the atoms for the purposes of the *puruṣa*. So in this text it must be that it is *pradhāna* that is spoken of as "he," being figuratively referred to as conscious since he is as if conscious.

Answer : It is just as natural to take "he" as referring to the *puruṣa*, the enjoyer, and to treat the implied agency as figurative.

Objector : If *puruṣa* is taken to be intrinsically the enjoyer, experiencing of pleasure or pain constitutes no real change in the *puruṣa*. But if you who follow the Vedas admit that the Self is a creator, you must admit that the Self undergoes intrinsic change and so becomes subject to faults like impermanence, etc.

Answer : No, since on our view the creative agency is manifested through the presence or absence of adjuncts consisting of name-and-form by means of ignorance. We speak this way so that talk about bondage and liberation of the Self in the *śāstras* becomes intelligible. In reality however the Self is neither agent nor enjoyer, whereas the Sāṃkhyas, understanding that agency is superimposed on the Self, do not, because they do not follow the Vedas, hold the parallel view about enjoyership. Too, by assuming that *pradhāna* is a real thing distinct from the Self they become misled by sophistry and mislead others, so that endless disputation occurs among the various schools (who admit differences as real). We do not argue in the same spirit- as these sophists, but only so that those seeking liberation can understand the true meaning of the Upaniṣads by ignoring these other theories.

In any case, no distinction can be found between enjoyership and agency. What distinctive attribute is it that the *puruṣa* has allowing it to be called enjoyer, but that *pradhāna* lacks so that it is merely agent ?

Sāṃkhya opponent : It is the property of mere consciousness (*ciṅmātra*), so that *puruṣa* can change internally as its experiences differ but does not become transformed into something different. *Pradhāna,* on the other hand, does transform into other things.

Answer : That is a merely verbal distinction. If *puruṣa* is originally mere consciousness, and then a new property—some specific experience—comes to qualify it and then disappears, after which *puruṣa* becomes pure consciousness once more, well, likewise, *prakṛti* also is originally (unmanifest) *pradhāna,* then becomes *mahat,* etc., and then these disappear, upon which *prakṛti* is pure *pradhāna* again. So where is the difference ? But if *puruṣa* remains pure consciousness while experiencing, then there is no real experiencing in it at all.

Sāṃkhya : The peculiarity of experiencing is that it involves a change in pure consciousness.

Śaṃkara : Then fire, etc., which undergo change of attributes, ought to be called "enjoyers," which is absurd.

Objector : Well, enjoyership may belong to both *pradhāna* and *puruṣa.*

Answer : That repudiates the Sāṃkhya theory that *pradhāna* acts for the benefit of *puruṣa,* since between two enjoyers there is no dominance and subordination, just as two lights cannot illuminate each other.

Objector : The enjoyership of the *puruṣa* involves its being reflected in intelligence (*cetas*) in a sāttvic fashion.

Answer : Then *puruṣa* is not an enjoyer, only being reflected; nothing has affected it. And if *puruṣa,* being without attributes, experiences no bad (*anartha*) things, then what is it that the Sāṃkhya scriptures are composed in order to remove ?

Sāṃkhya : Those scriptures are composed to remove bad things superimposed through *avidyā.*

Answer : Then the hypotheses that *puruṣa* is only enjoyer and not agent whereas *pradhāna* is agent and not enjoyer, and that *pradhāna* is a real thing different from *puruṣa,* are useless and unwarranted opinions (*kalpanā*) and need not be paid any attention to by those seeking liberation.

Sāṃkhya : From (your) monistic standpoint also composing of scriptures is useless.

Answer: No, since the question cannot arise. So sophistry cannot arise at all.

BHAGAVADGĪTĀBHĀṢYA

We move now to works whose ascription to Śaṃkara has been questioned, beginning with the commentary on the famous epic poem, the *Bhagavadgītā,* most beloved of all classical literature to Indians far and wide. Perhaps because of the celebrated nature of the *Gītā* a good deal has been written on Śaṃkara's interpretation of the text, although one would suppose that rivalry among the various Vedānta schools would as likely focus on differences in interpretation of the Upaniṣads and the *Brahmasūtras,* which are equally common ground. The *Gītā,* unlike the Upaniṣads on which Śaṃkara comments or the *Brahmasūtras,* appears to have been most influenced by Sāṃkhya thought, which adds still another dimension to the polemics.

First, as to Śaṃkara's authorship of the work. That it is Śaṃkara's has been questioned, by Hacker and others, on the basis of discrepancies between the accounts in this work and in the *Brahmasūtrabhāṣya* concerning God's role and the workings of *avidyā.*[39] Ingalls[40] and Raghavan,[41] however, maintain the work is authentic. Both point out that Bhāskara quotes this work word for word. Furthermore, Ingalls suggests that to test Śaṃkara's authorship of any work one should examine the arguments propounded there to see if they are found in any of (what he considers to be) the four unquestionably genuine works of Śaṃkara, that is, *Brahmasūtrabhāṣya, Upadeśasāhasrī,* and the commentaries on the *Bṛhadāraṇyaka* and *Taittirīya.* The *Bhagavadgītābhāṣya* passes this test, Ingalls claims.

Mayeda has examined the question of authenticity using Hacker's criteria and has concluded that there is no reason, on those criteria, to reject Śaṃkara's authorship.[42] However, this is largely a matter of lack of evidence against, rather than positive evidence for. One does not find in this work the term *avidyā* used in ways characteristic of later Advaita. On the other hand, one doesn't find it used synonymously with *nāmarūpa*, as that term hardly appears in the *Bhagavadgītābhāṣya*. The terms "*ānanda*" and "*vivarta*" are not found in this work used in ways later Advaitins use them, and "*īśvara*" appears frequently as in Śaṃkara's clearly genuine works. The ratio of use of "*māyā*" to "*avidyā*" is about 1 to 3 in both this work and the *Brahmasūtrabhāṣya*.

A second strand in discussions of this work concern Śaṃkara's success in interpreting the meaning of the *Gītā*. Some writers have taxed him with willful distortion of the *Gītā*'s sense, notably P. M. Modi, who has written voluminously to this effect.[43] Particular points that arise in this attack concern the relation of karma and *jñāna* to *mokṣa*—many writers find that the *Gītā*, unlike Śaṃkara, teaches that action is either the primary way to liberation or at least a viable one to knowledge. Again, it is claimed that the *Gītā* makes no distinction such as Śaṃkara's between *nirguṇa* and *saguṇa* Brahman.[44]

"E" references are the edition by H. R. Bhagavat in *Works of Shankaracharya* (2d edition : Poona : Ashtekar & Co., 1929). "T" refers to the translation by A. Mahadeva Sastry (Madras : V. Ramaswamy Sastrulu & Sons, 1972; first published in 1897).

Introduction (E1-2; T1-6). Śaṃkara explains that it is the twofold *dharma* of *pravṛtti* and *nivṛtti*—works and renunciation—maintenance of which by men will preserve the order that God gave to the universe. When *dharma* gave way to *adharma* Viṣṇu incarnated himself as Kṛṣṇa and came on earth and taught Arjuna without any purpose of His own but merely to help people, whom He expected to heed His teachings. This teaching is what Veda-Vyāsa arranged into the *Bhagavadgītā*.

Śaṃkara finds that, despite previous commentaries, the meaning of the *Gītā* is difficult, and he proposes therefore to give a brief commentary (*vivaraṇa*) on it.

The purport of the *Gītā* is that the supreme state (*niḥśreyasa*), complete end to *saṃsāra* and its cause, will come from *dharma* which involves Self-knowledge preceded by renunciation (*saṃnyāsa*) of all karma. He quotes several passages from the *Anugītā* (Aśvamedha Parvan of the *Mahābhārata*).

The dharma of activity (*pravṛtti*) leads its practitioners to the gods, etc. When practised in a spirit of devotion to God (*īśvara*), without concern for results, it produces purity of mind (*sattvaśuddhi*), and thus indirectly conduces also toward the supreme state.

II.10 (E8-12; T22-29). The story up to this point shows that when a man is confused by grief and delusion he accumulates merit and demerit that produce *saṃsāra*. Seeing that Self-knowledge preceded by renunciation of karma is the only way for him to avoid *saṃsāra*, Kṛṣṇa sets out his teachings in what follows.

Here some (the Vṛttikāra, according to Ānandagiri) say: Liberation cannot be attained merely by Self-knowledge preceded by *saṃnyāsa*; it requires knowledge coupled with the performance of prescribed actions, such as the *agnihotra* sacrifice. *Gītā* II.33, II.47, IV.15 are cited as examples of texts favoring this interpretation.

Śaṃkara : No. In II.39 Kṛṣṇa distinguishes between the standpoints of karma and of *jñāna*. In II.11-31 he sets out the true nature of the Self from the standpoint of *jñāna*, calling it the "Sāṃkhya" standpoint, and later he develops the doctrine of performance of actions and calls it the "Yoga" standpoint. One cannot follow both paths at the same time, since the "Sāṃkhya" way is based on belief in nonagency and unity whereas the "Yoga" way is based on belief in agency and multiplicity. The *Śatapatha Brāhmaṇa* also carefully distinguishes these two paths and assigns them to two distinct classes of people. That these are distinct is also shown by the following: Arjuna asks (III.1) which path is the right one, presupposing that he thinks them genuine alternatives.

Why did the combined-paths doctrine arise? One reason might be that since we find persons who know the Self continuing to act, a confusion might arise along these lines—but this appearance of activity on the part of the wise man cannot be viewed as part of the path, since his knowledge assures him that he is not an agent at all. Again, one might start an *agnihotra*, say, intending to get to heaven, but part way through attain Self-knowledge—though he continues the ritual it is no longer an action in the relevant sense. Then there are texts (IV.15, III.20) that seem to counsel action, but these are easily explained: either they suggest that Janaka and the rest of the ancients acted even though they had knowledge—in which case their "acts" were merely for the edification of others and were not interested ones; or if they did not have Self-knowledge then their actions conduced to purity of mind and thus indirectly to the attainment of Self-knowledge.

II.16 (E14-15; T34-37). Śaṃkara interprets this passage as denying that both causes and effects are real, even though they are perceived, because they do not exist forever.

Objection : Then nothing at all exists!

Answer : Not so. A content (*viṣaya*) is real if we never fail to be conscious of it; it is unreal if we ever fail to be conscious of it. What satisfies the former requirement is existence: we never fail to have consciousness of existence, though the kind of existence—pot, cloth, etc.—changes every moment and so shows those things to be unreal. Specifically, every simple experience involves a qualifier (*viśeṣaṇa*) and a qualificand (*viśeṣya*)—in "the pot exists" *pot* is the qualificand and *existence* is the qualifier.

Objection : When we have been conscious of a pot and it disappears, we fail to be conscious of *pot*, but we also fail to be conscious of *existence*, so it is equally unreal.

Answer : You are still conscious of existence, only it is now resident in another qualificand, that is, the Self. You are always conscious of the Self, whether you are conscious of any other qualificand or not.

Objector : But the qualifier and the qualificand must both be real throughout our experience, since they both relate to the same thing.

Answer : Certainly not. In the experience "this is water," referring to a mirage, *this* is (relatively) real but *water* is not, even though both terms have the same thing (the mirage) as their extension.

II.21 (E18-21; T43-48). This verse, says Śaṃkara, asserts that the enlightened man (*vidvān*) does not act at all, and so in particular does not kill. It has been shown that the Highest Self is unchangeable, and since the enlightened man is identical with his Highest Self, the conclusion follows that actions enjoined by scripture are intended for the unenlightened.

Objection : Knowledge too is meant for the unenlightened, since there would be no point in imparting it to one already knowing it.

Śaṃkara : No, the point is that when the unenlightened man understands the injunction to perform the *agnihotra*, for example, there is something left that he thinks he is to do and can do, that is, perform the *agnihotra*. For the enlightened man, on the other hand, when he has heard the truth, there is nothing that he thinks he is to do and can do, since he realizes he is a nonagent.

Objection : No one can know the Self as nonagent, immutable, etc., because the Self is unreachable by any of the sense organs.

Answer : No. Scripture (*Bṛhadāraṇyaka Upaniṣad* IV.4.19) tells us that It can be seen by the *manas*. So the possibility of knowledge of the Self must be admitted. This knowledge precludes any further action; it leads one to renounce all action (as indicated in *Gītā* V.13).

Objection : That passage does not indicate renunciation of *all* acts, since it teaches renouncing actions "by thought," so it does not teach renunciation of acts of speech and of the body, only of mental acts.

Answer : No, since acts of speech and of the body depend on activity of the mind. And other ways of trying to construe that passage are of no avail.

II.25 (E23; T51). "The Self is . . . unthinkable. . . . " The rule is that a real thing can only be a content of thought (*cintaviṣaya*) if it lies within the scope of the organs (*indriyagocara*). Since the Self is beyond the organs It is unthinkable.

II.69 (E38-39; T77-79). The duty of the enlightened man is to renounce.

Objection : There is no impelling *pramāṇa* (*pravartaka pramāṇa*) to indicate that activity (of renunciation).

Answer : There need be none. Since the very nature of a *pramāṇa* is to lead to Self-knowledge, such knowledge is naturally indicated, but no action is enjoined, since when knowledge is acquired the instruments of action—organs, objects—no longer are present. The Veda teaches that the Self is not a percipient of objects and as a result of that teaching ceases to be authoritative, just as dreams cease to be authoritative in the waking state.

III. Introduction (E41-44; T82-89). Arjuna's next question (in III.1) is this : "If you think that knowledge is better than action, why do you tell me to act in this way (viz., to fight in this war)?" The question only makes sense if there is a clear distinction between knowledge and action. But some (viz., the Vṛttikāra), who interpret the whole *Gītā* as teaching the combined-path view (*jñānakarma-samuccaya*), then take this third chapter as teaching that only one path is worthwhile. This is inconsistent. He might try to explain the inconsistency away by saying that householders, but not others, are unable to achieve liberation through knowledge alone (Arjuna being a householder), but this is also inconsistent, since he (the Vṛttikāra) explicitly says at the outset that the combined-path view is taught for *all* the *āśramas*. Again, he might say that what is meant is that for the householder, unlike the *saṃnyāsin*, knowledge must be combined with actions enjoined by scripture to be efficacious—in the case of *saṃnyāsins* knowledge combined merely with action enjoined in *smṛti* is sufficient. But how can any sensible person accept such an *ad hoc* explanation ? No special reason is given why the householder should be restricted in this manner. Is it rather that the poor householder must practice both the actions prescribed by scripture *and* those prescribed by *smṛti*, then ? ! That would be too hard on him !

Perhaps, then, the idea is that *only* householders—not *saṃnyāsins*—can attain liberation, since the other *āśramas* have *nityakarmans* to perform ? No, since the texts recommend renunciation of actions for all seekers of liberation, and the suggestion is that one should progress either stepwise or all of a sudden to the *saṃnyāsin* state.

In any case, liberation is not the result of any action, and so no action will help him.

Objection : Performance of *nityakarmans* is required, since omitting them will breed sin.

Answer : No, since sin only occurs for those *āśramas* prior to the fourth, the *saṃnyāsin*, stage; no one supposes that the *saṃnyāsin* who omits the worship of the sacred fire incurs sin as does the *brahmacārin*. Anyway, sin cannot arise from mere omission of action, for something cannot come out of nothing.

IV.11-14 (E64-66; T123-127). These stanzas explain God's attitude toward man's deserts. God rewards men precisely in accord with the way in which they seek Him. If they do not pursue liberation they don't get it; if they seek pleasure they get it, etc. God never rewards out of affection or aversion, or out of delusion. Indeed, He created the four castes (*varṇa*) according to the distribution of *guṇas* and karma on the part of their members—in Brahmins *sattva* predominates, in Kṣatriyas *rajas* predominates intermixed with *sattva*, in Vaiśyas *rajas* predominates intermixed with *tamas*, in Śūdras *tamas* predominates.

Objection : Since You created the four castes You must be non-eternal and bound by Your effects !

Answer : No—it is only from the standpoint of *māyā*: in reality I am no agent and thus unbound. I have no *ahaṃkāra*, am not attached to the fruits of acts such as creation, and thus do not enter *saṃsāra* because of them, as ordinary mortals do.

IV.18 (E67-70; T128-134). "He who sees inaction in action, and action in inaction, he is wise among men, he is the disciplined doer of all actions." Śaṃkara interprets this to mean that both activity (*pravṛtti*) and inactivity (*nivṛtti*) require an agent, thus presuppose that *avidyā* holds sway; through this ignorance people fall into error and confuse action with inaction and vice versa.

Objector : But we never see action as anything else than action—so it is not a case of erroneous knowing.

Answer : It is like the illusion we have, on board a ship, that the trees on the shore are moving when in fact they are stationary. We impute to the Self action, when in fact It is unable to act; it is only the body that can act. Likewise, inaction—failure to act or cessation of activity—is also falsely attributed to one's Self; since the Self is unable to act It is likewise unable to cease acting.

Some commentators interpret this stanza differently. According to them, it means: one who sees that the *nityakarmans* are not actions, since they do not produce any effects, and one who sees that the failure to perform *nityakarmans* is action, since it produces results like going to hell, etc.—these are the wise, etc. But this interpretation is wrong. For Kṛṣṇa has just told us (IV.16) that these wise ones win liberation by correct knowledge about action and inaction; now even if performance of the *nityakarmans* could produce liberation (which we deny), at any rate the mere knowledge that they don't produce any effect can hardly produce liberation. Furthermore, the interpretation pictures Kṛṣṇa as using figurative language to say what could easily be said directly, and produces possible misunderstanding thereby; our interpretation makes the Lord's meaning straightforward and direct.

IV.21 (E71-72; T136-138). The *saṃnyāsin* is allowed in this verse to "do mere bodily action." What does this mean? Not that he is allowed to any old action of the body, but rather that he only does the minimal amount to secure the maintenance of the body.

V. Introduction (E82-86; T154-159). Arjuna will now ask (V.1) which, *saṃnyāsa* or yoga, is the better.

Objection: The question is irrelevant since Arjuna has already been told that *pravṛtti* and *nivṛtti* are required of distinct classes of people.

Answer: Yes, from your point of view it is irrelevant, but from Arjuna's point of view it makes excellent sense, since he is asking which of the two *he* should follow, and both have been enjoined. Furthermore, the answer (V.2) will be that both *saṃnyāsa* and yoga lead to liberation, but that yoga is the better of the two—now from what point of view can this answer make sense? Since neither *saṃnyāsa* nor yoga is efficacious for one who has already attained Self-knowledge, obviously the question is understood as applying only to those who have not reached the state of Self-knowledge.

Question: Are both *saṃnyāsa* and yoga quite impossible for one who knows the Self?

Answer: Yoga certainly is, for it requires a belief in the Self as agent, which is precisely what the Self-knower knows to be wrong. As for *saṃnyāsa*, we must distinguish two kinds of *saṃnyāsa*. One kind is the sort practised by the realized self—of course that is appropriate for him being taught as such by the Lord. The kind of *saṃnyāsa* we have to do with here, however, consists in renouncing only some actions (not all as in the case of the Self-knower). It is with respect to this kind of *saṃnyāsa* that the Lord answers Arjuna's question: for one who does not know the Self, *karmayoga* is better than *karmasaṃnyāsa*, since the latter is more difficult to follow, involving *yama* and *niyama*, etc.

VI. Introduction (E97-99; T179-182). In V.27-29 the Lord has briefly described *dhyānayoga*, the meditative processes by which one immediately gains right knowledge. A householder should practice *karmayoga* until he is able to practice *dhyānayoga*.

Objection : Why not continue to practice both ?

Answer : Because VI.3 divides *yogins* into two classes and advises action for only one of them.

Objector : No, the distinction drawn there is between those who don't practice yoga at all and those who do.

Answer : No, since the passage explicitly identifies the second class as persons who have attained to yoga. Anyway, in VI.37-38 we are told about the ruin that befalls those who are failures in yoga. On your view a householder practices both performance of actions and renunciation of them together; if he failed at the latter, he would not necessarily be ruined, for he would still get the fruits of his good actions. The assumption there must be therefore that the two things are incompatible, that *dhyānayoga* is meant for the *saṃnyāsin*, not the householder.

Opponent : Those actions, performed by the householder, have been offered to the Lord and therefore bring about no results other than liberation; failure in them surely leads to ruin.

Answer : The description of *dhyānayoga* in VI.10, 14, etc., precludes that they should apply to householders.

Opponent : But VI.1 says that the *karmayogin* is both a *saṃnyāsin* and a yogi.

Answer : That verse merely praises abandonment of expectation of fruits (***phalākāṃkṣāsaṃnyāsa***), which is an external aid (***bahiraṅga***) to ***dhyānayoga***.

XIII.2 (E189-197; T318-335). XIII.1-2 teach that the one Lord is the knower of all objects.

Objection : If God is the only knower, then either God is subject to bondage in *saṃsāra*, or else there is no *saṃsāra* at all (there being no subject other than God to experience it). Neither conclusion is acceptable to scripture or to experience. So this reading must be wrong.

Answer : Both God and the individual selves appear to be *saṃsārins* subject to bondage due to adjuncts produced by *avidyā*. Just as a pillar is mistaken as a man through ignorance without any essential quality of the man being transferred to the pillar, so consciousness (=God, the knower) is mistaken as embodied, but no bodily qualities actually qualify consciousness.

Objection : The analogy fails, since although pillar and man are both objects of consciousness and can be mistaken for one another, the body and consciousness are not both objects of consciousness. So, the cases being dissimilar, we should conclude that consciousness really does become embodied.

Answer : No, for then the knower would have *all* the attributes of the known and would, for example, become unconscious ! Why should some qualities of objects actually pertain to the knower whereas others don't ? And the analogy isn't useless—it serves its purpose, in that the two cases agree in the relevant respects, even if not in all respects—no analogy is perfect, or it would cease to be an analogy.

Objector : The knower, you say, possesses ignorance (*avidyā*); therefore He must be bound, a *saṃsārin.*

Answer : No, since *avidyā* is produced out of *tamas*, from whence it gets its veiling capacity; it disappears upon illumination. It is like an eye disease, which temporarily leads us to see what is not the case; the perceptions had while diseased are not essential properties of the perceiver, as they are due to the diseased condition. In any case the objects of knowledge are not properties of the knower, any more than the objects lit up are properties of a lamp.

Objection : Well, then, if there is neither *saṃsāra* nor *saṃsārin* scripture serves no purpose.

Answer : Yes, it has no purpose for the liberated self; but for those saddled with *avidyā* it has a purpose to serve.

Objector : Scripture only has a purpose to serve if there is something really to be avoided and something to be achieved, as well as a real means to accomplish it. Since from the Advaita point of view these are lacking, scripture is useless.

Answer : The Self cannot really have different states. If the Self really could be bound and liberated, it would have to be either simultaneously or successively. It can't be so simultaneously, since the states are mutually contradictory. So it would have to be that the Self was successively bound and then free. But either these states are or are not caused by something else. If they are not caused by something else there can be no liberation. And if they are caused by something else, they cannot be inherent in the Self really. So the dualistic hypothesis won't stand scrutiny. Anyway, if bondage were real it would have to have no beginning but an end, and liberation would have to have a beginning but no end—and this is contrary to experience.

Anyway, scripture is meant for the ignorant, not for the wise, so the objection about the uselessness of scripture has no force. Even if an ignorant philosopher might think himself bound by injunctions meant for someone else, that would not change the situation.

Objection : Nevertheless a man, even though he knows the Self, may still think himself enjoined by scriptural commands, thinking that he has to obtain certain ends and avoid others.

Answer : No, he can only think so prior to Self-knowledge, which regularly follows observation of scriptural injunctions but does not precede it.

Objection : Those who think the Self to be independent of the body, as well as those who think the two are identical, are not interested in injunctions : so for whom will the scripture be relevant ?

Answer : For those who know about the Self through scripture but who do not yet directly know the Self in its essential nature.

Objector : If the wise do not perform Vedic ritual others may emulate them and refuse to perform it, and then no one will follow scripture.

Answer : No, since very few attain Self-knowledge, and ignorant men do not necessarily emulate the wise.

Objector : Even the pundits, the learned, think "I am so-and-so," "this is mine," just like ordinary bound *saṃsārins*.

Answer : Then they are not really learned. There are other pundits who think their self is distinct from God's, and think that in order to achieve liberation they must understand the distinction between knower and known, followed by direct knowledge of God; they also are ignorant, even though they may be learned in all the *śāstras*.

Opponent : Whose is this *avidyā* ? (i.e., in what does it reside ?)

Answer : Whoever sees it.

Opponent : And who is that ?

Answer : The question is pointless, as much as asking when one is acquainted with the owner of some cows, "Whose are these cows ?."

Opponent : No, it is not like that; the cows and their owner are both objects of perception, but *avidyā* and its owner are not both objects of perception.

Answer : Well, apparently you know who the owner is ! So there's no point in asking. You must know the Self by inference, since you cannot directly perceive yourself and *avidyā* at the same time —for you cannot both be the perceiver and perceived; and nothing else can perceive both, for that would lead to infinite regress.

Opponent : If the Self cognizes *avidyā* It is then tainted by it.

Answer : No, it is a figure of speech to say that unchanging consciousness is the cognizer of *avidyā*; as we have already seen, the Lord has taught that the Self is intrinsically without any relation to *avidyā*.

XIII.5-6 (E198-199; T337-339). A variety of Sāṃkhya elements are distinguished in stanza 5, and certain psychological attributes in stanza 6. Śaṃkara explains the former in the usual way and carefully emphasizes that psychological attributes—desire, hatred, pleasure, pain, etc.—are objects and not consciousness.

XIII.12 (E202-203; T344-349). The verse describes Brahman as "not said to be either existent nor nonexistent" (*na sattannāsaducyate*).

Objection : The Lord has shouted that He is going to explain what is knowable—it is unbecoming now to say that it neither exists nor does not exist.

Answer : No. In the Upaniṣads we find it described as "not this, not this," etc.

Objector : There is no real thing that is beyond expression and is yet knowable—that is a contradiction.

Answer : Nor is it nonexistent, since it is not a content of cognition. It is beyond the senses and can only be known by verbal testimony. Since scripture declares Brahman to have these apparently contradictory properties it is no contradiction to speak thus.

Objection : Scripture is itself contradictory when it says this, as in other places.

Answer : No—the other places you have in mind may be mere *arthavāda* passages of praise. In any case, it is appropriate not to speak of Brahman as existent, for everything said to be existent is immediately taken by all to be associated with some genus (*jāti*) or motion or quality or relation, but Brahman is associated with none of these.

XIII.23 (E210-211; T362-365). This stanza says that the Self-knower is not born again.

Objection : How can karmic effects of acts done in a previous life, in this life before realization, or even afterwards, be avoided ?

Answer : Deeds performed without desire and egotism are without karmic results, as the Lord has been saying.

Opponent : All right, but that still leaves the results of previous acts to be worked off.

Answer : Here we must distinguish between those karmic results that have already begun to work in this life, and the ones that have not. The latter are nullified by Self-knowledge, but the former must continue until exhausted; so the Self-knower's body continues until death working off the karma begun in this life—then he is not reborn, as the stanza states.

XVIII.48 (E276-278; T477-482). The stanza says that one should not abandon one's *svadharma*, the duty one is born with. Śaṃkara understands this to mean that a nonknower of the Self should stick to performing his own duty, since he cannot give up action altogether; on the other hand, the Self-knower, since he can give up action altogether, should do so, including his *svadharma*.

Now the Sāṃkhya and Buddhist philosophers cannot, because of their metaphysical views, allow that entire renunciation of actions is possible, so they should recommend without qualification giving up *svadharma*, and thus they would advise counter to the advice given here by the Lord.

Vaiśeṣika : But our metaphysical theory does not have this difficulty. On our view one can give up all actions; for on our view the self is intrinsically immobile, a substance in which actions arise and disappear.

Śaṃkara : This view is mistaken, since it allows that the nonexistent becomes existent, and the existent becomes nonexistent, which contradicts what Kṛṣṇa has said (e.g., in II.16). On your view a double atom (*dvyaṇuka*) does not exist, then it is produced and exists for a time, and then is destroyed and becomes nonexistent. You say that production is due to a combination of three kinds of causal factors. But then cannot an absence—like a hare's horn—come into existence, being a nonexistent just like your double atom prior to production ? How can a causal factor relate to what is nonexistent to occasion its coming into existence ? And if it can, why can it not relate to an absence ? And why should prior absence alone occasion the existence of something—why shouldn't other kinds of absence (Śaṃkara lists an impressive group) do so too, since they are indistinguishable from prior absence ? Actually the same argument refutes Sāṃkhya and Buddhism too; all these theories propose that what is nonexistent becomes existent, which is unreasonable.

The only alternative, which is ours, is to view causation as illusory, to accept that change is always a product of *avidyā*, that the Self is unaffected by it. Then it will be the case that the ignorant man, viewing action as an attribute of his self, is unable to renounce all actions, but the wise man, realizing that the Self is nonagent, will be unable *not* to renounce all actions.

XVIII.50 (E279-281; T484-489). *Objection* : How is knowledge of the Self possible ? Knowledge requires a content with a form, but nowhere is it admitted that the Self has a form (*ākāra*).

Answer : Its form is extreme purity, extreme clarity, and extreme subtlety. *Buddhi* is as pure, and so can take on the form of the Self's consciousness, and in turn the *manas*, the sense organs, and the body take on that form and thus come to think of the body as the self.

Objection : The *buddhi* cannot grasp the Self since it is formless; therefore Self-knowledge is impossible.

Answer : It is impossible for those not properly prepared; for those who have been properly prepared, it is impossible to see anything but the Self. Self-knowledge only requires the discontinuation of perception of the various forms of external objects—since the Self is known all the time it is not something that has to be acquired fresh. The Self—consciousness—is known immediately; even those who hold that awareness (*jñāna*) is without form (*nirākāra*) and thus not perceptible directly must admit that since objects are known *by* awareness it must be perfectly well known, as much so as pleasure, etc. One seeks to know objects with his awareness; one doesn't have to seek awareness in the same fashion. Thus no effort is needed, and no injunctions to act, to get Self-knowledge, which we already have; all that is needed is to remove the notion of the not-self as the Self. So it is easy to have Self-knowledge.

XVIII.66 (E288-293; T499-516). Śaṃkara reviews the arguments for viewing Self-knowledge alone as the path to liberation.

Objector : Liberation is gained by action only, since it (liberation) is eternal. Listen: not doing the *nityakarmans* breeds sin and leads to hell, so one must perform these acts. By doing so, coupled with avoiding prohibited (*pratiṣiddha*) acts as well as those acts (*kāmya-karman*) predicated on desires, one stops further karmic results, and when the results of past karma are burned off no more cause exists for rebirth and liberation is attained without further effort.

Counterobjection : But the results of past karma have not necessarily been worked off at the end of one's life; some have not at all started to work themselves out yet.

Objector's reply : Either one works those effects out precisely in performing the *nityakarmans*, or else the *nityakarman* destroys past sins.

Śaṃkara : These explanations are not satisfactory. Present acts cannot destroy past sins. As for the notion that the very performance of the *nityakarmans* constitutes the working out of karmic effects, they might constitute a way of working out those effects that had already started—that produced this body, etc.—but what you have to show is that they could constitute the working out of those results of past karma that have not started working themselves out yet. If you mean to suggest that *all* effects of past deeds have started to work themselves out in this life, then performance of *nityakarmans* is unnecessary—one merely has to wait, doing nothing, and one will be liberated.

Furthermore, if the idea is that it is the trouble one goes to, and the pain stemming therefrom, when performing *nityakarmans* that constitute the working out of past karma, then the same thing can equally be said about the *kāmyakarmans*, since they too involve trouble and pain. So one should infer that *nityakarmans* produce karmic effects quite as much as *kāmyakarmans*, because they are alike in the relevant respects.

So we should accept the *Gītā*'s message, namely, that the paths of knowledge and of action are intended for distinct classes of people and cannot be combined. Action is only possible for one confused by *avidyā*; it is impossible for one who knows the truth.

Objection : It is not true that all actions involve confusion by *avidyā*. It is true that we must regard the body, etc., as the self in order to act, but this notion is not *avidyā*, it is merely figurative (*gauṇa*). *Avidyā*, that is, false knowledge, occurs when we mistake a post for a man, etc., but here when we say "the body is the agent-self," etc., we have in mind that the body *belongs* to the self, and our way of expressing ourselves is intended to figuratively make that point.

Answer : Wrong. For one thing, figurative expressions are merely intended to praise; they do not lead to any real results. To say "Devadatta is a lion" does not produce a lion, but merely extols Devadatta's fierceness, etc. Secondly, in genuinely figurative language the speaker knows that the things spoken of are not as the figure would imply if taken literally: thus someone saying "Devadatta is a lion" in a figurative way must know that Devadatta is a man, not a lion. So, if saying "the body is the self" is figurative, the speaker must know that the body is not the self, and would not then regard the acts of the body as really belonging to the self. Likewise, if Devadatta hears himself described as a lion figuratively, he knows he is not literally a lion; similarly, if one hears that his body is his self in a figurative sense he would infer that the body's acts are not his (self's). For all these reasons no real purposes of the true self can be accomplished by the body if the identity in question were merely figurative.

Objection : Scripture speaks this way about the self, so it must be really efficacious.

Answer : No. Scripture is authoritative only in matters pertaining to things beyond human experience. Within the field of human experience the ordinary *pramāṇas*—perception, etc.—hold sway. Since it is evident to anyone that the notion of "I" applied to the body, etc., is the result of an illusion, not a figurative expression, scripture cannot affect the matter. A hundred scriptural passages might say that fire is cold, but they would not make fire cold; rather, we should interpret the texts in some alternative manner.

Objection : If actions require *avidyā*, then when *avidyā* ceases scripture, which enjoins acts, will be false.

Answer : No, for it conveys true knowledge about the Self, about Brahman.

Objection : If scripture concerning acts is no authority the same scripture concerning Self-knowledge is no authority either.

Answer : No, since nothing can remove true Self-knowledge. And we do not even admit that scripture concerning action is useless or ultimately misleading, since one can teach the truth by using false means, just as one can bring about correct results by telling falsehoods, for example, when one induces a child or a madman to drink milk by telling him his hair will grow, etc.

Another objector : The self is an agent, in the same way that a king is said to fight when in fact it is his soldiers, not he, who are acting, or as the patron is said to sacrifice when it is the priest, not he, who is performing the various acts. A person or thing is termed agent when the results of an action accrue to him. Even a magnet is the agent in making the piece of iron move, even though it does not itself move.

Answer : No, when we speak of the king or the patron as agent we know they are capable of action and may in fact perform certain acts themselves; then the extension of that agency to the activities of the soldiers or the priest is a figure of speech, and since a figure of speech does not make the connection (between the soldier's acts and the king, for example) real we conclude that in the same way the figurative extension of "agent" to the Self does not make the Self a real doer of actions. It all becomes clear when we notice that all actions are the result of *avidyā*. *Saṃsāra* itself, then, being a product of *avidyā*, it is right to say that it ceases upon true knowledge.

MĀṆḌŪKYOPANIṢADBHĀṢYA with GAUḌAPĀDAKĀRIKĀBHĀṢYA or ĀGAMAŚĀSTRAVIVARAṆA

A number of scholars have doubted that this commentary is the work of the author of the *Brahmasūtrabhāṣya*, beginning at least with Jacobi,[45] and including such stalwarts as Suryanarayana Sastri,[46] Belvalkar,[47] and de Smet.[48] Others have suggested that if this is the master's work it is flawed by youthful ineptness. Ingalls speculates that perhaps Śaṃkara began as a Bhedābhedavādin, then was influenced by Gauḍapāda's work to become an Advaitin.[49] Hacker makes a similar suggestion, only his idea is that Śaṃkara was first a Pātañjala Yogin (and even wrote the commentary on the *Yogabhāṣya* ascribed to a Śaṃkara), then heard or heard of Gauḍapāda and converted to Advaita.[50] Majumdar has attempted to indicate in detail the precise points where the author of this commentary misunderstands Gauḍapāda, concluding that the errors are so serious that the work cannot be by the same hand that wrought the Advaita masterpieces.[51]

In addition to the authority of tradition, followed by most Advaita interpreters, the ascription of this commentary to Śaṃkara has several modern champions. Vetter,[52] Hacker,[53] and Mayeda[54] all utilize Hacker's criteria. Hacker finds no serious discrepancy between the style of this work and that of Śaṃkara's genuine works, although he admits some differences in emphasis between Śaṃkara and Gauḍapāda, for example, over the antipathy of the latter, though not the former to such an extent, toward Buddhism. Hacker also finds in this commentary "two elements of a pre-illusionistic Vedānta tradition. One is the idea of the cosmic Virāj and Hiraṇyagarbha as corresponding to the body and the soul in man; the other is the doctrine of the *Prāṇa* as a cosmic and at the same time an anthropological entity."[55] The idea is found in other places in Śaṃkara's corpus as well, Hacker argues. Hacker also finds a "theory of *bīja* and *āspada*," which replaces "the theory, useless to his (Śaṃkara's) own mind, of the substratum of nescience";[56] the theory of *bīja* and *āspada* is also developed in the *Taittirīyopaniṣadbhāṣya*.

Mayeda, in addition to carefully testing the commentary against Hacker's criteria, considers several arguments offered by those who reject Śaṃkara's authorship of the work. Most of them turn on this author's apparently inadequate knowledge of Buddhism, as contrasted with the thorough understanding displayed by the author of the *Brahmasūtrabhāṣya*. Mayeda thinks that the author of this commentary intentionally misinterprets Buddhist terms so as to give Advaita readings to the passages on which he comments, but that he needed to know Buddhism to do that. Mayeda suggests that Śaṃkara similarly misinterprets Bhedābhedavāda in the *Brahmasūtrabhāṣya*, and Sāṃkhya terms in the *Bhagavadgītābhāṣya*. A final argument, stemming from the fact that manuscripts of this work start with an invocation (*maṅgala*), is easily met by pointing out that the *Bhagavadgītābhāṣya* and *Upadeśasāhasrī* (already demonstrated to Mayeda's satisfaction as being Śaṃkara's work) also have invocations.[57]

Despite these considerations, I retain serious doubts about the work's authenticity. A good many of the favorable arguments smack of special pleading intended to explain away what is used by their opponents as reasons for suspecting the ascription. Even the arguments from Hacker's criteria, although doubtless the weightiest among reasons for ascribing the work to Śaṃkara, stem largely from the absence of uses of Advaita terms characteristic of later Advaita. This line of argument will not avail, for example, against a reconstruction that postulates two Śaṃkaras, both Advaitins, one of which was responsible for this work and perhaps other Upaniṣad commentaries (the *Kaṭha* ?, the *vākya* commentary on the *Kena* ?) as well as perhaps works not on Advaita such as the *Yogabhāṣyavivaraṇa*, following Hacker's line of thought. I am not putting forth this hypothesis with any great seriousness, merely suggesting it is untested and compatible with most of what we now know.

"E" references are to the edition by H. R. Bhagavat, *Works of Shankaracharya* (Poona: Ashtekar & Co., 1927), volume two, part one, pp. 424-497. The translation indicated by "T" is by Manilal N. Dvivedi (Bombay: Tookaram Tatya, 1894).

COMMENTARY ON MĀṆḌŪKYA UPANIṢAD 1-6

Introduction (E424-425; T2-3). The subject matter, purpose, relation between them, and audience addressed are the same as for any Vedantic text. The first *prakaraṇa* (i.e., Book One) explains the word "*aum*" as conducive to Self-knowledge and deals with scripture. The second *prakaraṇa* shows the unreality of duality on the analogy of the rope-snake. The third shows the reality of nonduality by reasoning. The fourth *prakaraṇa* adduces and refutes those systems that hold views conflicting with Advaita.

1 (E425-426; T3-5). Now how can "*aum*" help achieve Self-knowledge ? Just as the Highest Self is the locus of the conceptual constructions (*vikalpa*) that It is *prāṇa*, etc.—like thinking a rope is a snake—so every kind of verbalization (*vākprapañca*) is just "*aum*," having as its content the conceptual construction that the Self is *prāṇa*, etc. Thus *aum* is the Self, being the word for Self. Nothing can exist apart from being named (*abhidheya*), and all names are modifications of *aum*. (Thus one understands the Self by understanding *aum*.)

2 (E426; T5-6). Indeed, name and thing named are one and the same; this is meant literally and is emphasized in order to show that it is possible to do away with both simultaneously, thus realizing Brahman as distinct from both.

3 (E426-427; T6-8). The first portion of "*aum*" is the state of waking (*viśva* or *vaiśvānara*), and the passage says it is conscious of

external things (*bahiḥprajñā*) (through *avidyā*, says Śaṃkara); seven members (explained as head = region of light, eye = sun, breath = wind, trunk = *ākāśa*, penis = water, feet = earth, mouth = sacrificial fire); nineteen mouths (the five sense organs, the five action organs, the five *prāṇas*, *manas*, *buddhi*, *citta*, and *ahamkāra*); and its results are confined to gross things.

Question : Since the point is to describe the inner Self (*pratyagātman*) why has the text wandered into describing it in terms of external things?

Answer : The whole universe, both inner and outer, is described in these passages, the difference being merely verbal. If we do not take it that way we shall be open to the Sāṃkhya interpretation, which is inconsistent with Brahman's unity.

4 (E427; T9-10). The second portion of "*aum*" is the dream state (*taijasa*), with the same members and mouths. It is conscious of what is "within" (*antaḥprajña*) and is confined to subtle results.

5 (E427-428; T10-12). The third portion of "*aum*" is deep sleep (*prājña*), in which there is no desire, no dreams, where all becomes one, made of consciousness (*prajñāna*) and bliss (*ānanda*). Its results are blissful.

6 (E428; T12). This (pure *prājña* or consciousness) is God, all-knowing (*sarvajña*), the creative source as well as the final resting-place of all beings.

COMMENTARY ON GAUḌAPĀDAKĀRIKĀS, BOOK ONE, 1-9

1 *Kārikās* 1-5 (E429-431; T13-17). These stanzas explain the preceding text. Their subject is the same as that of the Upaniṣad itself. The person who realizes that enjoyments and enjoyer are the same is not affected through enjoying, since It knows not modifications to differentiate It.

2. *Kārikās* 6-9 (E431-432; T17-19). Analogies are proposed to explain how *puruṣa* can produce *citta* through *prāṇa*—just as the snake is in the rope even before it is manifested, so all beings are in *prāṇa* before they come into existence. Sparks from a fire, rays of the sun, the spider who spins his web from himself are also relevant as analogies. The first part of *kārikā* 7 ("creation through expansion of the self") is explained by Śaṃkara as meaning that some hold that God flows (*sṛṣṭi*) into creation. As analogy for the idea that creation is like a magic show Śaṃkara offers a description of the rope trick.

COMMENTARY ON MĀṆḌŪKYOPANIṢAD 7

3 (E432-434; T20-25). The text deals with the "fourth" (*turīya*), the fourth part of "*aum*." It is not conscious of either external

or internal or both, or indeed of anything; it is not an object of any ordinary apprehension through thought or perception. It is the Self Itself.

The fourth is not mere absence either, though it can only be described by negative terms. But since it is the negation of the other three parts it follows that no added effort or knowledge is needed to realize the fourth, any more than one needs to do or know something further in order to be free from the snake illusion; all one has to do is to know the rope as rope.

COMMENTARY ON GAUḌAPĀDAKĀRIKĀS 10-18

4. *Kārikā* 11 (E435; T27). "*Viśva* and *taijasa* can be both causes and effects." Specifically, *viśva* is cause and effect of the nongrasping of reality (*tattvāgrahaṇa*), *taijasa* of the grasping of things in a fashion other than they are (*anyathāgrahaṇa*). "*Prājña* (is) cause only" in that its only function is to cause ignorance of reality.

Kārikā 12 (E435; T27). "*Prājña* knows nothing," that is, it is not conscious of anything external and dual, "whereas *turīya* is always seeing," is conscious of everything everywhere. And since it is always seeing it is "omniscient."

COMMENTARY ON MĀṆḌŪKYOPANIṢAD 8-11

(E437-438; T30-33). The four parts of *ātman* just identified correspond to the four parts of the word "*aum*," since, as we have seen, objects and their names are identical.

COMMENTARY ON GAUḌAPĀDAKĀRIKĀS 19-23

Kārikā 23 (E439; T34). If one meditates on the first letter (*a*), that is, if he makes that letter his intended object (*ālambana*), he is identified with *vaiśvanara* and is carried to *viśva* (the waking state). Likewise, if he meditates on the second letter he is carried to the dream state, and on the third letter, to deep sleep.

COMMENTARY ON MĀṆḌŪKYOPANIṢAD 12

(E439-440; T34-35). The *turīya* is the partless (*amātra*) Self, indescribable, all bliss, and nondual—so It is the same as that Self with the three parts corresponding to the waking, dream, and deep sleep stages.

COMMENTARY ON GAUḌAPĀDAKĀRIKĀS : BOOK TWO: UNREALITY (VAITATHYA)

6. *Kārikās* 1-3 (E441-442; T37-39). The point of Book Two is to prove by reasoning (*upapatti*) what the first has shown by reference

to authority. The argument is phrased by wise men as follows: All things seen in dreams are unreal (*vaitathya*), because they are inside (*antaḥsthāna*) the body in a subtle ("covered up") condition. That is, since an elephant can be seen in a dream but obviously cannot really be inside the body, it must be unreal.

7. *Kārikā* 4 (E442; T40). The precise form of the argument is this: Objects seen in the waking state are unreal, because they are seen, like things seen in dream. The argument is valid even though it is granted that dream objects are unlike waking ones in certain respects.

(E443-444; T40-43). The example given of something that is "nonexistent at the beginning and at the end" is a mirage.

Objection: The argument is incorrect, for things seen in the waking state, like food and drink, are used to assuage hunger and thirst, whereas dream objects do not do so.

Answer : No. One who has just eaten and goes to sleep may dream he is hungry, and, likewise, one who has just been dreaming of eating a meal will wake up to find himself hungry.

Kārikā 8. Śaṃkara understands this stanza as answering an objector who argues that the example in the above inference, that is, things seen in dream, is fallacious because "unestablished" (*asiddha*). Things seen in dream are quite unlike those seen in the waking state since they transcend experience (*apūrva*)—for example, one dreams of having eight hands and the like. Śaṃkara's answer is that the objection is irrelevant, since "transcending experience" is a property of the cognizer (the dreamer), not of the objects of his cognition.

9. *Kārikā* 13 (E445; T44). How the self "conceptually constructs" experience is explained as involving especially words and *vāsanās*.

11. *Kārikā* 32 (E449-450; T51-54). "Nothing originates . . . ." Śaṃkara says that this verse, declaring "the highest truth," summarizes the preceding discussion and takes the opportunity to set forth the teaching in his own words. Where there is no duality there cannot be, on pain of contradiction, origination, etc., any more than a snake can, on pain of contradiction, originate from or in a rope.

Objection : If so, scripture should teach the absence of duality, not nonduality, for they are opposed. And so, since there is no *pramāṇa* to show the reality of nonduality the conclusion of *śūnyavāda* is reached, since no duality exists.

Answer : No, since a snake, despite its opposition to the rope, nevertheless seems to exist there.

Objector: We do not accept the example, since the rope is as imaginary as the snake !

Śaṃkara : No, since when the snake is sublated the rope remains, or at any rate the imaginer (*vikalpayitṛ*) does.

Objector : But if there is no operation possible due to the very nature (of the Self), how can scripture dispel the idea of duality ?

Answer : All duality is merely superimposed by *avidyā* on the Self through judgments like "I am happy," "this is mine," etc.

Objector : Then since the Self's nature is evident, what role is there for scripture ? A *pramāṇa*, such as scripture, only functions if there is something to accomplish that has not already been accomplished.

Answer : Its function is to remove the obstructions produced by *avidyā*, which preclude us from a better state, by dispelling duality through teaching (e.g., by "not this, not this," etc.) the characterlessness of the pure Self.

Kārikā 36 (E451; T56). "As if inert," that is, declaring himself as the Self only and not what he thought he was or has become.

Kārikā 37 (E451-452; T57). The wise person should become a completely retired *paramahaṃsa* and should leave provision of food, etc., entirely to chance (*yadṛcchā*).

BOOK THREE : NONDUALITY

12 *Kārikā* 1 (E452-453; T58-59). This book tries to prove nonduality by reasoning (*tarka*).

Kārikā 2 (E453; T60). The "nonmiserable state" is in fact Brahman, the unlimited, partless, infinite consciousness.

Kārikā 5 (E454-455; T62-64). The stanza states that when one *jīva* is bound or freed it doesn't follow that all *jīvas* are bound or freed, any more than when one part of *ākāśa* is soiled it follows that all of *ākāśa* is.

Objection (*by the Sāṃkhya*): But you believe (wrongly) that there is only one Self and so cannot maintain the above thesis.

Answer : We do believe there is only one Self. There is no basis for your doctrine of the plurality of selves.

Sāṃkhya : The basis is that *prakṛti* cannot serve another's purpose; since it does so, we postulate the selves as the things that it serves.

Answer : But you do not believe that *prakṛti* and *puruṣa* are related in an inseparable manner; indeed, the *puruṣas* are viewed as ever free, and it is only the *buddhis*—aspects of *prakṛti*—that are subject to bondage or liberation. So the "serving another's purpose" is easily accounted for just by the fact that there is something else other than *prakṛti*—and it may as well be a single Self.

The Vaiśeṣikas, to be sure, do maintain that desire, etc., inhere in the selves, that is, are related to them in an inseparable manner.

But they are wrong, for some of the qualities in question—that is, traces (*saṃskāra*)—cannot be in an inseparable relation with a self that has no parts and no size—or else memory will be continuous and occur simultaneously with perception. (If you say it is occasioned by contact of *manas* with *ātman*,) contact between the internal organ and the self cannot occur, for selves are entirely without touch (*sparśa*). Anyway, qualities (*guṇa*) such as desire cannot be inseparably related to a substance such as a self, since qualities are evanescent, whereas the self is permanent. Or if you insist that the qualities are permanent too, then liberation will be impossible. Again, if inherence (*samavāya*) is distinct from substance it will require some third relation to connect them; if not, then everything will be eternally related to everything else to which it is related at all.

Kārikā 7 (E456; T65). *Objection* : The space in a pot is as real as space *per se*.

Answer : No, for the space in a pot is not a modification of big space (*mahākāśa*); no more are *jīvas* modifications of the Self.

14 *Kārikā* 18 (E460-461; T73). Śaṃkara says that there is no conflict between the Advaitin and the dualist, any more than there is conflict between a man seated on an elephant and a madman on the ground who thinks he is on another elephant and riding against him.

17 *Kārikā* 42 (E439; T89). Śaṃkara glosses "*laya*" as deep sleep (*suṣupti*).

Kārikā 44 (E439; T90). To wake someone up from *laya* involves disciplining him by discriminative self-insight.

BOOK FOUR : THE PEACE OF THE FIREBRAND (ĀLĀTAŚĀNTI)

18 *Kārikā* 1 (E471; T92-93). This book is intended to show the mutual inconsistencies of the other systems and thus demonstrate their falsity. This first stanza salutes the originator of the Advaita view (*darśana*) and tradition (*saṃpradāya*). The text intends us to understand that consciousness and its objects are ultimately non-different.

19 *Kārikā* 3 (E472; T94-95). The two parties are identified respectively as the Sāṃkhya and the Nyāya-Vaiśeṣika schools.

20 *Kārikā* 9 (E473; T96-97). The "own-nature" (*svabhāva*) of a thing is explained as that which belongs to it completely from the beginning, its essence, inborn and not artificially produced. This own-nature does not change.

Kārikā 10 (E473; T97). The own-nature of a *jiva* is that it is the Self; if it imagines otherwise that does not cause it to abandon its own nature for some other.

22. *Kārikā* 19 (E475; T100-101). The "*buddhas*" who explain the theory of nonorigination are, according to Śaṃkara, the learned Sāṃkhyas and Vaiśeṣikas who by their polemics indirectly prove the true thesis.

Kārikā 20 (E476; T103-104). The opponent offers the seed and the sprout as an example of a beginningless series of causes and effects, but this commits a fallacy that Gauḍapāda chooses to call "*sādhya-sama*," implying that the *hetu* or reason stands in as much need of proof as the *sādhya* or thing to be proved. Actually the fallacy has more to do with an example (*dṛṣṭānta*) that allegedly supports the inference but does not really do so, since it is not evident that the series of seeds and sprouts is itself beginningless, for seeds require causes; so do sprouts, and as for the series, since it is a thing (or considered as one) it too requires a cause, and so forth.

23. *Kārikā* 22 (E476-477; T103-104). Śaṃkara displays dialectical arguments to prove nonorigination. For example, the following: if *x* is by its own nature existent, it can never become existent, and if it is both existent and nonexistent by nature nothing will be produced since its contradictory nature precludes that.

24. *Kārikā* 25 (E478; T105-106). The reason why what the opponent takes as an occasion is not real is that, for example, a jar, which is the occasion for our identifying something (*prajñapti*) as a jar, cannot really be occasion since it is not real. Thus the "cause" is "no cause," as the stanza puts it.

Kārikā 28 (E479; T107-108). This section, proving the illusoriness of external objects, consists of Vijñānavāda arguments. But in this stanza those arguments are turned against the Vijñānavādin's conclusion. The Vijñānavādin believes that the mind (*citta*) is causally efficacious even though objects are not; but his arguments apply equally against the causality of mind. The Śūnyavādins are fools who wish to hold the universe in their hands.

25. *Kārikā* 41 (E482; T113). Here Śaṃkara attributes both experience of the waking and dream worlds to construction (*vikalpa*), calling both worlds error (*viparyāsa*).

32. *Kārikā* 83 (E491; T128). Śaṃkara lists the erroneous notions about things held by several schools, explicitly identifying as "nihilists" those who hold that the self doesn't exist and the Digambara (Jains) who hold that it both does and doesn't exist.

33. *Kārikās* 87-88 (E492-493; T130-131). Śaṃkara identifies the three states described in these stanzas as respectively the stages

of waking, dream, and deep sleep and distinguishes them from the fourth (*turīya*) state, which is the highest truth (*paramārthasatya*).

34. *Kārikā* 90 (E493-494; T132). Śaṃkara takes this stanza to say that of the four preliminary things only the thing to be known, namely, Brahman, exists from the highest standpoint (here called the *agrayāna*), though all should be studied by the aspirant (*bhikṣu*). Of the other three, the things to be avoided are the three stages of waking, dream, and deep sleep, the things to be attained by a pundit free from desires for children, wealth, and fame are the three proper means to knowledge—theoretical knowledge, innocence, and concentration. And the things to be developed are the faults called *kaṣāya*—passion, aversion, delusion, etc. But none are real things.

Kārikā 99 (E496; T136). Śaṃkara pointedly remarks that despite some resemblances—denial of the existence of external objects, etc.—the Advaita theory is different from that of the Buddha, since that is not nondualism.

DAKṢIṆĀMŪRTISTOTRA

This brief hymn (*stotra*) is held traditionally to have been commented on by Sureśvara in the *Mānasollāsa*. If the *Mānasollāsa* is actually Sureśvara's work we might have reason to accept Śaṃkara's authorship of the hymn. But as that ascription is doubtful (see below under Sureśvara), and as we have no real reason to think that Śaṃkara wrote any hymns at all (though we have no particular reason to think he didn't either), the matter must be left in suspense.

"ET" refers to the edition and translation by T.M.P. Mahadevan in *The Hymns of Sankara* (Madras : Ganesh & Co., 1970).

1 (ET 5). The hymn is addressed to the south-facing Lord (*dakṣiṇāmūrti*), incarnate in the guru, who by *māyā* as in a dream sees the universe, which exists within Him like a city in a mirror, as manifested outside, but who when awake sees only His own, nondual Self.

2 (ET 7). Respect is paid to the south-facing Lord who, like a magician or a yogi, makes manifest the universe by His own will, the universe, which is in the beginning undifferentiated like a sprout in its seed, but which becomes differentiated into spatial and temporal states when imagined under the influence of *māyā*.

3 (ET 9-10). To that south-facing Lord whose light, the nature of existence, illuminates objects that are as if nonexistent, who causes those who resort to Him to understand (the Self) directly through the Vedic text "that art thou," on the direct understanding of whom there will be no returning to this ocean of transmigration.

4 (ET 11-12). To that south-facing Lord whose consciousness moves out through the visual and other organs like the light of a great lamp set in the belly of a pot with many holes, so that the whole universe shines because He shines in the awareness "I know."

5 (ET 13-14). To the south-facing Lord who destroys the great delusion, apparently produced (*kalpita*) by the power of *māyā*, found in people who talk much and think of the self as the body or the senses, etc.

6 (ET 15-16). To that south-facing Lord who in deep sleep when the sense organs are withdrawn becomes the one existence veiled by *māyā* like the sun or moon in an eclipse, and who on waking is aware that He has slept.

7 (ET 17). To that south-facing Lord who, shining within as "I" unchanging through childhood, youth, and old age, dream, waking, and deep sleep, manifests Himself to His followers by the blessed *mudrā*.

8 (ET 19). To that south-facing Lord, the Self, who dreaming or waking, deluded by *māyā*, sees differences such as cause and effect, owner and owned, teacher and pupil, father and son.

9 (ET 20-21). To the south-facing Lord whose eight-fold form comprises the whole universe—earth, water, fire, air, space (*ambara*), sun, moon, and self (*pumān*)—beyond whom nothing exists for anyone who seeks.

10 (ET 22-23). By hearing, reflecting, and meditating on the universe's being completely Self, and by reciting it, one will naturally attain Lordship (*iśvaratva*) along with the supreme splendor of the universal Self, and will achieve unimpeded divine power involving the eight forms.

PAÑCĪKARAṆA

Belvalkar believes this small treatise is properly ascribed to Śaṃkara, arguing on the ground of a traditional line of commentaries on it beginning with Sureśvara. However, he admits "there is nothing in the work itself that warrants its ascription to Śaṃkara . . . ."[58] The *Vārttika* on it, supposedly by Sureśvara, being clearly redolent of Tantra, is extremely suspect.

"ET" refers to the edition and translation by members of the Ramakrishna Mission Sevashrama (Mathura: Mathura Printing Press, 1962).

1 (ET 1-2). The term "*virāj*" is used to stand for the collection of all the quintuplicated (*pañcīkṛta*) five elements (*mahābhūtas*) and

their results. This is the gross body of the Self. The waking state (*jāgarita*) is the state where the sense organs produce knowledge of objects. The Self, conceived (*abhimāna*) as both the waking state and the gross, body is called "*viśva*." These three (*virāj*, *jāgarita*, and *viśva*) are together represented by the letter *a* in "*aum*."

2 (ET 2-3). The five nonquintuplicated *tanmātras* and their result, that is, the subtle body (*liṅga*), together comprise what is called "*hiraṇyagarbha*." The subtle body has seventeen parts—five *prāṇas*, ten organs (of sense and of action), the internal organ (*manas*), and the *buddhi*.

3 (ET 3-4). When the sense organs are withdrawn, ideas (*pratyaya*) arisng from traces (*saṃskāra*) produced in the waking state with their contents are called the dream state (*svapna*). The Self conceived as both (the subtle body and the dream state) is called "*taijasa*." The three (subtle body, dream state, and *taijasa*) are represented by *u* in "*aum*."

4 (ET 4-5). Nonknowledge (*ajñāna*) of the Self, which causes both the gross and the subtle bodies, along with the reflection (*ābhāsa*) (of the Self) is called "*avyākṛta*" or unmanifested. This is the causal body of the Self. It neither exists (*sat*) nor doesn't exist, nor both exists and doesn't exist; it is neither different from, nor not different from, nor both different and not different from, the Self. This nonknowledge is neither made up of parts, nor without parts, nor both, and it is only removable by knowledge of the identity of Brahman and the Self.

5 (ET 5-6). When all awareness of qualifications (*sarvaprakārajñāna*) stops and the *buddhi* stands still in its causal nature, it is called "deep sleep." The Self conceived as these two (viz., deep sleep and the causal body or nonknowledge) is called "*prājña*." The three (viz., nonknowledge, deep sleep, and *prājña*) are represented by the letter *m* in "*aum*."

6 (ET 6-7). Now *a* goes into *u*, *u* into *m*, *m* into "*aum*," and "*aum*" into "*aham*," that is, "I." I am the Witness-Self, isolated and having the nature of pure consciousness only, I am not nonknowledge nor even its result, but I am Brahman alone, eternally pure, enlightened, liberated, and existent. I am the highest bliss, one without a second, the inner consciousness. This remaining in a state of nondifference is what is called "*samādhi*."

7 (ET 8-9). (The above is evidenced) by scriptural sentences such as "that art thou," "I am Brahman," "Brahman is consciousness and bliss," "This Self is Brahman," etc.

APAROKṢĀNUBHŪTI

Belvalkar is inclined to regard this work as having "a fairly satisfactory claim to Śaṃkara's authorship" since it is "honored by many commentaries." He expresses doubts about the ascription of the commentaries to their traditional authors, however, and remarks "Even the original work does not rise very much above the commonplace, and may have been an early effort of the Ācārya."[59] Ingalls[60] and Mayeda[61] reject Śaṃkara's authorship of *all prakaraṇa* or expository works except for the *Upadeśasāhasri*. Hacker, in addition, finds evidence from colophons suggesting the work is spurious.[62]

"ET" identifies the edition and translation by S. Venkataramanan in *Select Works of Sri Sankaracharya* (2d edition; Madras: G. A. Natesan & Co., n.d.).

2 (ET 39). Direct (*aparokṣa*) experience (*anubhūti*) is here explained as a means to liberation. It should be studied zealously.

3 (ET 39). By performing the duties of one's caste and station (*svavarṇāśramadharma*), by asceticism and by worship of the Lord (*hari*), men will obtain the fourfold (requirements of) nonattachment, etc.

4 (ET 40). Pure nonattachment involves having the same attitude toward all objects from Brahmā down to inanimate things as one has toward crow droppings.

5 (ET 40). Right discrimination means determining that the Self is eternal and everything perceptible is not.

6 (ET 40). Control of mind (*śama*) is the abandoning of subconscious impressions (*vāsanā*). Control of body is the restraint of external fluctuations (*bāhya vṛtti*).

7 (ET 40-41). Abstention (*parāvṛtti*) is turning away from objects. Resignation (*titikṣā*) is enduring all frustrations.

8 (ET 41). Faith (*śraddhā*) is devotion (*bhakti*) to the sayings of scripture and teacher. Concentration (*samādhāna*) is fixing one's mind on reality.

9 (ET 41). Desire for liberation (*mumukṣatā*) is the intense thought "How and when, O Lord, shall I be liberated ?"

10 (ET 41-42). One desiring welfare for oneself, after satisfying the above-mentioned requirements, should begin an inquiry (*vicāra*) in order to establish knowledge.

11 (ET 42). Knowledge cannot arise except through inquiry, just as perception is impossible without light.

12-16 (ET 42-43). Examples of the kind of inquiry meant are provided: for example, "Who am I ?"

17-21 (ET 44-45). An analysis is given of the misidentifications common among ignorant men between the self and the body.

22-40 (ET 45-51). It is shown how the self differs from both gross and subtle bodies.

41 (ET 51). *Objection* : By distinguishing the self from the body all you have shown is that the world (*prapañca*) exists, as is indeed stated by the Tārkika (the logician). What is the point of that ?

42 (ET 51). *Answer* : We have so far shown that the self and body differ. Now we shall show that the distinction of the body as different is unreal.

43-46 (ET 52-53). Consciousness is by nature one, and everything else is unreal, like the rope-snake. Everything is Brahman-Ātman and nothing else.

47-55 (ET 53-55). The Vedas declare this.

56-86 (ET 56-65). Many illustrative analogies are offered to show the unreality of duality, including (56-57) dreams; (59-60) the disappearance of the pot, the silver, and the earring when one knows that it is (respectively) clay, shell, and gold; (61) the blue of the sky, the mirage, the man in the post; (62) the ghost in an empty place, the city of the Gandharvas, the double moon; (63) waves of water, vessels of copper; (74) the house in the lumber, the sword in the steel; (75) reflections in the water; (76) apparent movement of things seen by one on a ship; (77) yellow seen by a jaundiced man; (78) dizziness; (79) the wheel-of-fire; (80) big things seem small when far away; (81) small things seem big when close up; (82) glass mistaken for water; (83) charcoal mistaken for a jewel; (84) apparent movement of the moon when clouds are moving; (85) motions perceived by one in a faint.

87-89 (ET 65-66). In the way illustrated thus, the Self is mistaken for the body, but the mistake disappears when Brahman is realized.

90 (ET 66). *Objection* : But even when the Self has been realized the results of karma already begun (*prārabdha*) cannot be avoided.

91 (ET 66-67). *Answer* : No. Once knowledge of reality (*tattvajñāna*) has arisen there can be no results of *prārabdhakarman*, just as after waking there is no dream.

92 (ET 67). It is acts done in past lives that are called *prārabdha*. But since there is no past life, those acts don't exist.

93 (ET 67). The (waking) body is superimposed (*adhyasta*) as much as the dream body is. But an illusion is not alive, and therefore it can't act.

98 (ET 69). In speaking of the destruction of karma when the

Self is realized the Vedas use the plural case ending (*karmāṇi*) (and not the singular or dual) to indicate that *prārabdhakarman* (in addition to the other two kinds) is destroyed.

100-103 (ET 70-71). Here is a fifteen-step process of meditation leading to liberation, consisting of (1) forbearance (*yama*), (2) observance (*niyama*), (3) renunciation (*tyāga*), (4) silence (*mauna*), (5) place (*deśa*), (6) time (*kāla*), (7) posture (*āsana*), (8) subduing the root (*mūlabandha*), (9) equilibrium of the body (*dehasāmya*), (10) fixed vision (*dṛksthiti*), (11) breath control (*prāṇāyāma*), (12) withdrawal of the senses (*pratyāhāra*), (13) attention (*dhāraṇā*), (14) contemplation (*dhyāna*), (15) *samādhi*.

107-109 (ET 72-73). "Silence" is explained as either (a) the silence of Brahman, which defies expression and with which the seeker should identify himself, also known as *sahaja*, or (b) literal silence of speech.

110 (ET 73). "Place" is that by which the universe is pervaded.

111 (ET 73). "Time" is another name for Brahman since all creatures from Brahmā on down are manifested in the twinkling of an eye (*nimeṣa*).

112-113 (ET 74). "Posture" is explained as the condition in which Brahman is blissfully contemplated, and the posture called "*siddha*" is that in which the perfected ones repose.

114 (ET 74). "Subduing the root," that is, control of *citta*, is proper for *rājayogins*.

115 (ET 75). Bodily equilibrium is not just stiffening the body, but absorption in Brahman.

116-117 (ET 75). Fixed vision is not necessarily just studying the tip of one's nose, but directing one's vision in some fashion that will cause the distinctions of seer, sight, and object to cease, for example, by realizing that the whole world is Brahman.

118-120 (ET 76). Breath control isn't just pressing the nose but has to be understood more deeply as control of all the life forces.

124-126 (ET 77-78). *Samādhi* is forgetting all fluctuations by making them unmodifiable and then of the form of Brahman. One should practice this until one can do it instantly at will. Then one is a *siddha* and king of yogis (*yogirāj*), though the real nature of *samādhi* cannot be reached by word or thought.

127-128 (ET 78-79). Obstacles to *samādhi* are listed.

129 (ET 79). One's consciousness becomes what he thinks on; one should think on the fullness (*pūrṇatva*) of Brahman and so become full.

130-134 (ET 79-80). Those who, having once realized Brahman, give it up are, though human, like animals, whereas those who develop what they have achieved are the best of men. They become identical with eternal Brahman, as Śaunaka, Śuka, and others have, whereas the others, clever in their talk and swayed by passion, merely fight about words and transmigrate over and over.

135-142 (ET 81-83). The meditation on the clay and the pot, illustrating how to identify with and thus become the cause, should be repeated.

143-144 (ET 83-84). The steps outlined detail a scheme called "*rājayoga*." Those whose passions are only partly rooted out should combine this yoga with *haṭhayoga*. But those whose internal organ is ripe will easily and quickly reach perfection by practising the above yoga alone with faith in their teacher and in God.

ĀTMABODHA

This is a very popular short treatise that has been commented on by a number of Advaita luminaries. Belvalkar is inclined to view it as genuine, but without giving any particular reasons.[63] As with the *Aparokṣānubhūti*, Hacker and others suggest the work is not Śaṃkara's.[64]

"ET" references are to the edition and translation by P. N. Menon, *Atma Bodha of Sri Sankaracharya* (2d edition: Palghat, 1964).

1 (ET3). The work is for those who have satisfied the four requirements.

2 (ET 4-6). Compared with other means Self-knowledge is the one direct means to liberation, a necessary condition for it as fire is for cooking.

3 (ET 9-10). Action, not being opposed to *avidyā*, cannot destroy it, but knowledge can.

5 (ET 14-15). The *jiva*, tainted with ignorance but having been made pure by repetition of his knowledge (*jñānābhyāsa*), dies of itself as the clearing-nut does in water.

6-8 (ET 16-19). Analogies of dream, shell-silver, bubbles in water adduced.

9 (ET 20). The various individuals are imputed (*prakalpita*) to eternal Viṣṇu as bangles are to gold.

11 (ET 23). Just as differences of taste, color, etc., are superimposed (*āropita*) on water, so distinctions of caste, name, stage of life, etc., are superimposed on the Self.

12-14 (ET 24-29). The three bodies—gross, subtle, and causal—are explained. The gross body is a fivefold combination of elements;

the subtle body consists of five *prāṇas*, ten sense organs, *manas*, and *buddhi*; the causal body is *avidyā*.

15-16 (ET 31-36). The doctrine of the five sheaths (*pañcakośa*) is explained. By reason one should husk the sheaths to discover the grain that is the inner Self.

17 (ET 40). Though the Self is eternal and omnipresent, It does not shine in everything, but only in the *buddhi*, where It is reflected as if from a mirror.

25 (ET 54). Mixing (*saṃyojya*) parts of existence (*sat*) and consciousness (*cit*) with the fluctuations of *citta*, by nondiscrimination of them the idea "I know" arises.

42 (ET 81-82). By rubbing contemplation on the wood of the Self the flame of knowledge will arise that will consume all the fuel of *avidyā*.

43-44 (ET 83-85). When *avidyā* is destroyed by knowledge the Self will manifest itself, just as the sun does when darkness is dispelled at dawn. The Self always exists but seems not to because of *avidyā*. When *avidyā* is destroyed It is discovered, like the necklace on one's neck.

49-53 (ET 93-102). Liberation while living (*jīvanmukti*) occurs when the knowing one (*jñānin*) gives up the adjuncts that previously limited him and, giving up all attachment, enjoys the bliss of the Self, unaffected by the adjuncts even though they are all around, just like the sky. Knowing everything he can move about like a deluded person but unattached. When the adjuncts are (eventually) destroyed the sage (*muni*) merges into Viṣṇu.

58 (ET 107). Brahmā and the others, residing in a portion of the bliss that is Brahman's in Its infinite form, become blissful themselves in proportion to their respective portions.

59 (ET 108-109). All real things (*vastu*) are united with Brahman. Practical affairs (*vyavahāra*) are imbued with consciousness. Brahman pervades all, as milk pervades butter.

63 (ET 114-115). Brahman is different from this (universe). There is no other than Brahman. If anything shines other than Brahman it is false (*mithyā*) like the mirage.

ŚATAŚLOKĪ

The *Śataśloki*, consisting of one hundred stanzas, is "remarkable for the easy familiarity with which it marshalls forth Vedic and Upaniṣadic texts in support of Advaitic conclusions".[65] Belvalkar regards it as probably Śaṃkara's. Hacker and Mayeda reject it.[66]

"ET" refers to the edition and translation by S. Venkataramanan in *Select Works of Sri Samkara* (2d edition: Madras: G. A. Natesan & Co., n.d.).

1-2 (ET 85-86). Salutation to the guru.

3 (ET 86-87). Scripture holds that knowledge of Brahman comes through experience (*svānubhūti*) and reasoning (*upapatti*).

4-13 (ET 87-93). The Self is distinguished from what is not-Self as Witness from agent or enjoyer.

14 (ET 93-94). There are two kinds of nonattachment: the former springs from disgust occasioned by noting that one's desires are not usually satisfied; the latter springs from knowledge and involves rejecting the objects of desire.

14-21 (ET 93-99). Renunciation is examined.

22-25 (ET 99-102). Verses on creation and dissolution.

26-32 (ET 102-106). The ways of *māyā.*

33-38 (ET 107-111). Dreams and waking experience compared. The reality or unreality of things depends only on the length of time they last. Everything has construction (*kalpanā*) as its root.

42 (ET 113). First comes *jivanmukti* or liberation while living, and then final liberation. These are the result of practice (*abhyāsa*) and the discipline of knowledge (*jñānayoga*) and require the advice and assistance of a guru. Practice is of two kinds, bodily—including postures, etc.—and the other, equivalent to the discipline of knowledge, which involves abstention (*uparati*).

43-46 (ET 114-116). *Jīvanmukti* characterized, and the stages of attaining final liberation.

47-49 (ET 117-118). Upaniṣadic analogies to illuminate the nature of Brahman.

50-54 (ET 119-122). The reflection analogy explored.

75-82 (ET 136-141). Dreaming is reviewed. By analogy it is concluded that everything is merely created by experience (*dṛṣṭisṛṣṭi*), that the world is as unreal (*mṛṣā*) as a juggler's illusion.

83-86 (ET 141-144). Action and knowledge and their results are contrasted.

87-90 (ET 144-147). Self-illumination; the operation of the *prāṇas.*

91-101 (ET 147-154). The saving knowledge and how it leads to liberation.

ĀTMAJÑĀNOPADEŚAVIDHI or PRAKARAṆA or BĀLABODHINĪ or ĀTMAVIDYOPADEŚA

Belvalkar classes this as a work which is "usually, but not convincingly, supposed to belong to Śaṃkara's authorship."[67] Hacker concludes from colophons that it is not genuine.[68]

"ET" refers to the edition and translation by Swami Jagadananda (Madras: Sri Ramakrishna Math, 1953).

PART ONE

I.1 (ET 1-2). The teaching is meant for those who have satisfied the four requirements.

I.2 (ET 2). Everybody knows that the seen is different from the seer. But what is the Self?

I.3-6 (ET 2-5). The body is not the Self.

I.7-9 (ET 7-8). The sense organs are not the Self.

I.10 (ET 8). The internal organ (*manas*) is not the Self.

I.11 (ET 8). The *buddhi* is not the Self.

I.12-14 (ET 8-10). The Self is not *prāṇa*, because *prāṇa* is without consciousness in deep sleep.

I.15 (ET 8-10). *Objection*: *Prāṇa* appears to be without consciousness in deep sleep because the sense organs have temporarily stopped functioning, not because it is not conscious.

Answer : No, for the senses cannot stop functioning while their owner (*svāmi*) is functioning, just as the king's officers cannot cease working as long as he is working. So, the sense organs do not belong to *prāṇa* but rather to *jīva.*

I.16-17 (ET 11-12). The senses operate toward their respective objects when the *jīva* comes out (*bahiḥ nirgatya*) in the waking state when karma occasions it to wake from sleep. When the results of that karma have been exhausted the *jīva* draws in all the organs of object consciousness (*viṣayavijñāna*) produced from connection with its adjunct, *buddhi*, and then experiences dream or deep sleep.

I.18-20 (ET 13-14). So, the *jīva* experiences the three states successively, going to waking and sleep due to its karma, and to deep sleep in order to remove fatigue.

I.21 (ET 15). Now *prāṇa* functions in all three states—otherwise the body would be taken to be dead when asleep.

I.22-24 (ET 15-16). The ego (*aham*) is likewise not the Self but rather an object of perception, like a jar, etc., since it does not exist during deep sleep and has various qualities.

I.25 (ET 17). The reason why the body, etc., are taken for the Self is because of that want of discrimination between seer and seen.

PART TWO

II.1 (ET 19-20). The nature of the Self is described according to various Upaniṣads.

II.2 (ET 20-21). The all-pervading Self, without parts, cannot have the *buddhi* as its locus (*ādhāra*), but It is said to reside in the heart of everyone since It is qualified by all *buddhis*.

II.3-7 (ET 21-25). *Objection* : The Self cannot be properly called a "seer," for the act of seeing involves subject, object, desire, or aversion. Furthermore, if It is a seer It cannot see all the *buddhis* at once, since an act involves instruments that are independent of the agent; so if It sees It must only see a limited number of objects or in succession.

II.8 (ET 25). And why did you say (in II.2) that It is qualified by *buddhi(s)* ?

II.9-11 (ET 25-27). *Answer* : As for the last point, a relation between them (Self and *buddhi*) is possible since they are both subtle, transparent (*svaccha*), and partless. And though they cannot be connected as varnish with wood, not having form, there is a connection due to superimposition, since the *buddhi*, though nonilluminative like a gem, appears to be so because of the proximity of the illuminating Self.

II.12 (ET 27-29). And so, just as the sun, though without notions, desire, etc., still can be said to illuminate things just by its proximity to them, likewise the Self is called a "seer" since, though devoid of ideas of subject, object, desire, or aversion, It is naturally illuminative and is in proximity to objects. So only the ignorant impute agency to the Self, agency in an act of knowing; It does not know in that way.

II.13-18 (ET 30-32). Likewise, the Self is an "agent" only as a magnet is, which moves metal only by its proximity. In the case of the Self it is the proximity occasioned by Its being the Witness that allows the ignorant to impute agency to It.

II.19 (ET 32-33). *Objection* : If the Self is pure consciousness how can one know It by means of the *buddhi* ?

II.20 (ET 32-33). *Answer* : The Self cannot be known by the intellect any more than the sun can be illumined by color.

II.21-22 (ET 33-34). And also because the *buddhi*, being an object of knowledge, cannot also be a knower, just as two lamps cannot be illuminated by each other.

PART THREE

III.1-9 (ET 35-45). Waking, dream, and deep sleep are explained and distinguished from each other and from consciousness.

PART FOUR

IV.1-6 (ET 46-48). The Self is thus not these states but the fourth (*turīya*), consciousness only. The fourth is not another state but rather the Witness of the three states through Its proximity. If *turīya* were a fourth state the result would be emptiness (*śūnyatā*), since then the Self could not be known (and likewise therefore the not-Self). And the doctrine of emptiness can't be right, since superimposition requires a (positive) substratum (*āspada*).

IV.8 (ET 49-51). *Question* : How can the three states give us knowledge of the pure Self?

Answer : Since It persists in all three states, whereas each of them does not persist.

IV.9 (ET 49-51). *Objection* : But in deep sleep consciousness does not persist.

Answer : No, objects do not persist then, but consciousness does, as one reports on waking that he has been asleep.

IV.10 (ET 52-53). For this reason the Self is not dependent on a *pramāṇa* (for our knowledge of It), because only noneternal and limited things are so dependent. Who would be the *pramātṛ*—the one who uses the *pramāṇa*? It can only be the Self itself (and It doesn't need a *pramāṇa*!)

IV.11 (ET 52-53). *Objection* : The Self is proved by scripture (*āgama*).

Answer : No, not even by it. The Vedas are proof of the knowledge of unity of Self and Brahman, not by making Brahman an object of a *pramāṇa*, but by negating the properties of not-Self that have been superimposed on the Self.

ĀTMANĀTMAVIVEKA

The *Ātmanātmaviveka* is another spurious work, not specifically mentioned by Belvalkar or Hacker.

"E" refers to the edition by H. R. Bhagavat, *Minor Works of Samkaracarya* (2d edition: Poona Oriental Series 8, 1952), pp. 405-414. "T" refers to the translation by Mohini M. Chatterjee in *A Compendium of the Raja Yoga Philosophy* (edited by M. N. Dvivedi) (Bombay, 1885).

1-2 (E405; T34). Everything that is seen (*dṛśya*) is not-Self. The Self is the seer. The distinction between Self and not-Self is set forth in many books and is explained here.

3-10 (E405-406; T34-35). Frustration comes to the self from its taking on bodies, which is in turn produced by karma, which in turn arises from passion, etc., which are produced by the ego notion (*abhimāna*), which comes from lack of discrimination, which is due to lack of knowledge (*ajñāna*). *Ajñāna* is not produced by anything, being the beginningless mixture of *sat* and *asat*. It has the three *guṇas* as its nature and is said to be by nature contradictory to knowledge because it leads to the experience "I am unknowing." This nonknowledge will not cease until the unity of the Self with Brahman leads to cessation of *avidyā*.

11 (E406 ; T35-36). *Objection* : The *nityakarmans* lead to cessation of *avidyā*, so what is the point of knowledge ?

Answer: Actions, etc., cannot lead to the cessation of *avidyā*, since action and knowledge are contradictory.

12 (E406; T36). Knowledge is gained from discussion (*vicāra*) of the distinction between Self and not-Self. Who are ready for such discussion ? Those who satisfy the fourfold requirement of discriminating eternal from noneternal things, being nonattached to enjoying the fruits of actions here and hereafter, possessing the six properties of *śama*, etc., and desire for liberation. Nonattachment is explained as having the same disinclination against objects like garlands, women, etc., as one has against vomited food, and this should extend to the higher spheres from heaven to the Brahmaloka.

12-16 (E406-407; T37). Of the six qualities, *śama* is restraining the internal organ so that it only engages in listening (*śravaṇa*), reflecting (*manana*), and meditating (*nididhyāsana*). These are illustrated and explained.

17-18 (E407-408; T37). *Dama* is the restraint of the external senses, explained as the ten organs of sense and action, and they should be restrained from doing anything other than participating in listening, reflecting, and meditating.

Uparati is refraining from actions prescribed in scripture. Or, it is just that state of the internal organ in which it is limited to listening, etc.

Titikṣā is bearing with equanimity opposites such as heat and cold as well as bodily cuts, etc. Or, it is pardoning those one is capable of punishing.

Samādhāna is when an internal organ practicing listening, etc., considers things capable of producing impressions (*vāsanā*) but finding faults in them returns to the *samādhi* involved in listening, etc.

Śraddhā is faith in the guru and in the Vedantic sentences.

18-20 (E408; T37-38). Those *brahmacārins* who satisfy the fourfold requirement are obligated to engage in the discussions mentioned. Householders are also advised to do so, for it leads to improvement.

21 (E408; T38). What is Self? It is that which is different from the three bodies, from the five sheaths, which witnesses the three states, and is *sat*, *cit*, and *ānanda*.

22 (E408; T38). The three bodies are the gross, subtle, and causal bodies. The gross body is the effect of the (*mahā*) *bhūtas* that are *pañcīkṛta* (composed of the five subtle elements); it is born of karma and subject to six transformations including birth, etc.

23 (E408-409; T38-39). The theory of *pañcīkaraṇa* is explained.

24 (E409-410; T39-40). The subtle body is the effect of the elements not *pañcīkṛta* and it has seventeen marks. These seventeen include five sense organs, five action organs, five *prāṇas*, *manas*, and *buddhi*. Each organ is explained. *Vāc* (the action organ of "speech") is explained as something other than speech but in which speech is located and which itself occurs in eight places, that is, breast, throat, head, upper and lower lips, palate, tongue, and the muscle that binds the lower jaw to the tongue. The inner organ (*antaḥkaraṇa*) is explained as having four parts—*manas*, *buddhi*, *citta*, and *ahaṃkāra*. They have different loci—*manas* is in the root of the throat (*galānta*), *buddhi* in the *vadana*—the mouth or face, *citta* is in the navel (*nābhi*), and the *ahaṃkāra* is in the heart (*hṛdaya*). Their functions are (respectively ?) doubt, ascertainment, retention (*dharaṇā*), and egoism.

The *prāṇas* are likewise located differently. *Prāṇa* itself is in the heart, *apāna* in the rectum, *samāna* in the navel, *udāna* in the throat (*kaṃṭha*), and *vyāna* throughout the body. Also they have different functions—*prāṇa* goes out, *apāna* goes down, *udāna* goes up, *samāna* breaks up (? -*samīkaraṇa*, lit. "makes things [food ?] the same") and *vyāna* circulates within the body.

25-28 (E410-411; T41). These *prāṇas* have five more *upavāyus*, that is, *nāga* (vomiting), *kūrma* (opening the eyes), *kṛkara* (appetite), *devadatta* (yawning), and *dhanañjaya* (digestion or nourishment). The presiding deities (*adhipati*) of each of the seventeen are identified.

Among these (seventeen), that having the nature of an effect and possessing the power of agency is known as the *prāṇamaya* sheath (*kośa*), whereas that having the nature of an instrument (*karaṇa*) and possessing the power of desiring is called the *manomaya* sheath, and that having the nature of an agent and possessing the power of knowledge is called the *vijñānamaya* sheath. Collectively all this is called the subtle body (*liṅgaśarīra*; the etymology is explained).

29-31 (E411-412; T41-42). The causal body is the cause of the other two bodies; it is beginningless, *anirvacanīya*, is accompanied by a reflection (*sābhāsa*), responsible for the notion that Brahman and Self are not the same—that is, it is nonknowledge (*ajñāna*).

All three bodies, constituting the not-Self, are impermanent (*anṛta*), nonconscious (*jaḍa*), and by nature frustrating (*duḥkhātmaka*). Impermanence is not being found to be a thing (*vastu*) in all the three times (past, present, and future). To be nonconscious is to be a thing free from the knowledge of either true or false contents.

The three states (of which the Self is witness) are waking, dream, and dreamless sleep.

37 (E412-413; T43-44). The five sheaths are named. The *annamaya* sheath is the gross body. It is so-called since the food eaten by the father and mother is transformed into semen and blood, which is in turn transformed into the shape of a body. This body wraps up the Self like a sheath, concealing the Self as the sheath conceals the sword.

Prāṇamaya sheath is the next sheath, so-called because the combination of the five action organs and five *prāṇas* make the Self appear to speak, move, hunger, thirst, etc.

The third sheath is *manomaya,* which makes the Self appear to perceive, doubt, suffer, etc., because it consists of the five organs of sense combined with the internal organ.

37-38 (E413; T44). The *vijñānamaya* sheath is the five sense organs combined with the *buddhi*. It is commonly known as the *jīva,* which, through being considered as agent and enjoyer through *avidyā,* goes to other worlds and returns thence.

The final sheath is *ānandamaya*. It is the *antaḥkaraṇa* in which *avidyā* dominates, and it produces fluctuations (*vṛtti*) that are pleasant (*priyamoda*), joyful (*pramoda*), etc., thus showing the Self—which lacks desires, enjoyments, pleasure, and joy—as having these experiences.

39-41 (E413-414; T44-45). The reasons why the Self is different from the three bodies and five sheaths and why it is the witness of the three states are detailed. The expression "*saccidānanda*" is also explained.

TATTVABODHA

This work is regarded as spurious by Belvalkar.[69]

"ET" refers to the edition and translation by L. Simha (Sialkot, 1877).

1 (ET 1). Invocation to Vāsudeva, the Lord of the yogis and the guru who give knowledge.

2-9 (ET 1-3). The four requirements are explained.

10-28 (ET 3-9). The Self is differentiated from the three bodies (gross, subtle causal), the five sheaths, the three states (of waking, dream, and deep sleep) and is characterized as reality, consciousness, and bliss (*saccidānanda*). All of these notions are succinctly explained.

29-33 (ET 9-11). The order of creation in twenty-four categories is set forth. First came the five elements, from which the five sense organs, the four internal organs (*manas*, *buddhi*, *citta*, and *ahaṃkāra*), five action organs and five *prāṇas* arise. From the tamasic form of the five elements through quintuplication arise the gross body. Quintuplication is explained as (1) dividing the tamasic nature of each element into two; (2) dividing one of the two halves into four equal parts; (3) combining the undivided half of each element with one-eighth of each one of the other four elements.

34 (ET 11). The *jīva* is explained as the self attached to the gross body and limited by *avidyā*; it views God as different from itself under the influence of *prakṛti*.

35 (ET 12). God is the Self limited by *māyā*, which is a different limitation from *avidyā* or at least conceived as such by the *jīva*. As long as this conception on the *jīva's* part is maintained, transmigration will continue.

36 (ET 12). *Objection* : If *jīva* and God are so different, how can "that art thou," etc., produce knowledge of their identity?

37-39 (ET 12-13). *Answer* : Because the literal meaning (*vācyārtha*) of "thou" involves the conception of a gross and/or subtle body, but its secondary or implied meaning (*lakṣyārtha*) is of pure consciousness, free from limitations. Likewise, the literal meaning of the word "that"' is God—qualified by omniscience, etc.—whereas its implied meaning is pure consciousness free from limitations. Thus the sentence in question identifies *jīva* and God through indication by means of their implied meanings.

40 (ET 13). The nature of a *jīvanmukta* is described—he is one who knows even in this life that he is nothing but pure consciousness.

41-46 (ET 14-15). Three kinds of karma are explained. *Āgamin* karma is what is done by a knower (*jñānin*) after attaining knowledge. *Sañcita* karma is the stored-up results of past births that is the seed of indefinite numbers of future births. *Prārabdha* karma is what has brought the present body into being and produces experiences in this world, and which is destroyed when those experiences are finished. *Sañcita* karma, on the other hand, has to be destroyed by certain knowledge (*niścayajñāna*) that one is Brahman; in this way also *āgamin* karma is destroyed. In addition, those who worship, serve, and praise a knower get his meritorious karma, whereas those who blame or hate him and do him injury get his bad *āgamin* karma.

47 (ET 15). Whether one dies in Banaras or in the house of one who eats dogmeat, no matter; only if one knows the Self does one become liberated and go beyond *saṃsāra*.

DAŚAŚLOKĪ

The *Daśaślokī* is a hymn attributed to Śaṃkara. Its importance largely derives from Madhusūdana Sarasvatī's (sixteenth century) important commentary on it titled *Siddhāntabindu*.

"ET" refers to the edition and translation by T. M. P. Mahadevan and N. Veezhinathan (Madras: Sankara Vihar, 1965).

1 (ET 1). I am not the elements or sense organs or the collection of them, since they are transient (*anaikāntika*). The one in deep sleep, established as one, the one remaining, isolate, bliss (*śiva*)—that I am.

2 (ET 6-7). For me there are not caste (*varṇa*) or rules of conduct for caste and stage of life, nor is there attention (*dhāraṇā*), contemplation (*dhyāna*), or yoga, etc., since the superimposition of "I" and "mine" on the not-Self has been destroyed. The one remaining, isolate, bliss—that I am.

3 (ET 9-10). In deep sleep, they say, there is neither mother nor father, gods nor worlds, not Vedas, sacrifices, nor places of pilgrimage; for in deep sleep I am not voidness, but am the one remaining, isolate, bliss.

4 (ET 12-13). Sāṃkhya, Śaiva, Pañcarātra, Jaina, Mīmāṃsā, etc. —none of these doctrines holds good, for by a particular experience (*viśiṣṭānubhūti*) (it is known that) the Self is pure. The one remaining, isolate, bliss—that I am.

5 (ET 17-18). I am not locatable, since I am all-pervading like space (*viyat*), single and partless. I am the one remaining, isolate, bliss.

6 (ET 19). Without color or size or form am I, for I have the nature of light. The one remaining, isolate, bliss—that I am.

7 (ET 21). (There is) neither teacher nor teaching nor pupil, neither you nor I nor this universe. Understanding of one's true nature does not allow alternatives (*vikalpa*). I am the one remaining, isolate, bliss.

8 (ET 23). I have nothing to do with the three states of waking, dream, and deep sleep. Since they are of the nature of *avidyā*, I am the fourth (*turīya*). I am the one remaining . . . .

9 (ET 26). Since (the Self) is all-pervading, the final goal, self-established, and not located in anything else, the whole world, being different from It, is unreal (*tuccha*). I am the one remaining . . . .

10 (ET 28). (The Self) is not one—whence could there be a second other than It? It is neither isolate nor nonisolate, neither void nor nonvoid, because it is nondual (*advaitaka*). How may I explain what is established in the Vedānta (texts)?

VĀKYAVṚTTI

Traditionally ascribed to Śaṃkara, this is a work dealing with the interpretation of "that art thou" and making use of the form of teacher-pupil exchange so tellingly utilized by Śaṃkara in the *Upadeśasāhasrī*.

Edition and translation ("ET") by Swami Jagadananda (2d edition; Madras: Sri Ramakrishna Math, 1953).

1-2 (ET 2-3). Invocation to Viṣṇu.

3-4 (ET 3-4). A pupil comes to a teacher and asks what is the means of liberation.

5-6 (ET 5-6). *Teacher*: Good question! Liberation comes from that knowledge of the identity of the *jīva* and the Highest Self which arises from sentences such as "that art thou."

7 (ET 6-7). *Pupil*: What are these—*jīva* and Highest Self? How can they be identical, and how can such sentences show that they are?

8 (ET 7). *Teacher*: You are the *jīva*, and you who ask "who am I?" are Brahman itself.

9 (ET 7-8). *Pupil*: I don't even know what these words mean—how can I understand what "I am Brahman" might mean?

10-27 (ET 8-19). *Teacher*: You're right—you must know the meanings of the words to understand a sentence composed of them. You must understand that the Self is not the body but the Witness of the nature of reality, consciousness, and bliss. No more are you the sense organs, the internal organ, the *buddhi* or *prāṇa*. Rather, you are like the light that illuminates all these; as a lamp must be different from what it illuminates, so must the Self be different from everything else. Now, it is this witnessing Self that is the meaning of the word "thou" (in "that art thou").

28-36 (ET 20-25). As for the word "that," it means nothing else but Brahman, known in the Upaniṣads in various ways (listed here).

37-48 (ET 26-34). Now as to the meaning of the whole sentence "that art thou." This meaning is not to be understood as relational (*saṃsarga*) or qualificational (*viśiṣṭa*), but rather as partless (*akhaṇḍa*) single essence (*rasa*) only. The two words mean precisely the same thing. Understanding the sentence means knowing that neither word means anything other than the other one. More technically: each of the two words "thou" and "that" have a literal meaning (*vācyārtha*), "thou" meaning consciousness connected with internal organ (*antaḥkaraṇa*) and illuminated as object (*ālambana*) of the idea and word "I," whereas "that" means that which has *māyā* as its limitation, which is the cause of the universe, omniscient, etc. Now since the literal meanings of the two words are incompatible, in explaining the meaning of the sentence "that art thou" one resorts to implied or secondary meanings of the words (*lakṣyārtha*). And one does this by leaving out certain aspects of the literal meaning. Thus one can make sense of the sentence.

49-53 (ET 35-38). One should listen, etc., to scripture and practice restraint (*śama*), etc., until the meaning of the sentence "I am Brahman" becomes firm. When this happens, then by grace of scripture and teacher the cause of *saṃsāra* will be completely destroyed. Then when one's bodies (gross and subtle) are dissolved, freed from subtle objects, and released from karma, one is immediately liberated. When karma not yet arisen (*anārabdha*) is thus destroyed, one yet remains, because of *prārabdha* karma, liberated in life (*jīvanmukta*) for some time, until he comes to isolation (*kaivalya*), from which there is no return, which is the highest abode of Viṣṇu.

VIVEKACŪḌĀMAṆI

This is a sizable work, extremely popular among Advaita adepts. Ingalls argues that it is not genuine Śaṃkara since it propounds theories not found in Śaṃkara's unquestioned works. For example, "the author of the *Viveka-cūḍāmaṇi* makes an absolute equation of the waking and dream states after the fashion of Gauḍapāda. Śaṃkara may liken the two to each other, but he is careful to distinguish them. Again, and most decisive of all, the *Viveka-cūḍāmaṇi* accepts the classical theory of the three truth values, the existent, the nonexistent, and that which is *anirvacanīya* . . . . Now, Paul Hacker has pointed out that when Śaṃkara uses the word *anirvacanīya*, he uses it in a sense quite different from that . . . ."[70]

Hacker,[71] interestingly enough, finds reason to affirm the genuineness of the work on the basis of colophons, but Mayeda, like Ingalls following out the criteria Hacker proposes elsewhere, holds it to be spurious.[72]

Edition and translation ("ET") by Swami Madhavananda (2d edition: Calcutta: Advaita Ashrama, 1966).

1 (ET 1). Invocation to Govinda, the Sadguru.

2-13 (ET 2-6). A human birth is rare, rarer is a male birth, rarer still a Brahmin birth. More rare progressively are knowledge of scripture, discrimination of Self from not-Self, and most rare is liberation, which requires the merit of a hundred births. Three things require God's grace—a human birth, desire for liberation, and the case of a perfected person. So, a male who has mastered the Vedas and does not strive for liberation commits suicide—he is the greatest fool of them all. Only Self-knowledge can yield liberation. Actions cannot do so; at best they can yield purity of *citta*.

14-27 (ET 6-10). Only one who satisfies the four qualifications (an *adhikārin*) can achieve liberation. They are explained.

28-30 (ET 10-11). These four qualifications should be practised with intensity, as only so will they yield the ultimate result, namely, liberation. Even if they are initially pursued with only moderate intensity, through the guru's grace they may eventually lead to the desired results when combined with nonattachment, etc. If they remain languid, however, the various practices are merely appearances.

31-32 (ET 11-12). Devotion (*bhakti*) is the chief factor among those causal factors leading to liberation. It is defined as the seeking after one's own real nature (*svasvarūpānusaṃdhāna* or *svātmatattvānusaṃdhāna*).

32-40 (ET 11-15). One who satisfies the four requirements should approach a teacher and ask him for instruction in the means to liberation.

41-47 (ET 15-18). The teacher replies that there is such a means, and that it involves consideration of the meaning of the Vedānta texts together with faith, devotion, and meditation.

48-49 (ET 18-19). *Pupil* : What is bondage, and how did it come? How is liberation achieved? What is Self and not-Self and how can one discriminate between them?

50-68 (ET 19-25). *Teacher* : Bondage is *avidyā*, and the only means of gaining liberation from it is through direct realization—one cannot get it by Yoga or Sāṃkhya or actions or learning (*vidyā*).

69-70 (ET 25-26). The cause of liberation is, first, complete nonattachment to any noneternal things, then *śama*, *dama*, *titikṣā*, and renunciation (*nyāsa*) of all actions enjoined in scripture. Then come hearing (Vedantic sentences), thinking on them, and constant meditation on the truth. This leads to the supreme *nirvikalpa* state, that is, *jīvanmukti*.

71-92 (ET 26-34). The Self distinguished from the gross body.

93-107 (ET 34-39). The Self distinguished from subtle body, *prāṇas*.

108-123 (ET 40-46). *Avidyā*, or *māyā*, is the power (*śakti*) of God, and is made up of the three *guṇas*. *Rajas* has the power of projection (*vikṣepa*), which, constantly active, creates the modifications of the *manas* such as frustration, etc. Its properties include lust, anger, envy, jealousy, etc. *Tamas* has the veiling (*āvṛtti*) power, which makes things appear otherwise than they really are. It causes transmigration and also is the cause of the initiation of projection. Its properties include ignorance, sleep, and stupidity. *Sattva*, finally, is clear as water but in conjunction with the others conduces to transmigration until it is purified. The properties of mixed *sattva* include humility, restraints and observances, faith, devotion, desire for liberation. The properties of pure *sattva* are peace, bliss, self-realization, etc. Another name for *avidyā* is the undifferentiated (*avyakta*), the causal body, whose special state is deep sleep.

124-135 (ET 46-51). Description of the Witnessing Self, which illuminates all modifications of the *manas*, unchanging and different from *prakṛti*, etc.

136-168 (ET 52-66). How discrimination removes bondage by successively leading us to distinguish each of the sheaths from the Self, culminating in the *manomaya* sheath.

169-171 (ET 67-68). The *manas* is *avidyā*. When it is destroyed everything else is destroyed, since it is the necessary condition of the manifestation of anything. The whole universe is the projection of the *manas*. *Saṃsāra* does not really exist.

172-183 (ET 68-73). How the *manas* produces bondage.

184-191 (ET 73-76). The *buddhi* with its fluctuations and the sense organs form the *vijñānamaya* sheath. It is also called the *jīva*. It is this which appears to act as agent, impelled by karma born of past desires; it is this which is born and dies, and has experiences of waking, dream, pleasures, and frustrations. It is a limitation of the Highest Self, which shines within and appears to act and experience through that limitation.

192-193 (ET 76-77). *Pupil* : Since *avidyā* is beginningless, transmigration must go on forever—so how can liberation occur ?

194-211 (ET 77-84). *Teacher* : Good question ! But since it is only through error that the Self appears involved with *avidyā*, when the error disappears all the effects of *avidyā*, including transmigration, disappear also, like the snake erroneously seen in the rope. Now, the *vijñānamaya* sheath is not the true Self since it changes, is unconscious, limited, a sense object, and is not always present (for example, in deep sleep). Within it lies the *ānandamaya* sheath, a blissful reflection of the prototype of bliss, the Self, which spontaneously manifests itself to those experiencing the results of meritorious acts as a pleasant feeling. It is untrammeled during deep sleep, less evident in dream and waking. But it is not the Highest Self either, since it changes, is a modification of *prakṛti*, is the effect of past acts. So all five sheaths must be eliminated by reasoning on the basis of scripture.

212 (ET 84). *Pupil* : But when these five sheaths are eliminated nothing remains. What (positive) real thing is left when the Self-knower realizes his identity?

213-240 (ET 85-95). *Teacher* : Clever question! There is one positive thing left, namely, the Self. Even though It is not perceived then, the Self is the presupposition of all experiences of whatever sort; It is pure consciousness; It is Brahman. Now the Upaniṣads assure us that all the things in the universe are effects whose cause is Brahman; therefore since effects are identical with their causes, it follows that everything is Brahman, and since the Self is Brahman, that the Self is the one positive, real thing—the only existent, the only consciousness, the only bliss.

241-249 (ET 96-100). How "that art thou" is to be interpreted so as to yield the same message.

250-264 (ET 100-106). How to meditate on "that art thou."

265-267 (ET 106-107). Even after realizing the truth the beginningless subconscious impression (*vāsanā*) that one is agent and enjoyer remains, which causes transmigration. Liberation is the attenuation of the *vāsanās*.

268-444 (ET 108-172). Verses that counsel the Self-knower in careful meditations designed to attenuate the *vāsanās*.

445-463 (ET 172-179). *Prārabdha* karma continues to bear fruit during this period, though *sañcita* is destroyed by Self-knowledge and *āgamin* fails to affect the Self-knower. Indeed, none of the three kinds —even *prārabdha*—are even considered by the wise man who is forever concentrated on the identity of Self with Brahman and knows nothing else. Everyday acts, with respect to which *we* may consider *prārabdha* karma as causes, are experienced by the Self-knower as memories, just as one remembers objects seen in a dream. Certainly such karma cannot be attributed to the Self; and it cannot even be attributed to the body except by superimposition, since the body itself is unreal. Scripture speaks of *prārabdhakarman* only to answer ignorant questions about how the body continues to exist after Self-realization, but one cannot infer the reality of the body of the Self-knower from that.

464-580 (ET 179-223). The remainder of the work consists of repetition of ideas already expressed for the Self-knower to continue meditating on prior to final release.

SARVAVEDĀNTASIDDHĀNTASĀRASAṂGRAHA

Belvalkar finds this work "nongenuine."[73]

Edition and translation ("E" and "T") are by Swami Tattwananda, *The Quintessence of Vedanta* (Ernakulam : Sri Ramakrishna Advaita Ashrama, 1960).

1-4 (E1; T1-2). Invocation to Govinda, the guru, and to Gaṇeśa. (In some versions there is also an invocation to Advayānanda, the guru.)

5-15 (E1-3; T2-3). Every work must begin by setting forth who is fit to study it, its subject matter, its relevance, and its purpose. Those who satisfy the four requirements (set forth elsewhere), who reason well, are intelligent and learned in the scriptures are qualified to study this text. Its subject matter is pure consciousness as marked by the identity of *jīva* and Brahman. The proof of this identity provides the relevance. And its purpose is liberation.

16-47 (E3-7; T3-10). The first of the four requirements is discrimination between the eternal and the noneternal. It leads to nonattachment by indicating the defects in the noneternal—and when the faults in a thing are recognized, who seeks it further? Examples :

48-49 (E7-14; T10-17). Verses on the temptations of worldly things and exhortations to become nonattached to them. Nonattachment leads to the six virtues.

95-103 (E24-25; T17-19). Tranquillity (*śama*) has three kinds: (1) the internal organ fixed on reality alone (*vastumātra*), having abandoned its own modifications, is the highest peace, marked by the *nirvāṇa* of Brahman. (2) Where the series of ideas (*saṃtāna*) is the instrument of knowledge (*dhī*), this is the medium peace, marked by pure being only. (3) When the internal organ abandons objects and devotes itself to scripture, that is the other (third) peace, which is *sattva* mixed (with other qualities).

104-150 (E15-21; T19-27). Serenity (*prasāda*) is gained by the practice of virtuous actions and attitudes, as well as yoga.

151-209 (E21-29; T27-38). Renunciation (*uparati*) is the abandoning of all actions. By its practice one realizes one's true Brahman nature, since Brahman is devoid of action or indeed of any qualities. Thus the seeker after liberation must give up all actions, even ritually prescribed ones, and follow the path of knowledge alone. The paths of action and of karma are incompatible.

210-217 (E29-30; T38-40). Faith in the guru and in the Upaniṣads leads to liberation. The Vedas (including the Upaniṣads) are deserving of faith since they speak the truth, and they speak the truth since they are the word of God. The guru, being one with God, is also trustworthy.

218-225 (E30-31; T40-41). Concentration (*samādhana*) is complete absorption in what scripture says.

226-296 (E32-43; T41-53). Desire for liberation (*mumukṣutva*) has four forms. (1) The very eager aspirant is one who is willing to renounce everything including pleasures. (2) The second order is the seeker who has indirect knowledge of Brahman, who perceives the threefold sorrows and desires to leave his family. (3) The third form is one who thinks "there is plenty of time for liberation—why hurry ? First I shall enjoy the world." (4) The lowest form is one who thinks liberation is a lucky accident. A brief dialogue between an aspirant and his guru is provided.

297-309 (E43-45; T53-55). Superimposition (*adhyāropa*) is to attribute what is not real to something real, for example, a snake to a rope, or being silver to a shell. *Avidyā* is its cause; it neither is nor is not but is *anirvācya*. Likewise, it is neither the same as Brahman nor entirely different, just as a lamp is not the same as its light nor is it entirely different. It has a collective (*samaṣṭi*) and distributive (*vyaṣṭi*) aspect. Its collective aspect, dominated by *sattva*, is known as *māyā*.

310-315 (E45; T55-56). Pure consciousness with *māyā* as its adjunct dominated by *sattva* is known as unmanifest (*avyākṛta*, *avyakta*) or as God (*īśvara*). God is omnipresent, omnipotent, and omniscient.

316-326. (E46-47; T56-58). In its distributive aspect *avidyā* takes the forms of various individual selves, dominated by *rajas* and *tamas*. Thus the distributive aspect is inferior to the collective one. Now pure consciousness when limited by *avidyā* in Its distributive aspect becomes known as the inner Self (*pratyagātman*), and when It identifies itself with that aspect and so comes under the sway of the *guṇas* it is known as *jīva*. This distributive aspect is the causal body, and the inner Self is otherwise known as *prājña* when it is identified with the illuminator of this causal body. This causal body of *prājña* is the same as the *ānandamaya* sheath, specially exhibited in deep sleep. *Prājña* is blissful in nature, as everyone knows upon waking up; since bliss is common to all, there is no real difference between God and *prājña*, the collective and distributive aspects of *avidyā*, at that stage.

330-333 (E47-48; T59-60). God, in conjunction with *māyā*, creates the whole universe, for He is both material and efficient cause; as pure consciousness He is efficient, and as limited by *māyā* He is material.

334-337 (E48; T60). The creation of the five elements.

338-341 (E48-49; T60-61). The constitution of the subtle body.

342-349 (E49-50; T61-63). The internal organ (*antaḥkaraṇa*) is the result of the interaction of the five sattvic parts of the five elements. It has four functions: (1) as *manas*, to imagine (*saṃkalpa*), (2) as *buddhi*, to ascertain (*niścaya*), (3) as ego sense (*ahaṃkāra*) to have a notion of ego (*abhimāna*), (4) as *citta* to be conscious (*cintana*). The *buddhi* is the agent, and the *manas* is its instrument. The self that through delusion identifies with them is subject to transmigration.

350-354 (E50-51; T63-64). The *buddhi*, *manas*, and sense organs taken together constitute the *vijñānamaya* sheath.

355-374 (E51-54; T64-68). The *manas* together with the five sense organs constitutes the *manomaya* sheath.

375-408 (E54-58; T68-73). The *prāṇas* and action organs taken together are known as the *prāṇamaya* sheath.

The subtle body, which lies within all the last three sheaths is known by different names suggesting its various roles, for example, Hiraṇyagarbha, Sūtrātman, *prāṇa*, *taijasa*. These are explained. How the gross elements arise from their subtle origins is explained.

409-416 (E59; T74-75). Quintuplication is explained.

416-429 (E59-61; T75-77). The presiding deities for each sense.

430-433 (E62; T78). The creation of the universe.

434-456 (E62-65; T78-82). Four different kinds of beings—womb-born, egg-born, sweat-born and seed-born. The *annamaya* sheath.

457-509 (E65-73; T83-94). The nature of Self. How superimposition can occur on something (the Self) that is not perceived (review of arguments in opening sections of Śaṃkara's *Brahmasūtrabhāṣya*). *Māyā* as *mūlāvidyā*.

510-519 (E73-74; T94-95). By knowledge one destroys ignorance (*ajñāna*), but not by actions.

520-580 (E75-82; T95-108). Refutation of false views about the nature of the Self—(1) that one's son is one's Self (i.e., that one's welfare lies in one's children); (2) that the senses are the Self; (3) that *prāṇa* is the Self; (4) that the internal organ (*manas*) is the Self; (5) that knowledge and ignorance are both properties of the Self; (6) that the Self is void (*śūnya*).

581-611 (E82-87; T108-114). Refutation of *śūnyavāda*. (1) In deep sleep something exists, which shows that when the internal organ is reabsorbed into the unmanifest something (positive) exists. (2) Something cannot come from nothing. (3) No proof is required of the Self—It is instinctively known to all.

612-631 (E87-90; T115-119). The Self is eternal, self-illuminating, blissful.

632-634 (E90-91; T119). *Pupil* : If the Self is blissful then why do people strive for pleasure (since they already have it) ?

635-672 (E51-56; T120-126). *Teacher* : Because people do not know the nature of their Self and so suppose that the sources of pleasure lie in external objects. Now clearly pleasure is not a property of external objects, since it is we (not external objects) who experience it when we grasp external objects through our internal organ (*manas*). But it is clear also that it is not an intrinsic property of the *manas* either, since it does not always accompany activities of that organ. So the truth is that a person experiences pleasure when, as a result of past meritorious actions, he acquires some object he desires and gets a reflection (*ābhāsa*) of the bliss that is intrinsic to the Self. This is confirmed by noting that pleasure has degrees, which shows its dependence on the amount of merit operating, as well as on the fact that pleasure eventually disappears as the meritorious karma is exhausted, and that pleasure is always mixed with frustration, showing its dependence on karma.

673-699 (E96-100; T126-132). But it is not that bliss or existence or consciousness either are properties of the Self, for the Self is without diversity and has no properties. It is *by nature* bliss, existence, consciousness. It is nondual.

700-792 (E100-113; T132-150). "That art thou" analyzed.

793-794 (E114; T150-151). *Pupil* : Surely merely listening to "that art thou" isn't enough to obtain liberation. What else must one do—how many ways can one attain *samādhi* ? What are the obstacles to realization ?

795-818 (E114-117; T151-156). *Teacher*: There are two kinds of aspirants to liberation, the fully qualified and the only moderately qualified. For the former, merely hearing "that art thou" and understanding it as explained above produces final realization. But the other kind should practice hearing, consideration, and meditation until all wrong ideas about the Self are dispelled. And the question of *samādhi* comes up in connection with this meditation.

819-898 (E117-129; T156-171). There are two kinds of *samādhi*, *savikalpa* and *nirvikalpa*. *Savikalpa samādhi* is so-called because one is still aware of the distinctions between knower, known, and knowing, whereas in *nirvikalpa samādhi* these are absent.

Now *savikalpa samādhi* has two kinds—having to do with the body and with the scripture. The former involves progressively meditating on the differences between one's body, etc., and one's Self until one merges all objects of knowledge into Self-consciousness. The former proceeds through meditation on the words of scripture.

899-921 (E129-132; T171-176). *Nirvikalpa samādhi* is meditation on Brahman alone. The eightfold yoga (of Patañjali) is set forth.

922-923 (E133; T176). Obstacles to yoga enumerated.

924-937 (E133-135; T176-179). *Pupil* : Tell me the difference between *jīvanmukti* and *videhamukti*: let me understand.

938-1006 (E135-144; T179-191). *Teacher* : There are seven stages of knowledge (*jñānabhūmi*): (1) the desire to know; (2) inquiry (*vicaraṇa*); (3) attenuation of mental attachment (?) (*tanumānasin*); (4) attainment of *sattva* nature; (5) nonattachment (*asaṃśakti*); (6) *padārthabhāvanā* (text), but "absence of consciousness of all external objects (translation: the translator apparently reads "padārtha-abhāvanā"); (7) the fourth (*turiya*). Achieving this final stage, one obtains the bliss while awake that one normally only has in deep sleep. This is *jīvanmukti*. Even beyond this is *videhamukti*, where all that remains is silence.

ADVAITAPAÑCARATNA or ĀTMAPAÑCAKA

Belvalkar does not notice this work. It is edited ("E") by Surnath Kanjan Pillai in the *Journal of the Kerala University Oriental Manuscripts Library* 9 (1957), 3: 69-84; 4: 37-48, 95, and is reprinted as Trivandrum Sanskrit Series 190, 1958. There is a translation ("T") by K. R. Pisharoti in *Vedanta Kesari* 36 (1949-50), pp. 241-242, which is also found in *Prabuddha Bharata* 56 (1951), pp. 301-305. The summary provided below is taken from K. Raghavan Pillai's Introduction to his edition.

1 (E4; T241). Study the Veda always. This must be done at appropriate times. Perform the action enjoined by the Veda properly. Through the proper performance of Vedic action, perform the worship of God. Take the mind away from the idea of performing actions intended to achieve particular desires. Avoid sins like desire, anger, etc. Remember that the pleasures of life are faulty. Endeavor toward the realization of the Self. Leave the home.

2 (E9; T241). Seek the company of the good. Intensify your devotion to the all-powerful God. Cultivate mastery over the senses. Quickly renounce action, which has become too firm to give up. Approach a teacher who is good and learned. And daily attend on him. Seek after the one and imperishable Brahman. Listen to the declarations of the Upaniṣads.

3 (E15; T241). Think about the meanings of these sentences. Accept the conclusion of the Vedānta. Withdraw from hostile reasoning. Accept the arguments of those well-versed in the scripture. (Accept logic that is not antagonistic to the scripture.) Constantly dwell on the idea "I am Brahman." Destroy the haughtiness that steadily increases (along with the increase of knowledge). Renounce the identification of the Self with the body. Give up arguing with the wise.

4 (E20; T241). Seek to remedy hunger and sickness, hunger through begging for alms, and sickness through medicine. Do not try to procure tasty food. Do not be joyful if by chance delicious food, etc., is obtained. Yearn for detachment. Be neither kind nor cruel to people. Cultivate equanimity in experiences of the opposites like cold and heat, pain and pleasure. Do not speak futile words (i.e., words that do not contribute towards liberation).

5 (E23; T242). Sit comfortably in solitude. Concentrate on the supreme Brahman. Understand the omnipresent Self and see this phenomenal world as sublated by the true knowledge of Brahman. Burn the accumulated actions of previous lives in the fire of knowledge. As for subsequent actions they will not bind you. Experience the fruits of the commenced actions in this life. And then stay firmly established solely in Brahman.

VĀKYASUDHĀ or DṚGDṚŚYAVIVEKA

Belvalkar reports that a commentary on this printed in Banaras Sanskrit Series edition (B1944) ascribes the work to Bhāratītīrtha.[74] "The work has not . . . been included in the Vanivilas edition and so stands suspect." It is however printed in *Minor Works of Samkara* (H. R. Bhagavat, ed.), and comprises forty-six verses. Terms such as "*cidābhāsa*" and "*pratibhāṣika*" abound, suggesting a later origin than Śaṃkara's time.

UPADEŚAPAÑCAKA

This work is comprised of five stanzas beginning with "Vedo nityam adhiyatām."

MĀYĀPAÑCAKA

This consists of five stanzas describing *māyā* as "skilled in associating the dissociate" (Pisharoti's translation of *aghaṭitaghaṭanapatiyasi māyā*), that is, as that which maintains an apparent connection between things that are really unconnected.

LAGHUVĀKYAVṚTTI

Eighteen verses on Advaita themes. Uses expressions like "*nirvikalpakacaitanyam*" and "*savikalpakajīvo,*" which seem un-Śaṃkaran.

COMMENTARIES ON OTHER UPANIṢADS

There are commentaries on various Upaniṣads, notably the *Śvetāśvatara*, *Nṛsiṃhottaratāpanīya*, and *Kauśitaki Upaniṣads*, which appear to be erroneously ascribed to Śaṃkara. However, the evidence on these has not been systematically collected and studied.

MAṆḌANA MIŚRA

Traditionally, Maṇḍana Miśra was supposed to be both the pupil and the brother-in-law of Kumārila. Allen Thrasher, who has done the most careful work to date on this philosopher, thinks that tradition is unlikely. However, Maṇḍana certainly follows Kumārila in time, as well as Dharmakīrti and Prabhākara, all of whom Maṇḍana quotes.[1] Frauwallner gives Dharmakīrti's dates as A.D. 600-660;[2] Thrasher suggests 660 as the *terminus a quo* for Maṇḍana's date. Uṃveka, the Mīmāṃsā commentator who comments on Maṇḍana's *Bhāvanāviveka,* wrote his commentary between 760 and 790. Thus, Thrasher concludes, Maṇḍana must have lived around A.D. 660-720.[3]

Tradition also makes Maṇḍana a contemporary of Śaṃkara. This tradition Thrasher finds consistent with all that we can tell on the evidence available. Thrasher remarks: "Many of Śaṃkara's themes appear in Maṇḍana—for example, that the universe and its divisions have only a practical reality, not a final one, but that the practical reality lasts until liberation; that liberation is the manifestation of the soul's own form; that something unreal can lead to a real result; that the Upaniṣads deny all difference; that to allow any *pariṇāma* in Brahman would be to give it parts, and that reality must be free from all change whatever; that the *jīva* really is Brahman, but appears to be divided from it by false knowledge and by limiting adjuncts . . . ."[4] One might retort that this suggests that Śaṃkara got his ideas from Maṇḍana. Thrasher responds to this in continuing the passage quoted : "These common themes are so numerous that if Maṇḍana did write before Śaṃkara, Śaṃkara's intellectual contribution would shrink to the vanishing point. *Prima facie,* I do not find this very plausible . . . ."[5]

Rather, Thrasher is inclined to accept Advaita tradition, which makes Maṇḍana and Śaṃkara contemporaries, Maṇḍana perhaps the older of the two. Maṇḍana was evidently a Mīmāṃsaka earlier in his career, for he wrote several Mīmāṃsā treatises before he wrote the *Brahmasiddhi*. Thrasher indicates several passages in the *Brahmasiddhi* that he believes provide evidence that Maṇḍana knew of Śaṃkara's views when he wrote his Advaita work. Kuppuswami Sastri and Vetter have noted at least one of these (32.13-34.23).[6]

Advaita tradition goes further still, in that it identifies Maṇḍana with Śaṃkara's pupil Sureśvara. This has given rise to lengthy scholarly debate, which still goes on. There is plenty of reason to conclude that Sureśvara knows of Maṇḍana's work. The tradition is recorded in, if not original with, Mādhava's *Śaṃkaradigvijaya*, where it is said that Maṇḍana, Sureśvara, and Viśvarūpa are the same person.[7] Other authorities find this person is also the same as Bhavabhūti and Uṃveka.[8] One of the earliest of modern scholars to discuss the question was Mysore Hiriyanna, who found reason to doubt the identification.[9] His arguments were developed and added to by P. V. Kane,[10] D. C. Bhattacharya,[11] and S. Kuppuswami Sastri.[12] Others, however, most recently R. Balasubramaniam,[13] have pointed to the close similarity in thought and style between *Brahmasiddhi* I.28-31 and *Sambandhavārttika* 342-350 and 377-436. He also suggests another possible relationship among Maṇḍana, Śaṃkara, and Sureśvara; perhaps Maṇḍana wrote the *Brahmasiddhi* setting forth a non-Śaṃkaran brand of Advaita, then became converted by Śaṃkara, took the name of Sureśvara and wrote the Śaṃkaran Advaita works commonly attributed to Sureśvara. Although admitting discrepancies between views and attitudes displayed in Maṇḍana's and Sureśvara's works, Balasubramaniam is not convinced these are sufficient reason to rule out the possibility of the identity of their authors.

The only clearly Advaita work by Maṇḍana is the *Brahmasiddhi*. All of his other known works are either Mīmāṃsā or grammatical works, with the possible exception of the *Vibhramaviveka*, a treatise on theories of error, which appears to come down in favor of a form of the *anyathākhyāti* theory of Mīmāṃsā. In the *Brahmasiddhi* he mentions a theory called *anirvacanīyakhyāti*, which term later became the stock term for an Advaita theory of error. Thrasher has also discussed the issues raised by this and concludes that in the *Brahmasiddhi* Maṇḍana accepts both theories, applying them to explain different things.[14] If he is right, it suggests that Maṇḍana was not an Advaitin when he wrote the *Vibhramaviveka*.

BRAHMASIDDHI

"E" refers to the edition by S. Kuppuswami Sastri, Madras Government Oriental Series 4 (Madras : Government Oriental Manuscripts Library, 1937). (B1346). Summarized by Allen W. Thrasher.

CHAPTER ONE : ON BRAHMAN (BRAHMAKĀṆḌA)

I.1, including *kārikā* 1 (E1). Intelligent men differ about the texts of the Upaniṣads.

(1) Some say they are not instruments of knowledge (*pramāṇa*). For either (a) the Self is established by some other *pramāṇa*, in which case the Upaniṣadic texts are restatements (*anuvādaka*) (and not *pramāṇa*, for a *pramāṇa* must give new knowledge), or (b) it is not established by another *pramāṇa*. If it is not, one cannot grasp its connection with the word that names it, and if therefore it is not the object of a word (*padārtha*), it cannot be the topic (*viṣaya*) of a sentence (*vākya*).

Besides, the Upaniṣadic texts have no reference to action (*pravṛtti*) or to abstention from action (*nivṛtti*), and therefore are not an end of man (*puruṣārtha*) (and consequently, it would appear, not a *pramāṇa*).

(2) Others teach that the Upaniṣads are not a *pramāṇa*, under the pretext of saying that they are a *pramāṇa* for apprehending (*pratipatti*) that the Self is something that should be done (*kartavyatā*).

(3) Others think the Upaniṣads have a secondary reference (*upacāritārtha*). For, if the primary meaning (*śrutārtha*) is accepted they are contradictory to the Vedic injunctions (*vidhi*) to action, and also contradictory to perception and the *pramāṇas* based on it (because they deny the existence of diversity).

This book is begun to establish that the Upaniṣadic texts are *pramāṇa* for the Self as It is described in *kārikā* I.1, by means of refuting opposing views.

Verse 2 : "Bliss, one immortal, unborn, cognition (*vijñāna*), imperishable (or "syllable," *akṣara*), who is not all (*asarva*), who is all (*sarva*), fearless, we bow to the Lord of Creatures (*prajāpati*)."

I.2 (E1-2). (Discussion of "bliss") *Objection* : Brahman cannot be of the nature of bliss because, if It were, the activity of a person desiring liberation would be derived from a passion (*rāga*) for bliss. But activity based on passion is the seed of *saṃsāra* and so cannot result in liberation. Moreover, scripture (*Bṛhadāraṇyaka Upaniṣad* IV.4.23) says that it is the pacified and controlled person who sees the Self, and one acting from a passion for bliss cannot be such a one. Therefore the scriptural passages that describe bliss refer to the transcendence (*atikrama*) of all frustration. In ordinary life we observe that the word "pleasure" is used upon the cessation of frustration. Others say that pleasure *is* this cessation. You cannot object that in this case a stone would be blissful, because pleasure is an inner fluctuation that is experienced, or else it is the apprehension of the self as qualified by that (fluctuation, or perhaps by the cessation of frustration).

Answer : No, bliss (or pleasure) is not merely the cessation of frustration. We observe that a person up to his waist in a cool pond has pleasure in the lower part of his body and frustration (irritation) from the heat of the day in the upper part. Also, if pleasure were merely the absence of frustration, the denizens of one hell would have pleasure from the absence of the frustrations of the other hells. Moreover, we see that people not in a previous state of frustration may experience pleasure from contact with certain sense objects. Also, there is a difference of degree in pleasures, but none in the cessation of frustration.

I.3 (E2-3). *Objection* : Pleasure is produced by the removal of a desire (*kāma*), which (if unfulfilled) is frustrating.

Answer : No, we observe that people indifferent to a thing still may enjoy it when it is experienced. Nor does enjoyment produce desire and then produce pleasure by desire's extinction. For enjoyment does not necessarily extinguish desire. And the removal of a desire by seeing the object's faults does not produce pleasure. It is not true that the difference of degree in pleasures can be accounted for by the difference in degree of the previous frustrating desire, because it is things that come to us undesired and without effort that produce greater pleasure. In addition, we do not consider that the state before the awakening of desire and after enjoyment and the cessation of desire is pleasurable. Anyway, if an object produces desire when it is experienced, how can its enjoyment extinguish desire? In addition, sometimes the enjoyment of desired objects produces not pleasure, but frustration. In every case it is the previous experience of something as pleasurable that produces desires. Apparent exceptions can be explained as due to experience in previous births. The difference in the desire of different people is accounted for by their varying (previous) births, whereas there is no distinction in the cessation of desire. Sometimes people are frustrated by the cessation of desire, for example, if they have certain illnesses, and this is because they cannot experience certain pleasures. Everyone may experience that there is such a thing as (positive) pleasure. We think that the teachers have said that pleasure is the absence of frustration to encourage people attached to pleasure. The primary meaning of the word "bliss" is pleasure, as something other than the cessation of frustration. (This is how the word "bliss" should be taken where it occurs in the Upaniṣads with reference to Brahman, because) something for which the Vedic word (*śabda*) is the only *pramāṇa* should be understood in accordance with the word.

I.4 (E3). Not all wishing (*icchā*) is passion (*rāga*), and so activity toward the bliss of Brahman is not based on passion. Passion is an insistence (*abhiniveśa*) of nonexistent qualities (*guṇa*) projected by *avidyā*. But the wishing, the complacency of the mind (*cetasaḥ prasāda*), and the inclination (*abhirūci*) toward the truth that results from clarity in seeing the truth are not passion. If the activity of escaping from the suffering of *saṃsāra* and reaching the bliss of Brahman were passion, no one could ever escape *saṃsāra*. If all desire were forbidden by scripture, no activity would be possible, including activity for liberation.

I.5 (E3-4). *Objection* : If bliss is the experienceable in Brahman, then there will be the duality of agent (*kartṛ*) and object (*karman*) of action, and consequently also of action (*kriyā*) and means (*karaṇa*). But if it is not experienceable, it is as good as nonexistent, and cannot be an end of man (*puruṣārtha*).

Answer : The fruit of a *pramāṇa* (namely, valid knowledge itself, *pramā*) is not nonexperienceable, because the possibility of anything's being experienced is dependent on its being experienced, nor is it an object of experience in the same way the thing known is, because *pramāṇa* has only one fruit, and also there would be an infinite regress. It is experienceable as being self-luminous (*svaprakāśaka*). Likewise the agent of knowledge is experienceable as being self-luminous, because if it is not known one will not be able to have the connection (or reflective consciousness, *anusaṃdhāna*) between the agent, object, and fruit of *pramāṇa*, and so there will be no difference between what is known by oneself and what is known by someone else. Nor is it experienceable as the thing known (*karman*), because then it would be different from itself and would not be a Self (*ātman*, i.e., it would not be conscious—or perhaps, "it would not be itself"). Like the fruit and the agent of *pramāṇa*, the blissful nature of Brahman is experienceable as being self-luminous, and not experienceable as not being the object of experience.

I.6 (E4-6). *Opponent* : Properties (*dharma*) are of two sorts, positive (*bhāvarūpa*) and negative (*abhāvarūpa*). If bliss were a positive property of Brahman, it would differ from Brahman's consciousness (*vijñāna*), so that one of the two would be the substrate (*dharmin*) and the other the property (*dharma*). Thus there would be duality. Therefore, the word "bliss" in reference to Brahman means only the absence of pain, just as scripture calls Brahman "not coarse, not fine, not long", etc. (*Bṛhadāraṇyaka Upaniṣad* III.8.8).

Answer : No, in Brahman bliss and consciousness are identical with each other, as in the case of the moon a light (*prakāśa*) identical with pleasure (*ahlāda*) is communicated by two words ("pleasant" and "light"), or as in the case of the sentence "the sun is an exalted (*prakṛṣṭa*) light" the form of light and exaltation (*prakarṣa*) are not different from each other.

The supremacy of Brahman's bliss is not merely the absence from it of suffering in the form of dependence on means (*sādhana*) or of perishableness, for in things whose knowledge depends on scripture (*śabda*) we must follow scripture. Only if Brahman is positive bliss can worldly blisses be portions (*mātra*) of it, as scripture says. This is so by limitation (*avaccheda*) of its bliss.

The Self is bliss for the additional reason that It is the object of the highest love (*preman*), as scripture says. For every creature desires its own existence.

Bliss is experienced (*anubhava*) in deep sleep, as we know from our reflection (*parāmarśa*) upon waking that we slept well, and from scripture.

I.7 (E6). (Discussion of the word "one" in *Kārikā* I.1.) *Objection* (according to Ānandapūrṇa, by a Naiyāyika): The scriptural passages that teach oneness are metaphorical (*upacāra*); they say that in Brahman differences of genus (*jāti*), place, and time are absent. The text "The Self is all this" (*Chāndogya Upaniṣad* VII.25.22) is metaphorical, occasioned by the fact that everything is for the sake of Brahman. This is because

(1) there is a difference (*vyavasthā*) of enjoyment (*bhoga*) in different people; (2) t here is a difference between the transmigrating and the liberated; (3) the power of sight (*dṛk-śakti*, i.e., cognition in general) must have an object different from itself, because it is contradictory for it to function (*vṛtti*) on itself; and (4) we perceive objects to be different, and to possess the different qualities of pleasure, frustration, and delusion.

Answer : No. Scripture clearly teaches the real nonexistence of all diversity, and that diversity is based on *māyā*. We can only attribute to scripture the employment of secondary usage when there is a reason for it, and there is none visible here. Besides, scripture emphasizes the point by repetition.

I.8 (E7-8). *Answer to* (1): The difference of enjoyments can be accounted for by an imagined (*kalpita*) difference (of selves), just as pain, which is in the Self, is attributed to this or that limb of the body. Also, we see a difference of color or shape (*saṃsthāna*) in the various reflections of a face in different surfaces.

Answer to (2): We can use the same analogy just given: without a mirror the original appears without the faults of the mirror. Besides, imagined differences can produce real effects—death from an imaginary snakebite, illumination from a reflected sun.

Answer to (3) *and* (4): The seer (*draṣṭṛ*) is not different from the seen (*dṛśya*), because there is no contradiction in cognition's functioning on itself, in the sense that it is like a lamp self-luminous, as was explained above by the analogy of the fruit of *pramāṇa*. Indeed, if you deny the unity of seer and seen there is no way to account for their relationship. The various suggested alternatives do not stand examination. Therefore the seer transforms (*pariṇāma*) itself into, or appears (*vivartana*) in this or that way.

I.9 (E8-9). (Discussion of the words "immortal, unborn" in *Kārikā* I.1) (Against Vijñānavāda) The Self is not momentary cognition (*jñāna*), nor is liberation the cessation of cognition by the elimination of *vāsanās* and *kleśas*, or the production of pure cognition freed from the form (*ākāra*) or the objects (*viṣaya*). The Vijñānavādin says that only on this theory of his can there be something to be removed (*apaneya*) and something to be gained (*upaneya*) by the activities based on *śāstras*, so that neither *śāstras* nor activities will have a goal. But we say that the thing to be removed is beginningless *avidyā*. For all doctrines believe there is a beginningless *avidyā* to be destroyed.

Avidyā is neither absolutely (*atyanta*) real nor absolutely unreal, neither identical (*svabhāva*) with Brahman nor another thing. It is just for this reason that it is called *avidyā*, *māyā*, "false appearance." If it were either identical with Brahman or different it would be ultimately real (*paramārtha*), not *avidyā*. If it were absolutely unreal like a sky flower it would not enter into practical usage (*vyavahāra*) (i.e., it is precisely because *avidyā* is logically contradictory that we call it "ignorance" or "illusion"). Not being absolutely real, it can be destroyed; thus providing something to be removed. Likewise, it does not introduce a second thing different from Brahman.

I.11 (E10-11). To whom does *avidyā* belong ? To the *jīvas*.

Not to Brahman, because Brahman is knowledge (*vidyā*) itself and therefore is void of false imagination (*kalpanā-śūnya*). Mutual dependency, such as that of the *jīvas*, since the *jīvas* are different from Brahman only by false imagination (*kalpanā-avidyā*), is only a fault in reference to real things, not in reference to a thing that is mere *māyā*. If the object of *māyā* were not logically impossible (*anupapadyamānārtha*), it would not be *māyā*.

This mutual dependence is no fault for the additional reason that *avidyā* and the *jīva* are both beginningless.

Moreover, on this theory there is no need to posit a motive (*prayojana*) for the emanation (*sarga*) of the world, because *avidyā*, being an error (*vibhrama*), does not act with reference to a motive.

The dilemmas that some (atheists) raise—that the motive of emanation cannot be to show favor to others, because there are no others before emanation and the world is mostly frustrating, or that it cannot be something like Its own play (*ātmakrīḍādi*), because Brahman has everything It desires—do not apply to an emanation based on motiveless *avidyā*. Anyway, those who have their desires fulfilled may exert themselves toward play out of exuberance (*ullāsa*), whereas those who are afflicted by desire may be averse to play for that very reason.

A magician is not cruel or unjust (*vaiṣamya-nairghṛṇya*) in cutting up an illusory person. Nor are painters cruel or unjust because of the difference between intact and mutilated people in paintings. Nor are children in playing with clay images.

Anyway, rewards differ in accordance with works. Brahman does not cease to be a Lord (i.e., It does not become dependent) in doing so, because a Lord who gives different rewards in accordance with different service is still a Lord.

The objection (in Kumārila's *Ślokavārttika*) that an emanation from Brahman cannot be an impure modification of a pure *puruṣa* (i.e., Brahman) does not apply if the emanation is based on *avidyā*. Besides, there may, in fact, be an impure modification of something pure, for if there were no difference at all between original state (*prakṛti*) and modification the relation of these two would not be. For example, water, a liquid, has solid modifications such as hail, and unconscious cowdung a conscious modification in scorpions.

Anyway, the impurity of the *jīvas* is an error (*vibhrama*), as is their apparent difference from Brahman, like the apparent impurity and difference from the original of a reflection.

I.12 (E11-12). There is no cause (*hetu*) for *avidyā*, which is connatural (*svābhāvika*), beginningless, and causeless.

It can nevertheless be destroyed, because, first, the texts that teach the means to its destruction would otherwise be purposeless, and second, other beginningless things can be destroyed, as (on the Nyāya-Vaiśeṣika view) the beginningless black color of atoms of earth is destroyed by baking a pot.

Knowledge (*vidyā*), though eternal in Brahman, is adventitious in the *jīvas*. When they get it, they are released.

If *avidyā* belonged to Brahman, Brahman would be the transmigrant, and when it was released all would be released at once, which is absurd.

I.13 (E12-14). The means (such as listening to the Upaniṣadic texts, or meditation), even though they involve difference, destroy other differences before disappearing themselves, leaving nothing but pure Brahman. It is like the powder made from a certain nut (*kaṭaka*), which precipitates other dust from water before itself precipitating, or like the fluid (in the stomach), which digests other liquids and is itself digested, or like a poison (used as antidote), which destroys another poison and is itself destroyed. Thus we may interpret *Īśā Upaniṣad* 11: "Crossing over death by *avidyā*, by *vidyā* one obtains immortality." These means merely remove ignorance; they do not produce any positive result, which would be impermanent.

Another interpretation of Īśā Upaniṣad 11: *Avidyā* does not exist without *vidyā*. Even the vision of difference is not devoid of light (*prakāśa*), because in the absence of the light nothing would appear (*prakāśeta*). Therefore the highest light alone appears in this or that way, only bound up with *avidyā*. The *vidyā* of hearing of the unicity of the Self cannot be without the *avidyā* of the division of hearer, etc., and so by this *avidyā*, which is proximate to *vidyā*, one may cross over death.

Objection: Hearing, reflection, and meditation based on difference, which is unreal, are also unreal, and so how can they exist, and to what effect? (How can something unreal produce real knowledge?) Moreover, the apprehension of truth from something unreal is false, like that of fire by inference from steam falsely apprehended as smoke.

Answer: Unreal things may have real effects. Magic (*māyā*) is the cause of pleasure and fear. Unreal things may also be the cause of the apprehension of real things, as a drawing of a gayal teaches us about that animal, or written "letters" communicate the real spoken letters.

Objection: In their own form these things are real, not void. But in your doctrine the means to the knowledge of Brahman are unreal in their own form.

Answer: In the examples, the things are unreal in the form in which they communicate (*pratipādika*). Moreover, the means to the knowledge of Brahman are *not* unreal in their own form, because their own form is Brahman. Therefore Brahman itself, as bound up with *avidyā*, is the means for obtaining Brahman. This capacity of unreal things to produce real knowledge is not from similarity (of the gayal and its picture), or from convention (linking the written characters and spoken syllables). For in ordinary usage we say "this is a gayal," meaning the picture, and instruct children that the characters are syllables. Likewise an inference based on a mirror image, which is false, is not necessarily false itself. The apprehension of a difference of meaning from a vowel sound that participates in unreal differences of long and short may be true. An illusory snakebite may cause death, and one may also infer from the illusory snakebite real effects to come to him who thinks himself bitten.

I.14 (E14-15). *Against the Vijñānavādin* : The faults of there being nothing to be gained or lost by efforts for liberation that the Vijñānavādin urges against the Advaita are present in his own theory. If the Self is instantaneous cognition there is nothing to be removed, because something instantaneous ceases of itself, and there is nothing to be gained, because there is no distinction in a moment of being without and with something extra added (*atiśaya*). You cannot add to or remove anything from a stream of moments, either, because a stream is not a thing (*vastu*), whereas the transmigrant must be to be an agent and enjoyer.

Objection : The stream is neither absolutely unreal nor absolutely real; it is real by imagination (*kalpanā*). Efforts are for *its* liberation.

Answer : Then it is something imagined that transmigrates and is released, and the transmigration and release of something imagined must themselves be imaginary. Why don't you agree with this when *we* say it? Transmigration and release are with respect to something imaginary, not the highest absolute truth.

You cannot object to our Self that It is beginningless and endless, because even if one accepts instantaneous cognition your stream is beginningless and endless.

Moreover, there is this objection to your theory of the stream: Its final moment must either have an effect or not. If it does, it isn't final. If it doesn't, it is nonexistent, because it has no effect, which on your theory means it is powerless and therefore nonexistent. But if this moment is nonexistent, the previous moment is nonexistent by the same reasoning, and so on back *ad infinitum*. Should you say that the final moment produces the first moment in *another* stream, an omniscient one (*saṃtānāntara sarvajña*), well then, how is it *another*? For there is nothing that distinguishes one stream from another other than the relation of cause and effect.

I.15 (E15-16). *Objection* (*by a Naiyāyika*): Cognition is a quality (*guṇa*) of the self, not its essence. The attainment of Brahman is the self's abiding in its own form (*svarūpāvasthāna*), from which all specific qualities (*viśeṣaguṇa*) have been removed. For this state (of abiding in its own form) may fitly be called "Brahman," because it is "great" (*bṛhati*). If the essence of the self is cognition, it will, being omnipresent and not dependent on the body, etc., for cognition, be ever more a transmigrant, having cognition of all things knowable. Moreover, it is illogical to say that in liberation the self is cognition but does not cognize anything, because the verb "cognize" requires an object.

Answer : To this the verse says "cognition." Scripture says that the Self is cognition. Fire only burns what is brought into proximity to it and is capable of combustion. Mirrors only reflect what is brought near them. Similarly the Self only enjoys sense objects when It is in the body and they are brought near by the senses. On the Nyāya theory cognition arises in the self when it is in contact with the internal organ (*manas*). But if all selves and all internal organs are omnipresent, everyone will experience everything, so the difference of enjoyments is no better accounted for than on our theory. The response that it is brought about by deeds (*karman*) can be used by us equally well as by you. Anyway, once one has seen nondifference and everything has come to the state of being the Self (*ātmabhāvam āpanna*), there is nothing for the Self to see (and therefore no real problem of the difference of enjoyments), even though its nature is sight.

A liberation defined as the cessation of distinguishing properties, including cognition, would mean the absolute nonexistence of sight, but this is in no way different from the (Buddhist) position that liberation is a destruction (*uccheda*). Who would desire the nonexistence of the (or his) Self, which is dearer than everything ?

Objection: People are observed to desire their own destruction, because it may end various frustrations.

Answer : This does happen in those for whom every pleasure has been extinguished by grievous illness. But transmigrating beings are not in this situation, because they experience manifold pleasures. The cessation of frustration is a purpose of man, but not one's own destruction, which would end many pleasures. But for us, who hold that liberation is the highest and unadulterated bliss, liberation is an unequivocal (*ekāntika*) end of man.

I.16 (E16-18). [Gloss on the word "syllable" (*akṣara*) in verse 1.] Brahman is the word (*śabdātman*), specifically the *oṃkāra*, as scripture says. The *oṃkāra* is Brahman itself, not just a symbol (*pratīka*) of It, as a statue is a symbol of a god, a support (*ālambana*) for worship (*upāsanā*). The *oṃkāra*, according to scripture, is present in all speech (*vāc*), and speech is the Self of everything, because of scriptural authority to that effect, and also because of logic. For, modifications (*vikāra*) are accompanied by the form of their original (*prakṛti*), and all the universe is accompanied by the form of speech, because everything is known by cognition (*vijñāna*) that has a tincture (*uparāga*) of speech. We know this last point from the following considerations :

I.17 (E18-19). (a) Cognition of the word (*śabda*) accompanies that of the object (in verbal cognition). If it is not known, the object is not known, which is not the case with the sense organs (which need not themselves be known to be used to know an object).

(b) When one knows by means of an inference, one refers the inferential sign, for example, smoke, and the thing known, fire, to different loci (*vyadhikaraṇa*),[15] which is not the case with verbal knowledge (one says, "this is a pot"). The relation of qualifier and qualified (*viśeṣaṇaviśeṣyabhāva*) that belongs to the two words in "the lotus is blue" (*nīlam utpālam*) belongs to the object as well. But in the case of an inference from two marks, for example, "Since, even though it is upright, a crow settles on it, it is a post (and not a man)," one apprehends a third thing from two things that mutually delimit each other (*parasparavyavacchinna*). So verbal cognition and inference are not parallel.

(c) A judgment (*niścaya*) reflects the form of speech (*śabdarūpaparāmarśin*) even in cognition gained by some other *pramāṇa* than speech, whereas the cognition of fire does not have the form of smoke.

(d) Even the activity of babies for their mother's breast requires a judgment of the verbal form "this." Judgment cannot be free from the tincture of the form of the word. Therefore even babies have cognitions tinctured by the form of words, as they participate in the impressions (*bhāvanā*) of words in former births.

(e) There are objects that belong solely to verbal usage (that are in everyday use?—*vyavahārika*), that have no nature other than an appearance (*vivarta*) of language (*śabda*). Other objects should be considered to be the same because they belong to the same class (*tatsāmānyāt*, i.e., they also are the objects of words). For example :

(i) Injunction (*vidhi*) and prohibition (*niṣedha*). These are nothing substantial (*avastuka*), because they refer to no activity or abstention from activity (*pravṛtti-nivṛtti*) in any particular one of the three times past, present, and future. Therefore they are a mere intuition (*pratibhā*) conducive to activity or abstention from activity.

(ii) Sentence meaning (*vākyārtha*). Conjunction (*saṃsarga*) is nothing over and above the things conjoined, and the things conjoined are nothing over and above their form as unconjoined. (Therefore sentence meaning as a separate thing or complex whole is unreal.)

(iii) A collection (as a complex whole comprised of parts). The same reasoning applies as for the sentence meaning.

(iv) Nonexistent things such as the circle of fire made by a whirled firebrand (*ālātacakra*), by the same reasoning.

In all these the reality that is speech (*vāg-tattva, śabda-tattva*) appears in this or that way (*tathā tathā vivartate*) because no cognition can be without a support. Examples ii-iv are examples of cognition with constructions (*vikalpa-pratyaya*) that cannot exist without the tincture of the form of language.

(f) Even if (we grant that) there is cognition prior to language, it becomes more vivid (*sphuṭatara*) and becomes distinct (*vivekavatī*) after the entrance of language. Take for example the application of names to the notes of the scale, or the names given by herdsmen to their animals.

(g) Conversely, when the form of language is withdrawn, things even if one is conscious of them are as good as unknown, for example, when a man sees grass, etc., when walking along a path.

Therefore, that consciousness is consciousness depends on the form of speech, or else (Maṇḍana's final conclusion, presumably), consciousness simply *is* the power of speech (*vāk-śakti*). Some say (Maṇḍana probably agrees) that even when the power of speech is withdrawn there remains a subtle (*sūkṣma*) power of speech. In any case, the awareness of objects in cognition depends on the form of speech. So, since every object of cognition is accompanied by the form of speech, everything is a modification of speech, as pots of clay, or an appearance (*vivarta*), as reflections of the moon in rippling water.

I.18 (E19). (Another interpretation of "*akṣara*" in verse 1, here interpreting it to mean "imperishable":) Brahman does not undergo change (*vikāra, pariṇāma*). Scripture calls It "immovable" (*dhruva*) and "eternal" (*nitya*). If It changed in Its entirety It would be destroyed. If It changed in part (*ekadeśa*) It would have to have parts and would be neither eternal nor one.

I.19 (E19-20). [Gloss on the word "not everything" (*asarvam*) in verse 1:] *Objection*:[16] Brahman is identical with everything (*sarvātmatā brahmanaḥ*). This is shown by scriptural passages such as "having all smells, having all tastes" (*Chāndogya Upaniṣad* III.14.2). Also, if the objects of enjoyment, whose nature is light (*prakāśa*), were different from Brahman, they would not appear (*na prakāśeran*), and, being inert (*jaḍa*), they would not be experienced.

Answer: To this we respond, "not everything." Scripture denies all diversity. If the diversity of the world is real and is the nature of Brahman there can be no deliverance, because one cannot separate a thing from its nature. Also, if, as we say, there is only one Self, Brahman, there would be no difference among Selves of enjoyments, and no difference of bound and released. Therefore Brahman is not identical with the diversity of the world (*prapañca*), but the diversity is simply the display (*vilāsita*), the play (*krīḍita*) of *avidyā*.

I.20 (E20). [Gloss on the word "everything" (*sarvam*) in the verse:] Although Brahman does not have everything as Its self, everything has Brahman as its Self. Everything has positive reality (*rūpa*) through the positive reality of Brahman and is not simply void (*śūnya*). If everything were void, if the nonexistence of diversity were the highest truth, this would be equally so in bondage and in liberation, and so everyone would be freed from all eternity (*nityamuktiprasaṅga*).

In addition, *avidyā* is not merely absence of apprehension (*grahaṇābhāva*), because this (nonapprehension of the things in the world) is equally present in liberation, and also nothing would appear (during transmigration). *Avidyā* is therefore apprehension (of the object) otherwise than as it is (*anyathārthagrahaṇa*) and the superimposition (*adhyāsa*) of a nonexistent form (*avidyamānarūpa*) on it. This is impossible with respect to the void; an error based on a void would be without a cause (*bīja*). Scripture also teaches that Brahman has positive reality.

I.21 (E20-22). [Gloss on the word "fearless" (*abhaya*) in verse 1:] *Objection* : Some (Cārvākas, probably) say that there is no pleasure unmixed with frustration, and that pleasure only remains pleasure so long as it belongs to a person who is frustrated.

Answer : We have already shown that pleasure is not merely the cessation of frustration. There is no fear (or "danger," *bhaya*) or distress (*kleśa*) in Brahman, as scripture repeatedly says. There is no connatural (*svābhāvika*) fear in Brahman, because that would contradict Its blissful nature. There is no fear that is adventitious, because there is no second thing other than Brahman.

(Another interpretation of "fearless"): There is no fear of the liberated person returning again (*punarāvṛtti*) to *saṃsāra* on account of the infinity of works accumulated in past lives, because knowledge destroys works like a penance (*prāyaścitta*), though they be infinite in number. This we know from scripture and from the fact that knowledge dissolves the distinction of agent, object, and result essential to actions. How could this distinction arise again? Not from *avidyā*, because *avidyā* is beginningless and therefore has no cause, because a cause cannot act on something already existent. Once destroyed, *avidyā* cannot act as a prior nonexistence for the cause to act on [because the only possible cause would be the Self, and that is unchangeable (*kuṭastha*), says Ānandapūrṇa]. On the other hand, it cannot begin again without a cause.

(The apparent cessation of *avidyā* in deep sleep and the fact that scripture calls deep sleep the attainment of Brahman are not objections to this.) In deep sleep only *avidyā's* projecting (*vikṣepa*) (of false appearances) ceases, but the influence (*saṃskāra*) of that projection and the nonapprehension (*agrahaṇa*) (of reality) continue. If this were not so, there would be no difference between deep sleep and the fourth (*turiya*). Scripture calls deep sleep the attainment of Brahman because projection is absent.

I.22, introduction to verse 2 (E22-23). *Objection* : What is the *pramāṇa* for Brahman ? Not perception (*pratyakṣa*), because its object (*viṣaya*) is difference (or "different individual things," *bheda*). Not inference, because that is preceded by perception. Not comparison (*upamāna*), because the object of comparison is a similarity (*sādṛśya*), which is based on difference. Presumption (*arthāpatti*) can be a *pramāṇa* only for the *reverse* of nondifference. That is, an *arthāpatti* comes in the form: No practical activity is possible without difference, for it is impossible to apprehend anything, even nondifference, without the difference of knower, etc. (Therefore difference exists.) Negation (*abhāva*) cannot be a *pramāṇa* for a positive entity like Brahman. Neither can it be a *pramāṇa* for the nonexistence of diversity, because it is impossible so long as perception, etc., exist (and function as *pramāṇas* for difference).

Neither can tradition (*āgama*) be a *pramāṇa* for Brahman. If it be a tradition set in motion by a qualified individual (*āptapranetṛka*), it would be dependent on other *pramāṇas* and therefore share their incapacity to act as *pramāṇas* for Brahman. If it be an independent (*svatantra*) tradition (i.e., the Vedas), it can be a *pramāṇa* only for injunctions and prohibitions, not for established entities such as Brahman. Statements of established facts are dependent on other *pramāṇas*. Moreover, in everyday life we see that words not aiming at something to be done have no purpose-and-meaning (*artha*).[17]

Moreover, we see that children learn the meaning of words from watching their use to produce activity.

If the object (*artha*, not in the sense of the abstract "meaning" but the concrete reference) of words such as "Brahman" that name Brahman can be known by other *pramāṇas*, language (*śabda*) cannot be a *pramāṇa* for It (because *pramāṇas* give only new knowledge). But if It is not known, It is not the object of a word (because to employ language one must know the connection of word and object, which is impossible if one doesn't know the object), and if It is not the object of a word, It cannot be the topic (*viṣaya*) of a sentence as being qualified. For the meaning of a sentence is the uniting of the objects of the words.

An entity in which all distinction (*avaccheda*) is dissolved cannot be the object (*gocara*) of apprehension, because every apprehension proceeds by the distinction (*vyavaccheda*) "It is this way, it is not that way."

I.23 (E23). *Answer* : Verse 2: "The sages say that It comes into currency (*prasiddhi*) from tradition (*āmnaya*), and that It is described via the dissolution of the diversity (*prapañca*) of difference (*bheda*)."
We will explain below (in Chapter Three) that scripture is not dependent even if it expresses already existent things.

I.24 (E23-25). Certain sentences are observed to have as their motive the production of pleasure, without regard to any activity or abstention from activity, for example, "A son is born to you." There may be a certain activity in the case of the employment of these sentences, but that activity is the intent (*tātparya*), not of the understanding (*pratipatti*) of the speech, but of its production (*utpatti*). The intent of the understanding is an already existent fact. Moreover, there can be no injunction of anything here as a means to an end, because the birth of a son is already accomplished, and the resulting pleasure requires no further activity to produce pleasure once one knows of it. Other examples would be the employment of unpleasant words by evil people to produce sadness, or informing a frightened person that the thing he is entangled in is not a snake but a rope, so that his fear may cease. Likewise, communications of events in distant places, whose aim is to quiet the curiosity of questioners, are not for any loss or gain (*hānopādāna*). In statements of existent facts that *are* for some loss or gain, such as "This road has thieves" or "This spot of earth contains a treasure," the language is not concerned with the loss or gain but solely with the existent fact. The activity or abstention from activity comes from the knowledge of the fact combined with the memory, ascertained earlier from other *pramāṇas*, that the thing described is a cause of benefit or harm. Such sentences as these are not mere substitutes for injunctions, such as "Don't go by this road," "Take this treasure." For, other *pramāṇas*, such as perception, may enter into activity or abstention, but they aim at or fulfill themselves in (*paryavasita*) nothing but accomplished facts.

I.25. (E25). *Objection* : Activity and abstention are intended by the speaker (which is not the case in perception and other non-linguistic-*pramāṇas*).

Answer : The fact of being the meaning of a word arises not from the intention of the speaker, but from the capacity of the word. If it were not so, even the obtaining of various desirable things with the treasure would be a meaning of the words employed, since it also is intended by the speaker. When one desires to know something by perception, etc., with activity or abstention in mind, activity and abstention are not the objects of perception, etc. Besides, if activity were the meaning of the words, everyone would have the thought of acquiring the treasure upon hearing of its existence, whereas some are indifferent to it.

The objector is wrong when he says that all language learning is from observing the use of injunctive words, as an examination of the learning of the words "a son is born to you" shows.

I.26 (E25-26). Let us grant that all utterances impel to action (*pravartaka*) and that one arrives at their connection (with their objects) from that action. Still, one must consider whether the words other than the specifically injunctive word (*vidhāyakapada*) aim at only their own objects, or their union with the thing to be done (*kāryārtha*), or at the union only of the meanings of the words. It cannot be the first, because if they aimed at only their own objects there would be no understanding of the object of a sentence, and so the employment of words would be purposeless. Therefore they do aim at some union with other objects. But since the use of words and their understanding is explicable merely by this (by *some* sort of union with other objects, whether they be something to be done or not), there is no *pramāṇa*[18] for any *particular* union (i.e., for union with a thing to be done).

Words must necessarily aim at the union of their objects, so that from this there results the cognition of a qualified (*viśiṣṭa*) already existent object. Otherwise, the association (*anvaya*) of the objects of words in everyday language would be based on the speaker's intention, and consequently there would be no connection in Vedic language, where there is no speaker.

If all the words are associated with the thing to be done there will be no mutual connection of the objects of words. In that case no prescription (*niyoga*) having as its object an object that is qualified will be understood, for the prescription will be accomplished by the object of a single word (i.e., the verb). The prescription comes *after* the application (*viniyoga*) (of the words ?).[19]

It is, in fact, possible to describe an entity unknown by any *pramāṇa* other than *śabda*—by the negation (*pratiṣedha*) of all particulars (*viśeṣa*). For, although one does not know the entity Brahman, nor its connection with the word of which it is the object, one does know words for particulars, and the word "not" (*nañ*). By the combination of these, scripture teaches Brahman by such words as "not coarse," etc. Thus verse 2 says, "By the dissolution of the diversity of difference."

I.27 (E26). Another explanation of these words of verse 2: The objector said that an entity in which all particulars have disappeared cannot be the object of apprehension. But it is precisely through the cessation of particulars that Brahman is described, as the entity gold is known through the abandonment of its particular configurations such as a lump, a necklace, etc.

I.28 (E26-28). *Problem* : Does the whole of tradition (*āgama*) describe Brahman via the dissolution of the diversity of difference, or only some part of it. (As will be evident from the discussion, this is also the question of the relationship of knowledge and works.)

On this point there are the following positions:

(a) All of the Veda, including the portions relating to works, teach the dissolution of something with respect to something. For example, the injunction "One who desires heaven should sacrifice," because it implies the existence of a self after death, dissolves the notion that the body is the self. Prohibitions and injunctions dissolve natural (*naisargika*) activities based on passion (*rāga*), etc., by prohibiting them or directing toward other activities, respectively. Thus they are accessory (*upayogin*) to qualification (*adhikāra*) for knowledge of the Self, because one who is not pacified and self-controlled is incapable of that knowledge. (According to Ānandapūrṇa, this is the position of Brahmadatta.)

(b) Works accomplish the destruction of desires (by fulfilling them). One who by works lasting a thousand years accomplishes the destruction of desire obtains the highest nondual Self from the state of Prajāpati (Brahmā).

In both (a) and (b) the whole tradition aims at the knowledge of the Self as the one thing to be done. There are also the following positions that say that knowledge is not the sole end of the Veda:

(c) The injunctions to action aim at qualifying a man for knowledge by first removing the disqualification of not having discharged the three debts.

(d) Works and knowledge are connected by "severality of connection" (*saṃyogapṛthaktva*). As the Veda says, "They desire to know by sacrifice" (*Bṛhadāraṇyaka Upaniṣad* IV.4.22). (The point seems to be that works may be made instrumental to the desire to know optionally, if the one who performs them so chooses. This is part of Maṇḍana's own position.)

(e) Works are connected with the qualification for knowledge as being a perfection (*saṃskāra*) of the person (*puruṣa*). (This is also part of Maṇḍana's own position.)

(f) Knowledge of the Self is a perfection (*saṃskāra*) of the agent (*kartṛ*) for the sake of qualification for the performance of works. (The usual Mīmāṃsā position.)

(g) Knowledge and works are unconnected and contradictory. (Śaṃkara or Sureśvara, probably.)

I.29 (E28-30). *Response to (a)*: Injunctions to works and injunctions to knowledge both have their own separate effects (*kārya*) mentioned in scripture. Moreover, because the expectancy (*ākāṃkṣā*) of means (*sādhana*) for knowledge is already satisfied, by the enumeration of the means of knowledge, such as celibacy and the like, the injunction to knowledge does not require injunctions of works (as an injunction to perform a certain sacrifice creates an "expectancy," a need to know the means of sacrifice, which is fulfilled by injunctions of means). If all injunctions and prohibitions have their fulfillment (*apavarga*) in the effect consisting of the dissolution of name-and-form, (they will have no further effect, and so) the rise and fall of creatures in *saṃsāra* will not be caused by works and so will be causeless (or "random"—*ākasmika*), as will also be release (*apavarga*—but in a different sense than just above). Therefore the *śāstra* (of the Vedānta) will be useless.

Objection : Injunctions of works enter into qualification for knowledge by their effects, such as heaven, just as instructions to go to villages along the way enter into the instruction to go to the city, which is the goal desired.

Answer : No, for in the example getting to the villages is not an object of desire, whereas the fruits of works *are* objects of desire, so there is no need to suppose another object, namely liberation. A speaker may describe the merits of the intermediate villages so as to induce us to get to the city at the end. But that is not the intent of his words; we learn that that was his intent from some other *pramāna*. But there is no other *pramāṇa* than language for the objects of Vedic injunctions; so we must accept the ends that are mentioned as the real ends—heaven, etc.—for injunctions to works, liberation for the injunction to knowledge. Moreover, if the instruction about going to the villages on the way is for the sake of getting the person to go to the final city, getting to the villages will not be the result of the instruction, because one might get to the city by another route. Similarly, if injunctions to works have as their end obtaining liberation, heaven, etc., will not be the end of the injunctions to works.[20]

Prohibitions may contribute to knowledge by preventing works based on passion, but injunctions of works do not do so. They are neither exclusive (*parisaṃkhyāyaka = parisaṃkhyānavidhi*) nor restrictive (*niyāmaka = niyamavidhi*), because their object is something totally nonestablished (*aprāpta*).[21] It is injunctions whose subject matter is already established that result in abstention (*nivṛtti*) from something else. Besides, there is nothing contradictory between performing the rite for gaining a village, which is the object of an injunction, and serving a king for the same end, so Vedic injunctions to works do not obstruct secular activities based on passion. Vedic injunctions do not obstruct activities for visible ends, for, if they did, they would prevent acting for a visible end such as the acquiring of wealth which is necessary for the performance of the very sacrifices that are the objects of Vedic injunctions. In fact, Vedic injunctions such as "Let him who desires heaven perform sacrifice" imply that the person they are addressed to is motivated by passion, for heaven. Activities (*pravṛttayaḥ*) with a visible end and works with an invisible end are equal in being thrown up by passion, etc., and in persistent attachment (*abhiniveśa*) to multiplicity (*prapañca*); there is no distinction by which one can say that those based on Vedic prescription (*niyoga*) are conducive to the knowledge of the Self and others are not.[22]

Should someone say that works are not a means (*upāya*) of desires (*kāma*), we reply again that randomness of the rise and fall of creatures and of liberation will result, as we said before. This idea has been refuted in the *Svargakāmādhikaraṇa* section of the *Mīmāṁsāsūtras* (VI.1-13). Moreover, this will render absurd the opponent's own position that Vedic works contradict worldly works because they have the same end.

I.30 (E30). *Response to* (*b*): The obtaining of desires does not destroy desire but increases it. It is not enjoyment but repeated meditation that sees the faults of sense objects, that destroys desire. One who had no means of satisfying his desires might desist from them and have recourse to the knowledge of the Self, but one to whom scripture has shown multiple means of satisfying his desires will apply himself to those very pleasures that naturally bear one away and would become averse to knowledge of the Self. The bliss that is in the Self, which has merely been heard about, is unable to reduce the fondness for that bliss, which has actually been experienced in sense objects.

Further response to (*a*): The Vedic sentence "One who desires heaven should sacrifice" does not have for its intent the dissolution of the idea that the body is the Self, because the sentence does not have that as its literal intent, and it cannot have that as its intent by implication (*artha* = *arthāpatti*) when the dissolution of the body and the senses is directly pointed out in the passage that begins "Not coarse . . . . " (*Bṛhadāraṇyaka Upaniṣad* III.8.8). It would be like inferring an elephant from its footprints when it has already been seen. Rather, if we were to look for an implied meaning, it would have to be that the Veda intends that knot of desire be firm (because no one without desire would be moved to act by this injunction). (But this is absurd.)

I.31 (E30-31). *Further response to* (*b*): Desirable things cannot destroy desire. There is, besides, no proof that they could enter into another result without regard to their individual results. If all works aim at knowledge, there is but one qualification, and so all works must be performed by the same person (the one desiring liberation), which is impossible.

Response to (*f*): What proof (*pramāṇa*) can the opponent give for the connection of knowledge to action ? There is neither mention in the context (*prakaraṇa*) of any injunction to action, nor syntactical connection (*vākya*) resulting from invariable (*avyabhicārin*) connection (*sambandha*) with works. But there is a separate statement of the fruit of knowledge, namely, "He does not return again" (*Chāndogya Upaniṣad* VIII.15.1). There being no reason to believe that this statement has a meaning other than the literal one, it is not a mere supplementary statement (*arthavāda*), and on the basis of it, it is clear that there are separate qualifications for knowledge and for works (because they have separate fruits).

I.32 (E31-32). *Objection*: The statement "He does not return again" is in the present tense (not in the optative, and therefore not an injunction). There being a visible fruit of injunction to Self-knowledge, namely, procuring activity for works whose fruits may be enjoyed in other bodies, there is no need to look for an invisible fruit of Self-knowledge and so no need to construe the statement of non-returning as a statement of this fruit, after changing its form (into the customary optative, thus, "Let one who is desirous of non-returning perform knowledge of the Self").

Answer: No, because the Person (*puruṣa*) described in the Upaniṣads is other than the one that is an agent and enjoyer. The latter is known to everyone by perception, there is no need for *śabda* as a *pramāṇa* for him. (*Śabda* only teaches what other *pramāṇas* can't.) This one, the *jīva*, is indeed one with the supreme Self. But to the *jīva*, and to him alone,[23] belongs the form of agent and enjoyer that is bound up with *avidyā* and ascertained by perception. This form is the cause of activity of works. That (form or Self) that is self-luminous and void of all divisions is what is desired to be known from scripture, and It is incompatible with works, for one who knows the bliss of the nondual Brahman cannot desire anything as the result of works, since all his desires are fulfilled, nor can he act for It, because the means of action are absent. Passages such as *Chāndogya Upaniṣad* I.1.10 and *Bṛhadāraṇyaka Upaniṣad* III.8.10 and IV.4.2, in which the knowledge of the Person described in the Upaniṣads (the supreme Self) seems to be prescribed as accessory to works, can be better interpreted.

I.33 (E32). *Response to (g)*: From the supposition that knowledge and works are contradictory, having as their spheres the nonduality and duality respectively, there would result the nonproduction of knowledge, because the division of *pramāṇa*, object and agent of knowledge is contradictory to the apprehension of nonduality. Should you deny this contradiction, saying that they are not simultaneous, the means (*upāya*) that involve duality coming before the knowledge of nonduality and ceasing immediately upon that knowledge, we respond that then there is no such contradiction as you allege between works and knowledge.

I.34 (E32-34). *Opponent* :[24] Works are useless in the knowledge of Brahman, because Brahman is not something that must be accomplished (*sādhya*), and as scripture says (*Muṇḍaka Upaniṣad* I.2.12), "That which is not made is not (obtained) by what is done (*kṛta*)." Neither do works have any utility (*upayoga*) in the *production* (*utpatti*) of knowledge, because that depends solely upon the *pramāṇas*. They are not accessories (*sahakārin*) to knowledge, because knowledge has nothing to accomplish besides itself. Liberation cannot be such a thing to be accomplished, because if it were it would be impermanent. Nor can the thing to be accomplished be the removal of the cause of bondage, because the cause of bondage is *avidyā*, and the arising of knowledge is itself the exclusion (*vyāvṛtti*) of *avidyā*.

Objector : The arising of knowledge may be the exclusion of that *avidyā* which is defined as nonapprehension (*agrahaṇa*), but not of that which is positive erroneous cognition (*viparyāsajñāna*).[25] Now, one positive entity (*bhāva*) cannot be the exclusion of another positive entity.

Opponent : Erroneous cognition, being caused (*nimitta*) by nonapprehension, ceases when its cause ceases.

Objector : A nonexistence cannot be the cause of anything. The cause of erroneous cognition is beginningless, motiveless *avidyā*, as was said before (at I.11). There is no room for asking about a cause for *it* (because it is beginningless). Error (*viparyāsa*) and its influence (*saṃskāra*) are established as mutually cause and effect of each other (and therefore need no further cause). Therefore the cessation of error is something *to be accomplished* by knowledge. In that task it might require works as an accessory.

Opponent : Persons in whom right cognition with regard to mother-of-pearl has been produced after a previous error do not make a separate effort for the removal of error, nor do they need any accessory. The destruction of the previous entity is nothing other than the arising of another, contradictory entity, not a mere void. Otherwise the destruction would have no cause. Knowledge is contradictory to error; on its production error is destroyed.

Objector : Works are causes of bondage. They are ended by knowledge, which requires an accessory.

Opponent : When knowledge cleansed of all particulars (*viśeṣa*) has arisen, the worldly usage (*vyavahāra*) of the division of works and fruits is impossible. Also, *Muṇḍaka Upaniṣad* II.2.8 equates works as equivalent to error and doubt: "The knot of the heart is broken, all doubts are cut, and his works waste away, when that is seen in its completeness."

Objector : Knowledge requires something else for perfect clarity (*vaimalya*).

Opponent : No, doubt and error, which are the blemishes of cognition, are impossible in knowledge that has arisen from a *pramāṇa*.

Objector : Some knowledge other than verbal knowledge is necessary to know Brahman, one that is direct (*pratyakṣa*), without any apprehension of separation (*vibhāga*), and beyond all conceptual constructions (*vikalpa*), because verbal knowledge, which grasps the connection of separate objects of words (or, "which grasps the connection of the objects of inflected words," *vibhakta-padārtha-saṃsargodgrāhin*), cannot have the nondual Brahman for its object. In the production of this there is dependency upon works, adoration (*upāsanā*), etc.

Opponent : What is the distinctive feature on account of which this other knowledge is sought ? Not vividness (*spaṣṭabhātva*), for knowledge is for the pervasion (*abhivyāpti*) of the object, and that is obtained when verbal knowledge arises.

Objector : For direct perception, since all right cognition (*pramiti*) has perception as its goal.

Opponent : This is not so, because once the thing to be known is known, nothing else is necessary.

Objector : Another *pramāṇa*, then.

Opponent : But a *pramāṇa* is necessary for establishing its object (not for establishing an object already established by another *pramāṇa*).

It cannot be necessary for establishing it a second time, because that could be done by the first *pramāṇa*. You may say that the very existence of another *pramāṇa* or a special pleasure might be the cause of a need for another *pramāṇa*. But this special pleasure results also from the vision (*darśana*) produced by the first *pramāṇa*. Since there exist other *pramāṇas* that can know a thing seen by direct perception, there would be an equal need for them to be employed upon an object known by perception; there is no difference among *pramāṇas* in their giving certainty.

Objector : Perception's object is something nearby, and therefore something capable of being abandoned or gained, whereas this is not so of the objects of other *pramāṇas*. (Therefore perception is of more practical utility.)

Opponent : In this case it is not another *pramāṇa* that is necessary, but some cause of bringing the object known closer.

Objector : Language (*śabda*) and the other *pramāṇas* besides perception have for their object the universal (*sāmānya*), whereas perception has for its object the particular (*viśeṣa*).

Opponent : Then the object of perception is not arrived at by language (and so it can't help to make it better known). Moreover, if Brahman is not arrived at by language, how is it that adoration (*upāsanā*) of Brahman goes on ? One cannot make one thing immediately present by adoration of another thing. The injunction of sacrifice and the like is for the sake of making the Self that is Brahman immediately present in that form presented by Vedic language, as blissful, sinless, etc. If this were not the true form of Brahman and it were possible that Brahman were not the end of man, the injunction will have a false object (*asad-artha*). Therefore, once the Self has become clear (*prakaṭa*) from Vedic language, which is free from doubt, no other *pramāṇa* is needed.

Objector : Even when one has arrived at the identity of the Self and Brahman from the scriptural statement "That art thou," the properties of a transmigrant are still observed, and something else is required to stop them.

Opponent : No. One who has seen Brahman as It is cannot be conjoined with properties caused by false vision (*mithyā-darśana*). Various passages of scripture confirm that these properties, and the state of embodiedness, come from false (*mithyā*) conceit (*abhimāna*). Therefore he who does participate in these properties has not arrived at the identity of Brahman and the Self.

I.35 (E35-36). Response to the entire previous discussion (in I.34): Even when the reality (*tattva*) has been determined with certainty (*niścita*) from a *pramāṇa*, false appearances do not necessarily cease. For example, the error of seeing a double moon, or of confusion about directions (*digviparyāsa*), does not cease in a person who has ascertained the truth from the speech of a qualified person (*āpta*). Similarly, false appearances continue even in the case of one who has arrived at the reality of the Self from tradition, free from doubt, because of the force of powerful traces (*saṃskāra*), accumulated by the repetition of beginningless false vision. For their cessation something additional (to verbal knowledge) is necessary. From ordinary experience that thing is known to be repetition of the vision of reality, and from the Veda it is known to be sacrifice, etc. (i.e., both repetition of the vision of reality and sacrifice and other good works help to eliminate the traces). Repetition creates a firm trace of its own and obstructs the previous traces. Sacrifice, etc., does the same thing in some unseen (*adṛṣṭa*) manner. Or else, as others say, sacrifice, etc., does so by destroying impurities (*kaluṣa*) that get in the way of the highest good (*śreyas*); for the purpose of obligatory rites (*nityakarman*) is the washing away (*kṣaya*) of sins.[26]

Objection : False appearances may continue, but certitude comes from the *pramāṇa*, and practical activity (*vyavahāra*) conforms to reality (*tattva*) and to certitude (*niścaya*). So there is no activity (*pravṛtti*) whatever on the part of one who has arrived at the reality of the Self. (The appearances continue, but not any activity, including meditation or sacrifice and other works.)

Answer : Even after the vision of reality has arisen certitude may have a false object, if the trace already produced by false vision is strong and a strong trace of true vision has not been implanted. For instance, we observe that one confused about the directions who doesn't keep in mind the truth told him by a qualified person may become confused again, because his activity is just as before. Or a person who previously became afraid of a rope, thinking it to be a snake, may again become afraid if he does not continuously keep in mind the *pramāṇa* by which he learned it was a rope. Therefore repetition of the vision of reality makes for the subjugation or elimination of the stronger trace produced by the repetition of beginningless false vision. Thus scripture says "He is to be thought about, to be meditated upon" (*Bṛhadāraṇyaka Upaniṣad* II.4.5) and prescribes means such as celibacy, sacrifice, and other things. Otherwise this instruction would have no meaning.

Objection : Knowledge of reality comes from tradition when it is assisted by celibacy and other means. (The opponent is now willing to grant that activity may have some use in producing knowledge, before it is produced, but he still wants to deny the idea that it exists and has a function even after the arising of knowledge.)

Answer : No, for apprehension arises from language by itself. Tradition, whose purpose is the understanding of reality, is not mute before certain special means, nor does it fail to give certitude, because it is free from all doubt. If it were not a source of certainty one could not even learn about the means from it.

(Some more examples of the continuation of false appearances and their effects after the gaining of certitude.) Even if one knows with certitude that a play is not reality, the actors on the stage are the causes of emotions in the audience via false appearances. Even if he knows with certitude that molasses is sweet, the false appearance that it is bitter continues in a sick man. Thus even one who knows with certitude that Brahman is the Self needs the means for the cessation of error.

The employment of means does not make liberation an effect (*kārya*). Just as the manifestation of reality by means of a *pramāṇa* does not make liberation an effect, neither does the special manifestation (that of the reality of the Self) by the means. The scriptural passages (that state that liberation comes from knowledge, not mentioning activities or means) refer to the state of the completion of practice, (not to verbal knowledge by itself). Or else let them apply to verbal knowledge, insofar as the knowledge of which language is the means is the cause of the later knowledge.

I.36 (E36). *Response to* (*c*): One does not have to have discharged the three debts (of sacrificing to the gods, begetting a son, and teaching the Veda) before embarking upon knowledge as an inflexible rule, because *smṛtis* such as *Gautama Dharma Sūtra* I.3.1 and scriptural passages such as *Jābāla Upaniṣad* 4 and others allow an option as to what stage of life (*āśrama*) one may enter after one's period of studying the Veda. Moreover, various passages in scripture teach the abandonment of works. *Manu* 6.35, which seems to teach that one must have discharged the three debts before entering upon knowledge, actually teaches that one who in fact has taken up householdership but considers that by the knowledge of the Self everything he needs to do is accomplished (*kṛta-kṛtya-tā*) and therefore neglects the discharge of the three debts incurs a sin that prevents the rise of knowledge, by not doing what is enjoined.

I.37 (E36). *Acceptance of* (*d*): This is the proper position. Even actions that have no necessary reference to another *effect* (*kārya*) have a severalty of connection (*saṃyoga-pṛthak-tva*), and therefore are accessory to knowledge. Thus scripture says, "Brahmins desire to know

Him by recitation of the Veda, by sacrifice . . . ." (*Bṛhadāraṇyaka Upaniṣad* IV.4.22). However, they are for the sake of production of knowledge, not by serviceableness to some effect (of knowledge), because knowledge has no effect other than itself.

Acceptance of (e): Or else, works are a perfection (*saṃskāra*), because *smṛti* says that knowledge arises in one who is perfected: "And also the work of the *āśramas*, because they are enjoined" (*Brahmasūtra* III.4.32).

I.38 (E36-37). *Objection* : The means for producing knowledge are obvious (*dṛṣṭa*), such things as quietude, self-control, etc., which destroy the distraction (*vikṣepa*) of the mind, for only in one who is concentrated (*samāhita*, cf. *samādhi*) and who uses repetition (*abhyāsa*) does clarity (*prasāda*) of knowledge arise. But if these means are sufficient by themselves to produce knowledge, how can such things as sacrifice (and other external actions, such as gift-giving) be means ?

Answer : What you say is true. Even celibate hermits obtain knowledge without such means as sacrifice. But knowledge is manifested quicker by these special means, and slower without them. (Note that this implies that the householder's state is more conducive to knowledge of Brahman than the hermit's.) Thus *Brahmasūtra* III.4.26 says: "There is dependence on all (means), because of scripture, like the horse." The scripture in question is *Bṛhadāraṇyaka Upaniṣad* IV.4.22 (see just above for translation). The *sūtra* means that as one may reach a village without a horse, but gets there faster with one, so one may gain knowledge by repetition, but works are required to gain it quicker and without difficulty.

I.39 (E37). *Objection* : Knowledge is the very form of Brahman, not something different from It. But Brahman is eternal and not an effect. So how can anything "be required" for knowledge ? (Things "are required" to produce effects.)

Answer : A piece of rock crystal whose form has been concealed by an adjunct (*upādhana*=*upādhi*) "requires" the removal of the adjunct for the sake of the manifestation of its own form, but the form of the crystal was not removed by the presence of the adjunct, nor was it produced as an effect by the adjunct's removal. So the form of the Self "requires" (means). (Brief *excursus* against the Buddhist doctrine of momentariness.) The form of the crystal was not destroyed or produced, because it is impossible that for no reason a moment (of clear crystal) should come into being that is like a previous (moment of clear crystal) but has several moments (of colored crystal) intervening. When fire has ceased a succession (of moments) of wood does not arise again from the coals.

Objection : (The example of the crystal is not parallel to the knowledge of the Self.) It is the cognition of the crystal (not the form of the crystal) that "requires" the removal of the adjunct. But cognition is an effect, and different from the crystal (unlike the knowledge that is identical with Brahman). For the human effort exerted for the removal of the crystal is for the sake of cognizing it.

Answer : (In fact, it is the form of the crystal that requires the removal of the adjunct, for the following reasons:) Cognition is not aimed at for its own sake, but for establishing the nature of the object. For one performs practical activity with the object, it is not based on bare cognition, since then one could perform it even with false cognition. (It is not cognition as such that permits successful practical activity, but cognition specified by the object as it really is.) Therefore cognition is aimed at for the sake of the nature of the object, and consequently activity for the sake of cognition is for the sake of the object and is required by the object. (And so the object—the form of crystal or the form of the Self—even though it is not an effect (at least, in the case of the crystal, of any activity in the situation we are presently considering), may still "require" something else.)

Cognition does not produce any modification in the object (for the sake of which the object might "require" it). For cognition and object are not connected. [If being cognized produced a real modification in the object, namely what the Mīmāṃsā calls "being revealed" (*prakaṭya*)] it would result that all things would be known by everyone. Finally, a change is impossible in things cognized that are in the past or future.

Therefore an object, such as crystal or the Self, which is *as it were* concealed requires an effort that it may be *as it were* manifested. (Note that this emphasizes the weakness of the sense in which the object "requires" an effort with means for it to be known.)

I.40 (E37). Verse 3: "Therefore he is described as being a universal (*sāmānya*) in which all different individuals (*bheda*) are absorbed, as gold as pointed out by the absorption of individuals such as bracelets, etc."

I.41 (E37-38). Because, as verse 2 says, It is described by the disappearance of particulars, Brahman is described by those who know It as a universal. It is the universal Being (*sattā*), according to passages such as "This is the great unborn *Ātman*, defined as Being (*sattālakṣaṇa*),"[27] or "Being (*sattā*) alone is the womb of all beings, the highest original form (*prakṛtiḥ parā*)."[28] It is like the description of the reality of gold by the absorption of its particular forms, such as bracelet or ring.

The words "in which all different individuals are absorbed" refute those who say that such a thing does not exist because there is no universal without particulars (e.g., Kumārila in *Ślokavārttika, ākṛtivāda*, verse 10.). It is quite true that Brahman is not strictly speaking a universal, but It is called a universal metaphorically because of the disappearance of all particulars in it. But you cannot prove that a thing that has no particulars of necessity does not exist, because there are particulars (such as atoms) that have no further particulars.[29]

CHAPTER TWO : ON REASONING (TARKAKĀṆḌA)

II.1 (E39-44). *Opponent* : Vedic tradition (*āgama*) is against perception, which presents us with the mutual difference of things; therefore it cannot be a *pramāṇa* for nonduality.

Answer : Verse 1: Perception does not negate, but merely affirms; therefore it cannot deny oneness.

Objection 1 : Neither Vedic tradition nor perception, etc., is dependent on the other, and so there is no reason that if they come into conflict tradition, and not perception, should lose its authoritativeness. Therefore there is no need to attempt to remove apparent conflicts between them as you are proposing to do.

Objection 2 : If there is a conflict, tradition is the weaker, because it is dependent on perception for its existence.

Objection 3 : The *pramāṇa* language (*śabda*) may depart from truth without preceding damage to its means, namely, words, whereas perception never departs from truth except as a result of damage to its means, namely, the sense organs. Therefore in a conflict perception is the stronger of the two.

Objection 4 : That which has an "opportunity for explanation" (*avakāśa*) is stronger than that which does not, and the Vedic statements of oneness have the opportunity to be explained away by some other application, such as having a secondary sense or being meaningless but useful for repeated recitation (*japa*), whereas the evidence of perception cannot be so explained away, and so must be accepted.

Objection 5 : Perception is stronger than language, because the Vedic language is self-contradictory, but perception is not.

Objection 6 : Perception is stronger than Vedic tradition because tradition is experienced later in the individual's life, and because before one understands the meaning of a verbal communication one must first apprehend the world through perception.

Objection 7: Even if perception and Vedic tradition are equal in strength of authority, one must try to remove apparent contradictions between them, because there can be no option in regard to an objective thing (*vastu*).

Response to objections 3 and 6 : Tradition is stronger than perception, because in the temporal sequence of *pramāṇas* the later are stronger than the earlier. The knowledge of nonduality depends on that of duality and follows it in time, but sublates it. Tradition is stronger because the faults of the agent that can exist in the case of perception cannot exist in the nonpersonal Vedic tradition. All perception is vitiated by the influence (*saṃskāra*) of *avidyā*. Perception is a *pramāṇa* with respect to practical life, but not in giving final truth.

Response to objections 2 and 6 : Language is not dependent on perception for its being a means of knowledge, but for its being established, that is, for being heard. Perception itself depends on other things to be produced. We see that later cognitions that require certain earlier cognitions may be stronger than them and sublate them. For example, we may first mistake a distant grove of trees for a herd of elephants, and then, after looking more carefully, without approaching nearer, see that it is a grove. Similarly, the cognition of higher numbers requires that of lower.

Response to objection 5 : The Veda is not self-contradictory, because duality is not taught in it, but is temporarily assumed as the basis for a later apprehension of nonduality.

Response to objection 3 : Perception and language may equally vary from the truth, and so one cannot decide on this basis which of the two has the stronger authority.

Response to objection 4 : The lack of any other opportunity for explanation is equal in the cases of both language and of perception. For if the texts of the Upaniṣads don't apply to establishing the truth of nonduality, they cannot be explained as having any other application. If it be possible either that tradition is stronger or that tradition and perception are equal in strength, one should not say that a Vedic passage has a secondary meaning or no meaning merely because it is contradicted by another *pramāṇa*. One should say so only when no reference in the literal sense of the words can be found, because every *pramāṇa* is independent in establishing its object. In a conflict one can just as easily assume an imaginary or metaphorical object for perception as for tradition, and just as easily assume perception has no object. When two *pramāṇas* are independent in producing the apprehension of an object, the later is stronger in authority.

Additional response to objection 5 : The Vedas are not self-contradictory in teaching duality in the parts that enjoin to works, and teaching nonduality in the Upaniṣads. For injunctions to works do not teach duality as a truth, but merely assume a duality already experienced.

II.2 (E44-45). Perception may either: (1) posit (*vi-dhā*) the

essence of an object, (2) exclude (*vy-ā-vṛt*) other objects, or (3) do both (a) simultaneously or (b) with exclusion followed by positing or (c) with positing followed by exclusion.
Only on the acceptance of (1) will there be no contradiction between perception and the Vedas.

Verse 2 : Alternatives (2), (3a) and (3b) are impossible because one must have posited some definite positive thing before one can negate.

Here a problem arises: how are we to explain how we negate things that we don't believe exist ? There are two possible explanations: First, we may say that we deny the presence of a certain already established object, quality, or the like, in a certain established locus, for example, of a lotus in the sky. Or second, we may say that we deny the objective externality of things that have obtained a form in the intellect (*buddhi*). In any case, a negation without regard to an already posited locus and object of negation would be asserting Buddhist voidness as the ultimate truth or would be a negation of everything with respect to every possible locus.

II.3 (E45-46). Alternative (3c) is also impossible, because (verse 3) there cannot be two successive operations (*vyāpāra*) in one act of knowledge (*buddhi*), because the act of knowledge produced by a *pramāṇa* is instantaneous.
Besides, perception illuminates objects that are proximate, and therefore it cannot in addition illuminate nonproximate objects such as the negandum.

II.4, including verse 4 (E46-47). It is not true (as the Buddhist theory of *apoha* maintains) that the positing of one thing as having a certain definite nature is itself the exclusion of the things that are other than it. For in every perception, if this were true, we would perceive the difference of the object of perception from absolutely every other thing that is different from it, whether or not each of these other things were the sort of thing that could be perceived by the same sense at the same place and time. (For example, the perception that something is blue excludes that it is yellow, but it does not exclude that it is sweet, which may or may not be true, that it is made up of invisible atoms, etc.)

II.5, including verse 5 (E47-48). Difference cannot be the essence (*rūpa, svabhāva*) of anything, as the Buddhists say it is. For difference is one single thing, but it resides in two things as differentiating them from each other. But if it is the essence of these things, they will be identical with it, and thereby with each other, and will not be different. On the other hand, if difference is not the essence of things, they are not by essence different. If, again, difference *is* the essence of things, then, since it is reciprocal nonexistence, which is a subdivision of nonexistence, things will be by their essence nonexistent. In addition, if difference is the essence of things, nothing can be one, and therefore no wholes can exist, because wholes are made up of unitary parts. The (Buddhist) opponent may object to our trying to show by these alternatives that the notion of difference is unable to stand logical scrutiny, saying that difference is not a thing (*vastu*), so that one cannot ask whether it is identical with things or different from them, but that it is simply based on the beginningless influences of logical constructs (*vikalpa*). But this is exactly what *we* say: we say that difference does not really exist but is simply the projection (*vilāsita*) of beginningless *avidyā*.

II.6, including verse 6a (E48-50). Things are not dependent for their natures on their relation (in particular, difference) to other things. If they were, all things would be mutually dependent and nothing would ever get established. "Relation" is a quality of human thought, and the natures of things are established by their own proper causes, and not by human thought.

Objection : Difference is not a single thing that resides in the same manner in two different things; rather, it differs from thing to thing, residing in one thing as its essence, and in the other via relation, and establishes them as different.

Answer : No, relation is created by human thought, which relates one already established thing to another already established thing for a specific purpose. If relation is necessary for establishing the nature of an object, then the prior causes of a thing are not sufficient to produce it—to produce it requires in addition something subsequent to its production, namely, its relation of difference from a counterpositive (*pratiyogin*)—all of which is absurd. Difference cannot be the essence of a thing for the additional reason that difference is understood as being relative to something else, and therefore extrinsic to the thing.

II.7, including verses 6b-7a (E50-52). Words of relation, such as "father/son" or "short/long," are indeed relative, but not the objects themselves. We apply these relation words to objects in virtue of their different participation in the same action. For example, the application of the words "father" and "son" depends on the different roles two people play in the action of procreation, in which both are involved. Similarly, the words "long" and "short" are applied because of a difference of less and more in the similar action of pervading space. The *existence* of the effect is caused not by "relation" but by the *action* of the cause.

One cannot prove that the difference of things is real from the difference of their effects or their uses in purposeful actions (*artha-kriyā*) because this assumes the reality of difference at the start of the argument, begging the question. Moreover, one cannot prove a real difference of things from a difference of purposeful action because one object may produce several purposeful actions, either simultaneously or successively.

Objection : We can tell there is a difference of things from the difference of their effects, because otherwise there is no property that distinguishes seeing an effect and not seeing it.

Answer : We ourselves admit such a distinguishing property, but as an object of imagination or construction (*kalpanāviṣaya*). It cannot really exist, because it can neither be identical with the object it resides in, nor different. Just as the Buddhist says that the similarity, and therefore the unity, of cause and effect is imagined (*kalpita*), so we may say the difference of effects is imagined. And as you say several causes may cooperate to produce one effect so we may say that one cause may have several effects. One may with equal justice say that the difference of effects from the cause and from each other is imagined, as we do, or that the unity of an effect is imagined (as you do).

II.8 (E52-54). The simultaneous presence of contradictory purposeful actions is not a proof of difference. For what does it mean for them to be contradictory? Not the impossibility of their occurring together in the same locus, because that is precisely what needs to be proven. Nor does it mean their being mutually exclusive by nature (*parasparavyavacchinnātmatā*), for we observe mutually exclusive properties in one locus, such as burning and cooking in fire. If this differentiates things from one another, no single thing with several properties can exist. Neither is contradiction to be of the nature of reciprocal nonexistence, for then the supposed contradictory actions, being nonexistences rather than existences, would not be real properties. Moreover, since in absolutely nonexistent things like sky flowers both of any set of contradictory actions are absent, they would both be present, because each is simply the absence of the other. Neither is contradiction the relationship of destroyer and destroyed, because the destroyer must come into being before it can destroy something, and until it does destroy it it is coexistent with the destroyed. Nor can we say that those properties are contradictory of which one is something positive and the other is its exclusion, because a positive property and its exclusion may reside in different parts of one thing.

Nor do we know the existence of difference in things from the fixed distinction (*vyavasthā*) of purposeful actions (*arthakriyā*). For, what is this "fixed distinction"? It cannot be, firstly, the diversity of effects, for we just saw that one thing may have diverse effects. Secondly, it cannot be the fact that a certain thing can be produced from one thing and not from others, because "otherness" is exactly what needs to proven. Nor, thirdly, can it be the power of producing a certain effect and its absence; for we have seen that one single thing may have contradictory properties, being connected in different times and places with a certain property and its absence. With regard to an infinite thing (such as Brahman, it is implied), it is logical that it should possess different, contradictory, finite properties. If the relation of a thing and its properties is one either of difference or indescribability (as identical or different), there is no reason they shouldn't be different in regard to their infinitude and finitude. If, to take the sole remaining alternative, their relationship is that of identity, the case may still be like that of a short stretch of time residing in a long one. If someone (the Buddhist believer in instantaneousness) should not allow that a long time is a single thing, we may give the further examples of a fire's simultaneously burning one thing and not burning another, but cooking it; or of its burning or cooking one thing and doing *another* act of burning or cooking on it; or of a cause, such as a seed, which in producing a certain effect, such as a sprout, does not produce another effect of the same cause, and thus is both productive and nonproductive.

We do not know the reality of difference from the distinctions of application to purposeful actions, for example, the application of milk to producing curds and not of sand, because we see that the same thing may be applied to different purposeful actions when accompanied by certain accessories. If you reply that it is the accessories that create the difference of application, then this is just our doctrine that difference is something extrinsic (*aupādhika*), not something ultimately real.

If difference is deduced from the universal difference supposedly caused by instantaneity, then, everything being equally different from everything else, everything may be applied to every use, or else nothing to any use. The Buddhist opponent may then say that the fact that it is not so derives from an imagined unity (between similar sorts of things acting as causes). But we may with equal justice say that the difference of application is brought about by an imagined difference of objects.

II.9, including verses 8b-9a (E54-56). Since, because of the previous arguments, it is possible for a single thing, such as Brahman, to have diverse contradictory effects, just as a fire does, there is no need to assert a real diversity of things. This is what the *Puruṣasūkta* (*Ṛg Veda* X.90) says.

Even if you imagine a real difference on account of the difference of effects or of the fixed distinction of purposeful actions, this does not explain why certain causes produce certain effects and not others. You may reply that it is because certain things have certain definite capacities that can't be known *a priori* or explained by logic. But then isn't it easier to assume one thing, Brahman, and say that It has the capacity, incomprehensible by logic, to produce many diverse effects, which in turn have fixed distinctions among themselves and always produce only certain effects and not others ?

II.10 (E56-57). *Objection* : One cause does not, in fact, have several effects, because the difference of effects is based on a difference of powers (*śakti*), which are the real, direct causes.

Answer (verses 9b-10a): If one thing may have many powers residing *in* it, without affecting its unity, can't it have many effects residing *outside* it without affecting its unity ?

Opponent (*mainly Kumārila*): Difference can be known by the *pramāṇa abhāva*. For difference is identical with reciprocal nonexistence and a nonexistence can only be known by the *pramāṇa* of the same name (viz., *abhāva*).

II.11, including verses 10b-11a (E57-58). *Answer* : No. *Abhāva* only acts with reference to some particular locus of negation and some particular negandum, thus "This is not that," or "That is not in this." But this *assumes* difference, which is what *abhāva* as a separate *pramāṇa* is posited to establish, so there is the logical fault of "mutual dependence." Also, knowledge of nonexistence is not from the bare absence of knowledge of something, but from the absence of knowledge when all of the causes of knowledge are present except the object, and the perception of some other object in its place. But this again *assumes* the difference of objects. This is true whether the knowledge of nonexistence is like an inference from the difference of objects, or from the difference of cognitions.

We have already shown that *perception* can't grasp difference immediately. Nor (contrary to the Nyāya-Vaiśeṣika view) can a second perception of the locus helped by the first perception of it and the remembrance of the negandum prove the nonexistence that is difference. For, this once more assumes the difference of locus and negandum, the very thing to be proven.

II.12, including verse 11b (E58-59). We do, in fact, see a single form in things conceived of as different, because perception, etc., do not apprehend difference, and there is no separate *pramāṇa abhāva*, as we have just shown. Every *pramāṇa* tells us that something *is*, and not that something is not or that something is different and nothing else. Thus every *pramāṇa* apprehends the common form Being (*sat*). It is not true that this common form is only produced by a second, construction-filled (*savikalpaka*) cognition, called "identification" (*anusaṃdhāna*). For, in that case even as ingle thing considered by identification with reference to its connection with different places and times would not be one. In addition, as Kumārila says, we can see other universal forms directly, for example, cowness in a herd of cows.

II.13, including verse 11b (E59-60). (Against Bhedābhedavāda, probably mainly that of Kumārila, but also perhaps that of the Jains and some Vedantins:) The existence of two cognitions, reflecting nondifference (*abheda*)—that which is continuous—and difference (*bheda*)—that which is discontinuous—does not show the ultimate reality of difference, but only its empirical reality. For, a cognition must derive from a *pramāṇa* and be in accord with logic to reflect reality, and we have shown that the cognition of difference does neither. Therefore, neither difference nor even the cognition of difference exists ultimately, but only empirically (*vyavahāra*). It is error, *avidyā*, indescribable (*na nirucyate*) as existent or nonexistent.

Four alternatives can explain the fact of these two cognitions: (1) universal (*sāmānya*) and particular (*vyakti*) are two different things that are joined together (the Nyāya-Vaiśeṣika view); (2) the thing is one, made up of both universal and particular (*viśeṣa*) (the view of Kumārila and the Jains?); (3) the particulars (*viśeṣa*) alone are the real things, nondifference is imagined on the basis of them and having them as its reference (the Buddhist view); (4) nondifference alone is ultimately real, and difference is imagined because of beginningless *avidyā*, having nondifference as the basis and reference of the imagination (Maṇḍana's own view).

II.14, including verses 12b-13a (E60-61). *Response to* (1): Universal and particular are not two different things, because we apply universal and particular terms to the same thing (*samanādhikaraṇya*), expressing identity (*parasparātmatva*), not relation (*sambandha*), saying, for example, "The pot is existent." If we did really apprehend universal and particular as different, everyone would agree on this doctrine, but they don't; rather, everyone apprehends them as identical. Moreover, we immediately perceive (*pratyakṣa*) both universal and particular together. But, if they were different, we would comprehend one of them mediately (*parokṣa*) via the other, as fire from smoke in inference.

Your special sort of relation, inherence, which supposedly unites universal and particular, is illogical, because two things must be either identical or different. The representation of two things as one is self-contradictory.

II.15 (E61-62). *Objection* : Inherence can conceal the difference of two things, as the conjunction of fire and iron conceals their difference.

Answer (including verses 13b-14a) : Then one thing may also appear as many, as in the case of "variegated color" (*citrarūpa*) (which the Nyāya-Vaiśeṣika accepts as a separate color), or the cognition of a city that is a unity but appears witht he forms of the various things in the city (a Buddhist account).

II.16, including verse 17 (E62-64). Everyday usage (*vyavahāra*—here clearly meant both as practical activity and as verbal usage) is not a criterion of what really is. You the opponent (Nyāya-Vaiśeṣika, Mīmāṃsā ?) may say that qualities (*guṇa*) and universals (*jāti*) are *upādhis* different from substances (*dravya*), but yet in sentences such as "the cow is white" we identify both a universal, cowness, and a quality, white, with a substance, the individual cow. But the content of thought and that of verbal usage are the same. Therefore thought also is not a sure guide to reality, and the thought of difference is not a proof of its reality.

The awareness of the continuous and the discontinuous may be explained not by an objective reality, but by a defect in the knower, just as we see visual errors may arise solely from defects of the subject, such as eye disease or strong emotions, without any exterior cause. *Avidyā* is this defect which accounts for the apprehension of difference, and it resides in the individual.

II.17 (E64). *Response to position* (2): To say that the thing is one but comprises two elements, the continuous (*avyāvṛtta*) universal and the discontinuous (*vyāvṛtta*) particular, is self-contradictory and therefore impossible. No cognition that is self-contradictory, for example, doubt, can be a *pramāṇa.*

(Verse 18) If there is no contradiction in essence, that is, reciprocal nonexistence, between universal and particular, they are simply one thing, and there is no difference between them; if there is a contradiction, they are simply two.

II.18, including verse 19 (E64-65). You cannot say that the difference comes not from a difference of essence but from a biformity in the cognition, the object itself remaining one, for either the cognition grasps two forms, in which case there are two objects, or it grasps one form, in which case there is only one object.

II.19, including verse 20 (E65-66). *Objection* : If universal and particular are not different, why is a second cognition necessary to know one of them after first knowing the other ?

II.20, including verse 21 (E66-67). *Answer* : Since according to your doctrine the essence of the object is compounded of universal and particular, the essence of the object does not carry over into other objects, and therefore you must say that the particulars alone are real.

Objection : That which carries over into other objects may not be the object itself, but it may be a component part (*aṃśa*) of it; otherwise the cognition of something shared with other objects would be an imagination without a cause (*nirbīja kalpanā*).

Answer : This "component part" may be the thing itself, and then it will be different from the particular. Or it may be some other thing than that thing, and the absurdity will result that there are three things, universal, particular, and that which possesses them. Therefore this "part," being neither the thing itself nor another separate thing, is the object of imagination, indescribable as identical with the thing or different from it (*tattvānyatvābhyām anirvacanīya*).

Objection : The part is neither the thing itself nor another thing nor not a thing at all, because nonexistent things like sky lotuses cannot be portions of anything. (In other words, the opponent tries to define the relationship of the part to the object in purely negative terms, to avoid the contradictions that will follow if it is described positively as identical or different. He implicitly denies that the "indescribability" of the relationship means that it is purely imagined.) Since the universal portion of an object may carry over into other things, the thing itself carries over (and therefore things are partly identical with each other, because the portion is not different from the object itself).

Answer : But since the other portion, the particular portion, does not carry over, the thing itself doesn't carry over. Moreover, if the thing is a collection of universal and particular, then, if *both* portions don't carry over, the thing itself does not carry over at all, and therefore things are really just different from each other, and not the same at all.

II.21, including verse 22 (E67-68). On the other hand, since one portion, the universal, that is, such forms as (being an) existent, a substance, and the like, does carry over in all things, everything will be identical with everything else, and this is just our doctrine of non-difference. For example, a horse sharing such universals as those just named with a cow, will carry over into a cow and be identical with it and vice versa. If you say that the particular does not carry over, then only difference will be real, as we proved before. There is no way to avoid the alternatives of absolute difference and absolute nondifference.

II.22, including verse 23 (E68). The same argument works against those (the Digambara Jains) who say that there is ar elation of difference and nondifference between the substance and its modes (*paryaya*). They seek to establish both the nondifference of substance, for example, of gold, by the indifference of one whose desire is merely for gold to what forms it is in, and the difference of modes, for example, of a plate and a necklace, by the joy and sorrow of those who want one or the other mode when it is changed into another mode. But in fact, either the thing carries over into another thing, in which case it will be the substance that is the thing, since the other portion, the mode, is absent; or if the thing itself does not carry over, the thing itself will be just the modes, since the same substance is found elsewhere. A portion isolated out of a thing is merely imaginary, because the object is mixed (*citra*) on this account, and the portion is not mixed (and therefore not the object and therefore not real. It is important to note that "thing," *vastu*, has the double meaning of both "object" and also "reality.")

II.23, including verse 24 (E68-69). In addition, if, as you say, substance is not merely different, but also nondifferent from its modes, then if some mode were destroyed and another produced, the substance itself would be in the old mode, abide as itself, and be produced in the new mode. It would follow that there would be a confusion (*saṃkara*) in the reactions of joy, sorrow, and indifference of those who want the new mode, the old mode, and the substance. But in fact there is a fixed distinction among them. You hold that neither difference nor nondifference is absolute. But if *nothing* is absolute, the nonabsoluteness itself is not absolute, and therefore you cannot say that nondifference is not absolute, and so you cannot avoid the confusion of reactions.

II.25, including verse 26 (E69-70). Now let us examine the remaining options of the four (that were stated at II.13) : (3) difference alone is real, and (4) nondifference alone is real.

Response to position (3): It is impossible that difference alone is real and that the imagination of nondifference is based on it. For difference is relative and can't be apprehended without first apprehending some second thing as different from the first. But this in turn depends on previously having apprehended difference. Therefore difference cannot be apprehended. But if it is not apprehended, it cannot be the basis for the imagination of nondifference.

The apprehension of nondifference, on the other hand, does not depend on a previous apprehension of nondifference, nor on the apprehension of difference. Therefore, having apprehended nondifference, taking it as basis, there is, on account of the inability to ascertain it as it is, the imagination of difference. The cognition of identification (*anusaṃdhāna*) "this is that" does not imply difference, because it may be applied to what all agree is a single object, but considered with reference to different places and times.

II.26, including verse 27 (E70-71). Everyone can experience for himself that the first perception grasps the bare object and is without constructions (*vikalpa*), whereas the cognitions with constructions[30] that follow plunge into particulars. Moreover, it is self-contradictory to say that the first perception grasps the object along with its particulars, but that the particulars, not yet being linked with words, are not noticed. A thing must either appear in a cognition or be absent from it.

II.27, including verse 28 (E71). We have shown that neither (1) nor (2) is possible, that is, (1) neither are universal and particular different things, and (2) nor are they portions of a single thing. Therefore either the universal or the particular must be false. This can't be the bare object.[31] For, as we see in everyday errors, such as the mistaking of a piece of shell for silver, we are never mistaken about the bare reality "this," which appears (i.e., it is constant in the first, erroneous, cognition "this is silver," and in the later correct cognition "this is shell.") The particulars, silver and shell, on the other hand, are not constant.

Objection : It is in the *manas* alone that error resides. Therefore the different sensory cognitions are not errors, and they establish difference.

Answer : No. The senses themselves may err, because we find that errors may correspond to the defects of the sense organs.

II.28, including verse 29 (E71-72). *Objection* (*a Buddhist*) : Entities have mutually exclusive individual marks (*vyāvṛttasvalakṣaṇa*). Therefore reciprocal nonexistence is either their essence or an attribute of them. Otherwise the phrase "mutually exclusive" would lack an occasion for its use, and so would be meaningless.

Answer : Reciprocal nonexistence cannot be the essence of things, because if one thing first exists independently, another whose form is its nonexistence may also exist, but if everything is by essence reciprocal nonexistence, nothing at all can exist, because everything's existence is dependent on everything else. If, on the other hand, you say that reciprocal nonexistence is an attribute, that is, an extrinsic property (*upādhi*) of entities, then in their *essence* they don't differ. If you say that reciprocal nonexistence is not a something (*kaścit*), which could be either the same as entities or different, that is just our position: if reciprocal nonexistence is not anything, then nondifference is proven.

We see that nondifference is the basis of difference, as a face is the basis of its various reflections. The reflections are not real new different things, because their dimensions differ from the original and from each other (and therefore they are a sort of error).

The cognition of oneness in a collection, such as a forest of trees, is not *ultimately* based on difference, because then there would be an infinite regress, and nothing would ever be one. Whenever we do stop, that cognition will be of unity, not of difference, and therefore it will not have difference as its basis.

II.29, including verses 30-31 (E72). Difference, for example, that of reflections, always appears as penetrated by the nondifference, for example, of the original object. Therefore difference is false. Similarly, the difference of the universe (*viśva*) is penetrated by the nondifference expressed by "this," "that," "object," "thing." In the case of differences such as that of the trees in a forest, even if we were to grant that the difference were not false, still, the case is different in that the unity expressed by such words as "forest" is not in each tree severally.

II.30, including verse 32 (E72-73). If the essences or individual natures of things are mutually exclusive, the proponent of the reality of difference must explain the appearance and practical usage of nondifference. (a) It can't be from similarity (*sādṛśya*), because things are *ex hypothesi* utterly unconnected. (b) It can't be from mere failure to note exclusion, because if exclusion isn't noticed in things that are mutually exclusive, when *will* it be noticed ? (c) It can't be from the fact that perception is not final knowledge (*niścaya*, here used as equal to *savikalpa jñāna*). For we observe that there is practical usage (*vyavahāra*, including *verbal* usage) based both on difference, for example, of a cow from other cows, and on nondifference, for example, of the universal cowness. Therefore nondifference occurs not just on the level of perception (which Maṇḍana apparently thinks must be *nirvikalpa*), but also on that of practical usage (which is dependent on *savikalpa* cognition). (d) It can't be because different things may perform one purposeful action, excluding those which don't perform it. Purposeful actions are just as different from each other as everything else is, and every exclusion is different from every other exclusion.

You may try to avoid these problems by saying that mutual exclusion is not the essence of things. But then how can it belong to them as the same in all of them ?

Objection : It may have as its basis beginningless traces (*saṃskāra*), rather than being dependent on any particular feature residing in the object.

Answer : But then there would be no restriction as to what things appeared nondifferent from each other. Therefore you must assume certain real capacities in things by nature different from each other, which capacities produce the idea of nondifference. But these capacities are on your hypothesis contrary to the [utterly different natures of the entities that possess them (i.e., they are the same whereas the objects are different)]. It is more economical to assume one single thing that by its greatness appears as many.

II.31, including verse 33 (E73). This idea is as good as the other three positions (see II.13), all of which say that usage based on nondifference is in accordance with appearance, not reality. (1) Those who teach a conjunction of universal and particular must admit that there is usage based on the false identification of universal and particular, which are different. (2) Those who teach a mixed object must say that both usages (of difference and nondifference) are according to appearance only, since the thing itself is mixed and its nature does not carry over—as was said above. (3) Those who teach absolute difference must say that the usage of nondifference is in accord with appearance only. So it is just as reasonable for us to assume that the usage of nondifference is in accordance with reality and that of difference with appearance.

CHAPTER THREE : INJUNCTIONS (NIYOGAKĀṆḌA)

III.1 (E74). We will now refute those who say that the Veda is a *pramāṇa* only for things to be done that are the objects of injunction (*vidhi*, *codanā*), not for things already in existence, and that therefore what the texts of the Upaniṣads teach is the injunction "One should perform knowledge of the Self"; they do not teach the Self directly.

Now, there may be three sorts of knowledge of the Brahman-Self that might be the object of such an Upaniṣadic injunction : (1) verbal knowledge, from language (*śabda*) (refuted below, III.2-46); (2) immediate manifestation (*sākṣātkaraṇa*) without constructions (*vikalpa*) (refuted below, III.47-68); and (3) meditational knowledge, called *dhyāna*, *bhāvanā*, or *upāsanā*, consisting in a continuous succession (*saṃtāna*) of verbal knowledge (refuted below, III.69).

(1) *Refutation of verbal knowledge of the Self as the object of an injunction*

III.2, including verse 1 (E74-75). The verbal knowledge of Brahman cannot be enjoined, because this knowledge arises directly from hearing Vedic sentences about Brahman, without any need for an injunction.

III.3, including verse 2 (E75-76). If to understand the meaning of a sentence an injunction were needed, we would need an injunction to understand the sentence communicating the injunction, and another to understand the latter injunction, and thus would enter an infinite regress.

III.4, including verses 3-4 (E76). The end of an injunction is activity, posterior to the hearing of the injunction, but the understanding of the injunction is simultaneous with hearing it.

If the indicative sentences of the Upaniṣads give knowledge of Brahman, there is no *need* to enjoin the knowledge; if they do not, there is no *use* in enjoining a verbal knowledge that can't be obtained. Nor can the injunction add "certainty" (*niścaya*): if indicative language can't give it, some other *pramāṇa* than language is necessary, not an injunction.

III.5, including verses 5-7 (E76-77). *Objection* : An injunction of knowledge serves to avert the suspicion that there is no intended meaning, as in the case of *mantras* meant solely for recitation (*japa*).

Answer : No, because according to the *Mīmāṃsāsūtras* the meaning of words should be taken to be the same in the Veda as in secular language, unless proven otherwise. Just as an injunctive word has a meaning by itself without depending upon another injunctive word to establish that it is not meaningless, so we can observe that the indicative words about Brahman have a meaning in themselves and do not require an injunction to reassure themselves they are not meaningless.

III.6, including verses 8-9 (E77-78). *Objection* : An injunction is necessary to know that Self-knowledge is a human good (*puruṣārtha*).

Answer : No, injunctions inform us of *future* results, but the result of knowledge, that is, the pervasion of the object by the knower, its becoming clear to him, occurs immediately.

Liberation can't be a future fruit, because it is not something accomplished by a cause; if it were, it would cease. Liberation is something positive—unsurpassable bliss and lordship (*aiśvarya*)—and, though negative effects, such as (liberation defined as) the posterior nonexistence of connection with the body, etc., can be unending, effects that are positive can't. If you say that liberation is the cessation of the *causes* of bondage, which is the object of an injunction, we respond that the cause is *avidyā*, and its destruction is nothing other than knowledge. Liberation is abiding in one's own form, which is not something to be effected. If you (trying to preserve the need for an injunction, which always has an effect in view) say that we may accept that liberation is an unending (positive) effect on the strength of scripture, we reply that one shouldn't interpret scripture as contrary to ordinary experience as long as it can be explained otherwise.

III.7, including verses 10-12 (E78-79). *Objection* : Even though there may be no fruit of the knowledge of Brahman subsequent to that very knowledge, an injunction is still necessary for the texts about Brahman to be authoritative (*pramāṇa*). For if they merely state what is already in existence, they must merely repeat (*anuvāda*) what can be known from another *pramāṇa*, and therefore are not themselves an independent *pramāṇa*.

III.8, including verses 13-14 (E79). *Answer* : The Veda is an independent *pramāṇa* if it tells something unknowable by another *pramāṇa*, even when it gives information about something already existent.

III.9, including verses 15-16a (E79-80). Perception and inference are independent *pramāṇas*, even though their object also is something already existent. Vedic language, not being derived from the thoughts of any person, is an independent *pramāṇa*. Human language, on the other hand, communicates first that a man has a certain thought, and only then does it communicate the object of that thought.

III.10, including verses 16b-17a (E80-81). *Objection* : With regard to already existent things, which can be known both by language and by other *pramāṇas*, there is a suspicion that one of those other *pramāṇas* may contradict language. Therefore language about things already existent depends on the other *pramāṇa*, on its noncontradiction of language, to ratify its validity. Being dependent, it is not an independent *pramāṇa* by itself. On the other hand, injunctive language, about things to be done in the future, communicates what cannot be known by any other *pramāṇa* and is therefore independent as a *pramāṇa*. Therefore an injunction to know Brahman is necessary to establish the validity of the Upaniṣadic sentences about Brahman.

Answer : If the possibility of being contradicted by another *pramāṇa* makes a *pramāṇa* cease to be independent, why can't we say that the other *pramāṇas* are dependent on language, inasmuch as they may be contradicted by it ?

III.11, including verses 17b-18 (E81). Besides, the fact that two *pramāṇas* may each grasp the same object does not make one dependent on the other, because we see that perception and inference may both apprehend the same object, and that several senses may apprehend Being (*sattā*), qualityness (*guṇatva*) and substance (*dravya*). In the case of secular language it is the very fact of its object being apprehended by another *pramāṇa* that makes language a *pramāṇa*; how much less can nonpersonal Vedic language, whose object can't be known from other *pramāṇas*, be prevented from being an independent *pramāṇa* about things already existing.

III.12, including verses 19-20 (E81-82). If (as the school of Prabhākara assumes) it is being a "command" (*niyoga*—a Prābhākara technical term) that makes language an independent *pramāṇa*, then commands in secular language would necessarily be independent and valid *pramāṇas*, whereas we see they may be dependent or invalid.

III.13, including verse 21 (E82). *Objection* : Human commands are preceded by a desire to communicate the desire of ends and means, which desire, being a thought of a person, does not exist in the nonpersonal Veda.

Answer : Then it is the presence or absence of a personal thought that is the cause of the dependence or independence of language as a *pramāṇa*, not whether or not the sentence refers to something already accomplished, or whether or not it can be known by another *pramāṇa*.

III.14, including verses 22-23 (E82). *Objection* : Vedic language intends a command (*niyoga*), unknowable by any other *pramāṇa*, whereas injunctions in secular language intend the "application" (*viniyoga*) of means to ends, which can be known by other *pramāṇas*. Therefore Vedic language is an independent *pramāṇa*, whereas secular language is dependent.

Answer : No, because words have the same meanings in the Veda and in secular language.

III.15, including verses 24-27a (E82-83). *Objection* : Commands can only be known from the Veda, whereas applications can be known from other *pramāṇas*.

Answer : In saying this, you are admitting that it is not the mere *possibility* that an object may be known by some other *pramāṇa* that causes language to be dependent, but the fact that, as is the case in secular language, language is employed only after something has been known by another *pramāṇa*. For, you have just assumed that the application of means to ends may be known both by the *pramāṇa* language and by other *pramāṇas*. In the case of human verbal communication, it is a speaker who talks of what is possible to be apprehended, and who would not speak of something without having known it, who is regarded as reliable. Conversely, it is one who speaks of what it is impossible to apprehend, or who might speak of something without having known it, who is unreliable, whose speech is not a *pramāṇa*. The Buddha is an example. (The implication seems to be that at least in the case of human language, it is that whose object is a thing that might be "apprehended"—that is, by another *pramāṇa* than language—that is *pramāṇa*, not that whose object can't be apprehended by another *pramāṇa*.)

III.16, including verses 27b-28 (E83-84). Therefore the sole cause whether or not language is dependent as a *pramāṇa* is whether it is personal or nonpersonal. And, whether its object is something already existent or something to be done in the future is irrelevant to whether it is dependent. If, as *Mīmāṃsāsūtra* I.1.5 says, "The relationship of word and object is natural (*autpattika*)," it is not necessarily true that language is preceded by thoughts of persons based on other *pramāṇas*, and is therefore dependent. The effort of *Mīmāṃsāsūtra* I.1.4 and commentary to show that no other *pramāṇa* for *dharma* is possible than Vedic impulsion (*codanā*) is not meant to show that Vedic language is independent and a *pramāṇa*, but to show that no other pretended *pramāṇa* for *dharma* is possible, lest someone accept something like the words of the Buddha as such a *pramāṇa*.

Objection : But then, for the Veda to be a finally authoritative *pramāṇa* we must prove that any other *pramāṇa* for the things it communicates is impossible, and so the Veda's being a *pramāṇa* is dependent on the absence of any other such *pramāṇa*.

Answer : Even if it depends on the absence of another *pramāṇa*, it is not dependent on another *pramāṇa*. Anyway, if the language of the Veda ceased to be a *pramāṇa* merely because another *pramāṇa* for its object were possible, the same would hold true for ordinary *pramāṇas* such as perception, inference, and the like (which is absurd). Moreover, you maintain that Vedic language teaches certain already existent things *by way of* teaching things to be done. Now, another *pramāṇa* might be possible for these already existent things, and might contradict Vedic language. And so the Veda would cease to be a *pramāṇa* equally on your opinion as on ours. But in fact, as we said before, it is not whether or not another *pramāṇa* is possible for the same object that determined the dependency of a *pramāṇa*, but whether or not it is personal, that is, preceded by the thought of a person.

III.17, including verse 29 (E84-85). *Objection* : The presence of an injunction is necessary to supply the action of a verb, without which the remaining words of a sentence are not connected.

Answer : Then the verb "is" may be supplied where necessary.

III.18, including verses 30-32 (E85-86). *Objection* (*Prābhākara*): The meaning of "is" is that something is apprehensible by a *pramāṇa*; therefore sentences of which "is" is the verb must convey an object whose knowledge is dependent upon another *pramāṇa*, and so these sentences cannot be by themselves an independent *pramāṇa*.

Answer : No, because a *pramāṇa* may be in contact with an object in any one of the three times, past, present, and future, and so its existence may give the ideas "was," "is," and "will be," not just the idea "is" alone.

III.19, including verses 33-34a (E86-87). *Objection* : In inference it is precisely the *present* contact with a logical mark (*liṅga* = *hetu*) that lets us know the possibility of something's being knowable by perception in the past, present, or future, and therefore we have the idea of the three times.

Answer : No, because there are objects knowable only by inference, never at any time by perception.

Anyway, if the meaning of "is" is the existence of a *pramāṇa* (other than language), this will be equally true in the case of the Veda (which will then not give us knowledge otherwise inaccessible, which knowledge we agree it does give us).

III.20, including verses 34b-35a (E87). *Objection* : Inference and Vedic language differ in that the object of inference can be reached by another *pramāṇa*, but not so Brahman as the object of Vedic language, because it lacks any distinctive qualifying attributes (*viśeṣa*) to act as logical mark.

Answer : No, because once *avidyā* is absorbed Brahman may also be known by direct vision (*sākṣātkāra*).

III.21, including verses 35b-36a (E87). If it is solely the fact of being known at present by a *pramāṇa* that constitutes Being, then everything that is known at present will itself be present, there will be no threefold temporality in objects.

III.22, including verses 36b-38 (E87-88). Is that which constitutes Being (a) being connected with a *present pramāṇa*, or (b) being connected with *any pramāṇa* ?

If (a), we would always say of any object of memory (considered as a *pramāṇa*), "It is," whereas we actually say neither "It is" nor "It is not" (but rather "It was").

If (b), objects once known and then destroyed would exist and serve purposeful action, and we would never desire to know if something once known still exists.

III.23, including verse 39 (E88-89). *Objection* : Then it is capability (*yogyatva*) of being joined with a *pramāṇa* that constitutes Being.

Answer : This "capability" is nothing but the nature of the object, and therefore there is no need to make the existence of a *pramāṇa* a condition of the existence of the object. Similarly, when we say a blue object is one capable of being known as having the form blue, the knowledge of blue is not a condition of the word "blue."

Conclusion : Since "is" therefore denotes the nature of the object, a sentence in which the meaning of "is" predominates communicates, without dependence on another *pramāṇa*, the nature of the object.

III.24 (E89-91). Even if there are many natures of objects, and not a single (universal called) "Being," our present point still stands—that it is not the connection with a *pramāṇa* that causes the use of the word "is."

(*Against Prabhākara, Nyāya-Vaiśeṣika, and the Buddhists, who deny the reality of Being considered as the highest universal* :) Nonetheless, there is, in fact, only a single Being; otherwise the same word "is" could not be applied to an infinite number of objects, since we see that homonymous (in the Scholastic sense—*sādhāraṇa*) words, such as "organ" (*akṣa*)[32] apply only to a limited number of class characteristics (*jāti*) or extrinsic indicatory marks (*upalakṣaṇa*). This universal subsumes the three universals supposed by the Nyāya-Vaiśeṣika to be the most inclusive true universals, namely, being a substance, being a quality, and being a motion (*dravyatva, guṇatva, karmatva*). "Being" thus has one meaning, not three separate ones. Besides, there is no reason to say that such categories as universal, particularity, and inherence (*sāmānya, viśeṣa, samavāya*) cannot be said to "be" in the same way as substance, quality, and action. You can't say we apply the word "is" to them metaphorically, because metaphorical usage requires something in common, and that common thing would be precisely what is meant by the term "Being." Being must be one, not just a term applied to several properties, one or the other of which every sort of entity (*padārtha*) must have. For a collection requires some single thing to unify its members, and if the single thing is merely the fact of having the word "being" applied to them, we cannot be sure it includes *all* entities. And if there is no common element that includes all entities, we will not be able to know whether any system's set of categories includes all entities, and consequently to tell whether that system is true.

Objection : The single all-inclusive thing necessary is being susceptible to a *pramāṇa*, or else capacity for purposeful action (*arthakriyā*).

Answer : Then there is no need for a number of properties to define being, and the two things you suggest may be merely indicatory marks (*upalakṣaṇa*) of Being, which is a single property common to all things that are. Also, if there were several occasions (*nimitta*) for the use of the word "being," we could be in doubt as to which was in question, as in the case of the word "organ"—but we see it is not so.

But in fact the single thing that is Being is neither (1) the *pramāṇa*, nor (2) purposeful action. (1) It cannot be the *pramāṇa* either (a) as true qualifier (*viśeṣaṇa*=*jāti*) or (b) as indicatory sign (*upalakṣaṇa*). It is not (a) the *pramāṇa* as qualifier, because as explained in III.18, a *pramāṇa* may refer to *past* things, because a *pramāṇa* is known after it has completed its operation of producing knowledge, so cannot qualify that knowledge; and because one may have doubt about the existence of some things even though we know there is no *pramāṇa* by which we might know them, whereas there can be no doubt whether or not a thing is qualified in a certain way once we know the qualifier is absent. It is not (b), the *pramāṇa* as indicatory mark, because the relationship of indicatory sign and thing indicated remains even after the sign has perished, but "is" is not applied to things that have perished or whose existence is in doubt.

The single unitary thing that is Being (2) cannot be purposeful action. If it were, we couldn't use the word "being" for anything before seeing its effect. If it is the *pramāṇa* itself that is the effect, the idea "it is" would come not from the *pramāṇa* by itself, but from something else (i.e., the subsequent second-degree apperception of the *pramāṇa*).

Moreover, every object is qualified by being as qualifier (*viśeṣaṇa*), and the object cannot be qualified by its supposed efficaciousness (*arthakriyā*), namely, *pramāṇa*, because they aren't simultaneous. If having an effect is not a qualifier but an indicatory sign of being, it would again result that what is past exists.

(*Reprise and summary of previous argument on being, with no new material.*) Neither purposeful action nor *pramāṇa* can be made the criterion of being or nonbeing, because the idea of being is already present in them—there would be an infinite regress. Therefore Being (*sattā*) equals the nature of object(s), and it is one.

III.25, including verse 40 (E91). *Objection* : But a definition of "capability" (*yogyatva*) (to be joined with a *pramāṇa*, i.e., of being) other than "having the nature of object," is possible, namely, the existence of a cause of a *pramāṇa* (*pramāṇa-hetu-sadbhāva*).

Answer: No. A treasure trove buried in the earth, without present perception, inferential sign, anything that can't be explained without assuming it, or living witnesses, is inaccessible to all *pramāṇas*, and yet we may wonder whether such a thing "is" or "is not."

III.26, including verse 41 (E91-92). Besides, because it is the function of *pramāṇas* to distinguish what is and is not, nonbeing can also be the object of a *pramāṇa*, and therefore the existence of a *pramāṇa* can't be the definition of being.

III.27, including verses 42-43a (E92). We know nonexistence, for instance, that of thorns in a spot we are considering stepping on. This is not (1) simply the knowledge of other things present, because we can perceive other things even where there *are* thorns and before looking at the spot of ground. Nor is it (2) the bare absence of determination (*pariccheda*) of thorns, because that exists even before we examine the place, and anyway we can't reflect upon this absence unless it is already assumed that absences are objects of knowledge.

III.28, including verses 43b-44a (E92-93). Nor is the knowledge of nonexistence merely (3) the absence of determination of the object when the other causes of determination are present. For there is no difference in that absence whether or not the thing inquired about *can* in fact be the object of *pramāṇas* (which also is against your own suggested definition of being as the existence of a *pramāṇa*).

III.29, including verses 44b-46 (E93). Neither is the knowledge of nonexistence merely (4) the knowledge of the spot isolated from other things. (a) If it is the isolation of the *knowledge* from other things than the spot, there would never be any need for a closer examination of the spot after a rough glance at it. (b) If it is the isolation of the *object* of knowledge, then (1) if the object is isolated in its own proper form, then the knowledge of this, the proper form, would be present even if it were mixed up with other things. If (2) it is isolated in conjunction with a qualifier, the only possible qualifier would be the *absence* of thorns (which is against your hypothesis).

III.30, including verses 46b-47a (E93-94). What is the object of the cognition and the verbal expression "is not" ? If you say it is the nonexistence of a *pramāṇa*, why can't it be the nonexistence of the object itself, for both are equally nonexistent?

III.31, including verses 47b-51a (E94). *Objection* : The idea and verbal expression "is not" are errors, arising in the absence of the idea and verbal expression of "is."

Answer : No, because this nonexistence is present even when there is no awareness, as in deep sleep, and so in deep sleep we would have the idea of the nonexistence of the whole universe.

Error requires the apprehension of a locus (*viṣaya*) of superimposition and of the thing superimposed, but nonexistences, such as the nonexistence of the idea and verbal expression "is," can't be a locus or thing superimposed.

III.32, including verses 51b-53a (E94-95). Even if we grant for the sake of the argument that being is capability for a *pramāṇa*, still the statements of the Upaniṣads are not dependent on another *pramāṇa*. For the existence of the object of the texts of the Upaniṣads, that is, Brahman, may then be defined as Its fitness for a *pramāṇa*, specifically tradition (*āgama* = *veda*). And, because this is the *only* *pramāṇa* for Brahman, it is independent of any other. Nor is another *pramāṇa*, other than a sentence saying this object exists, necessary to tell us about the object as qualified, because that is included in the existence of the object.

III.33, including verses 53b-58 (E95-96). Even if we were to grant that a *pramāṇa* for Brahman other than Vedic language is possible, tradition is still a *pramāṇa* for it.

Language is still a *pramāṇa* even when it is connected with another *pramāṇa*, as in the case of a qualified person communicating his knowledge. It is indeed dependent—on the speaker's knowledge—as far as the object goes, because the hearer does not think "This object is thus," but "This person has such-and-such knowledge." It is independent insofar as it is a *pramāṇa* for the latter apprehension, which in turn gives rise in the hearer to the former. One may, to be sure, reject human speech as regards its being a *pramāṇa* without necessarily rejecting its object, on the grounds that this speech is dependent if its object is something beyond the senses that no human being could know. An example would be the words of the Buddha. Similarly one rejects the speech of a liar on the grounds that one knows from some *pramāṇa* that he does not tell things as he has seen them. But a qualified person's speech is rejected neither in respect to its being a *pramāṇa* nor in respect to its object. If a qualified person's speech were not independent as regards its being a *pramāṇa*, there would be no practical activity based on words, but there is. Thus, even if the *object* of the texts of the Upaniṣads can be known by another *pramāṇa*, they are still a *pramāṇa*.

Indeed, the Vedānta texts do bring us to a *pramāṇa* other than themselves, one that is supernatural (*alaukika*), without the division of knower and object of knowledge, self-luminous; and they may be dependent, as regards their object—not as regards their being a *pramāṇa*—on this.

III.34, including verses 59-64 (E96-98). Therefore being is not the fact of being knowable by a *pramāṇa*.

Objection : We have the idea of a universal when we recollect (*avamarśa*) a form previously seen, as when seeing one cow we recall another and think, "This is the same." But we do not have this recollection of one "being" with respect to another one seen later.

Answer : The "recollection" may be either (a) the appearance of the previous form of the mind (*buddhi*), or (b) the identification (*anusaṃdhāna*) of earlier and later in the form "This is that."

(a) Between two things with the same universal one never sees a complete identity like that of seeing the same individual twice. Yet one sees a common universal shared by all existent things, by their difference from absolute nonexistence. Something may share one universal with one thing and another universal with another.

III.35, including verses 65-67a (E98). In regard to (b), we say that "identification" is not from the bringing together of two things, but from the appearance of a nondifferent form, because it may be performed with reference to the same object at the *same* place and time. Nor do we have this cognition with reference to a jug and a cup, which nonetheless share the universal clay. When the common traits are more numerous and more in evidence than the differences, we say that it is "that" (sort of thing).

III.36, including verses 67b-68a (E98-99). "Being" is not occasioned by connection with something else (namely, a *pramāṇa*) that serves as its qualifier, as in the case of words like "having-a-stick" or "cooking." The application of a qualifier precedes the idea of a thing as qualified, whereas the idea of a *pramāṇa*, being inferred from its effect, knowledge, is apprehended *after* being is apprehended. Since the idea of being and the idea of a *pramāṇa* are not simultaneous, they are not connected (as qualified and qualifier). There is a difference of time as past, present, and future on the basis of the time of connection with the *pramāṇa*, but this connection is not a true qualifier of being, but an extrinsic adjunct (*upādhi*).

III.37, including verses 68b-69a (E99). The argument has been assuming that there is no connection of the meanings of words without an action, and that "is" can stand as the word for that action. But now Maṇḍana says, against III.17 : It is not true that there is no connection of the meanings of the individual words in a sentence without an action. Such sentences as "The man (is) the king's (servant)," or "The trees (are) in fruit" communicate the relation of one thing to another, not the existence of anything.

III.38, including verses 69b-70a (E99-100). Still, even if there is in fact no connection of words into a sentence without an action, there is no problem in getting the indicative sentences of the Veda to communicate Brahman without reference to an injunction, because certain sentences in the Upaniṣads communicate the existence of Brahman as cause of the world by stating the origination of the world from It.

III.39, including verses 70b-73a (E100-102). *Objection* : In secular language the connection of the meanings of words is dependent on another *pramāṇa* (i.e., it is the knowledge gained from another *pramāṇa* that is expressed in the sentence); where there is conflict with other *pramāṇas*, in nonsense sentences, there is no connection of word meanings. But in Vedic language, whose objects other *pramāṇas* can't arrive at, the connection of word meanings depends on an injunction.

Answer : No. (1) The *hearer* does not employ the other *pramāṇas*; otherwise language would be useless. (2) The fact that the hearer may use the other *pramāṇas* to determine that the things referred to by the words are susceptible to connection is true with reference both to secular and to Vedic language—which destroys your distinction. (3) It is the desire to express (*vivakṣa*) that produces the connection of words, not a *pramāṇa* other than language, because that's what conveys the meaning to the hearer, and that's what makes the speaker speak. (4) We understand the speech of a liar, although there is no other *pramāṇa* for the meaning he communicates, since it is untrue. (5) We can understand the connection even where the meaning of the sentence is contradicted by other *pramāṇas*. Otherwise there would be no difference between meaningless and false sentences. (6) Even if it is the fact that the speaker has knowledge gained by another *pramāṇa* that gives the word-meaning connection, nevertheless the place of the other *pramāṇa* may in the case of the Veda be taken by the object described, Brahman itself. In addition, introducing an injunction won't solve the problem any better, because there is no other *pramāṇa* for it any more than for the content of Vedic indicative sentences. Since the Veda has no speaker, there is the difficulty that there is no person whose having a *pramāṇa* for a certain thing is conveyed by the Veda, in the case of both indicative and injunctive sentences alike. (7) In Vedic and secular language equally, we conclude by presumption (*arthāpatti*) from the meaninglessness of words by themselves, not the presence of another *pramāṇa* in the speaker's mind, but the connection of the meanings of the words into a whole. (8) Or, if secular and Vedic language are different in this regard, then in secular language we may arrive by presumption at the presence of a *pramāṇa* in the speaker, but in Vedic language words may convey their meaning independently (either of another *pramāṇa* *or* of an injunction).

III.40, including verses 73b-78a (E102-103). By presumption (*ākṣepa* = *arthāpatti*) we deduce the connection of the meanings of the words in a sentence from the fact that without such connection a series of words does not communicate any new object. There is no need to introduce a similar presumption of the connectedness of the meanings of words from the fact that otherwise the injunctive word would be useless. Besides, if the object corresponding to the injunctive word in a sentence is not knowable by another *pramāṇa*, one cannot know the connection of that word and the thing it refers to, and so cannot know how to act in obedience to the injunction.

III.41, including verses 78b-80a (E104). *Objection* : The connection of the injunctive word and its object is learned by a child not from the word directly, but is inferred to be in the minds of others by observing the use of it by an older person and the action of another person brought about by its use. But this knowledge and use on the part of the child's elders is still dependent on the word.

III.42, including verses 80b-85a. (E104-110) *Answer* : If it is inferred, language is not the sole *pramāṇa* for it. All use of language is preceded by inference (in learning it), as in your example. Therefore inference and language are like the seed and the sprout; neither is first. Moreover, because every understanding of a word is preceded by an inference by which its meaning is learned, the word is purely repetitive, and therefore not a source of new knowledge. Injunction (*niyoga*), for instance, is knowable by a *pramāṇa* other than language. The *learner's* knowledge of the object (in his case injunction) is not solely from the word, even though the observed *hearer's* knowledge of it may be (at that particular time).

Inasmuch as the learning (*vyutpatti*) of the relation of the injunctive word and its meaning arrives only at the existence of some cause of activity or another, there is no reason to infer a special nonsecular (*alaukika*) cause of activity in the Veda different from those we see in secular speech (such as the *niyoga* of Prabhākara). In fact (as the Mīmāṃsā principle states), words should be taken to have the same meaning in the Veda as they have in secular speech.

Objection : We know the existence of the nonsecular cause of activity by two successive inferences, first, the inference of some cause of activity or another, and then, second, an inference from the absence of everyday secular causes of activity to the Vedic cause of activity's being of another, nonsecular, sort.

Answer : Then the nonsecular cause is also known by *inference*, and not just by language. Anyway, the fact that the activity prescribed by the Veda is a means of happiness is a cause of activity (and therefore Prabhākara's *niyoga* is unnecessary). Also, if one cannot know the thing corresponding to the Vedic injunctive word by some *pramāṇa* other than language, one cannot know the connection of the word with it, and therefore the use and meaning of the word. For one can know the relation of two things only if both things are already known.

Objection : It is the power (*śakti, sāmarthya*) of the word that is the connection of the word. But the word is connected not with the object but with the idea of the object, because the effect of this connection defined as power cannot be the object, because that is already in existence, and so it must be the idea, which is not already in existence before the use of the word. In our case, that of learning the use of injunctive words from watching the activity of elders, this idea is learned by inference from the observed activity. [The point—implied, not expressed—seems to be that one can know in advance, by *pramāṇas* other than language, the idea conveyed by injunctive or other words, but not the (individual) object to which they refer. Therefore language is the sole *pramāṇa* for that, in the case of Vedic injunction, at least.]

Answer : If we infer the idea of a nonsecular cause of activity from the behavior of others, we also can thereby infer, at the time we first learn the use of a word, the cause of activity itself, because it qualifies the idea, or else we remember it as something previously known by another *pramāṇa*. In either case it forms the object of a *pramāṇa* other than language.

Objection: We can infer only the existence of the idea of the object, not that this idea is *pramāṇa* or memory (and so we can't infer the object itself).

Answer : No, because an idea must fall into one of five sorts of cognition—memory, *pramāṇa*, doubt, error, and conceptual construction (*vikalpa*). But of these this idea can only be *pramāṇa*; so there still is another *pramāṇa* for the existence of a cause of activity besides language. In addition, the child's own knowledge is not purely verbal, but inferential, and therefore *he* knows the cause of activity by a *pramāṇa* other than language.

Objection : The child's knowledge of the object of the injunctive word is not *pramāṇa* unless it is from a verbal communication free from defects. Therefore the child's knowledge does depend on the word, though indirectly through the speaker's valid cognition.

Answer : No, because the definition of verbal knowledge is knowledge from a word (and this the child does not yet have of that particular word). The knowledge of the object (the cause of activity) is not arrived at solely through the speaker's knowledge. One person cannot know by means of another's knowledge.

As to the necessity that a verbal communication must be free from defects if it is to be a *pramāṇa*—specifically, in the case of human communication, that the speaker must have a *pramāṇa* for the thing he asserts—this is a *criterion* for judging whether the sentence is a *pramāṇa*, not the cause of its being a *pramāṇa*. The possibility of the speaker's having a *pramāṇa* for the thing he asserts establishes that the sentence is a *pramāṇa* in the sense that the absence of that possibility sublates it. As we said before, human language is dependent on other *pramāṇas* as regards its being a *pramāṇa*, not as regards its object. Language connects directly with its object, not solely with the idea in someone's mind. This is the meaning of *Mīmāṃsā-sūtra* I.1.5, "But the connection of word with object is innate (*autpattika*)." Therefore there is a connection of the word and the object by themselves (to the exclusion of the idea), and this connection is their mutual fitness (*anyonya-yogyatā*). This can't be grasped unless the object is known, and the object can't be known except by another *pramāṇa* than language.

The fact of being apprehensible by another *pramāṇa* is not part of the meaning of a word (in particular, of the optative termination [*liṅ*]). For, one determines the meaning of a word both by positive and by negative concomitance (*anvaya* and *vyatireka*), not by either alone. Now, the optative ending is used when something is cause of welfare (*śreyo-hetu*) and not used when something is not a cause of welfare. Something accessible to another *pramāṇa*, on the other hand, may or may not be a cause of welfare; there is not negative concomitance, though there may be positive concomitance. If both positive and negative concomitance were not necessary in determining the meaning of a word, such things as the universal Being would enter into the meaning of the word "*śiṃśapā*" (the tree *Dahlbergia sissu*).

Objection : But if the cause of activity (*pravṛtti-hetu*), being a cause of welfare, is known by a *pramāṇa* other than language, yet, in the case of Vedic injunction, cannot be known by any *pramāṇa* other than Vedic language, the Veda will cease to be a *pramāṇa* with respect to it.

Answer : No, something apprehensible by more than one *pramāṇa* may, in certain special circumstances, be apprehensible by only one *pramāṇa*. Besides, a thing apprehensible by only one *pramāṇa* is still real. Thus, that certain actions whose fruits are far-off are causes of welfare is knowable only from the Veda, although there are other *pramāṇas* for knowing that actions whose fruits follow immediately are means to welfare. Besides, even in everyday life some actions, like ploughing, produce a far-off result, and so the distinction between Vedic and secular causes of activity as having respectively far-off and immediate results is not invariably valid. (Therefore worldly and Vedic injunctive language have the same meaning.) The meaning of the optative termination is merely the general fact of being a cause of welfare, at some time or another.

Another reason that the word is connected with the object directly, not just with the speaker's idea, is that we infer, from facial expressions and other signs, such things as pleasure at the same time we infer their experience by a person. We do not need a separate *pramāṇa* for pleasure in addition to that for its experience. Similarly we do not need a separate *pramāṇa* for the object in addition to language as the *pramāṇa* for the speaker's idea, because we know them both together.

Even if there is a separate *pramāṇa* (i.e., inference) for the *object* of the speaker's idea (the object being here some cause of action), still, since it is inferred, it is known by some other *pramāṇa* besides language.

III.43, including verses 85b-87a (E110). *Objection* : We do not say that the connection of words depends on an injunction (*vidhi*) on the grounds that otherwise the injunction will be useless (*vṛthā*), but on the grounds that the injunctive word as a *pramāṇa* communicates its object (i.e., *niyoga*) as itself also being a *pramāṇa*, and as such it causes us to posit by presumption something previously unknown, namely, the conjunction of the objects of the words, which does not need to be previously known by another *pramāṇa*, as it would if it were the object of a word.

Answer : No, because the same problem as before (cf. III.40) would arise: words depend on our knowledge of their connection with their objects, and that depends on our knowing the objects. If it were not so, one not already conversant with the use of the injunctive word would be moved to act. So *pramāṇas* other than language must enable us to know the object of injunction. Besides, language itself can let us know of the conjunction of the objects of words; why bring in the (nonsecular) object of the injunctive word ?

III.44, including verses 87b-91a (E111-112). What *is* the object of the injunctive word, we ask. (1) Not Vedic action, such as sacrifice itself, because that is known by language such as "he sacrifices." (2) Not the connection of the objects of words, because we see *that* even in secular language and in sentences that are not injunctive, by means of the proximity of words that are in various grammatical cases indicating various relations of their corresponding objects. Also, we see in the case of secular, noninjunctive sentences not only the conjunction of objects of words, but even activity caused by the sentence; so there is no need of an injunctive word to give rise to activity. (3) Not a *pramāṇa* to tell us the action has the capacity to realize the fruit, because the word itself may tell us that.

III.45, including verses 91b-95 (E112-113). Another argument why the Veda is a *pramāṇa* only for actions. *Objection* : Sentences have no object (*artha* as both use *and* meaning) unless they are employed for action (*pravṛtti*) or abstention from action (*nivṛtti*), and an injunction is necessary to fulfil this need.

Answer : In the case of the Upaniṣads, the injunctive word would be "one should understand it as being of this sort." But from such an injunction the only result possible is knowledge of the object's proper form—which is obtainable from the indicative sentence without an injunction.

III.46, including verses 96-100 (E113-115). *Objection* : The injunction to know in the Upaniṣads is not an originative injunction (*utpattividhi*), which would tell the proper form of the object as other originative injunctions tell the proper form of a rite. Rather, it is an injunction of eligibility (*adhikāravidhi*), which tells us the connection of an action with a desired end. An injunctive word is necessary in a sentence of this latter sort to get a person to act, and thereby for the sentence to have an object.

Answer : No, an originative injunction tells the proper form of a rite and the general fact of its being a means to a human good (*puruṣārtha*), and thus creates the expectation (*ākāṃkṣā*) of a particular human good that the injunction of eligibility supplies. Now, in the case of the injunction to know the truth (*tattva-pratipatti*), the object of the injunction is not the truth of the Self, because that is not an action. On the other hand, the *knowledge* of the truth of the Self is not related to the qualification, because it is things already known that are related to the qualification, because they take part in the actual performance of the action enjoined, not the means by which we know the things.

Discussion of (2) (*in* III.1), *the suggestion that it is immediate manifestation* (*sākṣātkāra*) *that is enjoined* :

III.47, including verses 101-105a (E115-118). *Objection* : The reality of the Self is not the object of verbal knowledge, because the language that is a *pramāṇa* is in the form of sentences, and the object of a sentence consists in the conjunction of diverse objects of words, whereas in the Self there is no duality. Also, the knowledge of the Self lacks the duality of agent and object of knowledge. Thus there is no ordinary (*laukika*) *pramāṇa* to produce it, and therefore it is enjoined by the Veda along with its means, such as self-control, meditation, and the like.

Answer : The awareness of the reality of the Self, being nondual and without differentiations (*avaccheda*), is one's abiding in one's own form, which is unsurpassable bliss in which all sorrow and other evils are extinguished, and so an end of man.

But, precisely because it is an end, it cannot be enjoined, because only means are enjoined, not ends. They are enjoined because otherwise we wouldn't know they produced some particular desirable thing. Now, one acts because of desire for something, a desire that arises spontaneously without need for an injunction. Neither can the object of injunction be how (or that) the thing is to be brought about (*ittham-bhāva*, which, according to the commentators, is equal to *itikartavyatā*), because activity with respect to that also arises from the object without need of an injunction, just like the activity for the end. We can know from other *pramāṇas* than Vedic injunctive language that something is desirable, and therefore act for it once we know the means are available; injunction serves solely to tell us the means.

Whatever definition you give of injunction, it will require some cause, and none other is possible than being a means to something desirable. Its cause cannot be its mere enunciation by the optative termination, because nothing causes activity by merely being named; rather, naming is the cause only of the idea of something, not activity. Also, if activity came merely from the word alone, even someone unversed in the meaning of the word would be moved to act upon hearing it.

Neither is the object of the injunctive word a prescription (*niyoga*), something that is the cause of the idea "I should do this"; for this is nothing but the fact of being thought to be a means of something desirable. Everyone invariably acts for something when he thinks that it is a means to something desirable and does not act when he does not think it is. This being true in secular usage, there is no justification for positing some nonsecular cause of action knowable only from language in Vedic usage such as the idea "It is to be done."

Moreover, this prescription (*niyoga*) can't come from language alone, for it must, if it is to be anything other than the fact of being a means to something desirable, either belong to someone who lays down an injunction, or be independent (of any person, i.e., derived from the Vedic word itself). But the fact of being something to be done (which the follower of Prabhākara gives as the definition of *niyoga*), is neither of these, but belongs to the *object*.

Objection : It resides in the object, but comes from prescription.

Answer : Still, the word can't be a *pramāṇa* for the action's being something that has to be done, because that still resides in the object, whereas the word directly denotes prescription, which is not in the object.

Also, one can't arrive by presumption at the to-be-doneness in the object from the presence of prescription, because in secular usage we see unqualified people give prescriptions of things that shouldn't be done.

Nor can you say that prescription is something to be carried out (*kārya*), which in turn requires carrying out its object (and therefore the word is *pramāṇa* with respect to the object indirectly). For in secular usage we understand the to-be-doneness only with respect to the object, not with respect to the prescription. For example, if we are ordered to milk the cow and it has already been milked, we don't milk it again to fulfil the prescription. Conversely, the other person has not fulfilled the prescription in this case, since it was not given to him, although he has effected its object.

III.48 (E118-119). *Objection* : There can be the enjoinment of the knowledge of the nondual Self, because it is a *means*—of gaining liberation. Since all our knowledge about liberation comes only from Vedic language, none from reason (*tarka*), one can't argue that if liberation is effected by knowledge as a means it may have an end, for the Vedas tell us that it has no end. Or else, since liberation is the result of a knowledge without an end, it itself is without an end. This is possible even if you say (as the Buddhists do) that knowledge is a series of instantaneous cognitions.

III.49, including verses 105b-106 (E119-123). *Answer* : If liberation is defined as the prior nonexistence of the body, organs, and *buddhi*, we reply that nonexistences cannot be results.

If liberation is defined as "the attainment (*prāpti*) of Brahman," we reject the definition. Let us examine various alternative definitions of "attaining" in this context :

(1) Attaining Brahman is like someone reaching a village. No, because Brahman is omnipresent and also is not different from him who would attain it.

(2) Attaining Brahman is nonseparation from it, like the nonseparation of the nectars of various flowers from honey or of rivers from the sea. No, for the same reasons as in (1), and also because nonseparation is the mixture of the parts of one thing with the parts of another, and Brahman is partless.

(3) Attaining Brahman is the effect's reaching the state of being the cause. No, because the effect is at all times the cause. Nor can you revise the definition to mean the destruction of the form of the effect, because liberation is not a destruction of one's self, which would

be undesirable, but immortality. Anyway, the effect, as an effect, does not really exist.

(4) Attaining Brahman is transformation (*pariṇāma*) into Brahman's form. No, because nothing is different from Brahman, and in particular the *jīva* and Brahman are identical insofar as they are consciousness (*caitanya*). Nor can you define the form of Brahman into which the *jīva* becomes transformed as Brahman's special Lordship, because this Lordship would be either inferior to Brahman's or equal. If it were inferior, it could come to an end at Brahman's wish. If it were equal, there would result the absurdity of there being two or more supreme Lords, whose wills might conflict. Moreover, scripture speaks of none but Brahman emanating the world.

(5) Conclusion: Therefore attaining Brahman is the manifestation (*avirbhāva*) of one's own form (*svarūpa*), like the manifestation of the proper form of a piece of rock crystal upon the removal of a red flower next to it. Therefore, liberation is not an effect. It is nothing different from knowledge. Knowledge, when it arises, automatically excludes its negation, ignorance, which in turn is identical with transmigration.

III.50 (E123-128). (Consideration of certain Vedic passages that imply the reality of difference and therefore apparently support the alternative definitions [1-4] in the preceding section.) *Re* (1): Those passages of scripture that speak of a "path" are talking about gradual liberation in stages (*kramamukti*) in which an individual goes first to the world of Brahmā, who is an effect, gains knowledge of Brahman there, and is liberated at the destruction of that world at the time of the great dissolution (*mahāpralaya*). For Brahman cannot have a special place to which one might go. Alternatively the "nonreturning" (*apunarāvṛtti*) spoken of in connection with the one who goes to the world of Brahmā may refer to nonreturning until the time of the great dissolution, after which one returns from the world of Brahmā to a new cycle in a new universe.

Re (2): The scriptural passages that talk of "nonseparation" are referring to the absence of discriminatory cognition (*vivekajñāna*) once Brahman is known.

Re (*part of*) (4): The scriptural passages that teach the emanation of the world from Brahman as its cause do not aim to teach causality in the literal (*yathāśabda*), primary (*mukhya*) sense, which would imply duality, but to teach the identity of all things with their cause, Brahman. The effect is no separate real thing from its cause, for, insofar as it is an effect, it cannot be either identical with or different from its cause (and so is illogical). It is just a construction (*vikalpa*).

In the same way as reflections are not *produced* from their original, nor words, sentences, paragraphs *produced* from syllables, since they have no separate identity from them, are neither different nor non-different from them, and so are just the objects of imagination (*kalpanā*) based on them, so difference is a construction based on Brahman.

Re (*another part of*) (4): The scriptural statements about the Lordship that is reached by the knower refer not to liberation but to a result of the knowledge of the Brahman with qualities (*saguṇa*). Or else, they may refer to liberation, but then the fact that they say that the liberated obtain all enjoyments refers to the manifestation of the form of Brahman, which *is* everything, which includes all enjoyments in itself as identical with It. Such (negative) things as sorrow, delusion, and the like are not the form of Brahman, but are projected (*adhyasta*) by *avidyā*.

Brahman's Lordship and knowledge do not depend on the real separate existence of something to be ruled or an object of knowledge, but on Brahman's already existent power of ruling (*iśanaśakti*) and form of knowledge (*jñānarūpa*), just as fire has the power of burning and illuminating regardless of whether a suitable object to exercise these powers on is present or not.

One "obtains all desires" in liberation by obtaining Brahman, which is the highest bliss, not by obtaining actual particular blisses, such as that of intercourse with women.

The Lord (*bhagavān*) identifies (in *Bhagavadgītā* X) with Himself things in which the imagined limitation of his own knowledge, Lordship, etc., is not very great.

Another opinion : Some think that the passages designating the higher Brahman by words based on name-and-form are not literally intended, but are for the sake of meditation. Similarly the passages ascribing to Brahman omniscience, Lordship, etc., are not literal, but are for meditation.

III.51 (E128-129). *Objection* : Granted that liberation itself is not something to be accomplished (and therefore not the object of an injunction), still, the exhaustion (*kṣaya*) of the causes of bondage, that is, past works, is something that may be accomplished, as it is accomplished by penances (*prāyaścitta*), and this exhaustion is necessary for liberation. The knowledge of the Self may be a means for this exhaustion. Moreover, the exhaustion of past works, being a destruction, is without end, even though it is an effect, so there is no need to fear an end of liberation.

III.52, including verses 107-108a (E129-130). *Answer* : The knowledge of the Self, immediately and by itself, dissolves (*pravilaya*) the usage of *avidyā* (*avidyāvyavahāra*), and thereby all works, because they are projected by *avidyā*. The verse that may be claimed to contradict this, *Chāndogya Upaniṣad* VI.14.2, "For him there is just this much delay, until he is not released, then he attains," can be explained satisfactorily in either of two ways : (1) The shedding of the body comes *swiftly* after Self-knowledge, not with a substantial delay, or (2) The passage *assumes* the delay, but *teaches* that the delay has as its limit the destruction of the body.[33]

III.53 (E130-134). *Objection to* (1) of the previous paragraph: But then it is illogical for the Bhagavadgītā (II.54 ff.) to give the characteristics for what it calls "the man of stable insight" (*sthitaprajñā*). *Objection to* (2): If all works are exhausted it is impossible there be any delay.

Answer in favor of (1): The Gītā refers to an aspirant at a particular stage, not to a perfected person. *Answer in favor of* (2): The separation from the body follows not immediately, but upon the exhaustion of works that have already begun to bear their fruit (*ārabdhakārya*). Therefore some people obtain liberation immediately upon knowledge, others after some delay. Just as trembling at a serpent may continue after the knowledge that it is really a rope, because of the influence (*saṃskāra*) of the fear, so the body continues for a while because of traces (*saṃskāra*). In a similar manner a potter's wheel keeps spinning after the potter has ceased moving it, because of the *saṃskāra* of motion. But the mere fact that it continues does not mean that it continues long. Nothing besides the knowledge of the real rope already possessed is necessary to make the trembling caused by the imagined serpent stop; the root cause having ceased, the effect eventually ceases. Likewise, the body eventually ceases once the Self is known.

The "man of stable insight" (*sthitaprajñā*) may thus also be explained as one who knows the Self and pays no attention to the body, which is but a mere shadow or appearance (*chāyāmātra*). This is "liberation while living" (*jīvanmukti*).

The act by which a given body has been produced, because it has already begun to produce its effect, has the appearance of continuing to ripen in that same body. The acts whose traces have not yet begun to produce their effects, which have not yet reached a state of activity, cannot produce an impression that would continue even after the knowledge of the Self. The remainder of the effect (of the trace) may be explained as due to the impression either (1) of the cause that has already reached a state of activity (e.g., a past deed, or fear), or (2) of the effect (e.g., embodiment or trembling), or (3) of both. In any case the impression of the effect continues after the cause is gone.

Just as an arrow already in motion may be stopped, works that have already begun to be enjoyed can be destroyed; we do not need to await their destruction by enjoyment. For example, there are expiatory rites for works whose ripening is indicated by dreams or the like. Therefore the persistence of the body after knowledge has been obtained is from the impression (*saṃskāra*) alone (not from the past works).[34] This is a mere appearance of ripening of works, which does not affect or bind the liberated person. The impressions of *avidyā*, being themselves *avidyā*, are swallowed up by knowledge, in that they no longer bind. Consequently nothing further, such as enjoyment, is needed for liberation but knowledge.

III.54 (E134). *Objection* : If the bondage that continues after the knowledge of the truth is merely apparent, why are meditation and the like necessary even after knowledge of the truth has arisen from language ?

Answer : Verbal knowledge, which is indirect, and the appearance of diversity, which is directly experienced, are not mutually exclusive. Therefore verbal knowledge must be supplemented by direct knowledge produced by meditation, which is contradictory to the appearance of diversity.

Moreover, verbal knowledge being the result of a *pramāṇa* and lasting but an instant (*kṣaṇika*), may be supplanted by a repetition of error. Therefore the knowledge must be continuously repeated, and this repetition is meditation.

Therefore knowledge is in itself the destruction of the causes of bondage, rather than being the cause of their destruction (i.e., there is no injunction to knowledge, because an injunction is of a means as a cause of the end, its effect).

In the same way, the scriptural passages that say that sins subsequent to knowledge do not adhere to the knower [according to the commentator Ānandapūrṇa, these are due to "carelessness" (*pramāda*)] do not mean that this nonadhesion is an effect of knowledge (so that knowledge could be prescribed by an injunction as a means to effect nonadhesion as an end).

III.55, including verses 108b-114a (E134-136). (Reply to the first objection in III.47) Brahman is indeed the object of verbal knowledge. You yourself, opponent, say that the knowledge of Brahman is the object of injunction. But one cannot prescribe what is not known, and Brahman is known from no other source than language.

A knowledge of the Self that is the object of injunction cannot be a *pramāṇa* for the reality of the Self. For, if injunction (*vidhi*) is understood as prescription (*niyoga*), and it is solely the prescription that is to be accomplished, the prescription and the word that denotes it complete their operation in producing the prescription, and so they cannot go on from there to establish an object (*vastu*). If you say that the prescription tells us that its object (namely, the action) is to be done, then it exhausts itself in that; it still does not touch the essence of a thing (because it deals solely with an action).

The injunction of a cognition does not establish the essence of a thing, but merely that the thing should be thought of in a certain manner, just as in the case of *arthavādas*, which do not teach the reality of the events they describe, but something else (usually, according to the Mīmāṃsā, the "glorification" of a certain rite).

The essence of a thing is not something that can be enjoined, because it is not something that can be performed, an action, but something already existent. The individual form (*svarūpa*) of a thing is established by its connection with Being (*sattā*) in one of the three times, whereas the action that is the object of injunction is not in any particular time.

When an act of apprehension is the object of injunction, the general rule that an injunction is a *pramāṇa* both for the act and for everything that qualifies it does not hold true. For, apprehension may be by superimposition of a certain appearance on what is really otherwise. Therefore Brahman is not established by the injunction to apprehend It.

III.56, including verses 114b-115a (E136). *Objection* : No cognition has an erroneous object, because a cognition that did not imitate the form of its object would have no object at all. Therefore error comes about by the mere negative failure to discriminate an object of present perception (e.g., mother of pearl) and an object of memory (e.g., silver), because of some common trait.

III.57, including verses 115b-123 (E137-138). *Answer* : No, it is the present fragment of mother of pearl that we consider silver and direct our action toward, not remembered silver. The mere failure to grasp the nonproximity of the remembered silver does not account for the regularity of action, because the mere absence of this discrimination is present with respect to other things than mother of pearl, such as clods of earth not presently seen. One cannot superimpose anything (including things remembered) on something that is not in contact with a sense organ. It is because it is silver that it is cognized, and because it is cognized *in* the mother of pearl that one moves toward that.

Should you respond that there is not just an absence of the awareness of the distinction of silver and mother of pearl, but a positive cognition of their identity, this is granting our doctrine of (positive) error.

III.58, including verses 124-129a (E138-140). In addition, memory must either (1) by itself discriminate its object from an object of *pramāṇa*, or (2) simply present the object without so discriminating it. But (1) is obviously not the case in your model of error, and, if one accepts (2), all memory of one thing while one is looking at another thing with common traits would produce error. But this is not so, because in some cases there is neither error nor *pramāṇa* but doubt whether it is the same thing or not.

Objection : Error occurs where only one thing is remembered, but doubt where more than one thing is remembered.

Answer : No. (1) There can be error when more than one thing is remembered (as being similar, but you think the thing before you is one of those things in particular). (2) Also, sometimes one may remember only one thing, and see traits common to it and the thing perceived but still have neither doubt nor error. (3) Again, there are errors not born of a memory of something previously perceived, such as that of a second moon in an astigmatic person. (4) In addition, one may remember one thing but still have the erroneous cognition of another, for example, a thirsty man may upon seeing shell recall water, but still think that it is silver.

III.59, including verses 129b-131 (E140). Not all error is based on similarity, for example, the error of a jaundiced person who takes what is white as yellow and what is sweet as bitter. Error can't be from the mere fact of similarity with the other thing and failure to notice the difference, because, since everything has some similarity with everything else, there would be no regularity in the arising of such errors. Therefore errors arise from specific defects in the sense organs.

III.60, including verses 132-139a (E140-142). *Objection* : The thing remembered is discriminated from the thing being perceived by its own cognition (i.e., by memory itself), but sometimes one does not apprehend the distinguishing properties (*viśeṣa*) in it. (The point is that one is aware that silver is a memory content, but does not note the differences between silver and the thing in front of one at present.) Thus there may be an absence of doubt when two alternative things are remembered, and neither doubt nor error when only one is.

Answer : Still, this doesn't explain how there can be error when two things are remembered. Also, in memory one may indeed apprehend the distinguishing traits.

Objection : In memory the difference of place and time of the thing remembered from the present object of perception is grasped, but in error it is not grasped.

Answer : No. Something known at many places and times, and even at the place in question, may still be discriminated from what is being perceived. Also, one can't remember an infinite number of places and times so as to grasp their difference from the present thing.

Objection : In error one doesn't discriminate the thing remembered from the thing present because of the fact that one does not apprehend that one is remembering, whereas in memory one is conscious that one is remembering and so one discriminates then.

Answer : Well, then, memory discriminates its object by itself from what is perceived and present, and in that case error cannot exist ever; but if it does not discriminate its own object, there would always be error when we see common traits and do not recognize that we are remembering (as was said at III.58). (Therefore error is not a mere failure to grasp the difference of time and place.) The discrimination (of memory from perception) "I am remembering" is therefore something in addition to memory. Besides, even if we do make this discrimination of memory and perception, we may still have an error of recognition (*pratyabhijñābhrama*), "This is the same one."

Moreover, perception is also discriminated by the very act of discriminating memory from it; and therefore when what is perceived is discriminated from what is remembered we should have an erroneous cognition that it is a memory, not that it is a perception.

If this nondiscrimination of what is remembered from what is perceived is the idea that what is in fact not present is present, then this is teaching the very same (positive) false object of memory that we preach. This is not just a failure to apprehend absence of proximity, because there is no such false memory in errors caused by a defect in a sense organ rather than in the *manas*. And as said before (III.57), there would not be the regular order in errors by which we move toward only the thing present to us.

Moreover, error can't just be the failure to grasp the object in some aspect, because no cognition can grasp the totality of an object, and therefore all cognition will be erroneous.

Also, errors such as seeing a double moon or confusion as to the directions of space (*dig-moha*, dizziness ?) continue even after they have been corrected by another *pramāṇa*.

III.61, including verses 139b-149a (E142-144). The theory that error is a nonapprehension of difference cannot explain the phenomenon of the sublation of error. The form of this sublation is, for example, "This is not silver," that is, the denial of a raised possibility (*prasajyapratiṣedha*). But nonapprehension is an absence (*abhāva*), which does not raise any possibility. What is denied is not just silver or the object present to the eye, but their (positive) identification, which requires a (positive) cause, which is our "erroneous cognition" (*viparītakhyāti*).

Nor is it merely a nonapprehension that is sublated when denying an error, because all cognitions (whether false or true) have the form of sublating a nonapprehension.

Moreover, a person may remember silver and see the common traits in the object present to the eye, and not apprehend the distinction of the two—but also not apprehend their nondistinction. Later he may see the object clearly, and apprehend the distinction, but this is not the sublation of an error. Nor is this cognition doubt, if one does not remember two possible alternatives.

Objection : A combination of the nonapprehension of the distinction and the consciousness of proximity in time (of the thing remembered) makes the thing in contact with the eye appear as silver or vice versa.

Answer : This is just our position of erroneous cognition, which is precisely the appearance of something as that which it is not. Ignorance (*ajñāna*) of the truth is a *condition* (*nimitta*) of this, but the (false) cognition of proximity is its *cause*. It is the latter that is denied.

Also, on your theory error, defined as nonapprehension of difference, is based on nonapprehension—a vicious circle.

In a dream there is no second thing to the dreamer, no external object whose distinction from the remembered object could be overlooked. If you say that in a dream there is a nondiscrimination of the remembered object as remembered, then the noticing of hitherto unnoticed qualities in an object is a case of the sublation of error, since these have not previously been discriminated.

III.62, including verses 149b-151 (E144-145). The opponent's theory is opposed to our actual experience, because in error we think "This white thing is silver," thus attributing both the present whiteness and the remembered silver to the same locus.

(A defense of the self-validity [*svataḥ-prāmāṇya* of cognition—against III.56].) The very arising of the cognition that a certain thing is so blocks the arising of a doubt about the object known; that is just what it is required for.

A *pramāṇa's* lack of invariable concomitance (*vyabhicāra*) with its object (viz., that it does not always exist where the object exists) does not prevent the *pramāṇa's* being a *pramāṇa*. For, it is the "determination" (*pariccheda*) of the object that the *pramāṇa* brings about that makes it a means of valid knowledge, not whether or not it is invariably concomitant. When an object is properly determined, that itself rules out doubt; it does not require invariable concomitance. If this viewpoint is not accepted, you must test your own knowledge of invariable concomitance to see if it itself is invariably concomitant, and thus you begin an infinite regress. Therefore the form of cognition by itself establishes its own validity.

III.63, including verses 152-157a (E145-146). (Against the idea that the absence of defects in the senses is necessary to the validity of knowledge.) The absence or presence of defects in the senses may be the cause of distinguishing *pramāṇa* from error as much on our theory that error is a (positive) false apprehension as on yours that it is a failure of apprehension. On our theory the defects are more powerful than on yours, because they produce not only failure to apprehend, as in your theory, but also error. One cannot infer the existence of an effect (such as *pramāṇa*) from the existence of its cause (such as a sense organ without defects), but one *may* infer (on our theory) the nonexistence of an effect (wrong cognition) from the nonexistence of its cause (the defect). So the theory of false cognition is preferable.

III.64, including verses 157b-161a (E146-147). On either theory of error the external object in contact with the senses may be said to lose its character of being the "objective support" (*ālambana*) of cognition, since its proper form does not appear, or it may be said to be the objective support, since, on either theory, some of its forms appear and some don't. [So the opponent cannot say that in our theory of error the external object ceases to be the objective support of cognition, and that cognition will then be without support (*anālambana*)—a Buddhist position that both we and our Prābhākara opponent reject.] Moreover, to either theory it could be objected that, if erroneous cognition lacks an objective support, even *pramāṇa* may lack it. Equally on both theories one may say that there must be an objective support on the grounds that *something* produces practical activity toward the supposed object (i.e., the shell produces activity directed towards silver).

III.65, including verses 161b-165a (E147-148). *Objection* : Although the intent of an injunction is action, an injunction of knowledge may establish the nature of a thing, just as, although the injunction of sprinkling the rice intends an action, nonetheless the injunction is for the sake of the substance rice. Similarly the action of knowing is directed toward the thing known. So we know the Self from the injunction to know the Self, as the existence in the rice of a perfection (*saṃskāra*) is known from the injunction of sprinkling, or the fact that sacrifice is a means to heaven from the injunction "He who desires heaven should sacrifice."

III.66, including verses 165b-171a (E148-151). *Answer*: An injunction of knowledge makes an object appear, but it may appear with its own form or with the form of something else, as we have shown. Now the end of an injunction of knowledge of the Self must be the dissolution of the appearance of that which is not the Self; so necessarily it must be possible for the Self to appear with the form of the diversity of name-and-form.

Objection: But there are two sorts of *avidyā*, that which "covers" (*ācchādika*) the light and that which "projects" (*vikṣepika*). The former is found alone in deep sleep and is defined as dissolution (*laya*); the latter is found in waking and dreaming. The fruit of the injunction of knowledge is the destruction of covering *avidyā* (and not of projective *avidyā*—which would correspond to Maṇḍana's notion of error as a positive falsehood).

Answer: No, projective *avidyā* is more necessary to be destroyed, because it produces all suffering, whereas dissolution is praised in scripture many times as bliss, because it is the end of various sufferings. Covering *avidyā* equals nonapprehension; projective *avidyā* equals false apprehension. The former is the cause; the latter its effect.

Objection: But you can divide these two not in that manner, but as nonapprehension and imperfect apprehension. (Hence one does not need the theory of false cognition to explain the facts of error.)

Answer: No, imperfect apprehension is still knowledge (*jñāna*, here apparently meaning not just "awareness" but "valid cognition"), rather than *avidyā*. Besides, no cognition grasps the object in its entirety. To repeat, it is not the mere nonapprehension of nondifference that must be stopped, but the apprehension of difference, that is, a false cognition, because it causes suffering.

Objection: But when one can see a visible fruit of an injunction if it establishes the object—the Self—in Its own true form, why should we suppose the invisible fruit of its establishing the Self under a form that doesn't really belong to It?

Answer: An injunction must serve an end of man, but apprehending a thing as it is and otherwise than it is may both serve ends of man. Apprehending the Self as free from sin, etc., may make one free from suffering, liberated while living; but so may apprehending it as such by continual meditation, even if it weren't such; for continual meditation may produce the practical activity of a thing that doesn't exist.

Only in this way can there be no contradiction of perception and the other *pramāṇas* (i.e., apparently, only if one says that an injunction may present an object with a form other than its own proper form can one avoid a contradiction between scriptural passages such as "One should worship speech as a cow," which apparently represents speech as a cow, and perception, etc.). Moreover (you should want this to be true, because if all injunctions represent things under their own form), the injunction to know the Self as nondual will establish the voidness of phenomenal diversity as the highest truth, and injunctions of works would apply to objects established by practical usage based on the imagination of something nonexistent. Therefore the injunction of the knowledge of the nondual Self is in order only as not being the highest truth.[35]

III.67, including verses 171b-173 (E151-152). Injunctions to "know" or "cognize"[36] the Self do not necessarily mean to cognize it as it is, for the word "cognition" (*jñāna*) is qualified in various ways—"false cognition," "right cognition," "doubtful cognition."

Besides, there cannot be an injunction simply such as this, "Cognize the Self," that is, in Its true form. For, either that form must be already established by another *pramāṇa* (in which case an injunction is not necessary), or, if it isn't so established, the injunction to know it will be impossible of fulfilment. Vedic language may enjoin cognition of it under a certain form, but the injunction does not tell us if that form is the true one.

III.68, including verses 174-179 (E152-153). If knowledge has a visible result there is no need for an injunction to get someone to act for it. One who desires to experience the form of the Self (which is the result of knowing It) acts toward that end spontaneously.

One cannot even enjoin knowledge as a *means* to that experience, because the experience is a visible fruit of the knowledge, and one wanting the fruit acts for the means, knowledge, spontaneously, without an injunction.

Even though that experience of the Self and the knowledge that is the means to it are not things in this world (*alaukika*), and are known only from Vedic language, one acts spontaneously for them, if one wants them at all, once one has learned of them from Vedic language, and therefore there is no need for an injunction.

III.69, including verses 180-183 (E153-155).

Refutation of (3) *of* III.1, *the possibility of an injunction of the continuous repetition of the knowledge obtained from Vedic language.*

One cannot maintain that apparently indicative sentences in the Upaniṣads in reality are injunctions of a continuous stream of cognitions, a reflection (*anucintana*), a meditation (*dhyāna*), for the very same reason as before—that an injunction cannot establish the true form of an object.

It is, however, possible that such a stream of cognitions may be enjoined after the form is known from an indicative sentence. But there is still no need for an injunction, because the visible fruit of the first knowledge and that of its repetition is the same—direct vision (*sākṣātkāraṇa*)—and one does not need an injunction to act for either knowledge.

Repeated practice of knowledge may produce greater clarity of knowledge in everyday life. Continuous concentration (*bhāvanā*) may make even a nonexistent object be experienced, how much more so when applied to a real object.

Certain scriptural passages that seem to enjoin a meditation on the Self can be better explained. *Chāndogya Upaniṣad* III.14.1 really enjoins a meditation on the Self as extrinsically limited by name-and-form, which leads to lordship, or if to direct vision, only by stages. Other passages really intend the cessation of doing meditation on other things than the Self.

Therefore, since none of the three knowledges (in III.1) can be the object of an injunction, one understands that the Upaniṣads are a *pramāṇa* for the Self as an already existent object, not for a knowledge to be performed as the object of an injunction.

Mīmāṃsāsūtra I.1.2 : "Dharma is the meaning, marked by impulsion" (*codanālakṣaṇo'artho dharmaḥ*) does *not* mean that the Vedas teach only things to be done and that the Upaniṣads, teaching an already existent object, are for the sake of some injunction.

Just as the Veda is an independent *pramāṇa* for certain actions to be performed, so it is an independent *pramāṇa* for the knowledge of the Self, which is something already existent.

CHAPTER FOUR : ON REALIZATION (SIDDHI)

IV.1, including verse 1 (E156). *Objection* : The sentences of the Upaniṣads cannot be a *pramāṇa* for an otherwise unknown object such as Brahman. Because a sentence communicates the conjunction of the objects of the words in it, and the ability of a word to communicate its object depends on the hearer's knowledge of its relation to its object. This in turn depends on a previous knowledge of the object.

The object must therefore be known by another *pramāṇa*. So, Brahman being known by no other *pramāṇa* than language, neither single words applied to It nor sentences can give knowledge of It. On the other hand, if It *is* known from another *pramāṇa*, Vedic language is redundant (and therefore not a *pramāṇa*, for a *pramāṇa* must give *new* knowledge). Therefore the purpose of the Upaniṣads is not to be the cause of knowledge (*pratipattihetu*), but for employment in recitation (*japa-upayoga*).

IV.2, including verse 2 (E156-157). *Answer* : We see in secular usage that a sentence communicates a hitherto unknown particular form by communicating an already known class characteristic conjoined with a collection of already known qualities, which collection is not shared by other things. This is what *every* sentence does insofar as it is a *pramāṇa*. In the Veda, the Upaniṣadic sentences work in the same way to communicate Brahman as a hitherto unknown object. The class characteristic in the case of Brahman is that of a cause, or of Being, and the conjunction of the objects of such words as "From whom these beings are born . . . . " (*Taittirīya Upaniṣad* III.1) or "Not coarse, not subtle, not long . . . . " (*Bṛhadāraṇyaka Upaniṣad* III.8.8) communicates a particular form.

IV.3, including verses 3-4 (E157). Besides, Brahman is not entirely unknown already, because since there is nothing over and above Brahman, Brahman is the object of every cognition. For the cognitions of particulars are accompanied by the form of the common characteristics, and Brahman is the true thing that is left over when diversity is absorbed.

The new thing the Upaniṣads communicate is the nonexistence of diversity. Both diversity and negation are already known; the Upaniṣads communicate their conjunction.

The other *pramāṇas*, being associated with *avidyā*, do not present their conjunction. Therefore it is a new truth for which tradition (*āgama*) is the only *pramāṇa*.

IV.4, including verses 5-11 (E157-159). *Objection* : A sentence that does not produce activity for an end of man, but merely communicates something already existent, is not a *pramāṇa*.

Answer : The fruit of a *pramāṇa* is not necessarily something that is an end of man, because a *pramāṇa* may sometimes produce indifference. Whatever is a cause of valid cognition is a *pramāṇa*.

Besides, the knowledge that the state of being a *jīva*, which involves suffering, is not real, and the cessation, identical with this knowledge, of that false cognition, is by its nature an end of man. Even the false cognition continues for a while, by virtue of its trace, but it does not affect one as before, and eventually ceases by repetition of the verbal knowledge in meditation.

Moreover, the mere production of knowledge by itself can be an end of man for people agitated by curiosity about a thing.

Further, an end of man is not necessarily the object of activity or abstinence from activity, for *pramāṇas* such as perception have as their objects not activity but already existent objects, yet the *pramāṇas* are ends of man.

Objection : The *pramāṇas* are ends of man insofar as they are helpful for getting accomplished things that are useful toward ends of man.

Answer : Even if we grant this, Brahman is an end of man in itself (i.e., not for another action) as being supremely blissful and the cessation of all sufferings.

It is precisely because Brahman is an end of man that the Upaniṣads teach It as nondifferent from the person instructed, saying "That art Thou"; if It were different, It would not be an end of man. Knowing his identity with It, and thereby becoming identical with It, all evil is extinguished and he becomes the supreme good (or the Highest Śiva, *paramaśivabhāva*, probably a punning compliment to Śiva) and reaches the perfect end of man.

Objection : The *pramāṇas* are accessories to activity with respect to the objects they give knowledge of. (So the Upaniṣads must either be accessory to activity or else they are not a *pramāṇa*.)

Answer : This is true in the case of the Upaniṣads also, because once one knows Brahman one acts to make it directly seen (*sākṣātkāraṇa*).

SUREŚVARA

We know little about Sureśvara on the basis of firm historical evidence. Tradition, as has been noted, makes Sureśvara the same as Maṇḍana, holding that Maṇḍana took the name Sureśvara after he and his wife became Śaṃkara's disciples following a crucial debate. The same traditional accounts go on to tell of Śaṃkara assigning to Padmapāda and Sureśvara the responsibility of commenting on his most important works. Finally, there is the question of which of the *pīṭhas* Sureśvara was given charge of. One tradition associates him specifically with the *maṭha* at Śṛṅgeri, Śaṃkara's birthplace. On the other hand, in the *guruparamparās* of *all* the *pīṭhas* Sureśvara's name appears, and a different tradition holds that Sureśvara was indeed given control of all of them.

Sureśvara's date clearly depends on Śaṃkara's, as well as on one's views on the question of Sureśvara's identity with Maṇḍana.

Of the works ascribed to Sureśvara, a clearcut case can be made for three: the two commentaries on Śaṃkara's *bhāṣyas* on the *Bṛhadāraṇyaka* and *Taittirīya Upaniṣads* and the *Naiṣkarmyasiddhi*. He is also credited with the commentary on the Dakṣiṇāmūrti hymn that is titled *Mānasollāsa*, and with a *vārttika* on the *Pañcīkaraṇa* sometimes ascribed to Śaṃkara. Manuscripts of works titled *Svārājyasiddhi* and *Kāśīmokṣavicāra* also bear his name.

BṚHADĀRAṆYAKOPANIṢADBHĀṢYAVĀRTTIKA

This is one of the longest works of Indian philosophy, running to some 11,151 stanzas, "half the length of the Rāmāyaṇa" says Mahadevan.[1] It begins with an introduction, referred to as *Sambandhavārttika*, whose purpose is "to set forth the relation (*sambandha*) between the two sections of the Vedas . . . through a criticism of the position taken by the Mīmāṃsakas and the other Vedāntins."[2] Van Boetzelaer reports that the tradition is that Śaṃkara first asked Sureśvara to write the *Taittirīya Vārttika*, afterwards the *Bṛhadāraṇyaka Vārttika*.[3] Vidyāraṇya explains why Sureśvara wrote commentaries on these particular Upaniṣads : "In honour of his teacher, Śaṃkara, who belonged to the Taittirīya recension (*śākhā*) of the *Yajurveda*, Sureśvara took up the *Taittirīyopaniṣad-bhāṣya* for explanation; and as his own *śākhā* was the Kāṇva of the *Yajurveda*, it was but appropriate that he took up the *Bṛhadāraṇyaka-bhāṣya* for his Vārttika thereon".[4]

"E" references in the following summary refer to the edition of the *Sambandhavārttika* by T. M. P. Mahadevan (B2390; Madras 1958), and for the rest of the work to the edition by K. S. Agase in the Anandasrama Sanskrit Series (B2386; volume 16, 1892-1894). "T" references in the *Sambandhavārttika* summary are likewise to the Mahadevan translation in B2390; the remainder of the work is untranslated. The summary is by S. Subrahmanya Sastri as revised by K. H. Potter.

BOOK ONE—INTRODUCTORY SECTION : SAMBANDHA-VĀRTTIKA

This section is an extended commentary on Śaṃkara's introductory comments, especially with respect to the proper understanding of the relation between the *karmakāṇḍa* or portion of the Veda dealing with action, and the *jñānakāṇḍa* or portion that provides knowledge of Brahman or the Self. It consists of about 1135 stanzas (1136 1/2 in Mahadevan's rendering), and the numbering adopted here corresponds to that in the Mahadevan text and translation here followed.

1 (ET 1-6) 1-9. Sureśvara gives several renderings of the word "*upaniṣad.*"

2 (ET 6-11) 10-19. One who is eligible for Vedantic study must have abandoned action altogether, be anxious to be rid of *saṃsāra*, and know that there is only the one Self. Even Vedic recitation and other ritual acts are to be abandoned by such a person. It is clear, therefore, that the class of persons who are eligible for Vedantic study is entirely distinct from the class of those who are enjoined to perform ritual acts.

3 (ET 11-15) 20-25. *Objection* : Nothing can be obtained except through actions. Just as heaven, etc., are obtained through actions, not to speak of worldly results, so liberation too is to be obtained through the kinds of actions enjoined in such Vedic texts as the one that enjoins us to "meditate," etc.

Answer : No. Worldly results and heaven are things that originate. Liberation, however, is eternal, it is Brahman itself and not the result of any action.

4 (ET 16-18) 26-31. *Objector* : But liberation has not been obtained yet, and so it must originate, like the gaining of heaven.

Answer : No. It is not a fresh thing to be brought about somehow; rather, it is the removal of error. When a person's disease is cured we do not say he has obtained something new, but merely that he has been restored to his natural healthy state. Scripture need not enjoin liberation, but it merely wakes a person up to the realization of his actual nature.

5 (ET 20-28) 32-45. *Objection* : Yes, but it is only by actions that one can wake up to the natural state of his self. The Vedas teach that only through action can one obtain any human goal, and indeed they indicate which actions are in point through injunctions and prohibitions. Statements in scripture that speak of existing things should be construed as subsidiary to injunctions, on the authority of Jaimini's *Mīmāṃsāsūtras*. Actions lead to liberation as follows: one shuns prohibited (*niṣiddha*) and optional (*kāmya*) actions and performs the required rituals (*nityakarman*). By so doing, one's past merit and demerit will be destroyed, and when there is no karma left to produce further births, liberation is obtained. Knowledge of the Self is not necessary Thus texts that appear to teach that knowledge is the means to liberation must be understood as explanatory (*arthavāda*), following the Mīmāṃsā rule (cf. *Mīmāṃsāsūtra* IV.3.1).

6 (ET 28-31) 46-50. *Answer* : No. The nature and causes of liberation on the one hand and of worldly prosperity (*abhyudaya*) on the other are contradictory to each other. You admit that realization of the true nature of the Self is liberation. But didn't the Self have that nature all along ? If so, what are actions supposed to be for ? If not, it couldn't be the Self's nature, since it would depend on causes. If the nature of the Self involves actions there can be no liberation at all.

7 (ET 31-39) 51-69. *Objection* : Actions are required in order to remove the sources of bondage arising from sensory contact.

Answer : What is supposed to be the cause of that contact ? If it is accidental, then, there being no control over what is accidental, there will be no liberation. If the contacts are the result of (past) merit and demerit, how can they produce contact in a Self that is by nature unattached (*asaṅga*)? Or if the Self is not unattached, again there is no hope of liberation.

Objection : The Self is potentially an agent and an enjoyer, but it is the actualization of the results of these traits that constitutes bondage. When merely the potentiality (*śakti*) remains but all actualization of them is stopped, liberation ensues.

Answer : Is this "potentiality" essentially connected with its results or not ? If it is, there can be no liberation in the fashion you describe. But since there is liberation, the "potentiality" cannot be causally related to its effects. Again, if the potentiality is essentially identical with its results neither can exist without the other. Furthermore, if the "potentiality" exists at the time of liberation then its effects cannot be ruled out, any more than the sun can exist without giving off heat.

8 (ET 40-57) 70-107. You say one gets liberation by abandoning the prohibited and optional actions. But even the most careful person will find it impossible to accomplish this—at least, it will be very difficult, and thus no one will follow your path.

Opponent : Nevertheless, that *is* the path, no matter how difficult.

Answer : No. Action is only a dubious means to liberation, and one wants a method that provides certainty. That method is through Self-knowledge. In any case, there is no Vedic maxim to the effect that one should abandon prohibited and optional acts in order to get liberation. In fact, scripture clearly says that liberation is obtained through knowledge. Now actions can at best only be a doubtful means to anything, since no matter what one may obtain by abandoning prohibited and optional acts one may also experience the results of present and future sins. Only through knowledge can one find a sure way to liberation. Ritual acts may purify the agent and ready him for Self-knowledge, but one who knows the truth of the Veda will realize that action is futile. A person may even be born free from desire because of previous (yogic) practice; he is eligible for Self-knowledge immediately. For one who is without attachment and desires knowledge actions are pointless, as is seen in cases such as those of Vāmadeva, Maitreyī, and Gārgī, all of whom gained Self-knowledge without performance of ritual actions.

Even if one avoids prohibited and optional actions in this life he may, on death, go to heaven because of his past good deeds, and thus he will not get liberation thereby. The same reasoning shows that the performance of the required actions (*nityakarman*) is not a sure means to liberation. Again, one cannot be sure that one will get liberation at the end of any one lifetime, for some very sinful deeds, such as killing a Brahmin, need more than one lifetime for their karmic results to be worked out.

Nor is it the case that the performance of required actions fails to incur any karmic results. This is indicated by Āpastambha (*Āpastambhadharmasūtra* I.20.3) when he explains that good deeds produce good results.

So, once the Self is supposed to be an agent and an enjoyer there is no possibility of liberation. Thus the Self-knowledge that we contend leads to liberation is not the knowledge of that self which is the agent in sacrificial actions, etc., and which might be the subject of explanatory sentences subsidiary to injunctions (as the opponent argued in section 5 above). Knowledge of the true Self cannot be a subsidiary to action.

Objection : In order that a sacrificer can even make sense of his ritual actions he must know that his self is capable of transmigrating into future bodies; so self-knowledge is subsidiary to action.

9 (ET 58-64) 108-121. *Answer* : That transmigrating self is only known by one who is ignorant of the truth, for its nature involves relation with something that is not a self, that is, bodies. Knowledge of such a self may be subsidiary to action, but that knowledge leads to karmic processes and bondage. The Self-knowledge we speak of is knowledge of the pure Self; Its association with anything else is ignorance—agency, enjoyership, action, and experience of its fruits, body, sons, wife, etc., indeed all things making one eligible for action are products of ignorance. Any notion of the nature of one thing as residing in another is a sign of ignorance.

10 (ET 65-72) 122-140a. It is a self that identifies itself with something different from itself that is eligible for actions. That identification arises from ignorance, and true Self-knowledge removes that ignorance. That knowledge arises from the Vedānta. *That* knowledge removes ignorance and is not what makes one eligible for actions. Thus scriptural sentences that speak of the result of *that* knowledge cannot be taken as explanatory (*arthavāda*) and subsidiary to injunctions to act. Or, if we admit that such sentences are explanatory and auxiliary, they are auxiliary, not to injunctions to act, but rather to major texts such as "that thou art," that is, the scriptural sentences in question are explanations of existent things (*bhūtārthavāda*), not of nonexistent things (*abhūtārthavāda*) that have to be obtained through acting. Action is an obstacle to liberation, not its means. The seeker of liberation, being nonattached, will avoid action; the Self-knower, recognizing no differences cannot act.

11 (ET 73-83) 140b-161a. *Objection* : Agency, etc., constitute the nature of the seeker.

Answer : No. The *pramāṇas* tell us otherwise, and furthermore, if it were so there could be no liberation.

Objection (from a materialist): There is no liberation, since the self is constantly changing in its experiences from moment to moment.

Answer : The Self is eternal and not constantly changing. It has no shape, etc., as do the particles of nature. Thus there is no possibility of prior absence (*prāgabhāva*) in the Self, as there is in a composite material thing. Having no parts, there is no question of change in the Self. Indeed, the Self is the witness (*sākṣin*) of agency, etc., which are therefore not Its attributes. It is not the object of the *pramāṇas*, which can grasp only those composite things that exist for the sake of something else. For the same reason, desire, aversion, etc., are not qualities of the Self; rather, they are properties of the internal organ (*manas*), and indeed they too are the products of ignorance. If desire, etc., were caused by oneself, that self would not desire what is evil; if they were caused by God we couldn't be sure of getting rid of them. The released self cannot rid himself of desire, etc., lacking such instruments for the purposes as a body, etc. Thus it must be ignorance that is the cause.

12 (ET 83-89) 161b-174a. *Objection* : If what you say is true the *karmakāṇḍa* is invalid; but if so, everyone must lose faith in scripture, including the Vedānta.

Answer : No. All *pramāṇas*, including scripture, are valid until Self-knowledge is acquired; after that, they all cease to be applicable. The injunctions prescribed in the *karmakāṇḍa* are valid for the man still under the sway of ignorance, but they fail to apply to the realized man.

Objection : Granted that agency and nonagency are not possible together, why cannot they apply in sequence and in either order— a man sometimes acting, sometimes thinking?

Answer : No. Knowledge is the nature of the Self, not action. Thus whereas action may precede knowledge, the reverse order cannot occur, any more than fire, which is naturally hot, can by itself become cold.

Objection : Reality has the nature of difference-cum-nondifference (*bhedābheda*), so there is no problem.

Answer : One thing cannot possess a self-contradictory nature.

13 (ET 88-96) 174b-188a. *Objection* : Is the world (*saṃsāra*) different from Brahman or nondifferent? If different, Brahman becomes limited. If nondifferent, either Brahman has parts (like the world) or knowledge will be unnecessary (since we will already have it, being in *saṃsāra*=Brahman) ! And if Brahman is itself ignorant, that is a serious fault in It; while It is free from ignorance, knowledge has no purpose.

Answer: Ignorance is imputed (*prakalpyate*) to Brahman by the ignorant *jiva*; from Brahman's point of view ignorance doesn't exist. Ignorance is not intelligible when examined using *pramāṇas*; it is not a real entity, and thus no one can have valid knowledge of it. Still, the Bhedābhedavādin has to make a number of assumptions to substantiate his view, whereas the Advaitin has to make only this one postulation, of ignorance.

Objection : The world of plurality is known to everyone, so it is real, and not the nondual (*advaya*).

Answer : Merely being commonly known is not a valid reason to assume the existence of something. Indeed, all of ordinary experience is false.

14 (ET 97-111) 188b-217. *Objection* : But ordinary perception is immediate, whereas the Self-knowledge gained from scripture is not.

Answer : What do you mean by "not immediate" ? The content of Self-knowledge is the most immediate thing of all, the inner Self. And perception depends on consciousness, which is the Self, so that scripture tells us of the most immediate means of all. Indeed the immediacy of perception depends entirely on the greater immediacy of consciousness, the Self itself.

You argued earlier (section 5 above) that since scripture, etc., speak only of action it is only actions that lead to liberation. We admit that actions may constitute an indirect means to liberation; what we deny is that they constitute a direct means thereto. Actions may help gain release, either by producing desire for Self-knowledge or by purifying the aspirant. And scripture, etc., clearly do not speak *only* of action; Self-knowledge is also spoken of there. If you mean that scripture does not *enjoin* Self-knowledge, we have answered that before and will address it again.

Objection : The Vedas do not teach Self-knowledge in texts such as "The knower of the Self is free from sorrow." Such texts are eulogies of that self which is the agent in ritual actions.

Answer: Why do you resort to secondary meaning (*lakṣaṇā*) when it is inappropriate ? The primary meaning is quite clear and acceptable, when we realize that the text in question refers to the true Self and the agent-self.

Objection : All of what you say is sheer imagination. I do not find from experience that knowledge produces such a result as you claim.

Answer : You may legitimately raise such a doubt if you satisfy the conditions for eligibility for knowledge, hear a sentence like "that art thou," and do not realize Self-knowledge. Of course, it is possible too that, hearing the sentence, one does not understand what the words in it mean. But if one does, the truth must come to him, like the realization "I am the tenth man."

Thus we conclude that renunciation of all actions is a subsidiary cause of liberation, since it helps one to understand the meaning of the great sentences (such as "that art thou").

15. (ET 111-115) 218-226. The gods, afraid that men would get liberated, confused men and as a result men took up ritual action. That one should abandon all actions and thus gain knowledge is attested to in scripture and tradition (*smṛti*).

16. (ET 116-126) 227-246. *Objection* : Without something to be accomplished (*kārya*) there can be no eligibility (*adhikāra*) for knowledge. [Thus, since a *kārya* requires an act (*kriyā*), action leads to liberation.]

Answer : Do you mean that *kārya* is required to establish eligibility for acquiring the means to knowledge, or for knowledge itself ? Since the means to knowledge, that is, hearing the great sentences of scripture, results from the prior abandonment of actions, the first alternative is inapplicable. And with respect to Self-knowledge, since it is an existing entity there is no question of "eligibility" as there is in the case of things gotten through injunctions.

There is no need for injunctions in the case of Self-knowledge. Vāmadeva got knowledge while he was still in his mother's womb—clearly no one enjoined anything on him there ! The situation is analogous to that of the son of a king who happened to be brought up in the family of a hunter and who thought that he, too, was a hunter. The recollection that he was a king removed his huntership. Likewise, for the ignorant the recollection that one is Brahman—through hearing "that art thou"—removes ignorance along with its products. Thus there is no question of injunction here.

What could an injunction accomplish, after all ? The purposes of injunction are precisely four—(1) origination (*utpatti*), (2) obtaining something (*āpti*), (3) purification (*saṃskāra*), and (4) modification of something (*vikāra*). Liberation cannot be any of these, since it is not brought about at all. The knowledge seeker is not caused—by an injunction or anything else—to get something, but is rather awakened, as a sleeping king is by his bards. The master is not ordered to act by his servant.

Injunctions have their scope with respect to *dharma*, as is clear on examining the *Mīmāṃsāsūtras*, which deal only with future results of human activity. Relating to a different subject matter, the evidence of Mīmāṃsā cannot controvert the Vedānta.

17. (ET 126-135) 247-267. Brahman, the content of all Vedantic texts, is not something with relation to which we can speak of a productive operation (*bhāvanā*). Where the question of the proper

instrument (*karaṇa*) and the method of proceeding (*itikartavyatā*) arise, injunctions are appropriate; but liberation is not something that can be produced, so injunctions are out of point.

Objection : If the only obstacle to release were indeed ignorance (*moha*) you would be correct. But if the bound self (*saṃsārin*) is a part (*ekadeśa*) or a modification (*vikāra*) of the Self liberation cannot be gotten solely by removing ignorance, but must involve action as well.

Answer : Even on those construals of the transmigrating self liberation still is not produced by action, since the real Self already exists; rather, liberation is revealed through the destruction of the binding ignorance. However, neither of the two relations proposed as holding between *jīva* and Self are correct. No causal relation can connect these two. Either *jīva* and Self are identical or they are different. If they are identical there can be no causal relation between them. If they are different the only liberation would involve destruction of the *jīva*. Such "liberation" does not involve action in any case.

18 (ET 135-145) 268-288. Again, completeness (*pūrṇa*) is perfection (*niḥśreyasa*), and anything short of complete appears only because of ignorance; thus liberation comes from removal of ignorance by its opposite, knowledge, and not by action, and so injunctions are useless. Appeal to Jaimini (in section 5 above) won't help, for in the *Mīmāṃsāsūtra* passage (I.2.1) "since scripture (*āmnaya*) has action as its subject" the word "scripture" refers only to the *karmakāṇḍa*, not to the Upaniṣads. Since the Upaniṣads have an altogether different subject matter they cannot be viewed as subsidiary to the injunctions in the *karmakāṇḍa*. Other Mīmāṃsā passages are likewise interpreted to show that the Upaniṣads are not subsidiary to injunctions.

Objection : They should be viewed as subsidiary, on the rule that where a single sentence meaning (*ekavākyatā*) is possible, splitting the sentence (*vākyabheda*) is precluded.

Answer : That rule only applies to cases where a single sentence meaning is possible. Since injunctions relate to a subject matter entirely distinct from that which the Upaniṣads relate to, the rule does not apply.

Objection : But you yourself argue that the *karmakāṇḍa* is subsidiary to the *jñānakāṇḍa* !

Answer : Yes, but that doesn't mean they have the same subject matter. *Karman* is subsidiary to *jñāna* in that, whereas actions may or may not be used as a means to knowledge, meditation is an action that does serve as a means to knowledge; thus the rule here relates to the cooperation between two sentences (*vākyaikavākyatā*) and not to single sentence meaning. Cooperation between two sentences can occur even when each sentence has its own distinct subject matter.

Objection : Since the beginning and end of the Vedas agree the whole Veda must have one subject matter. Thus the one who is eligible for release is the one who follows the injunctions prescribed there, rather than your view according to which eligibility involves renunciation of all actions.

Answer : No one could possibly follow all the injunctions found in the Vedas in one lifetime ! Thus no one will be eligible for release !

19 (ET 145-150) 289-298. *Objection* : You specify desire for liberation as one of the conditions of eligibility for release. But if liberation is not validly understood it cannot be desired; yet if it is validly understood there is no need for desire.

Answer : We find that some persons desire pleasure unattached to any particular place or time. Furthermore, on our view, as opposed to yours, knowledge unlike action yields immediate results rather than results at some future time. If knowledge had only future results, like action, then the kind of doubt you raise might arise—that is, as to whether there are any eligible persons, because the future result might not actually occur. But since the result of knowledge is immediate no such doubt need arise.

Objection : Where does this knowledge come from ?

Answer : From the removal of bondage.

Objection : That bondage is either past, present, or future. If it is past, it is not an obstacle, and if future, it does not now bind. But there can be no present bondage for one who validly understands.

Answer: One may have studied the Veda and understood its meaning, yet not be liberated because of a present obstacle; the *Chāndogya Upaniṣad* gives as analogy the case of the man who walks over buried treasure without knowing it.

20 (ET 150-155) 299-308. *Objection* : Liberation is eternal pleasure (*atyantikasukha*), so of course it is desired. And I agree that the *karmakāṇḍa* is subsidiary to the *jñānakāṇḍa*; actions purify the self that is seeking liberation. So the two sections of the Veda complement each other. It is not that one who performs actions seeks one goal, heaven, whereas the Self-knower seeks another, liberation. In scripture the term "heaven" is used synonymously with "liberation."

Answer : No. If "heaven" merely means any sort of happiness then one would not be inclined to perform ritual acts supervening on other actions that produce happiness. "Heaven" must mean conditioned pleasure and so is different from liberation, which is unconditioned. Again, if liberation (=heaven) is accepted to be the result of optional (*kāmya*) actions it could be attained by a single act, which would render senseless all the other injunctions in scripture. In any case, scripture (*Muṇḍaka Upaniṣad* I.2.7, I.2.12; *Chāndogya Upaniṣad* V.10.7) shows that one does not get liberation through action.

21 (ET 156-158) 309-312. *Objection*: It would be quite rash to abandon acting, since scripture enjoins ritual acts.

Answer: It would be even more rash to ignore scripture, which indicates that one who is nonattached should renounce actions. And scripture is not inconsistent between these two; it is speaking to different classes of persons in the two sections.

22 (ET 158-168) 313-331. *Objection*: If that is true, why doesn't Śaṃkara say so directly? All he says is that scripture provides evidence for the existence of the Self.

Answer: Śaṃkara is proving that the Vedānta is valid. Only when that is shown can he go on to show the relation between the two parts of scripture. Or else Śaṃkara may think that there is no relation at all between the two sections, since they have different subject matters.

Objection: In any case scripture at best only indicates the required (*nitya*) and occasional (*naimittika*) actions as means to Self-knowledge; so the two parts of scripture cannot be entirely related.

Answer: All actions are connoted by the term "sacrifice" (*yajña*) (in *Bṛhadāraṇyaka Upaniṣad* IV.4.22), since even optional acts, which no doubt normally have purposes other than knowledge, may operate as means to knowledge.

Objection: No, optional acts are expressly condemned in scripture as being "transitory" (*Muṇḍaka Upaniṣad* I.2.7), etc.

Answer: True, but they are enjoined. The condemnation is not of the act as such, but of attachment to the fruits of such an act.

Now the passages on meditation (*upāsanā*) that appear in the *jñānakāṇḍa* suggest meditation as a way of getting ready for Self-knowledge, but they do not lead directly to liberation.

23 (ET 168-176) 332-342a. None of the six kinds of evidence can show that knowledge is subsidiary in meaning to action. (1) There is no express statement in scripture (*śruti*) to show that Self-knowledge is auxiliary to ritual action. (2) Nor is that shown by an inferential connection (*liṅga*) drawn from the meaning of the words used in scripture. (3) And it cannot be inferred from any needed syntactical connection among the words constituting the sentence (*vākya*), as is possible in such a case as "He who has a ladle made of *parṇa* wood hears no evil sound" (*yasya parṇamayī juhur bhavati na sa*

pāpaṃ ślokaṃ śrunoti, Taittirīyasaṃhitā III.5.7.1), where syntactical connection forces us to presume that the ladle is made of *parṇa* wood; mention of a ladle leads us to expect an account of the material of which it is made, but Self-knowledge cannot lead us to expect mention of action to which it is subsidiary, since knowledge completely undermines the presumption of agency. (4) Nor can it be inferred from context (*prakaraṇa*), since as we have said the contact governing knowledge is entirely different from that governing action. (5 and 6) It cannot be shown on the basis of name (*nāma*) or sequence (*krama*) either, since they operate only when inferential connection (*liṅga*) operates, and as we have seen it does not operate here.

24 (ET 176-183) 342b-356a. *Objection* (by a *kāmavilayavādin*) : We agree that action is subsidiary to knowledge; it is so just because as long as desires hold sway there can be no Self-knowledge. Thus actions are required so that all one's desires are fulfilled; one thus obtains a god-like state (of Prajāpati) and from there one can realize the Self.

Answer : No. Even a life of a hundred years will not allow one to fulfil all his desires; rather, they just become multiplied by experience of pleasure. Desires can only be eradicated when one recognizes their faults; then one abandons them, and abandons the actions that would fulfil them as well. Gaining the god-like state of Prajāpati does not open the door to liberation; all particularizations (*viśeṣa*) alike block progress to liberation, and the Prajāpati state is no exception. Prajāpati has no more nor less reality than a worm, since reality is without particularizations.

25 (ET 183-195) 356b-377a. *Objection* (by a combined-path theorist or *jñānakarmasamuccayavādin*): There are three ways in which knowledge and action can be combined, depending on whether the one or the other or neither are subsidiary.

Answer : It can't be that neither are subsidiary; as has been indicated, the two kinds of texts have entirely distinct subject matters and thus cannot function together to yield a common meaning, and they produce distinct kinds of results (liberation for knowledge, heaven for ritual action). And neither one can be subsidiary to the other, since they are mutually opposed in what they presuppose. Of course, other kinds of knowledge regularly assist action—for example, knowing that one is a Brahmin is helpful to performing ritual acts. But Self-knowledge isn't helpful in this way, since it completely undermines the idea of agency that is critical in performing action. Self-knowledge precludes action. The only combination possible between Self-knowledge and action is succession—action preceding

Self-knowledge, since action is the external means whereas knowledge is the internal means to liberation.

26. (ET 195-211) 377b-410a. *Objection* (by a *prapañcavilayavādin*): The *karmakāṇḍa* is subsidiary to the *jñānakāṇḍa*, since the *karmakāṇḍa* teaches the means by which all differences found in the world are dissolved (*laya*; *vilaya*). For example, the text enjoining one who desires heaven to sacrifice actually enjoins us to give up the notion that the body is the Self; prohibitions enjoin us to give up actions instigated by attachment, etc.; the injunctions to perform required and occasional ritual actions likewise enjoin us to stop performing optional actions. It is in scripture as it is in the world; commands and warnings are used to prevent actions or to change the course of things. In this way all the *karmakāṇḍa* texts prepare one for Self-knowledge by dissolving actions based on attachment.

Answer : No. For which person is the *karmakāṇḍa* supposed to teach the dissolution of worldly actions ? Not for the one who seeks liberation, as scripture says that the result of the actions it enjoins is heaven, which is a different state from liberation. But it does not teach dissolution for one who desires heaven either, since one must perform actions (not dissolve them) in order to reach heaven, on the authority of scripture itself. Does the teaching exist then for one who wishes to destroy the world altogether ? But nonexistence cannot be the result striven after. Finally, is it that the *karmakāṇḍa* teaches dissolution as a means to arriving at the true knowledge that in turn produces release ? But one can have true knowledge even while the world exists, and when it is dissolved, as in deep sleep, there is no Self-knowledge.

If the world is natural (*svābhāvika*) it cannot be dissolved; if it is a product it is removed by destroying its cause, not by destroying it. The only way the world can be dissolved is by removing its cause (ignorance) through knowledge; dissolving one's faculties into deep sleep happens periodically by nature and does not arise from scriptural teaching.

Again, if the idea is that the injunctions both enjoin dissolution of the universe *and* attainment of heaven this won't do as a way of explaining the scriptural texts—one sentence can't have two opposed meanings. Anyway, if injunctions have as their meaning the dissolution of the world there can be no hearing of the great sentences, etc., which are the means to liberation, and thus liberation, as well as heaven, will become accidental, and the scripture will lose its point.

Objection : Both *kāṇḍas* have liberation as their intent; heaven is not an accidental result but is an intermediate step on the way to liberation, just as one may go through a village to get to the town.

Answer : No, the analogy is not apt, since one does not desire to reach the village by which one reaches the town, but one does desire to gain heaven.

Objector : Well, heaven is desired as means to the final end of liberation, just as the village is desired to be reached in order to get to the town.

Answer : No. In the *karmakāṇḍa* one only hears about heaven, not liberation; one who only hears of the village will not go on to the town beyond !

27 (ET 211-221) 410b-427. *Objection* : But injunctions must be subsidiary to the texts on knowledge, since they help one become eligible for Self-knowledge.

Answer : No. Prohibitions help one become eligible for knowledge by producing a turning-away (*nivṛtti*) from actions stemming from attachment, etc. But how can (positive) injunctions destroy attachment ? None of the several kinds of injunctions could do that. A specifying injunction (*niyamavidhi*, which states the operation by which an already established activity is to be carried out) cannot destroy attachment. Neither can an excluding injunction (*parisaṃkhyāvidhi*, which excludes one of several alternative interpretations concerning which act is enjoined). The only relevant kind of injunction for your claim is the main kind of injunction that commands us to do something not established otherwise (*apūrvavidhi*).

Objector : Yes, and such an injunction may cause one to turn away from actions stemming from attachment, just as one who desires to acquire a village by performing a certain kind of rite (the *saṃgrahaṇī*) turns away from getting the same result by undertaking service to the king.

Answer : Again, your analogy is inapt. The *saṃgrahaṇī* rite may get you your village in the future, whereas service should get it for you in this life; thus they do not have the same result, and the one does not necessarily cause you to turn away from the other. Anyway, activity enjoined by scripture cannot very well remove all activity stemming from attachment, since, for example, one would then have no money and could not pay for the activity enjoined ! There would then be no actions at all resulting from scriptural injunctions, and the *karmakāṇḍa* would become useless.

28 (ET 222-228) 428-440a. *Objection* : The texts on knowledge are subsidiary to those on action.

Answer : That would have to be proved by recourse to the six kinds of proof (see above, section 22), but none of them suffice.

Objection : The proof arises from presumption (*arthākṣepa*)—one has to know the Self in order to be able to act as an agent in acts intended to produce heaven, etc.

Answer : Yes, one must know the agent-self, but one need not (and cannot) know the real Self.

Objection : Our thesis is proved from the passages (*Mānavadharmaśāstra* VI.35; *Taittirīyasaṃhitā* VI.3.11) that say that one must gain Self-knowledge before discharging the three debts (to gods, ancestors, and teachers).

Answer : No. Scripture indicates that even the *brahmacārin* may renounce (*Jābāla Upaniṣad* 4), and anyway, the texts you mention only show that one should discharge the three debts some time, not necessarily after Self-knowledge.

29 (ET 228-236) 440b-455a. *Objection* (by the Prābhākara or Niyogavādin) : The Self, being the meaning of a word (*padārtha*), like corn, etc., must be known through *pramāṇas* other than scripture. The Self can be recognized by examining the states of waking, dreaming, and deep sleep. Scripture's function is to suppress (*nirodha*) the *vāsanās* arising from those three states or to suppress the internal organ. When the *vāsanās* have been suppressed the Self, being self-luminous, shines without dependence on any *pramāṇa*. Thus the Upaniṣads are not *pramāṇas* of the Self, but only as enjoining something, that is, the suppressions of *vāsanās*, which are the sole causes of any relation between the Self and what is bad (*anartha*). Thus it is release from them that constitutes liberation, and nothing else.

The operation of words is impossible except as dependent upon the injunctive force (*niyoga*), and it is impossible that the injunctive force should relate to what already exists. Again, only something yet-to-be-experienced can be an aim of human activity. Therefore scripture is not a valid *pramāṇa* of the Self—*both* the *jñānakāṇḍa* and the *karmakāṇḍa* are auxiliary to the injunction to eliminate obstruction.

30 (ET 236-248) 455b-478a. *Answer* : That is not right. Even without an injunction to do so we find that men accomplish their ends by using *pramāṇas*. Through inference we can come to know that the *vāsanās* produce relations between the Self and what is bad, and that by suppressing them one will remove bondage. For you, as for the Buddhists, scripture is of no help at all in gaining liberation. Furthermore, since *vāsanās* are endless it isn't possible to suppress them.

Can direct Self-knowledge destroy ignorance, and so destroy the *vāsanās*, or not? If so, you accept our view. If not, how could meditation (*bhāvanā*) destroy them, since meditation is itself destroyed by frustration (*duḥkha*), etc.

The Self is not in fact the meaning of a word, or for that matter, the meaning of a sentence. Scripture gives us knowledge of the Self not by a direct meaning-relation with its words, but rather by denying such a relation.

There are no *vāsanās* in deep sleep, etc., and yet those states do not constitute liberation. As for the notion that the Self shines self-luminously without dependence upon any *pramāṇa*, we answer that only through a *pramāṇa* can one grasp its so shining.

Likewise, you yourself cannot grasp the injunctive force except through your consciousness, which is the Self. The Self is not to be established by *pramāṇas*, since all things are established only by the Self (i.e., consciousness), so It doesn't depend on anything else.

As for the notion that only what is yet-to-be-experienced can be an aim of human activity, it is experience that is the aim, not objects; experience, that is, consciousness or the Self, is constant whereas objects vary, so it is the former that is the ultimate human aim, as well as the content of all the *pramāṇas*. Thus it is clear that the Upaniṣads speak of It too. Indeed, all empirical usage, whether ordinary or based on the Vedas, is for the sake of the enjoyer, who is essentially consciousness. Yājñavalkya's words in the present Upaniṣad ("for the Self's sake everything is loved," etc.) illustrate this.

31 (ET 248-286) 478b-542a. *Objection* (by the Niyogavādin) : Only what is to be done (*kārya*) can be the meaning of scripture, and so scripture cannot concern the Self. Existing entities are known by the other *pramāṇas*; if scripture grasped them also it would have no function of its own and would be dependent on the others. Every word is attested to by common experience as pertaining to activity (*pravṛtti*) or its cessation (*nivṛtti*). We learn the meanings of words by noticing their capacity to elicit, etc., activity or inactivity.

Counterobjection : Other *pramāṇas* can grasp what-is-to-be-done (*kārya*).

Objector : No, the only means for knowing it is the Vedas. Now the Vedic sentences do not produce activity—if they did, everyone would act whenever they heard a sentence; rather it *indicates* or makes known (*jñāpaka*) activity.

Counterobjection : It is desires, etc., that make us understand which actions to perform on hearing words.

Objector : No. Desires, etc., are the causes of prompting (*preraṇa*) one to act; the sound of the words make known this prompting. For example, a student may be commanded to act by his master when there is no desire on his part, nor even any recognition of desire, etc., on the part of his master. Thus desires, anger, etc., become prompters to activity only as they are known through other *pramāṇas*. It is therefore the injunctive force indicating what is to be done that is what prompts us to activity.

Other counterobjections to the Niyogavāda thesis are considered, most of them turning on grammatical considerations relating to verb endings. The Niyogavādin shows how even indicative verbs have an injunctive sense or force, and thus that obligation is a pervasive feature of our language. It is the fundamental feature, to which other features are subservient in function. The injunction "one who desires heaven should sacrifice" is exhaustively analyzed.

32 (ET 287-301) 542b-569a. *Answer* : The Vedānta texts produce the modifications (*vṛtti*) of awareness in which the Self is reflected. The Self is self-evident.

Objection : If so the Vedantic texts have no use.

Answer : Their function is to dispel the ignorance that veils the Self. Both knowledge and ignorance are experienced in the Self; that is not incomprehensible, any more than what experience also tells us, that is, that in deep sleep there is consciousness but no cognizer. Both sections of the Veda tell us about what is beyond the reach of the senses, but the *karmakāṇḍa* tells us what is to be done, whereas the *jñānakāṇḍa* teaches the Self. Both parts are *pramāṇa*, but of different kinds of things. (Other ways of interpreting the relevant parts of Śaṃkara's comments are considered.)

Objection : Since the Vedantic texts are not injunctive, like *mantras* and *arthavādas*, they cannot be *pramāṇas*.

Answer : *Mantras* and *arthavādas* are subsidiary to injunctions, so it is clear why they don't constitute independent *pramāṇas*. But the Vedantic texts are not subsidiary to injunctions, so the analogy doesn't hold. There are three kinds of *arthavādas* : (1) *guṇavāda* or metaphor, where the literal meaning is incompatible with what is established by some other *pramāṇa*; (2) *anuvāda* or restatement, where the meaning is established by another *pramāṇa*; and (3) *bhūtārthavāda*, where the meaning is neither established nor precluded by other *pramāṇas*. In all three cases the *arthavāda*, even though subsidiary to an injunction, has its own meaning—so what is the objection to allowing Vedantic texts to have their own meaning?

33 (ET 301-315) 569b-602a. The function of a *pramāṇa* can relate only to what is existent and as yet unknown. If perception and the rest (excluding scripture) are claimed to relate to the Self it would have to be shown that their object is as yet unknown. How could this unknownness be shown? Not by another *pramāṇa*, since this would involve mutual dependence. So, perception and the

other nonscriptural *pramāṇas* cannot relate to the Self. But they cannot conflict with the scriptural (Vedānta) testimony, since consciousness is the locus of all awareness of any kind.

There is no rule that words can only by used to mention what is to be done. For example, "Be happy! You have a fine son" enjoins neither activity nor cessation of it. Yet such a sentence can give happiness. Again, telling a man who imagines himself to be bitten by a (nonexistent) snake "Don't be afraid, it's not a snake" does not issue an injunction not to be afraid; the fear vanishes when the truth is known. An injunctive force (*niyoga*) occurs only when a person who knows that something is to be done is moved to act to do it in order that he may get what the injunction advises. In the Vedantic texts, however, as soon as he hears the words the goal is realized and nothing remains to be done; an apt analogy would be telling somebody a story to satisfy his curiosity. Of course, a statement of fact *may* be followed by action; someone told "This road is infested with robbers" may leave the road, but that is because he desires to avoid being robbed—the statement itself does not prompt one to activity, rather the desire does.

Objection: "This road is infested with robbers" surely is intended by its speaker as enjoining the hearer against traveling the road.

Answer: No. The meaning of a sentence is not a function of the intention of the speaker but of what the words have the capacity to mean. Especially you (Mīmāṃsakas) should accept that, since according to you scripture has no speaker! And since a speaker may intend all sorts of things, his words would then have to mean all sorts of things. The case is analogous to the other *pramāṇas*: one who desires to avoid snakes turns away when he sees a snake, but the seeing is not the turning away.

34 (ET 315-324) 602b-620. What is your theory of meaning? (1) Do you hold that words have meanings independently of their use in sentences? (2) Or do you take it that words mean only future results (*kārya*)? Or (3) does word meaning depend on the words' connections with other words?

(1) If words have independent meanings, then how can they combine to yield sentence meaning? The combination would be semantically nonsensical.

(3) If word meaning depends on connection with other words, then since not all words are injunctive in sense your position will have to be abandoned.

(2) So, your view must be that words mean *only* future results. But if so, all words speaking of the same future result will become

synonymous, which is absurd. Further, declarative statements will become meaningless. Again, what about a word—a verb, say—that directly means a future result : on the theory in question it does not have independent meaning and so must depend on other words, but those words are either injunctive or not; if not, those words have no meaning themselves, but if so, those (injunctive) words require further words, *ad infinitum*. Indeed, if all words only have sense as related to future effects, then they couldn't combine into sentences, since they would lack expectancy (*anāpekṣatva*). As a result, an injunctive force (*niyoga*) cannot be the meaning of an injunctive sentence. Yet if not, how does it figure in producing sentence meaning? For example, in the sentence "sacrifice with *soma*," what relates the words "sacrifice" and "*soma*"? Either the words require *niyoga* to relate them, or they are related without dependence on *niyoga*. But we have shown that *niyoga* cannot operate without depending on other already meaningful expressions with which to combine to form a sentence. So the *niyoga* or connection with the expected future result is only one content of words, not the meaning of a whole (injunctive) sentence. This fits well the relevant passage in Śabara's (*Mīmāṃsāsūtra*)*bhāṣya*.

Objection : But one needs to know the future result in order to connect the injunction with sacrifice.

Answer : That is, I gather, one must know the future result before one knows anything. But then one must know the future result before one can know the future result, which is impossible.

Objection : No. One can know a future result without dependence on another knowledge of one.

Answer : Then the obligation of "sacrifice" can equally well be known without dependence on any other knowledge.

Objection : But sacrificing is onerous, and one needs to have a future result indicated in order to be motivated to sacrifice.

Answer : Merely indicating a future result is not enough; the future result must be connected with sacrificing by an appropriate syntactical indication (e.g., an injunctive verb ending); but then, since the *niyoga* depends on the verb ending and the verb ending depends (according to you) on the *niyoga*, there will be (the fault of) mutual dependence.

Anyway, what is obligatory—that is, what *is* the "future result" (*kārya*)? It is something that requires human effort for it to occur. But then it is the sacrifice that is the obligatory future result, and not *niyoga*.

Objection : But *niyoga* precisely *is* the obligatoriness.

Answer : Then it can't *have* obligatoriness ! Only what is not now existing can be obligatory, but according to you *niyoga* exists now.

So, the right theory of meaning is this : some words denote existing things, some future results; likewise, sentences may or may not have as their sense existing things or future results.

35 (ET 325-331) 621-633. *Question* : Then why does activity arise after hearing certain words ?

Answer : Well, if one desires something spoken of in what he hears, he will naturally act. There is no such thing as *niyoga* over and beyond the instrument (*karaṇa*), *modus operandi* (*itikartavyatā*) and the thing to be accomplished (*bhavya*). Indeed, what is *niyoga* ?

Niyoga is not (1) inducement (*preraṇa*); for inducement is a function of words that has *niyoga* as its sense, and the sense of words cannot be identical with the words.

It is not (2) internal effort (*antaras prayatna*), for effort is mental, and *niyoga* isn't.

It is not (3) action (*kriyā*), since action belongs to its agent, whereas *niyoga* belongs to the person prompted by the injunction to act, and these need not be the same.

It is not (4) the result (*phala*), since *niyoga* is not what is desired.

It is not (5) an instrument (*kāraka*) for obtaining a result, for *niyoga* is what is yet to be obtained, whereas the instrument exists already to obtain it.

And it is not (6) anything else, for there is no clear statement of any other alternative.

And it is not (7) something unqualified temporarily, since if someone says "pot," there being no temporal qualification, it must become a *niyoga* !

And it is not (8) something beyond the senses (*atīndriya*), since it is the operation (*vyāpāra*) of the person prompted to act, which certainly cannot be beyond the senses.

Objection : *Niyoga* is what is accomplished when sacrifice is carried out.

Answer : Not if *niyoga* is eternal, as I gather you claim.

Objection : *Niyoga* is the expected future result (*kārya*) that functions to produce the ultimate human purpose (viz., heaven).

Answer : Is this *niyoga* always present, or is it produced by human activity and then produces heaven, etc. ? If the former, since *niyoga* is always present, heaven, etc., should be also. If the latter, this contradicts your own view, for an eternal thing cannot be produced. Indeed, the expected future result must be identical with the sacrifice, etc., since they are what produce heaven, and they are produced by human activity, not *niyoga*. So *niyoga* is not identical with *kārya*.

36 (ET 332-342) 634-653. *Objection* (*by a Bhāṭṭa*) : Right. Sacrifice, etc., are the objects to which a person is induced, and the optative mood (in which injunctions are expressed) express inducement (*preraṇa*). *Niyoga* doesn't come into it, as you say.

Answer : Wrong ! The same difficulties arise for the theory that inducement is what an injunction expresses as we have shown arise for the theory that an expected future result is what it expresses. Furthermore, what is this "inducement"? It can't be the essential nature (*svarūpa*) of the injunctive mood, since its essence is to make known (*jñāpaka*) what is not known; again, other moods can express inducement. And inducement can't be the ability (*śakti*) of the injunctive mood, since the claim is that inducement is expressed by that mood, and the ability cannot be identical with what is expressed. Nor can it be the operation (*vyāpāra*) of the enjoiner. Since we are concerned with Vedic injunctions there is no enjoiner other than the Veda itself, and its operation consists in making known what is unknown, which is therefore identical with "inducement." The Vedas are valid through making known (*jñāpana*), not through inducing. However, we agree that sacrifice, etc., which are what injunctions are about, do lead to desired ends such as heaven, etc.

Objection : Even when sacrifice, etc., are performed heaven is not always seen to result.

Answer : True, but the same difficulty obtains on your own view, since even if *niyoga* were what is expressed by injunctions the results are not always seen to occur immediately thereafter.

Objection : But sacrifice, etc. (unlike *niyoga*), are acts, and must have immediate results.

Answer : No, not all acts have immediate results; consider service to the king. In any case, our theory is simpler than yours. On your view *niyoga* is interposed between the sacrifice and its result (heaven), whereas on ours it is not; so ours is simpler and thus better. And there are difficulties in relating sacrifice, etc., to *niyoga*—does sacrifice generate *niyoga* directly ? But then no sacrifice could fail to generate heaven immediately; and no other relation seems possible on your view.

37 (ET 343-364) 654-692. So, the *niyoga* theory is invalid as respects the *karmakāṇḍa*. It is also invalid in regard to the *jñānakāṇḍa*. Such a passage (in the Upaniṣads) as "the Self is to be seen" is not an injunction—the Self is not the kind of thing whose knowledge can be enjoined, for reasons already indicated.

If Self-knowledge is enjoined, what is the supposed content of the injunction? Is it (1) verbal knowledge (*śabda*), (2) contemplation (*bhāvanā*), or (3) direct experience (*sākṣātkāra*)?

(1) Since a text like "The Self is Brahman" gives us knowledge of its meaning merely by being heard, there is no need for an injunction on us to know it, any more than understanding an injunction "Sacrifice!" requires another injunction to understand it. Furthermore, the result of an injunction to know is an activity, but what is being enjoined is activity aimed at knowing the meaning of the injunction!

Objection: What is enjoined is activity designed to verify the interpretation of the text.

Answer: Is the interpretation to be based on the text or on something else? If on the text the injunction is useless. If it depends on another *pramāṇa* the Vedas would become dependent on something else for its validation.

Objection: The injunction is required to remove a meaning not intended.

Answer: No, since words of all sorts, Vedic or otherwise, don't require an injunction in order that they be properly understood. Likewise for sentences.

Objection: The injunction makes knowledge appropriate as the means to liberation, just as the injunction to sacrifice makes ritual acts appropriate as means to heaven, etc.

Answer: No. Knowledge is not an action and is not a means to an end. Liberation will result from knowledge whether or not an injunction is present.

Objection: A sentence that states a fact is not by itself a *pramāṇa*, since it only restates (*anuvāda*) what can be known by other *pramāṇas*; but if an injunctive context is inferred this will make the text an independent *pramāṇa*.

Answer: But sentences about Brahman are not restatements. They make known an existing thing not known through any other *pramāṇa*. In any case, the fact that two *pramāṇas* may know a given thing does not make the *pramāṇas* dependent.

Objection: But if we know *x* by one *pramāṇa*, where *x* is previously unknown, and then subsequently know it by another, the earlier *pramāṇa* is valid since its content was unknown.

Answer: This "unknownness" of a thing—how do you propose to establish its presence? Not by a *pramāṇa*, since *ex hypothesi* the *pramāṇa* *removes* the unknownness! And it surely can't establish itself.

38 (ET 364-371) 693-705. *Objection*: But *niyoga* (unlike

Brahman, apparently, according to your admission) is *only* known through verbal testimony as *pramāṇa*; thus verbal testimony is an independent *pramāṇa* specifically in regard to *niyoga*.

Answer : Ordinary injunctions (e.g., "eat this fruit") must then require Vedic texts to make them known !

Objector : The difference is that in ordinary (non-Vedic) injunctions the injunction relates to something about which we have knowledge by other *pramāṇas*; not so in the case of Vedic injunctions.

Answer : Precisely; so Vedantic statements are not dependent on other *pramāṇas*, since they are not about things about which we have knowledge by other *pramāṇas*.

Objector : No, it is the Vedic sentences involving words governed by *niyoga*, which are independent *pramāṇas*.

Answer : No—the same words and meanings apply in the Vedas as elsewhere; the optative case can't mean one thing in the Vedas and something else in other places.

Objection : Anyhow, the reason why we must construe Self-knowledge as enjoined is that we cannot understand the meaning of Vedic sentences providing it unless we postulate a verb governing all Vedic contexts.

Answer : A verb, to be sure, but not any particular kind of verb; declarative statements have verbs. In "that thou art" we have a verb, but it doesn't designate any action enjoined, since there is no expected result—*jīva* doesn't become the Self, nor does this sentence speak of any relation between them other than identity. Thus scriptural texts teach the nature of the Self directly, through secondary meaning (*lakṣaṇā*), even though the Self is beyond the scope of words.

39 (ET 371-379) 706-719. Even if reality could be made known by other *pramāṇas* than scripture, scripture doesn't depend on those other *pramāṇas*. When what it says is understood, it has validly made known its subject matter, and no further *pramāṇas* are needed, any more than understanding *niyoga* requires another *pramāṇa* to make known its nature. A *pramāṇa* only makes something known; whether something is to be done or not depends on the object, not the *pramāṇa*.

Objection : But *niyoga* is something to be established (*sādhya*), not already established (*siddha*) like Brahman; so your analogy fails against me.

Answer : Either *niyoga* gets established by action or it doesn't. If it does, your argument is wrong; if it doesn't, performance of actions is useless.

40 (ET 379-397) 720-755. Brahman (unlike *niyoga*) is only made known by verbal testimony (i.e., scripture), since other *pramāṇas*

only make known things on the presumption of their difference from the knowing subject.

Objection : But scriptural texts cannot constitute the *pramāṇa* unless something is adduced to explain how the several word meanings in a Vedic sentence conspire to yield a sentence meaning. In the case of other words conveying the knowledge made known by other *pramāṇas*, the production of sentence meaning from the word meanings arises from the speaker's intention, and so in the case of Vedic sentences, since they have no author, unless we postulate an injunctive sense (to relate the word meanings) they will be nonsense.

Answer : Why so ? Perhaps a verb must be postulated, but why an injunctive one ?

Objector : Only injunctive verbs indicate *niyoga* independently; other words are restatements (*anuvāda*) and cannot independently explain how sentence meaning arises from word meanings.

Answer : Do you mean that the meaning of an injunction will be known even if we do not understand the words ? That can't be right.

Objector : Yes. It is only the sentence that has the meaning associated with *niyoga*, not the words.

Answer : Then each sentence means something entirely different from any other, unrelated in any way, which is absurd. "Bring the cow" would be unrelated to "tie the cow." But "cow" is meaningful only when cowness qualifies other things than this one, and "bring" is meaningful only when things other than this one can be brought.

Objection : Still, we see that sentence meanings are learned this way: the grandfather gives a command to the father, and the son, seeing the connection between the command and his father's action, understands the relation between the optative mood and the *niyoga*.

Answer : The *niyoga* in this case is *inferred* from the father's acts—so it is not gotten from verbal testimony alone. Indeed, the inference is the critical aspect, as it must precede activity.

We conclude that *niyoga* is not necessary for anything. Words when properly related by expectancy (*ākāṃkṣā*), fitness (*yogyatā*), and proximity (*saṃnidhi*) give rise to sentence meaning without postulating an injunctive sense or *niyoga*.

41 (ET 398-401) 756-761. *Objection* : There are two kinds of injunction, originative (*utpattividhi*) and injunction as to eligibility (*adhikāravidhi*). In the *karmakāṇḍa* we find originative injunctions such as "Sacrifice !," in the *jñānakāṇḍa* such as "The Self is to be seen." We also find the other kind of injunction, as in "He who wants liberation should gain knowledge." The former kind makes known

what is not previously known; the latter kind makes one who is inactive active.

Answer : But Self-knowledge cannot lie within the scope of either. It is not the subject of an originative injunction, since such an injunction not only makes known what is not previously known, but goes on to indicate what should be done; as we have seen, Self-knowledge cannot be the subject of such an injunction. But Self-knowledge cannot fall under the second kind of injunction either, since the Self cannot be enjoined, whether it is the *jiva* or the *ātman*, since both are existing things.

42 (ET 401-420) 762-790. (2, from section 37 above) : Nor is the content of the supposed injunction contemplation of the Self.

Objection (by a Prasaṃkhyānavādin): What is enjoined is not Self-knowledge but the means to that through reflection (*manana*) and meditation (*dhyāna*) with their auxiliaries (such as calmness, etc.), more specifically through that effort called continued meditation (*prasaṃkhyāna*). Just as in the world we find that the study of the *śāstras* leads to enlightenment, so in the Vedas continued meditation is enjoined as a means to experiencing (*darśana*). It is as in medicine: a prescription may be known to cure various things, and then there may be doubt as to whether it cures typhoid (*kaṣṭajvara*), and so it is specifically stated (in *Āyur Veda*) that it does, that is, that it should be used in that case too. Granted, meditation does not immediately produce liberating insight; still, the Vedic authority indicates that it does, and nothing can prove otherwise, since Vedic authority outweighs all else in the absence of any *pramāṇa* to the contrary. (The Prasaṃkhyānavādin continues.) Now in the *karmakāṇḍa* the injunctions are primary, but in the *jñānakāṇḍa* it is the statements (such as "that art thou") that are primary, the injunctions to meditate being subsidiary to them, since unless it is first known what to meditate upon such injunctions would have no point. Thus the assertive statements give mediate (*parokṣa*) knowledge that has to be made immediate through continued meditation. The subsidiary injunction does not obscure the sense of the primary assertion; nor is there the problem of scripture meaning two different things by one and the same sentence, since meditation is enjoined by scripture as the operation by which scripture makes its sense known. This subsidiary injunction is not the only such aid—reasoning (*yukti*) likewise assists; but neither scriptural injunctions nor logic alone can produce immediate awareness of reality. Yet both are required so that the knowledge gained from scriptural assertions may validly yield immediate knowledge of the

Self. If scripture is not interpreted this way, then one who has heard of the Self but has not arrived at immediate experience of It would construe scriptural assertions as auxiliary (*arthavāda*). He will not arrive at immediate knowledge without continued meditation. It is analogous to the case of "Sacrifice with the *viśvajit*!," which is shown in the *Mīmāṃsāsūtras* (IV.3.10-16) to require the addition of the notion of desiring heaven (*svargakāma*), without which the injunction would be without validity since it leads to no result. Now just as the words "sacrifice" and "*viśvajit*" have their own meanings, no doubt, but do not function as *pramāṇa* unless one supplies "*svargakāma*," scriptural assertions and reasoning, while no doubt preserving their natural meaning, do not produce valid knowledge until associated with continued meditation.

43 (ET 421-438) 791-819. *Answer*: What is this continued meditation supposed to accomplish? Surely not the supposed reality of knower, knowing, and known, since they are nothing but pure consciousness (*saṃvit*). Nor can continued meditation remove the mediateness from the Witness-Self, since it is never mediate. And, since the Self is self established (*svataḥsiddha*), continued meditation is not needed to avoid its nonestablishment. As for the removal of ignorance—that is accomplished by *pramāṇas*, not by continued meditation. Continued meditation cannot effect the release of the Self, since It is always liberated. It is knowledge that removes ignorance, and that does not require any kind of practice, whether of meditation or anything else.

In any case, continued meditation cannot be the content of *niyoga*, for it is not itself an act, but rather it is the repetition of the acts of hearing (*śravaṇa*) and reflection (*manana*). And so it is those acts (at best) that may be enjoined, not continued meditation. Repetition is not enjoined, but rather the act is enjoined, which is then repeated; the result arises from the act, not the repetition.

You said that meditation and reasoning assist one who has heard of the Self from scripture. But that is not right, for it would make scripture depend on reasoning in order to be valid.

Objection: Reasoning is not a distinct *pramāṇa* from the others, but rather a part of a *pramāṇa*, the other parts of which are verbal testimony, meditation and the Self. Together, they make known the unity of the Self.

Answer: But none of them is then the *pramāṇa*, since it is the *pramāṇa* that reveals the truth. If all the supposed factors together produced the result, no one of them would assist the *pramāṇa*—but your view was that continued meditation does just that. Just as oil, wick, and fire in combination produce a lamp that is the illuminator, but the lamp is self-illuminating, so likewise a *pramāṇa* may be causally composed or conditioned by various things but by itself be quite sufficient for producing valid knowledge. None of these supposed factors are independent *pramāṇas*; if they were, scripture would be a restatement of what reasoning, etc., can provide, or else reasoning would be merely a restatement of what scripture yields.

44 (ET 438-453) 820-847. Continued meditation is repetition, but it cannot improve an object, any more than a *pramāṇa* can improve an object by repeatedly knowing it.

Objection : When an object is in the dusk repeated perception of it may make it clearer.

Answer : But there the object of each perception is different from the preceding one—first a thing, then a living thing, then a human living thing, and so on. Or if you insist that all these things are the same object and the perception is single, then it would follow that all the *pramāṇas*—perception, inference, etc.—are the same one since they can all grasp the same object.

Anyway, continued meditation is a causal factor (*kāraka*), not something that makes something known (*jñāpaka*).

Now, you argued that injunctions to continued meditation are subsidiary to assertions in the *jñānakāṇḍa*. But that can only be if they can function together to provide a consistent sense, which they cannot, since they speak of different things. The assertions speak of reality, whereas an injunction to meditate speaks of *niyoga*.

Objection : They are consistent since they have the same expected result.

Answer : Since you do not hold that heaven is that fruit I assume it must be liberation. But liberation is self-established and needs no injunction at all; and since scripture is eternal (on your view) it doesn't need anything such as continued meditation to establish its sense.

If continued meditation is supposed to produce a result, does it do it immediately or only after a time ? If the former, repetition is unnecessary. But there is no specification of a period of time after which it will produce its result, as there is (in scripture) with respect to other prescribed actions. Or else we must suppose continued meditation either has results in subsequent lives—in which case it is a primary act, not a subsidiary one—or else that it is subsidiary to ritual acts, not to scriptural assertions. In either case one who desires liberation will not feel any obligation to follow the injunction to meditate.

45 (ET 453-475) 848-884. Either scripture expounds the true nature of the Self or it doesn't. If it doesn't, it cannot be valid—but we agree that it is. If it does, then realization will arise from the experiencing of the Self, which results directly therefrom, and continued meditation will be unnecessary.

Other reasons are offered why there is no need for continued meditation, or indeed any dependence on any sort of injunction or *niyoga*. Nor is there any dependence on reasoning in order that the liberating experience be realized. Reason removes doubts but does not provide valid knowledge; if it did scripture would cease to be a *pramāṇa*.

Objection : You say that, for example, "that thou art" is the *pramāṇa* for the truth, since "that" means Brahman and "thou" means *ātman*. But either we already understand what "Brahman" and "*ātman*" mean or we don't. If we do, then "that thou art" is merely a restatement, whereas if we don't, we need some other *pramāṇa* to tell us what they mean.

Answer : We know the meaning of "Brahman" and "*ātman*" from ordinary usage (*laukikaprayoga*). But the statement "Brahman is *ātman*" (or "that thou art") is not merely a restatement, since the sense of the sentence goes beyond ordinary usage. It is analogous to the use of words such as "*apūrva*," "*adevatā*" or "heaven" (*svarga*), which have ordinary senses but are used in the *karmakāṇḍa* in special, extraordinary senses. And it's not the words that provide valid knowledge, but the sentence that is the *pramāṇa*. We learn the meanings of the constituent words of a sentence by finding out what happens when a word is left out or added; however, it is not the words subtracted or added but the sentences resulting that convey the meaning. Just as there are words, and word meanings they express, so there are sentences and sentence meanings they express. A sentence is made up of words, and a sentence meaning is made up of word meanings. Thus whether in the Vedas or in ordinary speech the sentence meaning is made up of word meanings properly juxtaposed; the difference, therefore, is that in the Vedas (some of) the words have extraordinary meanings, and so thus too do the sentences that they compose.

Objection : Since the relation of a word to its meaning is established by the usage of elders, verbal testimony cannot be a *pramāṇa*, for it has a beginning.

Answer : No. The meanings of words are beginningless.

Objector : If so, how could anyone hear the word "cow" and not know its meaning? Since that does happen, meaning must be conventional.

Answer : Not so; if someone doesn't know the meaning of a word, all that shows is that he doesn't have the capacity to understand the meaning, not that the word doesn't have the meaning. Anyway, how could meaning be conventional? Do we learn it from the elders? But where did they learn it from? Or did God establish meaning? But no one remembers Him, or anyone else, doing so.

Objection : Failure to remember a thing doesn't prove it didn't happen.

Answer : Nevertheless, in the absence of any evidence through remembering what has been experienced there is no basis for postulating anyone who established meanings; so we conclude they are beginningless. Thus scripture, that is, verbal testimony, is valid—both the *karmakāṇḍa* and *jñānakāṇḍa* parts.

46 (ET 475-483) 885-902. Now, men desire to attain what is worthwhile and to avoid what isn't. But human goals are of two sorts, (1) something not yet attained, like a village one is traveling to, or (2) something already attained but forgotten, like a piece of gold in one's hand. To attain the former one should follow the injunctions set forth in the *karmakāṇḍa*. But since what blocks one from attaining the latter is ignorance, the only way to obtain it is to become aware of the truth. Sentences in the *jñānakāṇḍa* like "you are Brahman" or "that art thou" remove the ignorance that hides the ultimate human goal of the second sort; thus they are valid means of knowing (*pramāṇa*), just as the injunctions are valid.

Objection : The cause of the knowledge "that art thou" is, by your admission, false (*mithyā*); so the judgment can't be valid.

Answer : Before one is enlightened the means is not known to be false; and after enlightenment it doesn't matter that it is, since one no longer depends on any *pramāṇa* once the goal has been reached. A false means may lead to truth—and for that matter a true means may lead to falsity! And if you mean that a true means must be "real" (*paramārtha*), then scripture would contradict itself, for it declares that only Brahman is real, and if scripture in addition were real this would undermine the scriptural declaration.

47 (ET 484-500) 903-938a. The sentence "that art thou" is to be analyzed differently from sentences whose subject and predicate are opposed to each other, or are different things in relation. The Self and Brahman are in fact identical, so the subject and predicate designate the very same thing.

Objection : Since both perception and scriptural authority as found in the *karmakāṇḍa* prove or presuppose difference between the self and Brahman, your view is impossible to substantiate. And neither you nor I accept the view of identity-with-difference between them, for identity and difference are contradictories. Now you can't argue that

Vedānta texts sublate perception and scripture, since one needs perception even to become aware of the syllables (of scripture), and since you yourself accept the *karmakāṇḍa* as valid. So the Vedānta texts must be either figurative, or else they counsel meditation.

Answer : The *karmakāṇḍa* is not opposed to the Vedānta texts, for they have different subject matters. And perception cannot go against the Upaniṣadic teaching, since its function is to reveal the identity of a thing, not to produce an idea of difference. Difference cannot be real, since reality cannot be dependent. So nondifference is the very nature of reality; indeed, even the apparent difference between a *pramāṇa* and its (real) object must be illusory, for all reality is nondifferent. Two absences (*abhāva*) cannot be related to each other, since being both absences they are nondifferent. Nor can an absence be related to a real existent by either contact (*saṃyoga*), inherence (*samavāya*), or identity (*tādātmya*). So absences are not real; only positive existents (*bhāva*) can be real, and there can be no relation between an absence and a positive existent. All there is is the positive existent, which is essentially nondifferentiated.

48 (ET 501-507) 938b-949. *Objection* : Absence is itself a *pramāṇa*, and what it grasps validly are absences of objects.

Answer : Certainly not. A *pramāṇa* must be something known that makes known what has previously been unknown. Now what could make known the absence that you say is a *pramāṇa*? Absence cannot make itself known.

Again, does an absence have qualifiers or not? If not there is no way of making it known, and if so, what is the qualifier? If it is a *pramāṇa*, it cannot be known by a *pramāṇa*—an object cannot be known by its own quality. If you say that the qualifier of absence is an object—as is suggested by the phrase "the absence of pot"—I say that that phrase makes no sense, since I have shown that there can be no relation between an absence and a positive existent.

Objection : Perhaps the things are opposed, but still we can combine into a phrase or sentence words that are opposed, for example, "darkness" and "light."

Answer : No we can't, since the one word sets up expectations that preclude the use of the other.

Objection : What is meant by "absence" is another, different thing (i.e., "absence of pot" denotes cloth, say).

Answer : Then it would follow that when I say "the pot is absent" I am saying "the pot is a cloth"!

So I conclude that perception cannot grasp absences or differences.

49 (ET 507-513) 950-960. *Objection* : Perhaps perception both

reveals the identity of an object and its difference from other things at the same time.

Answer : That would be to attribute contradictory functions to it at the same time.

Objector : All right, then let's suppose perception first grasps identity and then difference, or the reverse order.

Answer : Cognitions are momentary, and thus one cognition does not last long enough to perform a sequence of functions. In any case, it couldn't do so even if it did last long enough: to know that *x* is blue we would have to know that *x* is not yellow or red or purple or. . . , but to know that *x* is not yellow we would have to know that yellow is not blue or red or purple or . . . , so neither grasping of identity nor of difference can precede the other.

Objector : You misunderstand. Our view is that difference and nondifference are not incompatible, since they are the very nature of reality.

Answer : That description of reality involves a contradiction.

50 (ET 514-529) 961-989a. *Vaiśeṣika* : On our view difference is a quality—separateness (*pṛthaktva*)—which resides in real substances and is perceptible like other qualities such as colors, etc.

Answer : Is this separateness different from its locus (=substance) or not ? If it isn't, then it is just the substance. If separateness is different from its locus, however, the locus is not different, that is, nonseparate, that is, it doesn't have separateness, which contradicts the hypothesis.

Objection : The locus is separate and nonseparate (with respect to different things).

Answer : All right, but the locus is not for that reason differentiated, any more than a lily is composite merely because it has several distinct qualities. We cognize the different qualities, but the reality that supports that difference is the nondifferentiated locus. Likewise, we perceive differences among the various existent substances—cow, pot, etc.—but the reality that supports those different things, and is the *real* object of our cognition, is the underlying *existence* (*sanmātra*), which is undifferentiated.

Now what relation can connect properties with their real underlying loci ? Not inherence, since the property is not seen to be different from its locus, and inherence is supposed to connect two distinct relata. Not contact, for the same reason—what would connect the contact with its relata ?

It cannot be that difference is real and unity unreal, nor can it consistently be maintained that one thing can be constituted of both particularity and generality—so it must be that the general—non-difference—is real and the particular—difference—illusory.

Arguments pertaining to the unreality of absences—difference—are repeated. The conclusion is thus drawn that all differences are superimposed on the one existent consciousness. So the Vedānta texts do not conflict with the *pramāṇas*, which require consciousness for their very operation.

51 (ET 530-537) 989b-1005a. *Objection* : In order for a *pramāṇa* to function, its object must be unknown prior to its functioning. You argue that consciousness alone is the object, but it is known prior to the operation of any *pramāṇa*; thus no *pramāṇa* can function.

Answer : A *pramāṇa* destroys unknownness—therefore it cannot have unknownness as its object. When we say "Now I know the pot; I did not know it before," we recognize that the unknownness existed before our cognition—thus the unknownness is established, not by a *pramāṇa*, but by experience (*anubhava*). Likewise, the knownness of the pot after it has been validly known by a *pramāṇa* is given to us by experience. When we wake up from sleep we realize we did not know anything while we were asleep—the *pramāṇas* did not operate there, and yet we experienced unknownness.

Objection : When we are asleep we aren't aware of anything, and that's why we say "I did not know anything when asleep."

Answer : If it were so we couldn't report on our sleeping state afterwards.

Objector : We infer that we did not know anything on the basis of our present knowledge after waking up.

Answer : Awareness cannot be different merely because of a difference in time. Indeed, time, cognizer, *pramāṇas*, etc., all depend on awareness. They come and go, but awareness must continue throughout. Thus experience is self-established, and it is in dependence on it that the *pramāṇas* gain their validity.

52 (ET 537-546) 1005b-1023a. Now just as a pot, previously unknown though existent, loses its unknownness when grasped by a *pramāṇa*, so likewise the Self, being a real thing, only loses its unknownness when grasped by a *pramāṇa*, that is, scripture. It is only scripture that can be a *pramāṇa* with respect to the Self; perception and the others necessarily grasp things conditioned by ignorance.

Objection : You apparently suppose that achievement of Self-knowledge yields some kind of happiness or pleasure. But surely only the destruction of all sources of frustration and transmigration can properly be said to constitute the ultimate human aim, since to pursue positive pleasure involves attachment and thus duality of knower and known, etc.

Answer : The destruction of frustration is not the same thing as happiness, since one can experience pleasure and pain simultaneously. And those who are happy desire more happiness—thus happiness cannot be the mere destruction of frustration. For example, one who is not frustrated gains increased happiness from the birth of a son: this happiness cannot be derived from the destruction of the frustration arising from the nonbirth of a son, for he wasn't even aware previously of any such frustration. Thus the ultimate human aim is supreme happiness, and all creatures, animals too, desire it, though they do not know the means of getting it. The Veda is the means of coming to know the supreme happiness, and thus becomes a *pramāṇa*.

As for the contention that desire for supreme happiness is attachment, we deny that: not all desire is attachment. The teacher who desires a solitary place to meditate in is not thereby attached.

53 (ET 547-560) 1023b-1049a. *Objection* : If the supreme happiness, that is, Brahman or the Self, is an object of knowledge there is duality: if it is not known, it cannot be the goal we desire.

Answer : The pure Self is not the kind of thing that can become an object of knowledge; only things that are not themselves pure consciousness may be objects of consciousness. Even he who desires heaven desires liberation, but not vice versa. All are eligible for Self-knowledge provided they have the four prerequisites mentioned, for all desire the bliss of liberation.

Objection : Scripture cannot be the peculiar cause of Self-knowledge in the fashion you have stated. It is evident that a person acts only on the basis of previous knowledge; even a child learns which acts to perform by watching his elders act when ordered, say, to bring the cow; the child learns that it is the knowledge of cow that prompts one to act, since action is a conscious activity.

Answer : Then it would follow that the injunctive force of prescriptions arises from ordinary, not scriptural, sources, which is objectionable to you. Scripture, if it is relevant, must function to reveal something already established; a *pramāṇa* is not a causal agent but a revealer. In fact, what you leave out of your account is the desire of the agent for happiness. Injunctions, even Vedic ones, are only instruments for effecting desires. No one would go to the trouble to sacrifice if he didn't expect good to come from it and if he didn't desire that good. In any case, whether injunctions are causes or acts or results of acts they operate in the sphere of empirical or ordinary (*laukika*) affairs and thus can be established by ordinary *pramāṇas* (i.e., those other than scripture). Brahman, by contrast, is not within the sphere of ordinary *pramāṇas*, as is shown in texts like "*neti neti*" ("not this, not this"), etc.

54 (ET 560-602) 1049b-1137a. If you do not grant that the Vedic scriptures are *pramāṇas* with respect to what is real, the *karmakāṇḍa* will lose its meaning too. For the validity of the injunctions in the *karmakāṇḍa* depends on the assumption of transmigration and rebirth, of heaven, of various sorts of future results that are outside the range of the ordinary *pramāṇas*. Thus you must admit a self that remains through change of body, etc. So why do you not admit that the Vedas are *pramāṇa* with respect to Brahman ? The self understood as in Sāṃkhya or in Vaiśeṣika won't be satisfactory for your purposes—the Sāṃkhya self is not related to bodies, and the Vaiśeṣika self cannot be an agent, or if it is, it can never get liberated. Indeed, no version of the self that can be attested to by ordinary *pramāṇas* will do. So only scripture can grasp the true Self.

The nature of that true Self is now delineated in familiar fashion. The remainder of this section glosses Śaṃkara's *Bhāṣya*.

SECOND BRĀHMAṆA

3-27 (E301-306). "There was nothing here . . . ," that is, no effect existed (says the Upaniṣad), though the cause did, *pace* the nihilist (*nāstitvamukta*). "It was covered over by Death . . . ." This "death" is in fact the supreme God (*parameśvara*), likened to an ocean. The word "*asat*" ("nothing") does not designate nonexistence. Either it designates difference or nondifference from existent (*sat*) : if nondifference it is clearly existence, whereas if it is different from existence it still must exist since it is the locus of difference. Nonexistence cannot be spoken of. Posterior absence (*dhvaṃsa*) is unacceptable (as the designation of "*asat*"), whether it be construed as an act (*kriyā*) or a result (*phala*), since neither can destroy its own cause; nor can it be the thing that is destroyed, since how can one destroy that by which the destruction gains existence ? It (this "*asat*") cannot even be awareness (*vijñāna*), for awareness must have a cause; furthermore, there would be the unwelcome consequence (for the Yogācāra) that awareness would be eternal. And if the nihilist tries to prove his point by inference his proof will lack an example, since on nihilist assumptions nothing exists to be an example.

28-73 (E306-315). Perception, inference, and verbal testimony all establish only existence (*sat*), not nonexistence. The inference is: "The universe has an existent as cause, because it is an effect, like a pot." The opponent's argument is : "The universe has nonexistence as its cause, because it originates only by destroying its cause, like the seed producing a sprout." But that cannot be right, since before its origination the effect was not there to destroy its cause. If what is not originated can destroy its cause then both cause and effect must exist, since nonexistence cannot destroy anything.

In any case, whether the effect exists or not it cannot destroy its cause. If it exists, then destruction of the cause isn't necessary to originate it. And if the rule is that production of effect requires destruction of cause, then since destruction of a cause (say, destruction of clay to produce a pot) is itself an effect it should destroy *its* cause (viz., clay)! Just as motion is impossible without something that moves, so destruction is impossible without a locus. So no effect destroys its cause.

The cause in the case of a pot is clay, not the lump (*piṇḍa*) of clay. The lump is, like the pot, an effect of the clay; the pot originates even without the lump. Many effects cannot exist in one cause at the same time, so the clay may produce first a lump and then the pot; still, that which continues to exist (the clay) is the cause, and that which is newly brought about is the effect.

Objection : The cognition of continuity through change is an error (*bhrānti*) occasioned by the similarity between the stages.

Answer : When the same thing recurs we recognize it—that is, we perceive it, and since perception is superior to inference this perception overrides your inference. Anyway, on your thesis of momentariness no recognition is possible, but unless recognition is possible your alleged "cognition of continuity occasioned by similarity" is impossible, since you must at least recognize similarity!

74-107 (E316-322). "The effect exists before it is produced . . . ."; otherwise, like a hare's horn, it would not appear even when the conditions for its manifestation are present.

Objector : So what stops *every* existent from manifesting itself when "the sun comes up", that is, when the conditions for manifestation are present?

Answer : On the (Nyāya) view that there are three kinds of causal factors whose collocation (*sāmagri*) occasions a result, that contingency would occur—if the three causal factors operate always and everywhere then everything would occur always and everywhere. Or if their operation is required for production, still, since the operation is itself an effect, either no effect is ever produced or it will once again always be being produced!

"There are two kinds of covering. . . ." Likewise, there are two kinds of manifestation corresponding to the two kinds of covering—in one the clay manifests itself as pot, in the other the wall manifests itself in the light. In both cases what is already existent is manifested; ignorance (*ajñāna*) is removed, and something previously unknown is cognized. In both cases effort is exerted to gain knowledge, though the kinds of effects that are manifested are different.

125-227 (E326-346). The word "death" here signifies the supreme Brahman, which with the help of the causal ignorance (*ajñāna*) is the cause of the origination and dissolution of the universe. Brahman is called "*avyākṛta*," "undeveloped," when considered with *māyā* as primary cause, but when *māyā* is considered as subservient It is called "inner controller" (*antaryāmin*). Even though illusory (the *māyā*-clad) Brahman is the cause of the universe. Scripture, too, is illusory but gives us knowledge of the real, Brahman.

The word "death" in the passage here indicates *māyā* also. In other places the word is used to indicate knowledge and action, or water, or the *jīva*. Some creation myths are reviewed, myths concerning Hiraṇyagarbha, Virāj, and the *prāṇas*, and the derivation of the term *aśvamedha* (the horse-sacrifice) is traced.

THIRD BRĀHMAṆA

1-37 (E347-354). In the previous Brāhmaṇa it was shown that the result of meditation combined with action is attainment of identity with Hiraṇyagarbha as "death." Now the nature of that "death" by which one gains liberation is detailed. The combination of meditation with action doesn't produce attainment of the Brahmaloka if they are accompanied by attachment, etc. So meditation on *prāṇa* is introduced in order to remove such obstacles. A myth based on a previous life of Prajāpati is told, symbolising opposition between two kinds of organs—identified as "gods" (*deva*) and "demons" (*asura*). The gods are bent on providing śāstric knowledge and activity, the demons bent on breeding anger, etc. The battle between them is waged on the field of the mental modifications. The gods enlisted the chanter (*udgātṛ*) of the *soma* sacrifice in their cause, so that right knowledge and action is prefaced by meditation on *prāṇa*.

38-87 (E354-358). When *prāṇa* is termed "pure," etc., this is not just for the purpose of worship—*prāṇa* actually has these qualities. Of course they may be unreal considered from the highest standpoint; the concepts of real and unreal are the outcome of ignorance. God (*īśvara*) is reflected in ignorance (*ajñāna*) and thus becomes the substratum of the universe, controlling its destinies. But the world of ignorance is nondifferent from Brahman; the Self is everything. Knowledge by its nature stands on reality, and so cannot reveal unreal things.

130-191 (E374-386). Having decided that the *udgītā* (the chant) was the best means to defeat the demons, the gods began to examine it. They asked the deity presiding over speech (viz., Vāk) to sing a *mantra* on fire. Vāk began to sing. By the benefit derived from that, Vāk saves all the other *prāṇas* in the body.

When the demons realized that desire, anger, etc., were being driven away by the singing, they attacked the singer (*udgātṛ*), that is, Vāk, with their arrows—the natural instincts—and as a result Vāk began to speak falsehoods, etc. Finding this defect of falsehood in ordinary speech we can infer the same defect in its cause; the sins committed by the demons in the body of Prajāpati continue even now in his children (i.e., our organs).

Similar events occurred pertaining to the other organs. Now when all the organs were afflicted by defects, the gods approached *prāṇa*, the vital breath, and asked it to sing. The point of the story is to indicate what it is that should be meditated upon by one desirous of release, and that thing is *prāṇa*, because the special qualities of all the other organs and breaths rest on the vital breath. The demons were unable successfully to attack *prāṇa*, and so it was accepted as the object of meditation. By meditating on *prāṇa* as one's own self an individual attains the all-pervading *prāṇa*-hood and his organs achieve the nature of fire, etc., leaving their limitations behind. *Prāṇa* is Hiraṇyagarbha. The meditator should meditate so intensely on it that even when living he becomes the deity and after death reaches him. This cannot be achieved merely by knowledge—as in the case of the *jīva* realizing Brahman—since both the meditator and the deity are products of Brahman. Meditation drives out all the enemies of the meditator.

192-200 (E387-388). Or we may say that the fruit of meditation is liberation, since that is enjoined (in the seventh book below). The attainment of Hiraṇyagarbha is only a byproduct. When meditation is enjoined directly as leading to a certain result, other aspects conduce to special side-effects.

The remainder of this section explains the remaining passages in the Upaniṣad.

FOURTH BRĀHMAṆA

1-70 (E427-441). In the previous Brāhmaṇas the results of the combination of meditation and action were mentioned. But what is really intended is that the result is still *saṃsāra* since Prajāpati, who created the world, had his own weakṇesses—fear, etc. So aversion even to the results of Prajāpati-hood must be cultivated; such aversion makes one eligible for Brahman-knowledge, and without it one cannot be eligible. Vedic rituals bring about a purity of mind, and one with a pure mind will realize the nature of *saṃsāra* and become detached from it, even from being Prajāpati or Brahmā. One must realize that all results of action are perishable, adopt *saṃnyāsa*, and take up listening to Vedānta. Since even the required actions (*nityakarman*) lead to rebirth, one must abandon them as well.

When Brahman is not cognized things are created with the help of beginningless *māyā*. From Viṣṇu was born the Sūtrātman with capacities of knowledge and action, and from him came Virāj with the three worlds as his body. Creation after the great dissolution (*mahāpralaya*) is by Brahmā; after the intermediate dissolution (*antarapralaya*) it is by Virāj. Before creation he was alone; there were no worlds. If the world is realized as Brahman liberation results; if it is realized as different from Brahman *saṃsāra* results. When there is no notion of "I" and "mine" one obtains liberation.

The supreme Self, afflicted by desire, etc., took on the form of a *puruṣa*; thus we worship Him as *puruṣa*.

Virāj *puruṣa*, though endowed with superior knowledge and *karman*, became afraid like a child because of its *avidyā*. *Avidyā* is the cause of all fear. Just as our predecessor was afraid of being alone—through *avidyā*—so we, through the same cause, are also afraid of being lonely.

But though thus fearful, he examined his position like any other person and realized what was real. Having realized Brahman, burnt the big darkness of *avidyā*, and attained all the ends of man (*puruṣārtha*), he thought "why should I fear, since there is nothing different from me?" This shows that ignorance of the Self alone is the cause of fear.

71-166 (E441-460). *Question* : How, without scripture or teacher's initiation into the great sentences (*mahāvākya*), did Prajāpati get Brahman-knowledge? If it was without any cause, it may as well come to us in the same manner. If he was initiated in a previous birth then there's no point in indicating the means to Brahman-knowledge for us either. For if Brahman-knowledge in the previous life didn't remove *avidyā*, then it is hopelessly difficult to remove it !

Answer : For Prajāpati the merit of his good deeds and knowledge is such that it gives immediate recollection of the great sentences. Manu says that Prajāpati's knowledge, nonattachment, power, and merit are supreme and natural, which shows that he does not require a teacher. As for the complaint that indication of the means to Brahman-knowledge is pointless—since devotion, acquaintance with texts, etc., are found in different degrees among men and are required in varying amounts, instruction about them is necessary. It is like the case of perceiving color—a cat does not require illumination; yogis see color with their internal organs alone; but we men require all the means—illumination, internal organs, and senses as well.

Question : Then how is it that Prajāpati became fearful, given his natural inclination to liberation?

Answer : Prajāpati is an official of God, an *adhikārika puruṣa*. Though endowed with supreme knowledge and thus having realized Brahman, he is visited with fear due to the latent impression arising from the same feeling in past lives carried over by *prārabdhakarman*. The "fear" of being alone, due to a spark of *avidyā* remaining in him, caused him to become through his own imagination a couple—man and woman—and the couple, Manu and Śatarūpa, in turn created all the animals, etc., in the world by their union, as well as the other gods, the four castes, etc.

I.4.7; 167-222 (E460-471). *Avidyā* is ignorance of Self, and through its destruction one attains all the ends of man. Ignorance, arising from identification of Self with body, is the cause. Then come merit and demerit, which produce the body. These two are brought about by acts—enjoined, prohibited—and are the results of *kārakas*, means of action—desire and hatred, which operate through the notions "this is good" and "that is bad," etc. And these in turn require objects, since without objects no cognition arises. Thus the notion of existence of objects requires ignorance of Self; all *pramāṇas* reveal the Self, but they do not grasp the Self since It is veiled by ignorance.

The word "unmanifested" (*avyākṛta*, in the Upaniṣad) indicates that there is no destruction of what exists or beginning for what does not exist. The word covers *avidyā*, merit, demerit, traces, the Sūtrātman, the five elements, and the enjoyer. This *avidyā* was transformed into name-and-form. The world manifested itself only as name-and-form and not in its own form. Though the universe was manifest, the manifestation is not complete since the Self is not manifested. The Self is self-luminous, pure and free from *avidyā*; It is only apparently associated with *avidyā*, but associated thus It is the cause of the universe.

223-340 (E472-499). The division of known and unknown depends upon the luminosity of the Self, which is self-luminous. The Self realizes itself without any *pramāṇa*. It realizes ignorance by outward cognition, not inwardly. (A long section here refutes the Vaiśeṣika and the Buddhists on the question of self-validation and self-illumination.) The recollection after deep sleep—"I did not know anything"—is only a superimposition of ignorance and past time, since the Self is always immediate. It sees itself by Its everlasting intelligence in all the three states (waking, etc.) as well as in all other bodies. Since the internal organ, etc., are inert (*jaḍa*) and the products of ignorance, ignorance does not reside in them.

341-364 (E499-504). In the Self reflected in primal darkness (=*avyākṛta*) the world is born, is sustained, and perishes. The supreme Self, having ignorance as prominent, causes the universe; having intelligence as prominent, it causes the souls with the help of latent impressions (*bhāvanā*), ignorance, and *karman*. These last are located in ignorance and through that in the Self. Brahman alone, in the form of all the intermediate causes, is the cause. He is the *prāṇa* of the *Chāndogya*; He is *ākāśa* and truth (or reality, *satya*); the unmanifest (*avyākṛta*) of scripture is the Self itself.

365-397 (E504-511). Why should latent impressions, etc., produce the universe? To help the person who created them. First, they create air and *ākāśa* and then the other three elements. The manifestation of the unmanifest is the work of God (*antaryāmin*). Though without form He, like a whirlwind, induces the world into action. Resting on ignorance, He as Brahmā is the cause. That same Self is known by those affected by ignorance as the Witness, by those whose intellects are not ripe as inert.

The cause of the superimpositions of Witness on world and vice versa is ignorance, which has the nature of false awareness. At the time of creation, without external cause it is manifested as name-and-form. Thus God, Brahman, becomes object of usage (*vyavahāra*), since name is a genus of which "Devadatta", etc., are species, and "form" (*rūpa*) is a genus of which white, blue, etc., are species.

398-413 (E511-525). By "name-and-form" is not meant the combination (*samuccaya*) of the two, since the deaf only grasp the latter and the blind only the former. The sense is that there is no creation; thus the apparently conflicting scriptural accounts of creation are actually consistent, being intended only to help remove ignorance and desire. Even the (*Kāma*)*Śāstra* of Vātsyāyana is meant to divert the attention of the reader to what is good. And the Buddha, who says that things are noneternal, painful, and void, wants to cut off desire. Or, we may say that the common purport of scriptures is the generation of the knowledge of identity, since all *pramāṇas* give rise to knowledge of the unknown and what is unknown is just the Self on whom the universe is superimposed.

414-446 (E516-523.) *Objection* : How can there be superimposition on the Self, since the Self has no generic or specific properties? When *x* is superimposed on *y*, it is because the general features of *y* are cognized but the specific features (which differentiate it from x) are suppressed. But in the pure Self this is impossible. Furthermore, in error the nonawareness of the difference between y and x is necessary, but in this case we are presumed to know that the universe is different from the Self—so how can the awareness of nondifference occur?

Answer : We need not answer this objection, since on our view ignorance alone is the cause of error. It is for those who do not accept ignorance as the cause to answer this.

Objection : How can ignorance, not being a real entity, be the cause of *saṃsāra*? Since false awareness (*mithyājñāna*) actually occurs, let it be the cause!

Answer : False awareness isn't a real entity either; it is a product of ignorance.

Objector : But false awareness occurs—it is not a nonentity, so it must be real.

Answer : The "reality" of awareness is ascribable in virtue of awareness' taking the form of its object, not its nonsublatability. That awareness which by assuming the form of its object grasps that object removes ignorance. For a thing to be real is to exist independently in its own nature. Anything that exists through dependence on another is unreal. Thus an illusion, such as the shell-silver, is unreal. But so are all specific awarenesses such as "this is a pot," "this is a cloth," etc., for these depend on Brahman, the one existent, and hence they are unreal. Only the Self exists independently and is thus real. Therefore, through Self-knowledge duality perishes. When by knowledge of reality ignorance perishes false awareness also perishes, since it is a product of ignorance. Since error and doubt arise only with respect to what is not known, they must be products of ignorance. But they are also real insofar as they are an aspect whose substratum is Brahman. In their own nature, however, they are not real.

447-477 (E523-530). *Objection* : Error arises when we apprehend the general features of a thing but import through memory special features not actually present.

Answer : No, since there are other kinds of illusion—for example, when a man with jaundice sees a shell as yellow. Ignorance is the invariable cause of illusions, whichever sort it is—shell-silver, the sky looking like a blue lotus, mistaking one direction for another, dreams, etc.

478-493 (E530-533). Thus it has been established that *saṃsāra* is a superimposition of not-Self on Self.

Sāṃkhya : No, *prakṛti* (here, *pradhāna*) is the cause of *saṃsāra*.

Answer : The cause of the world is the Self in association with ignorance, that is, name-and-form. Real things do not remove ignorance; only knowledge can remove ignorance. The Self is pure and without a second; Its association with a second is due to ignorance, and by the negation of ignorance It is pure. God, *avyākṛta*, *prāṇa*, Virāj, the sense organs, etc.—none of these are present in the Self save through dependence on ignorance. The view (Bhartṛprapañca's) that the Self is an object of external perception is incorrect, as shown on the authority of the *Kaṭha Upaniṣad*.

494-514 (E533-537). The Lord, in association with ignorance, created the entire universe from Brahmā to a blade of grass, and entered it. The "entry" of the Self is Its association with ignorance. The implication to be drawn is that all *jīvas* from Hiraṇyagarbha to the blades of grass are one with Brahman. The adjuncts (*upādhi*) being illusory, there is no problem in Brahman's being nonattached. Sūtrātman, first born of God, was endowed with the twin capacities of knowledge and action and is called "Hiraṇyagarbha." Next to be created was Virāj *puruṣa*, Lord of the gross elements. Gods (*deva*) such as Indra, Agni, Varuṇa, etc., are his creations.

515-556 (E537-545). *Objection* : It was said that the universe was manifested. Now, no manifesting agent was mentioned, so the phrase "he entered into it" is not correct. Though the supreme Self is said elsewhere to be the creator It is not present in the context here—rather, what is present is only the unmanifest (i.e., *prakṛti*).

Answer : There is no difficulty in our reading. Though God is not mentioned, He is implied by the statement "the universe became manifest" since without an agent such an event would be impossible. Just as the universe is now associated with an agent, etc., so also before creation it had an agent, who was the witness of the unmanifest. Just as the word "village" means both the houses and the people living there in expressions such as "the village caught fire," etc., so the word "unmanifest" implies an agent of manifestation also. "The Self is pure, nondual, etc.," refers to the Self alone, but here the agent is also implied.

Objection : The Self cannot enter into the world since, being all-pervasive, He is there already. Only something spatially delimited can enter.

Answer : No, for it is not indicated that the person who "entered" underwent any transformation. (The commentary proceeds to gloss the answers to the conundrums discussed in Śaṃkara's commentary.)

557-574 (E545-548). *Objection*: You quote scripture to show that the Self is not subject to frustration, but your scripture is in conflict with perception, through which one perceives frustration in oneself, and perception is superior in authority to scripture.

Answer : We perceive the frustration present in the conditioning adjunct (*upādhi*, viz., the mind) of the Self who is identified with it. If the Self were subject to frustration, what witness could perceive it? It is that witness who is aloof, and He is the Self. This Witness sees the *buddhi* bound by pleasures and frustration, etc. "You are that reality" conveys the true nature of the Self that is Brahman. Perception cannot grasp the Self, as shown in the text "by what can you cognize the knower, etc." The judgment "I am frustrated" is a figurative expression, analogous to "I feel pain in my nose," etc. If the pain or frustration were really in the Self it would be experienced always, since the Self is all-pervasive. Or else it would never be experienced, since like intelligence that is the nature of the Self it could not be experienced.

Objection : According to the text "everything is dear for the sake of the Self" the Self must have pleasure as its attribute.

Answer : No, this applies to the Self only as conditioned by ignorance, as in "where another as it were, then by what can one see another, etc."

575-605 (E548-554). *Objection* : According to *tarkaśāstra* (i.e., Nyāya-Vaiśeṣika) the qualities of the self are desire, aversion, pleasure, frustration, etc.

Answer : *Tarkaśāstra* is no authority, since it conflicts with other *śāstras*. Anyway, scripture declares desire, etc., to be properties of the *buddhi*. The inner Self is not perceptible. Perception becomes a *pramāṇa* only in dependence upon the shadow of the Self; so it is not capable of grasping the Self. The analogy between the Self and, say, *ākāśa* is faulty; frustration is not a quality of the Self as sound is of *ākāśa*. The one Self cannot be both knower and known, being partless. Again, being without parts the Self cannot contact the internal organ (as in Nyāya) so that frustration be produced.

Objection : But an eternal thing may have parts; for example, Vajra (Indra's thunderbolt), etc.

Answer : No. Contact is always followed by eventual disjunction. Even Vajra is the result of contact, dependent on ignorance.

The destruction of ignorance alone is required for liberation. It is as when a stranger says "you are the tenth" to one who is puzzled that his team seems to be lacking a member—likewise by hearing, from scripture or teacher, "that art thou" one's ignorance is destroyed and one gains Self-knowledge.

606-656 (E554-564). The reflectionist model is defended; it provides a way of understanding how the Self "enters."

Two illustrations are provided to distinguish the two ways in which Brahman exists in ignorance and its products. Just as razors kept in a barber's box differ among themselves and from their container, so also the Self differs through the various nerves in accordance with which It is called seer, bearer, etc., and from the body. But on the other hand, just as the fire in a burning log pervades throughout the log, so the Self pervades bodies, etc., throughout. Again, the Self realizes two specific states—waking and dream—and one general state—deep sleep—all of which are due to our false identifications of the Self that actually pervade everything. We see general and specific features and record them through false cognitions such as "this is an object," "I am the seer," "this is a sense organ," etc. Such false notions should be abandoned.

654-670 (E564-572). *Objection* : Since people do see such features, it is contradictory to assert that they do not !

Answer : No, the idea is that they do not see reality. Reality is one without a second, and the point is that men do not see *that*; all perception of features is thus not seeing reality. No feature is all-pervasive; every feature contradicts some other. This is illustrated from scripture.

671-719 (E572-578). The text "all activities combine in the Self" is not an injunction to meditate on the distributive as well as collective aspects of the Self. Such a meaning in a text would be redundant, since inference can indicate the same; but in any case such meditation is impossible since the various aspects of the Self are not comprehensible in a lifetime, and the aspects of body, etc., are based on ignorance.

720-735 (E578-581). One must see beyond cause and effect to reach the changeless Self. The division of manifest and unmanifest (effect and cause) is illusory, like the supposition of the difference between day and night in the sun. Likewise the distinction between Self and not-Self is based on ignorance. The Self is self-established, the other established only in dependence on the Self.

Objection : By saying "the Self should be seen in the not-Self" you presuppose duality !

Answer : No. Rather by distinguishing the not-Self from the Self you perceive the latter in Its real nature. The not-Self cannot be established as different or nondifferent from the Self; thus it is false. Even the Self's nature as seer is false, since It is consciousness itself.

736-750 (E581-583). We have dealt with the true nature of the Self. Now we proceed to deal with the nature of the word "Self" (*ātman*). He is so-called because He pervades, He takes, He enjoys objects here, He exists eternally. He pervades all not-Self as the rope pervades the rope-snake, etc., that is, fully. Since He sees all the fluctuations of the mind in which He is reflected by His own luminosity, He is called "Self." Thus by seeing Him everything is seen, and so the Self alone is to be cognized.

751-808 (E583-595). "Some say (this) must be" an initial injunction (*apūrva vidhi*), others think it a restrictive injunction (*niyama vidhi*), still others an exclusive injunction (*parisaṃkhyā vidhi*). But Śaṃkara shows it is not an injunction at all because the knowledge allegedly enjoined is not dependent on human effort. An initial injunction is not possible, since the knowledge allegedly enjoined is already partly in hand.

Objection : Since the real Self is not fully experienced let the text constitute a restrictive injunction or even an initial one.

Answer : No. Meditation is the repetition of knowledge of one and the same object until the attainment of identity.

Objection : Meditation and knowledge are the same thing in this context; we are being enjoined to meditate, that is, to cognize; mental activity is required, involving the three aspects (agent, object, action) as in "one should sacrifice." The Self is to be known by the mind with the aid of repetition, the result being liberation. "Other enlightened followers of the tradition" say: Texts devoid of injunctions are not valid. Such texts are mere repetitions. Only actions can be enjoined, not substances of qualities, etc., Self-knowledge is obtained through the injunction pertaining to study of the Vedas. Self-knowledge should lead to identity with the Self; but the knowledge arising from words is always complex since derived from combination of word senses, so it will not reveal Brahman, which is partless. Therefore another knowledge, arising after verbal knowledge, is what is enjoined —thus meditation on verbal knowledge.

809-898 (E595-613). *Answer*: These views are not correct. An injunction will have results where there is something to do after one gains verbal knowledge—for example, in the *agnihotra* sacrifice, where human activity is effective in beginning it, etc. But liberation is not such a result. Only one who thinks himself an agent will act; for one for whom that notion has disappeared there will be no activity after he has realized his identity with Brahman. The verbal knowledge of the Self itself dispels ignorance.

Objection : Without an injunction, merely by knowing the inner Self through understanding sentence meanings, no one can dispel ignorance.

Answer : No, since from those very texts, which explain the nature of the Self, the realization arises and ignorance perishes. What else is needed?

Objection: Injunction is required to retain the Self-realization in memory.

Answer: No. Self-knowledge is always available to anyone, being his very nature. Even if repetition is required it will be easily obtained without recourse to an injunction.

Śaṃkara's comments on this section are then glossed.

899-920 (E614-618). *Objection*: If the Self is not to be meditated on, the text "He should be heard, thought, meditated (*nididhyāsana*) on. . . . " will be contradicted.

Answer: No. By the word "*nididhyāsana*" direct awareness is indicated, direct awareness of what is set forth in the next sentence (in the text, viz., "by knowledge of Self all else is known"). It is nonrelational Brahman that is made known by the (great) sentences.

921-947 (E619-623). Śaṃkara says "it is nevertheless true that it is a kind of injunction, that is, a restrictive one . . . ." But this admission is only offered in the context of the illogical view of the opponent. Just as in sacrificing the removal of the husk of the corn is to be accomplished only by striking it with the pestle though there are many ways of removing the husk, so in this case by counseling "meditation" on the Self other kinds of meditation—on not-Self—are rejected as a result. In point of fact meditation on the Self is a universal habit, since every judgment starts with recognition of the "I."

948-993 (E623-633). Some say that in the Self, which is general, all particulars are contained, and that Brahman is to be meditated on as both general and with particulars. Or again, that Brahman is the locus of several states, or the cause of various effects, or the whole comprising parts, like the spokes in a wheel. We do not approve of this since it is neither the intention of scripture nor is it reasonable. Brahman's completeness is that when It is known everything is known; It is not exemplified in general and particular aspects, mutually differing, as a cow or a tree is. Since there are innumerable such aspects they cannot be known either simultaneously or in succession.

When the Self is known nothing remains unknown; so it is the Self that is to be realized. The case of not-Self is different. By its knowledge neither its locus nor what is superimposed on it is known. So it is Self, not non-Self, that is to be known.

Relation involves unreality. Then how can what is not-Self be known at all? Because it is not different from Self. By knowledge of Self everything is known, since the Self is the reality of the not-Self.

994-1008 (E633-635). The word "*pada*" means footprints. By

the cognition of footprints we come to know the whereabouts of the cow. So also by the names and forms of the universe we understand Brahman. Ordinarily, identity with Self is not cognized because of contradiction. To repel ignorance the Self needs to be known through a *pramāṇa*. By itself It will not remove ignorance—if It could, *pramāṇas* would be futile and there would be no *saṃsāra*. So, first of all, the *jīva* should be identified as different from the body, the senses, etc., and then eventually be understood as Brahman.

1009-1028 (E636-639). *Question* : Having begun by saying that by knowing the Self everything is known, how is it that the passage concludes by saying "he obtains fame," etc. ?

Answer : Because that obtaining is not different from knowledge, since obtaining the Self is only the destruction of ignorance. The Self is eternally obtained; his "obtainment" is only the removal of ignorance. So by realizing the Self the knower obtains "fame," etc., but this is only an *arthavāda*, since freed selves do not want fame, etc., these also constituting bondage.

I.4.8; 1025-1054 (E639-645). *Bhartṛprapañca* (according to Ānandagiri): This section tells us that love toward objects is to be avoided and love of Self established. According to Śaṃkara the section provides an additional reason why the Self should be known, that is, lovability. Or else it is intended to reject the liberation of the Sāṃkhya, where there is no bliss. Scripture says that there is bliss in liberation. In the world a son is more lovable than riches, the body more than a son, the senses more than the body, *prāṇa* more than the senses, and the Self most lovable of all.

"Riches" (*vitta*) are of two kinds—worldly and divine. Love of either is not reasonable; a person suffering from pain longs for death. But in the Self love is natural, as heat is in fire. The Sāṃkhyas say that love of not-self is natural, since all things consist of the three *guṇas*. But this is not correct; external things do not actually possess these qualities, but it is because of our ways of thinking that we get likes and dislikes, just as the same sunrise confuses the thief, blinds the sore-eyed and pleases the lost traveler.

Why is the Self alone lovable? Because He is the innermost, as will be shown later. Being the innermost is natural for the Self. For us (says Bhartṛprapañca) who hold that the Self is the inner self of eight stages—body, light, Virāj, etc.—the Self cannot be said to be the innermost, as It is the inner soul for each of the eight. Love for the not-Self is due to an adjunct; which should be removed to provide scope for pure Self-love.

1055-1074 (E645-649). It was stated above that the Self, being all, is the only thing that needs to be known. The Self is complete, but as long as one sees another self he is not full. The remainder of this Book and the whole of the second Book are meant to explain this thought.

1089-1124 (E652-658). The questions here are: (1) Which Brahman (lower or highest) is it by the knowledge of which we become complete? (2) Through knowledge of what did Brahman become complete? Clearly, it must be the highest Brahman that is "full"; only when the word has this primary sense can it take on an implied sense.

Is Brahmanhood natural (*svatas*) or dependent (*paratas*)? Not the first, since then Brahman-knowledge would be futile. If the second, however, Brahman cannot be a product of karma since then It would not be permanent but transitory. If It is produced by knowledge the question arises: was Brahman's knowledge about Brahman or about non-Brahman? Not the first, since the same thing cannot be both agent and object. Not the second, because of infinite regress. The passage is intended to explain how none of these questions should arise.

1125-1202 (E659-673). *Bhartṛprapañca says, however*: Meditators who contemplate Sūtrātman as identity-cum-difference enjoy identity with that Sūtrātman, that is, a Brahmin gradually becomes liberated. But since the knowledge of identity-cum-difference does not lead to completeness, Brahman-knowledge is required. The content of Brahman-knowledge is just Brahman; all else is superimposed on It. Brahman is the reality of the whole universe, sentient and insentient. By knowing It we become the imperishable Brahman Itself. Before Brahman-knowledge we are Brahman but are ignorant of It; that is *avidyā*. Brahman-knowledge does not lead to further action; by it all actions come to a halt.

Answer: All of what you say is acceptable to us *vivartavādins*, or can be interpreted so as to be acceptable, except your notion that in the passage "Brahman became all by knowing all" it is the Brahmin—the meditator—who is referred to.

Bhartṛprapañca: But listen. The word *brāhmaṇa* in that passage must at best refer to the lower Brahman, not the highest, for the highest Brahman does not require any knowledge. Furthermore the passage uses the past tense, which is not suitable for Brahman, which is not subject to temporal passage. However, these very same arguments prove that it is not the lower Brahman either that is being referred to—the same difficulties prevail. So we must understand, by this occurrence of the word, the man who tries to become

Brahman, a person who by meditation and action has attained lower-Brahmanhood and who, through meditation of the highest Brahman, will in the near future become that highest Brahman. The use of the word *brāhmaṇa* to apply to him is appropriate in the light of his future attainment, just as we say "he cooks food" although the raw rice is not yet food, though it will be.

1203-1232 (E673-679). *Answer* : This interpretation is unreasonable since "becoming all" would be impermanent, being dependent on a means. If the removal of limitations due to *avidyā* is intended, then the notion of "becoming Brahman" is uncalled for, since even before knowledge all *jīvas* are Brahman by nature, and limitations are all superimpositions of *avidyā*. Non-Brahmanhood is a product of *avidyā* and perishes with knowledge of reality. Thus the attempt to find a secondary meaning, etc., as in the above interpretation, are all unnecessary.

Question : How is ignorance possible, since it is contradictory to Brahman?

Answer : From our experience "I am ignorant" it is clear that ignorance resides in Brahman. Furthermore, since Brahman-knowledge is enjoined we conclude that Brahman must be unknown.

Question : If ignorance resides in Brahman, how, being omniscient, can Brahman bring about ignorance in the *jīva* ? Anyone acting with any sense would not throw the mischievous *avidyā* onto the *jīva*. Anyway, this is bad logic: since *avidyā* is beginningless, it is not a product. Brahman is the only locus and there is nothing apart from It. Scriptural texts such as "*puruṣa* is all this," "the Self is all this" clearly deny anything other than Brahman. Thus your interpretation makes scripture futile.

Answer : No. The teaching is fruitful for Brahman. Though before knowledge Brahman was without bondage, yet through *avidyā* It is the locus of bondage. By knowledge of identity we get ignorance removed. When identity is realized the removal of ignorance is not possible, but for one who has realized Brahman liberation is not desired.

1237-1283 (E680-689). *Objection* : *Jīva* is different from Brahman as the *jīva* is enveloped by good and bad deeds that earn good and bad results. The authors of *tarkaśāstra* stress the difference. We see people engaged in removing frustrations. The Vedas teach the means for liberation, and surely God does not need to be liberated. All these reasons show the existence of *jīva* as distinct from God.

Answer : No. On that view there would be no need for Brahman-knowledge since by knowledge of the *jīva* itself one would become all,

Objector : Brahman-knowledge involves contemplating the *jiva* as Brahman.

Answer : If Brahman is not known, how can one meditate on Its identity with *jiva* ? If Brahman is known, all human ends are obtained through Brahman-knowledge and meditation is without point.

Objection : Brahman-knowledge is taught for some other purpose.

Answer : No. Other cognitions can serve other purposes, but not Self-knowledge. Because it is stated that "the Self is Brahman" we conclude that the identity is in reality and not only in contemplation. Attainment of Brahmanhood is impossible by mere meditation, which cannot remove ignorance. The name "Brahman-knowledge" will not be appropriate if by the knowledge of something else liberation is attained.

1284-1304 (E689-693). *Question* : What is the proof for the existence of Brahman ? If there is something else that proves Brahman then Brahman cannot be identical with everything as was claimed.

Answer : No. Acceptance of proof does not contradict the description of Brahman given. True, if any entity other than Brahman be accepted there will be contradiction. But proof functions to remove ignorance and reveal reality. Things require *pramāṇas* only before and up to the time of their knowledge, not afterwards. The past tense—"became" in "Brahman became all . . . ."—depends on ignorance and is not a statement of reality, for there is no connection of past, present, or future with Brahman. Only one Brahman exists; before the operation of *pramāṇas* It was not a knower, but rather the witness of the darkness of ignorance.

1305-1329 (E693-698). Scripture is useful inasmuch as it repels ignorance. Though ignorance is beginningless it is removed by knowledge. If this is not accepted all *pramāṇas* will be worthless. The inner Self is what is known. Brahman is not an agent but only a witness; hence there is no conflict. Scriptural texts that say that Brahman is not knowable mean that Brahman, being self-luminous, is not to be illuminated by anything.

Brahman, being untransferable and unconnected, has no real relation with *avidyā*. But *avidyā* is established only by the illumination of the Self. Since the universe and its origination, etc., are not real apart from Brahman, knowledge of them is false like a dream cognition. The locus and content of valid cognition is Brahman conditioned by the manifest and unmanifest universe. Thus when ignorance is removed its products also perish.

1387-1435 (E709-718). That Brahman (as *jiva*) by the grace of a guru realized its own self as Self and became Brahman by the removal of ignorance. The word "only" conveys the idea that Self alone is Brahman and Brahman alone is Self.

Objection : Scripture says "you cannot know the knower", so how can you assert that the Self knows itself?

Answer : The Self is not known as an object, but as the witness of cognitions. Of all cognitions that of the inner Self comes first, and as there is no difference between cognizer and cognized the Self is cognized by the Self, resulting in removal of ignorance and hence realization. The sentence "I am Brahman" is analyzed.

1436-1526 (E718-735). Knowledge requires no eligibility, since anyone who gets Self-knowledge becomes Brahman, whether he be god, man, or *ṛṣi*. The word "only" indicates that no other means (*sādhana*) is required for liberation. Brahman itself undergoes *saṃsāra* and is liberated by knowledge—thus the words "god," "man," etc., are used in their ordinary senses.

Objection : If Self-knowledge can be attained without eligibility it cannot arise.

Answer : No, since knowledge can be gained because of traces (*saṃskāra*) acquired in past lives, as in the case of Vāmadeva. The Vāmadeva episode is recommended here to make students believe. Vāmadeva saw Brahman and exclaimed "I was Manu ! I was the sun !," etc. This is the beginning of the Sūkta of Vāmadeva. The whole Sūkta is implied here.

Objection : Liberation might have been possible for gods and great men of the past, but not for men of our times.

Answer : No. Even now whoever gets Brahman-knowledge becomes all. When knowledge is attained even the gods cannot bring any obstacles.

Bhartṛprapañca says that without enjoying all the fruits of action liberation is not possible. Thus liberation can only come after all enjoyment. But this is not wise, as such enjoyment will take many lives. Thus scripture says that even the gods are not competent to obstruct liberation.

Objection : But men are debtors to the gods. It is said that they help them like herds of cows helping a human being. Thus if a man becomes Brahman his dependence on them will cease and thus the gods do not brook his independence. Further, God also can obstruct our endeavors, since He is all-powerful. Thus there is doubt about all our undertakings, whether action or knowledge.

Answer : No. The gods and God, being objects of worship, will not hinder the fruits of karma. Even to obstruct they need the agent's past karma. God, time, gods—we have to take each as principal or subsidiary causal condition according to the occasion, and which is the principal is not easily known. Though some say that in getting the fruit, *karman* is the cause, whereas other say the gods are, and yet others say nature is, scriptural passages concur in accepting *karman* alone as the cause. As for knowledge, the gods cannot hinder our gaining liberation by knowledge since knowledge itself *is* liberation. Time, gods, doubt, error, etc., all are products of ignorance. When ignorance is removed they all cease to exist.

Objection : Repetition (*abhyāsa*) is required before liberation can ensue.

Answer : No, for we cannot be sure how many times knowledge must be repeated, and so there will be no decision.

Objection : The Self is cognized by the notion of "I"; so scriptural advice to know is merely *arthavāda*.

Answer : No, the Self taught in the Upaniṣads is never cognizable by the notion of "I."

1527-1557 (E736-741). *Objection* : Since we find that even knowers of reality have desires, etc., knowledge does not remove ignorance.

Answer : This is because of *prārabdhakarman*, which continues even after knowledge like a wheel. This kind of karma does not perish even by knowledge.

Objection : If *prārabdhakarman* is not destroyed by knowledge the other kinds of karma won't be either.

Answer : Scripture speaks of liberation while living. Further, the tradition of Self-knowledge continues in the world (and would be lost if Self-knowers were not around long enough to communicate the tradition).

Others say that liberation comes from suppression of the functioning of the mind (*cittavṛttinirodha*). This is not reasonable, since as suppression of mental functions at *pralaya* does not bring about liberation it will not do so any other time either. Likewise, multiplying traces born of the notion "I am Brahman" will not cause liberation, since the results of traces are also impermanent.

1558-1599 (E741-749). Now the gods will cease to be creditors in respect of the knower, Brahman, as debtorship is the product of ignorance and agency, etc., have no place in one whose ignorance has been removed. The gift of light by the sun and of breeze by the air do not bind Him, since sun, air, and other gods are bound to do their duties. The scriptural passage that says that men are threefold debtors by birth is an *arthavāda*.

He who sees the god as different from himself does not realize reality. He is visited by ignorance and surrounded by its products, hence takes the place of a cow by his actions toward the gods. That is, just as a cow helps the ordinary man in many ways so also this ignorant person helps the gods. One cow sometimes helps one person, sometimes many when it drags a cart filled with many persons. So also one man sometimes helps the whole world. When one cow is stolen the owner, though he has many cows, becomes unhappy. What shall we say about him when all his cows are stolen ! That is the nature of Brahman-knowledge; it deprives the knower of his agency for all action. Therefore the gods do not like men getting Brahman-knowledge. Hence if we want Brahman-knowledge we must propitiate the gods carefully; only with their blessing can we get this knowledge. People who want to get liberation without satisfying the gods will be deprived of heaven, etc., as well as liberation. Even now we see *saṃnyāsins* who are external-object-minded.

1600-1664 (E750-762). Brahman thought that without the four castes we cannot perform actions and hence It created the Kṣatriya class comprising Indra, etc. Since the Kṣatriya is more powerful than the Brahmin the latter extols him sitting below the king's chair in the Rājasūya sacrifice. The king addresses the Brahmin as "Brahmā", and the Brahmin replies "you are Brahmin," thus giving back the fame earned by him. But at the end of the Rājasūya the king submits to the Brahmin as he is his cause. A king who ill-treats his cause—the Brahmin—courts unhappy results.

Again not satisfied with the creation of the four castes Brahman wanted to create *dharma* which will overrule Kṣatriyas and in the absence of which the warrior class might with its physical strength ill-treat the Brahmin. This *dharma* is the ruler of Kṣatriya also. It is above might; it rules over Kṣatriyas. Hence it is that though feeble and powerless one wants to conquer the strong race with the help of *dharma*. *Dharma* is truth (*satya*) and vice versa. Truth is the purport of scripture and *dharma* is the proper procedure in performing action. Both should coincide to make the performance fruitful as otherwise either the meaning of scripture or the performance of action may go wrong.

Dharma is also a god. It is a truth of Vedānta that the one Brahman assumes the forms of several gods.

Now the divisions of caste among men are described. Brahman or the Brahmin became fire among the gods and himself was among men as Brahmin without undergoing any change. Fire is the divine form of the Brahmin. So he helps the human form of the Brahmin. The Brahmin can obtain all he wants by propitiating fire. The

Brahminhood obtainable by Kṣatriyas and Vaiśyas is not natural; it requires the help of fire and of Brahmins. The distinction among castes is mentioned here only to assist in performance of actions. Fire is the important factor in (ritual) action and is also the god there. But it cannot give liberation, since knowledge alone is the cause of that.

1665-1714 (E762-771). He who has performed all actions but has no knowledge of Brahman cannot be liberated. The death of the ignorant is connected with darkness, but for knowers it is the removal of darkness. The supreme Brahman does not save one who has not known that Brahman, any more than the Vedas or any worldly work does. Even if the nonknower performs actions night and day for crores of *kalpas* he does not get liberation. But Self-knowledge alone saves him. The knower does not require actions, for the effects of action, being brought about naturally, perish. When the reality of the inner Self is known everything is known and infinite bliss is acquired. Whatever the knower wants he can have by Self-knowledge itself, since all the pleasures in the world are contained in the bliss of Brahman.

According to Bhartṛprapañca, however, the foregoing passage must be construed differently, as follows:

Objection : Now action will not lead to liberation as it is perishable and the gods hold him in bondage without providing him liberation. He cannot leave off actions, since they are eternal (or required, *nitya*). The Self without being seen will not provide liberation, and since the seeker is a servant of the gods he cannot strive for Brahman-knowledge. There is no combination of knowledge with action. The agent is subject to the three debts.

Answer (on Bhartṛprapañca's interpretation): He must meditate on the Self alone and perform action. The performance of *nityakarmans* together with meditation on the Sūtrātman, having an origin, may perish. But the state of Brahman, having no specific aspects, is eternal. By meditating on this Brahman the seeker gains eternal results. When he sees action as Brahman itself actions will not perish. The combination of action with knowledge is twofold: First, there is the combination of *nityakarmans* with meditation on Hiraṇyagarbha. Second, there is the combination of action with the causal Brahman (Sūtrātman). The result of the first combination is the removal of all desires, since by attaining Hiraṇyagarbhahood one's desires will all be fulfilled. After this both the gross and subtle bodies perish. Through the second combination one gets liberation.

1715-1779 (E771-782). *Sureśvara's answer to Bhartṛprapañca's interpretation* : This interpretation is defective. On Bhartṛprapañca's view the result of the second combination of meditation and action will never be over. Furthermore, scripture tells us that when desires perish liberation ensues. This is contradictory to Bhartṛprapañca's view. At the time of liberation (*kaivalya*) no karma should be left unfulfilled. Furthermore, the result of the first combination is the attainment of Hiraṇyagarbhahood, not the destruction of bodies.

Objection : After attaining Hiraṇyagarbhahood he enjoys all desires and then the two bodies (gross and subtle) perish.

Answer : No, since in that case Brahman-knowledge would be fruitless.

Objection : In the *Īśā Upaniṣad* the combination of action and knowledge is advocated—"He who sees *vidyā* and *avidyā* together," etc. . . .

Answer : No, for "death" in this passage means a natural event and "*vidyā*" means scriptural knowledge. By "death" one conquers natural tendencies, and by pure *vidyā* one attains liberation. So there is no room for the combination of knowledge and action. Self-knowledge alone is the cause of liberation in the Upaniṣad as well.

1780-1883 (E782-797). Now the text describes how the ignorant helps the gods like a cow, and whom he helps. The "ignorant" is the one who has not realized the Self. "Self" means the groups of body, mind, and senses and the self who identifies itself with them. By action he has produced his body as well as the gods to whom he gives oblations. Agency and enjoyership are likewise false. By Brahman-knowledge they will expire. Briefly, all are the products and causes of everything. The householders who perform *homa* and *yāga* are the products of the actions of the gods. By his (the householder's) daily chanting of the Vedas he produces enjoyment for the sages. Since he is always helping all *jivas*, they all desire that he should not die, and this is why they do not allow him to get knowledge of Brahman. He must repay his debts.

Question : Since men are free to take up action (*pravṛtti*) or to abandon it (*nivṛtti*), why do they take up action instead of abandoning it ? Their protection is assured regardless. *Avidyā* only veils reality, so it is not the cause.

Answer : Desire (*kāma*) is the product of ignorance. Having not gained his desires he wants to obtain them by other means. Before marriage one is single, but afterwards one begets sons, and they grandsons. One does not know reality. He becomes influenced by the senses and the objects, confounded by them and induced by desire to desire a wife, sons, and all the materials for action.

FIFTH BRĀHMAṆA

1-12 (E797-799). In the state of ignorance every person through his actions creates the universe and enjoys its fruits. Since each individual enjoys common objects as well as individual ones, enjoyment will not be possible without his having contributed toward its origination by his action. All actions whether meritorious or not naturally generate both common and specific results—actions of Sūtrātman down to those of a worm. In some cases, like seeing a dance, the action that causes is general, whereas in others, like seeing one's own child, the causative action is specific. Thus each man creates the universe by his knowledge and action. This will be explained in the *Madhu Brāhmaṇa.*

13-94 (E799-814). This section develops I.5.1-2, which speaks of various kinds of food. The commentary provides interesting insights on the use of foodstuffs in sacrifice.

95-206 (E814-833). I.5.3 identifies three foods as speech (*vāk*), life breath (*prāṇa*), and the internal organ (*manas*). The senses are but operations of the internal organ, since being touched in the back one knows that he is touched. Vyāsa is quoted in support.

Each of the three is explained as regards its relation to body, the outer world, and the gods (I.5.4-13).

207-263 (E834-844). Prajāpati (I.5.14-15) has two aspects—as the world, and as time. In the former aspect he has the forms of the three foods just discussed. In his time aspects his nature is the moon (*candra*)—he creates the fortnight, season, and year. As he has increase and decline (as moon) he is of the nature of riches. He causes the transformation of the world. On Amāvāsyā day only one of his parts remains. Through that he enters all *jīvas* and again is born on the first day of the waxing moon. Since through him Prajāpati enters all the *prāṇas* one should not kill on that day.

Worship (*pūjā*) of Prajāpati is also intended here, as mere knowledge does not effect the desired end. The adept should meditate that he is Prajāpati, and that his riches are Prajāpati's parts.

Sons and two kinds of riches produce the three worlds. One who desires liberation should renounce the three worlds.

Bhartṛprapañca : Sons and the two kinds of riches produce liberation.

Answer : Means that are independently causes of their respective effects should not be combined.

Bhartṛprapañca : But the world of human beings is obtained by ritual action (the *jyotiṣṭoma*), and one overcomes that by means of one's sons.

Answer: No. This world is obtained by sons, not by rites. The

Mahābhārata confirms this. Furthermore, in the Upaniṣads it is said that the fruit of actions is the moon world (*candraloka*), not the world of human beings. And then, if through one's sons one overcomes the results of karma Brahman-knowledge will become pointless.

The world of the fathers (*pitṛloka*) is obtained by action, and by meditation the world of Brahma (*brahmaloka*). Here "*vidyā*" (in the text "*vidyāya devaloka*") means meditation, not Brahman-knowledge. The world of the gods (*devaloka*) is the foremost of the worlds, and "conquering" (*jaya*) it is only obtaining it. If by "conquering" were meant abandoning it or any of the other worlds, then since the purposes of men (*puruṣārtha*) would be obtained, there would be no reason to say that such persons are eligible for performing actions.

264-301 (E844-851). Now with regard to *saṃnyāsa* taken according to the ordinary sequence (i.e., *brahmacarya*, *gṛhasthya*, and then *saṃnyāsa*), scripture recommends what is called *sampratti karman* (renunciatory action). I.5.17 indicates how this involves one's sons. *Saṃnyāsins* who take up *saṃnyāsa* directly from *brahmacarya* are not eligible, since they have no sons. This type of action is intended for those that because of old age and the resulting incapacity to perform ritual acts wish to place them with their sons. The son, after having been advised by his father in the fashion indicated in the text, is capable of obeying his orders and becomes a means for the father to attain the worlds mentioned.

302-390 (E851-868). *Bhartṛprapañca* : After performing this renunciatory action, if the father lives he must perform the *agnihotra*.

Answer : But this act in fact involves an injunction of *saṃnyāsa*, so the person who performs it must take up *saṃnyāsa* afterwards. *Kauśitakī Upaniṣad* is cited, as well as Manu. After taking up *saṃnyāsa* he should contemplate *prāṇa*, or he may live without any meditation. When he dies he becomes one with his son along with his *prāṇas*. The entry of the father into his son is not literal; it means that the son gets the determinations that his father had before performing this *sampratti karman*.

When his duties are transferred to his son the father becomes the divine *prāṇa*. After death he enjoys the fruits of his karma but remains in this world in the shape of the son and performs actions. Because the son fulfils the duties of his father he is called "*putra*" ("son").

The father who has contemplated on the divine *prāṇa* Hiraṇyagarbha merges with him. Mīmāṃsakas say that by sons, action, and lower knowledge liberation is attained. Bhartṛprapañca says that by these three the father is redeemed from the three worlds and gains liberation. Both these views are wrong, for scripture says that these are all optional (*kāmya*) actions. Therefore they are for those who have not yet realized Brahman.

SIXTH BRĀHMAṆA

1-45 (E868-876). This Brāhmaṇa gives briefly the products of ignorance, though that has been dealt with previously.

46-93 (E876-885). *Bhartṛprapañca* : Brahman is difference-cum-nondifference. Though the powers (*śakti*) of Brahman are many Brahman is one. Though the bodies of cows are different the genus (*jāti*) *cowhood* is the same throughout them. So the universe is by nature difference-cum-nondifference.

Answer : This view is corrupt, since difference and nondifference in one object is inconsistent. In fact generality (*sāmānya*) and particularity (*viśeṣa*) are both superimposed; hence Bhartṛprapañca's view cannot be maintained.

BOOK TWO—FIRST BRĀHMAṆA

20-25 (E890-891). Gārgya is a nonknower of Brahman, and so haughty; Ajātaśatru, having attained the highest end of man, is the guru. The story provides easy understanding of the *sūtra* about knowledge (*vidyā*).

Others, however, say that in this story the person who entered the body is explained. The opponent, Gārgya, is of the view that gods alone are agents and enjoyers in the body, whereas the *siddhāntin*, the king of Kāśī, emphasizes the agency and enjoyership of the *jīva*.

This is pointless, since it is inconsistent with the *siddhāntin's* espousal of the identity of *jīva* and Brahman as set forth in the previous chapter. Further, even if the gods are in the body the existence of *jīvas* is accepted—so what is the point of the *siddhāntin* ?

40-204 (E894-921). The story in the text is explained (II.1.1-16).

205-247 (E921-928). The author says that since the king has already promised to teach Gārgya Brahman he has to tell him the true nature of the enjoyer and what is enjoyed. The nature of what is known is unreal, since it is not associated with a person in sleep. One's nature is just consciousness. Since before he awoke there was no trace of karma in him it is clear that karma is not his nature.

The *buddhi* and other organs originate from karma, and their dissolution is also caused by karma. The enjoyership of the Self is due to the reflection of consciousness (*cidābhāsa*) and its agency is due to ignorance. The pure Self identified with each of these things is called respectively "enjoyer" and "agent." When the karma that produces waking ends one goes to sleep. Latent impressions (*vāsanā*) continue through that state, and when one awakes those impressions freshen and one is led by desire, aversion, etc., to perform more acts. Thus the beginningless ignorance gives rise to *saṃsāra*. But the *jīva* becomes one with its reflection and settles in the pure Brahman during deep sleep.

Here it is stated that by realizing the *jīva* in its pure nature by negating the body, senses, and object superimposed upon it, we must know that the Self is no other than Brahman. This is the meaning here. *Jīva* is in the *buddhi*, and Brahman is also said to be in the *buddhi* only to convey the identity of *jīva* and Brahman.

248-272 (E928-936). Others, however, interpret the passage this way: The *jīva*, before waking, takes away the awarenesses (*vijñāna*) called speech, vision, etc., by the *buddhi*, and settles in the *ākāśa* contained in (or conditioned by) the heart. The Self, having the latent impressions of the *buddhi*, gets out of this *ākāśa* through the nerves (*nāḍī*) and sees dreams with the help of the *buddhi*.

This interpretation is not correct, since it says that along with the latent impressions the internal organ is dissolved. It is better that *jīva* is the agent and when all are dissolved Brahman alone is made the locus of dissolution. "*Svapiti*" ("it sleeps") (in II.1.17) is interpreted in the *Chāndogya* as dissolution into a thing's own self, and this is only Brahman.

The three states of waking, dream, and deep sleep are all illusory. To illustrate this scripture says that everything seen in dreams is illusory. The whole world is moving in agony thinking that these states are real, like the person who is confused finding his path in a jungle. He who realizes that the whole universe is the Self, he alone is called "one who has fulfilled all obligations" (*kṛtārtha*). Perception and the other *pramāṇas* do not embrace Brahman. *Avidyā* is not in the Self really. It is illusion. By the traces awakened by karma the *jīva* falls to dreaming and like a magician he creates big and small things all of which are false.

293-318 (E936-940). The king and other things (seen in dream) are not the attributes of the dreamer, since he sees them. The king seen by the dreamer is different from the king who is sleeping on the couch in the palace. What is observed in waking is not observed in dream, and vice versa. So being mutually inconstant they are both unreal. There is no doubt about the unreality of dreams, since the dead people, etc., seen in dreams do not exist at that time nor is there space for streets, coaches, etc., inside the body. Nor does the dreamer go out and see during sleep, since without a body he cannot move.

The immutable, nonrelated Self that goes out is apparently related with unreal adjuncts. Being naturally nonrelated he can have no real connection with the not-Self.

Objection : How can the Self be pure, since It is wandering in dreams through the power of desire (*kāma*), and being the seer of them militates against Its purity?

Answer : No, since It is nonrelated to desires or even to ignorance. The next section proves that the Self is secondless, being seen in deep sleep. It is the immutable (*kuṭastha*) witness.

319-363 (E940-947). In what manner does sleep come about? There is a lump of flesh called the "heart" (*hṛdaya*) hanging from the neck "like a lotus facing downwards. The seats of dream are nerves colored blue, etc. For each sense organ ten nerves go out to fetch their objects." Each nerve has numerous subnerves. They start from the heart, and are called "good-making" (*hita*). Spreading Its various *vāsanās* the Self sees various objects in dream. After enjoying the dream one goes into deep sleep and sleeps in the Self, which pervades with general awareness all over the body. The seat of the internal organ (*antaḥkaraṇa*) is the heart; from here the *buddhi* controls the senses. By one's karma the modifications of consciousness are spread out; when the modifications are controlled one dreams. Through the nerves he gets to *puritāt* (a skin over the heart) and spreads throughout the body with consciousness, like a hot iron. The Self in itself has no birth or death; It is like the *ākāśa* in a pot; by association with the *buddhi* It gets born and dies.

In deep sleep the Self has no connection with the body. This state is beyond all the pains of *saṃsāra*, just like a child's who has no desire or hatred. Or like a king whose subjects are obedient. But a child has no discrimination, and the king might be a drunkard. Thus a third example is given—like a Brahmin who, having the experience of pure Brahman, has carried out his duties and attained final happiness. Being rid of modifications the minds of all three enjoy full happiness.

364-413 (E947-955). So far the king's question "where does he rest while sleeping?" has been answered. The next section (II.1.20) answers the second question, "from whence does he come out to the waking state?"

To explain this the example of the spider and its thread is given. Just as the thread does not exist independently of the spider, so also the world of not-Self does not exist independently of the Self. Talk about creation here is to assist the listener; in reality there is no creation. This has been fully explained by Gauḍapāda. Just as the spider does not require any external things to create threads, so also Brahman creates the world without any external means.

Objection : God is the creator !

Answer : If so, why doesn't he always create (even in *pralaya*)? Whether one adopts the identity-cum-difference view or the non-difference view, in any case the cause-effect relationship cannot be defended.

414-711 (E955-987). In the Upaniṣads the *prāṇas* are mentioned as being the seventeen—the hearing organ, etc.—which make up the subtle body (*liṅga*). "Worlds" (*loka*) are the different types of bodies of this world—divine, etc. The "selves" referred to here are the *jīvas*, whose birth is like that of sparks from fire. Since only through ignorance does the Self get the names of "*prāṇa*," etc., He is the pure Brahman. For the purpose of meditation His secret name (*nāma upaniṣad*) is now given. The effect of this is the arising of the knowledge of Self and nothing else. That secret name is "Truth of truth" (*satyasya satyam*). The first "truth" is *prāṇa*, that is, the whole world of name-and-form. Its reality derives from the reality of Brahman, its substratum.

Now the discussion on II.1.20 by Śaṃkara begins, and carries through to the conclusion of this section. The commentary does not add anything important to Śaṃkara's thought.

SECOND BRĀHMAṆA

1-31 (E987-992). This section expands on the *prāṇas*, the first to be created in the account alluded to in the previous section. *Prāṇa* is seated in the head preeminently, and throughout the body. It derives its strength from food, and with that strength supports the sense organs and satisfies them. Only by the strength gained from the intake of food can *prāṇa* stay in the body, and so food is the rope by which *prāṇa* is tied to the body. When the rope becomes weak because of the exhaustion of karma, the *prāṇas* leave the body and it dies.

THIRD BRĀHMAṆA

1-67 (E992-1003). This section dwells on the two forms of Brahman—the gross or corporeal, and the subtle or incorporeal. The gross form has parts, is perishable, dependent, limited spatially, cognizable by the senses; earth, water, and fire among the five elements belong here. Its essence is the sun. The subtle form is immortal, unlimited, indeterminate; air and *ākāśa* characterize it, and its essence is the person in the sun.

This is now developed with respect to the divinities. Just as the eye is the seat of the sense of sight, so also the sun is the seat of Hiraṇyagarbha. Hiraṇyagarbha is that deity that is the president of all the senses of all creatures; He is of the essence of air and *ākāśa*.

Bhartṛprapañca : The *jīva*-Hiraṇyagarbha is the essence.

Answer : No, for the essence should be something nonconscious, as we have here to do with the gross, not the subtle realm.

68-104 (E1003-1010). Now the text develops the distinction with respect to the body. The essence of the first three elements (earth, water, fire) is the sense of sight. Scripture says that when the body is formed in the mother's womb it is the eye that is first manifested.

Now the form of the subtle body (*liṅga*) is explained. It is filled with *vāsanās*, like a curious cloth of many colors, like a magical spell confusing the individual. The Vijñānavādins and Naiyāyikas believe this to be the self. The Vaiśeṣikas say that self is substance and the *vāsanās* are its qualities. Sāṃkhya says that *pradhāna* (*prakṛti*) with the three *guṇas* operates independently for the sake of the *puruṣa*.

Bhartṛprapañca ("some pseudo Vedāntins") says that all effects surrounding the *jīva*, whether gross or subtle, are included in the gross and subtle forms of Brahman. They are respectively "*sat*" and "*tyat*," thus the word for "truth," *satya*. The *prāṇas*, being such products, are *satya*; though devoid of name-and-form they are so because of their association with the elements. At this stage it is not possible to differentiate between the *jīvas* and their adjuncts. Then the nature of the Self (*puruṣa*) is described. When the gross and subtle natures are negated what remains of *jīva* is pure, supreme Self. The *jīva's* nature is a collection of *vāsanās*, here described by comparison with a cloth dipped in yellow-colored water.

105-148 (E1010-1017). *Answer to Bhartṛprapañca* : This is erroneous, since *vāsanās* cannot attach to intelligence, which is not matter and indeed a completely different kind of thing. Furthermore, *vāsanās* do not attach to cognitions of pots, etc., and the Self is always nonrelated or nonattached. It is foolish to say that the product of the five elements has no connection with *vāsanās*. Bhartṛprapañca distinguishes three groups: (1) the five elements, (2) the supreme Self, (3) *vāsanās*. This last group includes (the results of) *vidyā* or meditative actions as well as other latent impressions. Located in the subtle body they yet produce results in the Self. Though the Self is by nature qualityless, yet by karma it gets qualities and thus becomes a transmigrator through agency and enjoyership. But those like Bhartṛprapañca who think thus are mistaken, for on this view there is no room for liberation. Desire, determination, doubt, etc., are properties of the internal organ, not of the Self. The presumption of the three groups is not valid. *Jīva* belongs with Brahman; the *vāsanās* appear in the *jīva*, and there is no third entity. If the two forms (gross and subtle) belong to Brahman only through the *jīva* and not directly, then the tone of scripture would be different.

Objection: There are other forms in Brahman, but for the *jīva vāsanā* alone is the form.

Answer: Even so, for Brahman, which evolves as *jīva*, the *vāsanās* arise.

149-170 (E1017-1020). The person described as "existing in the right eye" (*dākṣiṇo'kṣan*) is the subtle body and not the *jīva*, since the *jīva* is identified as pure Brahman and is not the same as the subtle body. The teaching of "not this, not this" only applies to the *jīva* (cf. Book Four). The various *vāsanās* in the subtle body give different colors to the Witness as the blemishes do in jewels. The subtle body with *vāsanās* of desire is yellow, or it may be white like wool. The differences are due to the intensities of the three *guṇas*.

171-214 (E1020-1028). So far, truth (*satya*) has been explained. Now the highest reality (*paramārthasatya*) will be explained, the "truth of truth." As it is beyond speech or thought it is taught only by precept. How do the words "truth" and "of truth" reveal Brahman? Because they reject primal *avidyā* and its products such as names, actions, *prāṇas*, worlds, and all sorts of causes and effects. By rejecting all external objects the inner Self which is unrejected is shown to be the Supreme Reality. The word "this" (in "not this") refers to name-and-form. The not-Self rejected in Brahman does not exist anywhere else since, being the product of ignorance in a substrate, it does not exist at all. Objects that have sprung from ignorance of the real Self cannot exist either as Self or as independent of It. The word "this" (in "not this") does not refer to Brahman, since it gives existence and illumination to the not-Self and so cannot be negated. Moreover, It is self-luminous, and the negation (in "not this") is not only of ignorance and its products but also their negations. Hence there is no positive or negative existence in the Self. The repetition of "not this" signifies all that is desired to be known.

Question: After the gross and subtle forms have been negated there may still be something left unnegated.

Answer: No. That will lead to nihilism (*śūnyavāda*). The whole text is a teaching (*ādeśa*) of some new insight, and nihilism is not a thing to be taught. Since the not-Self is dependent on ignorance, its annihilation is by Self-knowledge alone. Thus by repetition of "not this" man attains the supreme state of Self-awareness.

215-254 (E1028-1034). The difference between Brahman and Its gross and subtle forms is rooted out by the negation. However, this negation does not have negation as its purpose; rather, it purports identity. How is this ? The duality is negated even before the Upaniṣads speak, since it is naturally inconstant, being absent in deep sleep. Therefore the two negatives ("not this, not this") by implication (*lakṣaṇā*) reveal the Witness, which gives light to the negations. This Witness is the immutable Self. The word "this" signifies Brahman. Thus identity of *jīva* with Brahman is the meaning of the sentence. This is its only possible meaning. The teaching of Brahman through positive means is not possible, for Brahman is qualityless. The *prāṇas* are said to be truth. Brahman is the truth of truth, so it is the superior truth.

FOURTH BRĀHMAṆA

1-38 (E1035-1040). He who is averse to all sense objects including Brahmaloka is eligible for Brahman-knowledge. In becoming purified through performance of the *nityakarmans* the mind remembers the sufferings of *saṃsāra* and searches for the means to remove them. He must take up *saṃnyāsa,* ordained in scripture as the means to Brahman-knowledge.

The not-Self has been rejected by "not this, not this." If the not-Self is nondifferent from Brahman then Brahman would be miserable. If the denial results in nihilism then Brahman will disappear. If there is a second entity then Brahmanhood will be lost.

To bring out the idea of pure Brahman from the text "all is the Self" (*sarvam ātmā*) this Brāhmaṇa, the *Maitreyī Brāhmaṇa*, comes next.

Though Yājñavalkya had achieved the supreme knowledge he had to take up *saṃnyāsa,* without which liberation is not attainable. Just as sons, etc., are the means of obtaining this world, so also *saṃnyāsa* is the means for liberation. To enjoin *saṃnyāsa* for liberation is why this Brāhmaṇa is begun.

39-70 (E1040-1045). Explanation of the first four sections.

71-147 (E1045-1057). Yājñavalkya, after praising Maitreyī's state of mind, began to teach her. First, in order that she attain nonattachment he says that for a wife the husband is dear, not because he is the husband but because he does her good. In the same way the whole world is dear only because it is his. There are worlds that are agreeable to some and distasteful to others. This is because they are agreeable to one's own taste and not because they are in themselves good or bad. The whole world of not-Self is disagreeable because it leads one to sorrow and confusion. The Self is never disagreeable to anybody at any time. But one's wife, friends, etc., are only agreeable sometimes. Therefore love of Self is not due to any causal conditions, but is natural. Therefore we must maintain our love of Self; by Its mere knowledge all sorrows disappear and bliss is attained.

In the text's "the Self is to be seen, heard, thought on and meditated upon" (*ātmā vā āre draṣṭavyaḥ śrotavyo mantavyo nididhyāsitavyo*) the word "Self" refers to the inner Self, being clearly intended. The knowledge of "I," being common to everyone, is not what is enjoined; the knowledge "I am all" is what is enjoined. In *Chāndogya Upaniṣad* VII the nature of *bhumān* is given, and then rejecting the ego principle's (*ahaṃkāra*) Selfhood Self-knowledge is emphasized by saying "in all the Upaniṣads *ahaṃkāra* is dismissed as self and contemplation of the Self is stressed". There too scripture says that all is Self.

In deep sleep nobody sees not-Self. In waking and dreaming everybody sees Self and not-Self, so what is enjoined is not meditation on these two but rather the discrimination between the two. To understand sentence meaning knowledge of the meanings of the words is required. The knowledge "the Self is all" is born on the strength of its object; it cannot be enjoined. If it is enjoined it will be like contemplation of the words as fire. But there is no injunction here, since knowledge is not a thing to be carried out by men. Hearing, thinking, and meditating are enjoined; they can be accomplished. But the fruit, that is, the knowledge or realization, cannot be enjoined. Self-knowledge is always there but will only be realized when the adjuncts are eliminated.

148-211 (E1057-1067). Though the identity of *jīva* with the supreme Self is an existent entity and injunction has no scope, yet the Vedantic scriptures are valid inasmuch as they reveal the identity that is not known by any other *pramāṇa*. Just as words wake a sleeping person, so the Vedānta removes the ignorance that obscures the identity.

212-249 (E1068-1074). The Self being the object of "seeing" the *pramāṇas* might be thought appropriate for grasping It. To avoid this the text says that It should be "heard" (*śrotavya*), thereby indicating the scripture alone is the *pramāṇa* for the Self. "Seeing" is not enjoined, but rather its means, hearing, etc., with the help of which the Self will be "seen," that is, realized. By enjoining thinking (*manana*) the text indicates that it is reality (*vastutattva*) that is being intended here, since where one speaks only of meditation (which does not require its object to be real) one does not also speak of "thinking on" or reflection. "Meditating," here mentioned, is realization of Self in contrast to "seeing," which is superficial knowledge. Thus the three—hearing, thinking, and meditation—converge into one and the same entity, that is, the Self. That *nididhyāsana* is not meditation but only realization is indicated by the word "*vijñānena*" (which is used as a synonym for "*nididhyāsana*" in that last line of this text).

250-297 (E1074-1082). The next section (II.4.6) says that he who thinks that the castes—Brahmin, Kṣatriya, etc.—are different from Brahman is ineligible for liberation. This is because such a one does not see what is, but sees what is not. The Self persists in all not-Self, but the not-Selves differ and so are unreal. The Self alone is to be seen as setting aside the not-Self. What persists is real; what differs is unreal, like the rope among snake, wreath, etc., superimposed on it. The examples of drum, etc. (II.4.7-9), show that the generality of drum sound is real, the particular sounds unreal. In the same way, reality (*sat*) that persists is real and the varying objects unreal. The mention of many examples is to stress the fact that all particulars dissolve into the biggest generality, that is, Brahman. The *Chāndogya* says that name and other entities up to *prāṇa* dissolve into *bhumān* = Brahman.

298-326 (E1082-1087). Not only in the state of existence is there unity of Self but also in the state of origination. To illustrate this the text (II.4.10) gives the example of fire, sparks, and smoke. The sparks and smoke are nondifferent from fire. In fact, all things being only consciousness, there is no difference. Just as the fire releases smoke, etc., without effort, so also Brahman releases *prāṇa* and other products without effort. Likening them to breath (in the text) is intended to substantiate this. Though the Vedas are not products of some person they are valid, and their validity is because of their being nondependent. When in such a text as "all is Self" the Vedas appear to be invalid, scripture, in order to protect their validity, says that the Vedas are products of Brahman and hence valid. Other works—*mantras*, *brāhmaṇas*, *itihāsas*, etc.—are also mentioned in the text as products of Brahman. In this list "*itihāsa*" ("stories") does not mean the *Mahābhārata*, but only the stories given in the Vedas. "*Veda*" here means the bulk of the literature consisting of *mantras* and *brāhmaṇas*.

327-485 (E1087-1113). Just as there are no things different from consciousness during origination and maintenance of the world, so also there are no entities during *pralaya*. To reveal this he cites the example of the rivers flowing into the sea though nondifferent from it. The dissolution of the elements (earth, air, etc.) is in Brahman through *avidyā*, since Brahman is the material cause of the universe. The Purāṇas say that this is the natural dissolution. Dissolution through Brahman-knowledge is final and has no return whereas the other dissolutions mentioned here are temporary and lead to rebirth.

To substantiate this Yājñavalkya says that just as a lump of salt dropped in a pot of water dissolves and cannot be taken out, yet can be tasted in the water, so also the mass of intelligence (*vijñānaghana*) called *jīva*, due to the realization of the Self's identity with Brahman becomes one with It and its individual name and form are eternally lost. The *jīva's* individuality, being conditioned on ignorance, senses, and body, is no more. There will be no individual name.

Hearing this, Maitreyī suspected the death of the Self, since her husband had said that the Self is a mass of intelligence and that It dies with knowledge.

To pacify her, Yājñavalkya explained that he meant by "mass of intelligence" the unity of the Self, and by "the death of the Self" the demise of the individual name and *jīva*-hood.

When the Self is confined to the body, etc., through ignorance the knower, the known, and knowledge are felt to be different entities. But this is only in the state of ignorance. All the senses are the products of gross elements, since each cognizes only the quality of the corresponding element. Otherwise they could have cognized all qualities in the way that the internal organ and the *buddhi* do, which are products of five elements. All movements of the body belong to the *buddhi*, which is the same as *prāṇa*. All sense organs are energies of *prāṇa*. The energies of action and knowledge dissolve in Brahman.

The text "Because when there is duality, as it were" does not allow the possibility of duality. It is possible to compare one thing with itself, as in "The Rāma-Rāvaṇa war was like the Rāma-Rāvaṇa war." Or else the comparison is with objects in the dream state.

FIFTH BRĀHMAṆA

1-49 (E1113-1120). The substance of this Madhukāṇḍa is this : helper and helped should have come from the same origin. All creatures of the world have created the earth to enjoy the results of their karma, and hence it is honey (*madhu*) for them. All creatures being the products of the earth are likewise honey for the earth. Therefore the relationship of enjoyer and enjoyed is common to both (earth and creatures) as both are products of each other.

So it is said that the earth and earthen products, the body and gods, are all the Self. *Dharma* in the series developed in the text is what is the cause of the fate of all and what helps us all.

50-147 (E1120-1134). Truth (*satya* in II.5.12) is the Vedic activity called *dharma*. Humanity (*mānuṣa*) (in II.5.13) is the two bodies--gross and subtle—belonging to ordinary *jīvas* as well as to Virāj and Hiraṇyagarbha. "Ātman" (in II.5.14) means the combination of Virāj and Hiraṇyagarbha. This *ātman* has no cause or effect, and no middle place.

This *ātman* is a king (II.5.15) as he shines with his own effulgence after Brahman-knowledge. Bhartṛprapañca says that what is said here is that we must concentrate on Brahman as the locus of superimposition of the world as the spokes in a wheel. But this interpretation is wrong, not being in accord with the text. There is no word in the text conveying meditation, only the mention of the illusoriness of the world culminating in the unity of Brahman.

The Brāhmaṇa closes with a small story designed to eulogize Brahman-knowledge.

BOOK THREE—SECOND BRĀHMAṆA

1-31 (E1147-1152). Death (*mṛtyu*) in the story told in the foregoing Brāhmaṇa (III.1) is the senses and their objects as associated with desires, aversions, etc. It was stated that the attainment of Agni and Hiraṇyagarbha brings freedom from death. But that is not final liberation since they also are subject to birth and death. Therefore the real liberation by Brahman-knowledge needs to be taught. Even Prajāpati, who has speech, mind, and breath, is not free since he has these three senses (*graha*), which are called here "deaths."

Now, is there a death of this "death" or not? Yājñavalkya says yes. Water destroys fire, which destroys other things. But there is no infinite regress, as the destroyer of the universe cannot be destroyed. "Death," which is of the nature of ignorance, is destroyed by knowledge. Thus Self-knowledge is the death of death.

32-165 (E1152-1176). *Objection* : For him who realizes the Self and then dies, is there the exit of the *prāṇas* from the body or not? If they leave the body then there should be rebirth. But if not, the person is not dead.

Answer : (III.2.11) No. Since ignorance has been destroyed there is no rebirth, and so the *prāṇas* do not leave the body but are absorbed into Brahman. It is only "name" that remains (III.2.12), that is, nothing remains of him. Since names signify the universal and not particular aspects they do not perish.

The next section (III.2.13) aims at revealing the cause of "death," that is, senses and their objects. Here the word *puruṣa* signifies the ignorant *jīva* and not the realized Self, since the latter has no karma left (and the explanation alludes to karma). The words "speech" (*vāc*), etc., mean the contributions of the gods in connection with each sense. When the person dies the gods withhold the help they give each sense while the person lived, and when he is reborn they again help the senses of the newborn body. Now, when the dying man has left all his component parts where does he exist? What is his support? Does he attain *prakṛti* or God or the three *guṇas* or any other thing or his own past deeds? Yājñavalkya led Ārtabhāga off to tell him the secret, which is that the dead *jīva* is supported by his karma as protected by God.

Karman also implies *avidyā* and traces (*bhāvanā*), since these are also required in producing the body. But since *karman* alone is the crucial factor on which the dead man relies we can boldly say that those who have merit get superior bodies and those with sins get inferior ones.

FOURTH BRĀHMAṆA

1-63 (E1208-1218). That self which is different from the body and who is the agent of actions is the subject of the *karmakāṇḍa*. But the Self who is the Witness of this self and is called the seer of knowledge is revealed here. That is, who is it that can teach Brahman-knowledge?

Objection: Brahman cannot be the person who teaches, since Its nature is Brahmanhood and thus It need not be taught. For a non-Brahmin, Brahmanhood is impossible.

Answer: Brahman alone, veiled by ignorance, is the person eligible to teach. This is here established by removing the illusion of difference between Brahman and *jīva*.

Now Uśasta Cakrāyaṇa asks Yājñavalkya: "Please tell me which is directly visible (*sākṣa-aparokṣa*) and which is the inner Self within all." By the word "direct" the seer (of visual, etc., sights) is excluded, and by "visible" the triad of seer, seen, and sight is excluded. The word "Brahman" eliminates the doubt whether It is one with a second. The word "Self" indicates that It is an object of human endeavor. The words "inner within all" reject the view of the Sāṃkhyas that there are many Selves, one in each body. This combination of terms indicates that it is the *jīva* that is Brahman of which Uśasta speaks.

64-187 (E1218-1239). Uśasta (in III.4.2) complains that Yājñavalkya promised to show the Self directly but (in III.4.1) has only proffered an inference. Yājñavalkya defends his position by remarking that, not being an object of the *pramāṇas*, the Self cannot be taught directly except by the process he has adopted. The remainder of the comment follows Śaṃkara.

FIFTH BRĀHMAṆA

1-60 (E1240-1249). *Question* : Why does Kahola come (in this section) and ask the same question that was asked by Uśasta ?

Answer : It is not the same question; though the wording is the same, its meaning is different in that this question is about the Self's freedom from hunger, thirst, misery, and the rest of the attributes of *saṃsāra*.

61-86 (E1249-1253). Of these, "grief" (*śoka*) is the cause of other qualities. It is restlessness of mind. Confusion (*moha*) is non-understanding, taking the one as many. Thirst and hunger are qualities of *prāṇa*. The restlessness in grief produces activity, confusion brings about destruction; so they are not compounded. "Old age" (*jarā*) is a stage of the body, whereas "death" is separation of the *prāṇas* from the body. These qualities belong to *prāṇas*, the mind, and the body, and are not attributes of the Self, for the Self is non-attached. They are associated with the Self through ignorance; they disappear on the advent of knowledge. Since the Self's association with *prāṇa* ends at liberation there is no trace of hunger and the rest, which are products of *prāṇa*.

Grief and confusion comprehend the products of the Sūtrātman, that is, Hiraṇyagarbha. Old age and death comprehend the products of Virāj. Thus we have here comprehended the whole universe, gross and subtle. By bringing in the Sūtrātman and Virāj it is meant that in all acts of worship (*upāsanā*) ordained in the Upaniṣads the dissolution of all effects—the universe—constitutes liberation.

86-114 (E1253-1258). Apprehending this Self, the Brahmins take up *saṃnyāsa* and go begging. The word "Brahmin" (*brāhmaṇa*) indicates eligibility here, since the other *varṇas* are not eligible for *saṃnyāsa*. This is the view of Śaṃkara. Sureśvara, however, thinks the three highest *varṇas* are eligible for *saṃnyāsa*. Since *saṃnyāsa* depends on the arising of realization, it is that which constitutes eligibility for *saṃnyāsa*, and so no restriction is appropriate; thus the word "Brahmin" here just means the person who has known the Self.

What kind of "knowing" is referred to here ? If it means complete Self-realization then *saṃnyāsa* cannot be enjoined. If it means verbal knowledge *saṃnyāsa* can be enjoined. Now if we change the reading (in the text) so that it says "taking up *saṃnyāsa* and realizing Brahman the Brahmin . . . .", *saṃnyāsa* will be a means to knowledge, since once having heard of Brahman in *saṃnyāsa* he can, by reasoning and meditation, realize Brahman.

115-148 (E1258-1264). "Abandoning desire for sons, wealth, and worlds" includes things gotten by worship as well. The desire for children and the desire for wealth are the same since for the married man the two are essential and both attain some end.

149-214 (E1264-1276). There are two kinds of *saṃnyāsa*—directly gained from *brahmacarya*, and progressive, or step-by-step. The latter is favored for those who have not enough aversion to objects in their boyhood. By performing actions enjoined for the intervening stages of life (*āśrama*) one gets purity of mind and can then get *saṃnyāsa*. *Saṃnyāsa* is ordained in many places in the Vedas.

The *saṃnyāsin* should undertake hearing, reflection, and meditation. "By hearing" (*śravana*) four kinds of cognitions are meant. First, understanding the senses of words; secondly, knowing which are the principal and which the subsidiary; third, which of those attributes constituting contraries is to be removed; fourth, understanding a sentence such as "that thou art." He then acquires the capacity to reflect on the coordination of positive descriptions and the negations of their opposites and on the single meaning of the sentence. The word "*paṇḍa*" means knowledge, and a knower is a "*paṇḍita*." By gaining stability in the Self through the *śāstras* and one's teacher he should meditate fixedly on the Self, thus removing the wandering of the mind in not-Self. Then he attains the status of a "sage" (*muni*) and will be a true Brahmin, being himself Brahman.

Question : How can such a one become a true Brahmin ? One has to get there indirectly through sacrificing, step by step.

Answer : No. All actions must be abandoned, as is indicated by scripture. Liberation cannot be achieved by any means, being the beginningless Brahman.

EIGHTH BRĀHMAṆA

1-29 (E1290-1295). In answer to Gārgī's questioning Yājñavalkya explains that *ākāśa* pervades the universe. Here by the word "*ākāśa*" the Self alone is meant, since nothing else can be the inner controller of all. But this inner controller is not the final unmanifest or immutable (*akṣara*), which has not been mentioned anywhere. Even in the First Book, where it is said that the universe was initially in the form of the unmanifest, only the inner controller was referred to.

30-72 (E1295-1302). Bhartṛprapañca says that knowledge, action, and traces are the causes of the body, thus what is referred to here is ignorance, without which these three would not operate. Controllership requires ignorance, since the Self is without qualities such as controllership.

Gārgī asks Yājñavalkya what pervades the *ākāśa*. When by Self-knowledge ignorance is expelled, the Self becomes immutable or *akṣara*. Sūtrātman is not easily known, and *ākāśa* is even more obscure. But *akṣara* is hard for even Bṛhaspati to know or speak of, since It is beyond all *pramāṇas*. It is neither known nor unknown, hence cannot be defined in words. Since It is said to be directly knowable it cannot be denied. Gārgī thought by her question to put Yājñavalkya to an impossible task.

Yājñavalkya's answer (III.8.8) is "this is that," meaning that It is known to the Witness. It is not differentiated, nor is It continuous in many things like a universal property. The word "that" indicates that the thing in question was previously referred to as "direct" and "free from thirst, hunger, etc." The word "this" indicates that It is "direct." Even a thing that is only an object of perception, like the sweetness of sugar, cannot be described in words. What shall we say about the inmost Self!

It is called "*akṣara*" because It is opposite to cause and effect, which are perishable because interdependent. By saying (in the text) "Brahmins say" Yājñavalkya wants to show that he has answered the question correctly, as well as to indicate that *akṣara* is beyond the scope of inference and can only be taught by the Upaniṣads. The Brahmins who have dispelled ignorance by Brahman-knowledge say this.

73-108 (E1302-1307). The question arises concerning the kind of negation to be understood from the adjectives that appear in the text describing *akṣara*—for example, "not large," "not small," etc. Is the negation here of the "absolute" (*prasajyapratiṣedha*) or 'restricted" (*paryudāsa*) variety? If the second meaning were intended it would imply that there is something that is nonlarge, and that would contradict monism.

Objection: But otherwise the denial leads to nihilism.

Answer: No, since all denials require a substratum. But even on the second interpretation (the "restricted" negation) there is no duality, since the adjectives negated, being mutually dependent, have no independent standing and thus no reality. So, it may be that using the "absolute" kind of negation it is intended to remove the ignorance that is the cause of the use of "large," "small," etc. Or it may be viewed as intended to reject the view that Brahman is both the whole and the parts. Or perhaps it negates in Brahman everything in the scope of the *pramāṇas*.

The word "*amātra*" indicates that *akṣara* is not a *hetu* in inference.

109-180 (E1307-1318). *Objection*: If everything is denied in *akṣara* how can we come to know of Its existence?

Answer: It is self-luminous. Even though there is no proof for It yet It exists, like a pot in darkness, veiled by ignorance. There is no proof for either the existence or the nonexistence of *akṣara*, for It is self-luminous.

But regarding the existence of the inner controller there is disagreement among disputants, and to remove this the Upaniṣad goes on to give reasons for its existence. The difference between *akṣara* and the inner controller is illusory, but the inference can only be in regard to the inner controller. Just as people can exist peacefully only when there is control by a powerful king, so only when there is control of this world can it exist without transgressing its limits. The sun and the moon are the creation of one who knows their uses, just as a powerful light on top of a mansion. That earth and heaven do not break apart or fall down, though they are heavy, presupposes a sentient ruler. The various parts of time—minute, hour, etc.—presuppose a controller. The systematic diversity of rivers—running east and west and vice versa—presupposes a controller. That men give things as gifts and thus gain heaven presupposes someone who rewards them, since nobody would part with money without a reward. And since the giver, the gift, and the donee may all perish, there must be someone to reward people in subsequent lives. We observe in ordinary life that service by itself does not earn any reward unless it comes under the survey of a superior person competent to reward the worker. The same rule applies in the case of Vedic acts. Therefore the regularity of reward for one's acts in subsequent lives cannot be merely due to the *dharma* arising from the act. And likewise, as was said before, cessation of *saṃsāra* cannot be had by action. If there were no controller we would not see in the world realized souls free from miserliness, Brahmins who have fulfilled their obligations, free from *saṃsāra* and with their aims accomplished.

NINTH BRĀHMAṆA

1-153 (E1318-1342). The *akṣara* by being reflected in ignorance becomes the controller. The *akṣara* is also called "*prāṇa*" in the *Kauṣītaki Upaniṣad*, where it is said that the senses merge in *prāṇa* during deep sleep. Scripture also says "He is Brahman," meaning *prāṇa*. The *akṣara* controls the Sūtrātman through the inner controller, which is ignorance with the *akṣara* reflected in it. Through the Sūtrātman it controls the whole universe. This *prāṇa*, then, pervades the whole universe in its individual aspect and in its aspect as the many gods.

Now the text proceeds to discuss the number and nature of these many gods according to a variety of classifications.

154-210 (E1342-1351). The word "bliss" (*ānanda*) is used here to indicate Brahman, as it is also in the *Taittirīya Upaniṣad*. But there is room here for discussion, since scripture says that Brahman is beyond the *pramāṇas* and since some theorists say that Brahman has no "bliss."

Opponent : . . . . "Brahman is bliss, but since It is consciousness as well It cognizes Its own bliss," etc.

Answer : This is untenable since "cognizing something requires a body and organs," etc. There is no difference between consciousness and bliss, both of which are Brahman's nature. The text "the released soul eats, plays, and is happy" should be taken figuratively to mean that He is all and so all happinesses are His. By being "all" it is not intended that He has all miseries too, as those are illusory. All worldly happiness is brought about by some means, but in liberation the Self is bliss. He is also consciousness. He is also endless (*anantya*). Such experience of happiness is known to us in deep sleep.

BOOK FOUR—SECOND BRĀHMAṆA

10-33 (E1360-1364). (The text tells of Janaka, who fell at Yājñavalkya's feet and said he didn't know where he would go after death and wanted to be told.)

Objection : It has been said that worshipers attain the nature of the objects of their worship. How could the king not know this ?

Answer : The king knew that, but worship also conduces to liberation, which is Brahmanhood, and the king did not know this.

Another objection : No, what the king didn't know is the path to liberation, and that is what he wants Yājñavalkya to tell him.

Answer : This is not correct, since there is no mention of a path in Yājñavalkya's reply, nor is there mention of Brahman-knowledge in the previous Brāhmaṇa. The question is not about the path but only about the destination. Further, it was stated in the previous Book that the Self is Brahman, and since the not-Self is the Self himself there is no possibility of going out and searching for a path. One cannot take a path to the highest Self. Since the whole universe is superimposed on Brahman, it has no other substratum than Brahman. Scripture says "the knower of Brahman becomes Brahman." There is no curtain dividing liberation from us other than the darkness of ignorance. We have to remove the curtain.

34-85 (E1364-1372). "This being who is in the right eye is named Indra," says the text. He is so called because he is the enjoyer of gross objects in the waking state. The right eye is more powerful than the left. He is *jiva*, the enjoyer. People call him "Indra," showing respect by omitting the original name, since the gods do not like people getting at the secret of the nature of the name. His wife lives in the left eye and is Virāj, the object enjoyed.

This division as enjoyer and enjoyed is only for one god. It is intended for meditating on Agni and Soma. The two (enjoyer and enjoyed) meet in the heart. The essence of the food we eat assumes the form of blood and serves as the food for these two. Their covering, formed by nerves, looks like a net since it contains numerous holes. The nerve that shoots up from the heart is their path to come to the waking state from the dream state. The nerves are very thin, like a thousandth of a hair. They carry the sense objects to the senses and through the mind they satisfy the *jīva*. All the gods (*devatā*) in the body pass through these nerves for the enjoyment of the *jīva*. The experiences of pleasure or pain are only their proximity to the shadow of the knowing Self (*cidātman*). This too is dependent on the gods, and these latter are subject to the food we consume. The subtler part of that food satisfies the *prāṇa devatās* and reaches the subtle body. The juice derived from the food nourishes the gross body.

Why is it said that the subtle body is nourished by the subtler part of food ? The words "*iva*" and "*eva*" (in the last sentence of IV.2.3) have to be interpreted as follows: just (*eva*) the gross body (*viśva*) is nourished by the gross part of the food, whereas the dreaming subtle body (*taijasa*) has what is as if (*iva*) the subtler part of the food. But the causal body has the subtlest part of the food, not just what is "as if" the subtlest part.

Bhartṛprapañca interprets this passage like this: The Sūtra located in the heart pervades the nerves which project outward. All the other gods also pervade the nerves, since the body and the senses are common to all of them. When for example the sun, the god of the eye, functions by helping, the other gods become subservient to it. Thus there are as many Prajāpatis as there are nerves. The bodily limitation of the *prāṇa* should be brought into Virāj, Virāj into Hiraṇyagarbha, and he in turn into the supreme Self. This latter view is the author's view also. The *viśva* is to be brought into *taijasa*, and *taijasa* into *prājña*, whom the aspirer should bring into the supreme Self. This pure Self is devoid of all senses and their presiding divinities; it is pure intelligence.

106-113 (E1375-1376). *Question* : How can the king give fearlessness to Yājñavalkya (in the last sentence of this Brāhmaṇa), since he has already attained that stage ?

Some reply : The sage had not attained Self-realization. Others say that the king wishes final release from the body (*videhamukti*) for the sage who has already attained *jīvanmukti*.

These answers are not reasonable. Yājñavalkya is entitled to be a teacher, so he must have attained Self-realization. As such, *videha-mukti* is not far off for him. The real answer is this: the king used these words to show that he had attained Self-knowledge.

THIRD BRĀHMAṆA

9-12 (E1378-1379). The text says either "Yājñavalkya went to the king vowing he would not talk (*na vādiṣya*)" or "...that he would talk extensively (*saṃvādiṣya*)." The latter meaning is more appropriate, according to Sureśvara, since if the sage had a vow not to talk the king would not have compelled him to talk, and there is no mention of any reason for taking such a vow.

116-155 (E1396-1403). The materialist objection raised in Śaṃkara's comment on IV.3.6 is here rehearsed, starting with an objection by one who believes the body is the self (*dehātmavādin*).

Dehātmavādin : The text "the Self is Brahman," being contrary to perception, should be interpreted figuratively. The body is the product of the combination of the four elements, and by combination intelligence is born. The thought "I am a man" shows that I, the Self, and man, the body, are one, just as a snake is black.

Counterobjection : But the Self is self-revealed and so intelligence cannot be a property of It.

Dehātmavādin : No, for the same proof that proves the existence of intelligence also proves it to be a property of the body.

Counterobjector : The body is seen as "this," and the Self as "I." How can the Self be a property of the body under these circumstances.

Dehātmavādin : Just as an ornament made of gold has gold as its property though it seems to us as something different, so the body has intelligence as its property even though it is seen as different.

Question : Then why is a dead body not seen to be conscious ?

Dehātmavādin : Because the body is the product of four elements, and when the air—one of the elements—gets out, consciousness goes out with it.

Counterobjection : The dream body—for example, a tiger—differs from the waking body—human. But because of the recognition "I dreamt," in waking we infer that the Self is the same in both states—so the Self is different from the body.

Dehātmavādin : The elements themselves create the dream body, parallel to the creation of consciousness in the waking body.

Counterobjection : Some yogis remember their previous births. Thus their Self must be different from their bodies.

Dehātmavādin : By the same principle you invoke we should be forced to the absurd conclusion that if someone remembers his past birth in a body having a head wound and now experiences a wound in the same place his body must be eternal !

Furthermore, we know that the helper and the helped are of the same species, as in the case of the eye and the sun, and unlike sound, which does not help the eye in cognizing. Therefore, elements help elements; this is the rule. Thus the luminous thing that helps the body should be an elemental thing, like the sun. And the Self should be of the same species as the sun, since like the eye the Self is inside the body and invisible.

We rest our case on perception. We do not accept inference as evidence, since the following question arises : if invariable concomitance is between two specific (*viśeṣa*) things (fire on the hill inferred from smoke there) there can be no positive example (*sapakṣa*). But if it is something general that has to be inferred (for example, fire in general inferred from smoke in general) then there is the proving only of what is already proved (*siddhasādhana*).

Question : How is it then that the body, supposed to be the Self, is conscious sometimes and unconscious at others ?

Dehātmavādin : Well, it is so in ordinary experience and so should be accepted, just as we find a glowworm dark in one place and lit up in another.

156-203 (E1403-1412). *Sureśvara answers* : How can one question that by which all the authors belonging to various systems establish their beliefs ? First of all, is it correct to say it is "contrary to perception," since there is no object other than Self for perception to grasp ? Everyone accepts that the validity of the *pramāṇas* is due to their grasping an object not already known. But before the *pramāṇa* arises we cannot know that an object is unknown or that it is not. The existence of unknown objects can be established only by pure consciousness, Brahman.

The one who sees the seer, the seen, and sight in dreaming, and their absence in deep sleep, is the Self, different from the body. If consciousness is a property of the body, then the conception of "I" must be in another's body as well as in one's own !

204-239 (E1412-1418). Further, the same body cannot be cognized both as "I" and as "this" because of their inconsistency. So, since the body is "this" it cannot be "I." Perception does not reach beyond the external object; it does not grasp the knower. The Witness, consciousness itself, cannot be known. Again, to suppose that consciousness arises from the elements is without proof, since there is no trace of the properties of the elements there. When the body dies the death of consciousness cannot be known by the inert body nor by the Self, since one cannot see one's own death.

If you do not accept inference as a *pramāṇa*, you cannot say that the helper and helped should be of the same class, or that consciousness is elemental. Again, if intelligence is in the body which is elemental, why is the sun, etc., needed for seeing an object ? Actually, the helper and the helped should be of different classes. A pot does not help a pot to be seen. The body is the product of the four elements; they are of different kinds, yet they help each other. Moreover, negation also helps the body, for example, the absence of thorns on the road helps the pedestrian. But negation belongs to a different genus.

240-275 (E1419-1425). As for the argument against the validity of inference—that it cannot prove either specific or general things—this is wrong, for what inference proves is both specific and general, thus there is no defect. Furthermore, since you invoke inference to establish the nonvalidity of inference there arises a self-contradiction. Without inference the ordinary activities of men, like drinking, eating, speaking, etc., will not be possible.

As for your remark that the body is naturally sometimes conscious and sometimes not, that is not right, for we find in daily life that happiness is brought about by praise and unhappiness by insult.

276-339 (E1426-1436). Now Janaka asks (IV.3.7) "Which is the Self ?". The word "*ātman*" is used sometimes to indicate the body, or the mind, or the Witness, or other things; therefore I ask you, which among these is the (true) Self ? The answer indicates that there are two entities that help a man. One is external light, the sun, etc., and the other is the internal light, the Witness (*sākṣin*). All illuminating objects are noneternal except the Witness, with whose aid the sun, moon, etc., illuminate things and by which we experience dreams. With this Witness' help the *pramāṇas* come to exist.

Since the Self is cognizable only in Its association with the *buddhi* and not separately, the word "*vijñānamaya*" is put here. The word "*maya*" here indicates abundance. Those who interpret "*maya*" as meaning "produced by" flirt with contradiction, since on their own interpretation the words (elsewhere) "*vijñānamaya*," "*manomaya*," etc., cannot mean "made of" or "produced by" *vijñāna* or *manas*, etc., since the Self is not a product. There is a rule that when a word's meaning is doubted we must decide according to the interpretation of the same word elsewhere.

"Among the *prāṇas*" indicates that the Self is different from the senses or "*prāṇas*." "In the heart" indicates the Self is different from *buddhi* (here = heart). "Within" the heart serves to distinguish the Self from the modifications (*vṛtti*) of the *buddhi*, which are not inside the *buddhi* but go out from the *buddhi*. He who witnesses all these modifications is the Self, by whose presence they arise and are destroyed.

340-378 (E1436-1442). The word "light" is used in the text to exclude the view of the Nyāya school, where the self is taken to be inert. *Buddhi*, etc., function for the benefit of others, but the Self does not. The Self, "light," is self-luminous and self-evident. Being consciousness It is reflected in *buddhi*, *manas*, senses, and the body and makes them all appear to be conscious, just as a green pearl thrown in milk makes it appear green. The cause of this illusion is ignorance. It is illumined by the Self, consciousness. Since the Self is nonattached, His being the cause, the Witness, etc., are due to this same ignorance. The reflections are successive—first in ignorance, then in the *buddhi*, *manas*, senses, and body in that order. Hence the view that "I" is the first illusion. The text "He is consciousness of the conscious" conveys the same idea.

Though the light of the Self is existent also in waking, because of the other illuminators there—*buddhi*, *manas*, senses, sun—it is not possible to show It to students. Therefore Yājñavalkya takes up dream cognitions to demonstrate the existence of the self-luminous Self, since only *vāsanās* are there to condition It.

471-495 (E1457-1464). *Buddhist* : The difference between a pot and a light doesn't exist. The pot in the light is momentary and differs from the pot in the dark. Or else consciousness alone is real and momentary. Everything is cognition. The relation of knowledge, knower, and known constitutes the impurity of consciousness, and pure consciousness is gained by wiping out this impurity. Your Self cannot be established by perception, inference, or scripture. But we have inference to support our view, since it is not opposed to perception and perception alone is valid.

Question : But aren't knowledge and its knower different ?

Buddhist : No. The difference is known only through construction-filled (*savikalpaka*) perception, which is erroneous. Construction-free (*nirvikalpaka*) awareness alone is valid, and it cannot grasp difference.

496-530 (E1465-1470). Those Buddhists who accept external objects (*bāhyārthavādins*, i.e., Sautrāntika and Vaibhāṣika) are now refuted. The external pot cannot illuminate itself; it requires light and does not shine in the dark. So light and pot are different. But a lamp likewise does not illumine itself, since like the pot it is illuminated by being known. This does not lead to an infinite regress, since the Witness is self-revealed. That the Witness is different from the ordinary knower has already been established. This Witness is conscious of both the ordinary knower and the *pramāṇas*. Thus supported, perception, inference, and scripture can all function in cognizing external objects.

531-652 (E1470-1493). *Vijñānavādin* : There are no external objects. That which is not found apart from x is not different from x. Objects are not found apart from consciousness, thus they do not exist apart from consciousness, any more than dream objects do.

Answer : If you do not accept anything different from consciousness then you have no example for your inference, since dreaming is also consciousness. But if you accept external objects we can establish our view by inference. And you do accept them. When you say that what appears as external is illusory, you accept them; when you use words in their ordinary senses to refer to objects you accept them, for "pot," "light," "knowledge" are not synonyms. You should recognize difference between an instrument of knowing, an object known, a knower, etc. In addition, you take a *pramāṇa* to cognize an as-yet-unknown object, so you must admit their difference. If your view were to imply that the end and means are the same, your *śāstra* will be purposeless and its author a fool. Furthermore, you must accept your opponent in argument as different from yourself.

If you say that the pot doesn't exist you must accept existence, without which denial is impossible. Thus the momentariness of things is impossible, since without existing they cannot be the causes of any useful purpose. The evidence from the fact of recognition shows that a thing must exist for at least eight moments.

Vijñānavādin : But the stream of momentary events (*saṃtāna*) is eternal.

Answer : Not for you, because this would admit a self, the agent of the eternal stream that survives through it. Either the stream is the same as, or different from, the individual members of it. If they are different, then the stream must be eternal with the above discomfiting result. If they are not different, then they must be eternal like the stream !

653-696 (E1494-1502). The relationship of cause and effect must be accepted between two momentary things since they belong to different times. If they belong to a single moment then that relationship cannot arise. Thus there is no evidence to prove that everything is knowledge. Nor can *śūnyavāda* be maintained, because there is no evidence. The Bhāṭṭas, who say that the self has two aspects—of knower and known—goes against the Upaniṣads, which emphatically say that the Self is without parts.

The Vijñānavādin cannot explain recognition of the form "This person is the same man whom I saw years back." He cannot invoke similarity (*sādṛśya*), since similarity is impossible between momentary things and there is *ex hypothesi* no permanent seer who experiences the similarity. Again, recognition doesn't only tell us that these things are in general like those were, but in some cases, such as the one quoted above, it reports that the individual is precisely the same one.

Vijñānavādin : The earlier cognition generates a residual impression that is responsible for the recognition later.

Answer : But since nothing lasts more than a moment on your view, nothing can persist long enough to be responsible for something else.

Furthermore, in your view the merit or demerit earned by one's good or bad deeds will disappear without giving results—so grief or happiness would come to people undeserved.

697-741 (E1502-1512). The view that cognition has different aspects is also wrong. Consciousness is pure and untainted. Objects are other than consciousness, for they are outside and cognitions inside the body.

Finally, *nirvāṇa* will never be accomplished, since there is no persisting person to enjoy it.

Now the inference of the Advaitin that "All ordinary affairs require external illumination, as daily life requires the sun" is examined. We say this is correct. Inference cannot be set aside as not evidence, since we see smoke, infer fire, and get the use of fire as a result. Thus inference receives practical support.

742-808 (E1512-1527). [The Buddhist contends that the *hetu* in a successful inference must be either (1) a thing's nature (*svabhāva*), (2) an effect (*kārya*), or (3) noncognition (*anupalabdhi*).] *Answer* : The nature of fire is hotness, but one cannot infer that what is hot is fire, since other things (hot water) are hot. Or if your idea is that wherever you have invariable concomitance (*avinābhāvatva*) it is through a thing's nature, then effects will become a thing's nature ! Smoke, an effect, is caused by fire, but it is also caused (on your view) by the previous momentary smoke; so it is not invariably concomitant with fire. Furthermore, there are some perfectly good inferences that are none of these kinds—for example, the inference that Kṛttikā (a constellation) will rise since Rohiṇī (another constellation) is rising. Various attempts to save the Buddhist theory by construing the word "*svabhāva*" in other ways are refuted. Noncognition *per se* is not a third kind of *hetu*, for we need to know the counterpositive by some means, and if the means is inference from another noncognition we get an infinite regress.

809-830 (E1527-1531). To return to the text (IV.3.8) : The *jiva*, when going to dream, passes the body, senses, etc., which are symbols of death. The Self's "birth" is His taking on a body, for He is eternal and has no real birth. His "death" is the departure of the subtle body. The word "evils" (*pāpma*) (in the text) signify both good and bad deeds of the past. As all good and bad deeds lead to embodiment, and bodies, even those of gods, are to be abandoned eventually, even merit is in this sense a "sin." Being enveloped by *avidyā* the *jīva* goes to the other world and returns again and again until its final release. From this it is plain that it is different from the body. All its attributes are merely illusory superimpositions. The states of waking and dream are visible, the existence of another world after death is made known by the Vedas.

831-912 (E1531-1544). ". . . Revealing his own lustre by his own light—(he) dreams." (IV.3.9) When the karma producing waking experiences is over one goes to sleep and sees the illusion of his dreams. Each individual by his own karma creates his dream world; he lays down his waking body, creates the dream body and the dream world only by his *vāsanās*. Here by "his own" the natural light of the Self is meant. One sees by this light all the activities of the mind. Having eliminated all the "lights" of the waking state he sees them in dream with his *vāsanās* alone. Knowership, knowledge, etc., are all seen as objects. In dream one is self-luminous, he makes the *vāsanās* shine without any accessories. He is the witness of all that shines there. Being only the witness he has no connection with the objects, nor any activity. This is what is meant by "he dreams." When he was awake he had the help of the sun, the mind, the eye, etc., which illumined objects. But in dreaming they are absent. The *vāsanās* are not accessories here; they are themselves the objects of his awareness. Ignorance, desire, and karma are the only accessories in the creation of dreams. The witness is detached from all. Even his witnessness is a superimposition. The self does not enjoy happiness in dreams; everything is phenomenal.

946-948 (E1549). It is commonly said one should not wake up a person in deep sleep. The reason is this: having left the waking nerves he has gone with the dream nerves. If he were woken up suddenly he might enter a wrong nerve and be deaf or dumb for life.

974-1013 (E1553-1559). The Self who was detached in dream becomes tranquil in deep sleep. Like water purified by the *kaṭaka* nut, the Self when rid of all impressions (*bhāvanā*) of *saṃsāra* becomes clear. No *vāsanās* are brought to the deep-sleep state. Though he becomes somewhat tranquil in dream he is most tranquil in deep sleep.

Here only ignorance persists, the seed of the other two states. How is this state gained ? Yājñavalkya explains that the *jiva* goes back and forth among the states of dream and waking. In dream, with the help of the *vāsanās,* he only *sees* good and bad, but there is no activity here, only witnessing. Good and bad are the results of good and bad deeds he performed while awake. But he is not attached to them in dream, as is shown by the fact that when he awakes he does not experience the results of his dreams; for example, having eaten in one's dream one may wake up and immediately feel hungry.

1014-1045 (E1560-1565). Bhartṛprapañca interprets this section as follows : By the word "*ananvāgata*" is meant detachment from karma, and by the word "*asaṅga*" is meant detachment from desires (*kāma*). So the text means "He is without any karma produced in that (deep sleep) state, because he is without any desires in this (dream) state." Desire is the cause of deeds, but there is no desire in the dream state; desires are located in the waking state and exist in dreams no more than chariots, etc., do.

Or, the word "*asaṅga*" may mean changelessness, since change is due to activity. How is this ? Because the Self is not the real agent. Its agency is due to *vāsanās,* which belonging to the mind tinge the Self "as the scent of flowers in the oil in which they have been boiled."

1045-1066 (E1565-1569). *Question* : How can one "wander and enjoy" in deep sleep? One is unconscious and cannot wander or enjoy.

Prima facie answer : The passage must be read "he does not wander (*acāritva*) and does not enjoy (*aratva*)."

Reply: But the Self is said to be nonattached even in dream later in the same passage; so what is the difference ?

Another prima facie answer : As the *Māṇḍūkya Upaniṣad* says, one enjoys bliss in deep sleep. Or else because of being in deep sleep identical with God he enjoys God's happiness. But still the Self is not touched by the good or bad of the dream or waking states while in deep sleep.

Sureśvara's answer : Each of the three stages—waking, dream, and deep sleep—are divided into three states. For example, in the waking stage the waking state is veridical knowledge, dream is error, and deep sleep is when, being overcome with desire, one is unable to discriminate between good and bad. Again, in the dream stage the waking state is when a man seems to work, etc. The dream state in dreaming is when one dreams in his dream. When he is unable to express after waking what he saw in his dream, that is deep sleep in dream.

Now in the deep sleep stage there are likewise three states. The waking state of deep sleep is when there is a modification (*vṛtti*) in the sattvic form of happiness, that is waking; when the form is rajasic, it is dream, and when tamasic it is deep sleep. So, even in deep sleep "wandering," etc. is possible.

1067-1146 (E1569-1570). In deep sleep one enjoys all bliss and comes back to dreaming with his *vāsanās*. But he does not go out of the body. If he did his body would die. Being "*asaṅga*" he is not associated in deep sleep with waking karma as in dreams. Waking is false like dreaming. Even in the waking stage his agency is false. He is only a witness, and so does not really enter either the stages of dream or waking.

Now (IV.3.18) an example is given. Just as a big fish swims from one bank of the stream to the other, and being different from the banks is "*asaṅga*," so also the *jīva*, wandering from dream to waking successively, is *asaṅga*, untouched by the "banks" of waking and sleep. For the Cārvāka, however, the two states could occur simultaneously.

1147-1187 (E1578-1583). Bhartṛprapañca interprets this differently. He says : Karma is located in the subtle body. The *vāsanās*, resulting from karma, tinge the Self. Therefore to discriminate the Self from karma and *vāsanā* the text involving the word "*asaṅga*" was adduced. *Avidyā* is located in the Self alone, and it changes the Self and gives it illusion. This Self-awareness, being overpowered by ignorance, cognizes sounds, etc., which is to say that the *avidyā* becomes sound, etc., as well as becoming the means of knowing sounds, etc. In dealing with dream, desire was discriminated from the Self. Now in this present text (the fish example) *avidyā* is discriminated from the Self. The Self sees the world built by karma through *avidyā*. By knowing that both are not the Self he gains liberation. Likewise the next example (in IV.3.19) of the hawk is intended to distinguish the Self from *avidyā*. When he goes into deep sleep and is merged with Brahman he is rid of *avidyā*, as it does him no harm.

This interpretation (of Bhartṛprapañca's) is not correct, since the senses and their objects are mere *avidyā* and not something different. Therefore to say that nonattachment (*asaṅga*) is discovered by the Self through the senses is incorrect. *Avidyā* is not really existent in the Self and hence you cannot say that *avidyā* defiles the Self's awareness. The rest of the section is intended to discriminate the Self from the dream and waking states, as explained.

1188-1204 (E1583-1593). Now we have to decide whether consciousness is elemental or eternal. The opponent's position is that it is a product of elements. The Self gets knowledge through contact of the senses with their objects. This is refuted following the manner of refuting the Dehātmavādin (E1396-1403 above).

Our position is this. In dreaming the gods have no hold on our senses. The Self leaves Its connection with the body when dreaming: there are no senses operating, only *vāsanās*. By the example of the fish we are informed that the Self is different from bodies. He is pure consciousness devoid of activity, and so also distinct from desire and karma. Therefore everything is a product of *avidyā*, by eliminating which the Self enjoys liberation. In waking the Self is seen accompanied by body and senses; in dream He is seen with ignorance and karma; and in deep sleep He is experienced as clear. To explain His true nature the example of the hawk is given. This example reveals the Self as pure intelligence, or perhaps it is an example to show His nature in deep sleep. Just as a hawk wanders in the sky in search of food and when tired goes to its nest, so also after wandering in waking and dream the Self comes to Brahman to take His rest. When He goes there He does not see dreams of any kind, or any kind of experience. Like the hawk the *jīva* takes rest in *avidyā* where consciousness is reflected. The Self is different from *avidyā* and its products. The relationship of *avidyā* with the Self is indefinable and false and so will be destroyed by Brahman-knowledge.

1205-1242 (E1593-1601). The nature of the Self is that which we experience in deep sleep, where ignorance, desire, and karma are absent. To demonstrate the Self's real nature and to explain the products of *avidyā* the next section (IV.3.20) dealing with the "nerves" begins. The products of ignorance are seen only by association with *avidyā*. Or else the section on the nerves is introduced to demonstrate that the waking and dream states are unreal. Mountains, etc., are seen in the nerves, which are very small, and so the mountains, etc., must be unreal.

There are several nerves projecting from the heart. They are as minute as a thousandth part of a hair, and are filled with the juices of food. The Self, who has these nerves as adjuncts during dream, thinks that He is red, yellow, etc. The subtle body is very minute and enters these nerves, and so takes on all kinds of colors according to the *jīva's* karma. Because of the *jīva's* false identification with the subtle body he experiences all kinds of things, all of which are unreal. The division of real and unreal in waking is like the division in dream, since everything in waking is also unreal.

The nerves are white when phlegm is predominant, blue and black when wind is predominant, and yellow when bile is predominant. When all of these are equal the nerves will be of a thick red color.

1243-1262 (E1601-1604). During dreams the *jīva* creates by his *avidyā* a new world and enjoys it. Though there is only one *avidyā*, still for each subtle body it is different. It appears before the Self in the manifold forms of horse, chariot, etc. Sometimes he thinks he is tortured or made to surrender. All this is false. When karma producing dream is exhausted he wakes up. He acquires other *vāsanās* in waking by other deeds and again dreams. Thus being tied up with *avidyā* the *jīva* seems to be agent and enjoyer. As the Self is changeless there is no element other than *avidyā*, which causes Him to be agent, etc.

1263-1287 (E1605-1609). These impressions (*bhāvanā* = *vāsanā*) reside in the reflection of consciousness (*caitanyābhāsa*). Both (impressions and reflection of consciousness) reside in the internal organ. Being the witness of the internal organ, the Self is taken to be the locus of *vāsanās*. When an individual meditates as a god he gets the notion of "I am the deity" in dream; when the Self is meditated on as free from delusion and its results, the meditator has the dream "The whole universe is myself alone." In this latter case consciousness alone is seen. The words "I am the whole universe" (*ahamevedam*) are capable of removing one's *avidyā*. This world of the Self is the most superior world gotten by knowledge, for the other worlds are imposed by *avidyā*. In other cases the meditation is "as if " one were god, or king, thus they are not the results of *vidyā*. But the wholeness-experience in dream is real, not just a dream. In "I am all this" (*ahamevedam*) the word "I" (*aham*) denotes the unity of the Self, the word "this" (*idam*) denotes all the products of *avidyā*.

1288-1357 (E1609-1620). Even when *avidyā* persists we have this dream experience, and it arises before the *pramāṇas* are invoked. Thus it shows the real nature of the Self.

In the next section (IV.3.21) the Self in deep sleep is described, where *avidyā* is in a latent state, untouched by desire, free from merit and demerit, and thus free from fear. This is the Self's real nature since there is no delusion, etc., which produce desire and karma. The example of the man and woman embracing illustrates this: before they were united they were aware of duality, but after embracing they are not aware of any external objects. In the same way, when *avidyā* is operant there is experience of duality, but when it is latent the *jīva* becomes one with pure Brahman.

The words in this section of the text are glossed, and some variant readings are mentioned.

1358-1406 (E1621-1629). The next section (IV.3.22) says that in the stage of deep sleep a father is not a father, etc., since ignorance is absent, ignorance, which is the cause of generation. All such relationships cease to exist in deep sleep, *avidyā* being absent in its operative state. The Self, being unattached, is in all states really free from such relationships. So in deep sleep the *jīva* is free from robbery and killing of Brahmins, and Chaṇḍālas and Pulkāsas become non-Chaṇḍālas and non-Pulkāsas, since karma does not operate there. The *jīva* in this state is free from all desires connected with caste (*varṇa*) and stage of life (*āśrama*), because merit and demerit do not operate in him at that time. Actually, the Self is never involved in these things; His only property is consciousness, and He has nothing to do with ignorance, desire, and karma.

1407-1495 (E1630-1643). Now the question arises : if the Self is intrinsically conscious He should remain conscious in sleep as well as when awake. But in deep sleep He doesn't. So He is not intrinsically conscious. In answer to this the next few sections (IV.3.23-31) say: when the *pramāṇas* operate one has awareness of specific things. But in deep sleep they do not operate, and thus the Self is conscious only of Itself. So He sees; indeed, His sight never fails. But because He has no senses or objects to see, He does not see. Since the mind is absent there are no mental operations.

Just as the sun does not do any work but its presence alone causes knowledge, so also the Self's presence is His being a witness without operating. The experience of perception in dreams by persons who have lost their eyes shows the Self's eternal perceptive nature.

In these sections the word "*vai*" shows this. By "he does not see" the text denies the Self's seership because of the absence of objects of vision and of the senses. By the words "He sees" the Self's intrinsic consciousness is implied.

1496-1536 (E1644-1651). There are two kinds of destruction. Of these, destruction without residue is intended by the words "*na hi*," whereas the denial of change is meant by "*avināśatvāt*." Thus the Self is established as changeless. "Because there is no second thing," adduced as the reason (*hetu*), means because of the absence of ignorance in its operating state, though it is there in its latent causal state.

1537-1638 (E1651-1668). Others (Bhartṛprapañca), however, interpret these sections differently. They say : it was declared by reasoning that the Self is of the nature of self-luminosity. Now if it be said that the Self does not see in deep sleep, no, we say, He does see. He is not an inanimate element. But He has no knowledge of individuals. The Self is not only producer of knowledge, but He is also the agent of experiencing (*saṃvedana*), the fruit of knowledge. Knowledge does not stop, for it is the quality of the Self and qualities exist as long as the substance persists. Thus knowledge persists as long as the Self exists, but the Self never dies since He is the Self of all and is single. All that is second to Him is not different from Him; He cannot kill himself. So, since the Self is shining in sleep with knowledge, He is permanent. The passage that says "He does not see" says that because of duality, that is, objects, He does not see.

Sureśvara : This interpretation does not give the real meaning. If knowing in deep sleep is an activity, like going or coming, it should perish. How is it that it does not perish ? You say knowledge in sleep is produced by the Self but does not perish, but that is self-contradictory, since everything that originates should perish.

Your idea that the Self is said in this passage to do two things—produce knowledge and enjoy it—is wrong, since the "seeing" element is restatement whereas the "does not see" is the predicate. Since the former is already made clear, the phrase "does not see" negates agency in knowing. The Self is not the agent of seeing; He is sight itself. His enjoyership too is His pervasion through the reflection of consciousness and is not real.

1639-1793 (E1668-1696). *Bhartṛprapañca* : Every object in the world has two aspects—difference and nondifference. These two are not opposed to each other. The Self also, being an object, is likewise different-cum-nondifferent.

Answer : This view is false. There is no difference in the whole when properly understood. Individuals are different from each other according to the specific qualities of each object. The universal properties of different classes are different. But difference and nondifference cannot be both the property of one object. On the opponent's view the scriptural texts that negate difference, such as "not this, not this," would become meaningless. Inferences supposed to establish difference-cum-nondifference are also corrupt, since on the opponent's assumption hypothesis, reason, and example cannot be completely different, which they should be if inference is to be valid. On the other hand, if all the things in the world are nondifferent, there can be no communication between one person and another.

1794-1812 (E1696-1698). As all the causal relations are due to *avidyā* the knowledge of reality destroys all of them, the Self alone remains, and now He becomes pure "like water" (IV.3.32). He is one. There is no internal difference in Him. By the word "water" difference from objects of different species is negated.

1813-1845 (E1698-1703). Having completed his teaching for liberation, the sage says (IV.3.32) "This is the highest world," that is, the Brahmaloka. Here "this" indicates the Self. The "world" mentioned here is not any world but consciousness itself. "Brahmaloka" is Brahman that is consciousness, not a world. In this way the sage instructed Janaka to get rid of ignorance, which brings all distress. This attainment is the most superior one. All other attainments are transitory, as they are caused by desire and karma, the offspring of *avidyā*. It is the supreme bliss, as happiness ends with it. To explain this the text says: "On a particle of this very bliss other beings live." All happiness rising from objects are only the bliss of Brahman conditioned by *buddhi* and its modifications.

1846-1886 (E1703-1710). The next section (IV.3.33) aims at instructing the king about the supreme bliss by grades beginning from human bliss. As desires decrease bliss increases, so that the pinnacle of happiness coincides with the extinction of desires. Knowledge of the Vedas is counseled as leading from each stage to the next.

Objection : Since a combination of Vedic knowledge and destruction of desires is here made equivalent to Brahman-knowledge, the position of combined-knowledge-and-action (*jñānakarmasamuccayavāda*) is upheld.

Answer : No, since the Vedic knowledge referred to destroys agency and karma.

1887-1975 (E1710-1723). In this way Yājñavalkya completed his answer to the king's question, but the king now (IV.3.34) again asks him to explain the way to liberation. The king realized that the talk of wandering from dream to waking is only an example of going to the next world from this body, and the explanation of deep sleep is an example of the state of liberation. So the king asks Yājñavalkya to explain liberation.

So Yājñavalkya proceeds to explain *saṃsāra* in detail. The Self is always conscious, so He awakes from deep sleep, and after living a lifetime alternating between the stages of waking and dream in a body—like the driver in a chariot (IV.3.35)—he becomes old and feeble and the subtle body drops off as a fruit falls from the stalk (IV.3.36). The senses, though located in different parts of the gross body, collect into one place that is *prāṇa*. When the subtle body proceeds it is waited upon by many gross bodies. Just as when a king goes to a town and the people there assemble to receive him with food and drink, so also people wait for the *jiva* with a body intended for his enjoyment according to his karma (IV.3.37). Likewise the king when departing is accompanied by various persons, good or bad (IV.3.38), so when the *jīva* prepares to depart he is accompanied by the traces of his good and bad deeds, as well as the *prāṇas* and organs, etc.

FOURTH BRĀHMAṆA

43-73 (E1731-1736). Now the *jīva* along with the senses assemble "in the heart" (IV.4.1) with the subtle body, which is the cause of all cognitions. The Self has no cognition, and Its association with the subtle body is like water saturated with salt being felt saltish. By the word "heart" the *buddhi* is meant.

"When the presiding deity of the eye turns back . . . the man fails to notice color." The sense of sight is an aspect of the sun, which aids the eye in its cognition. When the *jīva* comes to the heart this portion goes back to the sun, which is the withdrawal of aid, and this occurs because the karma that was giving enjoyment to the *jīva* is now exhausted. So the *jīva* no longer sees colors, since that sun-aspect has become one with the sun (IV.4.2) and the sense of sight has become one with the subtle body. Then persons nearby say "he does not see." Likewise with the other organs.

97-125 (E1740-1744). "The top of the heart brightens . . ." (IV.4.2)—this is the knowledge of *buddhi* due to karma. In this knowledge the dying man sees his future body in which he is to be born again. The text alludes here to the *vāsanās* lit with the reflection of consciousness, as one had in daily dreams; it is intended to instruct us that we must be careful to do good deeds and meditate on God so that we can have a good cognition.

The subtle body goes out through any nerve, since all are open to him. If he goes out through the eye he goes to the sun, if by the top of the head he goes to the Brahmaloka. As it rises up *prāṇa* and all the other senses follow it. The *jīva*, having knowledge of his future body, gets out with the *vāsanās* and remains conscious till he gets the next body. But he cannot have knowledge of everything since he is not independent. To get independent knowledge of the future body, etc., he must practice yoga. All the *śāstras* are intended to provide the knowledge of the various means that one can attain through body, mind, and speech either to gain uplift or to earn calamity. The *jīva* takes with him *vidyā*, karma, and "past experience" (*pūrvaprajñā*). These constitute the means of his attaining a future body. Here "*vidyā*" means ordinary knowledge, doubts, and errors, and not Brahman-knowledge. By "karma" is meant all actions done by body, speech, and mind, both śāstric and otherwise. By "past experience" is meant those latent impressions of past deeds the fruits of which have been or have not been enjoyed.

126-146 (E1744-1747). There are different views as to how the *jīva* leaves this body and takes another. The Jains say that it is like a bird going from one tree to another. Some say that the gods take the *jīvas* to other bodies. The Sāṃkhyas say that *jīvas* attain expansion and contraction in another body. The Vaiśeṣikas think that the internal organ alone flies from one body to another like a bird. The Vedāntin's view is that the senses and *prāṇas* are all-pervasive but undergo contraction in bodies as conditioned by karma. The next text (IV.4.3) gives as an example the progress of a leech from one piece of grass to another, contracting its body as it goes.

Does the *jīva* use the materials from the old body to construct the new one, or does he take new material for each body? The text (IV.4.4) indicates that, just as the goldsmith melts down old gold and uses it to make new ornaments, so the *jīva* uses old elements (the five material elements) to create new bodies according to karma, whether in this world or in the various other worlds of fathers, *gandharvas*, gods, etc.

147-184 (E1747-1753). In the next section (IV.4.5) the Self's original nature and characteristics dependent on *avidyā* are explained. The transmigrating self, whose nature is nontransient and innermost, is the witness. The not-Self has no reality apart from the Self. "Ātman is Brahman, and Brahman Ātman," and all else is unreal.

Saṃsāra is due to association with *avidyā*. When this association ends the Self is released. Though He is the *prāṇa* of *prāṇas* He becomes so by error; He thinks He is *prāṇa*, He thinks He is mind, etc., by ignorance alone. By ignorance there arise in the Self the elements—*ākāśa*, etc. Thus, though not an agent, He seems to become the speaker of words through *avidyā*.

In this section both the gross body and the subtle body are mentioned. The mind is filled with desires, hatred, etc., because of *vāsanās*. These are the Self's many sheaths. Being saturated with merit and demerit the self becomes "one with all" (*sarvamaya*), because he becomes soaked with what he does. Whatever he does, that he becomes, "by good deeds he becomes good, by bad deeds bad."

185-234 (E1753-1761). But desire is also the cause of karma, so the text says "the Self is full of desire (*kāmamaya*)." Ignorance is the cause of desire also. There is no activity without desire. When a desire becomes intense it is called "resolve" (*kratu*), and so the man acts according to this resolve. Depending on which actions he does, the mind wanders with the Self reflected in it. Thus the Self, though nonattached, is through superimposition connected with the subtle body and is said to go to other worlds, though it is actually the subtle body that goes. The words "what it works out, it attains" refer to the world attained, not to the object of desire.

235-250 (E1761-1763). Since it is said that the *jīva* goes according to the maturity of its mind, it is clear that desire is the most important cause of *saṃsāra*. After enjoying the results of its karma the *jīva* comes back to the body in this world to perform actions again. Thus, forgetting its real nature, it travels between this body and the future body without rest, like a water pot in a Persian wheel.

251-303 (E1763-1771). Up to this point *saṃsāra* has been explained. Now liberation is explained.

The man who has no desire—the cause of desire, ignorance, having been uprooted by knowledge—is not born again. Such a man does not see any not-Self object as real and hence has no desire. One who has no latent impressions deriving from the senses becomes desireless. To do this he must first become desirous of attainment (*āptakāma*) and desirous of the Self (*ātmakāma*). He has attained all bliss (i.e., all desires) by his Self-knowledge, since all the minor blisses form parts of the supreme bliss.

Thus by being desirous of the Self one becomes desirous of attainment, then desireless (*niṣkāma*), and finally without desire (*akāma*). Now being firmly one with the Self he has no *saṃsāra*. His *prāṇas* do not go out, since ignorance is the cause of *prāṇas* existence and travel and it is destroyed. Just as the rope is the reality of the snake's existence so that when the rope is known the snake's existence and destruction are not known, so the Self is the reality of *prāṇa's* existence: when the Self is known none of them exist. So the release of the already released is obtained.

304-323 (E1771-1774). He who realizes the secondless, pure Self as in deep sleep is the real knower of the Self; others are all fools. There is no difference between a dead and a living *mukta*. Hence scripture says "being already released he is released." His attainment of Brahman is only the departure of the separating ignorance.

324-375 (E1775-1782). Those who say that in liberation there arises cognition of eternal bliss should explain what this arisal of knowledge is. Was bliss there before the arising or not ? If it was already there then it is the nature of the Self and consciousness too is the Self's nature. So the Sāṃkhya view of distinction (*abhivyakti*) (between Self and not-Self) is refuted. The view of those who believe in *asatkāryavāda* or *ārambhavāda* (i.e., the Nyāya-Vaiśeṣikas) is likewise wrong, since nonexistents can never come into existence.

376-390 (E1783-1786). The next section (IV.4.7) says that when all the desires existing in the heart subside along with their objects then the mortal becomes immortal. In deep sleep also, desires dry out but their *vāsanās* exist. In liberation the *vāsanās* too dry out. This is indicated by the word "all (the desires)." The words "exist in the heart" show that desires are properties of the mind and not of the self as the Tārkikas say. Since the mind is a product of *avidyā*, desires die when the mind dies along with ignorance.

391-412 (E1785-1789). Bhartṛprapañca, however, interprets the passage otherwise. He says there are two kinds of desires, some in the mind and others in the self. The idea is that when the desires in the mind die out the self becomes immortal. But even then the desires in the self persist, and do not die. "The heart" here has two meanings: one is the heart, the other the *jīva* who is separated from Brahman by desires. When the desires die *jīva* becomes Brahman. The desires that reside in *jīva* do not perish, however, since they are identical with the *jīva* who is released.

413-501 (E1789-1803). *Answer to Bhartṛprapañca* : This view is against scripture. Why ? The first Book, after explaining the fruit of knowledge, that is, all becoming the Self, also explains the fruit of ignorance, that is, the knowledge of difference as cause, effect, etc. In the course of that explanation the first Book says that desires, etc., are the products of ignorance. Of the seven foods the mind is one and its property is desire—that is what was said. Furthermore, in the explanation of the unmanifest (*avyākṛta*), where name, form, and action are mentioned as products of ignorance, it is clear that desire, being part of name-and-form, is *avyākṛta* and thus not a property of the Self.

The view of Jaimini and Kaṇāda that desire is a property of the self is wrong, since it is against the teaching of the Vedas. Book One says that everything knowable in form is located in the mind, which supports all forms; that speech supports all that illuminates; and that *prāṇa* supports all activities. Further, it is said in Book Three that all name, form, and action are located in the heart and that the Self is pure. Thus the Upaniṣad indicates that *all* desires should be removed. The *Chāndogya Upaniṣad* is adduced in support also. Scripture overrides Kaṇāda's view as much as that of the Buddhists.

502-531 (E1803-1807). The person who has realized the pure Brahman will have no connection, no identification with the body. The body will be left, as a snake's outer sheath is left on the anthill, without any attachment. Though others say that that body is the body of a realized soul, the liberated one has no idea of "I" or "mine" in it. Just as the snake feels that the thrown-off sheath is not "I," so the wise one feels that "his" body is not "I" or "mine" since the connection with that body has been cut. When ignorance has been destroyed by Self-knowledge, the Self becomes bodiless, for the connection with the body was only through ignorance. There is no connection between the real and the imagined (*kalpita*) even when there is imagination. But in the absence of *avidyā* there is no imagining at all; so *a fortiori* there can be no connection.

The Madhyaṇḍinas read (in IV.4.7, in the phrase "*athāyamaśarīro-'mṛtaḥ*") "*anasthika*" (before "*aśarīras*") meaning "devoid of bones," that is, implying that the realized Self has no gross body. The word "*aśarīra*," "bodiless," negates both the gross and subtle bodies.

532-545 (E1807-1810). Now the king's questions have been answered according to his desired ends and he has become an enlightened soul, having attained all that is to be attained. He offers Yājñavalkya a thousand cows.

Question : Why didn't Janaka give Yājñavalkya all he has ? Why only a fraction ?

Some answer that the king wanted to hear the stanzas (below) from him and so did not offer him the whole kingdom for fear Yājñavalkya would stop with what he has already said.

Sureśvara : No, this is not a good reason, for scripture, being free from desire or hatred, will not indulge in such mean deviance. The reason is that the king wanted to hear the means to Brahman-knowledge such as *saṃnyāsa*, hearing, considering, and meditating.

545-560 (E1810-1812). Now some mantras (the stanzas referred to above) are given to prove that knowledge alone is the cause of liberation.

1 (IV.4.8) Knowledge, the path to liberation, is very subtle. Since its content is all-pervasive it is wide. Since it is based on the old Veda it is also "old" (*vitata*). "*Vitara*" is another reading, meaning that it is the cause of crossing over from *saṃsāra*. " . . . has touched me," that is, I have realized it through the guru's teaching. "Heaven" (*svarga*) here is Brahman-bliss and not heaven, since the context is that of liberation. By this knowledge those already released attain release, for ignorance is the only impediment, and knowledge is the only remedy.

561-598 (E1812-1818) 2 (IV.4.9). Those who are ignorant suggest various paths to liberation. Some say it is pure, others say it is blue, yellow, green, or red. They speak of the single, spotless, and pure Brahman in this way, like blind men touching an elephant.

Some say he who performs meritorious deeds and becomes pure minded attains Brahman. They suggest a combination of Brahman-knowledge with action as the means to attain the knowledge of identity.

This combination of action with knowledge can be accepted only in succession, not simultaneously. Scripture says that the abandonment of action alone is the means to liberation.

599-615 (E1818-1821) (IV.4.10-12). Those who stick to actions, though free from sensual pleasures, gain only the utmost darkness. According to the Madhyandinas "*sambhūti*" is read in place of "*avidyā*," but the meaning is the same. Those who indulge in meditations (*upāsanā*) gain the eight *siddhis* that are opposed to liberation. These *siddhis* lead to worlds that have no happiness. If one realizes the Self, which is the Witness of cognitions as Brahman, what will he desire ? For what purpose will the body be afflicted ? He has no desires.

616-623 (E1821-1822) (IV.4.13). The person who lives in the everchanging body who has realized the Self as Lord becomes the creator himself. He has done all that is to be done, and nothing is left for him to do.

624-656 (E1822-1828) (IV.4.14-16). If we realize Brahman here and now, because our sins have subsided we will have performed our duty. If not it is a "great destruction" (*mahatī vinaṣṭi*) for us. The great destruction is the persistence of ignorance. When one realizes the Self as Brahman then there is nothing to control one, one does not hate anything nor does he want to save himself from the outer world. Since he has overcome time he has no change—the years, etc., revolve under him, and he is the real nature of the universe. Since the cause of duality has been destroyed the knower is deathless. He is the "*prāṇa* of *prāṇa*," the life-giver of life.

657-767 (E1829-1832) (IV.4.19). To realize Brahman the mind alone is the instrument and nothing else.

Objection: If Brahman is seen by the mind then there must be dualities as between seer, seen, and sight.

Answer: In Brahman there is no non-Brahman, seen or unseen. In perception only positive elements appear and hence there is no possibility of difference being observed. If a man sees the superimposed duality he obtains the cause of going from death to death, that is, Hiraṇyagarbha; the cause is ignorance.

677-698 (E1832-1835) (IV.4.20). Therefore Brahman is to be seen "in one form only," as consciousness (*caitanya*) according to the scripture "*satyaṃ jñānam anantam brahma*" ("Brahman is truth, knowledge, endless"). It is clear now that Bhartṛprapañca's difference-cum-nondifference is baseless and runs afoul of this passage "Brahman is to be seen in one form only."

Objection : If Brahman is seen there must be difference between seer and seen, and if so how can It be said to be "nonobject" ?

Answer : First, it is seen by negating other objects. Second, it is only the object of mental operations (*vṛtti*) and not of consciousness (*cit*). Ignorance is destroyed by mental operations and Brahman shines, being self-luminous. Since the Self is the inner soul of the seer, seen, and sight and is itself of the nature of consciousness It cannot be an object. Just as the sleeping person is awakened directly by a word without his remembering the relationship between the word and its sense, so also by the text "that art thou" the Self is awakened. This is because the capacity of the word is inexplicable (*acintya*) and sleep is illuminated by the Self, which is consciousness.

699-769 (E1836-1847) (IV.4.21-22). "Knowing (*vijñāya*) the nature of" Brahman "the wise man should attain *prajñā*," that is, he should learn the sentence sense of great sentences such as "I am Brahman."

Some commentators interpret this another way. They say that by "*vijñāya*" is meant the verbal knowledge of the identity of *jīva* and Brahman, and by "attaining *prajñā*" it is meant that he must make that knowledge a direct realization by repeating the verbal knowledge. This realization is brought about by the mind, and so it was said above that the Self should be realized by the mind. When the *jīva* contemplates a deity as his own self he becomes one with it. Thus he contemplates Hiraṇyagarbha and after attaining identity with it he looks upon Brahman as self and become Brahman.

This view is corrupt. The activities of mind, speech, and body depend on the person. He can do them or keep quiet. But the knowledge of identity between Self and Brahman that arises from the Vedic text is not dependent on a person. The person whose mind is free from *tamas* and *rajas* and who possesses equanimity, control of mind, etc., directly sees the Self by the great sentences and then all his ignorance is removed. He becomes all-knowing. All his duties are over; he has attained the fruits of his labor.

770-834 (E1848-1857). Others interpret the stanza thus: After knowing, one must meditate. Since sentences in general generate only the relation of one word-sense with another, the great sentences give only the knowledge of related Brahman. To get direct knowledge of nonrelational Brahman one has to meditate, and it is this knowledge alone that removes ignorance.

This view also is not good. All *pramāṇas* generate knowledge of the unknown. Brahman is unknown, and the text must generate a knowledge of Brahman that is nonrelational. This is natural. So additional meditation is useless. Indeed, by meditating on a false object nobody gains the truth.

835-877 (E1858-1864). Our view of the meaning of this passage is this. One should get knowledge of Brahman from the Vedic text,

This is "*vijñāna*." By "*prajñāna*" is meant the realization of Brahman as "I am that."

Or, by the pervasion of *pramāṇa* called "*vijñāna*" knowledge arises, but there is duality of seer and seen. By the pervasion of the object, called "*prajñā*," that duality comes to an end.

Or, the knowledge derived from hearing and reflection is what is meant by "*vijñāna*." By "*prajñāna*" direct realization through the text is meant.

Or, "*vijñāna*" is knowledge of the Self as Brahman, whereas "*prajñāna*" is the knowledge of Brahman as Self. By the word "only" (*eva*) duality and mediacy in Brahman are eliminated, since these are due to ignorance and perish through Vedic knowledge.

Or, by "*vijñāna*" is meant knowledge of the word-senses in the great sentences. By "*prajñāna*" the knowledge of the sentence meaning is intended. The text "the Self should be known" enjoins only the knowledge of the real nature of *jīva* through inference. When this is known it is easy to get at the purport of the sentence.

Or, "*prajñā*" is the knowledge of Brahman, the aim of man. The injunction ("the Self should be known") says that this knowledge should come after knowledge of the Self ("*vijñāna*").

Or, when "*prajñāna*" is ordained without mention of an object the word "*vijñāna*" is given only to supply the object of *prajñā*.

Or, "*prajñā*" is Brahman. Knowing the Self ("*vijñāna*") you must know Him as the supreme.

878-891 (E1865-1866). Some commentators say that though at the time of the knowledge of the sense of a great sentence ignorance should perish, yet it does not do so since even after realization one sees desire, grief, etc., in the adept. Therefore there are two ignorances, one natural (*naisargya*), the other accidental (*āgantuki*). The accidental one perishes by the rise of realization, but though the natural ignorance perishes through knowledge yet it rises again and causes aversion, etc. Therefore to remove this natural ignorance one must practice knowledge repeatedly after "*vijñāna*."

891-935 (E1866-1874). This interpretation is not correct, since there is only one ignorance, not two. For realization, only that which is not known can be the content. The Self is such. Ignorance is located only in consciousness (*cit*). The knower is not the locus since he is always known. When one Brahman-knowledge is obtained by the great sentences all ignorance perishes, one becomes all-knowing and has attained everything to be attained. If ignorance that has perished can come out again there is no guarantee that it will not rise again after death. Ignorance that is necessarily removed by knowledge can never hinder knowledge from functioning. Further, when ignorance, which is the cause of all, is removed by knowledge how can it come back again? Destruction of ignorance is not its dissociation from Brahman but Brahman itself, and hence there is no possibility of its coming out of Brahman again. The one thing the great sentence has to do is to reveal the unknown. When this is done nothing remains. Ordinary knowledge of Self does not need any repetition since in the views of the Prābhākaras, Bhāṭṭas, Nyāya, and Vaiśeṣika it is possible without any injunction to repeat it. In the view of the Vedāntin, since the Self is consciousness, all the world including the *buddhi* is pervaded by It and hence contemplation is unnecessary.

936-961 (E1874-1878). Knowledge of Self derived from scripture cannot be ordained to be repeated. If the injunction be restrictive (*niyama*) or eliminative (*parisaṃkhyā*) the *karmakāṇḍa* will have no eligible person to address itself to. Since injunction concerning karma or its fruit would then not be possible, how much more difficult would be an injunction to repeat meditation, since when knowledge has been attained the difference between knower, known, and knowledge comes to an end. The knowledge that destroys ignorance does not require any instrument for destroying it.

962-979 (E1878-1882). The adept should not think of many words. Since it is tiring for the speech organ, words conveying the not-Self should be avoided. One should always meditate through the *praṇava* (i.e., *om*). By repeating it he will eventually get the desire for Brahman-knowledge. After getting that desire he should leave off repeating it and take up the few great sentences to get Brahman-knowledge. Too, there is conflict between the *karma-* and *jñānakāṇḍas* and when a person becomes eligible for knowledge he should leave off repeating the *karmakāṇḍa*.

Now the text begins to show how the *karmakāṇḍa* helps the rise of desire to know Brahman. The *jīva* called "*vijñānamaya*" and who is near the *prāṇas* is the supreme Brahman. Its attributes are all-controllership, omnipotence, and unchangingness.

980-1062 (E1882-1895). The person who was spoken of in the third Brāhmaṇa as self-luminous and free from desire and karma is now stated to be the Lord of all. Thus, the *jīva's* dependence upon Brahman is also denied here. Just as when it is said "the *ākāśa* in the pot is the great *ākāśa*" the attributes of both *ākāśas* are negated, so it is here. Brahman's Lordship is full, not like that of the sun or the emperor. His Lordship is over origination, sustention, and destruction. He is not an agent of karma nor enjoyer of its fruit. He is not born, etc., for those are the products of ignorance. Therefore He cannot become superior or inferior by karma, not being an agent; He is nonattached. Since He protects all creatures He is called "Bhūtapāla." Being himself the cause of all He, in the form of Prajāpati, Indra, etc., protects the world. Just as a dam protects the waters on both sides from mixing, so is the Self protecting the eternal values.

Brahmins wish to know such a person by repeating the Vedas. Since such a desire does not arise independently, the Upaniṣad gives us the means of acquiring such desires.

As actions are advised for getting one's desires, and knowledge for getting liberation, there is no sentence unity between the two *kāṇḍas* (*karma-* and *jñāna-*). Since recitation of the Vedas, etc., are laid down to inculcate *desire* for knowledge they cannot bring about knowledge, for which *yama* and *niyama* alone are the causes. Desire for knowledge is available to any stage of life without distinction. The word "Brahmins" (*brāhmaṇa*, in IV.4.22) implies the first three *varṇas*, which are all competent for Vedic study. "The study of the Vedas, sacrifices," etc., are individually the causes, or else this indicates the whole of the *karmakāṇḍa*.

The interpretation that Brahman is to be known by "study of the Vedas" (IV.4.22) is not right, since Brahman is revealed by the Upaniṣads alone, not by the *karmakāṇḍa*. All obligatory rites are implied in this text as to be done. These rites bring about purity of mind and the desire for knowledge follows. The optional rites (*kāmyakarman*) are also to be performed without desire for the fruit. Performed in this way they produce purity of mind.

The "austerity" (*tapas*) referred to here indicates forbearance of the pairs of opposites such as cold and heat, etc. "*Anaśaka*" suggests not taking tasty food. Even if one dies such a one is sure to get the fruit in a later life. By the purity of the organs earned in many lives he will get release in the first stage of life (viz., *brahmacarya*) itself. However, fasting unto death should not be undertaken by one who is able to undertake hearing and thinking (about Brahman) in this life. But it may be undertaken in Prayāga (Allahabad), etc., by inefficient persons, since death then brings him liberation.

1063-1143 (E1895-1907). Or, this text (IV.4.22) intends that the *brahmacārin* "becomes a sage" by "study of the Vedas" (*vedānuvacana*), the householder by "sacrifice" (*yajña*), and the forest-dweller, and the *saṃnyāsin* by "austerity." All stages of life performed perfectly lead toward liberation. A "sage" is a *saṃnyāsin* who undertakes meditation (*dhyāna*) after hearing and considering. By being a sage he gets Brahman-knowledge.

Now the text praises *saṃnyāsa*, speaking of the wise old men who had attained Brahman-knowledge and did not desire sons, actions, inferior knowledge, etc.

1144-1179 (E1908-1914). Some say that *saṃnyāsa* is for those unable to perform actions, such as the lame, the blind, etc. This is not so, as the text does not indicate that such men are eligible for *saṃnyāsa.*

Objection : Why should those who desire Self-knowledge abandon action ? Let them perform actions and not *saṃnyāsa.*

Answer : No, since action has nothing to do with the world of the Self, as is indicated by "not this, not this." Vyāsa tells us that neither good nor bad acts affect him.

1180-1300 (E1914-1936). The next section (IV.4.23) gives a *mantra* making the same point, that Brahman-knowers are not affected by action, and so one should know the Self. Having attained desire for that knowledge one should foresake desires, should attain tranquillity and the other prerequisite qualities and, by eliminating all that is not-Self, should realize the Self by the text "that art thou." The six qualities are explained. In *saṃnyāsa* abandonment (*uparati*) is natural, but begging for food and hearing the Upaniṣads are not prohibited for the *saṃnyāsin* since they are important for one to gain knowledge. But even in begging one should leave the idea of "I" and "mine."

1301-1345 (E1936-1943). "This is the Brahman-world, and you have attained it," says Yājñavalkya, and having been thus instructed Janaka gave him his empire and his self.

(IV.4.25) Only by Self-knowledge does one become accomplished (*kṛtakṛtya*). This Self is the "eater" (*annada*). By meditating on Brahman thus one gets prosperity.

(IV.4.25) In the last section the four foregoing books are summed up. The Self is all-pervasive, Brahman, beginningless and endless. All the stages of life are herein negated. Brahman is fearless, for ignorance is destroyed. And we come to know Brahman by these qualities, though superimposed on Brahman, just as we get the knowledge of number by learning figures.

FIFTH BRĀHMAṆA

1-30 (E1944-1948). In the Madhukāṇḍa Brahman was explained through scripture. Then in the Munikāṇḍa it was further explained by reasoning, and by discussion in the Fourth Brāhmaṇa. This *brahmavidyā* is now concluded in the *Maitreyī Brāhmaṇa*, called Nigamanakāṇḍa. It repeats the story told in Book Two.

BOOK FIVE—FIRST BRĀHMAṆA

1-62 (E1949-1959). The *Yājñavalkyakāṇḍa* is over. Now the Khilakāṇḍa begins. Though everything has been explained in the two *kāṇḍas* (*karma-* and *jñāna-*) some activities remain to be explained, and this is "*khila,*" that is, some rituals pertaining to the qualified Brahman not put forth above, which are good for prosperity and indirectly lead to liberation. Likewise, the *praṇava* needs to be explained further, along with control of senses, charity, sympathy, etc., which are aids (*aṅga*) for all ritual acts of worship (*upāsanā*).

In the preceding Book Brahman was explained through the relationship of cause and effect. Now both these are denied. The universe is not existent apart from Brahman, nor is it Brahman's nature, since the universe is inert. But the universe is not a nonentity. Therefore Brahman is full (*pūrṇa*), identical with the universe. It is not pervasive like cowness, nor is It a separate individual like an individual cow. It is self-evident, bliss, and full. All effects have for their reality the full Brahman.

Now we have to understand the fullness of the qualified Brahman by removing phenomenal difference through Brahman-knowledge, thus cognizing its nature of purity, Selfhood and bliss, fully nondual consciousness.

63-116 (E1959-1968). The polemic against Bhartṛprapañca follows Śaṃkara.

117-130 (E1968-1970). The text says "Brahman is *om*, *ākāśa*, *purāṇa*." These are *mantras* for use in meditation.

SECOND TO THIRTEENTH BRĀHMAṆAS

(E1970-1983) II.1-XIII.5. Qualifications for meditation (restraint of senses, charity, and sympathy) are illustrated in a story (Brāhmaṇa II). Then the following Brāhmaṇas enjoin meditation on the qualified Brahman as heart (III), truth (IV-V), mind (VI), lightning (*vidyut*) (VII), speech (*vāk*) (VIII), Vaiśvānara or the digestive "fire" (IX). Brāhmaṇa X briefly describes the soul's path from the body at death. Further meditative forms of qualified Brahman are set forth in Brāhmaṇas XI-XIII.

(E1983-1985) XIV.1-15. Here the Gāyatrī (the most important meditative stanza for ordinary worship) is analyzed.

BOOK SIX

(E2005-2073) I.1-V.25. This Book continues with subjects similar to those of the previous Book. Sureśvara's commentary follows the text closely and does not add materially to Śaṃkara's.

TAITTIRĪYOPANIṢADBHĀṢYAVĀRTTIKA

"A Vārttika has been defined as a work that examines what is said (*ukta*), what is not said (*anukta*), and what is not well-said (*durukta*) in the original."[5] This Vārttika on Śaṃkara's commentary on the *Taittirīya Upaniṣad* is a work in 1027 verses that attempts to fulfil the requirements specified, including the third one, which Sureśvara addresses by providing explanations of certain passages of the Upaniṣad alternative to Śaṃkara's interpretations but without rejecting them outright.[6]

"ET" references are to the edition and translation by R. Balasubramaniam, *The Taittirīyopaniṣad Bhāṣya-Vārttika of Sureśvara* (Centre for Advanced Study in Philosophy : University of Madras, 1974).

PART ONE : ŚIKṢĀVALLĪ (ON PRONUNCIATION)

32 (ET 15). *Introductory section, part* 7 : Śaṃkara has argued that "absences cannot really have qualities," etc. Sureśvara draws the conclusion that absences generally (i.e., posterior, etc.) are constructions (*kalpanā*) acceptable only for practical affairs (*vyavahāra*).

(Sureśvara does not comment on the long discussion in section 11.)

PART TWO : BRAHMAVALLĪ (THE BLISS OF BRAHMAN)

63-69 (ET 95-98). *Commenting on section* 7 : Sureśvara construes the objector as an *apohavādin* who believes that the only function a word has is to deny its negate. This objector then argues that words cannot give us any positive knowledge *ex hypothesi*, and since we don't know Brahman by any other *pramāṇa* the sentence in question ("Brahman is truth, etc.") is about nothing at all.

Sureśvara's answer : Nothing false (*vitatha*) is experienced except as it is dependent (*āliṅgya*) on the highest reality (*paramārtha*). So, all falsity is based on reality. So a word does indicate a positive reality—the word "lotus" gives rise to a thought of the flower, the meaning of that word. A word by itself cannot indicate the absence of something—that can only be done by a sentence. Nevertheless, after coming to know the thing meant by a word, one of course comes to understand the absence of what is contradictory to that. In the present case, what the sentence ("Brahman is truth, etc.") gives us directly is the knowledge of the relation (i.e., identity) between a property (truth) and its possessor (Brahman). The absence of an absence (*apoha*) is not derived from this sentence, however, but from some other means of knowledge (viz., presumption or *arthāpatti*). The idea of blue does not arise independently of the idea of a thing that is blue, any more than the idea of a qualified thing (a blue thing, a true thing) arises independently of the idea of its qualifier (blue, truth). From a word like "blue" or "truth" we derive the sense of the sentence (in which it occurs); and then through expectancy (*ākāṅkṣā*) we get to the notion of "the blue thing" or "the thing that is truth (viz., Brahman)."

70-73 (ET 99-101). Since all real entities (*vastu*) are known by perception it is not possible to establish the momentariness of anything. If a pot exists it is not destroyed, and if it is destroyed there is no locus for its "destruction"; if you say that it exists after its destruction as the locus of that destruction, then it wasn't destroyed after all! If you want to talk of the destruction of destruction, may you live a hundred years! Our view is that the pot is indestructible. Destruction does not destroy its locus, any more than motion can destroy the thing that moves. How can anything that depends on a locus *L* for its existence destroy that *L*?

(13) 135 (ET 129). That which is not apparently-created or -constructed (*akalpita*) cannot be limited (*pariccheda*) by what is apparently-created or -constructed (*kalpita*). Now time, etc., are apparently-created, as is attested by the "*vācārambha* . . . " passage, *Chāndogya Upaniṣad* VI.1.4 (=VI.4.1).

140-151 (ET 132-141). We cannot explain creation by referring to Brahman for Brahman is nondifferent from everything, unchanging, single, and neither an effect nor a cause. And nothing else can be the cause of the world, since everything else is an effect. Brahman cannot even be the cause of the world by Its mere presence, since then It would always be creating and nothing would get destroyed. Again, since Brahman is not in time it is not the case that Brahman created the world in the past or will create in the future—but Brahman, being the cause of time, cannot be limited by time. Anyway, Brahman is not involved in any action, so cannot create in any time—past, present, or future. To speak of Brahman as qualified by temporal predicates makes no more sense than to speak of an atom as a camel. The only cause of the world is *avidyā*. Again, there is no cause of what does not exist (*asat*), and what exists does not have a beginning, indeed, has no qualities at all that could originate or disappear. Birth, destruction, etc., are unchanging (*kūṭastha*); if birth needed a birth, or destruction a destruction, etc., there would be an infinite regress. All candidates for the role of cause of the world cannot serve, since they all arise from *avidyā*. Creation is only apparent, like the arising of two moons from eye disease, or the snake in the rope.

158-162 (ET 144-148). In the course of commenting on the section describing the order of creation Sureśvara here brings in the notions of Virāj and Sūtrātman. Virāj is described as "the god marked by spatial directions, etc., who wears a body consisting of the five elements and who arises in (or from?) the notion 'I am everything'." Before it was Sūtrātman, its cause, that has the form of the "compact form of knowledge" (Van Boetzelaer's rendering of '*prajñānaghana*') before it produces Virāj.

163-172 (ET 149-152). Herbs, constituted of the five elements, are born from earth moistened by rain and provide us with food. Digested food produces bodily fluid (*rasa*), and from that comes blood, from that flesh, from that fat, from fat bones, from bones marrow, from marrow semen. Sexual desire is poetically characterized as stemming from *avidyā*-conditioned passion as well as the karma of the one who is to be born (?-*janyakarman*). From the semen, conditioned by karma and *śruta* (=*upāsanā*? cf. *Kaṭha Upaniṣad* II.2.7) and entering the womb, comes the embryonic state (*kalala*) having the form of a bubble (*budbuda*). From this embryo comes the fetus (*peśi*) and thence a body (*ghana*), from which come limbs and thence hairs. This new human body is composed of the same elements and organs as its karmic predecessor was.

176-179 (ET 155-157). *Avidyā* is responsible for the Self, as Sūtrātman and Virāj, appearing as the limited self (*kṣetrajña*). However, it is impossible to prove *avidyā* by a *pramāṇa*, any more than it is possible to see the darkness in a cave with a lamp. The not-Self, which is the result of *avidyā*, can be said to *be avidyā*. Its nature is nothing other than the nongrasping (or concealing) of the Self. "*Avidyā*," "nonknowledge," is like "*amitra*," "nonfriend," that is, "enemy" (i.e., it is not the name of an absence of, but of something opposed to, knowledge).

182-198 (ET 158-165). This section describes the development of the foetus in the womb. The food eaten by the mother is divided into three kinds: solid food becomes feces, flesh and buddhi, and the sense organs; liquid food becomes urine, blood, and *prāṇa*; fiery food becomes bone, marrow, and speech (i.e., the organs of action). The sense organs evolve from the *ahaṃkāra* conditioned by former karma and knowledge (*śruta*) through traces (*bhāvanā*). As the gross body grows the subtle body does also. The condition of the *jiva* in the womb it finds painful and disgusting, remembering its previous experiences through impressions (*vāsanā*), and the experience of birth is likewise painful.

199-221 (ET 165-171). The misery of human life—youth to old

age—is likewise expressed vividly. After death the *jīva* is led along by his karma to another birth.

232-237 (ET 177-182). The utility of the theory of the sheaths, about to be explained, is indicated. It provides a method of indicating the Self by approximation, just as one can point out the moon by pointing to a tree branch. *Avidyā* leads us to divide the Self into the "Thou" and the "I." Now both (apparent) divisions can be understood as consisting of five sheaths (*kośa*), the *annamaya*, etc., indicating the subject or "I," food (*anna*), etc., indicating the object or "Thou." By dissolving these sheaths in their respective causes and then dissolving even the ultimate cause itself, one may understand Brahman.

238-241 (ET 183-186). Virāj is food, evolved from *prāṇa*. The *manomaya* (sheath) has the Veda—*Ṛg*, *Yajus* and *Sāma*—as its nature. The *buddhi*, which ascertains the meaning of the Vedas, is *vijñāna*. Bliss (*ānanda*), resulting from knowledge and action, is the innermost essence of the other four sheaths.

(13a) 5. 320-351 (ET 230-247). *Objection* : The bliss-sheath is the highest Self, because (in the next section, the Bhṛguvallī) the conversation between Bhṛgu and Varuṇa terminates when it arrives at this point; furthermore, scripture frequently identifies Brahman as having the nature of bliss. Finally, this very chapter is (sometimes) called the "Ānandavallī."

Answer : No, since bliss is an effect, something obtained. Again, God (*iśvara*) doesn't obtain His self by himself; no aspirant, no matter how clever, can mount onto his own shoulder. Since the *ānandamaya* sheath has form (*ākāra*), the doubt whether Brahman exists or not could not arise in the fashion it does so in the Bhṛguvallī. As for the opponent's objections : In the Ānandavallī—the present part—Brahman is taught first, and then when (in the Bhṛguvallī) Bhṛgu is taught by Varuṇa, he stops when he has finished teaching the means —the five sheaths—since the goal—Brahman—has already been explained. In the context it is only appropriate for Varuṇa to speak of what is dependent on his will; since Brahman is independent (*svātantrya*) knowledge of Him is not dependent on the agent's will, so there is no point in Varuṇa's speaking of that, as once the bliss-sheath is realized the rest takes place of its own accord.

Again, Brahman *is* of the nature of bliss, as scripture avers; the bliss is freedom from all difference. *This* bliss, however, is free of all distinctions of grades of happiness, etc., and is not a content of thought, and it should not be confused with the "bliss" of the bliss-sheath (*ānandamaya*). The Brahman-bliss fills all five sheaths, including the *ānandamaya*. The *ānandamaya* sheath involves an adjunct—the *buddhi*, which experiences joy as a result of knowledge and action. Again, this *ānandamaya* self is known in our dreams, in our love of our children, in acquiring desired objects, etc. As a result of merit produced by good actions the *buddhi* becomes stabilized (*svastha*) and joy is more and more manifested.

8.5 550-558 (ET 348-352). (25) Sureśvara uses the example of the tenth man to illustrate how a self can "attain itself," that is, come to realize who he is by dispelling his ignorance.

(26) Attaining Brahman by being informed is not like getting to a village by following directions, for in giving directions one is not given a description of the nature of the village, whereas in imparting knowledge of Brahman one does.

9 595-614 (ET 375-385). The text of the Upaniṣad here mentions that words and concepts cannot grasp Brahman. Sureśvara points out that although words cannot directly denote Brahman they can indirectly (through *lakṣaṇā*) reveal Its nature, by removing ignorance, just as by speaking to a sleeping man one wakes him up even though the sleeper doesn't understand the meanings of the words used in waking him up.

Thus from hearing scripture one understands "I am Brahman" and ignorance is destroyed, and the cognition (by which one understands this) also disappears thereafter, as the medicine goes away after curing the disease. After that all that remains is Brahman, which is consciousness, and no *pramāṇa* is needed for further consciousness of It. The Self is not an empirical object, so perception, etc., are not needed, as they are in the case of someone telling you that there are fruit trees on the bank of the river (since you need your senses to confirm this statement).

615-630 (ET 385-394). Brahman cannot be reached by word or concept; injunctions to us to know It are futile. Likewise, It cannot be meditated upon, for in order to meditate on something one must identify something as the object of the meditation that is previously known to us. Since Brahman is not known to us prior to realization it follows that we can't meditate on It. Again, though the subject matter of the Vedas though unworldly (*alaukika*) can be conveyed as the meaning of a sentence since it can arise from the combinations of the meanings of the words, Brahman, being non-relational, cannot be made known by a sentence directly. And one shouldn't suppose that therefore Brahman doesn't exist, for it is only through Brahman that *pramāṇa*, what is not *pramāṇa*, and what only appears to be *pramā* (*pramābhāsa*) can become evident to us at all.

There occurs now an extensive discussion with a *niyogavādin*, who holds that the Vedas enjoin Self-knowledge, and that it is through them as *pramāṇa* that Brahman comes to be known. Sureśvara's response begins by pointing out (1) that the declarative portions of scripture (*abhidhāśruti*) have independent validity, (2) that no injunction can have validity without consciousness (which is the subject matter of the declarative portions), (3) that injunctions command people to do things but do not explain the nature of an object, so an injunction cannot provide Self-knowledge, (4) that since a person cannot perform an act he is not competent to perform no matter how many injunctions are addressed to him, the critical awareness centers on the object, not the injunction or any act, (5) that as long as declarative portions of scripture are viewed as subservient to the injunctive portions, it cannot independently indicate the nature of the Self, (6) since the Self cannot be perceived, no injunction can be relevant to It.

631-634 (ET 395-397). The *niyogavādin* now argues that it is only in the context of injunction that an object can be made known, and that a declarative statement independently of such a context is only a repetition (*anuvāda*) and without validity.

Answer : No, since a real thing (i.e., the Self) already exists It cannot be enjoined, for an injunction can only speak of what is to be accomplished; and Self-knowledge does not need enjoining, for it will occur (according to you) as a result of the presupposed injunction that each man should study the appropriate portion of the Veda—it needs no additional injunction any more than, having been enjoined to act, one needs another injunction to gain knowledge of action.

635-638 (ET 397-398). *Niyogavādin* : This would be so if men knew, without an injunction, that Self-knowledge is the means to the desired end. But men do not know that except by an injunction; it cannot be known from any other *pramāṇa*, nor from a declarative statement (of scripture).

Answer: No, for knowledge manifests its object—here, the Self—without any intervening activity, so there's no scope for an injunction other than the one enjoining everyone to study the Vedas.

639-673 (ET 399-412). *Niyogavādin* : True, the knowledge arising from Vedantic declarative statements is not enjoined. Rather, a different knowledge, one that is not (mediate and relational) like knowledge arising from words (*śabdajñāna*) and yet is gotten by a means (*upāya*), *is* enjoined. Since Brahman cannot be the direct meaning of a sentence it cannot be understood from scripture, since scriptural sentences (like any sentences) have a meaning that is derived from the relations among the meanings of its constituent words and Brahman is nonrelational. Nevertheless, scripture is assuredly the *pramāṇa* for coming to know Brahman.

Objection to the Niyogavādin : If Brahman cannot be understood from the sentences of scripture the Vedas cannot be about Brahman.

Niyogavādin : Brahman is the subject matter of the Vedas (*vedārtha*), since by meditating upon the indirect, relational knowledge of Brahman one gains direct nonrelational knowledge. But Brahman is not the subject matter of the sentences of the Vedas (*vedavākyārtha*), for (1) the Vedic utterances are commands, and Brahman is not dependent on human effort and so cannot be the subject matter of a command; (2) furthermore, Brahman (unlike e.g., *dharma,*) is not the *denotatum* of any word (since It lacks the kinds of features that make denotation of it possible), and therefore *a fortiori* It cannot be referred to in a sentence; (3) even if Brahman could be denoted, there is nothing the sentence could say about It beyond what the words say, which is quite general (i.e., whereas in other cases a sentence specifies features of what is denoted by its subject term, here there are no features to be specified, Brahman being *nirguṇa*).

Answer : We have answered this above (at 595). We do not need a *pramāṇa* to tell us "this is the content of my awareness," "this is awareness," or "I am the cognizer"—these are directly given to the Witnessing consciousness, and *pramāṇas* are only needed to give us knowledge of what is other than given. Yet the differences among subject, object, and act of cognizing are illusory—the Self is unchanging and there is no other than It, so that even this witnessing is only construed as cognizing because of association with *avidyā*. Thus the Self is not the knower; it is the *buddhi* that is the knower. What the seeker has to do is to apply scientific reasoning (*anvayavyatireka*) to convince himself that all objects are mind only in all the three states and to discriminate them from the pure consciousness (*cinmātra*), which cannot be referred to in a sentence. Such a one then, upon hearing a sentence like "that art thou," has his ignorance dispelled completely so that the unconditioned reality is made known. That is, because of the coordinate relation (*sāmānādhikaraṇya*) between the words "that" and "thou," which serves to remove the incompatibility between their meanings, the direct nonrelational sense is made known to us, and so the nonrelational Brahman is conveyed by the sentence, contrary to what the Niyogavādin said.

Again, one does not need to be enjoined to remove his ignorance by this means, since ignorance, error, and doubt can only arise with respect to objects like pots, etc., for as we have just said subject, object, and act of awareness are directly known and do not require a *pramāṇa*—thus no error, doubt, or ignorance needs to be dispelled in their case, and so no additional understanding (beyond the nonrelational knowledge of Brahman) is required or need be enjoined.

674 (ET 418). *Niyogavādin* : We infer our conclusion as follows: The Vedānta texts are connected with an injunction, because they are sentences, like sentences about actions.

Answer : An inference to the effect that Vedānta texts require injunctions (such as the one just given) is faulty, since pervasion between the *h* and the *s* cannot be established (in this case, since not all sentences are connected with injunctions, even on the Niyogavādin's own presuppositions).

678 (ET 421). One should not deprive the Vedānta texts of their validity by making them subsidiary to injunctions.

Objection : On the contrary, Vedānta texts without association with injunctions are not instruments of knowledge (*pramāṇa*).

Answer : Then it will be impossible to know Brahman and injunctions would have no content, which contradicts your own view.

687-688 (ET 426-427). The Niyogavādin's position is that only injunctions have validity (*prāmāṇya*); words in the Vedic corpus have no independent validity.

Sureśvara : This is wrong. Among these are words like "milk" (uttered by one who already knows milk). If this word does not validly convey its own meaning, it cannot play its appropriate part in an injunction like "Sacrifice by offering milk" and even injunctions will lack validity.

Niyogavādin : "Milk" in such a context does not have anything to do with the act, but only with determining its result, that is, heaven.

Answer : It doesn't matter, it still must function independently to denote heaven or whatever.

691-692 (ET 429-430). *Niyogavādin* : Since only texts that command something to be gotten or given up (i.e., injunctions) are valid, the sentence "I am Brahman" is not valid, since it commands neither.

Answer : Injunctions are valid insofar as they successfully lead men toward their purposes (*puruṣārtha*). Since the knowledge of the identity of Brahman and the Self, conveyed by the text in question, is the highest human purpose, the text must be valid independently!

699-700 (ET 432-433). *Niyogavādin* : A word by itself has no validity because (1) it depends on something else to convey its meaning, and (2) it is a repetition (*anuvāda*).

Sureśvara : How do you know this—that is, by what valid means of knowing (*pramāṇa*)? You cannot say: from the nature of the word itself, since you contend words have no validity. And you cannot say: from an injunction, since an injunction cannot reveal the nature of words. So there must be another *pramāṇa* besides injunction. Again, a word cannot depend on "something else," for example, another word, to convey its meaning, for if it is not a valid instrument for conveying what it signifies, how can the sense of a sentence arise from combinations of words?

701 (ET 433). Indeed, how can *any pramāṇa* convince you that words are not valid means of coming to know their meanings? What *pramāṇa* can give you knowledge of the absence of validity (in words)? Not through perception, etc., for these cannot grasp absences (*abhāva*). Or is it through words (*śabda* = verbal authority)? If so, words are valid means of knowing, contrary to your assumption.

702-705 (ET 434-436). Scripture, as we have said, conveys Self-knowledge by progressively negating other things (like the sheaths, see above).

Niyogavādin: No, the Self must be known as different from not-Self items like sheaths, etc.

Sureśvara: Is this "difference" (*bheda*) a negative entity or "absence" (*abhāva*)? If so, it can have no relation with a sense organ and cannot therefore be grasped by any of the *pramāṇas*. And you cannot say that difference is known from noncognition (*anupalabdhi*), for absence of knowledge or *pramāṇa* cannot make anything known, and anyway you yourselves do not admit absences!

707-713 (ET 437-439). *Niyogavādin*: Your arguments presuppose that Self-knowledge leads to liberation, but that assumption is based on the validity of scriptural injunction.

Sureśvara: How do we know the validity of that scriptural injunction? By another injunction? Then there will be an infinite regress of injunctions. Anyway, you suppose that the injunction "Study your section of the Vedas" is known without dependence on another injunction, so here too you should admit that the statement of other scriptural texts is known without dependence on injunction. Either the statement (of Self-knowledge, e.g., "I am Brahman") or the injunction must depend on the other if they are to cooperate in the way you maintain. But if the statement is subordinate to the injunction, meditation on it will only give rise to ideas about heaven as is the case with other meditations on injunctions, and we will never come to know Brahman. On the other hand, if the injunction is subordinate to the statement it is useless, since the statement has the power to convey its own meaning.

714-720 (ET 439-442). All this does not mean that injunctions have no role to play on our view. They are necessary, prior to attainment of Self-knowledge, to direct seekers to reflect on the meanings of the words in the assertions that impart Self-knowledge. Since those reflections must be achieved and require causal factors to be made present it is appropriate that injunctions relate to them, unlike the case of Brahman, which is not something requiring causal factors, etc.

Niyogavādin : You don't understand: the injunction is needed to get the seeker to meditate (*nididhyāsana*) on the meaning of the scriptural assertion—for example, "I am Brahman."

Sureśvara : *You* don't understand. Once Self-knowledge is realized, since ignorance is already destroyed, there is no possibility of or need for an injunction to meditate. If knowledge could not by itself remove ignorance it couldn't do so in combination with an injunction either. This is why the wise man, who knows the bliss of Brahman, the unchanging nondual One, is without fear of anything at all.

NAIṢKARMYASIDDHI

This is an independent exposition of Advaita in 423 stanzas connected by a prose commentary. It is divided into four chapters or "books" of about 100 stanzas each. Alston points out that Sureśvara here follows the *Upadeśasāhasri* of Śaṃkara very closely and suggests that this work also "contains clear echoes of Śrī Śaṃkara's 'Gītā Bhāṣya'."[7] Jacob points out that at least thirty-six kārikās of this work are also found in the *Bṛhadāraṇyaka-Vārttika*.[8]

Hiriyanna remarks of this work : "The style is quite charming and the author handles philosophic arguments with equal ease whether it be in verse or prose."[9] It is, he says, "simple and clear and forms an excellent introduction to Śaṃkara's system."[10] He suggests that the stanzas were composed originally and form a complete and connected whole, the prose passage being added later.[11]

References to "E" are to the edition by G. A. Jacob, revised by M. Hiriyanna, in the Bombay Sanskrit and Prakrit Series Volume 38, 1925. "T" references are to the translation by Anthony J. Alston, London 1959.

BOOK ONE

Introduction (E1-5; T1-2). All beings, from Brahmā to a clump of grass, naturally wish to avoid frustration. The only material cause (*upādāna*) of frustration is the body, which is rooted in karma; karma in turn is rooted in prescribed and prohibited actions already performed. Actions, again, depend on attraction and aversion, which are themselves caused by superimposition of the ideas of goodness and badness. This superimposition is caused by our accepting the duality of things. Finally, this acceptance of duality rests on our noncomprehension of the self-evident nondual Self, and so that noncomprehension (*anavabodha*) is the ultimate cause of everything not worthwhile (*anartha*) and precludes our experiencing the bliss that is the nature of the Self. Therefore the eradication of noncomprehension achieves every human purpose.

The cessation of nonknowledge (*ajñāna*) comes from right knowledge (*samyagjñāna*), which comes only from the sentences of Vedānta scripture (*āgama*), since the Self, obscured by noncomprehension, cannot be grasped by the other *pramāṇas*. Thus this treatise (*prakaraṇa*) is begun as representing the collected essence of the entire Upaniṣads (*aśeṣavedāntasārasaṃgraha*).

1-3 (E5-6; T2-3). Invocatory verses addressed to God (*hari*) and the supreme guru, showing the authoritativeness of Sureśvara's tradition.

4 (E7; T3). The present treatise explains the nature of that single basis which is the inner character on which everything depends.

5-6 (E8; T3-4). My guru has well said what has to be said in exposition of the Vedānta; I do not write my work to gain fame or wealth but rather to improve my own understanding by exposing it for criticism by those wise concerning Brahman.

7-8 (E9; T4-5). *Avidyā* is the failure to understand that there is but one Self. Its seed is *saṃsāra*, its destruction is liberation, and this result comes from understanding the sentences of the Upaniṣads. The result does not come from action, since knowledge and action are incompatible.

9-21 (E10-15; T5-10). *Objection* (by a Mīmāṃsaka): Action alone produces liberation. One who performs the prescribed daily and occasional ritual acts (*nityanaimittikakarman*) and avoids acts that are forbidden (*niṣiddha*) or that arise from desire (*kāmya*) avoids breeding further results such as becoming a god, as well as avoiding lower births in hell. Through experiencing their affective results he gradually exhausts the stored up merit and demerit, and by performing the prescribed rituals he does not get the demerit that accrues from neglecting them. So knowledge is quite unnecessary. There are no injunctions to know either in scripture or in *smṛti*, and we admit no other authorities on this matter. Jaimini interprets scripture as entirely exhausted in injunctive purport. Words cannot make up a sentence unless they depend on a verb, and the verb signifies an injunction. Further, even if knowledge occurs the texts indicate that it must be combined with action in order that liberation be achieved. So, men of all stages of life attain liberation only through mental, bodily, and speech acts.

22-28 (E15-18; T10-13). *Answer* : Since action cannot destroy *avidyā* it cannot cause liberation. Anyway, is liberation supposed to be the result of one act or of all (enjoined) acts together? If it is the result of one act, then the rest of the Vedic injunctions would be useless, and if it is the results of all of them together, the result of every ritual action would be the same, which is contrary to what the scripture itself indicates, since it specifies particular results for particular acts.

29 (E19-20; T13-14). So liberation does not come from action alone. We now argue that it arises from Self-knowledge alone, and our argument also involves inquiry into the causes of activity in the largest sense of the word.

Here the following question arises: Everyone knows that in the case of many acts—for example, those prohibited in scripture, as well as natural acts like eating, etc.—a person naturally imagines (*parikalpyate*) particular things to be worth acquiring or avoiding, and then depending on ordinary instruments of knowledge (*laukikapramāṇa*) acts appropriately, all of this happening whether the object in question is, for example, a mirage, or veridical. Now the question is: in the case of those acts, whether prescribed ritual acts or those arising from desire, which breed future karma (*adṛṣṭa*)—does a person proceed on the same basis as before, or in some other way?

This question is important. If *pramāṇas*, whether ordinary or scriptural, ascertain actions to be done, then the renunciation of action is based on error (*bhrānti*). But if *all* acts are based on error about what is real, like the acts of one who tries to drink the water in a mirage, then we are right and you are wrong.

30 (E21; T15-16). Indeed, all action whatever depends on false awareness (*mithyājñāna*), since perception, inference, and scripture all agree that the Self never lacks supreme pleasure and that there is no unpleasantness in It; thus our wish to get the pleasant and avoid the unpleasant depends on natural ignorance about the Self.

It is not scripture that moves a man to action. His motives are natural; indeed, they are found in animals too. All scripture does is to illuminate.

31-35 (E22-23; T16-18). With respect to things that one does not already have and that are not unreal, scripture can indicate how to get or avoid them, and then by acting appropriately one may get or avoid them. But when one desires to get what one already has, or to avoid what doesn't exist, one cannot get or avoid them through action; since delusion alone is the obstacle (to one's knowing that one has got or not got them), the only "getting" or "avoiding" is through knowledge. Action cannot destroy ignorance—indeed, action depends on ignorance.

36-37 (E24-25; T18-20). *Objection* : Self-knowledge itself is caused by *avidyā*, since scripture, pupil, and teacher are all dependent on *avidyā*, and without them no one acquires Self-knowledge.

Answer : No. Self-knowledge depends only on the self-illumined highest reality in its nature; it only depends on scripture, etc., for its origination, but once having arisen it doesn't depend on them at all. But action depends on *avidyā* both in its nature and for its origination, since an act by nature requires an agent. Furthermore, even after an action has occurred it requires something as a locus to account for its being able to produce its fruit many aeons later. Whereas action thus takes time and needs help to produce its fruit, Self-knowledge produces its result immediately without dependence on time or other means. It cannot be sublated since it is the supreme *pramāṇa*, and it requires no other means to protect it against subsequent sublation. So right knowledge is the right way, and the only way, to destroy *ajñāna*, which is responsible for frustration.

38 (E25-26; T20). *Objection* : Right knowledge must sometimes be sublated by wrong knowledge, since we find that even in one in whom the highest understanding has arisen ideas of agency, enjoyership, desire, and aversion do occur, and this could not happen unless right knowledge had been suppressed.

Answer : No, since *avidyā* has by then been sublated, it cannot in turn suppress right knowledge. It is the impressions (*vāsanā*) arising from it that remind the knower of right knowledge.

39-44 (E26-29; T20-23). *Saṃsāra* continues as long as *avidyā* does, and ceases when *avidyā* does.

45-53 (E29-33; T23-26). Still, though actions do not produce liberation, in a sense they serve as accessory conditions for it. A man, because of having much merit and having a mind purified by performance of the *nityakarmans*, may have nonattachment arise in him, and glimpsing the truth he may become fearful of the results of *kāmyakarmans* as he previously was of hell; as a result he may confine himself to ritual action only, and by offering all his actions to God come to nonattachment to all beings from the Brahmaloka on down. So, with *rajas* and *tamas* polished away by performance of *nitya-karmans*, the internal organ becomes pure like a clear mirror, naturally reflecting the light of the inner Self, and thus its only remaining desire is to dissolve in that inner Self. Since the *buddhi's* remaining acts have now produced this desire to dissolve within, they then come to an end with their purpose achieved.

Again, the chain leading to liberation goes as follows : From performing *nityakarmans* comes merit, from that destruction of demerit, from that purity of *citta*, from that appreciation of *saṃsāra*, from that nonattachment, from that desire for liberation, from that the seeking of its means, from that the renunciation (*saṃnyāsa*) of all actions and their instruments, from that the practice of yoga, from that desire to dissolve in the inner Self, from that understanding of the meaning of the great sentences of scripture, from that the cutting off of *avidyā*, from that establishment in the Self.

54-66 (E33-38; T27-30). But it is not that knowledge destroys *avidyā* in conjunction with action, since knowledge and action cannot exist simultaneously, one being an end, the other a means, and since they are related as sublater and sublated, action having to do with what is unreal, knowledge having to do with the highest reality—conjunction of them would be like conjunction between the sun and the night. Just as the Kṣatriya does not perform ceremonies appropriate for Brahmins, and vice versa, so the one who denies that the body is his Self takes no notice of action at all.

Of course knowledge and action are sometimes conjoined, that is, when knowledge prompts one to act. But knowledge prompts one to action only when that knowledge is false. For example, when a man takes a tree stump for a thief he runs away, but when he knows the stump for what it is he does not run. So two kinds of knowledge need to be distinguished—the kind (false) that plays a subordinate role in prompting action, and the kind (true) that by its mere appearance destroys *avidyā* and is never a partner with action.

The reason why knowledge of the second kind is incompatible with action is that it cannot appear without destroying *avidyā*; since when *avidyā* is destroyed plurality is too, and since action requires a plurality of factors, it follows that action is incompatible with knowledge of that kind.

67 (E38; T30-32). Some (Brahmadatta, according to Alston and Hiriyanna) say: *Avidyā* is not destroyed merely by the knowledge "I am Brahman." *Avidyā* only disappears after one meditates at length and acquires mental conviction (*bhāvanā*).

Others (Maṇḍana Miśra, according to Alston and Hiriyanna) say: the judgment "I am Brahman" is relational (*saṃsargātmaka*) and so does not yield a true knowledge of the Self. But by meditation on the meaning of such sentences another kind of consciousness arises that is nonrelational and goes beyond the meaning of the sentence(s), and it is this knowledge that destroys *avidyā*.

But the knowledge produced by scripture destroys *avidyā* completely and immediately, and so there is no possibility of further acts such as meditation. So the combination of knowledge and action (as proposed by the above thinkers) is impossible.

68 (E39; T33). Now we turn to another type of view (the Bhedābhedavāda of Bhartṛprapañca, according to Alston), which also maintains the aforesaid combination of action and knowledge. For them, Brahman is everlastingly manifold.

69-71 (E39-40; T33-34). There are two varieties of this view, according as it is held that (1) *jīva* and Brahman are identical in *saṃsāra*, or (2) that they are different there.

If (1) they are identical, then failure to attain liberation is due to *avidyā* only, and since actions cannot destroy *avidyā*, the combined-path view is impossible. But (2) if they are different, then liberation is impossible, since of two different things—*jīva* and Brahman—one cannot become the other.

72-77 (E41-44; T35-39). Still another variety of this view agrees that liberation comes through knowledge only, but construes "knowledge" as something that results from an action, namely, meditation enjoined by the Vedas. But as we have pointed out, action requires plurality and so contradicts the very nature of the Self, so it cannot produce liberation. Furthermore, a Vedic injunction to meditate will have no effect on one who has abandoned everything but Brahman and sees no plurality everywhere. Again, all Vedic injunctions are addressed to men of specific castes, yet on the assumption of the Bhedābhedavādin of type (1) all people of whatever caste are identical with Brahman, so those injunctions will make no sense anyhow.

Bhedābhedavādin : The *jīva* may know that he is identical with Brahman and still identify himself with his body (and thus his caste).

Answer : If the alleged knower identifies himself with his body it shows he isn't a knower after all—so of course *he* can perform actions. And if the idea is that this "knower" is the yogī who is the self of all actions, then since action is natural to him it can't be the intent of an injunction, any more than one can be enjoined to breathe!

78 (E44-45; T40-41). *Bhedābhedavādin* : Anyway, since Brahman is both differentiated and nondifferentiated, a combined-path view is possible, for knowledge, has reference to Its undifferentiated aspect and action to Its differentiated aspect.

Answer : No, since difference and nondifference are inconsistent with each other. Furthermore, since presumably I can pick either property as truly characterizing Brahman, I choose His "undifferentiated" aspect and conclude that Brahman must be subject to frustration, being identical with all things including those subject to frustration; indeed, Brahman must be the supremely miserable thing, since all frustrations anywhere apply to It !

80-84 (E45-48; T41-44). Another reason why liberation cannot be attained through action is this : (1) the *prārabdhakarman* of a present birth can be exhausted by experience, and (2) the bad karmic results that are not scheduled to be experienced in this birth can nevertheless be destroyed through certain penances (*prāyaścitta*). But no one can exhaust results laid down by actions in infinite numbers of previous births, and in any case no one can avoid performing an occasional *kāmya* act. Nor does scripture ordain any such command as your position would require.

Objection : The karmic results can be destroyed by performing *nityakarmans*.

Answer : No. On your own view *nityakarmans* have no results. And scripture does not support the notion that *nityakarmans* destroy the results of previous *kāmyakarmans*. And the *kāmyakarmans* of this life don't destroy the results of *kāmyakarmans* of previous lives, any more than this life's sins eradicate the sins of previous lives.

85-89 (E49-51; T45-49). To return to the Mīmāṃsā objection (in stanza 16, see above, 9-21) he says that there are no injunctions to know in either scripture or *smṛti*. The reason might be thought to be that there are many passages speaking of ritual action but few speaking of knowledge. But we submit that this is not a numbers game; authoritativeness does not depend on preponderance of number of texts, and since there is only one Self and many actions it is natural that more texts speak of the latter than of the former. If on the other hand you seriously mean that you cannot find *any* texts, consider, for example, *Muṇḍaka Upaniṣad* I.2.12.

Objection : In texts like *Bṛhadāraṇyaka Upaniṣad* I.4.7 and II.4.5 scripture enjoins men to gain Self-knowledge through meditation.

Answer : No. True Self-knowledge is the very nature of the Self and cannot be subject to man's will. Not being the subject of an action it cannot be enjoined. Even if there could *per impossibile* be such an injunction, it could not be a direct or novel injunction (*apūrvavidhi*), but only a regulative (*niyamavidhi*) or restrictive (*parisaṃkhyāvidhi*) one, since we can meditate on the Self only after we have excluded the not-Self.

As for the remark that "we admit no other authorities"—that is the babbling of one whose mind is asleep. The Self is self-revealed and thus does not depend on any *pramāṇa*—including scripture—to give us knowledge of It.

91-96 (E52-55; T50-53). As for your claim (in stanza 17, see 9-21 above) that "Jaimini interprets scripture as entirely exhausted in injunctive purport," you misunderstand Jaimini. If Jaimini had thought that he never would have written the *Brahmasūtras*, for they are filled with passages that merely state the true nature of Brahman and explicate It further. So we assume that Jaimini believed that the two kinds of scriptural passages—injunctions and assertions—are each authoritative in their own sphere. A statement like "that art thou" can't be supposed to be an injunction.

Furthermore, it is just as hard to make room for ritual action on Jaimini's principles as on ours. Since Jaimini believes he is different from his body, he must be beyond the scope of injunctions to act, beyond the *pramāṇas*, beyond pleasure and pain, for there should be no relation at all between Self and body on his principles.

97-100 (E55-57; T53-55). And as for the Mīmāṃsā theory that "words can't make up a sentence unless they depend on a verb, and the verb signifies an injunction," that is wrong, since many scriptural sentences lack verbs signifying injunctions. And you cannot go around supplying such words indiscriminately, but only when the meaning requires them. Now in the sentence "that art thou" the verb "art" clearly is a copula and has no injunctive sense, and it is quite wrongheaded to misinterpret it to mean something else, just as it would be wrongheaded to misinterpret an occurrence of the word "run" to mean "give."

BOOK TWO

1 (E58; T57). In this Book the author will set right certain misunderstandings concerning the meaning of the great sentences of scripture, starting with those which relate to the word "thou" in "that art thou."

2-3 (E59-60; T57-59). *Objection* : There are four possible ways one might obtain the ultimate end: (1) by the not-Self suddenly disappearing; (2) by remembering a sentence that one had heard before; (3) by being reminded of a sentence one had heard before; (4) by merely hearing the words of the sentence. Among these, (1), (3), and (4) are merely due to chance; only in the case of (2) does Self-knowledge arise intentionally.

4-8 (E60-61; T59-61). *Answer* : The correct alternative is (4), since Self-knowledge arises directly from what is conveyed in the sentences themselves. Of course certain conditions must be satisfied in the one who hears them in order that the hearing occasion its result—the hearer must be nonattached from *saṃsāra*, must desire liberation and so have consulted a guru, must have learned to discriminate the Self from the not-Self by reasoning according to agreement and difference (*anvayavyatireka*).

9-23 (E62-66; T62-65). Sureśvara now reviews how reasoning as well as scripture attests to the difference between the Self and the not-Self, for example, the body, the internal organ (*manas*), etc.

24-27 (E66-68; T66-69). The one Self cannot function as subject and object simultaneously.

Mīmāṃsaka : When the Self is grasped by the idea expressed by "I" It is both subject and object.

Answer : No. The *manas* cannot have the Self for its object, since it itself is the object of the Self, like a pot.

Mīmāṃsaka : Your answer is in the form of an inference, but since inference depends on perception and our contention is that the Self is given in perception, your answer is beside the point.

Answer : But the Self is not given in perception. The thing corresponding to "I" is just an attribute (*guṇa*) of the internal organ. If that thing were the seer Itself it could not be an object, any more than knowing itself is an object. So, since perception does not corroborate your view, you should accept my inference as given above.

Furthermore, since the Self is without parts or activity the thing corresponding to "I" cannot be an attribute of It. Even if it could be such an attribute, it could not be known by the Self as object at the same time the Self is functioning as subject.

Objection : Then it comes to be object at some later time.

Answer : If by "it" you mean the subject, the Self, it cannot do so then any more than now.

28-45 (E68-74; T69-76). *Objection* : In the great sentence "I am Brahman" the word "I," according to you, refers to the ego sense; yet since it is expressly identified with the Self in the sentence, it cannot be not-Self, and so must be nondifferent from the Self.

Answer : Not all statements made using the term "I" are about the ego sense; for example, in "I am fair" the "I" refers to the body. What "I am Brahman" does is to *negate* the ego sense; just as "that stump is a man" negates the idea of stump, so "I am Brahman" negates the idea of the ego sense. And when the idea of the ego sense is negated, since it is the only root of our relation with duality, all duality ceases.

Furthermore, the ego sense is different from the Self in many respects—it is not eternal, it is subject to change, its knowledge is gained by inference and not by direct experience. Something with such properties cannot be identical with or even a characteristic of an entity whose nature is contradictory to them. Indeed, there is no real entity (*vastu*) other than the Self, whether it is taken to be nondifferent or different from the Self.

46-53 (E74-77; T76-79). Objects are constructions (*kḷpta*); the subject is *nirguṇa* Brahman; the ego (*aham*), both subject and object at once, enters the Self and causes error (*bhrānti*). All differences in the one pure consciousness are due to Its being appropriated by Its reflections. Just as the sun, whose light is reflected in the rippling water as various things, is appropriated by those things and made to share their shape, motions, etc., so the pure consciousness, the Self, is appropriated by the many *buddhis* and made to share their properties, being considered attractive or repellent, etc. In this way it is the *ahaṃkāra*, sharing the characteristics of Self and not-Self, which is the root of all evil, even though there is no real relationship between it and the Self.

54-56 (E77-79; T80-83). The word "I" in "I am Brahman" has a secondary or figurative sense, analogous to the sense that "I" has in the sentence "I knew nothing" spoken by one who has woken up from a deep sleep; in both cases "I" has as its secondary (*lakṣaṇa*) meaning the highest Self. And it is appropriate that the word whose primary meaning is the ego sense be secondarily used to speak of the Self, for the ego sense is internal to everything else except the Self, is extremely subtle, and imitates the vision of the Self, and it cannot exist without the Self.

57-73 (E79-84; T83-90). We have just finished considering the Self as conditioned by agency, that is, by ignorance (*ajñāna*), for if we had discussed the pure Self itself we could not have applied reasoning to It at all. Likewise, we shall now consider the Self as witness, even though once again witnesshood is itself imagined (*parikalpita*) through *avidyā*, and we shall deny to the Self in this condition all forms of agency.

Philosophers notoriously disagree on most points. Yet at least they all agree in being concerned with direct experience (*anubhava*).

Objection : If experience is accepted as the Self we will be at fault whether we hold that the Self is subject to modification or whether we deny it. If it changes, it is noneternal; but if it doesn't, it can't be a knower (*pramātṛ*).

Answer : When smoke rises is space (*kha*) divided or not ? If not, the smoke isn't rising. If it is divided, what is it divided by ? The idea that the Self can be an experiencer (*bhoktṛ*) is an error due to the ego notion (*ahaṃbuddhi*), like the idea that the hills are moving when actually the boat on which one rides is. The Self illuminates everything, but "illumining" is not the name of an act; thus though changeless the Self can still function as witness. This witnessing Self is beyond time; thus, the kind of knowledge we experience progressively is grounded in the intellect (*dhī*) which is subject to transformations (*pariṇāmin*). The witness does not see, hear, or desire; it is without action, without effort, feels no pain or pleasure, nor is it subject to delusion, imagination, or memory. It never sleeps.

74-96 (E85-92; T90-98). By contrast, the intellect has form, exists for another, is temporal, indeed momentarily destroyed, dependent, and limited. The sufferer (*duḥkhin*) is not the witness: to suffer is to undergo change, and if the Self were the sufferer what would witness the changes? It is the pot that is born, remains, and is eventually destroyed, and not the space it seems to contain; similarly, birth, life, and death pertain to the *buddhi* and to me. The intellect's awareness is confined to the particular contents of the moment to which its attention is entirely limited; all such states occur within the eternal, motionless Self, since all require the illumination of that Seer, though they differ according to their specific content. The Seer in the *buddhi* of the Caṇḍāla is the same as the Seer in the *buddhi* of Brahmā; the apparent differences between those *buddhis* is due to the objects that each one illumines.

The capacity for suffering before true knowledge (*bodha*) comes from one's own body, not another's. Since even it turns out to be illusory, how can the suffering arising from the bodies of others affect one after true knowledge is attained? The whole universe, along with the ego sense, comes and goes before consciousness, and is thus as unreal as the lights seen when one presses his eyeball with his finger.

97-102 (E92-95; T98-101). We agree with Sāṃkhya that the whole of *saṃsāra* can be shown by reasoning to be not-Self. But we disagree with them when they derive all of it from *prakṛti*, for *prakṛti* is not-Self and quite distinct from the self-revealed Self. Rather, we hold that the locus of the world is in the failure to understand (*anavabodha*) the Self, an ignorance that is accepted only because of failure to inquire thoroughly (*avicāra*). Through an inference—for example, "things don't exist except when knowledge does, but knowledge exists when things are absent"—the Self and the intellect cannot only be distinguished, but it can be shown that the not-Self is unreal and that all common knowing involving *pramāṇas* and their objects (*pramāṇaprameyavyavahāra*) depends on *anavabodha* as its locus and so cannot grasp the Self as object. For in order to be known as object a thing must be known as different from oneself—but since the Self is oneself, who can know It as different? So, the distinction between Self and not-Self arises only on the level of the *pramāṇas* and is based on *avidyā*.

103-109 (E95-98; T102-104). *Avidyā* can be removed through the vision of reality (*tattvadarśana*).

Question : How do you justify that contention?

Answer : Everyone recognizes that awareness based on falsehood (*apramā*) is sublated by awareness based on veridical knowledge (*pramā*). In ordinary knowing sublation produces awareness of what was not known before, but since the pure Self is not an object of ordinary knowing the result of awareness of It is merely the destruction of *avidyā*, which is indicated (by secondary meaning) as a "result." Ordinary knowing involves three factors—knower, known, and knowledge. But they are all objects and require a witness that is different from all of them.

110-119 (E98-102; T105-109). *Objection* : The witness will need another witness to witness it, so an infinite regress will result.

Answer : No, since the witness, unlike the factors of ordinary knowing, is self-aware. It does not require something external to It as they do. Everything other than the Self is a magic show of duality, only apparently established through lack of inquiry. Now if *buddhi*, body, and objects are all inconsistent with the Self they must, from the ultimate point of view (*paramārthatas*) be assumed to belong to the scope of the sixth *pramāṇa* (viz., *anupalabdhi* or nonapprehension) (i.e., they don't really exist).

Objection : By what argument (*nyāya*) do you establish that?

Answer : The awareness of the intellect is established only by locating it in the eternal, changeless, self-established pure consciousness. The body and objects such as a pot depend (for their being made known) on the awareness of the intellect. Thus all not-Self is a false superimposition (*mithyā adhyāsa*) on the pure Self. The seeker for liberation, hearing from scripture "*neti neti*" ("not this, not this"), resorts to isolation (*kaivalya*) and like one awakened from a dream becomes awake to the Self and a stranger to the intellect, etc.

BOOK THREE

Introduction (E103-108; T111-114). We have shown that all this world from Brahmā to a clump of grass, marked by the knower (*pramātṛ*), the object of knowledge (*prameya*), the instrument of knowing (*pramāṇa*) and its result (*pramiti*), is nothing but a false superimposition. Between the Self and this world there is no relation except through ignorance (*ajñāna*). Wherever some positive relation or identity is asserted to exist between the world and the Self, such a passage should be interpreted as an injunction to perform symbolic meditation, just as the assertion "this earth is the *Ṛg Veda*," etc., should be interpreted as enjoining one to meditate on the earth as the *Ṛg Veda*, etc.

Now ignorance must be ignorance of someone about something, it must have a conscious locus and a content that it conceals. We have shown that only two categories exist—Self and not-Self. The locus of *ajñāna* cannot be the not-Self, for it is itself *ajñāna*; if it were the locus the arising of it in itself would not be an event of any significance, and worse, there could be no obtaining of knowledge; ignorance is also the cause of the not-Self, and it is absurd to suppose that the cause can exist only as supported by its effect. The same arguments show that the not-Self cannot be the content of ignorance either. So the locus and content of ignorance must be the Self.

The arguments adduced against the not-Self's being the locus and content of *avidyā* do not mitigate against the Self's fulfilling those roles. The Self is not itself ignorance, for It is pure consciousness. Again, if the Self is the locus of ignorance the arising of ignorance in that locus is a significant event, and there can be obtaining of knowledge through the Self's reflection in the internal organ. Nor is the Self the effect of which ignorance is the cause, since It is not an effect of anything, being eternal and changeless.

Objection : How can the Self be the object that ignorance conceals, since ignorance and the Self are incompatible, the Self being intrinsically knowledge, nonrelational, and productive of the very opposite of ignorance?

Answer : The Self seems to become separated (into knower, knowledge, known) only through ignorance, just as the rope appears to be different from the snake; in reality the Self, like the rope, is quite unaffected. Thus all duality disappears when ignorance disappears, and this arises from a man who understands the meaning of the scriptural texts hearing them. Thus the present Book explains the meaning of the sentences of scripture such as "that art thou," etc., by applying the method of reasoning through positive and negative concomitance (*anvayavyatireka*).

1-3 (E108-109; T117-118). When a man understands that the text "that art thou" means "I am Brahman" he loses his ego sense and his sense of possession, having grasped something that is beyond the range of speech or thought, since it depends not only on the direct meanings of the constituent words (e.g., "that" and "thou") but on their secondary meanings as well.

4-5 (E110-111; T118-120). *Objection* : You have argued that in order to understand the meaning of scripture a man has to give up ritual actions and apply methods of reasoning to the texts *before* he can hope to hear them (from his guru and so achieve liberation). Now this practice you recommend—is it something enjoined by scripture, or is it a natural inclination on his part ? If it is an injunction, and he does all these things and then fails to achieve liberation, he loses much merit. But if he takes up the practice from natural inclination no such fault ensues.

Answer : Our view is that he takes up the practice as the result of an injunction, for example, as phrased in *Bṛhadāraṇyaka Upaniṣad* IV.4.23, which commands men who have attained equanimity, etc., and have by reasoning recognized that the not-Self is unreal, to "see the Self"—to such a man who then asks "who am I" (*ko'smi*) scripture answers compassionately "that art thou."

6 (E111-112; T120-121). *Sāṃkhya objector* : *Ajñāna* is the false awareness that causes us to think that the body, sense, etc., are the Self, and it can be overcome by reasoning. So sentences like "that art thou" are pointless.

Answer : Awareness based on difference is the effect of *avidyā*, since in the witness there is no difference whatsoever. One should let the texts destroy it.

7-8 (E112-114; T121-126). *Another objector* : Since false awareness is just absence of awareness, what is it that the texts destroy ? Absence of awareness is not a real entity, so what is the cause of *saṃsāra* ? Not your "ignorance," since it doesn't exist.

Answer : Everything is unknown before our first awareness of it arises in the *buddhi*; it exists (then) through the one existent, and it is that existent which is that unknown thing. That existent is the Self, the reality that manifests itself as both knower and instrument of knowledge when there is desire to know and is revealed by Its own power—that is the unknown thing we speak of.

9-18 (E114-119; T126-132). *Objection* : The meaning of any sentence, whether ordinary or scriptural, is relational. Thus the understanding we get from a sentence like "that art thou" is necessarily relational, and from it we derive the idea "I am Brahman," whose meaning is to be analyzed in the same fashion that we analyze a sentence like "the lotus is blue" (i.e., as meaning a substance qualified by an attribute). That being the case, the idea of the inner Self, which leads to liberation, requires us to meditate (*nididhyāsana*) on such texts until a meaning arises different from the actual (i.e., relational) meaning they have.

Answer : Consider the sentence "the *ākāśa* in the pot and the *ākāśa* in the sky have the same locus." Here the meaning of the sentence is not a subject qualified by a predicate, but rather an entity not actually mentioned in the sentence, that is, the pure *ākāśa* unlimited by pot or sky. Likewise in the sentence "that art thou" we understand *directly* something going beyond the literal meaning of the sentence. This is true even though "that art thou" is a subject-predicate sentence and the one about the *ākāśa* is not; both manage to convey something beyond their literal purport by the same mechanism, that is, apparently referring to several things in order to speak of a single thing. Thus "thou" can't mean the *jīva* (as it would naturally be supposed to) since it is qualified by "that," i.e., Brahman, and "that" can't mean not-Self because it is apposite to "thou"; in this way the changeless consciousness and interiority that is the Self is collectively indicated—these properties are not qualifications or distinctions but intrinsic to the Self. When predicated of the *buddhi*, the ego, etc., they may be discriminated and contrasted as qualities, but when predicated of the Self they are not limitations of the Self, the Self is not affected by discriminations and contrasts, since in the Self consciousness and interiority are Its very nature.

19-21 (E119-120; T132-133). The way that the *buddhi* knows is contrasted with the way the Self knows. The *buddhi's* knowing consists of ideas that come and go; some of them are true, some doubting, some false. This flow of ideas is superimposed on the Self through delusion. That the Self is the witness underlying the stream of ideas is clear when one recognizes that an idea cannot be aware of itself after it disappears, nor can an idea know itself as it arises.

22-28 (E121-124; T134-136). First one must distinguish the Self from the not-Self by reasoning, and then hear "that art thou" if one hopes to achieve liberation. For if one construes that sentence in its natural meaning it is evidently false. But when one knows that the meaning must relate to the inner Self and not the not-Self, the words "that" and "thou" will come to be known to denote the same thing.

29-32 (E124-127; T136-137) *Question* : But since the body, etc., have been shown by reasoning to be not-Self why does one continue to suppose that they are the Self?

Answer : One doesn't. Not-Self and ignorance denote the same things, and when ignorance ceases the body, internal organ, etc., likewise cease. Only as long as one is in ignorance does one suppose they are either Self *or* not-Self. When they are destroyed one merely remains in one's Self, free from ignorance, having a kind of awareness that cannot be the meaning of any sentence.

33-42 (E127-132; T137-141). Reasoning alone does not serve to destroy *avidyā*; hearing scripture is required. The Buddhists who neglect scripture, even though they utilize inference, nonetheless end up in a denial of the Self. Scripture indicates directly and simply the Self, which cannot be known by the other *pramāṇas*. It also provides absolute certainty—wherever doubts exist you may be sure that the not-Self is present. Upaniṣadic support for these remarks is cited.

43-46 (E132-133; T141-142). It is through the functioning of the ego (*ahaṃvṛtti*) that one comes to know that one is Brahman, but the ego sense manages this by dissolving itself.

Question : Then when the ego sense is known why isn't the Knower known directly ? It must be because there is a contradiction between scripture and sense perception.

Answer : No, there can be no such contradiction, for the two means relate to entirely different subject matters. The senses are outer-direct, do not relate to the Self; scriptural texts like "you are that Real" (*tat sad asi*) are inward-direct toward the Self.

47-56 (E134-138; T142-148). *Objection* : The Self cannot be validly indicated by such texts as "that art thou" alone, since they are merely declarations and so require *pramāṇas* to make them authoritative. The relevant *pramāṇa* is the injunctions of scripture.

Answer : These declarative sentences are themselves scripture and constitute the *pramāṇa* in question; they do not depend on the other *pramāṇas*, and they relate to a subject matter beyond the senses, functioning by removing the idea that the other *pramāṇas* have any validity at all, waking us up as words may wake a sleeping man. Since the Self is eternally conscious It needs no other *pramāṇa* to reveal It. Perception and the others are irrelevant to It, since they point outwards toward the not-Self. The contrasts between Self and not-Self are once again reviewed.

57-58 (E139-141; T149-154). *Objection* : We can know the Self by inference, specifically, by noting the behavior and features of the not-Self and inferring the contrasting features of the Self. So the scriptural texts are beside the point.

Answer : No, for inference gives us only mediate knowledge.

Objector : True, but what possible addition could scripture make to the mediate knowledge we get from inference ?

Answer : Inference merely establishes the existence of the Self, but the Self is actually beyond existence and nonexistence (*sadasad-vyutthita*) and so must be learned from scriptural texts.

Objector : If that's all you mean, everyone gets "knowledge" of that every time he falls asleep !

Answer : No, for even in sleep ignorance is present; if it were not so everyone would become liberated merely by falling asleep.

Objector : One is temporarily liberated when asleep, and then returns when he wakes up.

Answer : That undermines the possibility of final liberation, since there would always be the possibility of returning.

Objection : A man *is* liberated when he goes to sleep; it is a different man who "wakes up."

Answer : No, since we all recognize that we are the very same person who went to sleep and while asleep had no experiences.

Objector : Well, if ignorance is present in deep sleep we should be aware of it during our sleep; since we aren't, it follows that it isn't there at all.

Answer : It is there, but there is nothing to manifest it, no operation of the internal organ (*antaḥkaraṇa*), since the internal organ is dissolved during sleep.

59-62 (E141-145; T155-159). The internal organ is the object of the Self's witnessing consciousness directly, but the Self goes on to take on the ego as mask (*kañcuka*), thus becoming (apparently) related to external objects by judging them as "mine," etc. The Self, that is, knows objects as "this" through the condition (*upādhi*) of ignorance, and then, becoming associated with the ego, knows them as "mine."

Question : How do you know this difference between the pure Self's awareness and that of the Self as associated with the ego ?

Answer : By reasoning, since the object as witnessed by the pure Self neither hinders nor helps the Self, and so is judged as a mere "this."

Neither of these two kinds of awareness (of object as "this" or as "mine") arise when *avidyā* is absent, for example, in deep sleep; only when a man wakes up does he have even the awareness that he knew nothing while asleep.

63-70 (E145-148; T160-165). In II.2-3 above we distinguished four ways of obtaining liberation, that is, four kinds of hearers. We consider here the fourth kind, the man who has repeatedly heard the texts so that he may understand their meaning. One may well ask, how can a final hearing convey something to him over and beyond what he has already gleaned by reasoning based on hearing them ? The answer is that it is like the tenth man, who didn't know he was the tenth. Just so, one may distinguish the Self from the not-Self by reasoning but not be directly aware that he is that Self because of ignorance, ignorance that is without a support (*nirālamba*) and contradictory to all reasoning and thus not something that can be investigated (*vicāra*). The direct knowledge of the inner Self that does not arise from the other *pramāṇas* destroys any need for investigations. "That art thou" produces knowledge (*pramā*) in the aspirant for liberation just as "you are the tenth" produces it in the puzzled fellow who is counting the company as nine. Again, both knowledges are incorrigible once they arise.

73-75 (E150-151; T165-167). *Objection* : If the Self is nondual as you say, why do the Upaniṣads continually refer to the Self as agent, knower, etc.?

Answer : To deny an erroneous idea one has to use language initially in such a way as to refer to it in order to deny it. Thus to deny that a post (mistakenly taken for a man) is a man one can't just say "post . . . post. . . .", but he has to make initial reference to the man in order to say "that is not a man but a post." Likewise, in the statement "that art thou" the terms "that" and "thou" initially refer to erroneous notions but scripture must make use of them in order to deny the error through their apposition. The universals connoted by the two words are in opposition, but as scripture intends them they are freed from their ordinary senses and come to consistently denote the same entity, that is, the Self.

76-80 (E151-155; T167-173). *Objection* : Admitting that the words are not here intended in their direct meanings and that the sentence "that art thou" would constitute a contradiction if they were so intended, nevertheless, it is still possible that in the sense intended by scripture that sentence indicates a substance-attribute relation, as does the sentence "the lotus is blue."

Answer : No, since both terms mean the same Self, free from duality and mediacy; since Brahman and Self are identical there is no room for a substance-attribute construction.

Objection : But if the word "that," for example, means nondual Reality, since it has no connection with anything else such as notions of suffering and duality, how can it negate them ?

Answer : We do not claim that what the word "that" denotes directly destroys the ideas of suffering and duality. What we do say is that the word "that" causes ignorance to be removed so that there is a waking-up to the fact of nonduality. The sentence thus teaches the Self primarily, and by implication denies the relation of the Self to *saṃsāra*, etc.

81-86 (E155-158; T173-177). Even if someone should insist that the scriptural sentence contradicts perception, we can always reply "all right, take it as a theme for meditation." However, if the sentence refers to a real entity it cannot be about an action to be done, even a meditative one. But scripture can't contradict perception, since they pertain to entirely different subject matters; thus they can both be *pramāṇas*.

Objection : But suppose the two *pramāṇas* speak about the same thing in conflicting ways ?

Answer : This cannot occur between scripture and perception. If a thing is perceived with the senses it cannot be known through verbal testimony, and vice versa; again, fallacious perceptions are corrected by more perceptions, whereas fallacious testimony is corrected by further texts. Nor must *pramāṇas* cooperate in order to be accounted as valid; if *x* is a *pramāṇa* it is so in its own right.

87-89 (E158-160; T178-179). In all this we have been allowing for the sake of argument that a limited and suffering Self can be validly attested by some *pramāṇa*; we have argued that even if it can be, this does not contradict the validity of scripture. In fact, however, such a Self is not known through any of the *pramāṇas*, for the *pramāṇas* can only deal with objects, never with the subject itself.

Even if we concede for the moment that the Self can be known by *pramāṇas* as limited and suffering, and that thus the sentences of scripture are contradicted by other *pramāṇas*—how in that case do *you* propose to interpret those sentences ? If you say, as meditative (*prasaṃkhyāna*), the upshot will be much worse than any meditation could avert. For if it is valid knowledge that the Self is limited and suffering meditation cannot change it; as a result, if one goes on to hold that the Self can lose its suffering nature, the Buddhist view of no-self will result. Again, if meditation negates the limited, suffering nature of the Self, how can it produce right knowledge, since such knowledge will contradict perception and the other *pramāṇas* ?

90-93 (E160-161; T179-181). *Objection* : When one has discriminated the Self from the not-Self by reasoning on the basis of the scriptural sentences like "that art thou," one then meditates on the ideas that result. When properly performed this improves on the kind of knowledge the *pramāṇas* can give us and generates perfectly valid knowledge. For example, one can meditate on the body of a woman and see beauty where reasoning suggests only matter and impurity, and the same method produces improved knowledge of reality, the difference being that in this case the knowledge is true.

Answer : No. All that meditation can produce is greater concentration of the mind, not new knowledge.

Objector : Through spiritual conviction (Alston's translation of *bhāvanā*) collected from repeated meditation one brings *saṃsāra* to an end.

Answer : Not altogether, for then the cessation of *saṃsāra* is a result and so cannot be eternal. After all, the belief that one is the *jīva* lasts for millions of years and yet it can be rejected on your own account; do you suppose that a conviction based on a little meditation in one life will withstand all pressures ?

Objector : Its ability to withstand all pressures arises from its Vedic authority.

Answer : No, since all it can do is to reveal things as they actually are; it cannot change the nature of things. So effects, whether of actions or of meditation, cannot be considered stable.

94-104 (E162-167; T182-188). Again, supposing for the moment that there is some felt conflict between perception and scripture, the former telling us that the Self is frustrated, etc., the latter that the Self is pure, nondual, etc., one must surely pick scripture over perception, since what perception and the other *pramāṇas* produce are judgments subject to error and subsequent rejection, whereas what scripture speaks to is self-illuminating and so eternally valid. But, as we remarked above, in fact two *pramāṇas* cannot contradict each other, being each valid in its own sphere. To suppose that they do contradict each other is a result of our ignorance, since there is no contradiction in reality. We do indeed mistakenly interpret our sense experience in a secondary sense, thus supposing that it is the Self and not the ego that is the knower of empirical objects, etc. As a matter of fact this shows that all use of language to indicate the Self is false; the Self cannot be directly named, and only a few words have primary meanings that make more appropriate than not their use to indicate the Self in a secondary way. Still, a false means may point the way if the other conditions are right, in this case if one is suitably disciplined before one hears the sentence "that art thou."

105-106 (E167-168; T189). *Objector* : You still haven't explained how a word that has no connection whatsoever with something can nevertheless produce right knowledge about that thing.

Answer : It is just as when we wake somebody up from sleeping by uttering his name. There is no connection between the name and the sleeping person who is "out of" his body when asleep—yet he wakes up.

108-109 (E169; T191). *Objection* : A false means cannot be a valid means for producing truth; for example, inferring the presence of fire from haze (mistaken for smoke) does not produce truth.

Answer : Empirical objects are neither real nor unreal, and yet they produce results; thus something can be (relatively) "false" and yet produce something (relatively) "real."

111-112 (E170-171; T192-193). *Objection* : How could *avidyā* ever come into being at all, since it depends on the pure, changeless Self ?

Answer : Well, it does; regardless of *pramāṇas* or reality it just stands there as if it were the Self!

116 (E172; T194). The objection "how can *avidyā* exist ?" is not legitimate whether it is asked before or after knowledge. Before knowledge it is evidently there, and after knowledge it is known to be nonexistent in all times—past, present, and future.

123-126 (E175-177; T196-199). *Objector* : Knowledge derived from words is mediate, but it becomes indubitable through meditation.

Answer : If meditation on the texts following upon reasoning does not produce direct knowledge in the first place, how can mere repetition of it produce it later on ?

Opponent : *Brahmasūtra* IV.1.1 directs us to meditate repeatedly, but what it means is that by continuing to study one may understand what was not understood on the first hearing.

Objector : If you refuse to admit that there are scriptural injunctions to meditate then *saṃnyāsins* are as much outside the scope of Vedic teaching as Buddhists are, and thus are liable to fall from grace, in which case they cannot become free from karma.

Answer : But we do admit that scripture enjoins us to hear and study the great sentences, so this objection does not apply.

BOOK FOUR

1 (E171; T201). This book repeats more briefly what has been discussed heretofore.

19-35 (E184-190; T208-215). Sureśvara quotes a number of passages from Śaṃkara's *Upadeśasāhasrī* in support of his doctrines.

41-42 (E192-193; T217-218). Quotations from the *Gauḍapādakārikās*.

43, 65-66 (E193; T218; E200-201; T225-226). More quotations from *Upadeśasāhasrī*.

72-77 (E203-205; T227-230). Concluding words paying deep respects to Śaṃkara.

DAKṢIṆĀMŪRTIVĀRTTIKA or MĀNASOLLĀSA

C. Markandeya Sastri writes: "It is not easy to accept this tradition (that Sureśvara wrote this work) after a perusal of the contents as well as perhaps language of this book."[12] He cites R. B. Amarnath Ray's opinion that the Dakṣiṇāmūrti hymn itself and this commentary on it are the work of Abhinavagupta and his disciple, since the work appears to teach the Kashmir Śaiva brand of idealism.[13] It refers to the thirty-six categories of Kashmir Śaiva, as well as other peculiar features of the Pratyabhijñā system.

"E" references are to the edition by Maheshananda Giri (Sridaksinamurti Samskrta Granthamala 2, Agra 1963). "T" refers to the translation by A. Mahadeva Sastri in *The Vedānta Doctrine of Śrī Śaṃkarāchārya* (Madras 1899).

CHAPTER ONE

1-3 (E3-6; T1-2). The invocation is addressed to Vināyaka, Sarasvatī, Maheśvara, Sadāśiva. The (Dakṣiṇāmūrti) hymn is addressed to the guru's own Self, than which there is no greater wealth, that Self who, having entered into the universe It created, remains in the mind (*manas*) of everyone.

4-7 (E8; T2-4). A student asks his teacher several questions: We say that things "are" and "appear." In what does this existence, this appearing, reside ? Do they reside in things distributively, or in God (*īśvara*), the Self of all ? What is God ? What is self (*jīva*) ? What is the "Self of all" ? How should the *jiva* understand It ? What is the means to that knowledge ? What is the result of that knowledge? And how can *jīva* and God be one ? How can the Self be the knower and doer of everything ?

8-15 (E14-22; T4-6). The teacher answers: All worldly things, which exist within (*antas*), appear as if without (*bahis*) by *māyā*, as reflections in a mirror. Just as, in dreams, the world exists in one's Self but appears to be external, so it is in the waking state too. Both kinds of objects (dream and waking) are impermanent and insentient (*jaḍa*). In dreams objects appear by the light one's Self—there is no other light; so the same is true of waking objects. And just as a man awake does not see the things he saw when dreaming, so when he attains true knowledge he does not see the universe. (*Gauḍapāda-kārikās* I.16 quoted here). When one gains Self-knowledge through scripture, the teacher's instruction, yoga, and God's grace he sees the world as within himself, just as one who eats food regards it as within himself.

16-20 (E25-26; T6-70). "What is self (*jīva*)?" The Self-consciousness (*cidātman*) becomes God just as a man in dream becomes a king, but just as when he is defeated by the enemy and spends what seems to him a long period of penance in the forest, its length only his imagination, so in the waking state that Self as *jīva* imagines his own world, unaware of the passing of time. Even God Himself, deluded by *māyā*, seems to have only limited power and limited knowledge. To be "God" is to be in control; to be *jīva* is to be dependent.

21-31 (E30-43; T7-11). All *jīvas*, being identical with Śiva, have awareness (*jñāna*) and action (*kriyā*). Having thus the powers (*śakti*) of God we infer the *jīvas* are God. Consciousness self-illumines itself in all awarenesses, like the light of the sun; if it did not, the universe would be dark, there would be no awareness. And if God does not act, how could there be any other activity? For action is either motion (*pariṣpanda*) or transformation (*pariṇāma*): motion becomes manifested as the result of consciousness moving toward the outside, whereas transformation involves change of condition, that is, of consciousness in awareness. Śiva appears as the all-knowing in Brahman, etc., and as varying degrees of awareness in gods, animals, and men. But when the highest Self is directly known all beings from Brahma down to the lowest plant are mere constructions (*kalpanā*) as if imagined in dream.

CHAPTER TWO

1-6 (E40-50; T13-16). *Vaiśeṣika*: Atoms combining together constitute the material cause of the world; it is atoms, not God, that make up the world, and changes are due to qualities (*guṇa*) producing like qualities in things. There are three kinds of cause: inherence, noninherence, and instrumental cause. Each effect resides in the place occupied by its cause.

7-8 (E51; T16). *Sāṃkhya*: The three *guṇas*—*sattva*, *rajas*, and *tamas*—constitute *pradhāna* (i.e., *prakṛti*) and so are the causes of creation, maintenance, and destruction of the world.

9-14 (E55-62; T17-22). *Answer*: Since existence (*astitva*) is found in every created thing (but atoms are not created), where do the atoms come from? Everyone admits that the effect is contained in the cause; therefore existence (*sattā*) and illumination (*sphurattā*), found everywhere (are the cause, not the atoms). Furthermore, (contrary to Vaiśeṣika) change involves the production of properties different from the properties a thing had before; (sweet) milk becomes (sour) curd, (thus the Vaiśeṣikas cannot explain change). Whereas on our account cause and effect, part and whole, genus and species, action and agent, etc., are all constructions (*kalpanā*) of just the one Light (*prakāśa*). Again, consciousness cannot arise from either atoms or *prakṛti*, since neither are themselves conscious things, and consciousness must be located in a conscious locus. Rather, milk is transformed into curds by God's power of activity (*kriyāśakti*) in the form of time (*kāla*), whereas the world comes to be by His power of awareness (*jñānaśakti*), involving the forms of knower, knowledge, and known.

15-16 (E63-64; T23). Awareness may be construction-free (*nirvikalpaka*), which illuminates real things, or construction-filled (*savikalpaka*), which takes many forms according to its illuminating verbal designations (*saṃjñā*), etc. Other forms of consciousness include imagination, doubt, error, memory, (knowledge of) similarity, guess (?-*ūha*) and uncertainty (*anadhyavasāya*).

17-19 (E65; T24). The Cārvākas accept one *pramāṇa*, perception. Kaṇāda and Sugata (i.e., the Buddha) accept in addition inference. Sāṃkhya adds verbal authority (*śabda*), as do some Naiyāyikas, whereas other Naiyāyikas add comparison (*upamāna*) as well. Prabhākara adds presumption (*arthāpatti*) to these, and the Bhāṭṭas and Vedantins add negation (*abhāva*) as well as presumption. The Paurāṇikas add to these inclusion (*sambhava*) and tradition (*aitihya*).

20-30 (E70-76; T27-29). The six Vaiśeṣika categories are enumerated, with their subdivisions. (The list is without surprises, except that the internal organ (*manas*) is not counted among the minute (*aṇu*) things along with the four kinds of atoms.

31-41 (E78-85; T29-32). Another set of categories (attributed to "theistic Sāṃkhya" by modern commentators) is expounded : it involves *māyā* =*pradhāna*) (other names are provided), which, with Brahman's consciousness reflected in it, produces *mahat*, time (*kāla*), and *puruṣa*. From *mahat* comes *ahaṃkāra*. From tamasic *ahaṃkāra* comes *ākāśa*, earth, fire, water, and air, as well as their associated qualities (sound, smell, etc.). From sattvic *ahaṃkāra* comes the *antaḥkaraṇa* and the sense organs. The *antaḥkaraṇa* comprises *manas*, *buddhi*, *ahaṃkāra* and *citta*, which have as their contents doubt, certainty, pride (*garvas*), and memory. The *devatās* (gods) for each of these, as well as for the various organs, are enumerated. From the rajasic *ahaṃkāra* come the action organs. These together with the five *prāṇas* (breaths) make up the twenty-four categories of Sāṃkhya-śāstra (i.e., fourteen organs, five breaths, and five elements).

42-43 (E86-87; T33-34). The Paurāṇikas count thirty categories by adding to the above twenty-four the following : *mahat*, time, *pradhāna*, *māyā*, *avidyā*, and *puruṣa*. The professors of Śaivāgama add to these *bindu*, *nāda*, *śakti*, *śiva*, *śānta*, and *atīta*.

44-52 (E88-97; T35-38). All these (categories) are constructions (*vikalpa*) that exist previously in the Self and that are displayed by *māyā* having the form of desire, awareness, and action. This is why every creature is (a) God (*īśvara*)—all changes come from their desires, awarenesses, and actions.

Objection : Do you mean that there are many Gods, one for each universe in succession like the seed and the sprout?

Answer : No. God, though one, creates without any instruments outside Himself, just as ancient yogis like Viśvāmitra created heaven by their mere will. God needs nothing other to create, nor does He need *pramāṇas* or organs for His awareness. He has absolute freedom (*svacchandakaritā*).

53-57 (E98-102; T38-39). If God were only the instrumental cause (*nimitta*) of the world, He would be subject to change and destructible, like a potter. On the other hand, if He has eternal qualities of the sort the Vaiśeṣika posits, for example, eternal will, then He would always be creating incessantly. Then *saṃsāra* would never stop, and the teaching about liberation would be pointless. So God's creation is all a display of *māyā*, and all empirical experience including teachings about bondage and liberation is likewise through *māyā*.

CHAPTER THREE

1-7 (E103-112; T40-44). How is it that existence and illumination have come to be joined (in experience) with the objects (of the world)? Questioning thus through the example (*nyāya*) of the prototype and the mirror, the teacher explains : Existence and light come from God; objects are inert, momentary, and almost nonexistent (*asatkalpa*); they appear (to our awareness) through the illumination of the Self. Or again, our multifarious awarenesses and their objects are tied to the *ahaṃkāra*, like pearls on a string. We cannot distinguish the world from its illumination, any more than waves can be distinguished from water. This awareness of objects, which is expressed by "I know (this object)," turns back and resting in the Self is expressed as "(this object) is known by me." And since products (pot) rest in their causes (clay), the world, indiscriminable from illumination, must rest in the highest Lord.

8-9 (E113-115; T44-45). The workings of *avidyā* are illustrated by use of both the analogy of the reflection in a dirty mirror, and by the analogy of pot-space.

10-18 (E116-124; T45-48). There follows a discussion of the meaning of "that art thou." "That" denotes the cause of the universe, whereas "thou" denotes the *jīva*. The relation between them is identity, as the identity between a person seen at one time and the same person seen at a later time. "That" and "thou" stand in the relation of apposition (*samanādhikaraṇya*), whereas the things these words mean should have a relation of qualifier and qualified (*viśeṣaṇa-*

viśeṣyabhāva). But since God and *jīva*, the primary *denotata* of "that" and "thou" respectively, cannot bear such a relation to each other, these words must be understood in a secondary sense (*lakṣaṇā*). The kind of secondary meaning involved here is "partial" (*bhāgalakṣaṇā*), partially including and partially excluding the primary senses of the words.

19-25 (E126-135; T49-52). Various other ways of construing "that art thou" are rejected. The sentence does not mean that the *jīva* is a part or mode of God, since God is partless and without change. Nor does it merely praise God. It does not speak of mere similarity between *jīva* and God, nor does it impute a causal relation between them, or a relation between genus and species, or between substance and attribute. And it doesn't merely recommend meditation.

26-32 (E135-150; T52-53). The Self, when mixed with body, organs, breaths, and ego sense, is regarded by ignorant persons as the self, just as fuel burning is regarded as fire itself. This is further explained through the teaching of the sheaths.

32-40 (E150-158; T53-55). Calling God and self cause and effect is to speak of them in their accidental (*taṭastha*) definition, like defining the moon to be on the branch of a tree. But the essential (*svarūpa*) definition of the Self is *saccidānanda*. When one becomes steady in the awareness that he is one with the Light, the Self of all, he reaches isolation (*kaivalya*) or liberation. Even if he only once has by chance the idea that he is the Self in all, he is freed from all his sins and is adored in Śiva's realm as Śiva himself. That great Self delivers all from *saṃsāra*, for He is God Himself.

CHAPTER FOUR

1-6 (E150-157; T56-60). *Objection* : The pot, cloth, etc., shine as self-existent, not through God's light.

Answer : Stanza 4 of the Dakṣiṇāmūrti hymn answers this. If the "I" did not shine in awareness there would be self-awareness of the form "I know." Then nothing at all would shine. Objects cannot exist by themselves; they depend on God for their being. If objects could shine by themselves, they would be shining all the time, or none of the time, which is contrary to fact. Again, if both conscious and unconscious things were self-luminous then both would perceive each other, in which case tastes could be grasped by the eye, etc.

7-22 (E159-177; T60-66). God is spoken of as the knower inasmuch as he appears through reflection in the two sides of the *antaḥkaraṇa*—the *kriyāśakti* and the *jñānaśakti*—like the dull and clear sides of a mirror respectively. *Buddhi* is like the clear side of the mirror because *sattva* dominates in it; thus it can take on the image (*chāyā*) of an object. Likewise the sense organs, because of their connection with the *antaḥkaraṇa*. The connection is made through the *nāḍis*, enabling the senses to proceed toward external objects. The center of the *nāḍī* system is the *mulādhāra*, located between anus and penis; there dwells the highest power (*parāśakti*) called Kuṇḍalinī or Sarasvatī, mother of breath (*prāṇa*), digestion (*agni*), sound (*bindu* and *nāda*). From the *mulādhāra* the *suṣumnā nāḍī* extends to the head. On its left and right are the two *nāḍis* respectively named *iḍā* and *piṅgala*, and these composed the basis of the *nāḍī* system (*nāḍīcakra*). Other *nāḍis* are described, and the *Kaṭha Upaniṣad* quoted.

23-27 (E178-181; T66-69). When the self perceives objects through the sense organs impelled by merit deposited in the *buddhi*, then that is the waking state. When the organs are withdrawn the self is aware of the traces laid down by waking experience, and this is the dream state. When even the *manas* is withdrawn the state is called deep sleep. But the Self is throughout covered by *māyā* and appears deluded, ignorant, etc. When the Self wakes up It is illuminated as *saccidānanda* in the awareness "I slept happily."

28-38 (E181-197; T70-72). Everything shines by the light of God; thus Brahman is called "*saccidanantam*." God manifests Himself as the ego in everyone. The ego has three forms : construction-free (*nirvikalpa*), pure (*śuddha*) and impure (*malina*). The first is the highest Brahman, without differences, like *ākāśa* without dirt. The second, pure ego, is manifest at the time of discrimination (*viveka*), when God is free from embodiment, etc., as *ākāśa* is seen when all the stars have faded away (in the early morning). The third, impure ego, is the Self conjoined with body, etc., just as *ākāśa* looks as though it is without illumination when pervaded by darkness. One should meditate on the first of these three; then the Self shines fully.

CHAPTER FIVE

1-8 (E198-209; T73-77). *Cārvāka* : Perception is the only *pramāṇa*; the only real things are the four elements (*bhūta*). There is no liberation; *kāma* and *artha* are the ends of man. There is no God or world beyond this one. The body is the self, for it is what is perceived to be born, grow, change, decay, and die, and it is based on bodily differences that all ascriptions of state (such as caste or order) are based.

Others say that the self is the breaths (*prāṇa*), or the senses, or the *buddhi*.

9-28 (E212-236; T77-83). *Answer* : The body is not the self, since it is visible and constituted. Nor are the sense organs the self, since they are mere instruments, like a lamp. The breath is not the self either, since there is no consciousness in deep sleep yet breathing goes on. And the *buddhi* is not the self, for the *buddhi* is momentary and dependent on something else for its illumination. Finally, the self cannot even be the aggregation of all these things, since if that were the case, when one of them were missing there would be no consciousness, but as we know, there are conscious blind and deaf people, etc.

28-32 (E236-240; T84-85). The size of the self is all-pervading; if it were only the size of an atom, it couldn't pervade the body, and if it were the size of the body, the youth could not be the same as the old man he becomes. Further, the self would be perishable.

32-36 (E240-243; T85-86). The notion "I am in the body" is a delusion produced by great *māyā*, for once God (*sadāśiva*) is seen, that delusion vanishes.

CHAPTER SIX

1-12 (E245-256; T87-92). (*Mādhyamika*): Everything is momentary and void (*śūnya*).

(*Buddhist Logician*): Everything is a momentary particular (*svalakṣaṇa*).

(*Ābhidharma Buddhist*): External objects are aggregates of atoms, whereas men, etc., are aggregates of the five *skandhas*—(1) *rūpa*, including objects and organs; (2) *vijñāna*, consciousness; (3) *saṃjñā*, including names, qualities, motions, ideas, and natural kinds; (4) *saṃskāra*, attachment, *dharma*, and *adharma*, etc.; (5) *vedanā*, including pleasure, pain, and liberation (*mokṣa*) (or delusion [*moha*]). There is no self beyond these five. There is no God, no creator, for the universe is self-made, born of momentary *skandhas* and atoms, one momentary awareness after another. The identity of things through time is an illusion, as is the idea of self and that of external objects.

13-20 (E257-268; T92-95). The sixth stanza of the Dakṣiṇāmūrti hymn is addressed to the Buddhists in order to refute them. If the cause of the universe be void, then the universe cannot exist at all, and would never have even appeared to exist. But then whom should one seek out as teacher, what constitutes the bondage we seek to be liberated from, who could be responsible for the illusion?

As to the theory of the *skandhas*—an aggregate, like a pot, requires a cause, a maker, and cannot make itself. And if identity through time is illusory, why should one initiate acting, since to act presupposes a belief that the motives of the action can be satisfied. The self is no more a nonexistent than *ākāśa*; both have functions, *ākāśa's* being to provide space, the self's to provide consciousness.

21-32 (E269-283; T95-99). "The Self is recognized in deep sleep," we say, and the passive construction implies that the Self knows itself through itself. It is only *māyā* that precludes self-awareness in deep sleep; the Self always shines as the lord of the adjuncts such as the body, etc. Liberation is the removal of this *māyā*.

CHAPTER SEVEN

1-8 (E284-294; T100-103). *Question* : If the Self is to be established on the basis of recognition (*pratyabhijñā*), what is this recognition and what is its purpose ? Why isn't recognition counted among the *pramāṇas* ?

Answer : Recognition is a judgment of the form "this is the same thing as that" by which we cognize once again something we have seen before. In the case of the Self we recognize the omniscience, etc., of the Self by casting aside the notion that It has only limited awareness, etc.—notions produced by *māyā*. By remembering experiences in former births a newborn animal knows enough to seek its mother's breast. This proves that the Self must have been there then and must be here now in order to have husbanded the trace (*saṃskāra*) of the former experience.

9-20 (E295-310; T103-108). *Question* : Then recognition means memory. How can mere memory be authoritative in proving the existence of the Self ? For if memory be accepted as authority then anything's existence can be proved (since one can remember anything whatsoever).

Answer : Memory (is not itself recognition; rather it) provides us with the materials whereby we can recognize the persistence of the same entity (the Self) through time. Recognition is the right knowledge (*vidyā*) that unveils the Self from Its *māyā*; thus recognition underlies all the *pramāṇas*. It is the awareness that one is God.

21-33 (E315-328; T108-112). How the world is a result of false attribution is explained. The other theories of error—that in error the content is real, or that it is nonexistent, etc.—are refuted, and it is concluded that error cannot be defined—if it could be, there would be no error. The universe is superimposed on the Self through error, and when the error is removed the self-luminous Self, unaffected by this error, is recognized for what It is, that is, Maheśvara. This truth is attested to by *smṛti*, by perception, by tradition, etc.

CHAPTER EIGHT

1-12 (E326-345; T113-114). *Question* : If nothing actually exists apart from the Self, how can practical affairs (*vyavahāra*) come to be? Who is bound, who liberated? By what cause does bondage occur? What is the definition of *māyā*?

Answer : This has been answered in the foregoing, but it will be repeated in brief again as in this science repetition is no fault. To attribute causality to the Self is like saying Rāhu has a head. All notions of difference are false, caused by *māyā*. "False" means sublated by right awareness. Even the guru instructing his pupil is appearance only, though a false idea—as in the Upaniṣads—can cause enlightenment, as an image of God, a painting or a reflection can illuminate their originals. All practical affairs are the result of *māyā*. But *māyā* is sublated, like deep sleep, by Self-knowledge.

13-16 (E346-349; T116). "*Māyā*" is a name for an appearance that is contrary to reason. It is not nonexistent, since it appears; it is not existent, since it is sublated. It is not different from consciousness (*prakāśa*), and it is not identical with consciousness, since it is inert (*jaḍa*). It is not composite, since no parts caused it; it does not lack parts, since its effects are and are made up of parts. *Māyā* is like a harlot; she deceives a man only as long as she is not scrutinized.

17-28 (E350-360; T116-118). The mind (*manas*) is subject to the three states—waking, dream, deep sleep—and because of these it acts and is bound by the results. But the Self is not bound by the mind's doings, any more than the sun is affected by smoke, vapors, etc., covering it, though it looks as if it is, so the Self is untouched by *māyā* though It seems to be. It is like a boy whirling around and around and seeing a world containing hundreds of moons; so the *jīva* sees this whole universe revolving in various forms due to the *vāsanās*. By practicing yoga and freeing the mind from contents a man turns away (*nivṛtta*) from the world and becomes a *jīvanmukta*.

CHAPTER NINE

1-6 (E361-368; T119-122). *Question* : How does this *māyā* cease?

Answer : Through devotion to God. Eight of the thirty-six forms (*mūrti*) of God (mentioned at II.31-42 above) are visible to all, and it is contemplation (*bhāvanā*) of these that is taught. The body of Maheśvara is made up of the thirty-six principles, as is a man's body; the distributive (*vyaṣṭi*) mind pervades his body, and so should be thought of as the entire Self. By devotion to this distributive form one obtains the collective (*samaṣṭi*) form, as has been ten times taught in scripture.

7-20 (E369-376; T122-125). A number of parallels between the collective or macrocosmic, and the distributive or microcosmic, forms are now detailed.

21-48 (E377-397; T125-132). The eight limbs of (*Pātañjala*) Yoga are now reviewed, and it is explained how the yogi progresses.

CHAPTER TEN

1-25 (E398-416; T133-138). The nature of godliness is expounded through recapitulating the eight *siddhis* (as in Pātañjala Yoga). These powers come to one who sees his Self in all, though one should not seek them for their own sake.

PAÑCĪKARAṆAVĀRTTIKA or PRAṆAVAVĀRTTIKA

This is supposed to be a commentary on a work of Śaṃkara's, but the ascription of the *Pañcīkaraṇa* to Śaṃkara is extremely dubious, as was indicated above. There is no other good reason to suppose Sureśvara authored this *Vārttika* other than that the original was his teacher's work. Furthermore, the commentary as well as the original work involves several kinds of yoga—*mantra, laya, haṭha, rāja*—which suggest a different origin later than Śaṃkara's time. It is primarily concerned with the analysis of the sacred syllable (*praṇava*) "*om*" as a basis for discipline leading to union with *saguṇa* Brahman, and is thus not really concerned with Śaṃkara's Advaitic views, though it is not clear that it is necessarily incompatible with them either.

"ET" references are to the edition and translation published by the Advaita Ashrama (2d revised edition), Calcutta, 1972.

1-2 (ET 9-11). Concentration on "*om*" is here expounded for liberation seekers. The highest Brahman existed alone. Then, with its own *māyā* superimposed upon It, It became, as it were, the seed of the universe.

3-11 (ET 13-18). From Brahman arose *ākāśa*; from *ākāśa*, air; from air, fire (light); from fire, water; from water, earth. *Ākāśa's* only quality is sound; air has sound and touch; fire has those two plus color; water has those three plus taste; earth has those four plus smell. From these arose the great, all-pervasive principle called Sūtra. These elements also produce the gross (*sthūla*) elements, which in turn produce Virāj. This process is known as quintuplication. It proceeds as follows: each (subtle) element is divided in two, and one of these two is divided into four. To one-half of each element is added one quarter of each of the other four halved elements. Thus each resulting gross element is one-half constituted by a single type of subtle element, the other half constituted by four equal parts of each of the other types of subtle elements (e.g., gross *ākāśa* is one-half subtle *ākāśa*, with the other half composed of equal parts of air, fire, water, and earth). And so on.

The effect of the gross elements is Virāj, which is the gross body (*sthūlaśarīra*) of the disembodied Self.

12-13 (ET 18-19). The same Brahman appears in three forms because of error (*bhrama*)—in forms pertaining to the gods (*adhidaivika*), pertaining to the body (*adhyātma*), and pertaining to the elements (*adhibhūta*).

14-29 (ET 19-29). Awareness of objects arises from the sense organs aided by the appropriate gods. Awareness having sound, etc., for its content is called the waking state. There the aspects pertaining to the body are the organs—auditory, visual, tactual, etc.—the aspects pertaining to the elements are objects—sounds, sights, touches, etc.—and the aspects pertaining to the gods are the deities associated with each sense. This analysis is extended to cover the action organs as well as the sense organs. Speech takes sounds as objects and has Agni as its god; the hands take touches as objects and Indra is their god; the feet take places gone to as objects and Viṣṇu is their god; excretion takes excrescence as object and Death is its god; sex takes women, etc., as objects and Prajāpati is its god. The mind (*manas*) takes thoughts as objects and the Moon is its god. The *buddhi* takes as object what is ascertained (?-*bodhavya*) and its god is Bṛhaspati. The ego sense (*ahaṃkāra*) takes the ego as object and its god is Rudra. *Citta* has as object that which one is conscious of (*cetavya*), and its god is the knower (Kṣetrajña). Likewise, ignorance ("darkness," *tamas*) has as object its evolved forms (*vikāra*), and its deity is God (*īśvara*). Thus is to be understood the waking state.

30-31a (ET 29-30). The *viśva* (referred to in Śaṃkara's first verse) should be seen as (identical with) Virāj so that difference (*bheda*) will be removed.

31b-37a (ET 30-33). The subtle body is now explained. It has five sense organs, five action organs, and four internal organs, that is, the *manas*, *buddhi*, *ahaṃkāra*, and *citta*. The *manas* is that which considers (*saṃkalpākhya*), the *buddhi* ascertains (*niścayarūpa*), the *ahaṃkāra* provides awareness of self, and *citta* is that which conducts contemplation (*anusaṃdhāna*) of memory. There are also the five *prāṇas* and five subtle elements. These five groups (sense organs, action organs, internal organs, *prāṇas*, and subtle elements) together with *avidyā*, desire, and karma, constitute the eight parts of the subtle body of the innermost Self.

37b-38 (ET 34-35). Dream is explained as the state when the

sense organs are inactive, when consciousness (*sphuraṇa*) appears as both grasper and grasped and possessing awareness arising from traces laid down by the waking state. That which possesses the notion of both (the dream state and the subtle body) is called *taijasa*, which should be identified with Hiraṇyagarbha.

42-43 (ET 37-38). When the *buddhi* rests in its causal state—like a banyan tree in its seed—when all awarenesses are withdrawn, that state is deep sleep. That which has the notion of both (deep sleep and the causal body or ignorance) is called *prājña*, and one should identify it with God.

44-49 (ET 39-43). Pure consciousness (*cidātman*) appears through delusion as many—*viśva, taijasa, prājña*, Virāj, Sūtrātman or Hiraṇyagarbha, and Akṣara (God). But *viśva, taijasa*, and *prājña* should be viewed as one with Virāj, Sūtrātman, and Akṣara respectively, in order that the nonexistence of difference be established. How this is symbolized in the "*om*" analysis is recapitulated following *Pañcīkaraṇa*, verse six.

50-65a (ET 44-59). Sureśvara repeats the *Pañcīkaraṇa's* verse six, on the nature of the Self as contemplated in *samādhi*. This contemplation culminates in direct awareness of the Self and is not possible without renunciation of the whole world of empirical objects. When one has come to see the Self nothing remains to be known—the Self is peace, bliss, without a second. One who achieves it becomes a *jīvanmukta*, liberated while living. Even when in carrying on henceforth in life he sees duality he does not really see it, since he does not see it as distinct from the Self; he sees it as unreal, just as one may see two moons knowing there is only one. The illusion of the body lasts up to the final experiencing of the results of *prārabdhakarman*. Scriptural passages are adduced to support this. After *prārabdhakarman* is exhausted the liberated one attains the status of Viṣṇu, transcendent reality.

PADMAPĀDA

Padmapāda is said to have been Śaṃkara's first pupil, and one who stayed with his master throughout Śaṃkara's career. Eventually, tradition affirms, Padmapāda was made the head abbot of the Puri monastery, but he did not stay there and in fact is alleged to have saved his teacher's life in the affair with Abhinavagupta.

His only known authentic work is titled *Pañcapādikā*. This title should indicate that the work covered five *padas*, and indeed there is a tradition, reported by Venkatramiah,[1] that after Padmapāda's complete commentary (*Ṭīkā*) on the *Brahmasūtrabhāṣya* had been completed it was burned to ashes by an unsympathetic uncle, and Śaṃkara himself was able to remember the *Ṭīkā* on the first five *padas*—that is, on Book One and the first section of Book Two—and dictated it to Padmapāda. However, Venkatramiah points out, no one has been able to explain why the work so named now consists only of comment on the first four *sūtras* of Book One, part one, and indeed Vidyāraṇya, who reports the above-related story, says himself that he is "not quite sure of the authenticity of the incident but that he is relying only on report."[2]

There are, however, indications that Padmapāda's commentary originally covered more than its present extent.[3] Furthermore, the fact that the known manuscripts break off at the end of the comment on *sūtra* I.1.4 without any ending verses suggests that the present state of the work is incomplete.

In the summary that follows, "E" references are to the edition by S. Srirama Sastri and S. R. Krishnamurthi Sastri in Madras Government Oriental Series 155, Madras, 1958. "T" refers to the translation by D. Venkatramiah in Gaekwad's Oriental Series 107, Baroda: Oriental Institute, 1948. The section headings constituted of a roman numeral followed by an arabic numeral correspond to the headings in "T." The work begins with five verses of invocation, not summarized,

PAÑCAPĀDIKĀ

FIRST VARṆAKA

I.1 (E7-14; T1-5). Śaṃkara's opening sentence (in the *Brahmasūtrabhāṣya*) explains what the subject matter (*viṣaya*) and purpose (*prayojana*) of the *Brahmasūtras* are by implication.

Objection : The subject matter is how to gain knowledge of the unity of the Self, and the purpose is the getting rid of the cause of what is not worthwhile. So what is the point of Śaṃkara's passages about superimposition ?

Answer : It needs to be shown that the cause of What is not worthwhile is not real and thus can be got rid of by knowledge; if it were real, knowledge would not avail, since knowledge can only remove nonknowledge (*ajñāna*). The *sūtrakāra* (Bādarāyaṇa) himself indicates that this is the case in *Brahmasūtra* II.3.29.

Objection : Then why doesn't the *Brahmasūtras* begin with verse II.3.29 ?

Answer : That passage is an answer to an objection against an interpretation of the *sūtras* which makes their meaning converge (*samanvaya*) (on Brahman), and thus that interpretation must be introduced first to make the objection relevant.

II.6-7 (E15-19; T5-6). *Objection* : Why doesn't Śaṃkara start his work with an invocation ?

Answer : From the meaning of Śaṃkara's introduction it is clear he has the Highest in mind, so what he says counts in effect as an invocation.

III.8-9 (E19-21; T6-7). Now Padmapāda quotes the opening sentence of Śaṃkara's commentary, "it is evident that the 'I' and the 'Thou' are different . . . . " like darkness and light.

Objection : What is the nature of this difference ? After all, in a dimly lit room both light and darkness exist to some degree, so the "difference" can't be "nonresidence in the same locus."

Answer : "Difference" means that there is no mutual relation between them as there is, for example, between a universal and the particulars in which it inheres. Since the "I" is essentially unconscious whereas the "Thou" is untransformable and unattached, neither can really take on the nature of the other.

IV.10-12 (E21-23; T7-8). " . . . as well as their properties." Although when two things are superimposed their properties must be too, still it can happen that properties are superimposed without their substrata, for example, if a deaf man should say "I can hear."

Superimposition is the appearance of the form of something in something that does not (really) have that form (*atadrūpe tadrūpāvabhāsa*). Thus it is false (*mithyā*). The word "false" has two meanings: it may signify negation or inexpressibility (*anirvacanīyatā*). Here it signifies negation.

V.13-15 (E23-26; T8-10). "... it is a natural propensity ....", that is, men's judgments and the language in which they are expressed involve it when they think and speak of "I" and "mine."

VI.16 (E27-30; T11-12). *Objection* : Since superimposition is said to be the product of false knowledge, how can it be said to be "natural," that is, beginningless ?

Answer : It must be admitted that the power of *avidyā* exists in both external and internal things by their very nature. Otherwise false appearances are inexplicable. Now this *avidyā* does not obstruct the appearance of the real nature of insentient (*jaḍa*) objects, since their failure to appear arises merely from the absence of any *pramāṇa* (operating to manifest them). Both before and after the "silver" appears (in the case of the shell being falsely perceived as silver) the actual nature of silver is perceived even though *avidyā* exists. Thus *avidyā* is only the cause of the appearance of something of a different nature (from the nature the thing really has). On the other hand, in the case of the inner Self Its nonappearance is due to beginningless *avidyā*, since that cannot be explained in any other way. And so it is that *avidyā* obstructs the appearance of Brahman in Its real nature in the inner consciousness and becomes the cause of the appearance of something of a different nature like the ego sense, etc. In this way superimposition is both beginningless as concealing the Self and a product of false knowledge, though not in the sense of being an accidental effect (i.e., superimposition requires *avidyā* logically).

VII.17-18 (E30-32; T13-14). *Objection* : In "that is mine" (cited by Śaṃkara as a case of superimposition) the word "that" refers to the body and is related to the ego sense as its property. Where is the superimposition in that ?

Answer : Since the ego sense is a superimposition its auxiliary (*upakaraṇa*) must also be so. When one is crowned king in a dream the trappings of royalty have no existence.

VIII.19-22 (E32-37; T14-16). The next section (of the introduction, concerning superimposition) is subdivided as follows: first the doctrine of superimposition is established, then its nature is outlined and its possibility defended, and finally its existence is demonstrated.

Objection : The first two parts are unnecessary, then, for only what is defensible and possible can be established by a *pramāṇa*, and if something is established, for example, by perception, there is no need to defend its possibility.

Answer : In this case, however, it is not enough merely to point to a man saying "that is mine"; one has to show what the cause is of that notion. As in the case of the shell-silver or double moon, *avidyā* is not experienced directly, but only when the notion has been sublated. But here the sublation is not found. So here the definition must be given first and then it has to be shown that such notions as these fall under it.

Objection : Even so, all that needs to be done is to prove the existence of something falling under that definition, nothing more. One doesn't need then to go on to show its possibility !

Answer : True. But an object may be known to us and yet because of another *pramāṇa* be judged not real (i.e., impossible). Likewise, one might doubt whether superimposition on the interior Self is possible on the grounds of an accepted *pramāṇa,* and this doubt needs to be removed.

IX.24 (E39-42; T17-18). "Superimposition . . . is the appearance in the form of a memory . . . ." That is, the object that appears is not remembered but is of the same kind as an object that has been seen before. So the meaning is that there is an appearance, in a manner that resembles memory, of something given to us in the past by a *pramāṇa.*

X.25-26 (E42-44; T19-20). *Objection* (by an *akhyātivādin,* say the commentators): When there is knowledge of *x* and only *y* is in contact with the visual organ, this must *be* memory (not just something like memory). Because of some defect in the capacity of the organ, silver (rather than shell) is remembered but is not recognized as a case of memory, and then this remembered silver is identified with what is being perceived because of a failure to discriminate between perception and memory.

Objector to the akhyātivādin : It can't be memory, since, for example, a boy who has never tasted anything bitter may because of sickness taste bitterness in something sweet !

Akhyātivādin : He must have experienced bitterness in some previous birth; otherwise he could just as well taste some taste heretofore unknown.

XI.27-30 (E45-48; T21-24). *Padmapāda* : What does it mean to say that it is "not recognized as a case of memory"? In fact the quality of being a case of memory is almost never experienced along with the object remembered, and so the fact that a given case of memory is not recognized as such is not sufficient reason to differentiate error from valid cognition.

Even in the occasional cases where memory of an object is accompanied explicitly with an awareness that it is remembered, expressed as "I remember," the awareness results from our having realized that this is an object we have seen before and so properly termed a "remembered" object, and so even here there is no notion that "this is a case of memory," and thus even these occasional cases do not give the objector any grounds. Anyway, in the case of superimposition it is not the object of a past *pramāṇa* that appears—what appears is a present object. So the knowledge of *x* when only *y* is in contact with the sense organ is not a case of memory, but a case of superimposition.

XII.31-36 (E48-50; T24-27). *Akhyātivādin* : If that's so—if silver (*x*) appears but it is shell (*y*) that is the supporting object (*ālambana*)—they are opposed, and this is an unattractive view.

Another objector (an *Anyathākhyātivādin*, according to the commentators): Why is it unattractive? Being a supporting object only means fitness for ordinary practice pertaining to consciousness, and here the shell indeed is so fit—so why can't it be the supporting object?

Akhyātivādin : Is the appearance of the shell in the form of silver correct (*paramārthika*) or not? If it is correct, there should be no sublation of it, but there is.

Anyathākhyātivādin : The appearance of silver is occasioned by a defect (in the organ) and is a transformation (*pariṇāma*) of the shell.

Akhyātivādin : That's silly—sublation does not occur after milk is transformed into curds, and once something has transformed into something else it doesn't return to its original form, whereas the shell become "silver" returns to shell.

Anyathākhyātivādin : It may—the bud becomes blossom when the sun shines and returns to the bud state at night. Likewise here.

Akhyātivādin : No, since on that analogy there would be no sublation—rather we would say "the shell has resumed its former state!"

Another party (an *Ātmakhyātivādin*): You (the *Akhyātivādin*) say that the silver is produced from an idea (*pratīti*) occasioned by some vitiated (*duṣṭa*) cause. But that's wrong, since whichever idea produces the apprehension of silver cannot be the one in which the silver is manifested, since they occur at different times. And it can't be produced by some other awareness altogether, since then the valid cognition of some other person might also manifest the silver.

Akhyātivādin : It doesn't matter whose awareness it is, if it's occasioned by a vitiated cause it can't have an actual silver as its object, and so by elimination it must be due to the failure to recognize it as a case of memory.

XIII.37-43 (E51-55; T27-32). *Anyathākhyātivādin* : But it has been well argued above that such failure to recognize never occurs anyway.

Akhyātivādin : Then why does silver appear when there is sense contact only with shell ?

Padmapāda (?-*Anirvacanīyakhyātivādin*): It's not that memory minus the recognition that it is memory arises in distinction from the perception depending on sense-object contact. Rather there is one awareness arising from the sense organ in combination with the traces (*saṃskāra*). More fully: the faulty or "vitiated" cause, having its ability to produce awareness of shell restricted, activates the particular traces, and the two together produce a single awareness and a single result. As a consequence the false silver-in-shell appears as the supporting object. So a false cognition has a false supporting object, and it is that which is sublated, for no sublation of the awareness itself occurs. The part played by traces in various types of awareness is easily discerned—in inference and in recognition traces combine with sensed contents to produce the respective kinds of awareness; the difference is that in those cases the awarenesses are valid because they arise from nonvitiated causes, unlike the case of error.

So the silver is made of *māyā*. If it had been real (*pāramārthika*) it would have been grasped by everyone, since its cause would not be vitiated. Whereas, given that the silver is made of *māyā* it follows that only those whose organs are faulty perceive the silver. The fact of the silver's being sublated also suggests its *māyā*-nature—for we sublated it by saying "this was not silver," not (as would be suggested by the *Anyathākhyātivādin's* view) "this was a different silver than the one we supposed," or by the *Ātmakhyātivādin's* view "there is no silver independent of consciousness."

XIV.44-48 (E55-59; T33-36). *Objection* : The (Advaita) definition of superimposition underpervades its *definiendum*, since it fails to extend to dream and sorrow (*śoka*); in these two false awarenesses there is no contact (of the senses) with anything that could be confused with something else. Indeed, the only cause is *vāsanās*, and so these are cases of memory, not "like" memory.

Answer : They are not cases of memory, for an object *is* immediately manifested.

Objector : They are not memory-*like*, since these awarenesses arise merely because of the traces born of previous *pramāṇas*.

Answer : Memory is just the appearance of a content arising from a previous *pramāṇa*. But here the internal organ (*manas*), being disturbed by sleep, together with particular traces activated by *adṛṣṭa* produces an awareness that has a false object as its content.

And the power of *avidyā* residing in immediate consciousness as limited by that (internal organ) manifests itself having that (false thing) as its supporting object.

Objection : Then the manifestation of the dream objects is internal only. But in our dream experience we are aware of (the object in a) delimited place, just as we are in waking, so that an internal locus will not serve to explain dream.

Answer : There is no fault here. For in the waking state also valid awareness is experienced as immediately interior, so that there is no difference between the immediately experienced and the awareness of a content, since they are both manifested in the same way. So even in the waking state an object is experienced just as intimately connected with internal immediate awareness; otherwise what is not conscious couldn't be manifested in awareness. For example, a pot in the dark doesn't become manifested except when a lamp lights it up.

That objects appear in experience to be distinct (from awareness) even in the waking state is the result of *māyā*. The whole world has its single locus in consciousness, and consciousness is without parts, since it has no spatial distinctions. So it is what is limited by construction (*kalpitāvaccheda*) that is manifested as worldly distinctions such as being limited, being internal, being external.

XV.49-51 (E59-60; T36-37). *Objection* : The definition (of superimposition) overextends to include the superimposition of Brahman on names. Since it involves neither a faulty cause nor the manifestation of a false object, it is not a superimposition (yet on your definition it must be).

Answer : True, it is not a superimposition, but that is because it is not an awareness (*jñāna*) but rather an act of the internal organ (i.e., a meditative act), for it is something done out of desire through the influence of an injunction. Awareness is dependent on facts; it is not possible to produce it or avoid it voluntarily.

Objection : It is evident that memory is voluntarily produced and that it can be suppressed by the internal organ.

Answer : True, but the effort of will, or of the internal organ, is directed toward bringing about or inhibiting the causes (of memory's arising) such as opening or closing one's eyes, but they are not operative in the production of awareness. So the meditation on names as Brahman is only "superimposition" through an injunction and for a result, like thinking of another man's wife as one's own mother in order to avoid sexual desire for her.

XVII.56-59 (E62-66; T40-42). In the definition of superimposition, if the phrase ". . . in some other place" were not to appear the definition would be compatible with there being no locus of superimposition.

Objection : Why is that view wrong ? Sometimes we see, for example, hairs without their having any locus.

Answer : No, for the light parts are the locus.

Objection : Well, then, let it be that the silver (in the shell-silver illusion) is the locus of awareness and the awareness the locus of the silver in a beginningless interdependence, like seed and sprout.

Answer : No, it is not like the seed and sprout, for there seed 1 depends on sprout 1, which depends on seed 2, which depends on sprout 2, etc., but here we have only two things. Anyway, even in the seed-and-sprout case one cannot conclude that they serve each other as locus—clearly we shall continue to search for their material cause (i.e., their locus). So the analogy is pointless.

Furthermore, when sublation occurs it does not involve mere denial, but denial of something in some locus. When we find out that this is not a snake but a rope our denial of snake is a denial of snake in this (rope). Even when one denies someone else's fundamental metaphysical concepts one means to say that the ultimate cause of things is not that but something else.

Or else, one can say that the locus of all negations and illusions is the witnessing Self. But the superimposed object is not nonexistent.

XVIII.60-61 (E66-68; T42-43). *Objection* : Isn't your view that everything is nonexistent ?

Answer : Who said so ? Our view is that the world is *anirvacanīya* and of the nature of beginningless *avidyā*. Still, we agree that at the dawn of *vidyā* the false object disappears altogether. It is not the case that it is known to be somewhere else, as the Naiyāyika thinks—when one says "this is not a snake" one does not become aware of the snake somewhere else.

XX.64-66 (E69-71; T44-46). Śaṃkara offers two examples to show that his definition "agrees with ordinary experience." The shell-silver example is intended to show how the ego sense, being illuminated by consciousness, comes under the scope of "Thou" and is then superimposed on the pure consciousness. The double-moon case is intended to show that the difference between *jīva* and God, in the form of the non-Self-nature of the *jīva*, is only appearance.

XXI.69 (E73; T47-48). *Objection* : By what *pramāṇa* do you know that there is a fault having *avidyā* as its nature and which veils the manifestation (of Brahman)?

Answer : We know this from scripture and from presumption

of the *śruta* kind (*śrutārthāpatti*). For example, *Chāndogya Upaniṣad* VIII.3.2, *Muṇḍaka Upaniṣad* III.1.2, etc., tell us. Again, since in scripture it is the *vidyā* of Brahman that is said to give release, by presumption one must conclude that it is *avidyā*, involving failure to comprehend Brahman, that causes bondage.

XXI.72 (E75; T49-50). *Objection* : Neither scripture nor presumption can prove this when they are contradicted by some other *pramāṇa*. But here it is contrary to reason that something without parts and self-illuminating should not be naturally manifested in appearance.

XXII.73-81 (E75-82; T50-54). *Answer* : This happens because of the false notion "I am a man."

Objection : If the idea of "I" has the same locus as the body, then the existence of an independent Self is impossible to prove, since we do not have such an idea and since scripture and inference cannot prove if perception is opposed to them. If you say that there is no such opposition since the idea of "I" is a false one, we answer—how do you know this ? Not from scripture or inference, since if they are right in this, perception is invalid (since it proves the reverse), and if perception is invalid then so are scripture and inference. Therefore anyone who believes in the Self must admit that the idea "I" denotes the Self and not the body, etc., or else they would be unable to prove the Self. And so the statement "I am a man" is not a false notion, but a metaphor.

Answer : Even if the idea of "I" denotes the enjoyer distinct from the body, etc., still that is not known to people for sure (*anadhyavasāya*), and so the superimposition occurs. An analogy is that the sound "*a*," though it reveals its true nature to us, is still—through superimposition occasioned by lack of understanding of that nature—thought to be characterized by *being a short vowel* (or *being a long vowel*). Just as experience alone suggests that the syllable "*a*" is a short vowel, so it suggests that the ego is the Self.

Objection : The cases are not alike, since in the former case experience helped by reasoning (*tarka*) tells us that "*a*" is different from *shortness* but not vice versa, whereas in the latter case it is evident that both body and Self are distinct from each other.

Answer : No, since if *x* is different from *y*, *y* is surely different from *x*.

Objection : Well, it is jugglery (*indrajāla*) to suppose that one who knows that two things are different on the basis of valid means of knowing strengthened by reasoning may yet judge them identical and not be speaking metaphorically.

Answer : Yes, it is jugglery; it is the work of *avidyā*. And that's why it is not a metaphor. The idea of "I" is properly about the Self, but denotes the body also through *avidyā*; thus even if reasoning distinguishes the two, the "I" idea continues to point to both, since they are both given in immediate awareness (i.e., perception) that is not affected by mediate awareness.

XXIII.84 (E84-86; T56). "The Self isn't nonobject . . . for it is the object of our notion of 'I' . . . . "

Objection : How can the Self be an object (*viṣaya*)? An "object" must be something external (*parāgbhāva*) which is made known as "this," as opposed to the subject (*viṣayin*), which is internal (*pratyak*), self-illuminating, and "not this."

Answer : The ego sense is that which has the notion of "I", and it is well known that it is made known both as "this" and as "not this." Can anyone disagree with this ?

XXIV.85-87 (E87-90; T57-58). *Opponent* (a Prābhākara): Surely the ego notion is not made known as "this." The knower, known, and knowledge (*pramiti*) are all immediately given; however, the known (*prameya*) is given as object whereas the other two are not. *Pramāṇa*, the activity of the knower, is inferred on the basis of the result (*phala*). Now in "I know this" the cognitive activity of the knower relates to the object (*viṣaya*) and not to the Self. The Self does reveal itself as "I" both in the result (the awareness or *pramiti*) and in the *viṣaya* (the pot, etc.,) through the instrumentality of the experiencing of the *viṣaya*.

Answer (by someone else, say a Bhāṭṭa) : No, the idea of "I" has the Self as its *viṣaya*; it is also the knower of that idea. So the Self is known as both "this" and "not this."

Prābhākara : That can't be, for the Self has no parts—so one part can't be knower and the other known—and It doesn't change—so It can't be first one and then the other. What is external cannot be Self, and so the Self cannot be the "this." So *pramāṇa* is inferred from experience (*anubhava*) that manifests both the "this" and the "not this."

XXV.88-94 (E90-97; T58-66). *Padmapāda* : Is it that (1) Self manifests itself as consciousness whereas experience manifests itself as unconscious (*jaḍa*) ? or that (2) both Self and experience manifest themselves as consciousness ? or that (3) experience manifests itself as consciousness whereas the Self is unconscious ? The first alternative is wrong, since if experience is unconscious the world will not be made known.

Prābhākara : No, the Self—the knower—being conscious, with the help of experience It makes known an object as "this" and itself as "not this."

Answer : How can the Self make something known using experience which is *ex hypothesi* unconscious ? There will also be an infinite regress if the Self needs the result of *pramāṇa* (i.e., experience) to manifest both the object and itself.

Now, as to (2): On this view the Self manifests itself and so does not need experience to help. If something is conscious by nature it doesn't make sense to say that it is only mediately perceptible and needs something else for its immediate perceptibility. Finally, like two lights one does not need the other.

Finally, as to (3): The view that Self is unconscious and experience conscious, that will not do either. For if (3) were correct each experience should be different from every other one *qua* experience, and they should all instantiate *experienceness* just as cows instantiate *cowness*. But it is quite clear that the experience of blue and the experience of yellow differ because of the differences in their contents and not *qua* experience.

Prābhākara : The difference (between experiencings) is due to destruction or lack of destruction (i.e., when experience of *x* occurs experience of *y* does not).

Answer : But the destruction of experience cannot be established, since experience is not something that is born (and so it can't be destroyed). This incidentally refutes the (Vijñānavāda) theory of extreme similarity (*atisādṛśya*) being responsible for our failure to perceive the differences among distinct experiencings.

Thus we conclude that it is the Self alone that is conscious by nature, and It comes to be called "experience" when It is limited (*upādhīyamāna*) by different objects of knowledge.

Prābhākara : All right, let's accept that. It is then the ego sense that answers to the "not this," that is, the knower.

Answer : True, but the ego sense is not the Self (the ultimate knower) since if it were there could be no deep sleep, since the ego sense would manifest itself even in the absence of any object.

Prābhākara : We do experience the ego sense in deep sleep, but it is not experienced as "I" because of the absence of objects.

Answer : That cannot be right, for the thesis is that the ego sense is naturally conscious of itself; so it should naturally manifest itself whether an object is there or not. If it did in sleep we should therefore remember that when we wake up—but we don't do so.

Prābhākara : Well, we do remember it; we say "I slept well," and this shows we experienced the "I" in deep sleep as well as the pleasure that arose then.

Answer : True, we do say that, but the memory is (produced by

Self-awareness and) not produced from traces laid down by experiencing pleasure; rather it is because of the absence of any sense perceptions that we say this.

XXVI.95-97 (E98-99; T66-68). So, *avidyā*—denoted in various contexts as *nāmarūpa, avyākṛta, māyā, prakṛti, avyakta, tamas, cause, śakti, sleep, akṣara, ākāśa*—which has as its nature the blocking of the manifestation of the nature of Brahman, produces selfhood (*jīvatva*)—that of which the ego sense is a transformation (*pariṇāma*) having God as its locus; the ego sense is the locus of the powers of awareness and action, it is the only basis of agency and enjoyership, it is a light produced by its relation with unchanging consciousness and is self-illuminating; it is known immediately.

The ego sense is not an evolute (of *prakṛti*), for if it were it would have no relation to the Self and function as "this" only; but since it functions as both "this" and "not this" it is to be understood as falsely attributed to the Self because of its intimate relation with the internal organ (*antaḥkaraṇa*), just as the crystal falsely appears red because of its proximity to the hibiscus.

XXVII.98-100 (E100-102; T69-70). *Question* : Why is the crystal's red color false ?

Answer : Because if the rays of the eyes got to the flower they would reveal validly its red color. But one cannot validly perceive a color without its locus, nor even the reflection of a color without *its* locus.

Objection : The red color appears, but it is not that the crystal appears red.

Answer : Then the crystal's own color should also appear.

Objector : It is obstructed.

Answer : Then how could we see it ?

Objector : We see it because it is not discriminated from the red color.

Answer : Then we should see air (*vāyu*) when it is not discriminated from the color of a substance.

Objector : Then the red color actually qualifies the crystal !

Answer : No, for then when the flower is removed the crystal would continue to be red.

XXVIII.101-103 (E102-104; T70-72). The confusion of conscious and unconscious in the ego sense is immediately evident to the Self without taking It as an object. Thus the ego sense is viewed both as "this" and "not this."

(This case contrasts with that of a face reflected in a mirror.) There the point is that the face and its reflection are actually identical, so that the error comes in thinking them different (whereas in the crystal-flower case the redness of the crystal is similar to but not crystal-flower case the redness of the crystal is similar to but not identical with the redness of the flower). So by analogy in "I am agent" the "not this" (viz., the Self) is identical with Brahman (and not, as in the ego sense case, merely the apparent sharer of consciousness with Brahman).

XXIX.104-111 (E104-109; T72-76). *Question* : Why are they identical ?

Answer : For example, Devadatta has certain features when outside the house, and he is also recognized to have those same features when he goes inside. This recognition would not be possible if the "two Devadattas" were different; no more would it be possible to recognize Devadatta's reflection in the mirror if it were not identical with him—in that case we should have to say that the mirror transforms itself when the prototype (*bimba*) is nearby. Nor does the prototype leave its impression as does a seal, since the reflection is not (necessarily) the same size as the prototype, since there is no contact between the prototype and the mirror, and since if it were thus the mirror would continue to reflect the prototype even after it was removed.

Question : Perhaps the mirror is like the rolled-up mat that, having been spread out by some circumstance, rolls back up again as soon as the circumstance disappears.

Answer : The cause of the mat rolling up is the dispositional tendency (*saṃskāra*) it has gotten because of being rolled up for a long time, not the removal of any circumstance. So a mirror that had been in the vicinity of a certain object for a long time ought, by analogy, to remain with a tendency to reflect that object even when the object has disappeared—but we know that doesn't happen.

Opponent : Very well—the reflection is not a different object from its prototype; still, it is not really identical with the prototype, any more than the silver falsely found in a shell is really identical with real silver.

Answer : The cases are not the same, for in the shell-silver case the silver is sublated, whereas in the mirror-reflection case the reflection (though it disappears) is not sublated (i.e., we do not judge "this reflection is not my face").

Opponent : Well, doesn't "that art thou" sublate error ?

Answer : No, what it says is that the *jīva* (=reflection or *pratibimba*) has the same nature as Brahman (=prototype or *bimba*). If it were sublatory it would be negative—"thou art not" analogous to "(this is) not silver."

Prābhākara : How can some one thing that manifests itself completely in two separate places really be in both ?

Answer : We don't say that a single thing can really manifest itself completely in separate places at the same time, but we do say that such a thing is single. Its appearance as many is due to *māyā,* which is good at producing impossible appearances.

XXX.112-114 (E110-112; T76-78). *Objection* : Even when we apprehend the identity of the reflection with its prototype they still appear to be separate; likewise, even when we apprehend the identity of the *jīva* with Brahman their separateness still continues to be manifested; thus it cannot be got rid of.

Answer : Though Devadatta's knowledge that the reflection in the mirror is identical with his face cannot destroy the mirror—which is why the separation continues to appear—the *jīva's* knowledge sublating the difference between *jīva* and Brahman destroys all the adjuncts including the internal organ (*antaḥkaraṇa*) that is the reflecting medium.

Objection : Both the mirror image and the rose-colored crystal arise because there is a real object nearby—the mirror or the rose—whereas in the case of the supposedly false appearance of the *jīva* there is no such real object to serve as adjunct.

Answer : That's why scripture alludes to the case of the rope-snake.

XXXI.115-118 (E112-114; T78-80). *Opponent* : Even in the rope-snake case, though the snake is not there, the trace of some past experience of snake must be, and it acts as the adjunct.

Answer : Yes, and the difference is that in all three cases—mirror image, rosy crystal and rope-snake—traces must operate, but in the first two some other object is present whereas in the last one there is no such entity there. Still, from these three examples it is not made clear that the "prototype"—the face, the flower or the rope—may be unrelated to other elements in the situation. This point, however, is brought out in still another familiar analogy from scripture, that is, the example of the *ākāśa* in a pot, for there the "prototype"—the *ākāśa*—is unrelated to the pot, the adjunct.

Not that these examples are sufficient in themselves to prove the point; they merely assist the *pramāṇas* by removing doubts that may arise. And so we conclude that the Self is "not this" but is figuratively spoken of as "this" in practical affairs.

XXXII.119-121 (E114-117; T80-83). The mechanics of empirical perception are as follows: A functioning (*vṛtti*) of the internal organ (*antaḥkaraṇa*) in its object or "this" aspect points to an object (*viṣaya*). Apparent change (*vivarta*) occurs in both the consciousness and in the object that also manifests consciousness, so that the two come to appear as subject and object respectively of a cognitive act. The result of this act is an experiencing of the object, so that the result of the act has the same object as the act itself. As a result of its derived consciousness and its association with the functioning (*vṛtti*) the ego sense then assumes the role of knower (*pramātṛ*), and so it is said that the Self knows the object presented in the *buddhi*. This is also why, though the consciousness of the Self is all-pervading, it becomes restricted to a specific object and is differentiated as belonging to a specific person as his experience.

XXXIII.122-134 (E118-133; T83-100). *Objection* : If objective things like blue color are consciousness by nature (as is implied in the above) then how is that different from the Buddhist position ?

Answer: In this way: blue and yellow, etc., are mutually exclusive awarenesses, but immediacy (*aparokṣatā*) is not multiple in this way, since it is known as one while the manifestations of objects are different. So blue color, etc., are not consciousness by nature; if they were, then consciousness would appear as excluding other things, and that is not the case.

Furthermore, they (the Vijñānavādins) admit as different from the awareness of blue color a conceptual construction (*vikalpa*) that is immediate and has to do with what is internal, distinct from the external—that is, accounting for the "I" in "I know the blue." So they really admit that there are two things, mutually exclusive, that have the nature of grasper and grasped (despite their protestations to the contrary).

Vijñānavādin : No, our position is that "I know the blue" is constituted by three types of *vikalpa*—of "I," "this (blue)," and "(I) know," these all being mutually exclusive.

Padmapāda : If they are so different, how do they become related in a knowledge situation ?

Vijñānavādin : Indeed, they do not actually do so; since the (three) single *vikalpa* cognitions are momentary and pass away immediately, the complex cognition ("I know the blue") arises immediately thereafter along with *vāsanās* produced by the three. Momentary entities cannot act; only if "I" and "blue" were persisting beyond a moment could they actually come into relation.

Padmapāda : Then the awareness of ego ("I") must be a pure particular (*svalakṣaṇa*) lasting only a moment.

Vijñānavādin : Right. But the difference between the "I" awarenesses from moment to moment is not known to us (normally) because of the extreme similarity in the "I" awarenesses.

Padmapāda : If the nature of consciousness is to cognize difference, but difference is not cognized, then nothing will be known at all.

Anyway, there is no *pramāṇa* to prove that similarity is responsible for an awareness of a single thing.

Vijñānavādin : But since awareness of a single thing is (on our view) erroneous of course a *pramāṇa* doesn't prove it !

Padmapāda : Your position involves mutual dependence, for the illusoriness of unit cognition depends on similarity, which in turn depends on the illusoriness.

Vijñānavādin : True, but the same fault would occur even if the unit cognition were not erroneous, since if the postulation of similarity is contradicted by *pramāṇas* the unit cognition will be valid, whereas if the unit cognition is shown to be valid the postulation of similarity is too.

Padmapāda : No, for the validity of awareness is self-justified and doesn't depend on something else, so that the postulation of similarity is opposed to *pramāṇas*, since that postulation is only possible if we suppose that recognition is invalid.

Vijñānavādin : The momentariness of everything follows from the experienced fact that everything is destroyed the moment after it arises.

Padmapāda : The persistence of pot is proved by the experienced fact that it is recognized as still present at the moment after it arises.

Vijñānavādin : But persistent entities are not real, because they lack efficiency (*arthakriyākāritva*). For consider: a thing that persists, remaining the same in its nature, cannot produce any results either successively or all at once. Not successively, for since it is unchanging there is no cause for its not producing anything or everything at any time. And not all at once, for having done so it would have to vanish at the next moment (having exhausted its causal efficiency) and so would not be persistent after all !

Padmapāda : What is this efficiency that according to you is a necessary condition of existence ?

Vijñānavādin : It is the ability to produce awareness of its object in the next awareness in a series.

Padmapāda : If so, no awarenesses exist, since they are all self-revealed (*svasaṃvid*) and need no other awareness to produce awareness of their objects. Or if the series in question is different from the one characterizing the "cognizer" of the first awareness, then another's awareness cannot be grasped by the senses, and inference does not grasp what is real anyhow, since it only grasps universals. Or if, finally, the series is God's then God's knowledge becomes identical with that of the *jīvas*.

Vijñānavādin : What we believe is that causal efficiency means being the occasion of another moment.

Padmapāda : Then the last moment (before the end of the series) won't exist, and there will be no liberation. Or if "liberation" be construed as an awareness on the part of the omniscient (God), then the "last moment" will not be the last moment !

Reverting to one of your arguments above, that a persisting thing remaining constant in nature cannot produce effects successively; your argument is mistaken, since a cause cooperates with accessory conditions in producing things and so can produce different things because of differences in the accessories while remaining itself the same.

A discussion follows in which various opponents try to question the notion that a cause can cooperate with accessories.

Vijñānavādin : Our view is that the momentary cause (say, a seed) is competent to produce the effect (the sprout) without the help of any accessories, but the sprout only comes to exist in company with other things—things, however, that do not stand in the causal relation to the sprout, since they do not arise until after the cause operates and disappears.

Padmapāda : That can't be right. Your view says that cause C does not need accessories A to produce effect E, but that E occurs if and only if A occurs at the same time. Now either A is entirely accidental—in which case we best give up depending on causal relations since we can't depend on them—or else C plus A constitutes the real cause, that is, the collection of conditions (*sāmagrī*) sufficient for producing the effect.

Vijñānavādin : Well anyway, your view is really the same as ours; we hold that the awareness and its object are identical, and so do you.

Padmapāda : The difference, however, is that we hold there to be a permanent Self, and you don't.

Objection : (Since you hold that the object is presented immediately because it manifests consciousness,) you should hold that the object of inference is known immediately, since it too must manifest consciousness.

Answer : No, since in inference, unlike perception, the object is not operative in producing the functioning and so is not manifested in the inferential cognition—it may be far away or even absent at that time.

Objector : If the object is absent why should the inference infer it rather than something else ?

Answer : Because that object is related (by pervasion) to the *hetu* (which *is* immediately presented).

XXXV.136 (E135-136; T102-104). It is not that the Self becomes fit for superimposition only because It is the object of the "I" notion; It is so because It is immediately experienced.

Objection (by a Bhāṭṭa): It is known to us by a distinct awareness of which the Self is the object.

Padmapāda : Does that distinct awareness occur at the same time as the awareness, say, of the pot, or at a different time? If at a different time, then there is nothing to tell me which awareness (of pot, etc.) belongs to me and which to someone else. And it can't be simultaneous—the (Bhāṭṭa) knower-self (being without parts) cannot have two distinct objects immediately presented at the same time.

XXXVII.138-140 (E137-138; T104-106). *Objection* : Śaṃkara first explains superimposition and only then tells us that superimposition is *avidyā* whose opposite is *vidyā*—surely this is a perverse order of exposition !

Answer : No, for if Śaṃkara had started by expounding *avidyā* only the veiling aspect would have been brought out; by beginning with superimposition the positive potency (*vikṣepa*) of *avidyā* to distort reality is properly emphasized.

XLIV.166 (E160; T124). *Objection* : You say that superimposition is endless and yet you also contend that the study of Vedānta brings it to an end !

Answer : The meaning is that superimposition will be endless without the study of Vedānta.

XLVII.179-182 (E170-172; T132-135). *Objection* : Śaṃkara says one should "acquire understanding (*vidyā*) of the unity of the Self...," which sounds as if *vidyā* were something that could be acquired like a cow; but the implication is incorrect, since awareness of the unity of the Self arises at the same time it manifests its content.

Answer : That is normally so, but in this particular case the content is something that is counterintuitive to ordinary men, who do not find it easy to accept the unity of the Self. Thus they do not recognize Self-knowledge, even though it has arisen, and that is why *vidyā* requires *tarka* to make that knowledge certain. Logicians tell us that *tarka* is an accessory to the *pramāṇas*. *Tarka* is reasoning (*yukti*), specifically that which ascertains that the *pramāṇa* operates properly, that a sentence means what it does mean, what the content really is.

Objection : If so, the Vedantic teaching becomes invalid, since it. is no longer independent.

Answer : No; the teaching (viz., "that art thou," for example) is independently capable of producing indubitable Self-knowledge.

Objector : Then what's the point of *tarka* ?

Answer : It removes obstacles arising from the natural feeling that the doctrine of the unity of the Self is an improbably (or impossible) one

XLVIII.183-184 (E173-174; T135-137). *Objection* : Awareness of the identity of the *jīva* and Brahman is no different from the awareness that the self is distinct from the body. But since it is evident that bondage persists even when the latter awareness is acquired, it is also clear that the former one cannot remove bondage.

Answer : No, they are quite different. The knowledge of identity makes impossible the notions of enjoyership, etc., unlike the knowledge of difference from the body.

Objection : Then if *avidyā* disappears at the time knowledge of the identity of *jīva* and Brahman arises, the whole ego knot (*ahaṃkāra-granthi*, i.e., the body, etc.) should disappear, since it has *avidyā* as its condition.

Answer : No, for *avidyā* still remains as a result of the traces (*saṃskāra*), just as fear remains even after its occasion is past.

XLIX.185-186 (E174-175; T137-138). *Objection* : Not all the Vedantic texts expound *vidyā*. Some of them set forth various kinds of meditation (*upāsanā*) leading to progressive salvation (*kramamukti*), to divine powers (*aiśvarya*) and to the quick maturation of karma leading to heaven (*abhyudaya*).

Answer : True, but the object of these meditations is Brahman, so it is appropriate that exposition of Vedānta begins by explaining the identity of the *jīva* with Brahman, etc. Meditation on Brahman as limited by specific properties is enjoined for specific kinds of results in the other part of the Vedānta, but as that part is subordinate (to the section relating to *nirguṇa* Brahman) there is no defect.

SECOND VARṆAKA

I.1-2 (E180; T142). *Opponent* (an *Anārambhaka*): Since Jaimini (in the *Mīmāṃsāsūtras*) investigates the whole meaning of the Vedas as indicated by his opening sentence "Then therefore the inquiry into *dharma*," and since Brahman-knowledge is enjoined, it is included under *dharma*, and since there is no further doubt that would require further inquiry, the inquiry into Brahman (*brahmajijñāsā*) is already accomplished.

II.3-7 (E180-183; T142-145). Here some (*Ārambhakas*) say that there is a further doubt that requires inquiry into Brahman, and that doubt arises because some Vedic texts are not injunctions at all—for example, *Chāndogya Upaniṣad* VI.2.1, "Existence alone was this (world) in the beginning, my dear." Again, even injunctive texts that appear to enjoin meditation on the Self or Brahman cannot be construed that way, since the Self is not a thing that can change as a result of an action such as meditation—none of the functions of an act are appropriate with respect to It—It cannot be produced, gotten to, modified, or purified, since It already exists in pure form. Thus, since no action pertains to the Self, there must be a separate inquiry into It, and that is why the first *sūtra* here announces such an inquiry.

IV.10-11 (E184-185; T146-147). Others argue that, since the *pramāṇas* other than verbal testimony cannot grasp Brahman, and since verbal testimony (i.e., the Vedas) relates to something yet to be achieved and so cannot grasp Brahman, inquiry ends where the *Mīmāṃsāsūtras* end. In order to refute this notion this first sūtra is proposed.

V.12-15 (E185-187; T147-150). *Anārambhavādin* : Just from injunctive implication in "one should study one's own branch of the Vedas" one is enjoined to take up Vedantic inquiry. Though the Self cannot be the object of the injunction, nevertheless it is through meditation (on It) as enjoined by scripture that liberation is achieved.

VI.16-17 (E188-189; T150-151). Still another view is this: Brahman can be the content of Vedic injunctions. For example, when the Upaniṣad (*Bṛhadāraṇyaka Upaniṣad* IV.5) says that "all this is the Self," it doesn't mean merely to *state* that everything is the Self, since that would make the Self unconscious like the world, but rather that knowledge of reality arises from the elimination of non-Self, and so one should postulate (*kalpayati*) an injunction in connection with this passage that has the effect of "know all this as the Self."

VII.18-20 (E189-190; T151-153). *Anārambhavādin* : Even if there may be cases where postulating an injunction is appropriate, this can't be one of them (since the Self is not something to be achieved).

VIII.22 (E190-191; T154). Moreover, merely being enjoined to meditate on or know the world to be not-Self will not make the not-Self character of the world disappear.

IX.23-26 (E191-193; T154-157). *Ārambhavādin* : It is like the *mantras* (which are enjoined to be recited at the sacrifice to remind one of the factors involved in the sacrifice)—though the knowledge in question has already been achieved, one may be enjoined to acquire it again (so that liberation may ensue). So "all this is Brahman" can be construed as an injunction as well as expressing knowledge.

Anārambhavādin : This would result in contradictions—for example, Brahman would be both the primary object (because the knowledge expressed is of Brahman) and the subordinate object (because Brahman-knowledge is enjoined as a means to liberation). Again, Brahman will be both something to be achieved (in liberation) and something already achieved (as knowledge), something to be known for the first time (as the object of an injunction) and already known (since the knowledge is enjoined to be re-acquired).

X.27-29 (E193-195; T158-159). *Ārambhavādin* : If what you say is right, any injunction involving subordinate items will be useless (since contradictory). For example, since "sprinkle the rice with water" involves knowing the rice through some other *pramāṇa*—perception, say—on your reasoning this will constitute a contradiction.

Anārambhavādin : No, the analogy is not apt, since in the case under discussion ("all this is Brahman" construed as an injunction) the "subordinate item" is not known independently of the sentence, whereas in the example you allude to, the rice *is* known by perception prior to and independently of the injunction.

Furthermore, a part of a sentence (*avāntaravākya*, lit. "a lower sentence") cannot be (or express) a *pramāṇa.*

Ārambhavādin : Our opinion is that a statement like "Brahman is truth, knowledge, endless" (*satyaṃ jñānam anantaṃ Brahma*) gives us knowledge and may be also a subordinate item in an injunction.

Anārambhavādin : That is not right; the sentence you mention is complete in itself and provides knowledge, unlike subordinate items, for example, *arthavādas*, which are subsidiary to an injunction.

XI.30-32 (E195-196; T160-162). *Ārambhavādin* : But since immediate awareness (*anubhava*) does not come from verbal knowledge (*śabdajñāna*), an injunction is needed; verbal knowledge accompanied by an injunction can provide *anubhava*, the injunction being to the effect that one should meditate upon the verbal knowledge, a reminder of what the verbal knowledge provides.

Anārambhavādin : Then the injunction is hardly necessary, since the verbal knowledge is the *pramāṇa* and one naturally meditates on the truth once one has realized it.

XII.33-35 (E196-198; T162-165). The Ārambhavādin provides examples to support his opinion; these are rejected by his opponent.

XIII.36-37 (E199-200; T165-166). *Ārambhavādin* : Well, then, let us suppose that there are not two knowledges (an injunction and a verbal knowledge) but merely one, the injunction; it is by presumption (*arthāpatti*) that one arrives at the conviction of the truth that all is Brahman, presumption based on the truth that the injunctive knowledge must have an object.

Anārambhavādin : You've got it just backwards—surely the statement "all this is Brahman" naturally points to the truth, and it is crazy to set that aside to get at the same truth by presumption! Furthermore, the object of an injunction doesn't always have to be an actual thing; one may be enjoined to meditate, for example, "on speech as a cow," etc.

XIV.38-39 (E200-201; T166-167). *Anārambhavādin* : Therefore, we conclude that words like "Self," "Brahman," etc., refer to the self that is identical with the "I" notion, and that in the Vedas one is enjoined to meditate on It in ways that are conducive to liberation. So there is nothing further needed that would require an inquiry into the nature of Brahman.

XV.40-43 (E201-204; T167-169). *Padmapāda* : It might be so if Jaimini had commented on the whole of the Vedas; but he only concerned himself with that part concerning the effects of actions, not that part which describes reality. This is shown by his opening sentence, "then therefore the inquiry into *dharma*," in which Jaimini advises one who has finished study of the Veda not to leave his guru's abode but to remain and study *dharma*. That this is the correct way of understanding Jaimini is suggested by the fact that there are different views about what *dharma* is—some say it is *agnihotra*, others say it is other kinds of ritual action. Furthermore, the words "then therefore" suggest that one needs to understand what *dharma* is in order to use ritual action as a means to heaven, etc. But this proves also that *dharma* does not exhaust the meaning of the Vedas.

XVI.44-47 (E205-208; T169-172). Likewise, in Jaimini's second *sūtra* it is said "*dharma* is that object whose mark is *codanā*," not that *dharma* is the object whose mark is the Vedas in general.

Anārambhavādin : No. The point of using the word "*codanā*" is to indicate that by following the Vedic injunctions one will get to heaven.

XVII.48-51 (E208-210; T172-175). *Anārambhavādin* : Furthermore, both Jaimini and Śabara expressly state that action (*kriyā*) is the purport of the Vedas.

Padmapāda : True, they seem to say that, but in the context we must conclude they are referring to only a part of the Vedas when they speak thus, for Śabara also indicates that the need to inquire into *dharma* should lead one not to terminate his studies after studying the Vedas. Their statements should be read to show that the Vedas have some meaning, not that *dharma* is their only meaning.

XVIII.52-55 (E211-215; T175-178). Here some (Prābhākaras) say: The reason one should inquire into *dharma* is just that it is possible to interpret the Vedas in a wrong manner; thus the meaning of the first *Mīmāṃsāsūtra* is that one should inquire into the meaning of the Vedas and not only into *dharma*.

Padmapāda : If so, the first *sūtra* should have read "then therefore the inquiry into the meaning of the Vedas."

Prābhākara : The word "*dharma*" is used instead merely to indicate that the meaning of the Vedas serves human purposes.

Padmapāda : This doesn't fit with the subsequent *sūtras*, since the third *sūtra* and what follows it go on to justify the validity of the Vedas, and on your interpretation the person enjoined to inquire into the meaning of *dharma*, that is, the Vedas, already accepts the validity of the Vedas, so these *sūtras* would then be beside the point.

THIRD VARṆAKA

I.1-6 (E216-219; T179-182). *Objection* : The first *sūtra* means that an inquiry (*vicāra* or *mīmāṃsā*) into Brahman should be started, since that is the natural meaning of the word "*jijñāsā*."

Answer : No, the word "*jijñāsā*" means "desire to know" and need not be thought of as synonymous with exegesis (*mīmāṃsā*). Indeed, the natural sense of the word indicates the desire to gain knowledge resulting from inquiry, so that "*jijñāsā*" presupposes inquiry rather than naming it.

II.7-10 (E219-222; T182-184). *Objection* : Even so, the word "then" (*atha*) indicates the initiating of *jijñāsā*, since it announces that scripture (*śāstra*) should be begun to be studied in order to acquire Brahman-knowledge.

Answer : No one can desire to acquire Brahman-knowledge, since its acquisition precludes happiness, requiring cessation of all sense-object contact.

Objector : But with it one obtains bliss !

Answer : But one hasn't experienced that bliss, so no one will desire it in contrast to happiness of the sort that has been experienced. If that were so, furthermore, everyone would have long since abandoned sensory desires in favor of Brahman-knowledge.

Objector : Well, everyone knows that Brahman-knowledge produces supreme satisfaction (*paritṛpa*); thus a man who is satisfied will still desire this higher satisfaction, since desire arises from not being fully satisfied.

Answer : No, satisfaction breeds repulsion, since it destroys appetite for objects.

III.11-13 (E222-224; T184-187). *Objection* : Still, "then" does not indicate the unique antecedents, as is claimed by Śaṃkara, since they are already enjoined in the general mandate on everyone to study the Vedas, in which Brahman is the chief subject.

Answer : But all the general mandate enjoins is that people learn to recite the words of scripture; so that understanding the meaning of the Vedas is separate from the injunction to study them.

IV.14 (E224; T187). Even if we admit that understanding the meaning is the result of the general mandate to study, still that mandate can't be the reason why one desires to know Brahman, since prior to Vedic study the meaning is not understood. So we still need to know in advance who the *adhikārin* is, that is, who possesses the unique antecedents of the inquiry into Brahman.

V.15-17 (E224-226; T187-190). *Objector* : Then, since the mandate doesn't specify the *adhikārin*, it will become useless.

Prābhākara : Since it is the teacher who will benefit it is he who causes the general mandate to be enjoined on the student.

Answer : If so there will be no obligation on the student to study ! Furthermore, teaching is a noneternal or optional mandate, one among those that Brahmins may or may not perform, whereas Vedic study, like the sacred-thread investiture, is eternal, that is, obligatory upon the apprentice. So how can what is noneternal produce what is eternal ?

VI.18-20 (E226-228; T190-191). *Prābhākara* : The mandate to teach is not optional, since it is by teaching that the teacher earns his living.

Answer : That nonoptionality arises from the constancy of the teacher's desire for a result—that is, money, but it is still not obligatory in the relevant sense, since there are other ways of making money and one does not incur sin by not making a career of teaching.

VII.21-25 (E228-231; T191-195). *First objector* : Still, it *is* an obligatory mandate that a father should instruct his son; it must be that a teacher has an obligatory mandate to instruct his pupils.

Padmapāda : That latter "mandate" is only ancillary to the duty a man has to support his ancestors by instructing his son, investing him, etc. Furthermore, if the general mandate is understood as enjoined on the teacher to teach, and not the pupil to study, then if a teacher should suddenly die in the middle of the course of study the pupil will not be obliged or inclined to seek another teacher !

(This discussion concerning the proper interpretation of "then" in I.1.1 continues for several pages. Since it involves some very technical issues in grammar and exegetics it is not further summarized here.)

XV.52-54 (E245-247; T209-211). *Objection* : The word "then" indicates that the desire to know Brahman arises after the performance of purificatory rites.

Answer : That would be all right if the results of actions always purified a man in the same life and thus prepared him for Brahman-knowledge; but the purification may be due to acts performed in previous lives as well, as is attested by scripture.

XVI.55-56 (E247-248; T211-212). *Objection* : Very well, the precedence of ritual acts may include those in previous lives.

Padmapāda : Then there is no scriptural sanction for the view.

XVII.57-61 (E248-251; T212-215). And in any case, as Śaṃkara says, the results of inquiry into *dharma* and inquiry into Brahman are entirely different, so there is no basis for supposing any regular order of succession between their respective accomplishments.

Thus something must be postulated, denoted by the word "then," after which the inquiry into Brahman is to be taken up.

XVIII.62-66 (E251-253; T215-217). The four *adhikāras* or "unique antecedents" are explained.

XIX.67-70 (E253-255; T217-220). *Objection* : Since the scripture indicates that the results of meritorious acts are imperishable, discriminating men do not necessarily renounce the objects of enjoyment. Nor does desire for liberation arise merely from knowing that there is an unchanging, eternal Being. And these not necessarily occurring, there is likewise no regularity in such men practicing the virtues such as tranquillity, etc. Since the identity of the *jīva* with Brahman is unlikely—they are opposite in nature—no desire for liberation is likely to arise, especially as no positive pleasure will be found in that state. So the desire for liberation cannot be the cause of the desire to know Brahman.

Answer : The scriptural passages you interpret as indicating the imperishability of meritorious acts are mere *arthavādas*, being contrary to other scriptural passages that enjoy the support of reasoning. And scripture also indicates that Brahman is the supreme end of man.

(The remainder of this section is devoted to grammatical analysis of the words of the *sūtra*.)

FOURTH VARṆAKA

I.1-2 (E264-265; T229-230). *Objection* : "Is Brahman generally known to us or not ?" Because of this dilemma the present work has neither purpose, subject matter or relation. Something can be the subject matter of a given treatise only in case it has yet to be expounded. If Brahman is already known expounding It will be without purpose, and the exposition will lack a subject matter (in the technical sense). However, if Brahman is not already well known It cannot be expounded, since in order to explain something one must first have it in mind, that is, know it at least to that extent.

II.3-8 (E265-268; T230-234). *Answer* : "Brahman is known to us"—so the work has all three perquisites. (The rest of the section refutes various arguments purporting to show that all three need not or cannot be specified.)

III.10-15 (E268-272; T234-239). *Objection* : It is Vedānta only, and not the *śāstra*—that is, the Vedāntasūtras—that has the three perquisites, for it is Vedānta that concerns Brahman, whereas the subject matter of the Vedāntasūtras concerns the reasons why the Upaniṣads should be understood as producing Brahman-knowledge. *Answer* : The exegesis (*mīmāṃsā* or *vicāra*) assists one in understanding of Vedānta and thus of Vedānta's subject matter, that is, Brahman, just as preliminary sacrifices are auxiliary to the main one and so have heaven as their result too.

Objection : The analogy is incorrect, since in the sacrifice case the auxiliaries are necessary for the result, whereas in the present case one does not need exegesis to know Brahman—one can be enlightened directly by hearing a text, according to you.

Answer : Still, the exegesis removes doubts about the meaning of the text that is heard.

Objector : That must be wrong. A sentence that appears ambiguous has to be understood as expressing a single proposition (meaning), and ordinary methods of disambiguating a sentence having been applied, the sentence then produces knowledge of its meaning without further inquiry. You seem to suggest that scripture first produces doubtful or false awareness and then with the aid of exegesis produces certain knowledge, but that is not correct—rather scripture has by its own capacity the power to produce that knowledge before any such exegesis.

Padmapāda : It is true that the meaning of the sentence arises prior to exegesis of the *sūtras*. However, that meaning arises along with others that are contrary to it, due to the ambiguity of the words involved, etc., and as a result seems to belong in the category of doubtful assertions. In this situation exegesis sees to it that the contrary meanings do not arise when the sentence is heard and thus that doubt does not occur, and as a result it functions as an auxiliary to the understanding of the sentence, which is of course the direct cause of the certain knowledge. Since this is so, it is naturally important that the purpose, subject matter, and relation of the Vedānta-sūtras—that is, exegesis—be explained; otherwise one might not study it and so be deprived of the beneficial results of hearing the Vedantic sentences.

IV.16-23 (E272-277; T239-244). *Objection* : How is "Brahman . . . known to us"—that is, by what means?

Answer : Since it clearly (from context) does not mean a member of the Brahmin caste, or Brahmā, or the individual soul (*jīva*), etc., one concludes it means some other thing. The case is analogous to the word "heaven."

Objector : Nonsense: if that were so we would be able to know the meaning of any word merely by hearing it used, even though we had never heard it before and knew of it by no *pramāṇa*. The meanings of words like "heaven" are not made known merely from their use.

Answer : Suppose you understand all the other words in a sentence except one—you don't abandon all attempt to understand the sentence, but rather try to understand the meaning of that word from considerations of fittingness (*nigama*), etymology, and grammar.

Objector : No, these are appropriate in clarifying that a word is being used in an unusual sense—for example, from fittingness we may conclude that a certain meaning among others fits the context best.

Answer : Well, you admit that fittingness, etc., can be used to pick out one use from others; we add that even where a use has not been found prior to this point these means can be used to arrive at the appropriate one. And that is what Śaṃkara alludes to in concluding that from the meaning of the root "*bṛh*" (to become great) one may conclude to the features of Brahman.

V.24-25 (E277-278; T244-245). *Objection* : Even if one might get an idea of such an entity as Brahman through etymology, etc., still a mere word (*pada*) cannot establish the existence of anything, for it is not a *pramāṇa*.

Answer : True, and that's why there must be inquiry into it, through providing reasons such as the next one offered by Śaṃkara, "(2) because Brahman is known to each person as his Self . . . . "

VI.26-29 (E278-280; T245-246). As example of "mistaken opinions" the Lokāyata view is reviewed and criticized here.

VII.30-33 (E280-282; T246-247). And here those who think the senses are the self, or the internal organ, or *vijñāna*, or the void.

VIII.34-37 (E282-286; T248-250). Here the view of the Naiyāyikas that "there is an agent and enjoyer different from the body . . . . " is criticized.

IX.38-40 (E286-289; T250-254). And here the Sāṃkhya view "that that being is enjoyer only, not agent," as well as the theists.

X.41-43 (E289-292; T254-257). Thus there are all these conflicting opinions, and if one should inadvertently be misled by one of them he may miss gaining liberation. So there should be inquiry into Brahman—*brahmajijñāsā*—to avoid that.

FIFTH VARṆAKA

I.1-4 (E293-295; T258-260). It is clearly appropriate, then, that the *sūtrakāra* (i.e., Bādarāyaṇa) should go on to explain the nature of Brahman.

II.5-8 (E296-298; T261-263). Śaṃkara's commentary ("Brahman is the omniscient, omnipotent cause. . . .") expounds the essential definition (*svarūpalakṣaṇa*) of Brahman. Such definitions are of two sorts—indicative definitions (*upalakṣaṇa*) and descriptive definitions (*viśeṣalakṣaṇa*). An indicative definition speaks in terms of worldly properties existing separately (from the definiendum), and not in terms of the intrinsic properties (of the definiendum). So the descriptive definition (of Brahman) has still to be stated.

" . . . The world of name and form": each system of philosophy has its own categorial classification of things in the world; this represents the Advaita classification.

III.9-11 (E298-301; T263-265). All other kinds of change are comprised within the three alluded to here (viz., origination, maintenance, and destruction).

IV.12-14 (E301-303; T266-267). Śaṃkara in saying ". . . it cannot arise from an unconscious *pradhāna* . . . ," etc., suggests a way of proving the existence of God, namely, by inference through exclusion of all possible alternatives (*pariśeṣānumāna*).

V.15-17 (E303-305; T267-269). Kaṇāda and others think that this argument through inference by exclusion is sufficient by itself to prove the existence of God and ask what further purpose the Vedantic texts then have?

Answer: "This last argument by itself is not sufficient. . . ."

SIXTH VARṆAKA

I-II (E314-316; T277-278). "From (Brahman's) being the source of scripture" we conclude to Brahman's omniscience.

Objection: If so scripture is dependent on human intellects.

Answer: No; like Brahman it is changeless and eternal.

Objector: Then how can it arise from Brahman?

Answer: It doesn't "arise" in time, but it is dependent on Brahman, as the snake is dependent on the rope. The scriptures say that they were "breathed" by Brahman; breathing is a spontaneous activity.

Objection: Then how do you maintain that Brahman is omniscient?

Answer: Both names and forms depend for their manifestation (*vivartana*) on the power of awareness (*jñānaśakti*) of Brahman.

SEVENTH VARṆAKA

I (E317-318; T279-280). The alternative explanation of *sūtra* 3 is explained here. It is not a defect in a *sūtra* to be capable of expressing more than one meaning—indeed, this is an embellishment,

EIGHTH VARṆAKA

I.1-4 (E319-321; T281-283). "*Objection* : Scripture is not the means of knowing Brahman. . . . "

Objection to the objection : Since the Vedas are not written by human beings scripture needs no other *pramāṇas* to corroborate its validity.

Objector : True, but we find that *pramāṇas* sometimes conflict with each other—for example, when we see nearness and distance in a picture with our eyes but find this to be wrong when we attempt to verify it by touching the surface. Likewise perception and scripture conflict on certain points, and scripture must give way to perception. Furthermore, scripture is invalid since it is devoid of significance for human values. Since scripture (you say) relates only to something already accomplished it has no relation to action and thus no relation to future happiness or frustration, relevance to which exhausts the sphere of human significance. "All scriptural passages are . . . injunctive."

Furthermore, even in regard to objects that are not available to perception scripture, unless injunctive, cannot be a *pramāṇa*. For scripture can only illuminate its object by illuminating other objects that are grasped by other *pramāṇas* (since the object is *ex hypothesi* already in existence, if it has no relation to other things it is not graspable.)

II.5-6 (E321-322; T283-284). *Objector continues* : Now even if it is admitted that the Vedānta portion of scripture is ancillary to injunctions to meditate, still an omniscient, etc. Being cannot be proved, and so those passages should be understood as providing one with a description of the world-cause to use in the meditations enjoined in the general injunction that one should study his branch of the Vedas.

III.7-8 (E322-324; T284-288). *Answer* : The fourth *sūtra* answers all this by appealing to the congruence (*samanvaya*) among the Vedantic texts. What is this congruence? It is a connection among the words (of the Vedānta texts) that (1) does not involve any mutually limiting relation (*parasparānavacchinnārtha*); (2) does not presuppose an injunction (*ananyākāṃkṣā*); (3) requires no supplementation (*avyatirikta*); (4) has a single essence (*ekarasa*); and (5) relates to the uninflected stems alone. This connection (found in a sentence such as "that art thou") is like the connection between the words "this" and "that" in "this is that Devadatta," or as between the words "brightest" and "shining" in "the moon is that brightest shining thing." What is excluded by this "congruence" is a relation such as that between an action and its object.

IV.9-11 (E324-326; T288-290). *Objection* : The question related to the validity as exemplified in sentences such as those in the second sūtra ("Brahman is that from which birth, etc.")—so why are we now given a different illustration (by Śaṃkara) ?

Answer : He has a reason. In the second sūtra an accidental definition (*taṭasthalakṣaṇa*) of Brahman was offered; in a sentence such as "that art thou" the identity of Self and Brahman is being exhibited, not an accidental feature of Brahman.

Now, to revert to your objection about the dependence of scripture on other *pramāṇas*—this is to be initially answered by pointing out that Brahman is without form and so not apprehensible by the senses.

Objection : Yes, and since that is so scripture as a whole cannot be a *pramāṇa* by which to prove Brahman.

Answer : Even though words generally must relate to perceptible things, still, consider how a child learns the language. He does so by observing the behavior of those who hear a word. No other *pramāṇa* is involved at the time, and yet he learns to understand what the word means. Now once having learned how to use the word he may subsequently want to explain its meaning to someone else; he realizes that he understood the meaning himself by a *pramāṇa* other than verbal knowledge (viz., perception), and so in explaining how he can convey the meaning to someone else he (wrongly) supposes that two *pramāṇas* are involved—perception and verbal testimony; in fact, however, perception plays no role at all in bringing about the understanding of the meaning by his hearer. Therefore, at the time of understanding the meaning of a word it is not that one cognizes the word as denoting an object that is given to one by some other *pramāṇa*, but rather that verbal testimony produces the understanding without requiring anything else, and the perceptibility of its object is irrelevant.

V.12-13 (E326-328; T290-291). Anyway, how can one suppose that what is not of human origin and so requires the assistance of no other *pramāṇas* can be invalid?

Objector : As we said, because of the analogy of the picture, that is, *pramāṇas* sometimes conflict.

Answer : The analogy is faulty. The conflicting *pramāṇas* are alleged to be verbal testimony and perception, but the one—verbal testimony—is *ex hypothesi* without fault (because nonhuman in origin) and for the same reason there can't be any relevant faultiness in perception, say through a defect in the sense organ (since the object in question—Brahman—is not perceptible through the senses).

Furthermore, your implied analysis of the picture example is incorrect. In fact, touch corroborates sight in this case. For perception as *pramāṇa* provides knowledge of the picture free from the illusion of nearness and distance—an illusion that is produced by subtle shadings and that would disappear if those lines were deleted—and touch corroborates that perception.

Now just as scriptural injunctions are valid with respect to actions, their validity stemming from the fact that they discriminate something not otherwise known, so the scriptural statements concerning the actual nature (of Brahman) are valid with respect to the object of which they speak, since they too discriminate something not otherwise known.

VI.14-16 (E328-330; T291-294). *Objection* : Only injunctions are valid, since the subject matter of scripture is actions.

Answer : No, that will involve mutual dependence. The only way to prove that the Vedas have only actions as their subject matter is on the basis that only injunctive statements are valid, but the only way to prove that only injunctive statements are valid is to assume that the Vedas have only actions as their subject matter. It is awareness, not action, about which the question of validity arises; even in the case of perception, its validity stems from the fact that it makes something known that was not known before.

Objection : That is only because perception has nothing to do with actions. But for scripture, which does have to do with actions, the test of validity must derive from its satisfying some human purpose.

Answer : But there are two ways in which one may hope to have one's purposes satisfied. Either one hopes to perform some action that is capable of gaining him some desired end (or avoid some feared outcome), or else he hopes to remove an illusion that makes him seem not to have that which is already there (or to lack that which he already lacks). The first kind of end can be accomplished through action, the second only through knowledge. Both, however, lead to the satisfaction of human purposes—indeed, the latter kind leads to the highest human purpose.

NINTH VARṆAKA

I.1-2 (E331-332; T295-296). *Objection* : Even though scripture does provide proof of Brahman, still this occurs only in conjunction with injunctions to act, for otherwise communication would be impossible. Communication arises from human desire to obtain what he wants and avoid what he dislikes. Now obtaining and avoiding these does not necessarily come about merely by destroying their relation to pleasure and pain. Whereas one may obtain pleasure by recognizing the gold he forgot, or avoid pain by recognizing that the rope-snake is not a snake, one does not obtain pleasure and avoid pain merely by hearing scripture and appreciating the nature of Brahman. *Saṃsāra* still goes on as before. Meditation is still required after Brahman-knowledge. So even if we concede that in some empirical cases declarations have a human purpose, in the case of the Vedas that is not admitted, and the statements of Brahman's nature must be understood as subordinate to the injunctions to men to study and meditate upon Brahman.

II.3-4 (E333-335; T296-299). *Answer* : What is the source of that knowledge having Brahman as its object that is enjoined in injunctions to meditate ?

Objector : It is the continual calling to mind of the knowledge that arises from the study of the Vedas.

Answer : But we see no results arising from that !

Objector : By continually thinking on a desired object one may bring to pass a continual series of pleasures.

Answer : If so an injunction is without purpose (since one can have pleasure without it).

Objector : Our idea is that the injunction to continually think on it is laid down in order that one may gain direct realization (*sākṣāt-kāra*).

Answer : That is unreasonable : one cannot get a perceptual result (like direct realization) from verbal testimony, any more than one can get perceptual awareness of fire from inferential knowledge of smoke's relation to fire.

Objector : Direct realization does not arise from recalling only verbal knowledge, but rather from another awareness arising from that stream of recollections.

Answer : There's no proof of that.

Objection : Then let us say that what is enjoined is meditation (*dhyāna*) on that object made known by verbal testimony—in the very form in which it is thus made known—in order to produce immediate realization of it.

Answer : One does not directly realize the object on which he meditates if that object is beyond the range of immediate awareness. And even if we were to admit that it happens, that still wouldn't prove that the object is real—one can meditate on imaginary objects.

III.5-6 (E335-337; T299-300). *Another says* : What is enjoined is some extraordinary (*alaukika*) awareness not arising from verbal testimony.

Answer : We need to know what *pramāṇa* it is obtained by, and what its content is, in order to know what to say about it. But once we know that there will be no purpose to the injunction !

IV.7-9 (E337-339; T300-303). *Another opponent* : Brahman, which is beyond the world, must be meditated on, and the injunction is to that effect. By analogy with injunctions to meditate on certain divinities to get appropriate results, one is enjoined here to meditate on Brahman to achieve liberation.

Objection to this opponent : Since on your view liberation has a beginning it must have an end, which is wrong.

Opponent's answer : No, for scripture says "he does not return again" (*Chāndogya Upaniṣad* IV.15-6; VIII.15.1; *Bṛhadāraṇyaka Upaniṣad* VI.2.15).

Objection : But reasoning (*tarka*) leads to the opposite conclusion.

Opponent : If reasoning carries the day, we could conclude the nature of liberation by reasoning alone.

Padmapāda : As Śaṃkara says, " . . . knowledge cannot be viewed as a means conducive to some action designed to gain liberation," because liberation is not a result of action. If it were, like heaven it would be enjoyed in some body, but scripture tells us that liberation is disembodied. Again, if liberation is thought of as a high degree of pleasure resulting from action, then it would be noneternal as reasoning rightly intimates.

V.10-13 (E339-342; T303-304). Discussion of other scriptural passages bearing on this problem.

VI.14 (E342; T304-305). That liberation results from knowledge and not action is also agreed on by the Naiyāyikas.

VII.15-16 (E342-343; T305-306). *Objection* : Granted all this, we still contend that the knowledge of the identity of Brahman and *jīva* is not valid but imaginary; still, it is to be meditated on in order to achieve certain results that may themselves be understood as imagined.

VIII.17-19 (E344-345; T306-307). *Answer* : This is contrary to texts, such as "that art thou," which establish the identity as real.

IX.20-21 (E345-347; T307-308). *Objection* : Brahman in any case becomes the object of the verb "to know" and so It does have relation to action; so there is no reason It cannot be the object of an injunction.

Answer : No; the statements like "that art thou" do not provide knowledge of Brahman in which Brahman is the object of knowing, but rather they serve to remove from Brahman the distinctions born of *avidyā*; among those distinctions are those between knower, known, and knowing.

X.22-26 (E347-350; T308-311). Liberation is not something that can be produced. An action can produce something in one of four ways: by giving rise to it (*utpatti*), getting to it (*āpti*), changing it (*vikāra*), or purifying it. But action cannot produce liberation in any of these ways.

XI.27-34 (E350-354; T311-315). *Objection* : "But knowledge . . . is itself a mental act."

Answer : "No . . . they are entirely unlike each other." Knowledge involves an already existing object, action involves one that is yet to occur. For that reason, apparent injunctions (in the Vedas) like "the Self is to be seen, heard about, thought over, and meditated on" are not to be interpreted as injunctions but rather as *arthavādas*.

XII.35-37 (E355-357; T315-318). *Objection* : If the Vedas speak of anything other than actions they cease to be the Vedas.

Answer : The Self is clearly indicated by the Upaniṣads alone, not by any other *pramāṇa*, and so It has no relation with action.

XIII.38-40 (E357-359; T318-319). *Opponent* : *Mīmāṃsāsūtra* I.2.1 states that the Veda only speaks of actions, and that statements that do not do so are without sense. This is because it is through the action indicated that the denotative significance (*śabdaśakti*) is made known by inference; without the indication of action this inference would be impossible and we are then unable to understand the meaning of the words.

Answer : You don't properly understand the *Mīmāṃsāsūtra*. Consider : in the injunction "Devadatta, drive the cow. . . . " surely "Devadatta" is known to mean Devadatta even though by itself it does not prompt action; so Jaimini means, not that the words in declarative statements are without meaning, but that such sentences are without purpose. However, understanding that to be Jaimini's intent, it is still inapplicable, since one can hardly maintain that a sentence like "that art thou" is purposeless, as that sentence generates knowledge of the identity if *jīva* and Self.

XIV.41-46 (E359-364; T320-323). *Objection* : What you are saying is irrelevant. Of course a single word has various capacities to signify different things in different contexts—it may be an action or something else. But the context that supplies a univocal meaning to that word is, in the Vedas, invariably injunctive in character, as Jaimini and Śabara have both clearly stated, and as Śaṃkara has recognized (when he states the opponent's position as ". . . all scriptural texts are either injunctions, prohibitions or supplements to those two."

Answer : But there are many statements (even in the *karmakāṇḍa*) in which there is no word expressing action and yet it is clear what the words mean. And as for the statements of Jaimini and Śabara, they have been misconstrued—the context of the passages is confined to performance of sacrifices. Generally, the connection between words arises after the understanding of the words, and not the reverse.

XV.47-52 (E364-369; T324-327). Again, consider the sentence "a Brahman is not to be killed"; it does not enjoin an action, but rather enjoins refraining from an action; here the negative prefix attached to the word forms a new (contrary) meaning in connection with the word it precedes and has nothing to do with action.

"And you can't assume that the 'not' . . . itself denotes some other (opposed) action, for. . . what 'not' means is passivity—inaction. . . ."

XVI.53-54 (E369-371; T327-328). You objected earlier that since the Brahman-knower remains in *saṃsāra* statements of Brahman's nature are without purpose. However, we do not accept that: the Brahman-knower does abandon *saṃsāra* at the moment of realization, since *avidyā* ceases and because of that there is no longer any connection between the body and the Self. The apparent consciousness of objects that persists is due to the remaining karma, which has already begun to fructify (*ārabdhakarman*); it is like the continuing appearance of the double moon because of an eye defect even after one has recognized the error.

XVII.55-57 (E371-375; T328-332). Conclusion.

TOṬAKA (or TROṬAKA)

Advaita tradition makes Toṭaka a quiet young man named Giri, who became a devoted but not overly quick pupil of Śaṃkarācārya. He is credited with composing a work of 179 stanzas called *Śrutisāra-samuddhāraṇa.* Since practically all these verses are in the *toṭaka*, or anapastic meter, Paul Hacker speculates that the author of this work may be an unknown person, possibly a pupil of Śaṃkara, and that the person received the name "Toṭaka" because of the style in which the work was composed. There is also a brief set of eight verses, *Toṭakāṣṭaka*, ascribed to this person.

Hacker has compared the features of Toṭaka and Śaṃkara's Advaita and finds that they have striking similarities—Toṭaka, like Śaṃkara, does not speak of *vivarta* and fails to distinguish *pariṇāma* from *vivarta*; "*avidyā*" is used in Śaṃkara's way; "bliss" (*ānanda*) is absent in the description of Brahman. The form of the *Śrutisārasamuddhāraṇa* is like that of the Gadyaprabandha, or prose section of the *Upadeśasāhasrī*, a dialogue between teacher and pupil.

Hacker also mentions some reasons why Śaṃkara himself is not the author of the *Śrutisārasamuddhāraṇa*—the use of the Sāṃkhya theory of the *guṇas*, the invocation addressed to Viṣṇu as *iṣṭadevatā*, and an alien use of the word "*sphuraṇa.*"[1]

In the following summary "E" references are to the edition by R. Krishnaswami Iyer (Srirangam, n.d.). The work is untranslated. The summary is based on the German summary by Paul Hacker in B6956, pp. 156ff. The editor wishes to acknowledge the assistance of Ms. Edeltraud Harzer in preparing this material.

ŚRUTISĀRASAMUDDHĀRAṆA

1 (E1). The author bows to Hari, lord of the three worlds.

2-6 (E8-11). When one realizes that the world is ephemeral and becomes bored with it, one looks for something permanent. This cannot be discovered through ritual acts, for the impermanent course of the world is operated by deeds. Therefore the seeker wants to become a *saṃnyāsin,* to abandon all ritualism. The path brings him to a guru, who instructs him that the Self is not the body nor the internal organ nor the five sheaths, but an endless, qualityless consciousness.

7-13 (E12-18). The Self is changeless; the internal sense changes according to its different thoughts (*matibheda*). The relation between the two is illustrated by the analogies of reflection and limitation. The internal organ cognizes only when it is "colored" by objects (*uparāgam āpekṣya*). But all thought functions require an unchanging consciousness to make them evident. This consciousness is self-conscious (*svacit*), Self-consciousness (*ātmacit*). Thus the internal organ stands with external objects in requiring consciousness to make them known.

14-20 (E19-24). The internal organ has two practical (*vyavahāra*) functions—as object, and as subject, egoity (*ahaṃkāraṇa*). Foolishly, people misidentify it as the basis of ordinary life practices. First there is the notion "I see"; then the appropriate sense organ faces toward the relevant object, and so practical affairs are accomplished.

21-33 (E24-34). Is the ego sense a quality (*guṇa*) of consciousness (*citiśakti*) or of the internal organ or of both ? Not the first, for we have seen that it is the object of the Self, and a quality cannot become an object of its bearer (*guṇin*) or of other qualities, just as the qualities of fire (heat, light) cannot become objects of the fire or of each other. The Vaiśeṣika thesis that an eternal self can have non-eternal qualities is refuted. Thus the ego sense must be an attribute of the internal organ, standing in the same relation to the Self as do the other functions (sensing, etc.) of that organ.

34-45 (E35-46). What is the relation between the individual self and the highest Self ? They are identical, as the Upaniṣads attest. It is like the space in a pot and space *per se*—the former is not a part or transformation of the latter, and just as the pot-space gets its name from the pot, so the individual self (*jīva*) gets its name from the body.

The doctrine of creation of the world by the Self is also meant to convey the identity between self and Self. Actually, the world has no origin, since it is not true, and so teaching about creation could serve no human purpose if literally intended or understood.

46-106 (E46-96). Though the *jīva* is identical with the highest Self, a man requires something to awaken him to realization of that, just as Rāma, though really Viṣṇu, must be awakened to a realization of that by being praised as Viṣṇu. Now all the Upaniṣads teach identity, but "that thou art" is particularly apt for the purpose.

Some Vedantins object that "that thou art" has a different purpose. Some say (1) that it is an injunction to meditate on the highest Self by identifying It with the individual self. Others say (2) it is intended as a metaphor—it means "the individual self is like the highest Self." Others still say (3) it is a way of praising the Highest. Still others say (4) the Highest is but a variety of the individual self.

Toṭaka responds mainly to (1). For one thing, when injunctions are given, their injunctive force is clearly evident in the words, but there is no clearly injunctive word in "that art thou." Secondly, no one through worship or meditation can make something what it is not; worshiping, praising, meditating are all actions, and actions produce only impermanent effects; thus the self and the Self could never become identical by worshiping, etc. These points also meet (2) and (3). As for (4), the terms used in the Upaniṣads in alluding to the Highest show clearly that It cannot be reduced to the individual, that it is rather the other way around.

Toṭaka explains the meaning of "that art thou" in now familiar fashion.

107-115 (E96-102). The highest Self is explained not to be material in constitution; It is noncomposite, nonperishable, nondual.

116-132 (E103-117). The whole world of elements, objects, organs, etc., is unreal. Toṭaka appeals inventively (says Hacker) to a combination of *Bṛhadāraṇyaka* and *Chāndogya* teachings about the way in which the light of the Self sustains the world. Just as the gold is true, jewelry untrue, or the threads true, the cloth untrue, so whatever comes to be is untrue.

133-150 (E117-130). The reason the jewelry, cloth, and world are "untrue" is that nothing can be really produced. The product (*vikṛti*) is not separate from the original stuff (*prakṛti*), it is nothing in addition. So-called "products" are only forms (*ākṛti*) of the primal matter. Toṭaka challenges Sāṃkhya, which believes in real production, with the following argument: Was the specific character of the effect in the causal stuff before production or not ? If so, then the notion that by becoming associated with this new specific character a change has taken place is an erroneous notion. But if that character was not there before, then something new has arisen, and it will perish, having a beginning, and the Sāṃkhya view will not differ from Vaiśeṣika's. Toṭaka recapitulates the consequences of this in the manner of Gauḍapāda.

151-178 (E130-151). Brahman can only be characterized negatively, except for Its positive nature as consciousness.

HASTĀMALAKA

Hacker believes that it is dubious that a person with the name Hastāmalaka actually lived in Śaṃkara's time.[1] Tradition makes Hastāmalaka another pupil of Śaṃkara's and either the author or the addressee of the fourteen verse poem of *Hastāmalakaślokas*. We know nothing more.

Edeltraud Harzer has translated Paul Hacker's German translation, and since the work is short it may provide a fitting conclusion to this volume.[2]

HASTĀMALAKAŚLOKĀḤ

1. "Who are you, child ? Whose ? Where do you want to go ?
How do they call you ? From where did you come ?
Tell me that—that's for certain—for my
Pleasure; increaser of my joy are you !"
2. "I am not a man, nor god, neither a sprite;
Nor Brāhmaṇa, Kṣatriya, Vaiśya, Śūdra;
Nor householder, hermit, brahmacārin,
Nor pilgrim monk—, the awareness itself am I.
3. The inner sense organ is under management of the cause,
As cause lets the course of the world shine by the rays of the sun,
That which is like the space-ether, free from boundaries,
That which is the perpetual warrant, am I myself, my being.
4. As heat is for fire, the perpetual awareness is
For him essential; sensory stupor of activity
Effects by the One, that unchanging.
That which is the perpetual warrant, am I myself, my being.
5. As a reflection of a face in the mirror no being
Has a being-here (Dasein) without a countenance; so also is
The soul only a reflex of the spirit in the heart.
That which is the perpetual warrant, am I myself, my being.

6. When the mirror vanishes then also the reflection perishes;
Only the face remains, free from confusion, alone.
Thus remains, free from inner sense organ, the One without reflection,
That which is the perpetual warrant, am I myself, my being.

7. That really free from every thoughtfulness,
The thoughtfulness is for the thoughtfulness, whose
Nature is always closed to thoughtfulness;
That which is the prepetual warrant, am I myself, my being.

8. That which is pure spirit, radiating some light
Into many internal sense organs; that radiance—like the sun—
The one that is splitting itself on the waters of jugs,
That which is the perpetual warrant, am I myself, my being.

9. The sun bestows its light on all eyes at once,
Illuminating the things that seek light. Thus shines
The one awareness for many inner sense organs,
That which is the perpetual warrant, am I myself, my being.

10. The eye grasps only what is lighted by the sun,
The sun only the lightless things. The One
Makes shining that which is lighted by the sun for the eye;
That which is the perpetual warrant, am I myself, my being.

11. It wanders with the wandering waters, the sun;
It breaks itself in the lakes in the same way, manifold the One.
Thus breaks itself and flows in the hearts the One.
That which is the perpetual warrant, am I myself, my being.

12. That understanding covered by clouds of the dull man
Believes the sun to be lightless, covered with clouds.
Thus it seems to the foolish inner-sense-bound.
That which is the perpetual warrant, am I myself, my being.

13. That which does not touch any of the many objects,
That unity intertwined in all objects,
The eternal purity, clear and comparable to space-ether,
That which is the perpetual warrant, am I myself, my being.

14. Celebrations differ according to the encampment:
Thus you sit in the multitude of hearts;
Like moons wander along in the lowest waters—
Only in this way is your being changeable, O Viṣṇu !

NOTES

References given with "B" followed by a number are to items in Karl H. Potter (ed.), *Bibliography of Indian Philosophies* (Delhi : Motilal Banarsidass, 1970).

CHAPTER ONE

1. Cf. J. F. Staal, *Nambudiri Vedic Recitation* (Mouton : The Hague, 1961).

2. Sangam Lal Pandey, *Pre-Śaṃkara Advaita Philosophy* (Allahabad: Darshan Peeth, 1974), pp. 91ff.

3. *Brahmasūtra* I.4.20-22.

4. "*avasthites*."

5. S. L. Pandey, op. cit., pp. 21-27.

6. *Brahmasūtrabhāṣya* on III.3.53.

7. *Śabarabhāṣya* on *Mīmāṃsāsūtras* I.1.5.

8. J.A.B. Van Buitenen, B2853, p. 19, n. 53.

9. S. L. Pandey, op. cit., pp. 173ff.

10. Van Buitenen, B2853, pp. 19-23; also V. Bhattacharya, B1254.

11. For opinions, cf. V. Bhattacharya, B1254; Kane, B7789; Guha, B6664; Nakamura in *Acta Asiatica* (*Toho Gakkai*) 5 (1963), p. 69; Chintamani, B2054; V. A. Ramaswami Sastri, "Old Vṛttikāras on the Pūrva Mīmāṃsā Sūtras," Indian Historical Quarterly 10 (1934), p. 431 ff.

12. Cf. Van Buitenen, B2853, pp. 301-302.

13. Vedānta Deśika, *Tattvaṭīkā*, cited by Van Buitenen as on p. 149 of an unspecified edition.

14. On these issues cf. S. L. Pandey, op. cit.; Van Buitenen, B2853; S. Kuppuswami Sastri, "Bodhāyana and Dramiḍācārya—two old Vedāntins presupposed by Rāmānuja," Proceedings of the All-India Orientalists Congress 3 (1924), p. 465; Jacobi, B7535, p. 17; Kane, op. cit.; T.K.G. Aiyengar, "Upavarṣa and Bodhāyana," Journal of the Sri Venkatesvara Research Institute 2.1 (1941), pp. 1-8.

15. S. L. Pandey, op. cit., p. 180.

16. Ibid., p. 89.

17. Ibid., pp. 91-93, 203.

18. Van Buitenen, B2853, p. 28.

19. S. L. Pandey, op. cit., pp. 199-202.

20. Ibid., pp. 194-197.

21. On Bhartṛprapañca, cf. S. L. Pandey, ibid., pp. 210-226; Hiriyanna, B1044, B1045; P. N. Srinivasachari, B7303. On Brahmadatta cf. Hiriyanna, B1143, B1144; also "Two old Vedāntins" in *Indian Philosophical Studies II* (Mysore : Kavyalaya, 1972), pp. 17-25; S. L. Pandey, op. cit., pp. 238-243. On Bhartrmitra see S. L. Pandey, ibid., pp. 229-235.

22. At *Gauḍapādakārikābhāṣya* IV.100 and *Upadeśasāhasrī* II.18.2.

23. See the section on Gauḍapāda below for references to this literature.

24. For a discussion, see the section on Maṇḍana.

25. For example, consultation of Volume Two of this Encyclopedia, dealing with Nyāyavaiśeṣika (*Indian Metaphysics and Epistemology : The Tradition of Nyāya-Vaiśeṣika up to Gaṅgeśa*), ed. Karl H. Potter (Delhi: Motilal Banarsidass, 1976; Princeton: Princeton University Press, 1977) will suggest that writers such as Śrīdhara and Aparārkadeva of the 10th-12th centuries notice Maṇḍana's arguments but not Śaṃkara's.

26. For discussion of these influences see S. Kuppuswami Sastri's Introduction to B1346.

27. Cf., e.g., *Brahmasūtrabhāṣya* on II.2.32.

28. See J. L. Majumdar, B1259, B1260.

29. The number of those who have discovered close relations between Buddhism and Advaita is legion. See, e.g., Joshi, B2225; V. Bhattacharya's Introduction to B1254, B1231, B1247; Naga Raja Sarma, B6688; C. D. Sharma, B5807; L. de la Vallée Poussin, B5492; L. M. Joshi, "Gauḍapāda's rapprochement between Buddhism and Vedānta," *Ṛtam* 1.1, 1969, 11-22; Ganganatha Jha, B2112; Daniel H. H. Ingalls, "The study of Śaṃkarācārya," Annals of the Bhandarkar Oriental Research Institute 33 (1952), pp. 1-14.

30. K. A. Krishnaswamy Aiyar, B2078.

31. Others among the many who reject Buddhist influence on or even significant parallelisms with Advaita include: Purohit, B1242; Budhakar, B2081, B. K. Sengupta, B2188; Devaraja, B2245; Kawada, B5942; S. Roy, *The Heritage of Śaṃkara* (Allahabad, 1965); Anantakrishna Sastri, B4586; Mahadevan, B1256.

CHAPTER TWO

1. N. Veezhinathan, "The nature and destiny of the individual soul in Advaita," Journal of the Madras University 47.2 (1975), pp. 19-20, understands *sañcita* to include *prārabdhakarman.*

2. K. S. Iyer, B6629: 3 (1916-17), pp. 39-41.

3. Veezhinathan, op. cit., pp. 11-12.

4. Indian philosophers use this term to mean the place within the body where feeling, willing, thinking, etc., takes place. It does not necessarily denote the physical organ that goes by that name in Indian anatomy.

5. This is one of the points of divergence in the texts. Cf. Paul Deussen, B6623, Chapters 30, 32.

6. And in *Brahmasūtrabhāṣya* III.1.1, alluding to the same passage.

7. *Chāndogya Upaniṣad* V.10.1.

8. *Chāndogya Upaniṣad* VII. liberally illustrates the kind of rewards intended.

9. Cf. *Brahmasūtras* IV.3.10, 22, *Bṛhadāraṇyaka Upaniṣad* VI.2.15 and Śaṃkara's comments thereon.

10. Maṇḍana Miśra, *Brahmasiddhi* with Śaṅkhapāṇi's commentary, edited by S. Kuppuswami Sastri. Madras Government Oriental Manuscripts Series 4 (Madras 1937), pp. 123-124.

11. On V.10.6.

12. On IV.2.3.

13. *Taittirīyopaniṣadbhāṣya* II.189-200.

14. B1443, pp. 106-110.

15. B1559, p. 365.

16. Cf. K. S. Iyer, B6629, 1 (1914-15), p. 278.

17. *Bhagavadgītā* II.46.

18. *Bhagavadgītā* III.5.

19. *Muṇḍakopaniṣadbhāṣya* III.2.5.

20. *Gauḍapādakārikās* I.31-38.

21. See, for example, A. C. Das, B7010; G. R. Malkani, B7033; M. A. V. Rao, "Karma saṃnyāsa," Vedanta Kesari 20 (1933-34), pp. 345-352.

22. Cf., e.g., W. S. Urqhart, *Vedānta and Modern Thought* (London, 1928), pp. 172-190.

23. See, e.g., Nikhilananda, B1244; K. S. Iyer, B6629; Kumarappa, B2072.

24. See S. N. Mitra, "Advaita and morality—or Advaitic transformation of will," Vedanta Kesari 26 (1940), pp. 407-414; D. M. Datta, B7063 [cf. also Malkani *contra* Datta, in Philosophical Quarterly (Amalner) 30 (1957), pp. 201-206]; S. C. Chakravarti in Prabuddha Bharati 71 (1966), pp. 409-414.

25. Maṇḍana's views appear to be the subject of the entire ninth book of the *Pañcapādikā*.

26. See above, p. 30.

27. *Chāndogyopaniṣadbhāṣya* on II.23.1.

CHAPTER THREE

1. See above, p. 30.

2. E.g., *vidhi, codanā, niyoga.*

3. See Mysore Hiriyanna, "The doctrine of *niyoga*," in *Indian Philosophical Studies II* (Mysore : Kavyalaya, 1972), pp. 87-96.

4. An analysis that discovers twenty-six separate arguments in Sureśvara's writing is C. Markandeya Sastri, *Sureśvara's Contribution to Advaita* (Vemur: Sundari Samskrita Vidyalaya, 1973); see also V. P. Upadhyaya, B7113.

5. On *kāma-pradhvaṃsa-vāda* see M. Hiriyanna, B1045.

6. Cf. M. Hiriyanna, "Prapañca-vilayavāda—a doctrine of pre-Śaṃkara Vedānta" in *Indian Philosophical Studies II* (Mysore: Kavyalaya, 1972), pp. 28-35.

7. Hiriyanna, B1045.

8. This aspect of Śaṃkara's thought is emphasized in papers by Ganeswar Misra in his *Analytical Studies in Indian Philosophical Problems* (Bhubaneshwar: Utkal University, 1971).

9. See Kunjunni Raja, B6510A, pp. 70-72.

10. Ibid., Chapter 3.

11. Cf. N. M. Sastri, B2126. *Taittirīya Upaniṣad* II.1.1—*satyaṃ jñānam anantaṃ brahma*—is frequently cited as a *mahāvākya*. Other authcrities cite more—Sastri cites G. A. Jacob's report that a work title *Mahāvākyavivaraṇa* recognizes twelve great sentences.

CHAPTER FOUR

1. Caterina Conio, *The Philosophy of Māṇḍūkya Kārikā* (Varanasi: Bharatiya Vidya Prakashan, 1971).

2. V. Bhattacharya, B1254.

3. Introduction to B4586.

4. Ibid., p. 6.

5. Deussen, B6623.

6. The counterpositive of an absence is the thing that is absent. See Volume II of this Encyclopedia (cited in note 25 of Chapter One above), p. 53.

7. See this editor's article in a Festschrift honoring Daniel H. H. Ingalls' sixtieth birthday, forthcoming.

8. The term is used, but only in the innocuous sense of "a possible interpretation, not mine" or as "option" in the grammarians sense. Cf. P. K. Sundaram, *Word Index to the Brahmasūtrabhāṣya*, Volume II (Madras: Centre of Advanced Study in Philosophy, 1973), p. 830.

9. P. P. Subrahmanya Sastri's foreword to B1346. Cf. S. Suryanarayana Sastri's comments, B1362.

CHAPTER FIVE

1. It appears to occur first in the *Nṛsiṃhottaratāpanī Upaniṣad.*

2. E.g., *Brahmasūtrabhāṣya* I.4.15.

3. Krishna Warrier, B7136A, p. 251.

4. R. B. Joshi, B2225.

5. Krishna Warrier, B1736, p. 306.

6. P. D. Devanandan, B7012.

7. R. D. Ranade, *A Constructive Survey of Upaniṣadic Philosophy.* Poona Oriental Series 7 (Poona: Oriental Book Agency, 1926).

8. R. B. Joshi, B2225.

9. Ibid.

10. Ibid.

11. S. Sarasvati in B7178G.

12. D. H. H. Ingalls, B2173.

13. Ibid.

14. *Bṛhadāraṇyaka Upaniṣad* I.4.7.

15. *Pañcapādikā*, First Varṇaka, XXVI.95 ff.

16. E.g., at *Brahmasūtrabhāṣya* I.1.4.

17. E.g., *Bṛhadāraṇyakopaniṣadbhāṣya* II.1.20.

18. U. C. Bhattacharjee, B7969, p. 82.

19. *Bṛhadāraṇyaka Upaniṣad* IV.3.9.

20. *Upadeśasāhasrī* II.17.26-29.

21. At *Bṛhadāraṇyakopaniṣadbhāṣyavārttika* II.1.319-363.

CHAPTER SIX

1. This remark relates to the occasions (*nimitta*), not to the material cause, (*upādāna*), which must of course ultimately be real.

2. Maṇḍana accepts these; cf. *Brahmasiddhi* I.22 below.

3. *Bṛhadāraṇyakopaniṣadbhāṣya* II.1.20.

GAUḌAPĀDA

1. On these points, cf. Walleser, B7541; Barnett in Journal of the Royal Asiatic Society, 1910; V. Bhattacharya, B1254; Kunjunni Raja in Adyar Library Bulletin 24 (1960); S. L. Pandey, *Pre-Śaṃkara Advaita Philosophy* (Allahabad: Darshan Peeth, 1974).

2. Walleser, B7541.

3. S. L. Pandey, op. cit.

4. V. Bhattacharya, B1254, pp. lxvi-lxvii.

5. Ibid., pp. lxxii-lxxiii.

6. Despite misgivings; cf. the paper referred to in note 7, Chapter 4, above.

7. V. Bhattacharya, B1232.

8. B. N. K. Sharma, B1236, B1268.

9. V. Bhattacharya, B1254.

10. E.g., Venkatasubbiah, B1245, B1249; Ray, B1250; Mahadevan, B1256; C. D. Sharma, B5807.

11. Cf. Conio, op. cit., pp. 7 ff.; also V. A. Gadgil, "The Māṇḍūkyopanishad and the Gauḍapādakārikās," Journal of the University of Bombay 6 (1937-38), pp. 66-79.

12. V. Bhattacharya, B1231, B1247, B5707. But cf. C. D. Sharma, B5807; Divanji, B1252. Also Majumdar, B1259, B1260, who traces Gauḍapāda's Buddhism to the *Laṅkāvatārasūtra*; de la Vallée Poussin, B5492.

13. Kawada, B5942; S. Roy, *The Heritage of Śaṃkara* (Allahabad, 1965); L. M. Joshi, "Gauḍapāda's rapprochement . . . .", Rtam 1.1, 1969, 11-22; Mahadevan, B1256; Paul Hacker, "Notes on the Māṇḍūkyopaniṣad and Śaṃkara's Āgamaśāstravivaraṇa" in *India Maior* (Congratulatory Volume presented to J. Gonda), Leiden, 1972, pp. 115-132; Saccidanandendra Sarasvati, *Māṇḍūkyarahasyavivṛti* (Holenarsipur; the author, 1958).

ŚAṂKARA

1. Hacker, B2162; Mayeda, B1942B; Mayeda, "On the author of the Māṇḍūkyopaniṣad—and the Gauḍapādīyabhāṣya," Adyar Library Bulletin 31-32 (1967-68), pp. 73-94; "On Śaṃkara's authorship of the Kenopaniṣadbhāṣya," Indo-Iranian Journal 10 (1967), pp. 33-55; "Śaṃkara's Upadeśasāhasrī: its present form," Journal of the Oriental Institute (Baroda) 15 (1966), pp. 252-257; "The authenticity of the Bhagavadgītābhāṣya ascribed to Śaṃkara," *Wiener Zeitschrift fur des Kunde Sud- und Ostasien* 9 (1965), pp. 155-197.

2. Ingalls, "The study of Śaṃkarācārya," op. cit.

3. Cf. also Märschner, B1680.

4. Mayeda, B1942B.

5. The grounds for this statement are reviewed in S. K. Belvalkar, *Vedānta Philosophy* Part I: Lectures 1-6 (Poona, 1929).

6. In *Upadeśasāhasrī* II.18.2, as well as in *Gauḍapādakārikābhāṣya* IV.100, if we accept the latter work as authentic.

7. Belvalkar, op. cit.

8. Kunjunni Raja in Adyar Library Bulletin 24 (1960).

9. Cf. Allen Wright Thrasher, The Advaita of Maṇḍana Miśra's Brahmasiddhi. Ph.D. thesis, Harvard University, 197 .

10. Ibid. See below, under Maṇḍana Miśra, for references on the Maṇḍana-Sureśvara equation.

11. For more complete accounts based on this literature see, e.g., Baijnath, B6562; Seshadri, B2156; D. N. Pillai, *Śaṃkara the Sublime* (Calcutta, 1912); K. T. Telanga, *Shamkaracharya, Philosopher and Mystic* (Adyar, 1911); T. S. Narayana Sastri, *The Age of Śaṃkara* (Madras 1916; enlarged ed. 1971); Menon, B1522; Agamananda's introduction to Tattvananda (tr.), *The Quintessence of Vedānta* (Calcutta, n.d.; Ernakulam, 1960).

12. Belvalkar, op. cit., regards this story as "silly myth-mongering" (p. 233, note); Daya Krishna, B2268A, discusses its implications.

13. Consult A. Nataraja Aiyer and S. Laksminarasimha Sastri, *The Traditional Age of Sri Samkaracharya and the Math* (Madras 1962), as well as the works cited under the preceding notes.

14. An "ulcerated sore, or fistula," says K. T. Telanga, op. cit.

15. Ingalls, op. cit.; see also B2173 and B2177.

16. Hacker, "Śaṃkara der Yogin und Śaṃkara der Advaitin. Einige Beobachtungen," *Wiener Zeitschrift für des Kunde Süd- und Ostasien* 12-13 (1968-69), pp. 119-148.

17. Hacker, "Relations of early Advaitins to Vaiṣṇavism", *Wiener Zeitschrift für des Kunde Süd- und Ostasien* 9 (1965), pp. 147-154.

18. E.g., Ghate, B7609; Radhakrishnan, B8996; B.N.K. Sharma, B1242.

19. Thibaut, introduction to B1610. See Amalnerkar, B1613; Faddegon, B6672.

20. E.g., Modi, B1663, B1668; A. K. Banerjee, B6758.

21. Mahadevan, B2390.

22. Märschner, B1680; Hacker, B6956, p. 1918.

23. Ingalls, B2177, p. 295.

24. Van Boetzelaer's introduction to his translation of Sureśvara's *Taittirīyopaniṣadbhāṣyavārttika* (Leiden, 1971).

25. R. Balasubramaniam, Introduction to his translation of Sureśvara's *Taittirīyopaniṣadbhāṣyavārttika*, Madras University Philosophy Series 20 (Madras, 1974), pp. 15-16.

26. Ibid., p. 21.

27. Mayeda, B1942B; Mayeda, "Śaṃkara's Upadeśasāhasrī," op. cit.; Mayeda's introduction to his edition of *Upadeśasāhasrī* (Tokyo, 1873).

28. G. A. Jacob, preface to B2394, pp. 8 ff. Cf. Mayeda, B1942B, p. 188.

29. Mayeda, B1942B, p. 196.

30. Mayeda, "Śaṃkara's Upadeśasāhasrī," op. cit.

31. Cited in Mitra, B1688.

32. R. D. Ranade, op. cit., p. 24.

33. Hiriyanna, introduction to B1775, pp. iv-v.

34. S. C. Vidyarnava, B1770.

35. Budhakar, B2081; R. M. Sastri, B2064; Belvalkar, op. cit.

36. Mayeda, "On Śaṃkara's authorship of the Kenopaniṣadbhāṣya," op. cit.

37. Ranade, op. cit., p. 29.

38. *The Upaniṣads*, translated by F. Max Müller. Part II. Sacred Books of the East 15 (Oxford, 1884; New York, 1962), pp. xxvii.

39. Anam Charan Swain, "Authenticity of the Bhagavadgītābhāṣya attributed to Śaṃkarācārya," *Mysore Orientalist* 2.1 (1969), pp. 32-38, citing Hacker, B2162. Cf. also Karmarkar, B1587.

40. Ingalls, "Study of Śaṃkarācārya," op. cit., pp. 7-8.

41. V. Raghavan, "Bhāskara's Gītābhāṣya," *Wiener Zeitschrift für des Kunde Süd- und Ostasien* 12-13 (1968-69), pp. 281-294, esp. 283 ff.

42. Mayeda, "The authenticity of the Bhagavadgītābhāṣya," op. cit.

43. See, e.g., Modi B1582, B1583, B1585.

44. Cf. Mukherji, B9184; B.N.K. Sharma in Principle Karmarkar Commemoration Volume (Poona, 1948), 180-195; Ray, B6860 (=B1583A); K. S. Iyer in *Vedanta Kesari* 1 (1914-15), pp. 42-47.

45. In *Journal of the American Oriental Society* 33 (1913), p. 52, note 2; cited in Mayeda, "On the author of the Māṇḍūkyopaniṣad," op. cit.

46. Suryanarayana Sastri, "Some observations on the Māṇḍūkyakārikās" in *Collected Papers of S. Suryanarayana Sastri* (ed. T.M.P. Mahadevan) (Madras 1961), pp. 262-271.

47. Belvalkar, op. cit., p. 218.

48. R. V. de Smet, "The law of karma," *Indian Philosophical Annual* 2 (1966), pp. 328-335.

49. Ingalls, "Study of Śaṃkarācārya," op. cit., p. 12.

50. Hacker, "Notes on the Māṇḍūkyopaniṣad," op. cit.

51. Majumdar, B1260.

52. Tilmann Vetter, "Zur Bedeutung des Illusionismus bei Śaṃkara," *Wiener Zeitschrift für des Kunde Süd- und Ostasiens* 12-13 (1968-69), pp. 407-423.

53. Hacker, "Notes on the Māṇḍūkyopaniṣad," op. cit.

54. Mayeda, "On the author of the Māṇḍūkyopaniṣad," op. cit.

55. Hacker, "Notes on the Māṇḍūkyopaniṣad," op. cit., p. 130.

56. Ibid., p. 131.

57. Mayeda, "On the author of the Māṇḍūkyopaniṣad," op. cit.

58. Belvalkar, op. cit., pp. 226-227.

59. Ibid., p. 226.

60. Ingalls, "The Study of Śaṃkarācārya," op. cit.

61. Mayeda, introduction to his edition of *Upadeśasāhasrī*, op. cit., p. xi.

62. Hacker, B2142.

63. Belvalkar, op. cit.

64. Hacker, B2142; Ingalls, "The study of Śaṃkarācārya," op. cit.; Mayeda, introduction to his edition of *Upadeśasāhasrī*, op. cit.

65. Belvalkar, op. cit., p. 227.

66. Hacker, B2142; Mayeda, introduction to his edition of *Upadeśasāhasrī*, op. cit.

67. Belvalkar, op. cit., p. 227.

68. Hacker, B2142.

69. Belvalkar, op. cit., p. 229.

70. Ingalls, "Study of Śaṃkarācārya," p. 7.

71. Hacker, B2142.

72. Mayeda, "Śaṃkara's Upadeśasāhasrī," op. cit.

73. Belvalkar, op. cit., p. 229.

74. Ibid., p. 228.

MAṆḌANA MIŚRA

(Footnotes 15-36 by Allen Thrasher)

1. Allen Wright Thrasher, The Advaita of Maṇḍana Miśra's Brahmasiddhi. Ph.D. thesis, Harvard University, 1972, pp. 174-176.

2. Frauwallner, B9032, p. 137.

3. Thrasher, op. cit., p. 199.

4. Thrasher, op. cit., pp. 176-177.

5. Thrasher, op. cit., p. 177.

6. Thrasher, op. cit., pp. 178ff.

7. D. C. Bhattacharya, B1358, cites Canto VII of the *Śaṃkaradigvijaya* as the source of this identification. See also Balasubramaniam, "Identity of Maṇḍanamiśra," *Journal of the American Oriental Society* 82 (1962), pp. 522-532.

8. See D. C. Bhattacharya, B1358; also B. R. Gupta, B2408.

9. Hiriyanna, "Sureśvara and Maṇḍanamiśra," *Journal of the Royal Asiatic Society* (1923), pp. 259-263.

10. P. V. Kane, "The chronological position of Maṇḍana, Umbeka, Bhavabhūti, Sureśvara," *Journal of the Asiatic Society*, Bombay Branch, n.s. 3 (1928), pp. 289-293.

11. D. C. Bhattacharya, B1358.

12. S. Kuppuswami Sastri in *Proceedings of the All-India Oriental Congress* 3 (1924), pp. 480-481.

13. Balasubramanian, "Identity of Maṇḍanamiśra," op. cit.

14. Thrasher, op. cit.

15. *Vy-adhikaraṇa* also means "in different grammatical cases," i.e., in "from the smoke, it is fire," "smoke" is in the ablative and "fire" in the nominative. Both meanings are probably intended.

16. The commentator Śaṅkhāpani says that these are those who teach a real universe of diversity (*satya-prapañca-vādin*). They would presumably be a sort of Vedāntin, of the Bhedābheda sort, probably.

17. This argument seems to depend on the fact that *artha* means both "point," or "purpose," and "meaning." Thus statements without a point are also in the opponent's opinion without a meaning, and they have no point unless they are employed to produce action or its avoidance.

18. As there is a *pramāṇa*, presumably *arthāpatti*, for the existence of some sort of union with the objects of other words.

19. It is not clear what "*viniyoga*" means here. The commentators seem to take it as equivalent to *anvaya*, the connection of the objects of words in a sentence. This whole passage is somewhat obscure.

20. Maṇḍana here seems to be doing two things. First, he is affirming that the injunctions to works have an end in themselves, heaven, etc. Second, he is preparing the way for his own opinion that works may be made accessory to knowledge rather than secular ends.

21. In an exclusive injunction (*parisaṃkhyānavidhi*), something is enjoined with respect to some things so that everything else previously established (*prāpta*) is excluded. Thus the injunction "Five five-nailed animals should be eaten" limits the "established" eating of all five-nailed animals to five sorts of animals only. In a restrictive injunction (*niyamavidhi*) one thing is prescribed, where in

the absence of that injunction either one of two "established" options would be possible. Thus the injunction "One pounds the rice" eliminates the possibility that one might use the other possible way of removing the husks from the grain, namely, cracking them with the fingernails. In both these the question of some course of action has already arisen, they are "established." But it is otherwise with prohibitions, according to Maṇḍana.

22. This is directed not only toward the present point at issue, but against the Prābhākara idea of *niyoga* as the object of Vedic injunctions.

23. Cf. Maṇḍana's insistence elsewhere that *avidyā* belongs only to the *jīvas*.

24. From here to the end of I.34 there is a long discussion between an opponent (*pūrvapakṣin*) and an objector to him who represents Maṇḍana's views in part (see the statement of his viewpoint in I.35 and later at III.48-54), but with whom he does not entirely agree (an *ekadeśa-siddhāntin*, "one who states a partial conclusion"). The opponent apparently bases himself on Śaṃkara's views, but holds a stricter disjunction between knowledge and works than Śaṃkara. Perhaps he is Sureśvara. See also Vetter's discussion at n. 212, p. 113 of his edition and translation of the *Brahmasiddhi* (Wien, 1969). I introduce the *pūrvapakṣin's* arguments by the word "Opponent," and the *ekadeśasiddhāntin's* by "Objector," to call attention to the isolation of the argument, replacing the customary "Objection" before the *pūrvapakṣa* and "Response" before the *siddhānta*.

25. Cf. the distinction of two kinds of *avidyā* at I.9, I.20, I.21, III.61, and III.63.

26. The point is that one may either hold that sacrifices and the like produce a counter-*saṃskāra* in some way that is not obvious ("visible") and must be learned or inferred from scripture, as the injunction to sprinkle the rice grains before they are pounded has no visible purpose and so we must infer that sprinkling produces a *saṃskāra*, or else that sacrifices have an obvious purpose and *saṃskāra* in producing the destruction of sins previously committed, like the pounding of rice grains that they may be made into cakes. Thus Citsukha's commentary.

27. *Bṛhadāraṇyaka Upaniṣad* IV.4.24, where, however, the words "defined as Being" are absent. They are found in the *Vṛtti* on *Vākyapadīya* I.145.

28. Unknown quote. But cf. *Vākyapadīya* III, Dravya (1), 15.

29. *Viśeṣa*, "particular" is not being used here solely in the Nyāya-Vaiśeṣika sense of "ultimate particularity."

30. Note that Maṇḍana does not use the term *savikalpa pratyakṣa*. It is possible that he thought that all *pratyakṣa* was *nirvikalpa*.

31. *Vastu-mātra*, which, N. B., on Maṇḍana's view equals the universal !

32. I translate "*akṣa*" by "organ" because it often means, not specifically the eye, but any sense organ, and "organ" has the advantage of being an equivocal term in English.

33. According to the Mīmāṃsā, what a Vedic passage "assumes" or "repeats" (*anuvāda*) cannot be the point it wishes to teach.

34. The commentator Śaṅkhāpani says this is directed against Śaṃkara, with special reference to *Brahmasūtrabhāṣya* IV.1.15 and 19.

35. This sentence is a literal translation of Maṇḍana's sentence concluding the commentary on these verses. It is not clear what point it makes, whether *no* injunction, including that to know the *Ātman* as without duality, can deal with the highest truth, or whether the injunction to know the *Ātman* as without duality somehow misrepresents It, even though the *Ātman* is in fact without duality.

36. It should be kept in mind here that the Sanskrit root "*jñā*" has the usual root meaning "to know" in ordinary language, and covers any sort of cognition "Knowledge" as valid cognition" is *pramāṇa*. An injunction to know and to "cognize" the *Ātman* is the same (*jñānavidhi*). I have chosen cognize as the broader word in English.

SUREŚVARA

1. Mahadevan, B2390.
2. Mahadevan, B2390, p. xiii.
3. Van Boetzelaer, introduction to his translation of *Taittirīyopaniṣadbhāṣyavārttika*, op. cit., p. 3.
4. Balasubramaniam, Translation of *Taittirīyopaniṣadbhāṣyavārttika* (Madras University Philosophy Series 20, 1974), p. 9, referring to Canto 13 of *Śaṃkaradigvijaya*, verses 65-66.
5. Balasubramaniam, ibid., p. 10.
6. Cf. Balasubramaniam, ibid., pp. 12ff, for more on Sureśvara as Vārttikakāra.
7. Alston, B2400, p. 11.
8. Jacob, preface to the second edition (1925) of B2394, p. xi.
9. Hiriyanna, introduction to second edition of B2394, p. xxxi.
10. Ibid., p. xxx.
11. Ibid., pp. xxx-xxxi.
12. Markandeya Sastri, op. cit., p. 12.
13. Ibid., p. 12.

PADMAPĀDA

1. Venkatramiah, introduction to B2419, p. xv.
2. Ibid., citing *śloka* 116 of the *Sarvadarśanasaṃgraha*.
3. Ibid., p. xiv, note 2.

TOṬAKA

1. Hacker, B6956, pp. 28-32.

HASTĀMALAKA

1. Hacker, B6956, p. 33.
2. The following is an attempt at a metrical translation of the Hastāmalaka verses. It is to be noted that the inner sense organ (*buddhi*, *manas*, *dhī*) is designated by "sense (sg.)," "heart," etc.

In verse 3, lines 2 and 3, and in verse 13, lines 1 and 2 have been rearranged. For the meter see Hacker's introduction (ibid., III.2). (E. Harzer).

INDEX

ābhāsa (appearance, reflection) 84-85, 120, 169, 173, 242, 264, 319, 339, 342. *See also* reflection model

abhāva (negation, negative entity, absence)
  as a *pramāṇa* 97, 360, 380-81, 449, 553
  in Buddhism 250, 261-62
  in Nyāya-Vaiśeṣika 261, 305
  in nihilism 291
  mutual absence (*anyonyābhāva*) 378, 382, 385-86, 529
  nonproductive 206, 367, 405, 449
  not grasped by a *pramāṇa* 529
  of things believed not to exist 376
  perceptibility of 449-451
  posterior absence (*dhvaṃsābhāva*) 206, 388, 453
  prior absence (*prāgabhāva*) 66, 183, 305, 405, 425
  -rūpa (negative property) 350

abheda (nondifference) 147, 356, 381, 383-87, 397

Ābhidharma Buddhism 557

abhihitānvayavāda 57, 59

abhimāna (ego notion) 229, 329, 341, 369. *See also ahaṃkāra*

Abhinavagupta 16, 118, 551, 563

abhiniveśa. *See* attachment

abhyāsa (practice, repetition)
  of knowledge (*jñānābhyāsa*) 323, 370, 372, 471. *See also* meditation
  two kinds of 325

abhyudaya (heaven, higher ends of man) 255, 422, 581

absence. *See abhāva*

Acarya, Narayana Ram 120

act, action (*karman, kriyā*) 66, 92-93
  and knowledge (*jñāna*), relation between 192, 229-30, 255, 257, 272, 278-81, 285, 288, 296-98, 325, 339, 363-69, 422-24, 428-29, 431-32, 441, 531, 534. *See also jñānakarmasamuccaya*
  agent and result, distinction between. *See* difference
  as signified by verb 57, 397
  bodily (*kāyika*) 30, 297-98, 300, 515, 532
  desireless (*niṣkāma*) 511
  eligibility for. *See adhikāra*
  enjoined. *See* injunction
  expiatory (*prayaścitta*) 30, 359, 407-8, 536
  four kinds of results of 39-40, 427, 596
  meditative. *See* meditation
  mental (*mānasa*) 30, 126, 139, 297-98, 515, 532, 596
  occasional (*naimittika*) 30, 44, 184, 430, 432
  optional, desired (*kāmya*) 30, 44, 47, 184, 205, 207, 257, 306-7, 422-23, 430, 477, 518, 531, 533, 536
  organs of (*karmendriya*) 22-23, 34, 170, 237, 311, 319, 330-32, 561
  prohibited, proscribed (*niṣedha, pratiṣedha*) 30, 40, 47, 127, 179, 184, 205, 207, 229, 258, 306, 357, 360, 363-65, 422-23, 432-33, 458, 530-31
  purposeful. *See arthakriyā*
  regular daily (*nitya*) 36, 42-44, 47, 50, 176, 178-79, 182, 184-85, 195, 203-8, 229, 240, 272, 298-300, 306-7, 329, 370, 422-23, 430, 432, 457-58, 473, 483, 518, 530-31, 533-34, 536
  ritual. *See* sacrifice
  role of in liberation 38-46, 194-95, 207-9, 242, 295-96, 306-7, 336, 421-34, 473, 532-33
  sampratti (renunciatory) 476
  section of scripture on. *See karmakāṇḍa*
  stems from desire 404, 458, 478, 502, 530
  traces, residues. *See karma*
  vocal (*vācika*) 30, 54, 297-98, 515, 532

activity. *See pravṛtti*

adhikāra (eligibility, preparation)
  for action 207
  for studying a text 339
  for Vedic study. *See* scripture, entitlement to study
  four requirements for *brahmajijñāsā* or inquiry into Brahman 36-37, 122, 140, 218, 323, 326, 329, 331, 336, 339, 363, 421, 426-27, 429, 452, 586-87
  -ka puruṣa (official of God) 458
  two kinds of 342

Āditya. *See* sun

adṛṣṭa 171, 195, 233, 370, 532, 568. *See also* karma
  in Sāṃkhya 169
  in Vaiśeṣika 157, 169

Advaita Vedānta 5-19
  relation to other systems 19-21

Advaitapañcaratna (attributed to Śaṃkara) 19, 343-44

Advayananda 339

āgama. *See* scripture

Āgamananda 608

Āgamaśāstra (of Gauḍapāda). *See Gauḍapādakārikās*

Āgamaśāstravivaraṇa. *See Gauḍapādakārikābhāṣya* (of Śaṃkara)

Agase, K. S. 421

agent (*kartṛ*) 65-66, 88, 122-23, 168-69, 206, 222, 264
  difference from act and result. *See* act, agent, result, distinction between

aggregation of elements
  as self 192, 198, 223-24, 557
  in Sarvāstivāda 159-61, 557

Agni 461, 487, 494, 561

agni. *See* fire, digestive

agnicayana. *See* fire, sacred

Agnihotra, Agniṣṭoma (daily fire sacrifice) 44, 178, 184, 209, 229-30, 257-58, 278, 296-97, 464, 476, 584

agnosticism 7
agrayāna 113, 317
ahaṃkāra (ego sense, egoity) 20, 22, 60, 86-87, 126, 242-43, 299, 311, 326, 330, 332, 341, 484, 523, 538-40, 542, 545, 553-54, 561, 565, 572-74, 577, 599
-*granthī* 581
part of *antaḥkaraṇa* 553
three forms of 556
air (*vāyu*) 24, 27, 237, 287, 311, 318, 459, 481, 560, 574
aiśvarya (lordliness, divine power) 208, 388, 406-7, 417, 517, 581
Aitareya Brāhmaṇa 270
Aitareya Upaniṣad 28-29, 59, 270, 273-77
Aitareyopaniṣadbhāṣya (of Śaṃkara) 18, 27-28, 116, 270-77
Aiyar, A. Nataraj 608
Aiyar, K. A. Krishnaswami 21, 604
Aiyengar, T. G. K. 603
Ajātaśatru 477
ajātivāda (nonorigination, no-cause theory) 7, 21, 63-68, 72, 108-9, 111-13, 232, 296, 305, 313, 316, 480, 522, 599-600
ajīva in Jainism 163
ajñāna (nonknowledge, ignorance) 70, 78-79, 90, 240, 319, 329-30, 341, 413, 455, 531, 533, 539, 541, 543, 564. *See also avidyā*
ākāṃkṣā (expectancy) 186, 364, 403, 438, 443, 522, 591
ākāra, ākṛti (form) 55-56, 139, 162
in Vijñānavāda 352
of Brahman 305-6, 480-83, 524
ākāśa 24, 27, 83, 98, 108-9, 129, 133-34, 140, 160, 165-66, 171, 185, 192, 202, 209, 212, 219, 237, 259, 286-87, 292, 311, 314, 462, 481, 490, 560, 574. *See also* pot-space
as (color of the) sky 94, 120, 196, 222-23, 459, 478
mahā- (big-) 315
akāsmika (random) 364-65
akhaṇḍārtha (partlessness of sentence meaning) 57
akhyātivāda 566-68
akṣara (imperishable, the syllable *om*) 135-37, 140, 285-87, 348, 356, 358, 490-92, 562, 574. *See also aum*
ālambana (supporting object) 94, 255-56, 312, 335, 356, 414, 567
ālātacakra or *ālātaśānti* (wheel of fire) 83-84, 110, 112, 315, 321, 357
ālayavijñāna 159, 162
Allahabad. *See* Prayaga
Alston, Anthony J. 241, 530, 534-35, 548, 612
Amalnerkar, 608
Āmavāsya 475
anadhyavasāya (uncertainty) 553, 571
ānanda. *See* bliss
Ānandagiri 11-12, 105, 117-18, 256, 296, 466
Ānandapūrṇa Vidyāsāgara 351, 359, 363, 409
Ānandavallī (=Brahmāvallī chapter of *Taittirīya Upaniṣad*) 524
anārambhavāda 581-84
Aṅgiras 285
animal 25, 27, 121, 172
(re)births 259-60, 281
aniruddha 165
anirvacanīya 80, 115, 219, 330, 335, 565, 570
-*khyātivāda* 347
antaḥkaraṇa (internal organ) 22, 86, 196, 216, 330-31, 335, 341, 479, 546, 553, 555-56, 574, 576
antaryāmin (inner controller) 77, 134, 277, 455, 459, 490, 492
antinomianism 35-36, 40-41
anubhava (immediate awareness) 54, 92, 98, 123, 144, 320, 333, 351, 451, 539, 572, 583
Anugītā (Aśvamedhaparvan of *Mahābhārata*) 295
anupalabdhi 529, 541
-*hetu* 500
anusaṃdhāna (reflective consciousness, re-identification) 350, 381, 384, 397
anuśaya (karmic residual traces). *See* karma
anuvāda (restatement) 348, 389, 436, 441, 443, 447, 464, 526, 528, 612
anvayavyatireka (positive and negative concomitance) 252, 401, 527, 538, 542
anvitābhidānavāda 57-59, 443
anyathākhyātivāda 347, 567-68
apāna (inhalation) 274, 330
Aparārkadeva 604
Aparokṣānubhūti (attributed to Śaṃkara) 18, 320-23
Āpastambhadharmasūtra 423
apavāda 8, 174
apavārga 50-51, 194, 364
apoha(*vāda*) 55, 71, 250, 376, 521
apophasis 8
apratisamkhyānirodha 160
āpti (obtaining) 39-40, 196, 210, 427, 596
apūrva 31, 174, 313, 447
ārambhavāda 581-84
Āraṇya (one of the *daśanāmas*) 118
Āraṇyakas 3, 270
Aristotle 65
Arjuna 45, 295-96, 298, 300
Ārtabhāga 488
arthakriyā (purposeful action) 378-79, 386, 392-93
-*kāritva* (efficiency) 578
arthāpatti (presumption) 58, 97, 360, 366, 398, 405, 434, 521, 553, 583, 610
śrutārthāpatti 570-71
arthavāda (supplemental text, explanatory to injunction) 48, 51, 124, 175-76, 267, 275, 304, 366, 410, 422, 424, 436, 445, 466, 471 587, 596, 600
three kinds of 436
āsana (posture) 322
asat (nonbeing, nonexistence) 65, 75, 262, 395, 453, 511, 522. *See also* unreality; *abhāva*
-*kalpa* 554
-*kāraṇavāda* 141, 161, 166, 261-62
-*kāryavāda* 7, 41, 144-46, 149-50, 156, 158, 511
ascertainment, certainty (*nirṇaya, niścaya*) 330, 341, 370-71, 386, 388, 482, 545, 553
ascetic(ism) 45, 209, 259, 272, 320
"wandering mendicant" 256-58

asiddha (a fallacy) 313
Āsmarathya 10, 87, 135, 142
āspada (ground) 309, 328
āśrama (stage of life) 121, 323, 371-72, 506
duties of 37, 43. *See also* dharma, morality
enjoined by scripture 177
four ideal stages of life 34-35, 44-45, 219, 476, 490
Śaṃkara's list of 45
āśrama (retreat, monastery) 118
Āśrama (one of the *daśanāmas*) 118
astrology (*jyotiṣa*) 285
asura (demon) 455-56
Atharva Veda 284-85, 289
atheism 7, 556-57
atīta (a Śaiva category) 553
Ātmabodha (attributed to Śaṃkara) 18, 116, 323-24
Ātmajñānopadeśa (attributed to Śaṃkara) 18, 326-28
ātmakhyātivāda 567-68
ātman (Self). *See* Brahman
the word "*atman*" 463-64
Ātmanātmaviveka (attributed to Śaṃkara) 18, 328-31
Ātmapañcaka. *See Advaitapañcaratna*
Ātmaṣaṭka. *See Aitareya Upaniṣad*
Ātmavidyopadeśa *See Ātmajñānopadeśa*
atom, atomic theory 123, 152, 156-58, 161, 163, 166, 202, 353, 552
double, *See dvyaṇuka*
attachment (*rāga*) 30, 44, 234, 317, 329, 348-50, 363, 433
to life (*abhiniveśa*) 350, 365
Audulomi 10, 87, 142
aum (sacred syllable) 13, 89, 104, 107, 136, 174, 256, 310-12, 319, 356, 517, 520, 560, 562. *See also akṣara*
avaccheda (limitation, differentiation) 351, 361, 404
mutual (*anyonya-*, *paraspara-*) 357
-vāda. *See* limitation model
avasthā (state or stage) 88-91, 104, 106-7, 241, 275, 316-17, 328, 330-31, 333, 434, 459, 463, 478, 502, 508, 559. *See also* dream; sleep, deep; waking, *turīya*
aversion (*dveṣa*) 229, 279, 304, 317
a *kāraka* 458, 478
avidyā (ignorance). *See also ajñāna*
as causal body. *See body*, causal
as God's power 337
as reflecting medium 77, 498, 504
as superimposition. *See* Superimposition
beginningless, uncaused 70, 337, 352-53, 367, 468, 516, 546, 565
cannot be validly known 426, 523
cause of bondage, rebirth 6, 32, 195, 243, 269, 289, 336, 388, 503
cause of fear 457-58, 505
cause of God's qualities 148, 187, 332
cause of *jīva* 332, 574
cause of the world, of constructions, distinctions, change 50, 62, 67, 70, 76, 121, 125, 140, 146, 197, 221, 233, 235, 240, 269, 287, 299, 305, 382, 504, 522-23
coexists with *vidyā* 354
collective/distributive (*samaṣṭi*/*vyaṣṭi*)
aspects of 340
covering (*āvaraṇa*, *ācchādika*) 71, 79, 86-87, 115, 182-83, 251, 279, 302, 324, 337, 360, 415, 474, 565, 611
definition of 458, 531
destroyed by *vidyā* alone 33, 38, 50, 69, 195, 221, 228-30, 323, 329, 424
different for each subtle body 505
in Buddhism 21, 159-60
latent in deep sleep 505
locus of 80, 86, 88, 303, 352-53, 382, 425, 468, 503-4, 516, 542, 611
merges into *avyaktaprakṛti* 238
motiveless 353, 367
occurrence of the word "*avidya*" in scripture 78, 279, 354
ontological status of 20, 33, 80, 352, 381, 426
a Paurāṇika category 553
play (*krīḍā*, *līlā*) of 359
produced from *tamas* 302
productive of desires, pleasures 272, 280, 425
projective (*vikṣepika*) 71, 79, 87, 93-94, 115, 359-60, 377, 408, 415, 565, 569, 580, 611
relation to *māyā* 79-80
removal of. *See* liberation as removal of *avidyā*
required for action 307-8, 366
root (*mūla-*) 79-80
secondary (*tula-*) 79-80
single (not many) 505
unrelated to Brahman 304, 458
usage of term in Śaṃkara 115, 294-95, 311, 598
-vāsanā (impressions of *avidyā*) 409
-vyavahāra 408
avyākṛta 458-59, 461, 512, 574
avyakta 140, 337, 340, 574
-prakṛti. *See prakṛti*
awareness. *See jñāna*
Āyur Veda 444. *See* also medicine
ayutasiddha 158, 183

Bādarāyaṇa 4, 10, 12, 26, 31, 119, 175, 564, 589
Bādari 135
Badrinath 16, 18, 104, 117-18
Bahvṛcā Upaniṣad. *See Aitareya Upaniṣad*
bāhyārthavāda 498
Baijnath 608
Bālabodhinī. *See Ātmajñānopadeśa*
Balasubramaniam, R. 205, 347, 521, 608, 610, 612
Banara 16, 117, 333
Banerjee, A. K. 608
Barnett, L. D. 607
begging 257, 519
beginningless(ness) 70, 113
series. *See* seed and sprout
Belvalkar, Sripad Krishna 116, 308, 318, 320, 323-24, 326, 328, 331, 339, 343-44, 607-10
Bengal 18, 103-4
Bhagavadgītā 5, 11, 32, 45, 78, 118, 138, 178, 218, 266, 271-72, 294-308, 407-8

Bhagavadgītābhāṣya (of Śaṃkara) 18, 29, 40, 45, 78, 96, 116, 294-308, 530
Bhagavat, H. R. 181, 205, 255, 278, 280-81, 284, 289, 295, 310, 328, 344
Bhāgavata 165
bhakti (devotion) 320, 336-37
Bhāmatī (commentary on Śaṃkara's *Brahmasūtrabhāṣya* by Vācaspati Miśra) 17
Bhārati (wife of Maṇḍana Miśra) 15-16, 117-18, 420
Bhārati (one of the *daśanāmas*) 118
Bhāratītīrtha 344
Bhartṛhari 20, 54, 56, 59, 116, 118
Bhartṛmitra 12
Bhartṛprapañca 12, 40, 50-52, 87, 187, 193-94, 196, 201-2, 204, 461, 466-67, 470, 473-77, 481, 487, 490, 494, 502-3, 506-7, 512, 514, 520, 535
Bhāskara 11, 40, 118, 181, 217, 294
Bhāṭṭa Mīmāṃsā 15, 20, 57, 440, 499, 517, 553, 572, 580
Bhattacharya, Dinesh Chandra 347, 610
Bhattacharya, Umesh Chandra 88, 606
Bhattacharya, Vidhusekhara 64, 104-5, 603-4, 606-7
bhāva (state) 111, 367
(positive entity) 261, 449
-rūua 115, 350
Bhāvabhūti 347
bhāvanā (continuous concentration) 417, 434, 441, 534, 548, 559
bhāvanā (latent impression) 357, 459, 488, 501, 505, 523
Bhāvanāviveka (of Maṇḍana Miśra) 346
Bhāvaviveka 12, 103
bhaya. *See* fear
bheda. *See* difference
Bhedābhedavāda 40-41, 43, 50-52, 87, 118, 181, 309, 381, 425-26, 443, 467, 477, 507, 514, 535, 610
bhikṣu (monk) 289, 317
bhoga (experience) 23, 29-31, 33-34, 108, 231, 266, 351. *See also* happiness, pain
bhoktṛ (enjoyer, lit. "eater") 122-33, 134, 147, 1 458, 493, 506, 539
Bhṛgu 524
Bhṛguvallī (chapter of *Taittirīya Upaniṣad*) 205
bhūta. *See* element
bindu (a Śaiva category) 553, 556
birds, two, symbolizing two selves 136, 287-88
birth (*jāti*) 26-30, 32, 34, 202
physiology of 523
"three births" of *Aitareya Upaniṣad* 28-29, 276-77
blind leading blind, analogy of 128
blind man carrying lame man on his back, analogy of 154
bliss (*ānanda*)
ānandamayakośa 91, 131-32, 212-13, 215, 331, 337-38, 340, 524
and prājña 106
definition of 349
in liberation, Self-knowledge 343, 388, 404
of Brahman 7, 76, 115, 131-32, 136, 197-98, 205, 269, 285, 324, 337, 342, 348-51, 365, 367, 407, 419, 452, 492-93
of deep sleep. *See suṣupti*
relation to love 351
relation to pleasure, happiness 76, 197-98, 342, 348-50, 365, 429, 451-52
result of knowledge and action 213
the term "*ānanda*" 295
blood 26-27, 219, 331, 494, 523
Bodhāyana 11
body (*śarīra*) 121, 227, 306
as cause of the world 67, 78, 81-88, 123-24, 130, 133, 139, 141-44, 147, 151, 153, 170, 214, 219, 287, 292, 397, 406, 459, 480, 485, 522, 599
as reflecting medium 498
bodily act. *See* act, bodily
causal 319, 324, 330, 331, 335, 337, 340, 494
dead 495
dream 495, 501
equilibrium of 322
formation of the 523
not the self 122, 175, 218-19, 222-23, 326, 336, 458, 495-96, 556-57
physical or gross (*sthūla*) 20, 22, 24, 83, 140, 319, 321, 323-24, 330-331, 335, 336, 341, 473-74, 481, 487, 494
subtle (*sūkṣmaśarīra, liṅga*) 24-25, 27-29, 108, 140, 171-72, 179, 193, 202, 277, 287, 319, 321, 324, 330-331, 335-336, 341, 473-74, 480-82, 487, 494, 501, 503-5, 508-9, 561
watery 26-27
bondage. 6, 22, 32, 239, 336-37
See also saṃsāra
Brahmā 87-88, 235, 247, 320, 324, 363, 457, 459, 461, 530, 540-41, 580
brahmacārya 34, 36, 118, 208, 289, 299, 329, 370, 490, 518
lifelong 45, 256, 259
Brahmadatta 12, 363, 534
Brahmaloka 26-27, 137, 175, 179-80, 268-69, 281, 289, 329, 406, 476, 483, 507, 509, 519, 533
path to the. *See* path, *devayāna*
Brahman (ultimate world principle, Highest Self)
and Its states, relation to. *See bhāva*
as inner ruler. *See antaryāmin*
as pure consciousness 6-7, 20, 54, 75-76, 92, 188, 225-27, 233-34, 321, 504, 506, 514, 539, 542
as source of scripture 124, 485, 488
as support of world 136-37
as witness, seer. *See sākṣin, dṛk*
as word (*śabdabrahman*) 139, 356
=Atman 7, 61, 124, 132, 172, 188, 215, 232, 328, 338, 478, 480, 510, 528. *See* also *tattvamasi*
Bhedābheda view of 193, 204
bliss of. *See* bliss of Brahman
can It be an object of awareness? 76, 94, 110, 120, 122-23, 125-27, 145, 188, 210-11, 226, 232, 237, 275, 283, 328, 360, 409, 417-18, 452, 479, 496, 514-15, 525, 538, 540, 545, 572, 587. *See also* Self-knowledge.
can It be referred to or spoken about?

55, 59-61, 74, 125, 193, 242, 282, 327, 360, 369, 392, 417-18, 434, 459, 525-27. *See also neti neti*
definition *per accidens* (*taṭasthalakṣaṇa*) of 75, 205, 555, 592
disembodied 128
does It have efforts or desires? 132, 187, 213, 353, 425, 462
essential definition (*svarūpalakṣaṇa*) of 75, 205, 208-11, 330, 514, 555, 590
eternal, omnipresent 122, 137, 232, 327, 333, 342, 351, 372, 379, 424, 493, 519, 522, 590, 600
the (only) existent, "one without a second" 7, 21, 75, 213, 263, 317, 338, 448
"fixed in Brahman" (*brahmasaṃstha*) 256-57, 286
form of. *See ākāra* of Brahman
full (*pūrṇa*) 76, 78, 126, 269, 322, 421, 465-67, 517, 520
has absolute freedom, independence 524, 554
higher Brahman (*para, nirguṇa*) 26, 74-75, 77, 80-81, 107, 131, 137, 141, 173, 175, 187, 232-33, 277, 295, 465-466, 515, 527, 539, 581. *See also sākṣin*
how proved? 280, 348, 360, 396, 409, 417-18, 425, 434, 442, 451-52, 458, 466, 469, 478, 488, 531, 536, 545, 582, 587-89
identical with liberation. *See* liberation
inquiry into (*brahmajijñāsā*) 121-23, 343, 517-18, 581, 584-89. *See also adhikāra*
interior (*pratyagātman*) 120, 196, 311, 324, 340
relation to *jīva* 10, 28, 37, 41, 60-61, 73, 86-87, 132, 134, 136, 142, 159-61, 172, 174, 188-91, 193, 196, 219-20, 236, 315, 334, 406, 428, 461, 466, 483-84, 488, 505, 512, 517, 535, 555, 587, 599.
knowledge of. *See* Self-knowledge
lovability of 466, 484
lower (*apara, saguṇa*) 24, 26, 31, 50-51, 74, 77-78, 107, 137, 141, 175, 179-80, 186-87, 267, 272, 277, 281, 296, 407, 467, 515, 520, 539, 560. *See also* God
neither existent nor nonexistent 304 554
nondifferentiated, unmodified, partless 53, 148, 152, 168, 191-93, 197-98, 204, 213-14, 227, 237, 255, 311, 354, 358
nondifferent from, not dependent on *nimittas* 213-14, 354
nondifferent from world 259, 280, 406-7, 455, 478
nonagent 52, 126, 128, 167, 211, 227, 278, 292-93, 297, 299, 305, 308, 327, 422-25, 477, 502, 505, 517
not a product 49, 110, 122, 166, 196, 283, 372, 427, 468, 518, 522, 582
not subject to *duḥkha* or *saṃsāra* 6, 185, 196-27, 213, 231, 239, 244, 269-70, 293, 359, 423, 425, 489, 517
not a *śeṣa* 127, 231 -32
not *prakṛti* 130-36
not attained (*aprāpta*) 405-6, 525
omnipotent 122-23: 149, 407, 517
omniscient 110, 122-24, 129, 149, 232, 269, 468, 590
pure 122, 126, 145
sarvātman ("all-Self") 269, 359.
self-luminous, self-evident 76, 138, 267, 290, 314, 342, 434, 436, 445, 453, 458, 482, 495, 506, 515, 520, 527, 531, 536, 540
size of 135, 137-38, 167, 231, 425
states (*avasthā*) of. *See avasthā*
unchangeable (*kuṭastha*) 137, 227, 231, 287, 297, 302, 359, 479, 505-6, 517, 522, 540, 590, 599
union with 131-32, 174, 179, 187, 202, 268, 485-86
a universal 373-74, 418, 485
brāhmaṇa (Vedic directions for sacrifice) 3, 46, 485
brāhmaṇa (priestly caste). *See* Brahmin
Brahmanandin 12, 18
Brahmasiddhi (of Maṇḍana Miśra) 15, 17, 19, 56, 58-59, 99, 347-419
(*aham*) *brahmāsmi* (a *mahāvākya*) 232, 247, 319, 335, 470, 525, 528-30, 534, 538-39, 542
Brahmasūtras (of Bādarāyaṇa) 4-5, 9-11, 25, 75, 77, 87, 118-180, 294, 372, 550, 562, 588
attributed to Jaimini 537
Brahmasūtrabhāṣya (of Śaṃkara) 11, 15, 17-19, 23, 24-27, 31, 45, 51, 65, 69, 72, 74, 84-85, 89, 94-95, 115-16, 119-81, 217, 294, 308-9, 341, 564
Brahmasūtrabhāṣyaṭīkā (of Padmapāda) 563
Brahmasūtravṛtti (of Upavarṣa) 11, 18
Brahmasūtravṛttivārttika (of Sundara Pāṇḍya) 12, 18
Brahmavalli (chapter of *Taittirīya Upaniṣad*) 205, 521-30
Brahmin (*brāhmaṇa*) 30, 187, 192, 286, 299, 431, 467-68, 472-73, 489, 491, 518, 534, 588
killing a Brahmin, 423, 506
a true Brahmin 490
breath. *See prāṇa*
Bṛhadāraṇyaka Upaniṣad 25, 59, 75, 87-88, 107, 109, 124, 133-34, 136, 141, 144-45, 174, 177, 230, 254, 279, 290, 297, 348, 350, 363, 366-67, 370, 372, 418, 430, 453, 536, 582, 595, 600
Bṛhadāraṇyakopaniṣadbhāṣya (of Śaṃkara) 15, 18, 25, 48, 76, 95, 116, 180-204, 294, 436, 453, 461, 464-66, 480, 488 495, 520, 543
Bṛhadāraṇyakopaniṣadbhāṣyavārttika (of Sureśvara) 17, 19, 72, 180, 420-520, 530
Bṛhaspati 491, 561
(Gautama) Buddha 163, 317, 391, 396, 459, 553
buddha (enlightened person) 110-12, 114
used ironically 316
buddhi 22
activity of 225, 244, 341, 346, 544
and reasoning 280
and the sense organs 236-37, 479

as the discriminator of *jīva* from *ātman* 232, 234
as "heart" 199, 212, 497, 509, 613
as prototype in reflection analogy 86, 246, 251
as reflecting medium 20, 85, 199, 241, 245-46, 248, 264, 305-6, 324, 327, 498, 555-56, 577
as *upādhi* of *sākṣin* 246, 251
errors or constructions of 231-32, 239-40, 263-64, 376
immobile 237
in Buddhism 238
in the "cave" of the *Kaṭha Upaniṣad* 134
in deep sleep. *See suṣupti*
inert 232, 244
its order of creation 332
locus of desires and impressions 291, 229, 236, 462, 478
locus of merit 525, 556
=*mahat* 149, 143, 145, 293, 314, 353
material for 523
not the Self 199, 326-27, 334, 556-57
part of *antaḥkaraṇa* 330, 341, 553
part of subtle body 311, 319, 324, 330
part of *vijñānamayakośa* 331, 337, 341
=*prāṇa* 486, 497
product of karma 477
ruled by Bṛhaspati 561
role in dream production 478
size of 167
vṛttis of 497
Buddhism, Buddhists 8, 13, 19-21, 55, 64-65, 71, 79, 83-84, 93, 95, 105, 118, 150, 159-163, 181, 200, 243, 245, 305, 309, 356, 372, 376, 378, 385, 393, 405, 414, 434, 458, 498, 512, 545, 548, 550, 577. *See also* Ābhidharma, Dignāga, Mādhyamika, Vijñānavāda, Yogācāra
crypto-Buddhism 13
Budhakar, G. V. 604, 608

Caṇḍālas 260, 506, 540
Cārvāka (or Lokāyata, a materialist) 8, 19, 22, 122, 175, 181, 198, 244, 246, 291, 359, 503, 553, 556, 589. *See also dehātmavāda*
caste. *See varṇa*
catuṣkoṭi 113
cause, causality 7, 62-67, 113, 379-80, 463, 499
and effect, distinction between 41, 144-46, 149-50, 156. *See also satkāryavāda, asatkāryavāda, pariṇāma, vivarta,* etc.
inherence cause. *See samavāyikāraṇa*
instrumental cause. *See nimittakāraṇa*
material cause. *See upādāna*
nonorigination, no-cause theory. *See ajātivāda*
Nyāya-Vaiśeṣika analysis into three sorts 165, 305, 454, 552
Chakravarti, S. C. 605
chanda (meter, prosody) 133, 285
Chāndogya Upaniṣad 12, 25, 59, 88, 130-37, 141, 147, 165-66, 168, 171, 174, 176-77, 207, 230, 254-55, 259, 261, 263-67, 269-70, 287, 351, 358, 366-67, 408, 417, 429-30, 459, 478, 484-85, 512, 522, 571, 581, 595, 600
Chāndogyopaniṣadbhāṣya (of Śaṃkara) 15, 18, 17, 66, 85, 104, 116, 254-269
Chāndogyopaniṣadvākya (of Brahmanandin) 12, 18
Chāndogyopaniṣadvākyabhāṣya (of Draviḍācārya) 12, 18
change 62-67, 590. *See also pariṇāma, vivarta*
illusion of persistence through change. *See also ālātacakra* 454
charity (*dāna*) 256, 259 520
Chatterjee, Mohini M. 328
chāyā (shadow) 243, 556
-*mātra* (mere appearance) 408
Chintamani, T. R. 603
Christianity 37
Cidambaram 14, 17, 19, 117
Cidvilāsa 117
citta (individual consciousness) 82, 85, 106, 108, 111, 159, 234, 240, 311, 322, 330, 332, 341, 561
in Vijñānavāda 316
not conscious(ness) 246
part of *antaḥkaraṇa* 533
-*vṛtti* 324
-*vṛttinirodha* 471
color 264-65, 268, 291, 353, 560
conditions for seeing 458, 509
variegated (*citrarūpa*) 382
commentary 4-5
comparison (*upamāna*) 97, 286, 360, 553
concentration. *See samādhi*
conceptualism 55
Conio, Caterina 64, 606-7
Conjeeveram. *See* Kanchi
consciousness (*cit. caitanya, saṃvit*)
analogous to light 224. *See also jñāna, vijñāna, citta; prakāśa*
and bliss, relation between 76, 493
and superimposition. *See* superimposition
as the power of speech 54
between births 27-29
cidābhāsa 344, 477, 505
ciṅmātra 293
cidātman 494, 551, 562, 599
citiśakti 599
eternal 93, 167, 188, 225-26, 276, 284, 291
immediate. *See anubhava*
in Buddhism 21, 199, 498-500
in deep sleep. *See suṣupti*
not an act 92
not dependent on another 224
of the *jīva*. *See jñāna*
pure 21, 92, 154, 248, 445, 498. *See also* Brahman as pure consciousness; *jñāna, nirvikalpa* 21
reflective. *See anusaṃdhāna*
self-revealing, self-evident. *See svaprakāśa*
contact. *See saṃyoga*
contradiction 8, 378
self-contradiction 382
counterpositive (of an absence [*pratiyogin*]) 66, 377, 500, 606

creation 81-88, 106, 150-51, 185, 214-15, 325, 332, 341, 352-53. *See also* Brahman as cause; God as efficient cause
apparent creation (*kalpayati*) 107
creation of universe by each individual's acts 475
myths of creation 87-88, 273-75, 455-61, 560

dahāra 137-38
Dakṣiṇāmūrtimānasollāsa (attributed to Sureśvara). *See Mānasollāsa*
Dakṣiṇāmūrtistotra (attributed to Śaṃkara) 18, 317-18, 420, 555, 557
Das, A. C. 605
dama (detachment, restraint of organs) 36, 122, 272, 329, 336, 515, 520
Daśanāmins 16, 118
Daśaratha 247
Daśaślokī (attributed to Śaṃkara) 18, 333-34
Dasgupta, Surendra Nath 116
Datta, Dhirendra Mohan 605
death 22-24, 29, 33, 179, 182, 193-94, 202, 266, 453, 455, 474, 487-89, 497, 501
as a god 561
death of death 487
debts, three, to the gods 273, 363, 371, 434, 470-71, 473-74
dehātmavāda 495-96, 503
demerit (*adharma*) 31-32, 36, 44, 108, 128, 132, 206, 218, 228-29, 233, 258, 295-96, 299, 422, 458, 510, 531, 534
dependence 113, 149, 238
dependent nature (*paratantra*) 68, 111
mutual dependence (*anyonyāśraya*) 28, 240, 248-49, 352, 380, 578, 593
desire (*kāma*) 23-24, 34, 44, 49, 53, 201, 205-6, 226, 229, 235, 271-72, 280, 287, 304, 314-15, 349, 365-66, 429, 431, 435-36, 474, 479, 482, 502, 511-12, 561
for liberation (*mumukṣutva*). *See* liberation, desire for
a *kāraka*. *See* act, stems from desire
threefold (for sons, wealth, worlds) 278, 317, 489-90
De Smet, R. V. 308, 609
destruction (*nāśa, vināśa*) 506, 522
determinism and free will 29-31
Deussen, Paul 65, 78, 604, 606
deva. *See* gods
devadatta (yawning) 330
devaloka (world of the gods) 476
attained by meditation 181, 279
path of the. *See* path, northern
Devanandan, P. D. 78, 606
Devaraja, N. K. 604
dhanañjaya (digestion) 330. *See also* fire, digestive
dhāraṇa (attention) 322, 330, 333
dharma (duty, morality) 108, 121-23, 143-45, 176, 320, 391, 417, 427, 472, 584-85
varṇāśramadharma 176, 320
svadharma 256, 305, 320
dharma (in Buddhist sense of "entity") 111, 237, 350
dharma (property) 111, 350
Dharmakīrti 115-16, 346
Dharmapāla 103
dhyāna (contemplation) 322, 333. *See also upāsanā*
dialectic 8
difference (*bheda*) 6, 7, 34, 40-42, 50, 62, 68, 70, 114, 254-55, 257-58, 318, 353-54, 361, 373, 385-87, 409, 418, 527, 529, 559, 564
arguments against the reality of difference 71-73, 109, 147-49, 358, 376-84, 449-51, 507
as separateness. *See pṛthaktva*
between agent, act, and result 41, 220-21
between cause and effect. *See* cause
liberation as destruction of. *See* liberation
nondifference. *See abheda*
Dignāga's school of Buddhism 55. *See also* Vijñānavāda, Yogācāra
dik (spatial direction)
an effect? 166
dikviparyāsa (dizziness) 321, 379, 412, 460
discrimination (*viveka*)
awareness of (*vivekajñāna*) 406
of eternal from noneternal 122, 320
divinities. *See* gods
dizziness. *See dikviparyāsa*
doṣa. *See* fault
doubt (*saṃśaya*) 330, 394, 400, 411, 460, 482, 553
Draviḍācārya 12, 18, 191
dream (*svapna*) 13, 21, 24-26, 63, 72, 85, 89-91, 106-9, 146, 172, 199-202, 225, 228, 233-35, 240, 248, 252, 257, 265, 268, 286, 289, 298, 319, 321, 325-27, 338, 413, 460, 478-79, 484, 502, 504, 551, 556, 561-62, 568-69
as result of karma 90, 201, 234, 276, 290, 311-13, 318, 501, 505
analogy of 148, 152, 161, 321, 323, 499
three states of 502
Dṛgdṛśyaviveka. *See Vākyasudhā*
dṛk, dṛṣṭi (vision) 369-70, 444
dṛksthiti (fixed vision) 322
dṛkśakti (power of vision) 351
dṛṣṭisṛṣṭi 326
mithyādṛṣṭi (false vision) 369
tattvadṛṣṭi (vision of reality) 541
two kinds of 188, 196
duality. *See* difference
duḥkha (frustration) 110, 113, 128, 155, 168, 269, 285, 328, 331, 337, 348-49, 462. *See also* pain
Durgasaptatī (of Gauḍapāda?) 104
dvaitavāda (doctrine of duality) 264
Dvaita (Vedānta) 9, 14
Dvivedi, Manilal N. 310, 328
dvyaṇuka (double atom) 305
Dwarka 16, 18, 118

earrings, loss of, analogy of 128
earrings, disappearance of when known to be gold 321
earth (*pṛthivī*) 22, 24, 27, 88, 236, 287, 311, 318, 560
eating not a *nityakarman* 185
eclipse 318

effort (*yatna, prayatna*) 39, 226, 228, 439, 569
dependence of *dharma* on 123
necessity of it for liberation 209
ego, "I" 21, 121, 230, 251. *See also ahaṃkāra, abhimāna*
elements 108, 166, 171, 193, 201, 264, 332, 321, 458, 510, 556. *See also* earth, air, fire, water, *ākāśa*
gross (*bhūta, mahābhūta*) 24, 219, 318, 560
subtle. *See tanmātra*
empty terms 211. *See also* hare's horn
envy 337
Epics 25. *See also* Mahābhārata, Rāmāyaṇa
epistemology. *See* knowledge, theory of
error (*viparyāya, viparyāsa, bhrānti*) 7, 39, 42, 67, 79, 91, 120-21, 128, 178, 183, 189, 316, 367-68, 370, 385, 400, 409, 454, 460, 532. *See also avidyā, ajñāna*
theories of error (*khyātivāda*) 20, 69-71, 93-94, 347, 411-15, 539, 553, 558. *See also akhyāti-, ātma-, asat-, anyathā-,* and *anirvacanīya-khyātivāda*
excretion, organs of 22
exegesis of scripture (*mīmāṃsā*) 4-5, 46-53, 72, 585, 588
six principles of 430-31
external world, object (*bāhyārtha*) 306. *See also bāhyārthavāda*
existence of 161-62, 199-201
awareness of 311
eye 311. *See also* visual organ

Faddegon, Barend 608
fainting 173, 321
faith. *See śraddhā*
fatalism 29-30
fatigue 265
fault (*doṣa*) 228, 241
in the knower 38
in the (sense) organs 414, 456, 566
fear (*bhaya*) 128, 216, 231, 359, 456-58, 581
-lessness (*abhaya*) 228, 494, 519, 530
of doing evil 258
figurative language, figure of speech. *See* meaning, figurative; metaphor
fire, light (*tejas*) 24, 88, 292-93, 237, 263-66, 318, 379, 650. *See also* Agni, *prakasa*
digestive 135, 556. *See also agni*
five fires 259
sacred fire 229, 242, 258-59, 299, 311
sparks from a fire, analogy of 84, 191, 311, 485
wheel of fire. *See ālātacakra*
food (anna) 26, 28, 88, 171-72, 176, 185, 263-65, 480, 494, 518, 523-24
foodstuffs in sacrifice 475
matter as food for the gods 274
sheath of (*annamayakośa*) 91, 215, 331, 341, 524
three kinds of 475
forbearance. *See Yama*
forest-dwelling (*vanaprasthya*) 34, 36, 286, 289
fowler's son, analogy of 191
Frauwallner, Erich 346, 610
free will 29-31, 168
and determinism. *See* determinism and free will
frustration. *See duḥkha*

Gadgil, V. A. 607
Gambhirananda 205, 278, 280-81, 284, 289
Gandhāra, mean reaching, analogy of 230, 266
Gandharvas, city of the 286, 321, 510
Ganeśa 339
Gaṅgā, Ganges 117
Gārgī 423, 490-91
Gārgya 477
Gauḍa 13
Gauḍapāda 12-14, 18, 20, 33, 45, 63-70, 72, 79, 83-84, 87, 89, 91, 103-14, 116-18, 309, 335, 479, 600
Gauḍapādakārikās 12-14, 18, 81, 89, 103-14, 550-51
Gauḍapādakārikābhāṣya (of Śaṃkara) 18, 82, 103-4, 116, 118, 308-17
Gautama, author of *Nyāyasūtras* 187
Gautamadharmasūtras 371
gavaya 354
Gayatrī 520
gestation of foetus in mother's womb 27-28
Ghate, V. S. 608
ghost (*preta*)
in an empty place, analogy of 321
-ly state 281
Giri. *See* Toṭaka
Giri (one of the *daśanāmas*) 118
Giri, Maheshananda 551
God (*Īśvara*). *See also* Viṣṇu, Śiva, etc.
abode of subtle body 140
as cause of difference 77-78, 132, 554
as creator of *jīvas* 82, 87, 123, 164-65
as creator of *dharma* or universal order 295
as creator of scripture 164, 340
as "death" 453
as (non)different from *jīvas* 130, 133, 164, 168, 187, 276, 303, 332, 558, 574
as efficient cause of the world 77, 81-89, 123, 163-65, 172, 273-75, 340, 480, 554
as establisher of meanings of words 56, 448
as manipulator of karmic developments 31, 68, 70, 77, 123, 153, 164, 168, 174, 189, 213, 299, 311, 317-18, 455, 468, 488
as material cause of the world 77, 84, 163-65, 340
as obstructor of endeavors 470
as *saguṇa* Brahman. *See* Brahman, lower
as Witness. *See sākṣin*
the *devatā* of darkness 561
devotion to, faith in 295, 323, 531
does He have desires? 77, 106, 113, 164, 168
embodied? 132, 301-2

free from sin 132, 152-53, 164 168
God's play (*līlā*, *krīḍa*) 77-78, 106, 152, 359
grace of 168, 209, 336, 551
Īśvaratva 318, 553. *See also aiśvarya*
meditation on, worship of. *See upāsanā*
omnipotent 77, 87, 123, 148, 340, 470
omnipresent 137, 164, 340
omniscient 77, 87, 113, 123, 148, 152, 164, 183, 301, 311, 332, 340, 349
=*prājña*. *See prājña*
proofs of the existence of God 123-24, 590
qualified by *avidyā*, *māyā*, *upādhis*? 88, 148-49, 287, 332, 340, 461, 551-52, 554
reflected in *avidyā* 455, 552
śaktis of 337, 552-53, 555, 590
the term "*Īśvara*" 115, 295
thirty-six *mūrtis* of 559
gods (*deva*) 25-26, 108, 138-40, 188-89, 235, 270, 274, 289, 295, 427, 455-56, 461, 472, 481, 488, 492, 494, 504, 510, 553
Presiding (*adhipati*) 330, 341
their bodies 138-39
way of the gods. *See* path, northern
world of the gods. *See devaloka*
Govindānanda 11
Govinda Bhagavatpāda 14, 16, 117, 335, 339
grammar 244
arguments from 48
the science of (*vyākaraṇa*) 285
Grammarians (Vaiyākaraṇas) 20
grāhyagrāhaka (grasper and grasped) 199, 201
grasping, organ of 22
Guha, A. 603
guṇa 329, 337, 350, 482, 488, 538, 599
guṇatva. 390, 393
in Sāṃkhya 108, 128-29, 152, 155, 238, 466, 552, 598
in Vaiśeṣika 239, 315, 355, 382, 552
viśeṣaguṇa 358
guru (teacher, guide) 8, 37-38, 117, 272, 317, 325, 531, 559, 599
grace of 336, 469
as one with God 340
guruparamparā (teacher lineage) 420

Hacker, Paul 115-16, 118-19, 204, 217, 294, 308-10, 320, 323-25, 328, 335, 598, 600, 607-19, 613
happiness 26, 29. *See also* pleasure
hare's horn 161, 305, 454
Harzer, Edeltraud 598, 601-2
Hastāmālaka 16, 18-19, 601
Hastāmālakastotra 18-19, 601-2
hāṭhayoga 323, 560
"heart" (*hṛdaya*) 24, 133-34, 479, 494, 497, 512, 604
heat 236, 241
heaven (*svarga*) 8, 25-27, 30, 32-33, 38, 47, 49-50, 171, 194-95, 229, 256, 258-59, 273, 281, 296, 421, 423, 429-30, 432-33, 439, 440, 445-47, 513, 529, 588-89
hell 25-27, 171, 260, 281, 349. *See also Saṃyamanam*
hetu or *liṅga* in inference 392, 500
Himālaya 16
Hinduism 3, 5, 34, 37, 44
Hiraṇyagarbha 27, 50, 87, 179, 182, 185, 259, 277-79, 281, 307, 319, 341, 455-56, 461, 473-74, 476, 481, 487, 489, 494, 514-15, 562
Hiriyanna, Mysore 50, 347, 530, 534, 603, 605, 608, 610, 612
householdership (*gṛhasthya*) 34, 36, 45, 208-9, 256-59, 272, 289, 298, 301, 329, 371-72, 474, 518
humility 337
hunger and thirst 258, 270, 274, 489
hymn (*stotra*) 317

icchā (desire, wishing) 349
identity (*tādātmya*, *ekatva*) 150, 174, 194, 381
identity and difference 62-73, 147-48
identity statements. *See tattvamasi*
of *ātman* and *Brahman*. *See Brahman*, *tattvamasi*
of *jīva* and *ātman*. *See Brahman*, relation to *jīva*
of positive with negative 449
of Witness and ego 245
ignorance 7-8, 65, 73, 78. *See also avidyā*, *ajñāna*
illusion. *See* error
Indo-European languages 3
Indra 88, 133, 138, 235, 274, 461, 472, 493, 518, 561
thunderbolt of. *See* Vajra
inference (*anumāna*) 97, 99, 123, 142, 241, 275, 286, 354, 357, 360, 381, 389-92, 399-400, 434, 499-500, 528, 540, 553, 571, 579
critique of 496-97
pariśeṣānumāna 590
infinite regress (*anavasthā*) 157, 200, 226-27, 239, 292, 350, 386, 388, 394, 438, 498, 522, 529, 541
Ingalls, Daniel H.H. 80, 116, 118, 180-81, 294, 308, 320, 335, 604, 606-10
inherence. *See samavāya*
injunction (*vidhi*, *codanā*) 357. *See also niyoga*, *liṅ*, *karmakāṇḍa*, act
all scripture dominated by injunctive mood. *See karmakāṇḍa*, *jñānakāṇḍa*
as *pramāṇa*. *See* scripture, validity of
cannot provide Self-knowledge 526
exclusive (*parisaṃkhyāvidhi*) 365, 433, 464, 517, 536, 611
four purposes or results of. *See* acts, four kinds of results of
injunction to know Brahman 364-66, 487-91, 409-10, 414-17, 441-42, 484, 525, 530, 535-36, 581-83, 594-95, 600, 612
injunction to know the truth (*pratipattividhi*) 403
injunction to meditate on Brahman 51-52, 465, 530
negative injunction proscription. *See*

act, prohibited
of eligibility (*adhikāraviddhi*) 403, 443-44
of or in the Vedas. *See* scripture, Vedas
originative injunction (*utpattividhi*) 403, 443-44
possibility of 168-69
primary or initial (*apūrvavidhi*) 58, 185-86, 433, 464, 536
restrictive injunction (*niyamavidhi*) 18, 365, 433, 464-65, 517, 536, 611
to a Self-knower 43-44, 168-69, 184, 255, 271-72
source of force of 452
what can be enjoined 123, 126-27, 173, 195, 271, 388-91, 402-5, 432, 434, 437, 611
innocence 317
insects 25
rebirth as 260, 281
intention (*tātparya*)
awareness 22
of speaker 58, 437
internal organ 23-24, 87, 90, 121, 123, 170, 202, 228, 235, 254, 265, 277, 282, 284, 459, 462, 482, 505, 533, 540, 599. *See also buddhi*, *manas*, *antaḥkaraṇa*
as effect 166
as self 122, 599
in Vaisesika 169-70
invariable concomitance (*avyabhicāra*, *avinābhāva*, *vyāpti*) 414, 496, 500. *See also anvayavyatireka*
Īśā Upaniṣad 270, 278-79, 284, 354, 474
Īśopaniṣadbhāṣya (of Śaṃkara) 18, 278-80
īśvara. *See* God
itihāsa 485
itikartavyatā or *itthaṃbhava* (modus operandi) 404-5, 428, 439
Iyer, K. S. 23, 604-5, 609
Iyer, R. Krishnaswami 598

Jābāla Upaniṣad 135, 371, 434
Jacob, G. A. 217, 530, 605, 608, 612
Jacobi, Hermann 308, 603
jaḍa (inert) 108, 115, 331, 358, 459, 551, 565
Jagadananda 217, 326, 334
Jaimini 4, 31, 135, 175, 179, 422, 428, 512, 531, 537, 581, 584, 596-97
Jainism 8, 19, 71, 163, 333, 381, 509
Digambaras 316, 384
Janaka 296, 493-95, 497, 508, 513, 519
japa (repeated recitation) 374, 388, 481
jarā (old age) 489
jāti (genus, class-characteristic) 55-56, 351, 393-94, 418, 477. *See also* universal.
jāti. *See birth*
jaundice, illusion produced by 321, 411, 460
Jayanta Bhaṭṭa 11
jealousy 337
Jha, Ganganatha 255, 604
jīva (*ātman*, individual self)
as agent. *See* agent
as constructor of dream objects 89-90 501, 504
as "death" 455
as experiencer. *See bhoktṛ*
as *kṣetrajña* 287, 523
as transmigrator 24-25, 27, 29, 140, 151, 179, 276-77, 424, 478, 501-2, 508-11, 523. *See also* karma
as *vijñānamayakośa*, s.v.
beginningless 352
defined 109, 332
embodied in plants 172
how created? 82-83, 87, 108-9, 340, 480
in Jainism 163
in sleep. *See sleep*
locus of *avidyā*? 80, 352, 468
misinterpretations of 108
perceptible 366
proof of 275
a reflection. *See* reflection
relation to Brahman. *See* Brahman, relation to *jīva*
relation to God. *See* God
relation to its body 169-70, 287, 326, 487, 504, 510
relation to Witness. *See sākṣin*
relation to world 81, 151, 171, 214, 264, 551
subject of Self-knowledge 576
untrue 264, 418
jīvanmukti (liberation while living) 34-35, 43, 202, 324-25, 335-36, 342-43, 352, 408, 416, 494, 559, 562
jñāna (awareness, cognition) 24, 62, 75, 111-12, 373, 415-16, 569, 612
and action. *See* act and knowledge
false (*mithyā-*). *See* error
momentary 352, 355, 405, 450
in Nyāya-Vaiśeṣika 239, 353, 356
nirvikalpakajñāna 92, 110, 353, 386, 498
savikalpakajñāna 92, 353, 381, 386, 498
sākāra/nirākāra 306
true (*samyak*) 531. *See also pramā*, *vidyā*
-vidhi. *See* injunction to knowledge
jñānabhūmi (stages of knowledge) 343
jñānakāṇḍa (declarative section of scripture) 8, 46-54, 57, 204, 208, 270, 421, 428-30, 432-34, 436, 440, 443-44, 446, 448, 517-18
jñānakarmasamuccaya (*vāda*) (combined-path view) 20, 40-41, 45, 49-51, 270-71, 296, 298, 431, 508, 513, 535
jñānayoga (path of knowledge) 45, 325
jñāpaka (function of making something known) 53, 435, 440, 446
Joshi, Lal Mani 604, 607
Joshi, R. B. 78-79, 606
juggler (*indrajāla*) 325, 357
jyotiṣṭoma 475

Kahola 196, 489
kaivalya (isolation) 255, 335, 474, 541, 555. *See also* liberation
Kaladi 16, 117
kalpa 139-40

the science of ritual 285
kalpanā (constructing, construction) 68, 216, 237, 240, 262, 294, 318, 325, 351-52, 355, 407, 513, 521-22, 569, 582. *See also vikalpa*
kalpanāviṣaya (constructed object) 378, 539
nirbījakalpanā 383
kāma. *See* desire
Kamakoti Pitha (at Conjeeveram) 17-18
kāmaśāstra 16, 459
kāmavilayavāda 49-50, 431
kāmyakarman. *See* act, optional
Kaṇāda 157, 187, 512, 553, 590
Kanchi (Conjeeveram) 17-18, 118
kañcuka (mask) 546
Kane, P. V. 347, 603
Kāṇva recension of Śukla-Yajurveda 180, 421
Kapila 142-43
kāraka (function of prompting activity to obtain a result) 53, 439, 446, 458
kāraka (grammatical case ending) 211
karaṇa (instrument) 251, 290, 428, 43
karma. *See also* act, *adṛṣṭa*, *apūrva*
āgamin or *sañcīyamāna karman* 23, 29, 34, 338
and dreams. *See* dream
and *saṃnyāsa*. *See saṃnyāsa*
conditions world-creation 459, 503
demeritorious 27, 29, 205-6, 260, 500-501
destroyed by Self-knowledge 178, 189, 231, 266, 304, 423, 487, 531-33
how it controls destiny of the *jīva* 24-30, 171-72, 202, 231, 259-60, 328, 349, 423, 471, 477-79, 488, 501, 508, 511, 523, 530
karmatva 393
karmavipāka and *karmakṣaya* (maturation and exhaustion of karma) 22-23, 31, 42, 178-79, 201, 205-7, 259, 326, 342, 307-9, 422-23, 474, 536
karmic residues (*karmānuśaya*) 22-34, 36, 140, 171, 259-60, 306. *See also saṃskāra*, *vāsanā*
law of 29-30, 49-50, 189
locus of 503, 561
meritorious 26, 178, 189, 205-6, 500-501
prārabdhakarman 23, 29, 31, 34-35, 42, 178, 186, 189, 205, 231, 266, 288, 304-5, 321-22, 335, 338, 408, 458, 471, 536, 562, 597, 604
produced by effort 228
produced by *nityakarmans*. *See* act, regular daily
sañcitakarman 23, 29, 31, 266, 332, 335, 338, 408, 604
karmakāṇḍa (injunctive section of scripture) 8, 46-53, 57, 181, 191-92, 204, 208, 270, 421, 425, 428-29, 432-34, 436, 440, 443-44, 447-49, 453, 488, 517-18, 596. *See also* injunction
karman (grammatical object, objective) 248, 350
Karmarkar, R. D. 609
karmayoga 301, 306
kartavyatā (future result) 348, 434-35
kārya (effect) 7, 48, 196, 406. *See also* cause
kārya (something to be accomplished) 427, 435-39
kāryahetu 500
Kāśakṛtsna 10, 87, 142
kāṣaya (faults) 317
Kāśī, King of 477
Kāśīmokṣavicāra (attributed to Sureśvara) 19, 420
Kashmir 14
Kashmir Śaivism 16, 551
kaṣṭajvara (typhoid fever) 444
kaṭaka (clearing- or soap-nut) 43, 90, 323, 354, 501
Kaṭha Upaniṣad 134, 138, 140-41, 270, 280, 284, 461, 556
Kaṭhopaniṣadbhāṣya (of Śaṃkara) 18, 20-21, 310
Kauśītakī Upaniṣad 133, 141, 174, 476, 492
Kauśītakyupaniṣadbhāṣya (attributed to Śaṃkara) 19, 345
Kawada, Kumataro 604, 607
Kena Upaniṣad 281-83
Kenopaniṣad(pada)bhāṣya (of Śaṃkara) 18, 116, 281-84
Kenopaniṣad (vākya)bhāṣya (of Śaṃkara) 18, 281, 310
Kerala 16, 18, 117
Khilakāṇḍa (section of *Bṛhadāraṇyaka Upaniṣad*) 520
kleśa (hindrance, impurity) 111, 208, 289, 352, 359
knower (*jñātṛ*, *pramātṛ*) 6, 121, 235, 248. *See also jīva*
and knowledge, relation between 225
and known, relation between 42, 228
knowledge 62. *See jñāna*, *vidyā*, *pramā*
is it an act? 33, 38-40, 225, 244, 250-51, 284. *See also* act, incompatible with knowledge
not a result 227
role in liberation. *See vidyā*, *jñānayoga*, etc.
theory of knowledge 92-100
kośa (sheath), theory of 91, 109, 205, 324, 330-31, 338, 510, 524-25, 529
krama (a kind of exegetical evidence) 431
kramamukti. *See* liberation, progressive
kratu (resolve) 510
Krishna, Daya 608
kṛkara (-appetite) 330
Kṛṣṇa 5, 45, 295-96, 300
kṛttika 500
kṣātriya 299, 472-73, 534
Kumarappa, B. 605
Kumārila 4, 15-17, 20, 57, 59, 71, 116, 346, 353, 374, 380-81
kuṇḍalinī 556
kūrma (opening the eyes) 330

Laghuvākyavṛtti (attributed to Śaṃkara) 19, 345
lamp, analogy of 95, 199-200, 248, 334, 498
language 8, 357-58. *See also* meaning, *śabda*

acquisition or learning of 48, 57-58, 360, 362, 399-400, 435, 443, 592. *See also vyutpatti*
as communication 58, 361, 398, 400-1, 417, 437, 593
philosophy of language 46-61
Lāṅkāvatāra Sūtra 607
laya (dissolution) 110, 415, 432, 478
layayoga 560
leech 25, 510
length of life (*āyus*) 28-30, 32, 34
liberation (*mokṣa, mukti, niḥśreyasa*). *See* also *kaivalya*
and Brahmaloka. *See* Brahmaloka
and karma. *See* karma
and *saṃnyāsa*. *See saṃnyāsa*
as eternal pleasure. *See* bliss
as removal of *avidyā* 36, 39-40, 43, 125-26, 288
backsliding from 35, 42, 145-46, 153, 176, 359, 406
definition, nature of 32-38, 180, 205, 335, 338, 352, 405, 422, 489, 546
desire for liberation (*mumukṣutva*) 36, 122, 176, 218, 221, 320, 337, 339-40, 429, 452
eligibility for. *See adhikāra*
eternal, beginningless and endless 39, 125-26, 177, 195, 202, 206, 306, 405, 421-22, 595
four ways of obtaining liberation 537-38, 546
in Bhedābhedavāda 49, 51, 476-77
in deep sleep. *See suṣupti*
in Mīmāṃsā 32, 47, 476
in Nyāya 355-56, 595
in the womb 28-29, 277. *See also* Vāmadeva
is Brahman 421-22, 490, 493
is or requires Self-knowledge. *See* Self-knowledge
means of achieving. *See* paths
not an effect 32-33, 97, 196, 203, 238, 242, 286, 288, 371, 388-89, 405-7, 421-22, 427, 464
occasioned by hearing a *mahāvākya* 54, 247
possibility of 167, 169, 238-39, 315, 337, 422, 424, 470, 535
progressive (*kramamukti*) 27, 406, 581
properties of liberated one 37, 94, 180
role of action in. *See* act, *karmakāṇḍa, Self-knowledge*, injunction
role of meditation in. *See upāsanā*
science of (*mokṣaśāstra*) 148
while living. *See jīvanmukti*
life (*jīvana*) 29-32, 189
length of. *See* length of life
light (*prakāśa*) 24, 138, 287, 311, 354, 358, 552, 554. *See also* fire
lightning 25-26
limitation model (*avacchedavāda*) 599. *See also* pot-space
liṅ (optative) 48, 401-2, 404, 442
liṅga, a kind of exegetical evidence 430
liṅga=hetu. *See hetu*
liṅga. *See* body, subtle
locomotion, organ of 22
lokasaṃgraha (world-order) 37
Lokāyata. *See* Cārvāka
love (*prema*) 35-37, 351, 466
lust 337
lying 396, 398
lie-detection test 267

Mādhava 117, 347
Madhavananda 181, 335
Madhu Brāhmaṇa (section of *Bṛhadāraṇyaka Upaniṣad*) 475, 486, 519
Madhusūdana Sarasvatī 333
Madhva 14, 105
Mādhyamika (Buddhism) 13, 21, 162, 199, 557
Mādhyandina recension of Śukla-Yajurveda 180, 513-14
magic show, magician, analogy of 88, 90, 106, 146, 241, 273, 311, 317, 353-54, 478, 541
Mahābhārata 5, 476, 485
Mahadevan, T. M. P. 17, 317 333, 420-21, 604, 607-8, 612
mahat. *See buddhi=mahat*
mahāvākya (great sentences of the Upaniṣads) 51, 54, 59, 427, 457, 465, 515-17, 550, 583
interpretation of 59-61, 537
Maitreyī (Yājñāvalkya's wife) 141, 423, 483
-Brāhmaṇa (section of *Bṛhadāraṇyaka Upaniṣad*) 483, 519
Maitrī Upaniṣad 78
Majumdar, J. L. 20, 309, 604, 607, 609
Malabar 16
Malkani, G. R. 605
manas (intellectual organ)
as reflecting medium 498
control of 110
does it move? 237, 556
grasps external objects 342, 475
in Nyāya-Vaiśeṣika 315, 356, 553
in subtle body, transmigratory process 23, 171, 179, 319, 324, 330, 475, 561
locus of desire, aversion, etc. 425
locus of error, constructions 237, 385, 412, 561. *See also* dream
locus of meditation, worship 255, 297
locus of *taijasa* 106
mānasapratyaya 268
mānasika act. *See* act, mental
manomayakośa 91, 215, 331, 341, 497, 524, 559, 568
modifications of 337
not the Self 198, 275, 326, 334, 341
operator of sense organs 475
order of creation of 332
part of *antaḥkaraṇa* 341, 553
presiding divinity of 475, 561
a reflection of *buddhi* 20, 306
Mānasollāsa (of Sureśvara?) 19, 317, 420, 550-60
Mānavadharmaśāstra (the "Laws of Manu") 24, 285, 371, 434, 457, 476
Maṇḍana Miśra 14-17, 19-20, 27, 42-43, 51-52, 54, 56-59, 63, 71-72, 75-76, 79-80, 85, 90, 98-100, 116-8, 346-420, 534

Māṇḍūkyakārikās (of Gauḍapāda). *See Gauḍapādakārikās*
Māṇḍūkya Upaniṣad 12, 59, 89, 104-5, 502
Māṇḍūkyopaniṣadbhāṣya (of Śaṃkara) 18, 308-12
maṅgala (invocation) 121, 309
mantavya 123, 125, 127
mantra 104, 183, 219, 229, 388, 436, 485, 519-20, 582
  mantrayoga 560
Mantra Upaniṣad. *See Muṇḍaka Upaniṣad*
Manu 470
  "Laws of." *See Mānavadharmaśāstra*
marriage 229
Märschner, Käthe 607-8
materialism. *See* Cārvāka
maṭha 16-18, 420
māyā 559
  and deep sleep. *See suṣupti*
  as *avyakta* (*prakṛti*) 286, 553
  as dissimulation 289
  as God's power? 79, 554
  cannot cause real results 109
  cause of dreams 172, 240
  cause of *jīva* 60, 551-52
  cause of, nature of world-appearance 65, 68, 106, 113, 232, 317, 325, 551, 554, 568-69
  destroyed by devotion 559
  frequency of term in Śaṃkara 115
  in Vijñānavāda 20, 79
  jīva's power 81, 107
  a Paurāṇika category 553
  relation to *avidyā* 78-80, 140, 277, 299, 318, 332, 337, 340, 351-52, 455, 457, 553, 558-60, 574, 576
  seed of awareness 240-41
  scholarship on 78
Māyāpañcaka (attributed to Śaṃkara) 19, 344
Mayeda, Sengaku 115-16, 217, 281, 294, 309, 320, 324, 335, 607-10
meaning
  connection of words in a sentence 397-400
  figurative (*gauṇa*) 55, 59-61, 225, 263, 267, 292, 300, 303, 307-8. *See also* metaphor
  primary (*abhidhā*, *śakti*) 55, 242, 244, 348, 400, 426, 539, 596
  relational 543
  secondary (*lakṣaṇā*) 55, 225, 242, 244, 351, 426, 442, 483, 525, 539, 541-42, 555
  sentence-meaning (*vākyārtha*) 57-58, 252-53, 262, 357, 388, 393, 397-98, 402-3, 418, 443, 447, 484, 521, 543-44, 588. *See also tattvamasi*, *mahāvākya*
  single sentence meaning (*ekavākyatā*) 428-29
  theory of meaning 54-60, 99, 139, 334-35, 388, 391, 401-2, 437-39, 447-48, 521, 529, 531, 589, 596-97
medicine 256, 422, 444
meditation. *See upāsana*
memory, recollection 69, 94, 120, 186, 189, 226, 234-35, 249, 252, 315, 338, 392, 396-97, 400, 411-12, 460, 553, 558, 561, 566-69
  impossible in Buddhism 238
  memory of previous births 495-96
  memory traces 83
Menon, P. N. 323, 608
merit (*dharma*) 31, 44, 108, 128, 228, 233, 269, 295, 422, 457-58, 510, 531, 534. *See also* karma, meritorious
metaphor (*upacāra*) 59-60, 110, 125, 128, 130, 134, 184, 190, 211-12, 348, 351, 393, 436, 571, 600
metaphysics 74-91
milk and curds, analogy of 151, 379
(Pūrva) Mīmāṃsā 4-5, 11, 15, 19, 31, 38-40, 43, 47-49, 52-53, 55-56, 92-93, 99, 117-18, 127, 139, 183, 333, 346-47, 364, 382, 399, 410, 420, 427, 437, 476, 531-32, 536-38, 612
(*Pūrva*) *Mīmāṃsāsūtras* (of Jaimini) 4, 11, 124, 139, 143, 365, 388, 391, 401, 417, 422, 427-28, 445, 581-82, 584, 596
Mīmāṃsāsūtrabhāṣya (of Śabara) 438
mirage, analogy of 228-29, 286, 297, 313, 321, 324, 532
(dirty) mirror, analogy of 33, 60, 73, 85-86, 126, 234, 240, 242-43, 247, 264-65, 281, 317, 324, 351, 354, 533, 554, 574-76
Misra, Ganeswar 605
Mithila 19
Mitra 608
modesty 218
Modi, P. M. 296, 608-9
modification. *See vikāra*
moha (confusion, delusion, stupidity) 233, 317, 337, 428, 489
mokṣa. *See* liberation
momentariness (*kṣaṇikatva*) 21, 55, 150, 159-61, 200, 409, 522, 578
momentary cognition as self 122, 237-38
monism 7, 63
monotheism 7
moon 24, 27, 289, 318
  as fruit of actions 476
  as a god 581
  as time aspect of Prajapati 475
  double moon, illustration of error 42, 120, 216, 221, 257, 321, 358, 370, 411-12, 522, 562, 566, 570, 597
  way of the moon. *See* path, southern
morality 35-36, 44. *See also dharma*
  beyond. *See* antinominomianism
  moral obligation 41
motion 236, 552
  first motion in Vaiśeṣika 156-57
mudra 318
Mukherji, A. C. 609
mūlabandha (subduing the root) 322
mūlādhāra 556
Müller, F. Max 284, 609
muṇḍaka, meaning of the term 284
Muṇḍaka Upaniṣad 135-36, 138, 270, 284-89, 367-68, 430, 536, 571
Muṇḍakopaniṣadbhāṣya (of Śaṃkara) 18, 116, 284-89
muni (sage; silent meditator) 177, 324, 490, 518

Munikāṇḍa (section of *Bṛhadāraṇyaka Upaniṣad*) 519
mūrta (material) 108
mutual dependence, fallacy of. *See* dependence, mutual

Nāciketas 280
nāda (a Śaiva category) 553, 556
nāḍī (nerve, vein) 24, 90, 172, 266, 478-79, 494, 504, 509, 556
nāga (vomiting) 330
Nāgārjuna 96
naimittika act. *See* act, occasional
Naiṣkarmyasiddhi (of Sureśvara) 17, 19, 217, 420, 530-50
Nakamura, Hajime 603
name (*nāman*) 239, 250, 310, 323, 459, 487
  and form (*nāmarūpa*) 74, 79, 115, 123, 131, 135, 148, 171, 197, 214, 216, 219, 259, 261, 264-65, 286, 292, 295, 364, 415, 417, 458-59, 461, 481, 512, 574
  a kind of exegetical evidence 431
  nameable (*abhidheya*) 310
  secret (*nāman upaniṣad*). *See* truth of truth
Narada 136
Nārāyaṇa, author of *Māṇḍūkyopaniṣadṭīkā*
Narmada river 14, 117
nāstika (heterodox thinkers) 233
neti neti ("not this, not this") 54, 60, 74-75, 109, 173, 193, 230, 242, 304, 314, 453, 482-83, 541
Nigamanakāṇḍa (of *Bṛhadāraṇyaka Upaniṣad*). *See Maitreyī Brāhmaṇa*
nihilism 222-23, 291, 316, 453, 482-83. *See also* Mādhyamika, Cārvāka
niḥśreyasa. *See* liberation
Nikhilananda 605
nimeśa ("the twinkling of an eye" : a short period of time) 322
nimitta (*kāraṇa*, instrumental cause; occasion) 142, 213, 394, 413, 606
nirmāṇakāya (dream body) 201
nirodha (suppression, cessation) 186
  three kinds of in Sarvāstivāda 160
nirukta (science of etymology) 285
nirvāṇa 21, 500. *See also* liberation
  brahmanirvāṇa 339
niṣedha. *See* act, prohibited
nitya
  nityakarman. *See* act, regular daily
  nonapplicability of term 113
  pariṇāminitya vs. *kuṭasthanitya* 125
nivṛtti (inaction, abstention from activity) 295, 299-300, 348, 357, 361-62, 365, 403, 419, 433, 435, 474, 559
niyama (observances) 256, 258, 301, 322, 337, 518
niyoga (prescription) 48, 241, 362, 365, 387, 390, 399, 402, 404, 410, 434, 437-43, 445, 447
  Niyogavāda 48-49, 434-44, 525-30. *See also* Prābhākara
nominalism 55
nonattachment (*vairāgya*, *asaṅga*) 36, 40, 44-45, 113-14, 122, 195, 218, 286, 320, 329, 336, 339, 343, 422, 457, 483, 490, 502-3, 533
  two kinds of 325
noneternal (*anitya*), nonapplicability of term 113
nonviolence (*ahiṃsā*) 208, 218
Nṛsiṃhatāpanīyopaniṣadbhāṣya (of Gauḍapāda?) 104
Nṛsiṃhottaratāpanīyopaniṣadbhāṣya (attributed to Śaṃkara) 19, 345
Nyāya, Naiyāyika 8, 11, 19, 55-57, 71, 93, 100, 149-50, 192, 261, 315, 351, 353, 380-82, 393, 454, 481, 498, 511, 517, 553, 570, 589, 595
Nyāyasūtras (of Gautama) 164

object. *See also viṣaya*
  bare object 385
  object of injunction 404-5, 409
  object of Self-awareness 7
  supporting object. *See ālambana*
obligations to man, ancestors, and gods. *See* debts
om. *See aum*
omniscience 106, 292. *See* Brahman, God
  of *prakṛti* 129
optative mood *See liṅ*organs
  as self 122. *See* sense organs; action, organs of, internal organ
overintellectualism 3, 5-6

pada (footprint) 465-66
padārtha (meaning of a word) 348, 434
  as category in Vaiśeṣika 393
Padmapāda 11, 16-17, 19, 43, 72-73, 75, 79, 82-83, 86-87, 117-18, 420, 563-97
pain 26-27, 304, 494, 593-94. *See also duḥkha*
  location of 220
Pañcapādikā (commentary by Padmapāda on Śaṃkara's *Brahmasūtrabhāṣya*) 17, 19, 82-83, 563-97
Pāñcarātra 5, 333
Pañcīkaraṇa (attributed to Śaṃkara) 18, 318-19, 560, 562
Pañcīkaraṇavārttika (attributed to Sureśvara) 19, 318, 420, 560-62
Pandey, Sangam Lal 103-4, 603, 607
paṇḍita, etymology of 490
Pāṇini 136
pāpma (evil) 501
paradox 8, 34-35
paramahaṃsa 118, 218, 258, 314
parāmarśa (consideration) 351
  in inference 357
paramārtha, *-ika* (higher standpoint, reality) 34-35, 67, 108, 113, 197, 215, 352, 448, 521, 541, 567-68
parāvṛtti (abstention) 320
parental influence 27-28
parikalpita (imaginary nature) 263, 532, 539
  in Yogācāra 68

pariṇāma (*vāda*) 7, 66-67, 82, 84, 86, 142, 346, 352, 358, 406, 552, 567, 574, 598
pariṇāmin (evolver) 251, 540
pariniṣpanna (absolute nature), in Yogācāra 68
parivrājaka 118
part and whole 383-84
Pārvata (one of the *daśanāmas*) 118
path (*yāna*, *gati*) 208, 493, 513
  northern, way of gods (*devayāna*) 24-27, 175, 179-80, 255, 259, 281, 286, 288-89.
  southern, way of fathers (*pitṛyāna*) 24-25, 255, 259-60, 281
perception (*pratyakṣa*)
  an act 196
  and immediate awareness of Self 97-98, 241, 368, 426
  and memory distinguished 412
  as *pramāṇa* for Brahman? 360, 392, 495-96
  conditions of perceptibility of things 65, 369, 380-81, 412
  fallacious (*pratyakṣābhāsa*) 254
  grasps difference? 98, 360, 380-81, 449. *See also* abhava, perceptibility of
  a *pramāṇa* 97, 286, 389, 553, 556
  relation to inference 191-92
  savikalpakapratyaksa 386, 611. *See also jñāna*, *savikalpaka*
  scope of 97-99, 123, 192, 223, 252, 306, 348, 368-69, 374-76, 389-92, 416, 446, 462, 571. *See also śabdapramāṇa*; scripture
phala (fruit, result) 123, 161, 242
  niyoga is not a 439
  of *pramāṇa* 350, 352
picture or painting, analogy of 236, 240, 353, 559, 592-93
Pillai, D. N. 608
Pillai, K. Raghavan 343-44
Pillai, Surnath Kanjan 343
Pisharoti, K. R. 343-44
pīṭha. *See maṭha*
  Kāmakoti Pitha s.r.
pitṛloka (world of the fathers) 279, 476. *See also* path, southern
place (*deśa*) 322, 412
plants 25, 27, 172
  in rebirth 260
Plato 95
pleasure (*sukha*, *rati*) 76, 110, 113, 269, 288, 304, 306, 331, 342, 348-49, 359, 494, 593-94. *See also* bliss
  in Vaiśeṣika 239
polytheism 7
pot, disappearance of when known to be clay 321
pot-space analogy 33, 60, 83, 86, 88-89, 108-9, 129, 149, 151, 191, 286, 288, 315, 479, 517, 540, 544, 554, 576, 599
Potter, Karl H. 603-4
Poussin, Louis de la Vallée 604, 607
Prabhākara, founder of school of a branch of Mīmāṃsā 4, 15, 57-58, 346, 393, 399, 553
Prabhākara, father of Hastāmalaka 18
Prābhākara school of Mīmāṃsā 57, 390, 392, 414, 434, 517, 572-73, 575, 584-85
practice. *See abhyāsa*
prācūrya 132
pradhāna. *See prakṛti*
pradyumna 165
Prajāpati 87-88, 137-39, 277, 348, 363, 431, 455-58, 487, 494, 518, 561
  two aspects of 475
prajñā, *prājña* 85, 89, 104, 106-7, 110, 235-36, 277, 311-12, 319, 340, 494, 515-16, 562
  prajñānaghana 523
  pūrvaprajñā 509
prajñapti 111, 316
prakalpa (imputation) 425
prakaraṇa (treatise) 4, 105 (context), a kind of exegetical evidence) 431
prakaṭya (being revealed) 373
prakṛti or *pradhāna*
  avyaktaprakṛti 85, 88, 238, 279, 461
  = *avidyā* 574
  in Sāṃkhya 20, 33, 79, 86, 115, 123, 128-32, 134-35, 140-43, 145-46, 152-55, 164-65, 169, 238-39, 263, 278, 292-93, 314, 332, 337-38, 460, 481, 488, 540, 552-53, 590
  prakṛtilaya 279
pralaya (period of reabsorption between creations) 26, 88, 139-40, 145-46, 152, 156-57, 259, 406, 457, 471, 485-86
pramā (truth, veridical awareness) 226-27, 252, 350, 541
pramāda (carelessness) 409
pramāṇa (instrument of knowledge) 191, 418. *See also* perception, inference, comparison, *śabda*, scripture, *arthāpatti*
  alaukika 396
  conditioned by *avidyā* 7, 96-97, 418, 541
  for Self-knowledge. *See* Brahman, how proved
  give certainty 368-69, 381
  how known? 394, 397, 401, 572
  independent in establishing its object 375, 389-93, 396, 441-42
  must give new knowledge 348, 368-69 389, 436, 441, 451
  number of 97, 553
  pravartakapramāṇa 298
  proper scope of 96-97, 146-47, 161, 195, 249, 286, 307-8, 314, 369, 375, 394-95, 401-2, 435, 453, 469, 499, 532, 548-49, 591-92
prāmāṇya (validity, truth) 99, 148, 251, 400-1, 414, 451
  svataḥ/parataḥ 7, 226, 253, 413-14, 458, 528
pramātṛ (knower, subject of veridical awareness) 226, 539, 541, 572, 577
prameya (object of veridical awareness) 121, 161, 543, 572
pramiti (right cognition) 368, 541, 572
prāṇa (breath, vital airs)
  absorbs organs during sleep 170, 265, 492
  as *akṣara* 492
  as conceptual construction 108, 234, 310

as Hiranyagarbha 277, 288, 309, 456, 475-76
as reflecting medium 82, 85, 106
as seventeen components of subtle body 319, 324, 330, 341, 475, 480, 561
chief *prāṇa* 170
constituents of 332, 523
daughter of Kuṇḍalinī 556
eleven 170
five 319, 324, 330, 341, 475, 480, 561
held to body by food 480
in creation myths 87, 455
in liberation 511
in theistic Śāṃkhya 553
loci of in the body 330, 480
not the Self 133, 136, 141, 198, 287, 326, 334, 336, 341, 497, 557
omnipresent 492
operation of 325, 330
prāṇamayakośa 91, 215, 330-31, 341
presiding deities of 492, 494
products of 489, 524
qualities of 465, 489
role in transmigratory process 23-24, 179, 266, 476, 508-9
praṇava. *See aum*
Praṇavavārttika 560-62
prāṇāyāma (breath control) 322
prapañca (the world) 106, 321, 359, 361, 365
prapañcopasana (quiescence of the world) 108
vakprapañca (verbalization) 310
prapañcavilayavāda 50, 173, 432
prasāda 339, 350, 372. *See also dama*
prasaṃkhyāna. *See* meditation, *prasaṃkhyāna*
Prasaṃkhyānavāda 444-47
Praśna Upaniṣad 78, 137, 270, 289-90, 292
Praśnopaniṣadbhāṣya (of Śaṃkara) 18, 116, 289-94
prasthānatrayī (triple basis of Vedānta) 5
pratibhā (intuition) 357
pratibhāsika 344
pratibimba (prototype in reflection model) 86
pratīka (symbol) 356
pratisaṃkhyānirodha 160
pratiṣedha (denial, negation) 230
pratiṣedhakarman. *See* act, prohibited
paryudāsa (restricted negation) 491
prāsajya (absolute negation) 413, 491
pratītyasamutpāda 160
pratyāhāra (withdrawal of the senses) 322
pratyabhijñā (recognition) 200, 500, 558
error of recognition (*bhrama*) 412
Pratyabhijñā system of Kashmir Śaivism 551
prāyaścitta. *See* act, expiatory
pratyaya (idea) 224, 319
pravṛtti (activity) 22, 295, 299-300, 348, 357, 361-62, 365, 370, 388, 403, 419, 435, 439, 474
cause of 400-1
Prayāga (Allahabad) 117, 518
prayojana (purpose)
of creation 352-53
of a text 339, 564, 587-88
preraṇa (prompting to activity) 435-36, 439-40
pride (*garvas*) 218, 553
pṛthaktva (separateness) 450
pūjā (worship) 475
Pulkāsas 506
Purāṇa 268, 485
and Paurāṇikas 553
Puri (the town) 16, 18, 118, 563
Puri (a *daśanāma*) 118
puritāt ("heart") 172, 479. *See also* "heart"
Purohit, N. B. 604
puruṣa
cosmic. *See* Viraj
in Sāṃkhya 128, 130, 140-41, 153-54, 238-39, 295, 314
a Paurāṇika category 553
puruṣārtha (human purpose, end of man) 175, 255, 348, 350, 388, 403-4, 415-16, 418-19, 457, 476, 528, 556
Puruṣasūkta (*Ṛg Veda* X.90) 38
Pūrvamīmāṃsā. *See* (Pūrva) Mīmāṃsā.

quintuplication theory of creation (*pañcīkaraṇa*) 88, 265, 318, 323, 330, 332, 341, 560-61

Radhakrishnan, Sarvepalli 608
Raghavan, V. 294, 609
Rāhu 243, 559
Raja, K. Kunjunni 56, 116, 605, 607-8
rajas (the *guṇa*) 299, 337, 340, 515, 533, 553
Rājasūya 472
rājayoga 322, 560
Rāma 247, 600
Ramakrishna Mission Sevashrama 318
Rāmānuja 9-12, 14, 105, 119
Rāmāyaṇa 5, 17, 420
Ranade, R. D. 78, 284, 606, 608-9
Rao, M. A. V. 605
rasa (taste) 560
Ray, R. B. Amarnath 550-51, 607, 609
reasoning 146-47, 153, 253, 310, 544-45
red crystal, analogy of 82, 85-86, 93, 138, 202, 232, 240, 248, 265, 372-73, 406, 574-76. *See also tarka*, *yukti*
reflection model 20, 73, 77, 83-89, 94, 185, 214, 225, 231, 234-35, 241, 245-46, 248, 321, 325, 351, 386, 407, 417, 462, 539, 542, 554, 575-76, 599. *See also ābhāsa*; mirror; *bimba*; *pratibimba*; etc.
relation (*sambandha*) theory of relations 62-73, 377. *See also* difference; identity; inherence, etc.
between the two sections of the Vedas. *See jñānakāṇḍa*; *karmakāṇḍa*
requirement of a text 587-88
unreal 465
release. *See* liberation
renunciation. *See tyāga*; *saṃnyāsa*
renunciatory act. *See* act, renunciatory
repetition. *See abhyāsa*
Ṛg Veda 78, 285

Rohiṇī 500
rope-snake, analogy of 39, 68-70, 81-83, 86, 88-89, 93-94, 108, 125, 127, 138, 146, 196-97, 222, 228, 243, 256, 269, 310-11, 313-14, 321, 337, 340, 370, 408, 485, 511, 522, 542, 570, 576, 594
Roy, S. 604, 607
Rudra 561
rūpa (form) 239, 459
rūpa (color). *See* color
rūpaskandha 557

Śabara 4, 11, 438, 584, 596-97
śabda (verbal testimony, a *pramāṇa*). *See* scripture
śabdātman. *See* Brahman as word
śabdabodha or *śabdajñāna* (verbal cognition) 357, 368, 370, 387-88, 400, 409, 441, 464, 515, 526, 583
śabdādvaita 54, 59
saccidānanda 75, 330-32, 342, 555-56
sacrifice (*yajña*) 108, 121, 125, 139, 175-77, 189, 240, 256, 369-70, 372, 402, 415, 424, 430, 432, 438-40, 445, 474, 518, 528, 588, 597, 611
  animal sacrifice 172
  horse sacrifice (*aśvamedha*) 182, 455
Sadananda 117, 217
sadāsīti (a *mahāvākya*) 233
sadāsmi (a *mahāvākya*) 241
sādhanā (meditative means) 242, 255
sādhyasama (a fallacy) 111, 316
Sagara (a *daśanāma*) 118
Śaiva, Śaivism 119, 163, 333, 553. *See also* Kashmir Śaivism
sākṣātkāra (immediate manifestation, direct vision) 417, 419, 426, 441, 594. *See also* Self-knowledge; *anubhava*
  is *nididhyāsana* 465
sākṣin (Witness) 75, 92, 121, 127, 196, 203, 232-35, 238, 245-49, 251, 276, 283, 287, 319, 327-28, 330, 334, 337, 425, 445, 459, 462, 479, 482-83, 488, 491, 497-99, 505, 510, 514, 539-41, 544
śakti (potency) 149, 168, 380, 422-23
  as primary meaning. *See* meaning, primary
  āvaraṇaśakti. *See* ignorance, veiling
  equals *avidyā* 574
  for knowing 129
  of Brahman 477
  of the injunctive mood 440
  paraśakti 556
  a Śaiva category 553
  vikṣepaśakti. *See* ignorance, projective
salt dissolved in water, analogy of 266, 486
śama(*tva*) (tranquillity, self-restraint) 36, 122, 218, 242, 272, 320, 329, 335-37, 515
  two kinds of 339
samādhi, *samādhana* (concentration) 36, 110, 113, 216, 235, 317, 319-20, 322, 329, 340-41, 372, 562
  nirvikalpakasamādhi 35, 336, 342-43
  saṃnyāsa not a kind of 35
  savikalpakasamādhi 342-43
sāmagrī (collection of causal factors) 454
samāna (a *prāṇa*) 330
sāmānādhikāraṇya (grammatical agreement) 262, 381, 527, 554
samavāya (inherence) 149-50, 156-58, 164, 315, 382, 393, 449-50
samavāyikāraṇa (inherence cause) 166
Sāmaveda 254, 281
Sambandhavārttika (section of Sureśvara's *Bṛhadāraṇyakopaniṣadbhāṣyavārttika*) 347, 420-53
sambhava (inclusion) 553
saṃhitā (Vedic ritual formulae) 46
Saṃhitā Upaniṣad. *See Īśā Upaniṣad*
saṃgrahaṇī ritual 433
Saṃhitī Upaniṣad 205
saṃjñā (verbal designation) 553
saṃjñāskandha 557
saṃkalpa (wish, imagination) 268, 341
saṃkara (mixture, confusion) 384
Śaṃkara (ācārya) 6, 9-21, 23-26, 28, 30-31, 33-46, 48-52, 54, 56, 59-60, 65-66, 68-81, 83-85, 87-98, 103-4, 115-347, 364, 430, 489, 550, 560, 563-65, 570, 580, 585, 587, 589-90, 595-96, 598, 601, 611-12
  as author of devotional poetry 78
  his date 115-16
  his work 115-16
  a realist 79-81
  traditional accounts of his life 116-18, 420-21
Śaṃkara(*dig*)*vijaya* 117, 347, 610
saṃkarṣaṇa 165
Sāṃkhya 19-20, 33, 66-67, 85, 88, 93, 111, 115, 118, 128-30, 134-35, 140-43, 146-47, 152-55, 169, 193, 258, 278, 293-94, 304-5, 309, 311, 314-16, 333, 336, 453, 460, 466, 481, 488, 510-11, 540, 543, 552-53, 589, 598, 600
  standpoint, in *Bhagavadgita* 296
  theistic Samkhya 163, 553
Sāṃkhyakārikās (of Īśvarakṛṣṇa) 65
Sāṃkhyakārikābhāṣya (of Gauḍapāda) 104
saṃnidhi (proximity), as condition of sentence meaning 443
saṃnyāsa, *saṃnyāsin* 16, 34-37, 41, 43-45, 117, 175, 197, 203-4, 256, 270, 272, 278, 285-86, 288, 295-96, 298-300, 325, 336, 427, 457, 476, 483, 489, 513, 518-19, 550, 599
  and karma 35
  as means for liberation 483
  false *saṃnyāsa* 472
  two kinds of 300-1, 490
saṃsāra (cycle of rebirth, transmigration) 6, 22, 127-28, 153, 171, 181, 194, 218-21, 228-29, 235, 242-43, 266, 270, 272-74, 285-86, 295-96, 302, 308, 332, 337-38, 341, 348, 355, 364, 460, 478, 508. *See also* bondage
  appreciation of 534
  beginningless 112, 153, 159, 164
saṃsarga (relation, conjunction) 357
  relevance of a text 339
saṃsārin (transmigrator) 122-23, 171, 222
saṃskāra (trace, tendency) 22, 220, 241, 315, 319, 360, 367, 370, 375, 387,

408-9, 458, 470-71, 500, 558, 568, 575, 581
saṃskāra (purification) 30, 32, 39-40, 47, 126, 196, 364, 372, 425
a purpose of injunction 427, 611
a result of action 39-40, 596
saṃskāraskandha 557
saṃsthāna (shape, configuration) 351
saṃtāna (stream of consciousness) 160, 189, 243, 252, 339, 355, 499
of verbal knowledge 357
saṃvṛta, saṃvṛti 107, 113, 313
in Buddhism 262
saṃyamanam (Yama's world, hell) 24-25
saṃyoga (contact) 149, 158, 164, 223, 284, 449-50, 462
Sanatkumāra 136
Śaṅkhāpaṇi 610, 612
śānta (a Śaiva category) 553
sapakṣa, in inference 496
saptabhaṅgī (sevenfold preication) 163
Sarasvatī 556
a *daśanāma* 118
Saraswati, Balakrsnananda 104
Sarasvati, Saccidanandendra 79-80, 606-7
Śarīrakamīmāṃsāsūtras. *See Brahmasūtras*
Śarīrakamīmāṃsāvṛtti (of Upavarṣa ?) 11
Sarma, B. N. Krishnamurti 105, 607-9
Sarma, R. Nagaraja 604
Sarvadarśanasaṃgraha (of Mādhava) 612
Sarvajñātman 12
Sarvāstivāda 159-61
Sarvavedāntasiddhāntasaṃgraha (attributed to Śaṃkara) 19, 339-43
Sastri, A. Mahadevan 295, 551
Sastri, Anantakumar 64-65, 604
Sastri, C. Markandeya 550, 605, 612
Sastri, N. M. 605
Sastri, P. P. Subrahmanya 606
Sastri, R. M. 608
Sastri, S. Kuppuswami 347, 603-4, 610
Sastri, S. Laksminrsimha 608
Sastri, S. R. Krishnamurthi 563
Sastri, S. Srirama 563
Sastri, S. Suryanarayana 308, 606, 609
Sastri, T. S. Narayana 608
Sastri, V. A. Ramaswami 603
sat, sattā (existent, existence, being, reality) 109, 240, 259, 262-66, 296-97, 373, 381, 390, 393-94, 396-97, 410, 450, 459, 552, 554
criterion of 7, 75, 296
inference to establish existence 453-54
sat, cit, ābanda. *See* saccidananda
Śatapatha Brāhmaṇa 170, 180, 296
Śataśloki (attributed to Śaṃkara) 18, 324-25
satkāraṇavāda 66, 147-49, 261, 405, 454
satkāryavāda 7, 65-66, 111, 142, 149, 182-83, 454
sattā. *See sat*
as Brahman 75
in Vaiśeṣika 75
sattva (the *guṇa*) 129, 255, 299, 337, 339-41, 343, 553, 556
sattvaśuddhi 295,
satyaprapañcavāda 610
Śaunaka 285, 323
Sautrāntika 498
scorpion 145, 353
scripture (*śruti*; *āgama*; *Veda*; *śabda*). *See also jñānakāṇḍa*; *karmakāṇḍa*
and *smṛti*, weight of 143
as producing Self-knowledge ? 98-99, 124-25, 146-47, 173, 233, 254, 257, 272, 298, 328, 360, 366-67, 371, 387-90, 396, 403, 416-18, 426, 435-36, 442, 444, 447, 451-53, 469, 526-27, 531, 533, 545, 582, 591-93
authorless 58, 398, 443, 485, 591
composition of 3, 46
conditioned by *avidyā*, superimposition ? 97, 121, 208, 221, 418
contrasted with secular language 396-401, 442
entitlement to study 138, 140, 586
how it functions 99, 125, 271, 314, 328, 343, 435-36, 441, 469, 527, 530, 545
interpretation of. *See* exegesis; *niyoga*; Mīmāṃsā, etc.
is it entirely injunctive in force? 38, 47, 49, 124, 127, 173, 184, 242, 360 387, 390, 403-5, 417-18, 426, 435-36, 444, 526, 531-32, 582, 584, 596
primary purpose of 47, 50, 122, 208, 418, 585, 591, 594
recitation of 421, 474, 518, 585
relation to perception 98-99, 147, 241, 307-8, 369, 374-76, 389, 396, 401, 416, 426, 442, 452-53, 461-62, 571, 591-93
relation to reasoning and inference 99, 144, 146-47, 152, 396, 399, 401, 416, 442, 444-45, 452-53, 462, 545, 571
Sāṃkhya on 128-29, 293
validity of scripture as a *Pramāṇa* 47, 49, 53, 97-99, 123, 244, 254, 257, 262, 264, 307-8, 339-40, 348-49, 366, 375, 387-92, 396, 399, 401, 403, 418, 425, 430, 441, 447, 452-53, 484, 526-29, 531-32, 545, 570-71, 591-93
which texts are scripture? 3, 14
seed 292
and sprout, analogy of 111, 113, 153, 262, 316-17, 379, 399, 570, 579
(*bīja*) 106, 309
burnt, analogy of 34, 240-41
self (*ātman*). *See also* Brahman
highest (*paramātman*). *See* Brahman
in Buddhism 21
individual (*jīvātman*). *See jīva*
in Nyāya-Vaiśeṣika 284, 355-56
in Sāṃkhya. *See puruṣa*
self-control 218
Self-illumination (*svaprakāśatva*) 199-200, 226, 290-92, 325, 350, 396, 458, 578
analogy with fire burning itself 155, 162
as property of Brahman or pure consciousness 75-76, 95, 236
in Buddhism 201, 245
self-knowledge, Brahman-knowledge (*ātma-jñāna, brahmajñāna*)
and bliss. *See* bliss
as removal of *avidyā* 36, 39, 41-42, 50, 53, 186, 188-89, 229-30, 232, 298,

300, 306, 372-73, 403-4, 406-8, 424, 434, 457, 470, 472, 484, 597
enjoined? *See* injunction to knowledge
entitlement to. *See* *adhikāra*
how gotten. *See* scripture; *śravaṇa*
is it identical with liberation? 34-36, 40, 53, 125, 177, 189, 205, 285, 296, 323, 325, 406, 469, 487, 533
need for meditation after? *See* *upāsanā*
nothing can sublate it 308, 533
possibility of 96, 241, 305-6, 465, 470
pramana for? *See* scripture
relation to action. *See* act and knowledge, relation between
statements of. *See* *mahāvākya*
semen 26-27, 29, 219, 276, 331, 523
Sengupta, Bratindra Kumar 604
sense organs (*bhutendrīya*) 22-24, 34, 83, 90, 93, 121, 170-71, 194, 198, 227, 237, 282, 287-88, 306, 311, 318-19, 324, 330-31, 337, 341, 357, 412, 461, 475, 561, 612
as reflecting medium 498
material 486, 523
not self 326, 334, 341, 556-57
number of, in Samkhya 155
sense presentations 70, 121
sentence (*vākya*) 55
declarative. *See* *jñānakāṇḍa*
injunctive. *See* *karmakāṇḍa*, *niyoga*, injunction
meaning. *See* meaning
service to mankind 35-37, 259-60, 278
sex 117, 219
organs of 22
sexual desire 523
sexual intercourse 407
Sharma, C. D. 604, 607
sheaths. *See* *kośa*
shell-silver illusion 120, 196, 222, 321, 323, 340, 385, 410-11, 413-14, 460, 566-70
ship, illusion of trees moving from 299, 321
Siddhāntabindu (of Madhusūdana Sarasvatī) 333
siddhasādhana (begging the question) 496
siddhi (realization) 322, 417
eight powers in Yoga 514, 560
śikṣā (science of pronunciation) 285
Śikṣāvallī (a chapter of *Taittirīya Upaniṣad*) 205
silence (*mauna*) 322
Simha, L. 331
similarity (*sādṛśya*, *sārūpya*) 161, 200, 237, 360, 378, 386, 411, 454, 500, 553, 573, 577-78
sin. *See* demerit; *pāpma*
Śiva 419, 551-53, 555
Śivaguru 117
skandha 159, 507
skepticism. *See* Cārvāka
sky, blue dome of, analogy of 321, 460. *See also* *ākāśa*
sky-flower 352, 378
Sleep 337, 478-79, 515, 545-46
deep. *See* *suṣupti*
Ślokavārttika (of Kumārila) 353, 374
smell (*gandha*) 560
smoke 24, 27
path of. *See* path, southern
smṛti (traditional writings) 5, 133, 135, 139, 142-44, 220, 243, 372
snake and rope. *See* rope-snake
snakebite, imaginary, causing death 351, 354-55
snake, fear of, trembling at 408
śoka (grief) 489, 568
soma 438, 455, 494
son of a barren woman 109
sons, role in liberation 475-76
South India 18
space (*vyoma*, *ākāśa*, *kha*, *ambara*) 88, 108, 233-34, 236-37, 287, 318, 539
sparks, analogy. of *See* fire
speech (*vāk*) 59, 475
act of. *See* act, vocal
vācārambhanamātra (*vikāra*) 257, 261
vāk-śakti 358
vāg-tattva 358
speech, organ of (*vāk*) 22-23, 179, 228, 282, 330, 356, 488, 517, 523
speech-acts, theory of. *See* language as communication
sphoṭa 20, 56
sentence-*sphoṭa* 56-57
sphoṭavāda 57, 59, 139
word-*sphoṭa* 57
Sphoṭasiddhi (of Maṇḍana Miśra) 20, 56, 59
spider's web, analogy of 84, 90, 135, 151, 311, 479-80
śraddhā (faith) 36, 320, 329, 336-37
as worship of ancestors 30
in the guru 329
śravaṇa (hearing)
conditions of 537-38
four kinds of awareness 590
śravaṇa, manana, nididhyāsana 52, 318, 329, 354, 427, 445, 484, 489, 513, 544-45
Śrīdhara 604
Srinivasachari, P. N. 603
Śrī Vidyāratna Sūtra (of Gauḍapāda?) 104
Śrīvidyāsubhṛgodaya (of Gauḍapāda?) 104
Śṛṅgeri 16, 18, 118, 420
śrotavya 123, 125, 127
śruti. *See* scripture
Śrutisārasamuddhāraṇa (of Toṭaka) 18-19, 598-600
Staal, J. F. 603
sthitaprajña (man of stable insight) 408
studentship (*brahmacārya*). *See* *brahmacārya*
study (*pravacana*) 288
subject object relationship 6-7, 62, 67-71, 76, 113
sublation (*bādha*) 7, 39, 82, 230, 241, 290, 413, 533, 541, 566-67, 570
substance (*dravya*) 216, 315, 382-83, 390
and mode (*paryaya*) 384
substanceness (*dravyatva*) 393
substance attribute distinction 71
Śūdra 140, 299
Śuka 323
sun (*āditya*) 24-26, 267, 288-89, 311, 318
as god of the eye 494

as gross form of Brahman 480
as seat of Hiraṇyagarbha 481
person in the 480
rays, of analogy of 84, 234, 311, 327
reflection of in rippling water 84-85, 264, 277
way of the *See* path, northern
Sundaram, P. K. 606
Sundara Pāṇḍya 12, 18
śūnya(tā) (void, voidness) 122, 231, 248, 328, 341, 376
Śūnyavāda 159, 161-62, 166, 249, 258, 261, 313, 316, 341, 482, 499, 557, 589
superimposition (adhyāsa, āropa) 69-73, 76, 78-80, 93-94, 118, 120-21, 146, 174, 187, 222-23, 231, 234, 238, 240, 242, 255, 269, 276, 291, 321, 323, 328, 333, 338, 340-41, 359, 407, 410, 458-60, 468, 485, 510, 530, 541, 564-71, 579-80
Sureśvara 12, 15-17, 19-20, 28, 43, 48-50, 54, 59-61, 72-73, 75-76, 80, 83, 88, 90-91, 116-18, 204, 217, 317-18, 347, 364, 420, 562, 611
suṣupti (deep sleep)
as *ānandamayakośa* s.v.
associated with "*m*" in "*aum*" 89, 319
association with *prājña* 106, 236, 311, 319, 337, 562
bliss experienced in 7, 269, 311, 343, 351, 479, 493, 502-3
buddhi stilled during 319, 326, 562
compare with *pralaya* 139-40
ego doesn't exist during 326
equals *laya* 315
how it comes about 479
mahāsuṣupti 140
manas withdrawn during 24, 110, 201, 326
no liberation directly from 89
organs not functioning during 24, 90, 201, 216, 326
prāṇa and deep sleep 136, 265, 326
proof of continuity of *jīva* during172-73, 269, 351
pure consciousness experienced in 7, 76, 90, 93, 173, 216, 225-26, 261, 265, 328, 333, 478, 506, 558
relation to ignorance 90, 337, 415, 478, 502-3, 505-7
three states of 91, 502-3
traces still present or not ? 89, 360, 501
vāsanās cleared away during ? 90, 501
why one should not wake a person from deep sleep 90, 501
sūtra 4-5
Sūtrātman 50, 87, 341, 457-58, 461, 467, 473, 475, 489, 491-92, 494, 523, 560, 562
svabhāva, svarūpa (a thing's own nature, essence) 188-89, 315-16, 410
an essential feature 225
in Buddhism 71, 376-77, 385-87
svabhāvahetu, in Buddhist logic 500
svadharma 256, 305, 320. *See also dharma*
svalakṣaṇa 250, 385, 577
svaprakāśa(tva). *See* self-illumination
Svārājyasiddhi (attributed to Sureśvara) 19, 420
svarūpa (essential form). *See svabhāva*
svarūpalakṣaṇa (essential definition of Brahman). *See* Brahman
svarūpāvirbhava (manifestation of one's own form) 406
Śvetaketu 59-60, 130, 261, 265-67
Śvetāśvatara Upaniṣad 778, 131, 141, 143
Śvetāśvataropaniṣadbhāṣya (attributed to Śaṃkara) 19, 345
Swain, Anam Charan 609
symbol, in meditation 25-26
sympathy 520
syntax 55

taijasa 89, 104, 106-7, 236, 311-12, 319, 341, 494, 562
Taittirīya Āraṇyaka 204-5
Taittirīyasaṃhitā 430-31, 434
Taittirīya Upaniṣad 75, 91, 124, 131-32, 141, 165, 174, 204, 418, 493
Taittirīyopaniṣadbhāṣya (of Śaṃkara) 18, 116, 119, 204-16, 294, 309, 521
Taittirīyopaniṣadbhāṣyavārttika (of Sureśvara) 17, 19, 28, 420-21, 521-30
Tālavakāra Brāhmaṇa 281
tamas (the *guṇa*) 299, 3-2, 332, 337, 340, 515, 533, 553
Tamil 5
Tamil Nāḍu 117
Taṇḍin Brāhmaṇa (of the *Sāma Veda*) 254
Tāṅka 12
tanmātra (subtle element) 24, 171, 179, 319, 341, 560-61
origin of, in Sāṃkhya 155
Tantra 318
tanumānasa (attenuation of mental attachment ?) 343
tapas (austerity) 214, 240, 518
tarka (reasoning) 144, 264, 280, 314, 374, 405, 571, 580, 595. *See also* reasoning
as argument 123
Tārkikas ("logicians", i.e., Naiyāyikas) 164, 225, 244, 264, 321, 462, 468, 512, 580
taṭasthalakṣaṇa (accidental definition of Brahman). *See* Brahman
tātparya (speaker's intention) 361
tattva 108
Tattvabodha (attributed to Śaṃkara) 18, 331-33
tattvajñāna (knowledge of the nature of things) 231, 321
tattvamasi ("that art thou") 51, 53-55, 59-61, 73, 124, 130-31, 151, 177, 186, 234, 241, 245-47, 251-52, 267, 317, 319, 332-34, 338, 342, 419, 424, 427, 442, 444, 447-48, 462, 490, 515, 527, 537, 542-45, 547, 554-55, 580, 591-92, 595-96, 600
Tattvananda 339
teaching, mandate for 586
teaching, possibility of its leading to liberation 96-97
Telanga, K. T. 608
tenth man, story of the 185, 210, 234, 251, 253, 426, 462, 525, 546

theism 7, 163-64
Thibaut, George 119-20, 608
thirst. *See* hunger and thirst
Thrasher, Allen Wright 116-17, 346-47, 608, 610
time (*kāla*) 108, 322, 392, 397, 412, 522, 552-53
  as cause of the world 106
  as effect of *avidyā* 88, 166
  aspect of Prajāpati 475
Tīrtha (a *daśanāma*) 118
titikṣā (resignation) 36, 320, 329, 336
Toṭaka 16-17, 19, 598
Toṭakāṣṭaka 17, 19, 598
touch (*sparśa*) 315, 560
trace. *See saṃskāra*
tradition (*āmnāya*) 3, 9, 361, 370-71. *See also smṛti*
  oral tradition 3
tradition (sampradāya) 9, 315, 531
tradition (*aitihya*) 553
transformation. *See pariṇāma*
tree
  banyan or *aśvattha* 287
  peepul or fig 280-81
  śiṃśapā tree 401
  trees in the forest 386
tridaṇḍa, *tridaṇḍin* (triple staff; triple-staff holder) 258
triplication theory of creation 88, 264-65
truth (*satya*) 62, 96-97, 288, 472, 481-82, 486. *See also prāmāṇya*
  as attribute of Brahman 75, 213
  highest truth (*paramārthasatya*) 317, 482
  truthfulness 208
  truth of truth (*satyasya satya*) 75, 189-90, 480, 482
  two truths 118
turīya (the "fourth", a state of awareness) 13, 89-91, 104, 106-7, 233, 311-12, 333, 343, 360
tyāga (renunciation) 272, 297, 322

Udaṅka 231
Uddālaka Āruṇi 9, 59, 265-66
udāna (a *prāṇa*) 330
Udgītha (section of *Bṛhadāraṇyaka Upaniṣad*) 183, 455-56
Udgīthavidyā 174
ūha (guess?) 553
Uṃveka 346-47
universal (*sāmānya*) 60, 75, 150, 161, 369, 373-74, 381-83, 385, 387, 396-97, 477, 611. *See also jāti*
  in Vaiśeṣika 75, 382-83, 393
unreality (*vaitathya*, *mṛṣa*, *tuccha*) 64, 67, 1-7, 1-9, 352, 521. *See also asat*
  has real effects 354
  of the world 21, 310, 312, 325, 333
upādāna (material cause) 123, 530, 606
Upadeśapañcaka (attributed to Śaṃkara) 19, 344
Upadeśasāhasrī (of Śaṃkara) 18, 70, 82, 84, 88, 93-94, 97, 103, 116, 119, 217-54, 294, 309, 320, 334, 530, 550, 598
upādhi (adjunct) 74, 78, 82-83, 86-89, 129-31, 196, 288, 324, 372, 379, 382, 386, 397, 461-62, 481, 546, 573
upalakṣaṇa (extrinsic indicatory mark) 393-94, 590
upamāna. *See* comparison
upanayana (sacred thread) 30, 140, 197, 258, 586
Upaniṣad 3-5, 9-12, 19, 23-26, 46-47, 76, 78, 87, 107, 121, 123, 125, 131, 139, 143, 190-91, 193, 229-30, 257, 285, 293-94, 339, 348, 375, 387, 417, 428, 476
  meaning of the term 181, 207, 280, 421
uparati (abstention) 325, 329, 339, 519
upāsanā (meditation, worship). *See also* injunction to meditate; pūjā
  and *dhyānayoga* 287, 301
  and sacrifice. *See sacrifice*
  as mental act. *See act*, mental
  conditions for 41, 183, 255, 520
  duty to 108
  enjoined by scripture. *See* injunction to meditate
  how to meditate 177-78, 338
  need for, possibility of after Self-knowledge 177, 272, 370, 409, 416-17, 419, 55-57, 534-35, 594
  nididhyāsana 354, 465, 484-85, 518, 530, 543
  on *om*. *See aum*
  on the part of the gods 138-39, 270, 455-56
  parisaṃkhyāna 228-29
  prasaṃkhyāna 42-43, 51-52, 241, 444-47, 548
  results of 26, 107, 131, 180-81, 188, 207, 236, 242, 255, 272, 277, 279, 323, 369, 456, 464, 509, 514, 550, 581
  role of meditation in getting liberation 20, 26, 41, 50, 128, 177, 194, 242, 255, 281 336, 353-54, 368-69, 430, 456, 473-74, 535
  sampat 187-88
  supporting object of. *See ālambana*
  upāsanāvāda 278
  worship of God 50, 320
Upavarṣa 11, 18, 139
Urqhart, W. S. 605
Uśasta Cakrāyaṇa 488-89
utpatti (origination)
  a kind of result of action 39-40, 596
  a purpose of injunction 427
Uttaragītābhāṣya (of Gauḍapāda) 104
Uttaramīmāṃsā 4

Vācaspati Miśra 17, 79
Vaibhāṣika 498
Vaiśeṣika 8, 19, 55-57, 71, 75, 100, 147, 152, 155-59, 163, 165-66, 169-70, 193, 201, 239, 261, 276, 284, 305, 314-16, 353, 380-82, 393, 450, 453, 458, 481, 510-11, 516-17, 552-53, 599-600
Vaiṣṇava 119
Vaiśvānara. *See* Viśva
Vaiśya 299, 473
Vājasaneyaka 174
Vājasaneyakasaṃhitā 180
Vajra 462

Vāk (god of speech) 456
vākya. *See* sentence
a kind of exegetical evidence 430-31
avāntaravākya 583
Vākyapadīya (of Bhartṛhari) 611
Vākyasudhā (attributed to Śaṃkara) 19, 344
Vākyavṛtti (attributed to Śaṃkara) 18, 334-35
value, theory of 22-45
Vāmadeva 28-29, 133, 277, 423, 427, 470
Vāmadevasūkta 470
Vana (a *daśanāma*) 118
Van Boetzelaer 204, 420-21, 523, 608, 612
Van Buitenen, J. A. B. 603
varṇa (caste or class) 121, 204, 219, 260, 299, 323, 333, 472-73, 485, 589, 506
varṇa (morpheme, syllable, letter) 55, 139, 354, 571
varṇāśramadharma. *See dharma*
Vārttika, nature of 521
Vāruṇa 461, 524
Vāruṇi Upaniṣad 205
vāsanā (impression, tendency) 23-25, 28-34, 36, 68, 90, 94, 161-62, 189, 201-2, 234, 268, 287, 290, 313, 320, 338, 352, 434, 478-79, 481-82, 498, 501-3, 505, 509-11, 523, 533, 559, 568, 577
vastu (real object) 197, 229, 255, 261, 324, 331, 355, 374, 377, 384, 410, 522, 539
vastumātra 611
vastutattva 484
Vasubandhu 68
Vāsudeva 165, 331
Vātsyāyana, author of *Kāmasūtras* 459
Veda. *See* scripture
vedanāskandha 557
Vedānta 3-6, 9-10, 19, 71
Vedānta Deśika 11, 603
Vedāntasūtras. *See Brahmasūtras*
Vedavyāsa 295
Veezhinathan, N. 333, 604
veins. *See nāḍī*
Venkataramanan, S. 320, 325
Venkataramiah, D. 270, 563, 612
Venkatasubbiah, A. 607
verb
as critical part of a meaningful sentence 57, 442-43, 537
meaning of verb root 211
verbal endings 436, 438
verbal testimony. *See śabda*
Vetter, Tilmann 309, 347, 609, 611
Vibhramaviveka (of Maṇḍana Miśra) 347
vibhu (all-pervading) 202
vicāra (inquiry, discussion) 320, 329, 343
videhamukti 343, 494-95
vidhā (to posit) 375-76
vidvān (enlightened person) 297-98, 300
vidyā (perfect knowledge; understanding) 6, 21, 33-34, 41, 69, 74, 78, 80, 120-21, 128, 131, 143, 175, 183, 192, 195-97, 206, 221, 228-29, 240, 279-80, 336, 352-54, 474, 476-77, 509, 553, 558, 570, 580-81
higher v. lower 285-86
stages of *vidyā* 113
Vidyādhirāja 117
Vidyāraṇya 217, 563
Vidyarnava, S. C. 278, 608
vijñāna 83, 112-13, 160-62, 198-200, 210, 348, 453, 478, 515-16
ālayavijñāna s.v.
vijñānamayakośa 91, 131, 215, 288, 331, 337, 341, 497, 517, 524
vijñānaskandha 557
vijñānātman 138, 190
viṣayavijñāna 326
Vijñānavāda Buddhism 13, 20, 94-95, 159, 161-62, 250, 316, 352, 355, 481, 499-500, 573, 577-79, 589
vikalpa (conceptual construction) 21, 54, 65, 67-69, 106, 161, 199, 206, 237, 240, 264, 269, 310, 313, 316, 323, 358, 368, 377, 385, 387, 400, 406, 553, 577
internal external 107-8. *See also kalpanā*
vikalpaka (one who wrongly interprets) 68, 314
vikāra (modification) 39-40, 126, 190, 196, 356, 428
a kind of result of action 39-40, 596
a purpose of an injunction 427
vikṣepa (restlessness/distraction) 235, 372
vikṣepa (power of projection) 337, 360, 377. *See avidyā*, projective
violence 29
vipāka (maturation, fruition of karmic residues) 22, 28-29, 31. *See also* karma
Virāj 87-88, 185, 273-77, 286, 290-92, 309, 311, 318-19, 366-67, 455, 457, 461, 466, 487, 489, 523-24, 560-62
wife of Indra 494
virtue, moral 35-36
viṣaya (content, object of awareness) 6, 40, 93, 108, 111-12, 201, 296, 348, 352, 360, 395, 572, 576, 588
subject matter of a text 339, 564, 587
viṣayin (subject of awareness of an object) 120, 572
viśeṣa (particular) 369, 381, 477
as distinguishing property 411
in Vaiśeṣika 393
viśeṣalakṣaṇa 590
viśeṣaṇa (qualifier) 174, 297, 394
of absence 449
viśeṣaṇaviśeṣyabhāva (relation of qualifier and qualified) 357, 522, 554-55
viśeṣya (qualificand) 297
Viśiṣṭādvaita 5, 9-11
Viṣṇu 27, 87, 247, 267, 280, 295, 323-24, 334-35, 457, 561-62, 598, 600
visual organ 23, 196, 237
Viśva, Vaiśvānara 89, 104, 106-7, 135, 310-12, 319, 494, 561-62
Viśvāmitra 554
Viśvajit sacrifice 195, 445
Viśvarūpa 347
vitta (riches), two kinds of 466, 475
Vivaraṇa school 73
vivarta 54, 59, 65, 84, 115, 118, 352, 357-58, 376, 590, 598
the term 295
Vivartavāda 7, 67, 82, 467
Vivekacūḍāmaṇi (attributed to Śaṃkara) 19, 116, 335-38

vow 127
of chastity 176
Vṛtti (a kind of commentary) 5, 11
vṛtti (operation of the internal organ) 92, 234, 331, 436, 514, 576-77
bāhyavṛtti 320
Vṛttikāra 11, 40, 181, 187, 256, 296, 298
vyadhikaraṇa (in inference) 357, 610
vyakti (particular individual) 55, 374, 381-83, 385, 387. *See also visesa*
vyāna (a *prāṇa*) 330
vyāpāra (operation) 439
Vyāsa, author of Epics 5, 475, 519
Vyāsa, author of the *Yogabhāṣya* 118
vyavahāra (ordinary affairs, practical usage) 121, 197, 289, 324, 352, 357, 370, 381-82, 386, 435, 447, 452, 459, 521, 540, 559, 599
vyāvahārika (lower standpoint) 34-36, 67, 215
vyavasthā (fixed distinction) 378-79
vyāvṛtta (excluded, discontinuous) 378, 382
vyutpatti (learning meanings of words) 399

waking state of awareness (*jāgarita*) 13, 89-91, 106-7, 225, 228, 233, 235, 240, 248, 268, 310-13, 319, 325-27, 484, 556
dangers of sudden waking. *See suṣupti*
three states of 502
Walleser, Mac 105-7
Warrier, A. G. Krishna 606
water 22, 24, 88, 236, 264-65, 287, 311, 318, 560
and foam, analogy of 84, 147, 197, 219, 273, 286, 323
and waves, analogy of 321, 554
wealth 30
Weber, Albrecht 254
welfare (*śreyas*) 40, 402
whole and part 150, 190
will. *See* effort
wind. *See* air
withdrawal from the world 35
word (*pada*) 55, 108
homonymous (*sādhāraṇa*) 393
words and their meanings. 139, 193, 361-62. *See meaning*
words and syllables, relation between 407
world (*jagat*)
dissolution of. *See laya*
not a nonentity 520
modification of the Highest Self 191
unreal 240, 426, 520
worship. *See upāsana*

Yājñāvalkya 9, 141, 196, 435, 483, 486, 488, 490-91, 493-95, 498, 502, 508, 513, 519
Yājñavalkyakāṇḍa (of *Bṛhadāraṇyaka Upaniṣad*) 520
Yajurveda
Black 205
White (*śukla*) 180, 278, 421
Yama 24-25, 171, 280
yama (forbearance) 240, 256, 258, 301, 322, 337, 518
Yāmunācārya 12
year 25
yoga 3, 44-45, 173, 183, 278, 287-88, 300, 323, 333, 339, 423
asparśayoga 45, 105, 110
jñānayoga s.v.
karmayoga s.v.
Yoga standpoint, in *Bhagavadgītā* 296
(Pātañjala)Yoga 19, 35, 45, 92, 118, 163, 178, 186, 309, 336, 342, 560
Yogabhāṣya (of Vyāsa) 118
Yogabhāṣyavivaraṇa (ascribed to a Śaṃkara) 3, 9-10
Yogācāra 68, 70, 92, 453. *See also* Vijñānavāda
Yogasūtras (of Patañjali) 143
yogin 317, 495. *See also yoga*
yogyatva, yogyatā (capability, fitness)
between word and object 401
a condition of sentence meaning 443
for being validly known 394-96
yukti (reasoning) 123, 241, 441, 445-47, 580

Library of Congress Cataloging in Publication Data

Main entry under title:

Encyclopedia of Indian philosophies.

Includes index.
1. Advaita—Dictionaries. 2. Vedanta—Dictionaries. 3. Philosophy, Indic—Dictionaries.
I. Potter, Karl H.
B132.A3E52 181'.482 77-85558
ISBN 0-691-07182-9 AACR2

companion to
Enc. of Indian Phil.